Handbook on Knowledge Management 1

Springer-Verlag Berlin Heidelberg GmbH

Clyde W. Holsapple
(Editor)

Handbook
on Knowledge Management 1

Knowledge Matters

With 61 Figures and 62 Tables

 Springer

Professor Clyde W. Holsapple
University of Kentucky
Rosenthal Endowed Chair
in Management Information Systems
425B Gatton Building
of Business and Economics
Lexington KY 40506-0034
USA
cwhols@pop.uky.edu

1st edition 2003. 2nd printing

Originally published in the series:
International Handbooks on Information Systems.
2003.

ISBN 978-3-540-20005-5   ISBN 978-3-540-24746-3 (eBook)
DOI 10.1007/978-3-540-24746-3

Cataloging-in-Publication Data applied for
A catalog record for this book is available from the Library of Congress.
Bibliographic information published by Die Deutsche Bibliothek
Die Deutsche Bibliothek lists this publication in the Deutsche Nationalbibliografie; detailed bibliographic
data is available in the Internet at <http://dnb.ddb.de>.

© Springer-Verlag Berlin Heidelberg 2004
Originally published by Springer-Verlag Berlin · Heidelberg in 2004
Softcover reprint of the hardcover 1st edition 2004

Softcover-Design: Erich Kirchner, Heidelberg

SPIN 10957868   42/3130-5 4 3 2 1 0 – Printed on acid-free paper

Dedicated with love to Carol, Christiana, and Claire

Preface

The *Handbook on Knowledge Management* is an extensive, fundamental reference work for the knowledge management (KM) field. Written by a large, international array of KM practitioners, scholars, and luminaries, its 65 chapters address a host of issues and approach knowledge management from a wide variety of perspectives. These range from classic foundations to cutting-edge thought. They approach KM from both informative and provocative standpoints. They cover both theoretical and practical angles, historical and futuristic trends, human and technological dimensions, operational and strategic viewpoints. The chapters include first-hand experiences, best practices, thoughtful recommendations, stimulating insights, conceptual tools, and philosophical discussion.

As such, the *Handbook on Knowledge Management* serves as a portal for knowledge management, a starting point for any investigation or study of KM, an essential for the library of every KM practitioner, researcher, and educator. The content is designed to be approachable by KM novices and to offer value for KM experts. It is designed to be a fundamental, lasting benefit to the multifaceted KM community. The KM content is broad and deep. It is also designed to go beyond itself, by pointing readers in the direction of many fine complementary publications that focus on various specialized, narrow aspects of KM. The *Handbook*'s content is specially structured in a way that allows readers to examine it straight through, or study a particular section of interest, or consult the book as needed when a specific KM issue arises.

Organization

The *Handbook* is organized into two volumes: *Knowledge Matters* and *Knowledge Directions*. The first of these volumes establishes the fact that knowledge matters to an organization, being important to its success or even its very survival. This volume also covers basic knowledge matters such as the nature of an organization's knowledge resources, the processing of knowledge assets, and factors that influence an organization's conduct of knowledge management. The second volume examines directions that an organization can follow in its knowledge management initiatives, including various technological directions and competitive directions. It documents directions that diverse organizations have taken in their KM efforts and offers visions of directions that lie ahead.

Volume 1: Knowledge Matters

The chapters of Volume 1 are organized into four major parts. Part I examines the foundations of knowledge management including knowledge organizations, knowledge managers, knowledge work, knowledge fields, knowledge economy, and a knowledge management ontology. This ontology provides an outline for structuring the remaining seven parts of the *Handbook,* by recognizing three major components involved in the conduct of KM in an organization: resources, activities, and influences. It recognizes that there is an important role for technology to play in KM, and that the conduct of KM leads to various kinds of outcomes for the organization. Putting all of this together, it is instructive and stimulating to look at specific instances of KM in actual organizations and to ponder what is emerging on the KM horizon.

Part II is concerned with knowledge as a key organizational resource, as a strategic asset, and even as the intellectual capital of a nation. It presents varying viewpoints on the nature of knowledge and discusses a wide range of knowledge attributes. Knowledge maps and organizational memory are considered as means for dealing with some of an organization's knowledge assets. The embedding of some of an organization's knowledge resources in its culture is also considered. Issues concerned with accounting for knowledge resources are explored and contrasted with traditional accounting's focus on other kinds of organizational resources. Although knowledge resources are important factors in an organization's success, it is also vital to pay attention to effective use of these assets in action.

In Part III, we concentrate on activities that an organization engages in when operating on its knowledge resources. This begins with a consideration of processors that perform these activities, flows of knowledge occurring among these processors (i.e., among and within instances of the activities), and the transformations that result. An organization's efforts to acquire knowledge from outside itself or select it from within are examined. Efforts to generate knowledge are discussed in terms of such processes as problem solving, knowledge creation cycles, and sensemaking. Collaborative KM activities involve multiple knowledge processors. They are examined in terms of creating and facilitating communities of practice, and appreciating knowledge sharing proficiencies. Carrying multiparticipant knowledge activity to a higher level, the issues of blending KM with business processes and realizing organizational learning through knowledge management activities are considered.

Part IV is concerned with factors that influence the knowledge processing that occurs within an organization. The ontology identifies four kinds of managerial influences on KM: measurement, control, coordination, and leadership practices. Accordingly, there are chapters that concentrate on valuing KM behaviors, knowledge control issues (e.g., security, assurance), coordination strategies for leveraging knowledge assets, and leadership issues (e.g., qualifications, roles, responsibilities) and prescriptions. In an overarching vein, there are chapters that explore the relationship between trust and KM success, KM enablers and constraints, improving KM by identifying and transferring best practices in an organization, and strategic knowledge managing in the context of networks of organizations.

Volume 2: Knowledge Directions

In the companion volume, the *Handbook* continues with four more parts. Part V surveys technologies for supporting an organization's knowledge management activities. This begins with an overview tracking the role and evolution of commercial knowledge management software. Ensuing chapters focus on technologies for knowledge storage and assimilation, knowledge processes and meta-processes in ontology-based systems, technology for acquiring and sharing knowledge assets, knowledge searching technologies, knowledge distribution technologies, peer-to-peer computing issues for KM, technologies for generating new knowledge by deriving it from existing knowledge, and automated knowledge generation via discovery that finds previously unseen patterns in data or text.

Part VI is oriented toward outcomes of knowledge management initiatives. It begins with an introduction to the dynamic capabilities of firms, indicating that they can compete based on knowledge. The next chapter presents the knowledge chain model, which identifies nine KM activities that can form the basis for achieving organizational competitiveness through superior productivity, agility, innovation, and/or reputation. This is followed by a roadmap proposed for achieving knowledge management outcomes. The next three chapters concentrate on the KM outcomes of productivity gains, greater agility, and innovation. Part VI closes with a consideration of issues surrounding the valuation of outcomes from the knowledge management function, plus a practical guide for measuring the value of KM investments.

Experiences in the practice of knowledge management form the theme of Part VII. This begins with an analysis of the state of current practice of knowledge management in organizations. The analysis is based on a focus group of leaders of KM initiatives. Next, there is an extensive comparative study of successful KM implementations in best practice organizations. This is followed by a consideration of the knowledge strategy process in the context of case studies. Part VII closes with a series of chapters devoted to case studies of KM implementations in the following organizations: the United States Department of Navy, Dow Chemical, Ford Motor Company, Cisco Systems, Swiss Re, a Military Joint Task Force, and Microsoft Consulting Services. These cases offer many lessons learned from knowledge management in action.

In Part VIII, we consider the horizon of this still unfolding field of knowledge management. There is an exploration of what is happening and needs to happen in the way of knowledge management education as it begins to become visible on the university radar screen. Evolving business forms for the knowledge economy are outlined as KM becomes increasingly established in the business world. In a related vein, a vision of the knowledge organization of the future is advanced, seeing it as an intelligent complex adaptive system. Also on the horizon, there is an examination of commercialization as the next phase of knowledge management. Another chapter sees a convergence of electronic business and knowledge management that, when recognized, promises to reshape both of them. The book closes with reflections on the curious success of knowledge management that may well eventuate in KM becoming pervasive and invisible. These chapters provide a sense of direction for the future of the KM field and suggest where we might expect to see some of the pioneering efforts emerge.

Impetus and Roots

The *Handbook on Knowledge Management* has grown out of an interest in KM that has spanned four decades. My initial interest in the 1970s concentrated on the significance of knowledge in decision making. This yielded an appreciation of the different roles that descriptive, procedural, and reasoning knowledge play in the making of a decision. It also led to an architecture and prototype for incorporating all three into a single computer-based system for supporting decision-makers in a domain of interest. Decision support systems devised in this way integrated database management, solver, and artificial intelligence technologies to support the ad hoc needs of decision-makers. In the 1980s, it was shown how this integration, as well as the integration of other traditionally distinct software components, could be accomplished in a synergistic fashion.

By the mid-1980s, this decision support work broadened into a vision that saw organizations as essentially knowledge processing systems and with a great potential to enhance the knowledge processing capabilities and outputs of their knowledge workers by configuring them as nodes in a network of knowledge flows. Each worker would be equipped with a networked computer-based system that could function as an intelligent processor anticipating and supporting the worker's needs, tapping into and contributing to an organization's distributed knowledge resource base, facilitating integration and collaboration among knowledge workers.

This mid-1980s vision of the knowledge-based organization perceived it as a knowledge processing system having knowledge assets and populated by knowledge workers who employ their own knowledge processing skills (individually and in tandem) to produce value from those assets. Over the next decade, achievements of KM pioneers in a variety of organizations, plus the continuing onslaught of technological advances such as the World Wide Web, buttressed and enriched this vision. In the same time period, decision support systems became so ubiquitous as to be practically invisible, blending into the fabric of work in knowledge-based organizations. The growing challenge for harnessing technology in support of knowledge work was to better appreciate the nature of that work within and across organizations. This lcd me to investigations that were not primarily technological, but whose results contribute to a foundation for understanding and developing computer-based systems that enable or enhance the conduct of KM.

Over the early 1990s, these investigations yielded publications that examined connections between knowledge and such topics as organizational reputation, organizational learning, organizational coordination, organizational communication, organization design, organization infrastructure, and network organizations. My research from the latter 1990s into the new century has built on these efforts, leading to a collaboratively engineered KM ontology, studies of the essential knowledge-intensive nature of electronic business, and introduction of the knowledge chain model for analyzing organizational competitiveness along the four (PAIR) dimensions of productivity, agility, innovation, and reputation. In this latter phase, it became evident that the time is ripe for a basic KM reference work that integrates the myriad contributions of KM researchers into a cohesive structure. The *Handbook on Knowledge Management* is the fruit of that recognition and the cooperative, knowledge-sharing efforts of a host of contributing authors and reviewers.

Acknowledgements

I am very grateful for the participation of so many authoritative KM practitioners, scholars, and luminaries in contributing chapters to this book. The biographic sketches of these authors are testimony to their qualifications, and are symptomatic of the range and depth of coverage provided by the *Handbook*. I am also indebted to the small army of reviewers:

Maryam Alavi

Conan Albrecht

Suzie Allard

Elaine Allen

Sulin Ba

P. R. Balasubramanian

Julian Barling

Vedabrata Basu

Dustin Cavanaugh

Yolanda Chan

Hui-Wen Chang

Lei Chi

Mark Clare

Robert Cole

Ambrose Gerard Corray

Tom Coyne

Dan Davenport

Elsie Echeverri-Carroll

Rod French

David Gaines

Brent Gallupe

William Glick

Peter Gray

Sara Han

Edward Hartono

Mark Hefferman

Brad Heintz

Thomas Housel

Pamsy Hui

Lin Ji

Linda Johnson

Kiku Jones

George Kenaston

Jae Kyu Lee

Pengtao Li

Henry Linger

Mia Lustria

Rueben McDaniel, Jr.

James McKeen

Osman Meric

Partha Mohapatra

Joline Morrison

Satish Nargundkar

Mark Nissen

David Oehl

Ghanshyam Patel

Dennis Pearce

Chanisa Phangmuangdee

Lynda Pierce

Lisa M. Pirone

Jon Powell

Gilbert Probst

Arjan Ravan

Shereen Remez

Elsa Rhoades

Vernon Richardson

Melissie Rumizen

Sub Samaddar

Brian Schott

Larry Seligman

Sandra Smith

Maribel Soto

Frank Sowa

Valerie Spitler

Randy Stage

Rich Talipsky

Jean Tatalias

Eric Tsui

Robert Turner

Sony Warsono

Benson Wier

Michael Zack

John Zipfel

These persons generously donated their time to referee manuscripts submitted for potential inclusion in this book, offering insights, critiques, and suggestions. Their efforts contributed to the quality of this volume. I thank Karen Rivera and Edward Hartono for their assistance in preparing some of the chapters for publication. Finally, I thank Springer's Dr. Werner Mueller for his patience and guidance throughout the life of this project.

Clyde W. Holsapple, Editor

C.M. Gatton College of Business and Economics
University of Kentucky, Lexington, Kentucky, USA

Table of Contents

VOLUME 1: KNOWLEDGE MATTERS

PART I: FOUNDATIONS OF KNOWLEDGE MANAGEMENT

PART II. KNOWLEDGE: A KEY ORGANIZATIONAL RESOURCE

PART III. KNOWLEDGE PROCESSORS AND PROCESSING

VOLUME 2: KNOWLEDGE DIRECTIONS

PART V. TECHNOLOGIES FOR KNOWLEDGE MANAGEMENT

Contributors to Volume 1

Suzie Allard is currently chair of the American Society of Information Science and Technology's Special Interest Group on Digital Libraries. She is a Presidential Fellow and doctoral student in the College of Communications and Information Science at the University of Kentucky. Her professional background includes 18 years as a media consultant studying end-user reaction to various stimuli. She received the 2001 *American Communication Journal* Article of the Year Award for her article: "Erasing the Barrier between Minds: Freeing Information, Integrating Knowledge." Her research interests focus on digital libraries and knowledge management, particularly how the digital library environment facilitates knowledge creation and innovation by encouraging international information communication and document creation.

Debra M. Amidon is the Chairman and CEO of ENTOVATION International, Ltd. (Wilmington, MA) – a global innovation research and consulting network linking 80 countries throughout the world. She is the author of several books including *Managing the Knowledge Assets into the 21st Century, Global Innovation Strategy: Creating Value Added Alliances, Innovation Strategy for the Knowledge Economy: The Ken Awakening, Creating the Knowledge-Based Business,* and *Collaborative Innovation and the Knowledge Economy.* Considered an architect of the knowledge economy, her own specialties include knowledge management, learning networks, customer innovation, and enterprise transformation. Her presentations have been heard throughout the world and she has advised such diverse organizations as the National Research Council, the Agility Forum, the Industrial Research Institute, the European Union, the BBC, and the World Bank. With a seminal conference in 1987, she set in motion what has evolved to an expansive "community of knowledge practice" comprised of theorists and practitioners from diverse functions, sectors, industries and geographies. Ms. Amidon holds degrees from Boston University, Columbia University, and the Massachusetts Institute of Technology where she was an Alfred P. Sloan Fellow. Prior positions include service as Assistant Secretary of Education for the Commonwealth of Massachusetts, founding Executive Director of the Northeast Consortium of Colleges and Universities in Massachusetts, and Dean of Babson College. http://www.entovation.com

Alex Bennet, internationally recognized as an expert in knowledge management and an agent for organizational change, is the United States Department of the Navy (DON) Deputy Chief Information Officer for Enterprise Integration and the DON's Chief Knowledge Officer (CKO). During her 17 years with the DON she has served as Acquisition Reform Executive, Standards Improvement Executive, and Director of Communications, Education and Training for Acquisition Reform. She has over 500 published articles worldwide, primarily on Navy topics. Among her many awards and honors, Ms. Bennet is the recipient of the Department of the

Navy Superior Public Service Award and the National Performance Review Hammer Award from the Vice President of the United States. Ms. Bennet is a Delta Epsilon Sigma graduate of Marymount University and a Golden Key National Honor Society graduate of George Mason University. She holds degrees in Management for Organizational Effectiveness, English, and Marketing; graduate certificates in Total Quality Management, System Dynamics, and Defense Acquisition Management; a Master of Arts in Human Development; and is currently pursuing a Ph.D. in Human and Organizational Systems.

David H. Bennet is a cofounder, past CEO, and currently Chairman of the Board of Dynamic Systems, Inc. He has extensive experience in private industry, civil service and the military. He is the author of a comprehensive guide for the application of Integrated Product Teams (IPTs) that includes a 230-page book and flight simulator. Over 8,000 copies of the CD ROM have been distributed throughout the Department of Defense and industry. He has extensive experience in change management, organizational development, and systems thinking. He has recently co-authored several journal papers on the next generation knowledge organization. Mr. Bennet is a Phi Beta Kappa, graduating Suma Cum Laude from the University of Texas with Bachelor's degrees in Mathematics and Physics, and a Master's degree in Nuclear Physics. He also has a Master's of Liberal Arts from John Hopkins University. He is currently working on a doctorate in Human and Organizational Systems with a dissertation in knowledge management.

Richard Boland, Jr. is Professor of Information Systems and Professor of Accountancy in the Weatherhead School of Management at Case Western Reserve University, where he has received the Theodore M. Alfred Distinguished Service Award and the Research Recognition Award. He is also Senior Research Associate & Judge for the Institute for Management Studies, University of Cambridge. Previously, Dr. Boland was on the faculty of the University of Illinois. He holds BSBA and MBA degrees from Northwestern University and a Ph.D. degree from Case. His research interests are in the areas of qualitative studies of technology design and use, visual representation of knowledge, idea generation, and narrative as a cognitive mode. He has served as Editor of *Accounting, Management and Information Technologies* and Co-Editor of Wiley's *Series in Information Systems*. Dr. Boland's many publications have appeared in such periodicals as *Academy of Management Journal, Information and Organization, Organization Science, Management Science,* and *Accounting, Organizations and Society.*

Sven Carlsson is Professor of Informatics at Jönköping International Business School. He was previously Professor of Informatics at the School of Economics and Management, Lund University. His research interests include the use of information and communication technology (ICT) to support individual and group decision making, strategic knowledge managing, ICT support for knowledge creation and sharing, and design and redesign of e-business processes and electronic value chains and networks in turbulent and high-velocity environments. Professor Carlsson has been a visiting scholar at the University of Arizona and National

University of Singapore, and a visiting professor at the University of Southern California. His articles have appeared in such forums as in *Journal of Management Information Systems, Decision Sciences, Information and Management, Journal of Decision Systems,* and *International Journal of Technology Management.*

Yan Chen was in the doctoral program in the Department of Information Systems at the University of Maryland – Baltimore County when this research was performed. Her interests include knowledge management, information technology, and information systems management.

Susan D. Conway is Group Program Manager for Microsoft Consulting Services, Knowledge Management. She completed her bachelors and master level work at California State University, Northridge and has a Ph.D. in education from Columbia Pacific University. Her current work includes measurement and valuation of online communities and knowledge management. She has spent a number of years developing and managing corporate skills, resource allocation, and technical project management programs in large enterprises such as Texaco, Computer Sciences Corp, NCR, and Microsoft. Her skills management work was quoted in CIO magazine "The Skills that Thrill" (Jan. 15, 1997), http://www.cio.com/CIO/011597_skills_content.html

Leif Edvinsson is CEO of Universal Networking Intellectual Capital, holder of the world's first professorship on Intellectual Capital at Sweden's Lund University, and internationally recognized leading expert on Intellectual Capital (IC). As former vice president of Skandia of Stockholm, Sweden where he became the world's first corporate director of Intellectual Capital, he has been a key contributor to the theory of IC and oversaw the creation of the world's first corporate Intellectual Capital Annual Report. Mr. Edvinsson formerly was senior vice president for training and development of S-E Bank, and president and chairman of Consultus AB, a Stockholm-based consulting company. In light of his work in both training and IC, Edvinsson has been a special advisor on service trade to the Swedish Ministry of Foreign Affairs. He is also special adviser to the Swedish Cabinet on the effects of the new digital economy, special advisor to the United Nations International Trade Center, and co-founder of the Swedish Coalition of Service Industries. Mr. Edvinsson holds an MBA from the University of California, Berkeley. He is the author of numerous articles on the service industry and on Intellectual Capital, as well as the IC book *Realizing Your Company's True Value by Finding Its Hidden Brainpower.* He is a regular speaker before such organizations as the BBC, CIO, Conference Board, Economist, Handelsblatt, INSEAD, IMD, and APQC. In 1996, Mr. Edvinsson was awarded for his pioneering work on IC both by the American Productivity and Quality Center, USA, and Business Intelligence, UK. In 1998, he was named by the Brain Trust Foundation in England as "Brain of the Year" following in the footsteps of such illustrious former winners as Garry Kasparov (World Chess Champion) and Professor Stephen Hawking. In 2000, he was listed on top-20 list of the "Most Admired Knowledge Leaders" in the world. http://www.unic.net/

Omar El Sawy is a Professor in the Information and Operations Management Department of the Marshall School of Business at the University of Southern California. His Ph.D. is from Stanford University and he was previously with NCR Corporation. He teaches and consults in the areas of knowledge management, e-business, information systems management for global operations, and fast response management. Dr. El Sawy is a four-time winner of the Society for Information Management's international paper awards competition, most recently in 1997 for work on transforming value chains for the electronic economy. In 1997, he was a Fulbright scholar at the Swedish School of Economics and Business. He is the author of *Redesigning Enterprise Processes for e-Business* (McGraw-Hill, 2001) and articles in such journals as the *International Journal of Technology Management*, *Journal of Organizational Computing & Electronic Commerce*, *Information and Management*, and *MIS Quarterly*.

Martin J. Eppler is the Vice Director of the largest institute at the University of St. Gallen – the Institute for Media and Communications Management (www.mcm. unisg.ch). He is responsible for the Institute's market and research coordination, particularly in areas of Knowledge Management (www.knowledgemedia.org), Information and Content Quality (www.information-quality.ch), as well as strategy. Dr. Eppler teaches knowledge and communications management in the masters, Ph.D., and MBA programs of the University of St. Gallen, is a guest professor at the University of Lugano (both in Switzerland), and is on the board of a specialized new media consulting company. He studied communications, business administration, and social sciences at Boston University, the University of St. Gallen, the University of Geneva, and at the Paris Graduate School of Management (ESCP). His research examines issues such as information quality in knowledge-intensive processes, knowledge mapping techniques, knowledge strategy and knowledge branding, and personal knowledge management.

Dianne P. Ford received her B.A. Honours in Psychology (with a focus on developmental and social psychology) and her M.B.A. (with a focus on international business and organizational behaviour) from the University of Saskatchewan, Canada. She is currently a Ph.D. student in Management Information Systems and Organizational Behaviour at Queen's School of Business, Queen's University, Canada. Her research interests are in knowledge management, cross-cultural issues, organizational culture and leadership, trust, and adoption of technology.

Brian R. Gaines is Professor Emeritus at the University of Calgary where he was formerly Killam Memorial Research Professor, Dean of Graduate Studies, Associate Vice President (Research), and Director of the Knowledge Science Institute. His previous positions include Professor of Industrial Engineering at the University of Toronto, Technical Director and Deputy Chairman of the Monotype Corporation, and Chairman of the Department of Electrical Engineering Science at the University of Essex. He received his BA, MA and PhD from Trinity College, Cambridge, and is a Chartered Engineer, Chartered Psychologist, and a Fellow of the Institute of Electrical Engineers, the British Computer Society, and the British

Psychological Society. Dr. Gaines is Editor of the *International Journal of Human-Computer Studies* and *Knowledge Acquisition*, and of the *Computers and People* and *Knowledge-Based Systems* book series. He has authored over 400 papers and authored or edited 10 books on a wide variety of aspects of computer and human systems. His research interests include: the socio-economic dynamics of science and technology; the nature, acquisition, and transfer of knowledge; software engineering for heterogeneous systems; and knowledge-based system applications in manufacturing, the professions, sciences, and humanities. http://repgrid.com/reports/ http://repgrid.com/WebGrid/

C. Jackson Grayson, Jr. is founder of the American Productivity and Quality Center (APQC) and serves as its chairman. His academic experience includes professorships at Harvard, Stanford, Tulane, and SMU, and he was Dean of business schools at Tulane University and at SMU, where he became known for instituting innovations in business education. This extensive background in education led to the founding of APQC's Institute for Education Best Practices. Dr. Grayson became most widely known in 1971, when he was appointed Chairman of the United States Price Commission during the period of price-wage controls. Although few like controls, Dr. Grayson was accorded national recognition by the press, business people, and labor unions for fair and firm administration of the controls and for his work in helping to remove them. Later, as a co-sponsor of the first White House Conference on Productivity, APQC and Grayson actively fostered the national dialogue that led to the creation of the Malcolm Baldrige National Quality Award. Dr. Grayson is a CPA, has been on the boards of directors of a number of large corporations, has worked as a reporter for a New Orleans newspaper, a special agent of the FBI, a manager of a cotton farm in northern Louisiana, a member of an export-import firm, and an owner of race horses. He is the author of many articles and books such as *American Business: A Two-Minute Warning* and *If Only We Knew What We Know: The Transfer of Internal Knowledge and Best Practice*. He holds a bachelor's degree from Tulane University, an M.B.A. degree from the Wharton School of Business at the University of Pennsylvania, and a doctorate in business from the Harvard Business School. http://www.apqc.com

Meliha Handzic is a Senior Lecturer in the School of Information Systems, Technology and Management at the University of New South Wales, Australia where she has taught and researched in the areas of knowledge management and decision support since 1993. Dr. Handzic is also the inaugural leader of the *kmRg* (Knowledge Management Research Group) in the School of Information Systems Technology and Management at UNSW.

John C. Henderson is the Richard C. Shipley Professor of Management and the Chair of the Information Systems Department at Boston University's School of Management. He also serves as the Director of the Institute for Leading in a Dynamic Economy at Boston University's School of Management. He received his Ph.D. from the University of Texas at Austin. He is a noted researcher, consultant, and executive educator with published papers appearing in journals such as *Management Science*, *Sloan Management Review*, *MIS Quarterly*, *IBM Systems Journal*, *European Management Journal*, and many others. He is the co-author of *Knowledge Engine*, a book that examines how effective leaders leverage the firm's knowledge assets. His research focuses on four main areas: managing strategic partnerships, the impact of the mobile Internet on markets and organizations, valuing IT investments, and knowledge management.

Clyde W. Holsapple holds the University of Kentucky's Rosenthal Endowed Chair in Management Information Systems and is Professor of Decision Science and Information Systems. He has been recognized as *Computer Educator of the Year* by the International Association for Computer Information Systems, honored with the University of Kentucky *Chancellor's Award for Outstanding Teaching*, and recipient of the *R&D Excellence Program Award* presented by the Governor of Kentucky. His publication credits include more than a dozen books and 150 articles in journals and books, plus many conference proceedings papers. The books include *Foundations of Decision Support Systems* (1981), *Micro Database Management* (1984), *Manager's Guide to Expert Systems* (1986), *The Information Jungle: A Quasi-Novel Approach to Managing Corporate Knowledge* (1988), and *Decision Support Systems: A Knowledge Based Approach* (1996). His research articles have appeared in such journals as *Decision Sciences*, *Decision Support Systems*, *Operations Research*, *Communications of the ACM*, *The Computer Journal*, *Journal of Operations Management*, *Omega*, *Policy Sciences*, *Organization Science*, *Human Communication Research*, *Journal of Organizational Computing and Electronic Commerce*, *Group Decision and Negotiation*, *Expert Systems*, *IEEE Expert*, *Expert Systems with Applications*, *Knowledge Acquisition*, *Knowledge and Process Management*, *Knowledge and Policy*, *Database*, *Journal of Strategic Information Systems*, *Information and Management*, and *Journal of Management Information Systems*. Professor Holsapple has served in editorial positions for scholarly journals such as *Decision Support Systems* and *Management Science*, as a tenured faculty member at the University of Illinois and at Purdue University, and as Director of the *Kentucky Initiative for Knowledge Management* since its inception in 1988. His B.S. (mathematics), M.S. (computer science), and Ph.D. (management science) degrees are from Purdue University. http://www.uky.edu/BusinessEconomics/dssakba/

Rodger Jamieson is an Associate Professor in the School of Information Systems, Technology and Management at the University of New South Wales, Australia where has taught and conducted research in the areas of security and audit of information systems, including e-commerce and knowledge management systems, since 1982. He has been awarded the prestigious UNSW Vice Chancellor's Award for Teaching Excellence. Dr. Jamieson is also the Director of the *SEAR* (Security, e-Business and Assurance Research) group. He holds a Ph.D., as well as honours degrees at both Bachelor and Master of Commerce levels, from the University of New South Wales. He is a qualified Chartered Accountant, member of the Information Systems Audit and Control Association, and spent eight years with Touche

Ross & Co. and Coopers & Lybrand as a chartered accountant. Dr Jamieson has been a visiting faculty member at the University of Southern California, Sydney University, and at the City University Business School, London. He has won the UK Literati Club outstanding paper award and the IS Auditors' inaugural award for publication excellence.

Murray E. Jennex is an Assistant Professor at San Diego State University and President of the Foundation for Knowledge Management, LLC. Dr. Jennex specializes in knowledge management, organizational memory, system analysis and design, and organizational effectiveness. He has managed projects for Y2K and in applied engineering, business, and information systems development and implementation. He holds a B.A. in chemistry and physics from William Jewell College, an M.B.A. and an M.S. in Software Engineering from National University, and an M.S. in Telecommunications Management and Ph.D. in Information Systems from the Claremont Graduate University. Dr. Jennex is a registered professional mechanical engineer.

Robert A. Josefek, Jr. is an Assistant Professor of information and operations management at the University of Southern California. His Ph.D. is from the Carlson School of Business at the University of Minnesota where he also taught. Since 1997, Dr Josefek has been conducting a series of studies related to information technology skills and workforce management. His other research interests include technology strategy, economics, and investment.

K. D. Joshi is an Assistant Professor in the School of Accounting, Information Systems, and Business Law at Washington State University. She holds a BA in Mathematical Statistics and an MA in Operational Research from the University of Delhi. She also earned an MS degree in Industrial and Operations Engineering from the University of Michigan. Dr. Joshi holds a Ph.D. in Decision Science and Information Systems from University of Kentucky. She has worked as Data Archive Specialist at the Institute of Social Research. Her research articles have been published in *Decision Support Systems, Information Systems Journal, Journal of Strategic Information Systems, The Information Society, Information and Management, Communications of the ACM, Knowledge Management Handbook,* and *Handbook of Electronic Commerce.* Her research has been funded by the National Science Foundation.

Timothy R. Kayworth is an Assistant Professor in Information Systems at Baylor University's Hankamer School of Business. His current research interest centers on the management of information technology in organizations. He has published a number of articles in well-respected journals such as the *Journal of Management Information Systems* and the *DATABASE for Advances in Information Systems,* as well conference proceedings at *Americas Conference on Information Systems (AMCIS)* and *The International Conference on Information Systems (ICIS).* His work has included such topics as virtual team leadership, the role of the CIO, and the role of corporate IT infrastructure standards. Dr. Kayworth holds a Ph.D. in Information Systems from Florida State University.

Dorothy E. Leidner is Associate Professor of information systems and eBusiness at Texas Christian University in Ft Worth, Texas. Dorothy received her Ph.D. in Information Systems from the University of Texas at Austin, where she also obtained her MBA and BA. She has previously been on the faculty at Baylor University and at INSEAD. She has also been a visiting professor at the Instituto Tecnologico y des Estudios Superiores de Monterrey, Mexico, at the Institut d'Administration des Entreprises at the Universite de Caen, France, and at Southern Methodist University in Dallas, Texas. Dr. Leidner has published her research in many journals, including *MIS Quarterly, Information Systems Research, Organization Science,* and the *Journal of Management Information Systems.* She received the Best Published Article Award from OCIS division of the Academy of Management in 2000, the Best Scholarly Contribution award from *MIS Quarterly* in 1995, and the Best Paper Award from the Hawaii International Conference on System Sciences, Decision Support Systems Track, in 1993. She is co-editor of the journal *Data Base for Advances in Information Systems.*

Jay Liebowitz performed this work while serving as the Robert W. Deutsch Distinguished Professor of Information Systems at the University of Maryland-Baltimore County. He currently is the Knowledge Management Officer at the NASA Goddard Space Flight Center. Previously, he served as Professor of Management Science at George Washington University and the Chair of Artificial Intelligence at the US Army War College. He has been a Fulbright Scholar, IEEE-USA Federal Communications Commission Executive Fellow, and International Association for Computer Information Systems Computer Educator of the Year. Dr. Liebowitz is founder and editor of *Expert Systems with Applications: An International Journal,* published by Elsevier.

Doug Macnamara is President and CEO of Banff Executive Leadership Inc. He has over 25 years of experience in leadership, governance & executive development, strategic facilitation and overall organizational development. He has specialized in strategy formulation and implementation, wilderness/high risk environments, organizational leadership, branding, and sales/marketing/service development. He has served as Vice President of The Banff Centre and General Manager of The Banff Centre for Management, where he led the development of dedicated programming areas for Aboriginal Leadership and Management, as well as Community and Not-for-Profit Leadership. His background also includes several years at Royal Trust responsible for leading strategic planning, management development, and technical training. He holds degrees in biochemistry, environmental, and adult education. Doug is an active speaker and executive retreat facilitator on such topics as leadership, value, and systems. He currently serves as Chair of the Board of The Banff Mineral Springs Hospital and is a member of the Board of the National Geographic Television channel.

Yogesh Malhotra holds a professorial appointment at Syracuse University, prior to which he taught in the Executive MBA programs at Kellogg and Carnegie Mellon. Dr. Malhotra has published two books on knowledge management and served as editor or reviewer for more than a dozen leading research journals. His experience

includes roles of advisor and thought leader for Intel, British Telecom, Ziff Davis, Hewlett Packard, Arthur Andersen, South Korean technology companies, Government of Netherlands, and, U.S. Government Federal Agencies; founding Chairman and CKO of BRINT, the globally branded knowledge management and strategic innovation firm with clients such as IBM, Microsoft, Hewlett Packard, Ogilvy & Mather, Chiatt Day, Foote Cone, and Silicon Valley B2B enterprises; and, technology and innovation leadership roles with other world reputed companies in IT, finance and banking, healthcare, and manufacturing sectors. His works and interviews have received coverage in *Business Week, Wall Street Journal, Fortune, Fast Company, Business 2.0, CIO Magazine, Computerworld, Information Week, KM World,* and other worldwide media channels. He has delivered invited keynotes and speeches to senior most executives of Baldrige Quality Award winning companies; Silicon Valley tech firms and venture capitalists; national knowledge management experts of South Korea; and CIOs and top IT executives in the Government of Mexico.
http://www.brint.com/ http://www.yogeshmalhotra.com/

James D. McKeen is Professor of MIS at the School of Business, Queen's University at Kingston, Canada. He received his Ph.D. in MIS at the University of Minnesota and is the Founding Director of the Queen's Centre for Knowledge-Based Enterprises, a research think-tank for the knowledge economy. His research interests include IT strategy, user participation, the management of the IS function, and KM in organizations. Dr. McKeen's research is published in the *MIS Quarterly,* the *Journal of Information Technology Management,* the *Journal of Systems and Software, Communications of the Association of Information Systems,* the *International Journal of Management Reviews, Information and Management, Communications of the ACM, Computers and Education, JMIS,* and *Database.*

Robert E. Neilson is Chief Knowledge Officer and Professor at the Information Resources Management College of the National Defense University (NDU), Washington, D.C. Through graduate-level academic programs at NDU, he prepares senior military leaders to direct the information component of national power by leveraging information and information technology for strategic advantage. His latest books include *Collaborative Technologies and Organizational Learning* (Idea Group Publishing) and *Sun Tzu and Information Warfare* (NDU Press). As an Institute for National Strategic Studies Faculty Research Fellow, Dr. Neilson examines (1) knowledge management as a strategic enabler with the national security community, and (2) Information Operations in the 21st Century.

Brian (Bo) Newman is the founder of the original *Knowledge Management Forum,* one of the first virtual communities of practice in Knowledge Management. Speaking and writing to international audiences, he is recognized as a champion for solid theoretical foundations upon which to build the practice. His primary research concentrations have been on the dynamics of the knowledge life cycle and establishing improved models for understanding the ways knowledge is developed, stored, transferred, and used within organizations. His work draws on over 25 years of service to a wide range of organizations in both the government and the private sector. http://www.km-forum.org/

Carla O'Dell is President of the American Productivity & Quality Center and serves as director of its International Benchmarking Clearinghouse. Dr. O'Dell's work in knowledge management dates back to 1995, when APQC and Arthur Andersen conducted the nation's largest symposium on KM with more than 500 attendees. Based on issues raised at the symposium, APQC launched, under Dr. O'Dell's direction, its first knowledge management consortium study, Emerging Best Practices in Knowledge Management, with 39 organizations. She also led APQC's second study, Using Information Technology to Support Knowledge Management, with 25 of the world's leading KM organizations. Dr. O'Dell is co-author with Dr. C. Jackson Grayson of *American Business: A Two-Minute Warning*, which Tom Peters said "gets my vote as the best business book in 1988." Also with Dr. Grayson, she co-authored *If Only We Knew What We Know: The Transfer of Internal Knowledge and Best Practice* (Simon & Schuster. 1998). She publishes several business journal articles each year. A frequent keynote speaker at senior executive events who appears often on business television, Dr. O'Dell holds a bachelor's degree with Stanford University, a master's degree from the University of Oregon, and a Ph.D. in industrial and organization psychology from the University of Houston. http://www.apqc.com

Lorne Olfman is Dean of the School of Information Science and Professor of Information Science at Claremont Graduate University. He came to Claremont in 1987 after graduating with a PhD in Business (Management Information Systems) from Indiana University. Lorne's research interests include: how software can be learned and used in organizations, the impact of computer-based systems on organizational memory, and the design and adoption of systems used for group work. A key component of Lorne's teaching is his involvement with doctoral students; he has supervised 24 students to completion. Lorne is an active member of the Information Systems community and has published in such periodicals as the *Information Systems Journal, Journal of Management Information Systems, ACM Transactions on Computer Human Interaction, Decision Support Systems, Database, MIS Quarterly,* and *International Journal of Man-Machine Studies.*

Paul Romer is the Dean Witter Foundation Senior Research Fellow at the Hoover Institution. He is also the STANCO 25 Professor of Economics in the Graduate School of Business at Stanford University. Formerly, he was Professor of economics at the University of California at Berkeley and on the faculties at the University of Rochester and the University of Chicago. Dr. Romer is an expert in economic growth theory, is currently researching the determinants of long-run economic growth, policy decisions about science and technology, transfer policies, and entitlement issues. He a member of the board of editors of the *American Economic Review*, a Fellow of the Econometric Society, a research associate of the National Bureau of Economic Research, and the Royal Bank Fellow of the Canadian Institute for Advanced Research. His work has been widely covered in the business press and has appeared in such scholarly periodicals as *Econometrica, Journal of Political Economy, American Economic Review, Journal of Economic Theory, Quarterly Journal of Economics, European Economic Review, Economic Theory, Journal of Monetary Economics,* and *Journal of Development Economics.*

He studied mathematics and physics as an undergraduate at the University of Chicago. After starting his graduate work in economics at MIT, he returned to the University of Chicago where he received his Ph.D. in economics.

Subhashish Samaddar is Assistant Professor of Information Technology and Decision Sciences in the Department of Management at the J. Mack Robinson College of Business and Technology, Georgia State University. He holds a Ph.D. in Operations Management from Kent State University, and was formerly the State Farm Associate Professor of Information Management and Decision Sciences at Western Illinois University. His current research interests include planning, design, and control issues of modern organizational systems, information technology and application of OR/MS and artificial intelligence techniques to organizational problems. His recent articles have been published in *Management Science, Omega, Communications of the ACM, Interfaces, International Journal of Flexible Manufacturing Systems, International Journal of Computer Applications and Technologies, International Journal of Operations and Production Management, Human Systems Management,* and *Computers and Industrial Engineering.* Dr. Samaddar has worked as a systems engineer with ACC-Vickers and Babcock Ltd. and Tractors India Ltd. (a subsidiary of Coles of U.K.), and since 1999, he has worked as the Chief Knowledge Officer of VoiceCore Corporation.

Ulrike Schultze is Assistant Professor in Information Technology and Operations Management at Southern Methodist University. She joined SMU's Cox School of Business in 1997. Her research focuses on the impact of information technology on work practices and she has been particularly interested in knowledge work, i.e., the social processes of creating and using information in organizations. Dr. Schultze has written on hard and soft information genres, information overload, knowledge management, and knowledge workers' informing practices. Her more recent projects are in the areas of electronic business. Dr. Schultze serves on the editorial boards of *MIS Quarterly* and *Information and Organization.* She received her bachelor's and master's degree in Management Information Systems from the University of the Witwatersrand in Johannesburg, South Africa, and her Ph.D. in MIS from Case Western Reserve University.

Heather A. Smith is a Senior Research Associate in the School of Business at Queen's University, Kingston, Canada. She is also a Research Associate with the Society for Information Management, Chair of the IT Excellence Awards University Advisory Council, and Co-facilitator of Queen's Knowledge Management Forum. A recognized authority on IT and knowledge management, she works with organizations to identify and document leading edge practices and to bring the best of academic research to practicing managers. In this role, she works extensively with groups of CIOs and CKOs to facilitate inter-organizational learning. Her research is published in the *Journal of Information Technology Management, Database, Communications of the Association of Information Systems, CIO Canada,* and *Government CIO.*

J.-C. Spender is Dean of the School of Business & Technology at the Fashion Institute of Technology (State University of New York) in Manhattan, New York. His initial business experience was in nuclear engineering, computing, and banking. His academic interest has always been in the nature, sources, and extent of managerial knowledge. His Ph.D. thesis, eventually published as *Industry Recipes; An Enquiry into the Nature and Sources of Managerial Judgement* (Blackwell, Oxford, 1989), won the Academy of Management's A. T. Kearney Prize in 1980. Dr. Spender's recent work, directed towards a knowledge-based theory of the firm, aspires to be a footnote to Edith Penrose's *The Theory of the Growth of the Firm* (Wiley, New York, 1959).

D. Sandy Staples is an Assistant Professor of MIS in the School of Business at Queen's University, Kingston, Canada. Sandy received his Ph.D. from the Richard Ivey School of Business at The University of Western Ontario, specializing in MIS. His research interests include the enabling role of information systems for virtual work and knowledge management, and assessing the effectiveness of information systems and IS practices. Sandy has published articles in various journals including *Organization Science, Journal of Strategic Information Systems, Journal of Management Information Systems, Communications of the Association of Information Systems, International Journal of Management Reviews, Business Quarterly, Journal of End-User Computing,* and *OMEGA*, and he currently serves on the Editorial Advisory Board of the *Journal of End User Computing.*

Dan N. Stone, C.P.A., holds the Gatton Chair of Accountancy at the University of Kentucky and was formerly Senior Research Scientist for the National Center for Supercomputing Applications and a tenured faculty member at the University of Illinois. He received a joint Ph.D. degree in accounting and management information systems from the University of Texas at Austin in 1987. Dr. Stone is Editor of the American Accounting Association's *Journal of Information Systems.* He has published over 35 academic works, including articles, essays, short stories, and poetry in a such journals as the *Journal of Accounting Research, Decision Sciences, Accounting, Organizations, and Society, International Journal of Man-Machine Studies, Organizational Behavior and Human Decision Processes,* and *Auditing: A Journal of Theory and Practice.* He does research, consults, and teaches on the topics of knowledge management, accounting systems and controls, and technology in organizations.

John S. Storck earned his doctorate at Boston University after many years of industry and consulting experience, including positions as Vice President of the Chase Manhattan Bank, responsible for European operations and systems, and a manager in the Deloitte & Touche information systems consulting practice in New York, Madrid, and Milan. Dr. Storck is a professor in the Information Systems Department at the Boston University School of Management, where he has served as Director of the Master of Science Program in Management Information Systems. His research on the development of strategic knowledge management capabilities for global organizations examines the nature of individual and group work in the knowledge economy, with a particular emphasis on how communities of practice enhance knowledge diffusion and learning. His work on knowledge management has been published in the *Sloan Management Review* and the *IBM Systems Journal,* as well as in books and the trade press.

Jacky Swan is a Professor in organizational behaviour at Warwick Business School, University of Warwick, UK. She is also Director of the Innovation, Knowledge and Organizational Networks (IKON) Research Unit. Her research has focused on the role of networks in the design and diffusion of Information Technologies (including cross-national comparative analysis). Dr. Swan's current research in knowledge management focuses on the processes of knowledge creation and diffusion in innovation projects across a variety of industrial sectors. She has published widely in these areas in leading international journals and is also co-author of a forthcoming book *Managing Knowledge Work* (Palgrave MacMillan).

David J. Teece is an applied industrial organization economist who has studied and consulted on issues on technological change, technology transfer, and intellectual property for over 2 decades. He is the Mitsubishi Bank Professor at the Haas School of Business at University of California, Berkeley where he also directs the Institute of Management, Innovation and Organization. Professor Teece has a Ph.D. in Economics from the University of Pennsylvania and has held teaching and research positions at Stanford University and Oxford University. He has authored over 100 books and articles including, "When is Virtual Virtuous? Organizing for Innovation," *Harvard Business Review*, January-February 1996 (with Hank Chesbrough), *Fundamental Issues in Strategy: A Research Agenda*, (Harvard Business School Press, 1994) (with Richard P. Rumelt and Dan Schendel), "Profiting from Technological Innovation," *Research Policy*, 1986, and *Managing Intellectual Capital*, (Oxford University Press, 2000).

Sony Warsono is a faculty member of the Accounting Department and Magister Management at Gadjah Mada University, Yogyakarta, Indonesia. His research interests include investigating how knowledge assets influence firm value, and the impact of research and development joint ventures on business performance. He is presently working on a doctoral degree in accounting at the University of Kentucky.

Thomas Whalen is Professor of Decision Sciences at Georgia State University and holds a Ph.D. in Systems Science from Michigan State University. His research focuses on the application of approximate reasoning to decision making under generalized uncertainty, especially in the fuzzy area between ignorance and risk. Dr. Whalen has published more than 100 papers in major conference proceedings and academic journals, including *Human Systems Management, International Journal of Man-Machine Studies, IEEE Technology and Society Magazine,* and *IEEE Transactions on Systems, Man and Cybernetics*. He is a senior member of the Institute of Electrical and Electronics Engineers and a member of the board of directors of the North American Fuzzy Information Processing Society.

Youngjin Yoo is an Assistant Professor of information systems in the Weatherhead School at Case Western Reserve University. His BA and MBA degrees are from Seoul National University and his Ph.D. is from the University of Maryland. Dr. Yoo's research interests include knowledge management, virtual team management, and information technology for organizational transformation. His research has appeared in such publications as *MIS Quarterly, Journal of Management Education, Academy of Management Journal,* and *Information Systems Management.*

Foundations of Knowledge Management

Part I

Foundations of Knowledge Management

Part I of the Handbook on Knowledge Management *examines foundations for understanding the knowledge management field. In "The Rise of the Knowledge Organization," David and Alex Bennet trace an evolution of organizations that has led to the emergence of enterprises that focus on networking, knowledge creation, knowledge distribution, and knowledge application. These knowledge-based, knowledge-intensive, knowledge-centric organizations are systems of knowledge assets and knowledge processors. The central focus of this book is on the nature, operations, challenges, outcomes, and possibilities of these knowledge organizations.*

In Chapter 2, Jim McKeen and Sandy Staples report on a survey of practicing knowledge managers. It reveals characteristics of these key individuals who are responsible for designing an organization's knowledge management initiatives and for making them successful. The authors' analysis yields a portrait of the "typical" knowledge manager encountered in today's organizations as well as an identification of traits belonging to the knowledge management role in these organizations.

Chapter 3 delves into the nature of knowledge work performed within and across organizations. Here, Ulrike Schultze describes and discusses knowledge work from each of three perspectives: economic, labor process, and work practice. She also examines criticisms and affordances of treating knowledge work as a distinct category of work in today's organizations.

In "Knowledge Fields," J. C. Spender explores the knowledge-based theory of the firm. An organization's knowledge field is comprised of a dynamic synthesis of the incomplete, constrained, and fragmented knowledge at its disposal. Importantly, this field is shaped by those who create and inhabit it. The chapter portrays alternative views on how this structuring and contouring of a knowledge field is approached: a flat, emotionless, mechanical approach; an asset approach shaped by transaction costs; an approach in which organizational power structures among participants shape the knowledge field; and an approach that recognizes emotional dimensions and dependencies among an organization's participants in their continuing efforts to effect a useful synthesis of available knowledge.

Chapter 5 is concerned with the issue of how knowledge-based organizations form and operate in a knowledge economy. Here, Paul Romer outlines this new economy, contrasting it with the traditional physical economy of extracting, assembling, and producing material goods. A pivotal notion is the principle of increasing (rather than diminishing) returns that can accrue to knowledge-based organizations. "The Knowledge Economy," not only describes and illustrates this principle, but also contends that knowledge plays a crucial role in propelling economic growth and deserves the careful attention of policy makers.

Part I closes with "A Knowledge Management Ontology" which gives a common language for discourse concerning the domain of knowledge management. Constructed in a collaborative fashion, this ontology identifies and characterizes an organization's conduct of knowledge management in terms of several basic components: knowledge management episodes, knowledge resources used in these episodes, knowledge manipulation activities that operate on these resources, and influences on the manifestation and outcomes of knowledge management episodes. Parts II-VI of the Handbook *are structured along the lines of this ontology.*

Together, chapters in Part I make the case that knowledge matters to modern organizations, from their operations to their strategic planning. These knowledge-based organizations thrive on knowledge resources, processing, infusions, and flows. Their success depends on nurturing, knowledge-centric management that is attentive to a host of knowledge matters. Part I lays the foundation for considering these knowledge matters in the remainder of the volume.

CHAPTER 1

The Rise of the Knowledge Organization[*]

David Bennet¹ and Alex Bennet²

¹ Chairman of the Board and Chief Knowledge Officer, Dynamic Systems, Inc.

² United States Department of the Navy Deputy Chief Information Officer for Enterprise Integration and Co-Chair, Federal Knowledge Management Working Group

The progress of humanity has been predominantly due to the effectiveness of organizations to achieve human pursuits. Organizations have always made use of knowledge and technology to survive. With the rise of large corporations in the early twentieth century came a strong interest in research in management and organizational theory. The awareness of the importance of information and knowledge, followed by a constant search for ways to create, store, integrate, tailor, share, and make available the right knowledge to the right people at the right time, led to the birth of knowledge management in the 1990s. Knowledge organizations, currently in their embryonic form, focus on networking and knowledge creation, sharing, and application. The ultimate challenge of the future is to liberate and amplify the knowledge and creativity of all organizational members, which will enable the rise of the knowledge organization.

Keywords: Knowledge Organization; Bureaucratic Organization; Organizational Theory; World Class Organizations; Evolution Of Organizations; Intelligent Complex Adaptive System (ICAS); Learning Organization

1 Introduction

The progress of humanity over the past 30,000 years has been predominantly due to the effectiveness of the organizations used to achieve human goals. For example, religious goals have been achieved through organizational structures developed by the world's major religions. Economic progress throughout history has been driven by commerce and business organizations. Political organizations have both provided stability and been the catalyst for change.

Organizational systems have internal structures that mediate roles and relationships among people working toward some identifiable objective. These internal structures, together with cultural, leadership, and management characteristics, provide the ability to effectively interact with their environment and achieve desired goals.

Organizations have a much longer history than is usually understood. While a study of evolution demonstrates the ubiquitous role of interactions and relation-

---

* First published in *Knowledge Management: The Catalyst for Electronic Government.* Vienna, VA: Management Concepts, 2001. Reprinted with permission.

ships among all life, the beginnings of structure, function, and dedicated efforts to meet objectives through intention, planned action, and individual roles had to wait until homo sapiens reached the hunter gatherer/agriculture transition.

Since the early hunter gatherer, circa 35,000 B.C., the success of small bands of humans gathering berries, leaves, and grubs and occasionally hunting larger animals is clear from the world-wide distribution of archeological sites where human colonies lived. Environmental forces demanded specific actions for survival, leading to the development of culture via the need and propensity to cooperate. Thus began the first attempts at structure and organization, driven by the same forces that drive organizations 37,000 years later: threats and opportunities in the environment and a strong desire to survive and achieve goals.

As demonstrated in this human activity, organizations usually existed through a successful balance between the forces in their environment and their own creativity and adaptivity. The boundary between the organization and its environment is almost always porous, flexible, and foggy. This frequently unpredictable external environment is driven by physical, political, sociological, economic, natural, and technological forces.

Organizations, a product of homo sapiens' superb cognitive and linguistic capabilities, have always made use of knowledge and one of its offspring, technology, to survive during their hour on the stage of history. An early example of this occurs during the eighteenth through twentieth Egyptian dynasties (1550 to 1069 B.C.). The Overseer of All the King's Works – a man of science, an architect, and the authority figure – directed the massive labor force required to build a pyramid. "His palette and papyrus scrolls were the symbols of the authority of knowledge, and bureaucratic lists and registers were the tools of political and economic power." (Silverman, 1997). Knowledge, demonstrated by writing, provided the authority, and the use of technology (in the form of pulleys, levers and wheels) provided the means.

The success of the Taizong dynasty (626-49 A.D.) was a direct result of Taizong's strong leadership and management approaches built on a solid cultural and military base. While building and stocking the latest instruments of war, Taizong used literature to spread manners and guide customs. He instituted a system of state schools and colleges (one reserved for children of the Imperial family) and gave the highest positions in the government to those who passed literary exams. Thus, Taizong not only recognized the value of learning and knowledge, but also used it to expand the Imperial family's influence throughout the empire.

Throughout history, the environment has become increasingly complex, dynamic, and technologically sophisticated. In response, organizations have become more complex, more flexible, and more egalitarian, with success very much dependent on making optimum use of all available information, experience and insight.

The technology revolution of the late 1700s began with the invention of the steam engine and ultimately brought about factories and mass production. With the emergence of the tycoons of oil, railroads, steel, and automobiles came the rise of the modern bureaucracy and the great test of its precepts of specialists and rigid rules. While economically successful, it took a large toll on human freedom. Specialization, limited learning and initiative, and assembly lines made mechanical robots out of workers. As new technology was developed, it was frequently misunderstood or misapplied and ended up restricting employees rather than liberating their potential.

2 The Bureaucratic Organization

Max Weber (1864-1920) developed the formal theory recognized today as the bureaucratic model. Weber, a lawyer familiar with power politics, economics, and religion, migrated to sociology through his attempt to understand how capitalism came into existence. His world of ideas was multidimensional.

The bureaucratic framework created by Max Weber in the late 1800s called for a hierarchical structure, clear division of labor, rule and process orientation, impersonal administration, rewards based on merit, decisions and rules in writing, and management separated from ownership. The bureaucratic model was built on management power over workers in what Weber called "imperative control." The key success factors of Weber's bureaucracy rested on authority and its acceptance by workers, and on the design and management of processes and rigid rules and procedures.

Weber linked knowledge with power. He believed that "Every bureaucracy seeks to increase the superiority of the professionally informed by keeping their knowledge and intentions secret." (Gerth and Mills, 1946). Because the pure interest of the bureaucracy is power, secrecy would grow with the increase of bureaucracy. We still live with the legacy of this intent.

With the rise of large corporations in the early twentieth century came a strong interest in research in fields such as leadership, management, organizational theory, and capitalism. Frederick Taylor, Henri Fayol, Mary Parker Follet, Chester Bernard, Adam Smith, Herbert Simon, Abraham Maslow, etc. (the list goes on and on), all contributed to the foundational research and set of organizational concepts of the early twentieth century. This era created the formal foundation of management and organizational theory. Although the origins lay in Weber's bureaucracy, church and state autocracy and military leadership, these were all modified by the social, political, and capitalistic drives in the free world after World War II. The new theories and concepts such as Theory X, Theory Y, Theory Z, Charismatic and Transformational Leadership, General Systems Theory, and Organizational Linking Pins, became popular and a noticeable shift occurred from bureaucracy toward a more benign and malleable organizational structure. Tools such as Management by Exception, Span of Control, Kurt Lewin's Force Field Analysis, and Taichi Ohno's Toyota Production Line techniques helped both managers and workers implement change throughout their organizations. While some changes occurred, most organizations continued to be hierarchical. Knowledge and information were held close by supervisors and managers and protected as knowledge and information represented personal power and authority. Economic progress was relatively steady and, until the 1970s, fairly predictable. During this post-bureaucratic era, the key factors were a combination of Tayloristic time and motion management and participative management, slowly bringing some of the workforce into the arena of worker responsibility and empowerment.

As the affluence, mobility, and expectations of the workforce in developed countries continued to rise, coupled with the explosive growth of information and communication technologies, and the creation of knowledge, organizations found themselves in situations of restructure or collapse. The old mechanical metaphor would no longer serve in the nonlinear, dynamic, complex global web of the mid 1990s. Many organizations failed, some were acquired, and the best set about seeking the popular vision of the "world-class" corporation. The stage was now set for the rise of information and knowledge organizations, with the information organizations taking the lead via computers and communications technology in the early 1980s and 1990s and the knowledge organizations, currently in their embryonic form, focusing on networking and knowledge creation, sharing, and application.

Because we will use three terms extensively in describing the current and future organization, it is important to communicate what we mean by data, information, and knowledge. Data are discrete, objective facts about events, including numbers, letters, and images without context. Information is data with some level of meaning. It is usually presented to describe a situation or condition and, therefore, has added value over data. Knowledge is built on data and information and created within the individual. Knowledge, of course, has many levels and is usually related to a given domain of interest. In its strongest form, knowledge represents understanding of the context, insights into the relationships within a system, and the ability to identify leverage points and weaknesses and to understand future implications of actions taken to resolve problems. Thus knowledge represents a richer and more meaningful awareness and understanding that resonates with how the "knower" views the world. Knowledge is frequently considered actionable.

3   Organizations of the Year 2000

Time accelerates. Distance shrinks. Networks expand. Interdependencies grow geometrically. Uncertainty dominates. Complexity overwhelms. Such is the environment and the context within which current organizations must survive and thrive.

This situation is a result of many years of evolution driven by a number of major factors. Of significance is the increasing economic affluence of the worker in the developed countries coupled with their increased education level, resulting in a strong demand by workers to be recognized, respected, and allowed to participate and have determination in their work. Economics and technology provide both the means and pressures for mobility, thereby giving workers the freedom to leave their jobs for other, more challenging positions. While the last 50 years have seen many ups and downs in terms of employment, productivity, interest rates, investments, etc., the recent decades have provided increasing wealth and economic success.

Consistent with this history, every organization lives at the pleasure of its environment – economic, sociological, scientific, technological, and political. For example, state charters legitimize corporations, Occupational Safety and Health Administration (OSHA) and the Department of Labor mandate tight restrictions on both safety and personnel regulations, the Environmental Protection Agency (EPA) regulates organizational behavior relative to environmental impact, and the business media heavily influence corporate stock values depending upon local and temporal events. Technology plays a dominant role in determining both the landscape of competition and the cultural and educational needs of the workforce. It is arguably true that technology has played the strongest role in creating the present environment within which organizations must adapt and learn how to excel compared to their competitors. For example, tremendous increases in processing speed, communication bandwidth, miniaturization of technology (nanotechnology), and the development of complex algorithms and application programs have spawned the rapidly changing pace of society and the increasing need and capability for communication, collaboration, and networking, both virtual and real. The phenomenal rise of the Internet, coupled with the spin-offs of intranets, extranets, portals, etc., have created a networking potential that drives all of society and corporations in terms of speed, interdependencies, global markets, and the creation and spread of memes instantaneously throughout the world. Memes are ideas that become a part of the culture. Those organizations that have found ways to compete successfully within this nonlinear, complex, and dynamic environment may dominate their competitors by as much as twenty-five percent in growth rate and profitability relative to the average in their industry.

Specific characteristics of these "world class" organizations are key to their success. Consider the distribution of all organizations within the United States versus their normalized performance (i.e., the number of organizations having a specific level of performance plotted along the vertical axis and performance along the horizontal axis). This graph would likely be represented by the commonly known bell curve, with the high performing organizations represented at the far right of that bell curve. While most of today's organizations are far from this world class region, many are working hard to improve their performance, that is, efficiency, effectiveness and sustained competitive advantage, in order to improve their competitive status and in some cases prevent being acquired or going into bankruptcy.

Often the tools, methods, structures, and principles that the best organizations have found to drive high performance are neither new nor, in many cases, unique. For example, many of the ideas that Toyota created in the late 1940s and early 1950s relative to lean manufacturing in the automobile industry (although refined and improved) are still considered world class, and, in fact, Toyota is considered by many to be the leader throughout the world in automobile manufacturing (Womack, et al., 1990). Taichi Ohno created the Toyota production system just after World War II as a response to potential bankruptcy and changing consumer demands (Shingo, 1989). The system eventually included just-in-time supply parts delivery, floor workers in the factory taking responsibility for product quality and having authority to stop the production line, and teams of workers solving problems on the factory floor and learning cross-functional jobs to insure continuous production line flows. Recognize that it took Toyota more than twenty years to create its present system, and it is still being improved. Approximately fifty years later many of these early ideas are still considered best practices and used by manufacturing organizations worldwide. They represent a significant departure from the bureaucratic hierarchy chain of command and minimum freedom of the worker.

In *Built to Last*, Collins and Porras did a six-year study of eighteen companies that had outstanding performance over time periods between fifty and two hundred years. Reviewing their results, together with other research on long-lived world-class companies, we offer the following factors as representative of long-term, highly successful organizations:

- Continuous striving to improve themselves and doing better tomorrow than what they did today, always remaining sensitive to their customers and their environment.

- Not focusing on profitability alone, but balancing their efforts to include employee quality of life, community relations, environmental concerns, customer satisfaction and stakeholder return.

- A willingness to take risks with an insistence that they be prudent and have an overall balanced risk portfolio. In general, they were financially conservative.

- A strong feeling about their core ideology, changing it seldom, if ever. Their core values form a solid foundation and, while each company's individual values were unique, once created, they were not allowed to drift with the fashions of the day. This core value molded their culture, and created a strong sense of identity.

- Relative to their employees, these companies demanded a strong "fit" with their culture and their standards. Thus, employees either felt the organization was a great place to work and flourished or they were likely short-term. At the same time, they were tolerant of individuals on the margins who experimented and tested for possibilities.

Many current top organizations have made significant changes in the way they do business in the past decade and have been able to create performance through change management and deliberately develop the fundamental characteristics needed for success. These characteristics must provide those responses necessary to excel in today's environment. For example, time to market or the ability to quickly develop new products is a key factor in many industries because of the decreased production time created through technology, concurrent engineering, and agile manufacturing techniques. The use of simulation, integrated product teams, and world-wide subject matter experts operating virtually have been instrumental in bringing new knowledge and ideas together to rapidly produce products desired by a sophisticated and demanding market. Examples of this capability are: (1) mass customization where economic order quantities of one are being pursued and (2) agility, the ability of an organization to move rapidly in response to changing and unique customer needs. Creativity and innovation have come to the forefront as key success factors with organizations striving to develop and unleash these capacities throughout their workforce, using a combination of management, workers, customers, and the ability to pull collaborative teams together as a situation or problem dictates.

Employee involvement has now been accepted and understood by world class organizations and many "hope to be's." Examples are Wal-Mart, Hewlett-Packard, IBM, Texas Instruments, Motorola, and the Chaparral Steel Company. These world-class organizational structures have moved significantly away from bureaucratic decision making, and have modified their hierarchies to include team-based organizations and horizontal structures with minimum "white space." These firms encourage cross-communication by all employees, supported by technology such as e-Mail and groupware (Coleman, 1997), and reward employees who play a strong role in influencing organizational direction and decision-making.

These same organizations, working predominantly in the fast-moving world of information and knowledge application, recognize the value of decisions made at the lowest qualified level and the payoff from smart workers who know their jobs. However, for employees at all levels to use their knowledge to make effective decisions, they must understand the context within which those decisions are made. This context is provided through shared vision, clear values, and strong organizational direction and purpose, combined with open communication. As described by Peter Senge in the *Fifth Discipline*, smart companies put significant effort into transferring their vision, purpose, and goals to all employees. Good employee decision-making stems from understanding their work in terms of its impact on adjacent areas of the organization, as well as its direct impact on the customer. This requires effective empowerment and systems thinking and customer orientation and focus (Senge, 1990). Note how far we have departed from Weber's description of bureaucracy and its relative impotency in the current world context.

Nurtured by Total Quality Management (TQM) and Total Quality Leadership, the transfer of better business practices has recently become a hallmark of high-performing organizations. Many tools are continuing to be developed to help organizations create environments that make maximum use of employee knowledge and creativity. These practices include benchmarking, business process reengineering, lean production, value chain analysis, agility, integrated product teams, balanced score card, and, most recently, knowledge management.

The birth of knowledge management (KM), occurring in the early 1990s, grew from a recognition of the difficulty of dealing with complexity and with ever increasing competition spurred by technology and the demands of sophisticated customers. First came an awareness of the importance of information and knowledge, followed by a constant search for ways to create, store, integrate, tailor, share, and make available the right knowledge to the right people at the right time. Fundamental to this picture was a growing appreciation for the knowledge level of employees. Although still in its infancy, as indicated by the large number of meanings and uses of the words knowledge and KM, the field has pushed many organizations far from the classical Weberian bureaucracy. For example:

- The knowledge organization's focus on flexibility and customer response compared to bureaucracy's focus on organizational stability and the accuracy and repetitiveness of internal processes.
- Current practices that emphasize using the ideas and capabilities of employees to improve decision-making and organizational effectiveness.

> Bureaucracies utilize autocratic decision making by senior leadership with unquestioned execution by the workforce.
> - Current efforts to bring technology into the organization to support and liberate employee involvement and effectiveness. Classical bureaucracies use technology to improve efficiency and expect employees to adapt.
> - Current actions to eliminate waste and unnecessary processes while maximizing value added. Bureaucracy seeks to establish fixed processes to ensure precision and stability with little concern for value.
> - Current organizational emphasis on the use of teams to achieve better and more balanced decision-making and to share knowledge and learning. The axiom is "knowledge shared is power." Bureaucracies minimize the use of teams to maintain strong control and ensure knowledge is kept at the managerial and senior levels. The axiom is "personal knowledge is power."

As valuable as the above ideas are, their implementation continues to be a challenge to all organizations. Although many of these tools were originally touted as silver bullets, after they become popular, and as companies try them without fully understanding the difficulties of their implementation, they frequently achieve less than anticipated results. Michael Hammer, co-creator of Business Process Reengineering, has defined business process reengineering (BPR) as "the fundamental rethinking and radical redesign of business processes to achieve dramatic improvements in critical contemporary measures of performance" (Hammer and Champy, 1993). We find that ten years later, BPR is just now being understood well enough to provide a good chance of success, if applied to the right situation by experienced professionals. The unproven perception was that as many as seventy percent of BPR implementations failed to meet expectations. Many feel TQM suffered the same difficulties. As time progresses and more organizations learn how to successfully implement these tools, they are becoming more and more useful and contributing significantly to organizational improvement.

From the authors' personal experience, major reasons for the difficulty in applying these tools comes more from the lack of infrastructure support, and the inability to change culture than it does from the individual workforce and leadership. Research has indicated that the resistance from cultural inertia causes great difficulty in transferring the knowledge to effectively implement better business practices (Brown, 1999). Thus, we expect the road to a highly effective and efficient knowledge organization to be filled with bumps and potholes. Every change in the basic beliefs of the workforce, or of "the way the work gets done" is slow, erratic and painful. The move to a knowledge organization is no exception. But the move is occurring and will continue. There appears to be no other viable alternative.

For any new ideas to provide long-term value, they must be better understood and continuously improved through a process of ongoing learning. As our environment changes, our organizations must be molded, and sometimes even reinvented, into something that better fulfils an important need. Thus we see that in today's environment, no solutions can be independent of either time or context. This also applies to organizational structures. To the extent that this is true, there is not – and likely may never be – any single form of organizational structure that provides maximum overall effectiveness or that can even be offered as a model for reference. However, they all must be able to move quickly and make knowledgeable decisions coupled with effective follow through.

A significant challenge continuously facing the modern knowledge organization is how to harness the benefits of information technology. While the rapid growth and widespread influence of information technology has resulted in huge investments by many corporations, there has been some disillusionment with its hoped for increase in productivity. However, those companies that have recognized the close relationship between information technology and culture, using technology to support people in achieving corporate objectives, have found information technology highly effective in creating a competitive advantage. To achieve this not only requires selecting and adapting technology to an individual organization's needs, but also a carefully designed process that brings technology into the culture in a manner that the workforce finds acceptable and motivates them to make the necessary cultural changes to successfully imbed workflow adaptations.

In addition to the aforementioned challenges in applying information technology and the requisite culture change, there are a number of fundamental barriers that "to-be" knowledge organizations face as they attempt to become world class and to develop and maintain continuous competitive advantage. It is widely known that change management is a broad and challenging field that offers many theories and processes to consider, but no guaranteed solutions. Fundamentally, the process of change is highly situational and dependent not only on the environment, goals, and objectives of the organization, but on its specific history, culture and leadership. Each year finds a number of new books and journal articles offering the latest and greatest solutions to implementing change. To the authors' knowledge, there is no "solution" to implementing change because each situation offers its own set of unique challenges, pitfalls, and potentially successful tactics.

A major source of opposition to creating a knowledge organization is likely to come from middle management's unwillingness to give up its prerogatives of decision-making and authority. Because most of the workforce gets their direct information from, and usually develops trust in, their immediate supervisors, they are heavily influenced by the attitudes and actions of these middle managers. This barrier has occasionally been overcome when senior management has circumvented the mid-level and worked directly with the workforce (Carlzon, 1987).

Although communication is essential in stable times, it becomes critical and extremely important during times of change and uncertainty. Rumors, informal networks, official organizational policies, and rules, as well as personalities and fear of job loss or power changes, all heavily influence the accuracy, noise level and usefulness of communication. The classic solution seems to be to communicate as much as possible, as accurately as possible and as often as possible, keeping all of the workforce informed on events and changes in the organization. Although theoretically sound and occasionally successful, this practice may be difficult under conditions where major changes are needed, but the rationale for these changes is difficult for employees to understand and accept. Thus, building a knowledge organization under conditions less than life threatening is challenging at best.

Before the workforce will accept new practices, they must be willing to recognize and admit that their current efforts are inadequate. This usually requires a paradigm shift and a willingness to adapt new assumptions in terms of how the business works and what must be done. The resistance to this paradigm shift is usually high and often unrecognized by management. The historic paradigm that produced past success is so ingrained in the belief systems of most middle and upper managers, and the risk of adapting totally new assumptions about the business is so large, that the "double loop" learning required, as discovered and explained so eloquently by Argyris and Schon (1978) in their book *Organizational Learning: A Theory of Action Perspective*, is a major challenge.

Still another challenge faced by leadership is the willingness to give up some of its own authority and decision-making and to empower the workforce (including teams) to make decisions based upon local circumstances. This diffusion of information and knowledge from upper and middle management throughout the workforce means that they give up authority while maintaining responsibility – something very few people want to do. Yet, to successfully release the worker's knowledge and experience for organizational improvement, the context, direction, and authority to make local decisions must be made available to all personnel, and those same personnel must be qualified to accept the challenge of empowerment.

A knowledge organization must, of necessity, become a learning organization so that the entire firm will learn while it works and be able to adapt quickly to market changes and other environmental perturbations. Except for a few professional firms, most workers are not in the habit of continuous learning as part of their job. Unfortunately, many supervisors and managers believe that learning on the job is not appropriate. It is no surprise then that individuals who have worked for years without learning or even the expectation of having to learn on the job find it highly challenging and difficult to "learn how to learn" and to continuously keep updated in their area of expertise. Creating the emergent characteristic represented by a learning organization will take much more effort than simply offering courses and training to the workforce.

Another challenging final barrier particularly relevant to those firms seeking to become knowledge organizations is that of creating a culture in which knowledge and knowledge sharing are valued and encouraged. As discussed earlier, many workers consider knowledge as power and job security, and are frequently unwilling to share ideas and experience with their colleagues. The solution to this barrier is an area of current research and ideas are being offered and tested. As always, they are situation dependent and represent another step toward complexity.

The evolution of organizations has passed from cooperative hunting bands to farming groups to towns/cities to bureaucracies. These changes took almost ten thousand years, or about five hundred generations (Berger, 2000). Yet during the past fifty years (two generations), organizations have moved from enlightened bureaucracies to employee-centered, team-based, networked, information, and knowledge intense structures struggling to keep pace with change. Recall that we are speaking primarily of those firms at the right side of our bell curve. In one sense, we are moving back to small bands of people working together to solve their common and immediate problems. In another, everyone lives, works, and relates in a totally new and strange world.

At the forefront of organizational performance are the knowledge-based organizations that have successfully adopted several or many of the practices discussed above while concomitantly taking advantage of the new technological advances such as knowledge portals, intelligent search engines and agents, and knowledge repositories. These organizations have achieved high levels of efficiency and effectiveness, sustained competitive advantage and, above all, achieved an effective balance that satisfies stakeholders, customers, the workforce, the environment, and local community needs. While there is still much experimentation with organizational design and trial and error is on the daily menu, general patterns of success seem to be emerging. These patterns are creating new metaphors for organizations such as: agile production systems, living organisms, complex adaptive systems, self-organizing systems, virtual organizations, the spiritual workplace, and of course, the knowledge organization. Which of these metaphors, or new ones to be generated in the future, will become the successes of the year, fifteen to twenty years ahead, cannot be predicted. In all likelihood, the future organization will contain parts of all of them. One can certainly be confident that information, knowledge, and their intelligent application will be an essential factor in future success. However, speculation may be useful in describing potential/probable visions of what the future knowledge-based organizations will look like. A lighthouse in the darkness serves a mariner well, even if his course is not directly in line with it.

4 The Knowledge Organization

As in all forecasting, we must first identify our approach and our assumptions. Our approach will be to consider the most probable world-class organization circa 2020 A.D. Recognizing the distinction between probable, preferable, and possible, we concentrate on the most-likely characteristics of the leading organizations (i.e., what we believe to be the most probable). Even to do this, however, requires a number of assumptions relative to the environment and external forces. For example, we assume there exists relative stability and peace, historically represented by about twenty-five percent of all nations in conflict at any one time, throughout the world (Durant, 1968), and that information technology continues to advance at its current "Moore's Law" rate: doubling in processing power and speed about every eighteen months, while reducing size at the same rate. However, we recognize that bioengineering and the rapid improvement of nanotechnology may well accelerate processing ability and the impact of technology on organizations much faster than Moore's Law. While artificial intelligence will greatly improve the application of logic and processing to narrow, well-bounded problems, it will not compete with human cognition and consciousness in understanding, situational awareness and learning. Thus, we believe deep knowledge, broad scope of interests, and high adaptability are unique to homo sapiens. While the Internet represents a network that may potentially shrink the world, it may well take another track, with the Internet becoming saturated and chaotic. Thus, while the best organizations will almost certainly have become porous systems with multiple connections beyond their immediate organizational boundaries, they may do so through private networks versus the Internet, but they will do so!

The Information Age is intensifying interactions among processes previously isolated from each other in time or space. "Information can be understood as a mediator of interaction. Decreasing the costs of its propagation and storage inherently increases possibilities for interaction effects. An Information Revolution is therefore likely to beget a complexity revolution" (Axelrod, 1997).

The metaphor we choose to use for the future knowledge-based organization is best given as an intelligent complex adaptive system (ICAS). By complex, we mean that an organization that can take on a very large number of states. A complex system is made of a "large number of individual, intelligent agents," each with their own ability to make decisions and strive for certain goals. These agents (workers) have multiple relationships within the system and externally through its boundaries, and these relationships can become highly complex and dynamic. Groups of these agents may work together to form typically what are considered components of the system, and these components together may form the whole system or organization under consideration. The word "adaptive" implies that the entire system is capable of studying and analyzing its environment and taking actions that adapt itself to forces in the environment in fulfilling its overall (organization) goals. Intelligent complex adaptive systems may be highly unpredictable or superbly self-organized, depending on their precise internal structure and relation to their environment. They will exhibit a unity of purpose and a coherence of action, while being highly selective in their sensitivity to external threats and opportunities. They will be able to bring diverse knowledge located anywhere in the organization (or beyond) together to solve problems and take advantage of opportunities. They will possess a number of emergent characteristics noted above that permit them to survive and successfully compete in the future world.

Our view of the world-class organization of 2020 would encompass an intelligent complex adaptive system consisting of a combination of hierarchical management and individual, quasi-self-organizing agents who can be cross-coupled to each other as needed. The balance achieved between these two components of the system will depend upon the specific environment, mission, and leadership of the organization. This organization may operate reasonably close to what is known as the "edge of chaos" (Bennet, 1997). The advantages of operating near this edge are that the opportunities for creativity and innovation are maximized through the motivation and freedom of individual agents or components. Unfortunately, this edge is narrow, and there is always a danger that the organization may become chaotic with its agents and components going in locally divergent directions, yielding little overall benefit to the organization, and perhaps exacting a heavy cost. Innovation and creativity are essential to provide the large number of potential actions and ideas necessary to adapt to an environment that is most likely much more uncertain, dynamic, and dangerous than that encountered today. This "edge of chaos" will be obtained by much more emphasis on individual worker competency and freedom in terms of learning, making decisions, and taking actions in their area of responsibility coupled with multiple and effective networks that provide sources of knowledge, experience, and insights from others.

These dynamic networks will represent the main infrastructure of the new knowledge-based organization. Made available by increased bandwidth and processing power of both silicon and biotechnology, they offer the opportunity for a virtual information and knowledge support system that will connect data, information, knowledge, and people through virtual communities, knowledge repositories, and knowledge portals. The foundation and grounding of these future firms will be strengthened through a common set of strong, stable values held by all employees. Such values not only provide guidance that enhances empowerment but also motivates and strengthens the self-confidence of the workforce, thereby magnifying the effectiveness of the self-organized teams within the intelligent complex adaptive system.

Learning and knowledge will have become two of the three most important emergent characteristics of the future world-class organization. Learning will be continuous and widespread, utilizing mentoring, classroom, and distance learning and will likely be self-managed with strong infrastructure support. The creation, storage, transfer, and application of knowledge (and perhaps wisdom) will have been refined and developed such that it becomes a major resource of the organization as it satisfies customers and adapts to environmental competitive forces and opportunities. The last ten years have been called the decade of the brain, one in which neuroscience research has made large gains in our understanding of the mind-brain problem and, in particular, the role of consciousness in how we learn, perceive, and sense our environment.

The third characteristic of knowledge-based organizations will be that of organizational intelligence. Karl Wiig, in his seminal book *Knowledge Management Methods*, describes intelligent behavior as: "Be well prepared, provide excellent outcome oriented thinking, choose appropriate postures, and make outstanding decisions" (Wiig, 1993).

"Be well prepared" includes acquiring knowledge continuously from all available resources and building it into an integrated picture, bringing together seemingly unrelated information to create new and unusual perspectives and to understand the surrounding world.

"Provide excellent outcome oriented thinking" is to be continuously innovative and creative and use all relevant knowledge. It also includes reframing problems and utilizing different perspectives for their solutions, understanding situations beyond their appearances, and discriminating and characterizing as an aid to problem solving.

"Choose appropriate postures" includes adopting suitable behavior in a given situation and anticipating future changes, putting effort in proportion to the situation's importance, and coordinating all relevant parties to build consensus.

"Make outstanding decisions" consists of identifying objectives, considering alternatives and consequences, setting priorities, and selecting the best alternative. Intelligent behavior of subsystems within a knowledge-based organization can best be seen in the effective use of teams. Bennet has identified four fundamental processes that high-performance teams have mastered that lead to successful outcomes. They are innovation, problem solving, decision-making, and implementation of team decision. Guidelines are provided for maximizing the effectiveness of each process, thereby creating intelligent behaviors. For example, under decision quality, nine factors are considered as necessary for a good decision: shared vision, efficiency, risk, timing, balance, impact on product value, political consequences, decision scope, and worst case scenario (Bennet, 1997).

For an organization to behave intelligently as a complex adaptive system, it must achieve continuous, interdependent collaboration and interplay among all levels of the system. This means balancing the knowledge and actions of its agents to achieve both the lowest-level tasks and highest-level vision of the organization, creating a distributed intelligence throughout all levels of the system. This is done by using teams and communities to amplify local intelligence levels, accelerate quality decision-making, and foster innovation and creativity. However, this "future world class" organization will have overall direction and goals and have developed measures of performance that serve to cull out inadequate ideas, decisions, and actions. Selection of the best ideas and actions is as difficult as implementation of that selection. Evolution has taught us that complex organizations evolve through a process of the random generation of ideas and individuals, which are then modified by chance encounters and eliminated by others more fit to survive. The ICAS is a knowledge-based organization that learns from evolution by building in the equivalent characteristics that include: survival of the fittest (a threshold of performance); trial and error by mutations and genetics (brainstorming, innovation, and analysis and problem solving); and recombining by sexual reproduction and combination (systems thinking, collaborative decision-making, and implementation). These three will be replicated in future organizations by teams combining new ideas, employees coming in to offer new and different ideas and actions, and the system as a whole creating performance thresholds, which filter out the bad ideas and decisions.

This capability highlights the importance of both internal and external networks as they heavily influence the relationships and amplify knowledge diffusion among agents, components, and external systems. As these networks increase, the organization becomes more complex, harder to manage, and potentially capable of handling more complexity in its environment.

An effective ICAS will have a permeable boundary and optimize its results through partnering, alliances, and close relationships with customers and stakeholders. Thus, where in a bureaucracy, policy, rules and power are dominant, in the knowledge-based organization of the future, learning, knowledge, networking, and relationships will be dominant.

5   Conclusion

The knowledge-based organization of the future (what we propose as ICAS) clearly breaks away from the bureaucratic model described by Weber. The future world where knowledge shared becomes power and the entire organization behaves as an intelligent, self-selecting, self-adapting system continually integrating and processing incoming data and information to determine its actions, is clearly idealistic – but not beyond the possible. The present recognition and popularity of the importance of knowledge to organizational success is merely the beginning of creation of the truly intelligent organization.

As we move into the twenty-first century, the goal of an organization has rightfully moved away from the oppressive working conditions of the early 20th century. The ultimate challenge of the future is to liberate and amplify the knowledge and creativity of all organizational members. For in them alone lives the source and power of intelligence and wisdom, which will enable the rise of the Knowledge Organization.

References

Argyris, C. and D.A. Schon, *Organizational Learning: A Theory of Action Perspective*, Philippines: Addison-Wesley Publishing Co., 1978.

Axelrod, R., *The Complexity of Cooperation,* Princeton: Princeton University Press, 1997.

Bennet, D., *IPT Learning Campus: Gaining Acquisition Results through IPTs*, Alexandria: Bellwether Learning Center, 1997.

Berger, L., *In the Footsteps of Eve: The Mystery of Human Origins,* Washington, D.C.: National Geographic, 2000.

Brown, J.S., "Conversation." *Knowledge Directions: The Journal of the Institute for Knowledge Management*, 1, Spring, 1999.

Carlzon, J., *Moments of Truth,* Cambridge: Ballinger Publishing Co., 1987.

Coleman, D, *Groupware: Collaborative Strategies for Corporate LANs and Intranets.* New Jersey: Prentice Hall, 1997.

Collins, R., *Four sociological traditions,* New York: Oxford University Press, 1994.

Cummings, T. G. and E.F. Huse,. *Organization Development and Change,* (4th ed.), New York: West Publishing Company, 1989.

Daft, R. L.and R.M. Steers,. *Organizations: A Micro/Macro Approach,* New York: Harper Collins.

Durant, W. A. *The Lessons of History.* New York: Simon and Schuster, 1968.

Ebrey, P. B. (ed)., *Chinese Civilization: A Sourcebook,* New York: The Free Press, 1993.

Edelman, G., *A Universe of Consciousness: How Matter Becomes Imagination*, New York: Perseus Books Group, 2000.

Gerth, H. H. and C.W. Mills, C. W. (Ed. and Trans.), from Max Weber: *Essays in Sociology,* New York: Oxford University Press, 1946.

Hammer, M. and J. Champy, *Reengineering the Corporation,* New York: HarperCollins Publishers, 1993.

Handy, C., *Understanding Organizations*, New York: Oxford University Press, 1993.

McKelvey. B., *Organizational Systematics,* Berkeley: University of California Press, 1982.

Outhwaite, W.and T. Bottomore (eds.)., *The Blackwell Dictionary of Twentieth-Century Social Thought,* Malden, MA: Blackwell Publishers, Inc., 1994.

Roberts, J. A. G. *A Concise History of China.* Cambridge: Harvard University Press, 1999.

Senge, P. M., *The Fifth Discipline: The Art & Practice of The Learning Organization,* New York: Doubleday, 1990.

Shingo, S., *A Study of the Toyota Production System,* Cambridge: Productivity Press, 1989.

Silverman, D.P. (ed)., *Ancient Egypt,.* New York: Oxford University Press, 1997.

Skyrme, D. J., *Knowledge Networking: Creating the Collaborative Enterprise,* Boston: Butterworth Heinemann, 1999.

Wiig, K.M., *Knowledge Management Foundations,* Arlington, TX: Schema Press, 1993.

Womack, J. P., D.T. Jones, and D. Roos, *Machine That Changed The World,* New York: Macmillan Publishing Co., 1990.

Wren, D. A. *The Evolution of Management Thought.* New York: Ronald, 1972.

CHAPTER 2

Knowledge Managers: Who They Are and What They Do

James D. McKeen and D. Sandy Staples

Queen's School of Business, Queen's University, Kingston, Canada K7L 3N6

Knowledge management (the process) and knowledge managers (the people) are recent organizational phenomena. The latter (the knowledge managers) are those key individuals charged with the task of making the former (knowledge management) successful. Due to the recent emergence of these organizational initiatives, a study of knowledge managers – who they are and what they do – was thought to be instructive and revealing as well as being sufficiently current to enable organizations to either adopt or adapt their knowledge management strategy. A survey to reveal the characteristics of knowledge managers as well as knowledge management initiatives was designed and distributed to practicing knowledge managers, primarily from US and Canadian organizations. This chapter, based on the analysis of 41 completed questionnaires, reveals the backgrounds, goals, ambitions, initiatives, and challenges as self-assessed by these individuals. By pulling this information together, a profile of a "typical" knowledge manager is presented. The question that remains to be asked is "Are these the most appropriate individuals to lead the KM charge"?

Keywords: Knowledge Management; Knowledge Managers; Knowledge Manager Characteristics; Knowledge Manager Activities; Organizational Knowledge Management Activities

1 Introduction

The emergence of the knowledge management function all started with Peter Drucker's now famous quote in The Post Capitalist Society (1993) ...

> "The basic economic resource – the means of production – is no longer capital, nor natural resources, nor labor. It is and will be knowledge".

With such an endorsement and the instant legitimization that followed, organizations began the process of learning how to "manage" this new resource. Organizations higher on the information-intensive scale moved quickly. Positions were fashioned, systems were implemented, and metrics were created as titles such as "knowledge manager" began to dot the organizational panoply. With characteristic adherence to the adage "anything that can't be measured can't be managed", organizations began the search for value directly attributable to knowledge. Armed with oft-repeated success stories and evangelical exuberance, knowledge managers accepted the challenge articulated by senior management.

Knowledge management is an emerging management function. As such, we have an opportunity to study its evolution almost from the outset. The purpose of the study reported in this chapter is not only to explore the current organizational role of knowledge management but also to understand the knowledge managers themselves – their career aspirations, backgrounds, challenges, initiatives, and key challenges/problems.

This chapter is organized into the following sections. First, the research questions we investigated and associated literature are described. A description of the methodology we used to answer our research questions follows. The findings from our study are then presented and discussed.

2   Literature Review

There were two main objectives for our study. First, we wanted to develop a profile of knowledge managers. Second, we wanted to understand what activities they were working on in their organization. In order to help us meet our objectives, we looked for previous similar studies that had done similar things. We briefly review the studies we found below and describe how our study relates to and adds to the existing body of knowledge.

2.1   Previous Studies Examining Characteristics of Positions

Although we were unable to find any existing studies of the characteristics of knowledge managers, various organizational positions such as CEO (Shin, 1999), CIO (Feeny, Edwards, and Simpson, 1992; Stephens, Ledbetter, Mitra, and Ford, 1992), and CKO have been studied and we used those approaches to guide and inform our study. Below, we specifically review the existing studies on CKO's because they form the closest position to the focus of our study that has been empirically studied.

It has been estimated that the position of Chief Knowledge Officer (CKO) exists in about one-fifth of the Fortune 500 companies, although not all the positions carry the title of CKO (Stewart, 1998). Although the job of CKO is still relatively new for most organizations, it has existed in some firms since the early 1990's, with the big six accounting firms leading the way (Watt, 1997). As far as we could determine, there have only been two studies that examined the characteristics and competencies of CKO's (Duffy, 1998).

Bob Guns' study of 52 CKO's in the United States found that the CKO's came from a wide range of backgrounds and were generally hired internally because of a deep knowledge of the business (Duffy, 1998). The author of the study concluded that the skills necessary for a CKO are diverse. A CKO needs to be able to champion knowledge management (KM) initiatives and be able to energize the organization. He/she needs vision, change management skills, and strong interpersonal and communication skills. The CKO's studied were business-oriented in that they realized they had to produce concrete business results within a fairly short time period in order to survive and maintain support. Seven main challenges were identified:

1. Set knowledge management strategic priorities,
2. Establish a knowledge database of best practices,
3. Gain commitment of senior executives to support a learning environment,
4. Teach information seekers how to ask better and smarter questions of their intelligent resources,
5. Put in place a process for managing intellectual assets,
6. Obtain customer satisfaction information in near real-time, and
7. Globalize knowledge management.

Michael Earl and Ian Scott (1998) studied 20 CKO's from Europe and North America. They found that although CKO's had varied backgrounds, they shared similar personality traits. They tended to be outgoing, extroverted, and persuasive, as well as being high-achievement people. They were able to both play the part of actor on stage and be willing to be behind the scenes, influencing people. Communication skills were critical in terms of building support and commitment to KM programs. Earl and Scott (1999) found that CKO's had two main design competencies. They were both technologists and environmentalists. As a technologist, they understood how current and emerging information technologies could help capture, store, and share knowledge. As an environmentalist, they understood the need to create social environments that facilitated creating markets for conversations and sharing. Two leadership qualities also strongly emerged. CKO's were willing to take risks and enjoyed the newness of their tasks. This spirit of entrepreneurship also implied that they were visionary, while still being able to focus on producing deliverable results. As well as being entrepreneurs, CKO's were able to take on a consulting role, bringing ideas into the organization and listening to other people's ideas.

How is our study of knowledge managers different from the CKO studies? In the mid- to late-90's, appointing a CKO was thought to be the appropriate strategy to leverage the collective knowledge of organizations (Capshaw, 1999). A CKO is a senior executive position, commanding high annual salaries of $200,000 to $350,000 in the US (Herschel and Nemati, 2000; Hibbard, 1998). However, a 1998 study by the Delphi Group found that the use of CKO's was a small part of the knowledge management picture. Rather than a centralized, top executive-led strategy, a more typical strategy is to use a team of knowledge management experts who work closely with business units or are even a part of the business units (Cole-Gomolski, 1999a). The knowledge leaders in this strategy typically have titles like knowledge manager, knowledge architect, and knowledge analyst (Capshaw, 1999). This strategy is more consistent with the overall goal of sharing knowledge and involving all aspects of an organization. By specifically studying knowledge managers, we add to the overall knowledge management picture.

Although we were unable to find any empirical studies that have specifically looked at the characteristics of knowledge managers, Cole-Gomolski (1999b) suggested the following requirements for successful knowledge managers. She suggested a business knowledge comes first, although understanding technology is very important. Extensive business background (i.e. 10 years experience) is needed because knowledge managers have to be able to determine what information is worth sharing. A deep understanding of the business, along with IT expertise, are strong prerequisites for successful knowledge managers. Having an entrepreneurial spirit is also important since many knowledge managers have to develop their own vision and mandate (Cole-Gomolski, 1999b). TFPL (1999) conducted interviews, surveys, and workshops with KM practitioners and experts in Europe and North America to identify the skills needed for knowledge workers. While the focus of this was not specifically on knowledge managers, the findings were generally consistent with Cole-Gomolski's suggestions and the results of the CKO studies.

In their study of CKO's, Earl and Scott (1999) addressed several questions, including:

1. What do CKO's do? (What activities and interventions have they been engaged in so far?)
2. Is there a model CKO? (What capabilities and competencies do they require?)
3. Is there a typical CKO profile or personality?
4. What resources and support does a CKO require?
5. What are the early lessons of experience? (Are there any emerging "critical success factors" for CKO's?)

In our study, we address all of the above questions from the perspective of the knowledge manager. This enables us to meet our first objective. Our second objective was to identify the knowledge management activities that the knowledge managers and their organizations were working on, which is further discussed in the next section.

2.2 Previous Studies Examining Knowledge Management Activities

One of the few empirical studies that reports knowledge management activities was done by Ruggles (1998). Based on a study of 431 US and European organizations, he described what firms were doing in 1997 to manage knowledge, as well as what firms felt they should be doing, and what firms felt were the greatest barriers they faced. Creating an intranet, creating knowledge repositories, implementing decision support tools, and implementing groupware to support collaboration were the four most common projects being worked on. The three objectives that firms felt they should do, but hadn't yet done, were mapping sources of internal expertise, creating networks of knowledge workers, and establishing new knowledge roles. The three largest difficulties to implementing knowledge management initiatives were changing people's behaviour, measuring the value and performance of knowledge assets, and determining what knowledge should be managed.

Our study builds on Ruggles' (1998) work and provides an update to it. Specifically, we wanted to answer the following questions:

1. What are the most significant challenges to managing knowledge in the respondents' organizations?
2. How well are organizations performing knowledge activities?

The next section describes the methodology we used to address these research questions.

3 Methodology

3.1 The Questionnaire

A questionnaire was developed to collect data to answer our research questions. A variety of question types were used varying from open-ended questions to Likert-type scales. There were six sections in the questionnaire, roughly corresponding to the research questions. The sections gathering information about knowledge management activities, background on the knowledge management position, future knowledge management directions, information on the company, respondent's views of their job, and demographics about the respondent. To assess views about the respondent's job, we asked questions designed to measure job satisfaction, organizational commitment, ability to cope, and job stress. These constructs were measured with established instruments. Specifically, Warr, Cook and Wall's (1979) scale was used to assess job satisfaction. Job stress was measured using the scale developed by Rizzo, House, and Lirtzman (1970). Mowday, Steers, and Porter's (1979) scale was used to assess organizational commitment and ability to cope was measured using the instrument developed by House, Schuler, and Levanoni (1983). Table 1 reports the reliabilities of these scales, all of which are acceptable. The items were averaged together to obtain a score for the construct.

Table 1. The reliability of the Multi-Item Scales

Name	Number of items	Cronbach's alpha
Job satisfaction	11	0.92
Organizational commitment	7	0.93
Ability to cope	5	0.79
Job stress	5	0.85

Pre-tests of the questionnaire were done with 5 people, 4 of whom were experts in questionnaire construction and knowledge management issues. The fifth person was a practicing knowledge manager. The questionnaire was modified to reflect the suggestions of the pre-test participants. Both a web-based version of the finalized questionnaire and a paper-based version were prepared and used to collect data.

3.2 The Sample

In order to reach knowledge managers, we employed two strategies. First, the organizers of the Braintrust International 2001 conference helped us by sending notices to their participant list asking them to participate in the study. Braintrust is a practitioner-driven event that was developed by and for knowledge management practitioners so it was well suited to our goal of reaching knowledge managers. Potential respondents were offered two things in return for participation. In addition to being given a summary of the findings, the preliminary results were presented at the Braintrust International 2001 conference, held in San Francisco in February 2001. Our second strategy was to contact and invite participation from as many knowledge managers as we knew personally. Again, participants were offered a summary of the findings in return for participation.

These two strategies resulted in 41 responses from knowledge managers. These knowledge managers came from a variety of companies. Table 2 summarizes the demographic characteristics of the sample. Most of the sample was from North America with a fairly even split between male and female respondents. Most knowledge managers were in the '41-50' age group with an average age of 42.2 years. Very few of the respondents worked in a purely physical goods type industry, and most of the respondents worked in large companies (e.g. greater than 5,000 employees in the firm).

Table 2. Demographics of the Respondents

	Number	Percentage of Sample (valid responses)
Origin of Respondent		
• U.S.A.	26	70%
• Canada	8	22%
• Europe	2	5%
• Asia	1	3%
Age		
• 51-60	8	20%
• 41-50	17	44%
• 31-40	9	23%
• 21-30	5	13%
Gender		
• Male	18	46%
• Female	21	54%

Respondent's Type of Industry

- Services   21   55%
- Physical Goods / Products   4   11%
- Both Services and Physical Goods/Products   13   34%

Industry of the Respondent's Firm

- Financial Services   7   19%
- Government   6   16%
- Health and Social Services   1   3%
- High Technol-   7   19%
  ogy/Computers/Telecommunications
- Manufacturing   5   14%
- Pharmaceutical   2   5%
- Professional Services (Legal, Accounting,   8   22%
  Consulting)
- Other (HR Services)   1   2%

Size of Respondent's Organization
(number of employees)

- Less than 500 Employees   5   13%
- 501 to 1,000 Employees   7   18%
- 1,001 to 5,000 Employees   5   13%
- 5,001 to 10,000 Employees   3   8%
- 10,001 to 20,000 Employees   2   5%
- More than 20,000 Employees   17   43%

4   Results and Discussion

4.1 Knowledge Managers

According to our sample (see Table 3), knowledge managers are very well educated. Almost 90% held undergraduate degrees and 60% held graduate degrees (as well as undergraduate degrees). As undergraduates, half of the knowledge managers surveyed opted for a course of study in Arts and/or Humanities; a further third took courses in the sciences (general, computing, engineering); and an additional 17% earned an undergraduate degree in Business Administration. Their choice of graduate degree programs were logically more specialized and predominantly (one third of sample) focused on Business Administration. The rest of the sample selected from a broad variety of graduate programs.

We were interested to know what kind of background and previous work experience these knowledge managers brought to the KM position. The majority of respondents held managerial "line" positions (some at the VP or partner level in their organizations) before accepting the knowledge management role. Some (24%) had previously occupied more technical roles (systems/technical analysts) and a few (13%) brought project management skills to the KM position. While most knowledge managers had been with their current organization 1-5 years, the average was approximately 8 years. Only 13% of respondents had been with their current organization less than a year. Although we failed to ask directly, it appears that the majority of knowledge managers (approximately two thirds) were hired from within their organizations. Later on we will examine this trend further to discover more about hiring practices for the selection of individuals to fulfill the role of knowledge manager.

Table 3. Educational Background and Previous Experience

	Number	Percentage of Sample (valid responses)
Highest Degree Held		
• Diploma/Certificate	5	13%
• Undergraduate	11	28%
• Graduate	23	59%
Field of Undergraduate Study		
• Arts/Humanities	17	49%
• Computer Science	6	17%
• Business	6	17%
• Engineering	5	14%
• General Science	1	3%
Field of Graduate Study		
• Business	7	33%
• Arts/Humanities	4	19%
• Information/Library Science	4	19%
• Engineering	3	14%
• Computer Science	2	10%
Previous Job		
• Line	26	65%
• Staff	14	35%

Previous Job Experience (in total years for all respondents)

• Functional Business Manager	36	38%
• Systems/Technical Analyst	23	24%
• Partner/VP Level	14	15%
• Project Manager	12	13%
• Consultant	8	8%
• Librarian	2	2%
How Long with Current Organization		
• Less than 1 year	5	13%
• 1-5 years	17	44%
• 6-10 years	6	15%
• 11-20 years	7	18%
• More than 20 years	4	10%

4.2 The Nature of the KM Job

Table 4 presents the results of a number of questions examining the nature of the knowledge management position. It is clear that the KM initiative definitely has its genesis in high places. In 44% of the organizations polled, the CEO or equivalent ranking officer created the KM position. In a further 22%, the position was launched by a divisional manager or vice president and, in 31% of the organizations, a director level executive was responsible for introducing the knowledge management position.

Given the high level initial sponsorship of the KM position, it is not surprising to find that the reasons for creating this position are commensurate with senior ranks. "Leveraging knowledge content", "developing a knowledge strategy", and "promoting awareness of knowledge management" – the reasons stated by 77% of respondents – are very lofty goals. Given the newness of the KM position, this is perhaps to be expected. The incumbent in the KM role would be left to articulate specific achievable goals with appropriate timeframes.

While knowledge managers have been given substantial license to "carve out the KM role", it appears that they have not been equally blessed with the budgetary means to do so! In many cases, the KM budget is somewhat vague – often subsumed as part of another budget (for example, the IT budget). As a result, we were frustrated in our ability to successfully capture an accurate picture of the KM budget and/or the budgetary process. Based on anecdotal evidence we received, KM budgets appear to be "modest if not lacking, ephemeral, and extremely difficult to defend". Given this state of affairs, it is not surprising to find that the majority of KM positions (58%) in the organizations sampled have one or fewer (i.e. zero) supporting staff members. This likely reflects the developmental status of knowledge management within the majority of organizations.

Table 4. The KM Position

	Number	Percentage of Sample (valid responses)
Who Created the KM Position?		
• CEO/Chair/President	16	44%
• Director level	11	31%
• Division Manager/VP	8	22%
• I did	1	3%
Why Was the Position Created?		
• Manage/leverage knowledge content	14	37%
• Develop KM strategy	9	24%
• Awareness/promotion/communication of KM	6	16%
• Implementation of KM activities	6	16%
• Standardization of information	2	5%
• Improve virtual work	1	2%
How Many KM Staff Positions?		
• No staff	5	21%
• 1 staff	9	37%
• 2 staff	2	8%
• 3-5 staff	4	17%
• 6-10 staff	3	13%
• more than 10 staff	1	4%

Despite the difficulties in attempting to separate the *person* from the *position*, we asked our sample of knowledge managers a number of questions seeking their personal reflections of the KM position, their interest in seeking the position, and what they currently enjoy about the position. In Table 5, we report our findings.

We asked the knowledge managers if the focus of the job had changed since inception. Of those that felt that the focus had undergone a change, 28% felt that it had taken on a much more strategic focus for their organization while the other respondents felt that it had assumed more of a "support/maintenance" type, a "development" focus, or a "quality" or "research" type focus. The focal direction taken by the KM function is likely highly related to its origins. Given that the majority of KM functions were created by senior executives who articulated broad and strategic goals (see Table 4), it is appropriate that the change in focus for KM reflects a move towards implementation of the established mandate. Hence, we see *development*, *implementation*, and *change management* as the driving forces.

Given the newness of the KM position, we were interested to know how the incumbents were being evaluated. Not surprisingly, 21% claimed that they had no process for evaluation. Another 55% indicated that they were judged on attainment of established goals and objectives. Fewer respondents (11%) indicated that they were ultimately evaluated on the basis of customer satisfaction and fewer yet (8%) said that they were primarily evaluated on the basis of project delivery. These findings make sense. With its strategic level inaugural focus, the KM position appears to be changing focus (as indicated above) and gravitating to more specific and well-articulated goals. It is likely that, over time, the evaluation of knowledge mangers would migrate/evolve toward more deliverable objectives, as organizations will want to see measurable impact with maturity of the KM function.

Table 5. Knowledge Managers and the KM Position

	Number	Percentage of Sample (valid responses)
How has the focus of your position changed since inception?		
• Strategic focus	5	28%
• Support/maintenance focus	4	22%
• Development focus	3	17%
• Quality focus	3	17%
• Research/analyst focus	2	11%
• Cultural change focus	1	5%
How Are You Evaluated?		
• Meeting Goals/Objectives	21	55%
• No process for evaluation	8	21%
• Customer/employee satisfaction	4	11%
• Systems/Project Delivery	3	8%
• Usage of systems	2	5%
Time in Current Position		
• Less than 1 year	11	28%
• 1-5 years	26	67%
• 6-10 years	2	5%
What Skills Got You the Job?		
• KM concepts/theory/interest	23	26%

• Managerial Experience (problem solving, planning, project management, team experience, leadership, change management)	18	21%
• Technical Experience (IT, systems)	11	13%
• Organizational Experience (networking, culture)	9	10%
• Personal strengths (creativity, eagerness to learn, self-motivated, communication skills)	9	10%
• Knowledge of the business	6	7%
• Research/library skills	6	7%
• Consulting experience	5	6%

To underscore the newness of the KM function, most knowledge managers (68%) have been in the position between 1 and 5 years, with an average time in their current position of 2.2 years. In almost every case, the respondents are the first individuals to be appointed to the KM position. This means that Table 5 also indicates that the knowledge management function has existed 2.2 years on average and in 95% of the organizations, it has existed less than 5 years.

When asked "What skills do you think got you the job?", 80% of respondents replied

- knowledge of KM concepts (26%)
- managerial experience (21%)
- technical experience (13%)
- organizational experience (10%) and
- personal strengths (10%).

It appears evident that, other than their awareness of KM concepts, these individuals were chosen on the basis of their proven organizational competence and 8-year track record.

4.3 Organizational KM Activities, Challenges, and Capabilities

As pointed out at the beginning of this chapter, we thought that it could be insightful to redo the empirical work of Ruggles (1998) to see how much, and in what ways, organizations had progressed in terms of what KM activities they are doing, or feel they should be doing (see Figure 1). Ruggles (1998) found that the four most common KM projects *underway* by organizations were creating an intranet, creating knowledge repositories, implementing decision support tools, and implementing groupware to support collaboration. By 2001, over 90% of organizations sampled had implemented an intranet, 80% had created knowledge repositories, 50% had implemented decision support tools, and 56% had implemented groupware to support collaborations. In addition by 2001, the majority of organizations had created knowledge repositories, built data warehouses, and created internal networks of knowledge workers.

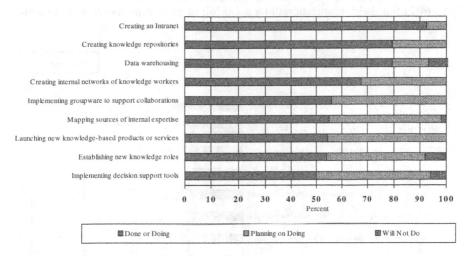

Figure 1. Key KM Activities

In 1998, the three activities that firms felt they *should do*, but hadn't yet done, were mapping sources of internal expertise, creating networks of knowledge workers, and establishing new knowledge roles. By 2001, 55% of organizations had completed mapping sources of internal expertise, 68% had created internal networks of knowledge workers, and 54% had established new knowledge roles. The three top tasks that organizations felt that they should do in 2001 were launching new knowledge-based products or services, implementing decision support tools, and implementing groupware to support collaboration. Out of the nine KM activities examined by Ruggles and this study, some organizations have consciously decided *not to* implement 4 activities: establishing new knowledge roles, data warehousing, implementing decision support tools, and mapping sources of internal expertise.

In 1998, the three greatest challenges to implementing knowledge management initiatives were changing people's behaviour, measuring the value, and performance of knowledge assets, and determining what knowledge should be managed (Ruggles, 1998). It appears little has changed since then. By 2001, the top two challenges were still changing people's behaviour and measuring the value and performance of knowledge assets (see Figure 2). Determining what knowledge should be managed had become less of a challenge while a new challenge moved up the importance scale – justifying the use of scarce resources for knowledge initiatives. We speculate later in the chapter that this challenge is likely to become even more important in the future.

Ruggles (1998) also examined the organizational capabilities of firms. In 1998, he found that approximately half of the respondents felt their organizations were good or excellent at generating new knowledge. This was the highest rated organizational capability. Accessing valuable knowledge from external sources and us ing accessible knowledge in decision-making were rated next, with about 1/3 of respondents saying their organizations did these things well. Almost no respondents (4%) felt their organization did a good job of measuring the value of knowl-

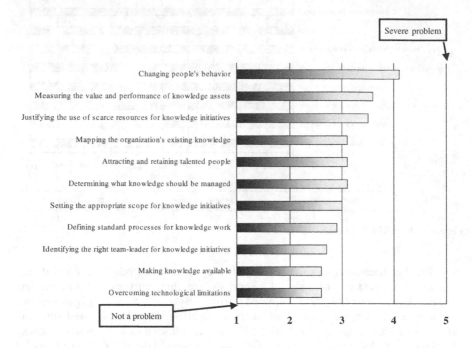

Figure 2. Key Organizational KM Challenges

edge assets and/or the impact of knowledge management. We found a similar pattern in our study. By 2001, the knowledge managers in our sample felt that their organizations had demonstrated two strong capabilities: generating knowledge and accessing valuable knowledge from external sources. Their weakest capabilities were: measuring the impact of knowledge management, measuring the value of knowledge assets and facilitating knowledge sharing through incentives. Clearly, these have been significant challenges for organizations in the past and remain so today.

4.4   The Satisfaction of Knowledge Managers with Their Current Role

Given that knowledge managers (at least those in our sample) have only been in the KM positions 2.2 years on average, it may be slightly premature to evaluate their overall job performance. Nevertheless, we examined four key elements related to job performance: coping ability, job stress, organizational commitment, and job satisfaction. **Coping ability** relates to one's capacity to make changes as deemed necessary to alleviate the pressures of the job; **job stress** refers to one's perception of job-imposed tension caused by the demands of the job; **organizational commitment** is the degree to which one experiences a positive bond with the organization that causes one to feel dedicated and loyal; and finally **job satisfaction** refers to one's contentment with their current job's ability to gratify their interpersonal needs for meaningful employment. While each of these measures a different construct, some tend to be related to each other. For instance, it is common to find high levels of perceived stress related to a low perceived level of ability to cope.

Figure 4 reports these four measures of job performance as rated by the knowledge managers that responded to our study. As can be seen, they are in a very healthy position. That is, they perceive a relatively low level of stress and a high level of coping ability. They also feel committed to their current organization and are relatively satisfied with their current KM position. Overall they seem to be content with their current organizational status.

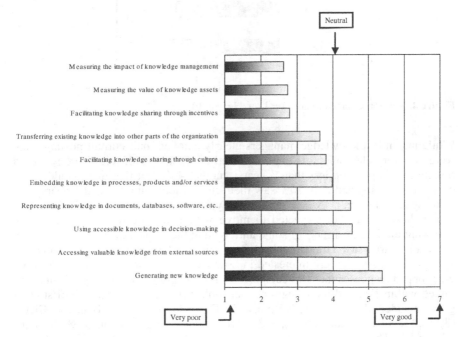

Figure 3. Organizational Capabilities

As shown in Table 6, it was clear from the responses to the question "Why did you accept the job?" that knowledge managers had accepted the KM position as a chance to "make their mark" within the organization. Their top responses were exceedingly positive including reasons such as "opportunity for learning", "desire to build something", and the "ability to influence/impact the organization". When asked "What do you enjoy most about your job?", it was clear from their responses that their experiences on the job had basically reinforced their reasons for accepting the job. For the most part, they felt that they were making a difference; they enjoyed the freedom to choose how to carry out the KM mandate; they felt they were working on the cutting edge; they enjoyed forging new networks of people; and they liked the ability to be creative and innovative.

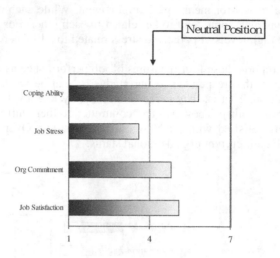

Figure 4. Key Job Characteristics (1 = Low; 7 = High)

While incumbent knowledge managers clearly enjoyed their current posting, they were also very clear about its expected lifetime. Exactly half felt that they would remain in this position less than 3 years; another 40% felt that they would move on within 5 years; and only 10% saw their current job going beyond 5 years. The next logical question is "where do you see yourself going from here?" Forty percent indicated that they expected to move within their current organization by "growing the KM position" ... some anticipating the chance of becoming a CKO. Almost a quarter saw a transition back into a line of the business as the next career step for them. As we were interested in how they saw their future careers in KM, we grouped responses into two categories – job categories where respondents continued within KM and job categories that took them beyond KM. This first category included the following responses: "Expand/Grow this job/maybe CKO" (39%), "KM Consultant" (19%), and "KM in another organization" (3%) for a total of 61%. The second category included the following responses: "line of business" (23%) and "technical position" (3%) for a total of 26%. If we divided the "Job is not a stepping stone/ I don't know" (13%) responses equally between the two categories, we would have 67.5% of the respondents expecting to continue within KM and 32.5% expecting to leave KM. Roughly speaking, two thirds of current knowledge managers expect to continue with a career in knowledge management. This finding reinforces the positive career orientation of knowledge managers as reported in Figure 4.

Table 6. Personal Motivation and Career Expectation

	Number	Percentage of Sample (valid responses)
Why Did You Accept the KM Job?		
• Desire to Impact the Organization	11	16%
• New Opportunities for Learning/New Challenges	10	15%
• Want to Create/Build Something	9	13%
• Empowerment/Influence/Independence	8	12%
• The People I Get to Work With	7	10%
• Already Doing It	6	9%
• Fun/Excitement	4	8%
• Professional/Career Development	3	4%
• No Choice!!	1	1%
What Do You Enjoy Most About Your Job?		
• Making a Difference	13	21%
• Variety and choice	13	21%
• Learning/Being on the Cutting Edge	10	16%
• Networking	9	15%
• Developing/Implementing Strategy	5	8%
• Chance to be innovative/creative	4	6%
• Passion/Excitement	4	6%
• Speaking Opportunities	2	3%
• Not sure?	2	3%
How Long Do You Expect to Remain in Your Current Position?		
• 0-1 year	8	20%
• 2-3 years	12	30%
• 3-5 years	16	40%
• More than 5 years	4	10%
Where Will You Go From Here?		
• Expand/Grow this job/maybe CKO	12	39%
• Line of Business	7	23%

• KM Consultant	6	19%
• Job is not a stepping stone/ I don't know	4	13%
• KM in another organization	1	3%
• Technical position	1	3%

4.5 Portrait of the Knowledge Manager and The KM Role

In this chapter, we have examined a number of dimensions of knowledge managers and the knowledge management role they currently play in organizations. By combining many of these findings, it is possible to construct a composite picture of both knowledge managers and the role of knowledge management. This, however, is a highly subjective undertaking and we do it out of interest and with no assurance or confidence that it is statistically valid. Read on at your own risk.

Based on our study, we find knowledge managers to be somewhat unique individuals characterized as follows:

- Highly educated
- Already a seasoned organizational performer and chosen for the knowledge management position based on their proven performance
- A "researcher" … seeks new knowledge, likes to learn
- Attracted to "being at the forefront of something new and exciting"
- Motivated more by a challenge than by formal power
- Receives intrinsic rewards from helping others … some altruism and/or evangelism
- A risk-taker … sometimes a maverick
- Sees knowledge management as a way to "make a mark within the organization".

Also based on our study, we find the knowledge management role to be somewhat unique. We would characterize it as follows:

- The KM role reports directly to the CEO … from 4 levels down!
- Modest budget … small staff … few entitlements
- Job description is "roll your own" variety … chances of a written job description are no better than 50%
- Role has existed just over 2 years
- Current KM was the first ever appointed in the organization
- Job was created by/for the current KM
- Original purpose was to "leverage the intellectual capital across the organization"
- Education, awareness, and promotion of KM philosophy is major preoccupation
- Changing the organization remains the key challenge
- KM role typically follows a "middle-out" strategy down and implement up

The individuals in our samples are truly the pioneers of knowledge management and as such, they carry significant responsibility. Given substantial license to fashion the KM role, they more than anyone else will be able to "put their mark" on their organizations with respect to knowledge management. As the first wave managers, they will cast the role for knowledge management within their organizations. They will assume the responsibility for hiring and training their staff and successors. They will build a strategy and direct its implementation. It is obvious that these incumbent knowledge managers, not only recognize this opportunity but also found themselves attracted to this challenge because of this opportunity.

Knowledge management can be interpreted as a religion. It has its well-known disciples and followers. It has recognized dogma not the least of which are the competing mantras of "KM as technology" versus "KM as people". Because of its newness, most knowledge managers are "spreading the gospel" and spending inordinate amounts of time and energy on the communication/education agendas. Knowledge management is a risk with a huge payoff – if it becomes widely accepted, early advocates will become legendary. If it becomes little more than a fad, these same advocates will be soon forgotten. This adds to the excitement and challenge particularly in financially-pressed times. This risk-reward balance is clearly foremost in the minds of today's knowledge managers.

Finally it is clear from our survey that the role of knowledge management has its origins at very high levels within the organizational hierarchy. This gives the incumbent knowledge manager significant credibility. As with many executive level initiatives, there will be a grace period – perhaps as long as 2-3 years. At the culmination of this period, the difficult questions will be asked and answers will be demanded. The fear that each and every knowledge manager wakens to late at night is the imminent question directed to him/her by the CEO – "Can you tell me the return we are getting on our KM dollar?". Answering this with accuracy and confidence presents the greatest challenge facing knowledge managers today.

5   Limitations of the Study and Ideas for Future Research

Readers should keep in mind the limitations of our study. Our results are based on self-reports from a relatively small convenience sample. Assessment of knowledge managers and their activities in organizations by other managers within the same organization would be a valuable future research direction because it could result in more objective assessments. Most respondents were from North America, which raises questions about the ability to generalize the findings to other areas of the world such as Europe and Asia. Earl and Scott's (1998, 1999) study of CKO's found few differences between European and North American CKO's, which provides some confidence that our results may generalize at least as far as Europe. We were unsuccessful in obtaining a meaningful picture of the financial resources available to knowledge managers. Pursuing this information in future research studies, as well as looking for objective measures of the impact of the activities of knowledge managers, would be very valuable to answer the critical ROI question. Future research should also study knowledge managers in more depth to understand what makes them effective and ineffective. Longitudinal field research, that allowed the inclusion of multiple perspectives, would be one valuable approach that could be used.

6 Summary

The role of knowledge manager in organizations is a new and growing phenomenon. Our study suggests that knowledge managers are well-educated and experienced individuals who are generally satisfied with their position and the freedom and latitude it affords. The primary goal is to guide their organization towards an understanding of knowledge as an organizational asset so that it can be managed for maximal benefit. As they see it, their key challenge is changing people's behavior. Despite considerable support from top management, they have little direct authority over employees so their levers for effecting change are negotiation, persuasion, and communication.

Our study has taken a snapshot of knowledge managers via a self-reported questionnaire. Information on the backgrounds, activities, and views of knowledge managers has been used to help us understand these pioneers. They undoubtedly play key roles in their organizations' quest for competitive advantage from knowledge. We hope our study is a starting point to help practitioners and researchers understand the practice of knowledge managers and, more importantly, the potential of the knowledge manager role in organizations.

References

Capshaw, S., "Spotlight on Knowledge Leadership: Where's the CKO?" *Inform*, July, 1999, 20-21.

Cole-Gomolski, B., "Knowledge 'Czars' Fall From Grace," *ComputerWorld*, 33, 1, January 4, 1999a, 1-13.

Cole-Gomolski, B., "Knowledge Managers Need Business Savy," *Computer-World*, January 25, 1999b, 40.

Drucker, P.A., *A Post-Capitalist Society*, New York: HarperCollins, 1993.

Duffy, D., "Knowledge Champions: What Does It Take to Be a Successful CKO?" *CIO*, 12, 4, 1998, 66-71.

Earl, M. and I. Scott, "What on Earth Is a CKO?" *London Business School Report*, 1998.

Earl, M.J. and I.A. Scott, "What Is a Chief Knowledge Officer?" *Sloan Management Review*, Winter, 1999, 29-38.

Feeny, D.F., B. R. Edwards, and K.M. Simpson, "Understanding the CEO/CIO Relationship," *MIS Quarterly*, December, 1992, 435-448.

Herschel, R.T. and H.R. Nemati, "Chief Knowledge Officer: Critical Success Factors for Knowledge Management," *Information Strategy: The Executive's Journal*, Summer, 2000, 37-45.

Hibbard, J., "Knowledge and Learning Officers Find Big Paydays," *Information-Week*, June 15, 1998, 170.

House, R. J., R.S. Schuler, and E. Levanoni, "Role Conflict and Ambiguity Scales: Reality or Artifacts?", *Journal of Applied Psychology*, 68, 2, 1983, 334 – 337.

Mowday, R.T., R.M. Steers, and L.W. Porter, "The Measurement of Organizational Commitment," *Journal of Vocational Behavior*, 14, 2, 1979, 224-247.

Rizzo, J., R. House, and S. Lirtzman, "Role Conflict and Ambiguity in Complex Organizations," *Administrative Sciences Quarterly*, 15, 2, 1970, 150-163.

Ruggles, R., "The State of the Notion: Knowledge Management in Practice," *California Management Review*, 40, 3, 1998, 80-89.

Shin, Y.K., "The Traits and Leadership Styles of CEOs in Korean Companies," *International Studies of Management & Organization*, 28, 4, 1999, 40-48.

Stephens, C.S., W.N. Ledbetter, A. Mitra, and F.N. Ford, "Executive or Functional Manager? The Nature f the CIO's Job," *MIS Quarterly*, December, 1992, 449-467.

Stewart, T.A., "Is This Job Really Necessary," *FORTUNE*, January 12, 1998, 154-155.

TFPL Ltd., "Skills for Knowledge Management," TFPL Briefing Paper, July 1999, URL = http://www.tfpl.com

Warr, P., J. Cook, and T. Wall, "Scales for the Measurement of Some Work Attitudes and Aspects of Psychological Well-being," *Journal of Occupational Behavior*, 52, 1979, 129-148.

Watt, P., "Knowing It All," *Intranet*, August, 1997, 17-18.

CHAPTER 3

On Knowledge Work

Ulrike Schultze
Cox School of Business, Southern Methodist University, Dallas, TX, USA

The management of knowledge and of knowledge work are regarded as the key challenges in the information economy and knowledge intensive firms. Even though the term knowledge work is used increasingly there is some ambiguity surrounding what constitutes knowledge work and who are regarded as knowledge workers. In this chapter knowledge work as a category of work is explored. Knowledge work is defined from different perspectives – the economic, the labor process, and the work practice perspective – and the implications of using knowledge work as a category of work in both research and practice are discussed.

Keywords: Work Classifications; Knowledge Work; Service Work; Informing Practices

1 Introduction

As economies move into the information age and post-industrial era, information and knowledge become important, if not the most important, resources in organizations (Bell, 1976). Knowledge and its application are regarded as the primary source of competitive advantage (e.g., Conner and Prahalad, 1996; Prahalad and Hamel, 1990). This era, or third wave (Toffler, 1980) distinguishes itself from the agricultural and industrial age before it, in that the largest portion of a country's workforce is engaged in the service sector of the economy which encompasses mainly human, technical and professional services (Bell, 1976). About 75% of workers today in the United States are employed in service sector jobs, which are expected to be the predominant type of employment in the next decade (Bureau of Labor Statistics, 1999). This implies an economic system that relies increasingly on knowledge and service work.

The concept of knowledge work is being used more and more in the literature, but frequently it is applied without careful definition. Nevertheless, a somewhat consistent theme of knowledge workers whose work inputs and outputs are high in information content (Davis, Collins, Eierman, and Nance, 1991; Straub and Karahanna, 1998), who apply "skilled mental labor" (Hellstrom, Malmquist, and Mikaelsson, 2001: 26) and "ply their trade through their intellective abilities and their specialized knowledge rather than their physical abilities" (Hayes, 2001: 79) has become apparent. Other attributes typically associated with knowledge work include mobility, flexibility, empowerment, teamwork, computer-mediation, application of esoteric and theoretical knowledge, and work that is in high demand in the information age.

The objective of this chapter is to review the definitions of knowledge work that have been proffered by the literature. Each definition offers a different lens through which we can see and study knowledge work. And, like any lens or pair of glasses, these definitions highlight and hide different aspects of the knowledge work phenomenon. Given that considerable criticism has been leveled against the concept of knowledge work, this book chapter will not only review the definitions of knowledge work from the economic, the labor process, and the work-practice perspective, but also contemplate the implications and affordances of the knowledge work concept.

2   Definitions of Knowledge Work

2.1 The Economic Perspective

The economic perspective emphasizes how knowledge work differs from other types of work. This perspective is concerned with creating classification schemes whereby occupations can be categorized and compared in order to address issues of policy, such as education and training, for instance, as well as issues of competitive advantage. Authors who define knowledge work from the economic perspective frequently draw on classification schemes that incorporate different types of knowledge that workers are expected to possess and differences in the nature of their work.

Machlup (1962) was one of the first to define knowledge work. In his effort to quantify the expenditure on knowledge and its contribution to the post-war economy, he defined knowledge work as the production and transmission of knowledge. Using census data, he classified the US labor force into knowledge and non-knowledge workers. Some occupations located in the manufacturing and service sectors were included in the knowledge work category, while all work belonging to the agricultural sector was regarded as non-knowledge work. His classification scheme required a somewhat arbitrary segmentation of professions. For instance, he excluded half of all physicians and surgeons from the knowledge work group, because he considered only half of their work to deal with knowledge creation and transfer. In the case of the doctors, knowledge work included diagnosing, giving therapeutic advice and making prescription.

In a report by the Organization for Economic Co-operation and Development (OECD), Arnal, Ok, and Torres (2001), divide occupations into two main groups: non-information and information workers. This distinction is supposed to reflect the different aspects of human activities, where non-information work produces goods and personal services, and information work generates and manipulates information. Service work is characterized by personal interactions with customers, and examples of service occupations include sales representatives, entertainers, artists and customer service representatives. In contrast, goods-producing work is characterized by physical labor and the manipulation of physical objects. Farmers, precision production craftsmen and factory workers are examples of people doing this kind of work.

Information work is subdivided further into knowledge, management and data work. The knowledge work category includes occupations that produce original knowledge or possess expertise that is not easily transferable. Occupations that qualify as knowledge work are engineers, scientists or computer scientists. In contrast to knowledge workers, data workers manipulate information, but they do not produce new knowledge. Examples of data workers are librarians, administrators, office clerks and counselors. Management workers include business owners, executives, legislators and senior officials.

In a similar vein, Drucker (1993) suggests that not all work with information qualifies as knowledge work. Some of it is service work. Service work, like factory work, relies on established procedures and has clearly defined deliverables. Clerical jobs such as data processing, billing, and answering customer queries are examples of service work. Service workers' tasks are fairly well defined, bounded, and frequently scripted (Leidner, 1993), which makes it possible to establish quantifiable productivity measures for them. This further relinquishes the need for high levels of education among service workers.

In contrast, knowledge worker's knowledge is frequently assumed to be tacit (Morris, 2001). This assumption implies the knowledge-based view of the firm, which conceptualizes firms as knowledge-bearing entities (Foss, 1996) or a body of knowledge (Spender, 1996). According to the knowledge-based view, a firm's boundaries are formed around irreducible knowledge differences. Grant (1996) argues that firms exist because of asymmetries in the economics of knowledge caused by the immutability of tacit knowledge and the risk of potential buyers expropriating explicit knowledge (also Grant and Baden-Fuller, 1995). Firms thus exist to create an environment in which the disparate specialist knowledge that is required to produce goods and service can be brought together in a way that provides incentives to cooperate rather than to behave opportunistically (Conner and Prahalad, 1996; Kogut and Zander, 1996).

Ironically, universal knowledge which has traditionally been considered as the highest grade of knowledge because it is 'true' at all times and in all places, does not have the same capacity for generating competitive advantage that local, specific and private knowledge does. Intangible firm-specific knowledge that enables the firm to add value to incoming factors of production in a relatively unique way is what gives organizations sustainable competitive advantage. Core competencies should ideally originate within the firm if they are to enhance the firm's competitiveness (Bierly and Chakrabarti, 1996).

Resource-based approaches therefore regard privately held knowledge as a basic source of competitive advantage (Conner and Prahalad, 1996). They argue that a company's competitive strength is derived from the uniqueness of its internally accumulated capabilities. To maintain sustained competitive advantage under the resource-based theory of the firm, the resource – also referred to as core or distinctive competence – must demonstrate four characteristics. It must be valuable, imperfectly imitable, rare among competitors, and have few strategically equivalent substitutes (Barney, 1991; Von Krogh and Roos, 1995).

The resource-based approach therefore implies that not all knowledge is equally valuable. Resources that can freely be purchased and traded in the market are limited in their ability to serve as a source of competitive advantage. Information and knowledge have typically been treated as a public good by economists, because once created, they can be reproduced and consumed by additional users at close to zero marginal cost (Grant, 1996; Poster, 1990). Thus, compared to service workers, whose work is scripted such that the only knowledge that is required for the job is assumed to be explicit, knowledge workers who are assumed to possess tacit knowledge are deemed more valuable to the firm.

Also, compared to service work, the tasks and final outcomes of knowledge work are not given. Knowledge work involves choices rather than right or wrong answers (Drucker, 1993: 85) and it makes room for creativity (Ledford, 1995: 55). Besides demanding high levels of education to begin with, knowledge work also requires thinking agents that are engaged in continuous learning and in the development of idiosyncratic and esoteric knowledge (Spitler and Gallivan, 1999; Sviokla, 1996). This learning and knowledge creation is frequently accomplished through collaboration among discipline-based experts that belong to communities of practice (Hayes, 2001).

Similar to Drucker (1993), Frenkel et al. (1995) approach their definition of knowledge work from the perspective of what kind of knowledge and skills are valued in the contemporary world of increasing computerization on the one hand and increasing ambiguity on the other. For instance, they highlight that theoretical knowledge becomes increasingly important in an environment in which symbols rather than physical objects are being manipulated. Their definition of knowledge work rests on three dimensions each of which is a continuum: form of knowledge (theoretical vs. contextual), creativity (high vs. low), and intellective, social and action-centered skill (high vs. low). Using these dimensions they distinguish between knowledge work and routine work, where knowledge work is characterized by theoretical knowledge, high creativity, and high social and intellectual skill. Using this three-dimensional framework, they classify the work of customer service representatives as routine work, and the work of an architect or a registered nurse as knowledge work.

In summary, the definitions of knowledge work that are based on the economic perspective highlight a few dimensions along which knowledge workers distinguish themselves from non-knowledge, data, service, and/or routine workers. These are:

- *The nature of the knowledge the workers possess*: Knowledge workers differentiate themselves from other categories of workers by possessing mostly abstract, theoretical, and esoteric knowledge, for which high levels of formal education serve as a proxy (e.g., Starbuck, 1992).
- *The nature of the knowledge they produce*: Knowledge workers distinguish themselves from other kinds of workers by producing new knowledge rather than merely manipulating existing knowledge. Because the production of original knowledge requires creativity, knowledge work differs from service work in that the workers are more empowered and able to use their intellective and social skills in a more autonomous and creative way.

It is also noteworthy that, seen from the economic perspective, knowledge workers are regarded as the most valuable of human resources in both economies and organizations. Furthermore, they are presented as the most privileged class of workers in that they are granted many liberties at work (e.g., creativity, poorly defined performance measurement). This creates an impression that knowledge workers form the "ruling class" (Donaldson, 2001) in the information age. As we see in the next section, this image of knowledge work is tempered somewhat in the labor process perspective.

2.2 The Labor Process Perspective

The labor process perspective of knowledge work concerns itself with the formation and composition of a new class (i.e., a class that is located between the blue-collar workers that make up the proletariat and the owners of capital that make up the bourgeoisie). Marx's theory did not account for the white-collar or knowledge workers who include professionals, technicians, and managers (Wuthnow and Shrum, 1983).

The definition of knowledge work advanced by the labor process perspective bears much resemblance to the definitions of knowledge work already discussed. For instance, Chamot (1987) divides the white collar workforce into (1) executives and managers who have supervisory authority, set policies, and see that they are carried out; (2) professional employees who usually have college degrees and occupy jobs that require the frequent use of judgment and application of specialized knowledge, and (3) clerical and support such as staff secretaries.

Furthermore, others have classified professionals and technicians as knowledge workers. Professionals are characterized by a systematic, scientifically-based theory, long formal education, autonomy, ethical rules, a distinct occupational culture, client-orientation, social sanction and authorization (Alvesson, 1993). Originally this class of work only included physicians, lawyers and priests, but now also incorporates, among others, accountants and consultants of various kinds. The inclusion of technicians in the knowledge work category is interesting, in that their work is quite physical in nature. Their work revolves around instruments and machines and they are employed in a variety of fields, including medicine, engineering, auto repair and computers (Barley, 1996). Since they require training in a science and technology on the one hand, and work on machines on the other, they straddle the industrial world of physical and the post-industrial world of cognitive work (Orr, 1996). This seems to justify their inclusion in the knowledge worker category.

From the labor process perspective, a key question surrounding knowledge work is whether this "middle grouping" will congeal to form a cohesive third class, also referred to as the service class or the new middle class (Smith and Willmott, 1991), or whether it will split into two groups with the managerial workers joining the capital owning class, and the technical-professional workers joining the working class. Wuthnow and Shrum (1983) highlight that there are ideological differences between the managerial and the technical-professional groups that could keep a coherent knowledge work class from forming. These differences are based on (a) managers typically having lower levels of education than professionals and technicians do, and (b) professionals and technicians being more dependent on government for jobs than managers are. To the extent that these differences are less material than the experiences managers, professionals, and technicians share by working in corporations and the common interest they have in differentiating themselves from the proletariat in particular, these occupational groups are expected to congeal into a new class.

Others who have approached knowledge work from the labor process perspective have focused on the changes in the nature of work. Some of this research highlights the increasing feminization, rationalization, and fragmentation of white-collar work that is associated with the increasing use of office technologies (e.g., Iacono and Kling, 1987; Kraut, 1987; Zuboff, 1988). This work suggests that the middle grouping of knowledge workers will not converge but split, with those engaged in more discretionary work aligning themselves with the owners of capital, while those engaged in the manipulation of information joining the ranks of the working class.

Kraft (1987) presents an example of fragmentation of white-collar work. Analyzing the work of programmers who he refers to as the "ultimate knowledge workers," he suggests that knowledge work will become increasingly proletarianized resulting in a split between the managerial and technical-professional groups of knowledge work:

> "One of the characteristics of knowledge work is that it is by definition intellectual labor. The core of intellectual labor is judgment and discretion. But I also have said that the overriding necessity of our production system is to eliminate human discretion and to transfer control to machines. In software work the anomaly has been confronted in a straight-forward and, I would say, an entirely predictable way: This prototypical mind work has been broken down into head and hand work and then the components parceled out to different workers. The trick has been accomplished in a way that will come as no surprise to management specialists. Some people make general decisions about design, hiring, expenditures, schedules and so on, whereas other people do the work. Programming, in short, has been industrialized." (p 108)

In summary, the labor process perspective defines knowledge workers as a "middle grouping" made up of professionals, technicians, and managers. It casts knowledge work in a system in which there are two dominant social classes, namely workers – or the producers of surplus value – and the owners of capital. The key question surrounding knowledge work in this context is whether knowledge workers will form a coherent third class, or whether they will be subsumed into the existing class system. Given this focus on class, the labor-process perspective is more focused on the ideological affiliations of the occupational groups that make up the knowledge work class, than on what knowledge the knowledge workers possess or what they do.

2.3 The Work Practice Perspective

The work practice perspective focuses on the work that knowledge workers *do* rather than on what they *know*. Blackler et al. (1993) argues that definitions of knowledge work that are based on what knowledge workers know are problematic in that the concept of knowledge is inherently ambiguous. Even though numerous definitions of knowledge work presented under the economic perspective incorporate aspects of what knowledge workers do, the work practice definition differs from these definitions in that it focuses primarily on knowledge workers' activities and practices.

Stehr (1994) classifies knowledge work into knowledge production and knowledge re-production. Stehr prefers the concept of knowledge re-production to knowledge transfer, which is the concept that Machlup (1962) used in his definition of knowledge work, because the distinction between creating and transmitting knowledge assumes that objective knowledge can be transferred easily and that there is no need to interpret it. Scientists and intellectuals are knowledge producers who contribute to the public fund of knowledge. However, the application and transfer of scientific knowledge is typically left to advisors, experts and counselors. Stehr (1994) sees their work as a form of knowledge re-production rather than a mere transfer of knowledge. In their capacity as interpreters and translators of knowledge, advisors, experts and counselors are engaged in a transformative, value creating activity. They acquire, manipulate, organize and communicate knowledge fitting it to a specific context, question, or problem. Their work is similar to that of an interpreter who translates statements made within one community, culture or tradition so that they can be understood within another (Bauman, 1987). Stehr therefore suggests that the mere transmission of knowledge is not enough to constitute knowledge work. To qualify as knowledge work, information and knowledge have to be (re)produced.

Drawing on the distinction between disciplines and professions, Fuller (1992) similarly differentiates between knowledge generation and application. He sees scientists as disciplinarians that generate original knowledge using the disciplining practices of their field, i.e. theories, methods and instruments. Lawyers and doctors, representing the professions, apply knowledge and pass it on. They serve as intermediaries between scientific knowledge and the general public.

Wikstrom and Norman (1994) add a third activity to knowledge work. They identify the following knowledge processes in organizations: generating new knowledge, making it productive, i.e., making it manifest in a service or product offering, and representing knowledge such that it can be transferred and shared. Similarly, Davenport et al. (1996: 54) define knowledge workers' primary activities as the acquisition, creation, packaging, or application of knowledge. Also, Snyder-Halpern et al (2001) define the following knowledge work roles: data gatherer, information user, knowledge user and knowledge builder. In their research, they show how nurses fulfill each of these roles.

In my own research (Schultze, 2000), I adopt a work practice approach and explore what knowledge workers do. In it, knowledge work is defined as the production and re-production of information. Ethnographically studying knowledge workers' practices of informing (i.e., the work of producing and re-producing information), my research highlights that knowledge workers are expected to "add value" to the firm. Adding value implies that knowledge workers need to add something of themselves, for instance, their own understanding, personal knowledge, and subjective point of view, to the informational objects they produce and re-produce. Thus knowledge work is depicted as a continuous struggle to objectify subjective insights, ideas, and hunches in order to produce information (i.e., objects that others recognize as being believable, reliable, and valuable).

I also identify three practices of informing that characterize the work of the knowledge workers I studied. These were also discernable in my work as an academic knowledge worker. The three practices of informing were labeled expressing, monitoring, and translating:

- Ex-pressing involves extracting knowledge and experiences out of the individual worker's mind and body, pressing these into words and then pressing these words into a coherent linear text. In expressing themselves, knowledge workers also press themselves out of the events that they are capturing in words. That means, they distance themselves from it and suspend their subjectivity in order to become a seemingly objective observer.

- Monitoring represents the task of seeing and seeking information without being seen, that is, without influencing the situation and/or the information that is being gathered. Rather than asking questions outright, monitoring involves the unobtrusive and continuous gathering of just-in-case information. By relying on monitoring as a practice of informing, knowledge workers have some measure of assurance that the information they gathered is unadulterated by their own interest and information gathering activity. They can therefore more readily claim the role of uninvolved bystander and objective observer.

- Translating entails a tacking back and forth between multiple contexts. For instance, it involves the interpretation of questions that are developed in the problem domain and the development of a feasible set of answers in the solution domain, but also the interpretation of other information that exists in the solution domain to refine the questions in the problem domain. Translating thus renders the information from one realm recognizable to the other. The balancing of induction and deduction plays an important part in translating, as does the balancing between subjectivity and objectivity.

Knights et al. (1993) define knowledge work as networking, thereby highlighting the social capital (rather than the intellectual capital) that knowledge workers apply in their work. Social capital includes existing relationships with people both inside and outside the firm. By highlighting the centrality of social capital in knowledge work, Knights et al. (1993) demonstrate the old adage of 'it's who you know, not what you know,' and therefore challenges the assumed importance of intellectual capital in knowledge work (also Alvesson, 2001).

In summary, the work practice perspective on knowledge work focuses on what knowledge workers do, rather than what kind of knowledge they possess. A common theme that runs through research adopting this perspective is that knowledge work is the production and reproduction of information and knowledge. Specific processes and practices that form part of knowledge work include generating new knowledge, interpreting and representing it, as well as expressing, monitoring, translating and networking.

3 Criticism of Knowledge Work as a Category of Work

There is some opposition to establishing "knowledge work" as a separate category of work, especially because of the privileged, powerful, and financially lucrative position that is afforded to this class of worker in the information economy (e.g., Alvesson, 2001; Knights et al., 1993). The term knowledge work is tautological because to act with knowledge is to be human (Cook and Brown, 1999; Stehr, 1992). And if knowledge is a prerequisite for *all* human work, then establishing knowledge work as a separate category intimates that some human activities do not require knowledge. Von Krogh, Ichijo and Nonaka (2000: 12) warn that "restricting the knowledge worker category to a certain type of professional employee will stifle a company's capacity to unleash the full potential of its human resources." They contend that "knowledge work is a human condition, rather than a privileged one" (p. 12). Consequently, they view humanness as the only qualifier for knowledge work.

Alvesson (2001) casts serious doubts on the justifiability of knowledge work as a privileged position. He maintains that both knowledge and its role in work processes such as the production of solutions to problems are ambiguous. In the face of ambiguity, identity and image construction through reputation and rhetoric become increasingly important. Thus knowledge intensive firms such as consulting or accounting firms *claim* that their workers have the required expertise and they *claim* that this expertise makes a difference in the production of solutions for the client. The symbolic value of knowledge and its espoused role in the production and reproduction of knowledge, information and ideas are then relied upon to construct an image of the firm's and its workers' knowledge-intensity.

Evidence for this argument can be found in the research of Hansen et al. (1999), which highlights how professional service firms use their knowledge management strategy as a positioning device. For instance, a consulting firm like McKinsey will limit codification of their consultants' knowledge, thereby preserving in key consultants the expertise that is necessary to solve a client's problem. Relying on a personalization strategy, rather than a codification strategy, creates an air of unique, highly specialized knowledge and implicitly promises the generation of solutions for which clients would expect to pay a premium.

Furthermore, Donaldson (2001) highlights that there is very little evidence that engineers, technicians, and academics have become "the ruling class" (p. 960). He argues that this is in part because there are limits to the efficient exchange of knowledge for rents, given that a buyer cannot assess the value of knowledge until it is shared with him/her, and that this very sharing of knowledge renders it a free good. Donaldson thus casts some doubt on the predictions and fears of the economic and labor process perspectives respectively.

This criticism of the concept of knowledge work raises questions about the implications of its use. What does the concept imply and what are the consequences? What are the affordances of knowledge work? In short, to what end can knowledge work as a category of work legitimately be used?

4   Implications of Knowledge Work as a Category of Work

Given the argument that all work requires the application of knowledge, the emergence of knowledge work as a classification of work needs to be understood with respect to the historical shift in the meaning of knowledge from craft-like know-how to an object, a resource, or a product. Drucker's (1993) discussion of the role of knowledge in economic development is helpful in tracing the evolution of the meaning of knowledge. In this work Drucker argues that the three waves of economic transformation the Western world has experienced were driven by the unique application of knowledge in its various forms. While others argue that investments in technology and capital were the driving forces behind these economic revolutions, Drucker considers these to be secondary causes and mere manifestations of different applications of knowledge.

Drucker thus argues that the *industrial revolution* entailed the application of knowledge to tradition and craft. The development and implementation of technology (i.e., tools, processes, and products) demystified craft and tacit knowledge. The industrial revolution changed the meaning of knowledge as it "converted experience into knowledge, apprenticeship into textbooks, secrecy into methodology, doing into applied knowledge" (p. 29).

The *productivity revolution*, which also marked the beginning of scientific management, was characterized by the application of knowledge to human work. Fredrick Taylor's time and motion studies were at the forefront of this transformation. Using scientific measures he rationalized skill, reducing all manual work, however 'skilled', to a mere set of repetitive movements. Any worker who was willing to do the work in the way that analysis showed it should be done was deserving of first-class wages. First-class work therefore no longer relied on the acquisition of skills through many years of apprenticeship. Indeed, long apprenticeships could be replaced by training, that is, the transfer of codified knowledge.

In the third revolution, which Drucker refers to as the *management revolution*, knowledge is applied to knowledge itself. Here knowledge is used to improve knowledge work. It is applied to guide innovation, define what new knowledge is needed and find ways of making existing knowledge more productive. Formal knowledge is seen as both a key personal and economic resource. As an economic resource, knowledge becomes a commodity and a utility that serves as a means of achieving social and economic results.

Aaronowitz and DiFazio (1994) summarize the change in the meaning of knowledge in a similar way. They note that the passage from an industry-specific labor process to computer-mediated work has changed the representation of knowledge. Whereas knowledge once resided in the process of steelmaking, for instance, it becomes a relatively "free-floating commodity to the extent that it is transformed into information that requires no productive object" (p. 17).

Fuller (1992) highlights yet another shift in the meaning of knowledge. He recounts that philosophers typically treated knowledge as being about things. Knowledge was thus regarded as immaterial propositions that transcend the material reality they represent. Over time, however, knowledge has taken on an economic presence as a thing. Consistent with the knowledge-based theories of the firm (Grant, 1996; Grant and Baden-Fuller, 1995), knowledge has been turned into a product that can be exchanged, accumulated, bought, and sold. In the information age, there is an increasing realization that knowledge is no longer just *about* the world, but that it is also *in* the world.

As mentioned earlier, the economic perspective of knowledge work assumes that the logical, rational, explainable and scientific know-why is superior to the situated practical know-how that blue-collar or agricultural workers have typically relied on. This is because theoretical knowledge is assumed to be rarer and more difficult to imitate than know-how. However, Stehr (1992), taking a work practice perspective, points out that skills and practical know-how are robust, specific and concrete whereas know-why is fragile, general and abstract. What this highlights is a difference in the perception of what is valued in the different theoretical perspectives of knowledge work; the robust, reliable know-how or the fragile, esoteric know-why.

In summary, it is important to acknowledge that the concept of knowledge work is part of a larger environment of meaning, in which theoretical knowledge that has been acquired through formal education is valued more highly than practical knowledge that had been acquired through experience on the job. It is against this backdrop that both researchers and practitioners need to decide whether the use of knowledge work is a desirable and defensible move.

5   Affordances of Knowledge Work as a Category of Work

Like any category, the knowledge work category acts as a kind of shorthand that allows researchers and practitioners to make claims about and develop initiatives for the disparate occupations that constitute this group of workers. What the concept of knowledge work does is highlight the similarities among disparate groups of workers – be they professionals, technicians, academics, or managers – while underplaying their differences. Thus, by referring to them as knowledge workers, the hierarchical distance between a manager and a trainee is underplayed. Similarly, the social distance between an academic with an advanced degree and a self-taught computer consultant is eliminated.

Focusing on the similarities among different occupational groups has the advantage of focusing on what is deemed to be important. For instance, if a company wishes to implement a knowledge management technology to which a broad cross-section of employees contribute, then it might be useful to refer to the intended users as knowledge workers in order to highlight that all of their knowledge is equally valuable, whether they are shop-floor workers or managers. Examples of where such a strategy has borne results are offered by Leonard-Barton (1995) who describes the benefits of viewing repetitive menial jobs from the standpoint of their potential for knowledge creation in her case study of Chaparral

Steel. Also, Von Krogh et al. (2000) argue that everyone in a firm has the capacity to be a knowledge worker; knowledge creation can occur between an untrained sales person and a new customer, for instance. Also, Cutcher-Gershenfeld et al. (1998) present how shop-floor workers in manufacturing environments are engaged in knowledge-driven work.

With respect to research, the affordance of the knowledge work category seems to lie in criticality (Golden-Biddle and Locke, 1993) or cultural critique (Marcus and Fischer, 1986). Critical research moves readers to re-examine their own taken for granted assumptions by using the research "to reflect not only on the members' world but more importantly on the world of the researcher" (Golden-Biddle and Locke, 1993: 614). One way of achieving this is through cultural juxtaposition.

In my own work (Schultze, 2000), I present not only the librarians, competitive intelligence analysts, and computer systems administrators as knowledge workers, but I also present myself, the researcher, as such. By so doing, this research highlights the fundamental logic underlying each of the practices of informing that were present in both my own work and the work of the knowledge workers I studied. This underlying logic was knowledge workers' endeavor to balance subjectivity and objectivity (in their relative sense), where subjectivity, tacit knowledge and the willingness to 'add one's self' are associated with being "value adding," and objectivity is associated with authority and safety against attacks on one's personal identity and competence.

In addition to showing the trans-situational nature of these practices of informing, my purpose in incorporating my own practices of informing into the research was to hold up as a mirror to academic knowledge workers the informing practices that were evident among the corporate knowledge workers that I studied. In this way, I hope to provoke reflection and self-examination about informing practices on the part of my readers.

6   In Conclusion

There are numerous definitions of knowledge work as a category of work. Arguing that there are different perspectives that act as lenses through which the knowledge work phenomenon can be viewed, this book chapter presented the economic, the labor process and the work practice perspectives on knowledge work. The economic perspective is primarily concerned with the occupations that are classified as knowledge work and how these differ from other occupations both in terms of the nature of the knowledge workers possess and the work that they do. The labor process perspective focuses on the position and alignment of knowledge workers within the established class system. The work practice perspective concerns itself with what knowledge workers actually do, thereby foregoing concerns over what they know and what they are supposed to know are role occupants.

Even though these perspectives focus on different aspects of the knowledge work phenomenon, there is some overlap among them. One of these is the meaning of knowledge, that is, what is regarded as knowledge and what kind of knowledge is valued. In the context of the information economy, knowledge-intensive firms, and the knowledge-based view of the firm – all of which fall into the economic perspective – the kind of knowledge that is valued is theoretical, abstract knowledge that is rare and difficult to imitate.

Given this rather narrow understanding of knowledge, there is considerable criticism of knowledge work as a category of work. A key objection to the concept of knowledge work is that all human endeavor requires knowledge, which would suggest that non-knowledge workers are less than human. Thus, by applying the category of knowledge work researchers and practitioners are not only setting up a system of difference but also a system of deference (Derrida, 1978).

Despite these criticisms of the knowledge work category, it does offer some affordances. For instance, the attributions of importance and high-status that are associated with the knowledge work category can be used strategically in knowledge management initiatives. For instance, by using the concept in an inclusive way and viewing everyone in the corporation as a knowledge worker, the corporation communicates to all its workers that their knowledge is valued. In the academic setting, the knowledge work category can be used to facilitate reflection and self-examination on the part of knowledge workers who read the research about knowledge workers who are engaged in occupations other than their own.

Acknowledgement

I would like to thank Valerie Spitler for her careful review of this book chapter.

References

Aaronowitz, S. and W. DiFazio, *The Jobless Future: Sci-Tech and the Dogma of Work*. Minneapolis: University of Minnesota Press, 1994.

Alvesson, M., "Organizations as Rhetoric: Knowledge-Intensive Firms and the Struggle with Ambiguity," *Journal of Management Studies, 30*, 6, 1993, 997-1015.

Alvesson, M., "Knowledge Work: Ambiguity, Image and Identity," *Human Relations, 54*, 7, 2001, 863-886.

Arnal, E., W. Ok, and R. Torres, *Knowledge, Work Organization and Economic Growth*, Labour Market and Social Policy Occasional Papers 50. Paris, France: Organization for Economic Co-operation and Development, 2001.

Barley, S.R., "Technicians in the Workplace: Ethnographic Evidence for bringing Work into Organizational Studies," *Administrative Science Quarterly, 41*, 3, 1996, 404-441.

Barney, J. B., "Firm Resources and Sustained Competitive Advantage," *Journal of Management, 17*, 1, 1991, 99-120.

Bauman, Z., *Legislators and Interpreters: On Modernity, Post-modernity and Intellectuals*. Cambridge, UK: Polity Press, 1987.

Bell, D., *The Coming of Post-Industrial Society: A Venture in Social Forecasting.* New York: Basic Books, 1976.

Bierly, P. and A. Chakrabarti, "Generic Knowledge Strategies in the U.S. Pharmaceutical Industry," *Strategic Management Journal, 17,* Winter Special Issue, 1996, 123-135.

Blackler, F., M. Reed and A. Whitaker, "Editorial Introduction: Knowledge Workers and Contemporary Organizations," *Journal of Management Studies, 30,* 6, 1993, 851-862.

Bureau of Labor Statistics, 1999, "BLS releases new 1998-2008 employment projections." URL=http://www.bls.gov/news.release/ecopro.nr0.htm

Chamot, D., "Electronic Work and the White-Collar Employee," in R. E. Kraut (Ed.), *Technology and the Transformation of White-Collar Work.* Hillsdale, NY: Lawrence Erlbaum Associates, 1987, 23-33.

Conner, K.R., and C.K. Prahalad, "A Resource-Based Theory of the Firm: Knowledge Versus Opportunism," *Organization Science, 7,* 5, 1996, 477-501.

Cook, S.D.N. and J.S. Brown, "Bridging Epistemologies: The Generative Dance between Organizational Knowledge and Organizational Knowing," *Organization Science, 10,* 4, 1999, 381-400.

Cutcher-Gershenfeld, J., M. Nitta, B.J. Barrett, N. Belhedi, S.S-C. Chow, T. Inaba, I. Ishino, W-J. Lin, M. L. Moore, W.M. Mothersell, J. Palthe, S. Ramanand, M.E. Strolle, and A.C. Wheaton, *Knowledge-Driven Work: Unexpected Lessons from Japanese and United States Work Practices.* New York: Oxford University Press, 1998.

Davenport, T. H., S.L. Jarvenpaa and M.C. Beers, "Improving Knowledge Work Processes," *Sloan Management Review,* Summer, 1996, 53-65.

Davis, G. B., R.W. Collins, M. Eierman and W. Nance, "Conceptual Model for Research on Knowledge Work," *Management Information Systems Research Center Working Paper 91-10, University of Minnesota, Minneapolis,* 1991.

Derrida, J., *Writing and Difference.* Chicago: University of Chicago Press, 1978.

Donaldson, L., "Reflections on Knowledge and Knowledge-intensive firms," *Human Relations, 54,* 7, 2001, 955-963.

Drucker, P., *Post-Capitalist Society.* New York: Harper Collins, 1993.

Foss, N. J., "Knowledge-Base Approaches to the Theory of the Firm: Some Critical Comments," *Organization Science, 7,* 5, 1996, 470-476.

Frenkel, S., M. Korczynski, L. Donoghue and K. Shire, "Re-constituting Work: Trends towards Knowledge Work and Information-Normative Control," *Work, Employment and Society, 9,* 4, 1995, 773-796.

Fuller, S., "Knowledge as Product and Property," in N. Stehr and R. V. Ericson (Eds.), *The Culture and Power of Knowledge: Inquiries into Contemporary Societies.* Berlin: de Gruyter, 1992, 177-190.

Golden-Biddle, K., and K. Locke, "Appealing Work: An Investigation of how Ethnographic Texts Convince," *Organization Science, 4,* 4, 1993, 595-616.

Grant, R. M., "Toward a Knowledge-Based Theory of the Firm," *Strategic Management Journal, 17*, Winter Special Issue, 1996, 109-122.

Grant, R. M., and C. Baden-Fuller, "A Knowledge-Based Theory of Interfirm Collaboration," *Academy of Management Journal*, 1995, 17-21.

Hansen, M. T., N. Nohria, and T. Tierney, "What's your Strategy for Managing Knowledge?" *Harvard Business Review*, March-April, 1999, 106-116.

Hayes, N. "Boundless and bounded interactions in the knowledge work process: the role of groupware technologies," *Information and Organization, 11*, 2, 2001, 79-101.

Hellstrom, T., U. Malmquist and J. Mikaelsson, "Decentralizing knowledge: Managing knowledge work in a software engineering firm," *Journal of High Technology Management Research, 12*, 2001, 25-38.

Iacono, S., and R. Kling, "Changing Office Technologies and Transformations of Clerical Jobs: A Historical Perspective," in R. E. Kraut (Ed.), *Technology and the Transformation of White-Collar Work*. Hillsdale, NY: Lawrence Erlbaum Associates, 1987, 53-75.

Knights, D., F. Murray and H. Willmott, "Networking as Knowledge Work: A Study of Strategic Interorganizational Development in the Financial Services Industry," *Journal of Management Studies, 30*, 6, 1993, 975-995.

Kogut, B. and U. Zander, "What Firms Do? Coordination, Identity and Learning," *Organization Science, 7*, 5, 1996, 502-518.

Kraft, P. "Computers and the Automation of Work," in R. E. Kraut (Ed.), *Technology and the Transformation of White-Collar Work*. Hillsdale, NY: Lawrence Erlbaum Associates, 1987, 99-111.

Kraut, R. E. "Social Issues and White-Collar Technology: An Overview.," in R. E. Kraut (Ed.), *Technology and the Transformation of White-Collar Work*. Hillsdale, NY: Lawrence Erlbaum Associates, 1987, 1-21.

Ledford, G. E. J., "Paying for the Skills, Knowledge, and Competencies of Knowledge Workers," *Compensation and Benefits Review, 27*, 4, 1995, 55-62.

Leidner, R., *Fast Food, Fast Talk: Service Work and the Routinization of Everyday Life*. Berkeley: University of California Press, 1993.

Leonard-Barton, D., *Wellsprings of Knowledge: Building and Sustaining the Sources of Innovation*. Boston: Harvard Business Press, 1995.

Machlup, F., *The Production and Distribution of Knowledge in the United States*. Princeton, New Jersey: Princeton University Press, 1962.

Marcus, G.E., and M.M.J. Fischer, *Anthropology as Cultural Critique: An Experimental Moment in the Human Sciences*. Chicago: University of Chicago Press, 1996.

Morris, T., "Asserting Property Rights: Knowledge Codification in the Professional Service," *Human Relations, 54*, 7, 2001, 819-838.

Orr, J. E., *Talking about Machines*. Ithaca: ILR Press, 1996.

Poster, M., *The Mode of Information: Poststructuralism and Social Context*. Chicago: University of Chicago Press, 1990.

Prahalad, C.K., and G. Hamel, "The Core Competence of the Corporation," *Harvard Business Review, 68*, May-June, 1990, 79-91.

Schultze, U., "A Confessional Account of an Ethnography about Knowledge Work," *MIS Quarterly, 24*, 1, 2000, 1-39.

Smith, C., and H. Willmott, "The New Middle Class and the Labour Process," in C. Smith, D. Knights, and H. Willmott (Eds.), *White-Collar Work: The Non-Manual Labour Process*. London, UK: Macmillan, 1991, 13-34.

Snyder-Halpern, R., S. Corcoran-Perry and S. Narayan, "Developing Critical Practice Environments Supporting the Knowledge Work of Nurses," *Computers in Nursing, 19*, 1, 2001, 17-23.

Spender, J.-C., "Making Knowledge the Basis of a Dynamic Theory of the Firm," *Strategic Management Journal, 17*, Winter Special Issue, 1996, 45-62.

Spitler, V., and M. Gallivan, "The Role of Information Technology in the Learning of Knowledge Work," in O. Ngwenyama, L. D. Introna, M. D. Myers, and J. I. DeGross (Eds.), *New Information Technologies in Organizational Processes: Field Studies and Theoretical Reflections on the Future of Work*. Norwell, MA: Kluwer, 1999, 257-275.

Starbuck, W., "Learning by Knowledge-Intensive Firms," *Journal of Management Studies, 29*, 6, 1992, 713-740.

Stehr, N., "Experts, Counselors and Advisers," in N. Stehr and R. V. Ericson (Eds.), *The Culture and Power of Knowledge: Inquiries into Contemporary Societies*. Berlin: de Gruyter, 1992, 107-155.

Stehr, N., *The Knowledge Society*. Cambridge: Sage, 1994.

Straub, D., and E. Karahanna, "Knowledge Worker Communications and Recipient Availability: Toward a Task Closure Explanation of Media Choice," *Organization Science, 9*, 2, 1998, 160-175.

Sviokla, J. J., "Knowledge Workers and Radically New Technology," *Sloan Management Review*, Summer, 1996, 25-40.

Toffler, A., *The Third Wave*. London: Pan Books, 1980.

Von Krogh, G., K. Ichijo and I. Nonaka, *Enabling Knowledge Creation: How to Unlock the Mystery of Tacit Knowledge and Release the Power of Innovation*. New York: Oxford University Press, 2000.

Von Krogh, G., and J. Roos, "A Perspective on Knowledge, Competence and Strategy," *Personnel Review, 24*, 3, 1995, 56-76.

Wikstrom, S., and R. Norman, *Knowledge and Value: A New Perspective on Corporate Transformation*. New York: Routledge, 1994.

Wuthnow, R., and W. Shrum, "Knowledge Workers as a 'New Class': Structural and Ideological Convergence among Professional-Technical Workers and Managers," *Work and Occupations, 10*, 4, 1983, 471-487.

Zuboff, S., *In the Age of the Smart Machine*. New York: Basic Books, 1988.

CHAPTER 4

Knowledge Fields: Some Post-9/11 Thoughts about the Knowledge-Based Theory of the Firm

J.-C. Spender

School of Business & Technology, Fashion Institute of Technology (SUNY), New York, USA

We explore a bounded and contoured metaphor for organizational knowledge, a territory with visible mountains of accepted ideas and hidden valleys of dissonant opinion. This 'knowledge field', a knowledge-based definition of the organization, is a dynamic synthesis of the inherently limited and fragmented bodies of knowledge that comprise its K-inventory. It is also structured and contoured by the emotions and feelings of those who inhabit the K-field and create it – feelings which arise, following Nussbaum (2001), from the patterns of individual and organizational power and dependency. Reflecting these notions, the KM literature is categorized according to the richness of the assumptions about knowledge. There is the naïve mechanical approach that equates knowledge, information, and data. Here the K-field is flat, frictionless, and without emotional dimensions. Next is the literature that defines knowledge as a corporate asset, scarce, narrowly held, but tradable, a K-field contoured only by transaction costs. Then we see knowledge shaped by the power structures among the actors constructing the K-field. The final section, influenced by New Yorkers' emotions after the WTC attacks, brings in dependence and the emotional dimensions of the actors' processes as they integrate the organization's knowledge inventory into a workable entity.

Keywords: Knowledge Field; Knowledge Management; Knowledge-Based Theory of the Firm; Emotion; Uncertainty; Dependence

1   Introduction

The idea of knowledge management (KM) has created considerable interest. It has drawn managers, consultants, economists, and business school academics into an unusual interaction. This may be because it leverages managers' earlier interest in core competencies, their communication, and their transfer. There is also awareness of knowledge as an important economic asset, and of the special problems of managing such assets. The major impetus, of course, is the ever-expanding impact of information technology on business, government and the global economy. But there are other intriguing indications arising from the curious nature of knowledge. Knowledge management may also help pull together ideas about corporate culture, networking, trust, and social capital, matters about which we have become even more conscious following the terrorist attacks and the shocks to our social and economic system.

But as we look at the KM literature it is immediately clear that it is neither homogeneous nor well integrated. There is no single set of terms or theoretical concepts – or even phenomena to be explained. Many writers, such as Stewart (1997), claim the readers' attention without justification beyond asserting that 'intangible assets are now the basis of the firm's competitive advantage', or 'in the Information Age we are all knowledge workers', etc. This does not help us understand much about knowledge, organizational or individual, or its management. And given the observation that 85% of the global 1000 companies are now 'doing knowledge projects' (Prusak, 2000), there is clearly much to be understood.

At the same time, the notion of knowledge as something 'out there', separable from the individuals and social systems that both know it and articulate it into reasoned purposive activity turns out to be increasingly less tenable. Recent experiences, especially the World Trade Center attacks, have reminded us of the fragile emotional and cultural nature of the environment in which we live and work. In particular, we have been reminded of our interdependence – so much so that many have argued the attacks have produced or revealed a huge upwelling of 'social capital'. It follows that a realistic theory of knowledge management must encompass a theory of the knowing self as well as integrating our ideas about the institutions and relationships that bind us into economic and social systems.

The purpose of this chapter is to add some clarity to the KM field by separating it into several different areas, each of which offers the promise of some level of coherence. I shall argue that each stands on rather different epistemological axioms. I shall focus especially on the topic of 'meaning' that I see as the difference between information and data. Both are types – or dimensions – of our knowledge. Information differs from data because it has meaning for specific actors. This definition begs the question of how we know what a particular piece of data means, the question of where meaning comes from. I shall argue that it comes from the practices that articulate knowledge into the actors' world. At the same time knowledge is very much about us, the individuals who know things and are members and agents of the social and economic systems we inhabit. Information is the precursor to considered activity in a particular context. Knowledge has meaning when it can be readily associated with the contextualized actions of our experience. The consequence, of course, is that knowledge is relativized, being removed from any system of universals – real or presumed – and relocated into historically and socially identifiable contexts. Clearly I have adopted a Kuhnian view, but I want to examine meaning and knowing more critically and move on from notions of abstracted knowledge to culturally contextualized activity.

Unlike many authors I presume meaning is inherently problematic and relative, and that data or signs are not necessarily meaningful. Meaning is never self-evident or simply buried in the data, ready to be revealed by purely objective or actor-independent methods. This is especially true when we look into ourselves and our social networks for meaning. It is not only recent disturbing events that cause many to ask themselves again those fundamental questions about the meaning of their lives and work. I argue that the rich promise of research into knowledge management is less to do with the relatively trivial operational issues of collecting, storing, and communicating data – even in the vastly greater quantities that now seem both possible and necessary – than with a new impetus to examine, and perhaps manage, the meaning and context of our work and organizational activity. I see this as a return to the agenda of Simon's best known work, Administrative Behavior (1947), in which he sought to meld a practical theory of the emotionally and morally engaged personality, with bounded personal knowledge, together with a rational theory of organization. It is certainly a good time for us to re-analyze our views of the relationship between personal values and organizational objectives, between national values and global objectives.

2 KM and Information Technology

The bulk of the KM literature, and its most accessible part, is about computer systems and applications. While there is no clear demarcation between organizational information technology (IT) and this kind of KM, the latter is typically about 'enterprise-wide data collection and collaboration management', management's determination to collect all the organization's data into a single coherent real-time database and then to connect workers across the organization, and to others outside the organization, in ways that enhance communication volume, timeliness, and precision. The objectives are greater efficiency and effectiveness, improved innovation, and better utilization of the knowledge already present in the organization. This literature proposes both a set of practices, for the most part familiar but occasionally novel, and an attitude or perspective about where to focus organizational resources and energy.

Many organizations have implemented new IT systems and have developed new information management practices. In some cases organizations' administrative structures have become much looser, with the new, more coordinated, IT facilities enabling teams and projects to form rapidly and organically around new challenges, administered through the new communication system rather than by co-locating workers or having the managers walk around. The resulting virtual teams often seem as real to their members as those that gathered for social occasions like the beer busts so celebrated in the 80s and 90s era of high-tech 'flat' or 'loose' organization. Enterprise-wide knowledge-bases can capture and relay information about project progress, but can also be set up to capture information about others, such as customers, suppliers, competitors. Published sources can be searched automatically for related materials, such as about the global economy or new technologies, which can then be added to the corporate database. Information can be 'pushed' to those whom it affects most immediately. Likewise experts or opinion leaders can be identified automatically by analyzing their email interactions with others. Informational networks can be mapped, analyzed, and managed. Above all, the knowledge in the organization can be better collected, codified, collated, stored, accessed, and communicated.

These moves ensure the organization is better grounded in the facts of the situation, more responsive to changes, better able to focus and harness the imagination of its members, and measure the effects of its actions. In the retail sector, point of sale information can drive manufacturing, inventory management, transportation, and advertising to significantly improve return on investment and competitive responsiveness. On the battlefield the ability of the new communications technology to disperse the 'fog of war' portends entirely new approaches to the management of military activity. In the financial sector there is the promise of both rapid response and, at last, a continuous real-time grasp of the firm's shifting financial assets and liabilities. Such organizations are likely to be significantly more efficient and effective, though many would point out that better information about the present does not necessarily lead to strategic advantage in terms of the imagining of tomorrow. But real-world competitive advantage is far more likely to result from the compounding of many small gains, and a powerful KM-oriented IT approach can prove to be a fertile foundation for these to be made, collected, and shared.

At this point we should note that these thoughts about responsiveness, efficiency, and so forth are actually located in a specific theoretical and epistemological context – that of classical organization theory. The underlying model is the mechanistic one envisioned by classical writers such as Taylor and Weber. The information being collected and transmitted is unproblematic in the sense that things mean what they say. The emphasis is on the organization as an entity whose existence is taken for granted and whose objectives are clear, in a context that is factual. We should note also that the organization's structure is an integral part of this information system. It is designed as a rational way of collecting and processing 'objective' data, of moving it around the organization and enabling the organization to address its given goals. While formal organization theory has much to say about the parsing and distribution of goals and sub-goals, and about the communication of commands and authority, it presumes systems for the collection of data about sub-group performance and comparing it against these sub-goals. Strategic gap analysis and accounting variances are part of this widely adopted approach to management (Ansoff, 1965).

3   KM and Organizational Assets

The impact of modern IT may do more than simply make the old mode of business more efficient. Teece (2000:3) argued that the increased power and reduced cost of information technologies, combined with the liberalization of product and labor markets, and the deregulation of international financial flows, is stripping away the traditional sources of competitive differentiation and exposing organizational knowledge as the strategic foundation of the new business model. This new model focuses especially on managing the organization's knowledge-assets – since only these remain to provide a basis for competitive differentiation.

At the same time we should note that some within the IT industry, most obviously Microsoft, have been able to reap the supernormal profits typically associated with creating effective monopolies, and that, presumably, we should apply Teece's comments to the industry's customers and their inability to capture some of these monopoly profits from their IT suppliers. In practice many in other industries, such as Amazon.com, apparel retailing, health care, insurance, and those using the Sabre airline reservation system, have been able to gain competitive advantage through novel use of IT. Under these circumstances they created more traditional types of competitive differentiation. But for those not able to build competitive advantage through new IT applications, in particular in competitive advantage through new IT applications, in particular in industries in which competitors can imitate everything enterprising firms do with IT – such as supermarkets and banks –the knowledge being managed within the system becomes crucial.

While managing has always been about directing and disposing the organization's assets, the potential novelty of a knowledge-based approach can only grow from the new phenomena and practices addressed. The assumption is that the management of knowledge assets differs from the management of the organization's more traditional assets, in particular those recorded on the firm's balance sheet. Differences may lie at several levels. There may be differences in the management of their creation, i.e. managing the production of ideas differs significantly from the management of the creation of goods and services. Innovation studies generally focus in this area. There may be interesting issues around the assembly, transportation, and storage of ideas both within and without the firm. There are likely to be significant differences in the marketing and trading of ideas. Finally, there may be some interesting strategic consequences of the differing modes of consumption.

While writers such as Leonard-Barton (1995) and Tushman & O'Reilly (1997) focused on the creation of knowledge assets, Teece focused on the difficulties of capturing their value once created. A major part of the challenge lies in establishing the property rights to a particular item of knowledge. Teece (2000:6) noted that the institutional apparatus of intellectual property systems has been strengthened in recent years, but it is still a complex and difficult area. The liberalization of global trade is still impeded by the widespread piracy of films, music, and computer software. Much research on how ideas are managed has considered only the management of patents, i.e. those ideas that can be gathered, identified and protected under the institutional fabric of patent law. Copyrights and trademarks can be similarly 'concretized' and turned into marketable property. The implication is a model with three classes of organizational assets: tangible balance sheet items, intangible items such as goodwill and brand value which can be shown on the balance sheet, and those intangible items such as employees' skills that cannot be captured and concretized. It is the last which managers refer to as those that walk out the door every evening – and maybe across the street to their competitors.

Simon (1947) pointed out that naive micro-economic theory shares important epistemological assumptions with classical organization theory. Knowledge is unproblematic in the sense that data is meaningful and freely available. Hayek argued that an unfettered market would be the principal source of the information necessary to optimal economic decision making. In practice, many have observed, the markets for data are riddled with imperfections and frictions. Transaction costs may be high, communication may be imperfect, data may be incomplete, and meaning may be incommunicable. Thus, competitive advantage may grow out of either (a) inherently mobile but well-protected knowledge or (b) inherently immobile or 'inimitable' knowledge.

When theorizing, there is a temptation to try to capture novel ideas or phenomena within well-known theoretical frameworks and so coping with threatening anomalies and 'saving the theory'. When using the apparatus of intellectual property rights and concretizing knowledge, we have an approach to knowledge management that saves micro-economic theory by treating knowledge assets as fundamentally similar to tangible assets. As a theory it is silent on the strategically vexing third category of organizational assets, those that cannot be concretized. It also denies the richer potential of the knowledge-based approach that can only be accessed by building on the differences between knowledge and tangible assets.

Many writers follow Arrow and note two characteristics that suggest fundamental differences between knowledge and other assets and therefore point to the limits to a micro-economic approach. First is the 'public' nature of knowledge, by which is meant its extensibility. Unlike the organization's more familiar tangible resources, knowledge is seldom consumed by its use. It can be communicated to others, or applied to the generation of goods and services, without being diminished. Hence it is difficult to calculate the returns to investing in the creation of knowledge. Knowledge is also extinguishable without being consumed. It disappears when it is overtaken and obsoleted by some new knowledge that has greater explanatory power and covers a greater range of phenomena (Popper, 1969).

Second is the observed economic tendency to increasing returns, especially those deriving from 'network externalities'. When others, initially ignorant and unable to benefit from a firm's goods and services, invest in learning how to use them, they become 'locked in' and the chances of them switching to another firm's products is reduced. The result is a market dynamic that differs from the more customary occurrence of diminishing returns and the classical competing away of quasi-monopolistic profits. Rather the market becomes one in which the winner takes all (i.e., it is inherently monopolistic). The crux is not the knowledge of the supplying firm, but the ignorance of its customers and their need to invest in dealing with their lack of knowledge. The dynamic is a consequence of the curious nature of knowledge, easy to distribute by copying and sharing, but only to those who already understand it. In contrast micro-economics is concerned with transactions and transfers of title to assets which are known to many but can only belong to one. Extensibility, extinguish-ability, and the transaction costs of generating and acquiring knowledge remind us that knowledge does not have the same distributive properties as tangible assets. The organization's knowledge is distributed across a 'field' or through a social space whose boundaries and behaviors are generally problematic, while its tangible assets are located at particular points. I suggest the unfamiliar distributive characteristics of knowledge escape the grasp of the conventional rationalist approaches and so push our knowledge-based theorizing in new and exciting directions.

4   KM and Organizational Power

In the sections above our rationalist inheritance leads us to assume information is 'objective' and not slanted, skewed, or otherwise biased by the personal interests or 'political' machinations of the people interpreting the downward flow of directive information or the upward flow of harvested performance data. In this sense classical theories presume the data field is 'flat' and visibility is perfect (i.e., everyone can know what is to be known), and the phenomena to be investigated do not grow out of differences in what is known (i.e., knowledge asymmetries).

In practice, of course, organizational data-fields are anything but flat. In the section above, we see they can be contoured by the transaction costs involved in creating, acquiring, or moving knowledge. But they are also textured by distinctions between what is and what is not acceptable, characterized by high mountains of the data, analyses, and discourses that fit with the organization's goals and culture, and by dark valleys of unacceptable discourse and notions that challenge the organization's sense of itself. The organization's culture is such that the mountain peaks and passes are visible from afar and known to many, while the valleys, ravines, and caves are often hidden, known only to a few, and are often come upon with surprise. Those who design organizational data collection systems understand well the reverse of the adage that knowledge is power. For power shapes knowledge, and data fields are typically designed to reflect the intentions of those whose organizational power is supported by the data collected – and to exclude data that might threaten that power. Data collection is also pragmatic; data is collected only when measurement systems exist. But the available measurement systems also reflect those with the power to bring them into existence or to suppress them. Databases and information systems are typically far from completely flexible. The reports required when the system was designed are often difficult to reorganize when times change and new managers seek new insights. New strategies, goals and objectives typically lead to the development of new measurement systems.

It is odd how little organizational politics and power are discussed in the KM literature, given how much has been written about the interactions between information, the technology that changes its availability, and the patterns of organizational power. Those with utopian expectations argue that IT is inherently democratizing, and wider information sharing will flatten the data-field and undermine the power patterns that distort it. In practice such flattening is highly unlikely, especially as improved communications generally lead to even greater centralization (Brown & Duguid, 2000:30). Indeed the decentralization of organizational power is normally so politically risky it is only considered when the alternative is a complete failure of the system. Commanders on the ground are only given the authority to act independently when communications with HQ are so inadequate that waiting for orders from 'higher up' would lead to certain defeat.

The reality is that new IT and KM techniques make constant oversight possible. Black boxes can be filled with data about flying aircraft, satellites collect data about soldiers' whereabouts and truckers' driving. Real-time data can be collected about the performance of customer service personnel or those writing software code. Video cameras backed up by visual recognition systems are increasingly widespread as organizational and national security equipment. The integration of these data-collection techniques into centralized and managerialist systems of organizational power might remind us of Braverman's concerns, or those of such early anti-technologists as Mumford or Ellul. To talk of power remind us that the uses to which data are put are seldom determined by purely 'objective' considerations. Organizational data-fields are highly contoured patterns of meaning shaped by the strategic choices of those with power over the organization.

In this section we have moved on from the rationalist models of the classical theorists towards a more realistic and complex world in which knowledge fields are manipulated to enhance and protect the patterns of organizational power. Knowledge management is not just the collecting, analyzing and distributing of information within a particular knowledge field, or of translating knowledge into value. It must also address the creation of the knowledge field and the management of the social system within which these information flows take place. It is part of organizational sociology and operates on both sides of the human/computer system interface.

5   KM, Consciousness, and Culture

Discussions of organizational power are typically grounded in Max Weber's concept of the person's power to make another do his/her bidding. We see how those with power might shape the knowledge-fields in which others are embedded to their own ends, but it tends to make us overlook our everyday functional dependence on the others who are part of the same field, who are integral parts of our lives. One of the older topics in organizational analysis is the examination of how those able to solve an organization's more difficult problems gather power there. But the contexts and consequences of our dependence on others have yet to be adequately explored in the management literature, in part because even to frame the question raises difficult issues – given our cultural disposition to individual responsibility and presumed self-reliance. Why would we want to examine the consequences of dependence on others when we are committed to an ideal of psychological and professional self-reliance?

In their attachment to rationalism, classical organization theorists assumed organizational roles were coherent, comprehensible, and complete, in the sense that rational actors can occupy them without difficulty. Simon (1947) showed us that these assumptions were extremely limiting, so much so that he felt there would be no need for a theory of administration were they correct. Yet we continue to assume that individuals sign on freely to their work in organizations, accepting the authority of those to whom they report in a simple exchange of their time and freedom for their wages, salaries, and advancement prospects. But who is so free of the power structures that make up our society? We are leery of examining too closely our own, or others', dependencies. But recent events make us acutely aware of the complexities and depth of our dependencies on others, within the family, the workplace and across our society.

Nussbaum (2001) has argued that the human condition is marked not only by a lack of knowledge, so that our species learns rather than knows and thus is actively involved in the production of our bounded individual and social knowledge fields, but also recognizes its dependence on objects and people beyond its control. Emotional development, she proposed, is a direct response to this fact – religious development too, of course. This suggests a new gloss on the developmental psychologists' notions that consciousness is internalized as a purely cognitive consequence of the interactions with the social context in which the child grows up (Spender, 1996:53). Activity theorists have not dealt so directly with emotion or the affective dimensions of human knowledge (e.g. Tharp & Gallimore, 1988). In Nussbaum's theory, the individual's emotions become the dynamic affective glue that integrates these interactions with others into the relatively integrated whole that we call the personality. Emotion is as central to our knowledge as our reasoning.

There is no reason to presume our knowledge of the world is intrinsically coherent. Whatever we know is certainly insufficient for us to ever see the world as 'all of a piece'. We are inevitably open to surprise. Our experience of the world is not integrated, in part because our ability to make sense of it, to give it meaning, is shaped by various theoretical 'lenses' and none of these is adequate to explain everything. Nor do we feel the same about everything. On the contrary, we have preferences and opinions about everything we know. We experience the world as pluralistic, fragmented, and emotionally and morally burdened. Integrating it into a workable whole is a profound human task that is both cognitive and emotional. The integration achieved cannot be static, a state in which we would be able to say that we know everything and are no longer open to surprise. Rather it is dynamic, tentative in a Popperian sense, to be held onto until some greater enlightenment obsoletes it, or it is blown apart by experience. We cannot achieve the level of functional integration that allows us to act purposefully towards the world without recognizing and resolving both the axiomatic inconsistencies between our perceptual lenses, and the contrasts between those objects and people over whom we have power versus those we cannot control but on whom we are nonetheless dependent. These conflicts and contrasts challenge our emotional abilities as they also challenge our cognitive abilities. We are aware of this every day of our lives. Without a functional level of emotional stability we lose sight of our goals and the meaning of our actions. Indeed the law may excuse us from being responsible for some of our actions when we lose that normal degree of emotional stability and integration.

In Spender (in press) I argued – following Adam Smith – that the core of a theory of the firm must lie in its grasp of the firm's integrating/transforming processes. We are inclined to think that integration and transformation happens at several discrete levels: to the employees who come together into a viable organization, or to the factors of production, as in Smith, or to the firm's integration (fit) into its markets, as in the classical theory of corporate strategy, or more generally into its socio-economic, political, and cultural contexts. The first step is to make integration/transformation the problem to which the theory of the firm is one's answer. The choice of integration problem characterizes the resulting theory. So in this chapter we are primarily concerned with the integration of the knowledge field that comes to define the firm as an operating entity. But, we must suspect that the various levels of integration and transformation are interlocked and enmeshed, that we cannot address one without entailing and addressing the others. The problems of integrating the constituent parts of the firm, whether they be people and equipment, or core competencies and complementary assets, or items of explicit knowledge and tacit skills, or tradable resources obtained at fair market prices and created sources of competitive advantage, cannot be separated from the task of integrating the firm into its social and political context. Because that is a context that is emotionally and morally burdened, as are the individuals in the firm, so the firm must also integrate its emotional and cultural activity.

I have argued elsewhere (Spender, 1989), as does North (1990), that culture is a collective social response to the uncertainties of human existence. Organizations also develop distinct patterns of knowledge. We call these patterns 'organizational cultures' and they arise because organizations are collectively cognizing entities which are also exposed to uncertainties, albeit of a rather different kind. While organizations are often treated as individual citizens at law, able to make contracts, own assets, and undertake liabilities, their a-social *gesellschaftlich* nature exposes them to uncertainties that individuals do not face. There is especially the awareness of the potential for eternal existence, for an organization does not age biologically and can forever adapt and replace its mis-functioning parts.

Organizations are also dependent on others they do not control, principally those economic entities that make up the markets for their goods and services, and for the inputs to their production processes. They are also dependent on the institutional fabrics in which they are embedded, such as those which regulate and enforce contracts, or allow knowledge to be concretized as patents. Their response to these dependencies may be to form cartels and pursue monopoly power, just as individuals combine and seek solidarity against those with power over them. But firms also respond emotionally in ways that reveal the need for leaders who collect, calibrate and focus the employees' feelings. Fitting emotions into the firm's actual context could mean that competitors are treated with respect – or they might be demonized. The hostility between Oracle and Microsoft is not simply a contrast of technologies, thin clients versus thick, or the consequence of competition between the two in the areas in which they meet. They have contrasting cultures energized by emotional commitments – just as both contrast with Apple. Many writers have argued that the organization's culture needs to be created, manipulated and managed. I would argue that this also applies to the emotional dimensions. The result is a rich source of meaning for those within the firm, enabling them to integrate and make sense of their actions and understand how they fit in to the larger whole. The collapse of an organization's culture certainly leads to cognitive problems, so that people become disoriented and no longer know what to do (Baumard, 1999), but it also leads to emotional problems. People feel the disorientation and lack of effective leadership deeply.

At the same time, there is no reason to assume, as many researchers do, that the emotional aspects of the field are 'flat'. Different people normally feel very differently about their organization. There is the same contouring with mountains and valleys as I suggested earlier. There may also be severe discontinuities, chasms, and rifts. There are groundswell movements – like shifting tectonic plates – as emotions gather and focus around objects, people and incidents and invest them with powerful historical and symbolic meaning. Leadership means perceiving these matters and harnessing them, so re-shaping the contours of organizational feeling.

Putting stress on the emotional geography of the knowledge field, as I have done in this section, raises interesting questions about the field's boundaries as well as about its contours. A K-field is populated by those over whom one has power, a notion consistent with organization theory, and by those on whom one is dependent but cannot control, a notion consistent with strategy theory. Together these comprise a distinct but limited group. One of the more puzzling concepts in strategy theory is that of the 'relevant environment', the parts of the firm's environment to which its strategists should pay attention. As we move towards a emotionally integrated knowledge-based theory of the firm, we see the relevant environment is that about which one has feelings that derive from relations of power and dependency. Having feelings and integrating them consumes energy, just as creating knowledge does. There is an analogy to entropy and binding energy. The people and things one has feelings about demarcate a knowledge field – others are 'off the radar'. No energy is expended integrating them into one's view of the world or theories of action within it. Much of the shocked reaction to the WTC attacks comes from the feeling that al-Qaida should have been high on somebody's radar screen and integrated into our national policies. We citizens were surprised, yet we knew they had strong feelings about us and that our government had explicit knowledge of their intention and ability to attack us, as they had done in the past.

The attacks gave us a new appreciation of the contours of our social knowledge. Aside from the revelation of our social capital, evident in countless stories of unsolicited help and kindness from one stranger to another, in New York at least we discovered our own strong feelings about our dependencies on those others, such as the firemen, police and EMS workers who died trying to save others. Their behavior revealed the meaning they attached to their work, and in many cases shamed those of us more closely focused on our own betterment. Our powerful feelings of grief about these public servants, as well as about those who simply worked in the buildings, for the most part people of whom one had no direct knowledge, made us all aware that our consciousness and sense of self is firmly grounded in a collective field of knowledge and meaning that we inhabit as citizens of New York.

6   Some Conclusions

This chapter seeks to parse the KM literature's discourse into relatively coherent parts on the basis of the epistemological assumptions that underpin them. In section 2 there is a purely mechanical approach in which knowledge, information and data mean the same thing, in which meaning is not problematic, and the writers' emphasis is on the technologies which enable us to collect and distribute data. In section 3 knowledge is still treated as an objectifiable asset that can be separated from those who know and use it, perhaps becoming concretized as a patent or even an organizational routine, but we saw its value as contingent on the functioning of the social and economic system in which it is applied. In section 4 we recognized a further interpenetration of knowledge and social context, and saw that meaning, which ultimately differentiates knowledge from mere data, is a product of social power. Every knowledge field will be come to be contoured in ways that reflect the historical patterns of power that underpin the social system in which that knowledge is articulated. These ideas re-connect us to the older literature on the sociology of knowledge (e.g., Marx or Merton).

Finally, in section 5, I adopted Nussbaum's concept of dependency to argue that all knowledge is unavoidably bound up with the actors who make it meaningful. A truly useful theory of knowledge must recognize that it has emotional and cultural dimensions that cannot be ignored without severely diminishing the discussion. I implied that knowledge cannot be properly comprehended as separated from the actors who apply it. A knowledge-based theory of the firm has to deal with the emotional and cultural aspects of integrating actors' activities together into functioning social entities such as firms and organizations and thence into an emotionally burdened social context. All of this is to do with building a theory that is relativized to the firm's historical socio-economic context. We move away from traditional notions of knowledge as objectifiable, grounded in some presumed universals, and mirroring the fundamental character and coherence of the universe. While I am agnostic on the ontological issues, I remain convinced that we should focus more on considered action under uncertain conditions if we are to understand economic behavior better. By uncertain I mean, following Knight (1921), that which is not known and so arrests reasoned action, rather than that which is known probabilistically (Spender, 1989:42). We define the firm as an instrument for integrating knowledge and activities so as to resolve uncertainty – rather than, for example, as a repository for knowledge (Teece, 2000:29) or intellectual capital (Stewart, 1997), or a system for minimizing transactions costs. This is not new, but in this chapter I added an emotional dimension derived from the patterns of social power.

I proposed the notion of a contoured knowledge field as a familiar metaphor to help counter the assumption of 'flatness' or naive objectivity that is embedded in much of the KM literature. Knowledge is highly shaped and fitted, not only to the activities that articulate it into the real world, but also to the power and dependency structures that characterize our social world. Knowledge fields are the underpinning patterns of meaning that allow us to see organizations as functioning entities which transform inputs into outputs. The knowledge embraces that already articulated into activity – whether planned responses or tacit organizational routines – and that which is lies in the background as potential activity – the capability to respond to new situations.

Only if we move on from inherently 'flat' and frictionless concepts of knowledge can we justify bringing such a problematic concept as knowledge into our discourse. The nature of human knowledge has puzzled the finest minds for centuries, and we are little wiser now than scholars were 2000 years ago.

References

Ansoff, I., *Corporate Strategy*, New York: McGraw-Hill, 1965.

Baumard, P. *Tacit Knowledge in Organizations*, Thousand Oaks, CA: Sage, 1999

Brown, J.S. and P. Duguid, *The Social Life of Information*, Boston MA: Harvard Business School Press, 2000.

Knight, F.H., *Risk, Uncertainty and Profit*, Boston MA: Houghton-Mifflin, 1921.

Leonard-Barton, D., *Wellsprings of Knowledge*, Boston MA: Harvard Business School Press, 1995.

North, D., *Institutions, Institutional Change, and Economic Performance*, New York: Cambridge University Press, 1990.

Nussbaum, M.C., *Upheavals of Thought; The Intelligence of Emotions*, New York: Cambridge University Press, 2001.

Popper, K.R., *Conjectures and Refutations; The Growth of Scientific Knowledge*, London: Routledge and Kegan Paul, 1969.

Prusak, L., "Victories and Challenges", *Knowledge Connections*, 2, 4, 2000, 1-3.

Simon, H.A., *Administrative Behavior*, New York: Macmillan, 1947.

Spender, J.-C., *Industry Recipes*, Oxford: Blackwell, 1989.

Spender, J.-C., Making Knowledge the Basis of a Dynamic Theory of the Firm, *Strategic Management Journal*, 17 (Special Winter Issue), 1996, 45-62.

Spender, J.-C., "Knowledge Management, Uncertainty, and an Emergent Theory of the Firm", in Bontis, N, and C. Choo (eds.) *Strategic Management of Intellectual Capital & Organizational Knowledge*, New York: Oxford University Press (in press), Chapter 9.

Stewart, T.A., *Intellectual Capital: The New Wealth of Nations*, New York, Doubleday/Currency, 1997.

Teece, D.J., *Managing Intellectual Capital*, New York: Oxford University Press, 2000.

Tharp, R.G. and R. Gallimore, *Rousing Minds to Life*, Cambridge, Cambridge University Press, 1988.

Tushman, M.L. and C.A. O'Reilly, *Winning through Innovation*, Boston MA: Harvard Business School Press, 1997.

CHAPTER 5
The Knowledge Economy[*]

Paul M. Romer[1] as interviewed by Joel Kurtzman[2]
[1] Stanford Graduate School of Business, Stanford, CA, USA
[2] strategy+business

The knowledge economy is one in which growth, value, and an improving standard of living are inextricably tied to knowledge, its creation, and its distribution. Knowledge processing replaces the processing of physical things on the center stage of production. Knowledge and knowledge processors are crucial enterprise resources, and their effective management is a key for economic success. This chapter examines the knowledge economy from the angles of growth, policy, and directions for improvement. Its insights are conveyed in the form of an interview.

Keywords: Competition, Government, Growth, Increasing Return, Knowledge Economy, Physical Economy, Policy, Property Rights, Training

1 Introduction

It is hard to label an economist who just turned 40 as venerable, but that is what Paul M. Romer's peers call the Stanford University economics professor. Professor Romer, who also teaches at the University of California at Berkeley while conducting research at the Hoover Institution at Stanford and the Canadian Institute for Advanced Research in Toronto, is best known for his theories about the dynamics of growth. In Professor Romer's view, knowledge is the unsung hero of the growth game. While most classical economists – not to mention Marx – focused on production, labor and capital, Professor Romer added knowledge and technology to the mix.

The classical approach operates well in the physical economy of resource extraction and commodity production, according to the professor. That economy is characterized by diminishing returns, since each additional ton of copper or barrel of oil is harder to find than the previous one and is – by definition – scarcer and therefore more expensive to extract from the earth.

The information economy is different, however. Large upfront costs are incurred to write a complicated piece of software or to discover specific gene sequences. But after the initial work is done, the cost of each additional "unit" is minimal or sometimes even nil. Software can be copied onto disks at very low

---

[*] Reprinted with permission from strategy+business, a quarterly management magazine published by Booz Allen Hamilton.

prices or sent out over the Internet. Each gram of protein produced by genetically altered bacteria only adds to the world's supply. As a result, while returns diminish in the physical economy, they increase in the knowledge economy – a cause for hope, according to Professor Romer.

There is another important tenet in the professor's world view. It is that the more we discover new things, the better we get at the process of discovery itself. Knowledge builds on itself. As a result, the capacity to create wealth and value increases over time, surely another reason for optimism.

Professor Romer's work is serious and academic. But while most economists have their cadre of on-the-one-hand, on-the-other-hand adherents and detractors, Professor Romer's work has so far attracted far more support than dissent among his peers, prompting speculation that he may someday be a recipient of the Nobel Prize for economics. Economist Paul Krugman and management theorist Peter F. Drucker are among Professor Romer's biggest and most public boosters. Professor Romer recently spoke with Strategy & Business at his Stanford office, in Palo Alto, Calif. What follows are excerpts from that conversation.

2 Economic Growth

S&B: For the most part, knowledge, like technology, has been taken for granted by economists who look at the factors that propel growth. But in your work, you assert that knowledge can raise returns on investments and that it is a factor of production, like capital, labor and raw materials. Does the information economy work differently from the classical economy?

Paul Romer: Let's back up. My work on growth can be traced back to an attempt to isolate the differences between the information or knowledge-based economy and what came before it. My belief is that those differences are important for our understanding of growth. Those distinctions matter to people running firms and they should matter to policymakers. They are issues that show up at a number of points in the economy. And since those issues are topical right now, it makes my work in this area a lot of fun.

S&B: What differences are you referring to?

Paul Romer: Let me articulate it this way. One feature of knowledge can be summarized by Isaac Newton's statement that he could see far because he could stand on the shoulders of giants. In other words, his notion was that knowledge builds on itself, which means that as we learn more, we get better and better at discovering new things. It also means that there's no limit to the amount of things we can discover.

This is a very important fact for understanding the broad sweep of human history and it is very different from what we are used to thinking about in terms of physical objects, where scarcity is the overwhelming fact with which we have to deal.

S&B: You say we are getting better at finding new things. What exactly do you mean by that?

Paul Romer: There are only a finite quantity of things with which we can work – basically, the matter in the earth's crust. We've had essentially the identical amount of physical stuff for millions of years. Now a lot in the language of economics – and in the popular language, as well – makes it appear as if we are wealthier today because we have more of this physical stuff. It makes it sound as if we have actually produced more physical things. But in truth, that is not right. If you think about it the way a physicist does, the law of the conservation of matter and energy states we have essentially the same quantity of things we have always had.

S&B: So what have we done?

Paul Romer: We have taken the fixed quantity of matter available to us and rearranged it. We have changed things from a form that is less valuable into a form that is more valuable. Value creation and wealth creation in their most basic senses have to do with taking physical objects and rearranging them.

Now, where do ideas come in? Quite simply, ideas are the recipes we use to rearrange things to create more value and wealth. For example, we have ideas about ways to make steel by combining iron with carbon and a few other elements. We have ideas about how to take silicon – an abundant element that was almost worthless to us until recently – and make it into semiconductor chips.

So we have physical materials to work with – raw ingredients – which are finite and scarce, and we have ideas or knowledge, which tell us how to use those raw materials. When I say there are always more things to discover, what I mean is that there are always more recipes that we can find to combine raw materials in ways that make them more valuable to us.

S&B: What you are saying sounds straightforward enough. What does it mean for the economy and for growth?

Paul Romer: The claim I made a moment ago about standing on the shoulders of giants tells us something important. It says that we can take advantage of a form of increasing returns in the process of discovery. Now it could have been – I suppose – that with each new discovery, it got harder and harder to make additional discoveries. In that case, we would – at some point – simply give up. Progress would be slowing down and eventually would come to a halt. Of course, this is not what we see when we look at history. From one century to the next, the rate of technological change and the rate of growth of income per capita has been speeding up.

S&B: This is contrary to discovery in the physical world, isn't it?

Paul Romer: Yes. The physical world is characterized by diminishing returns. Diminishing returns are a result of the scarcity of physical objects. One of the most important differences between objects and ideas, the kinds of differences that I alluded to before, is that ideas are not scarce and the process of discovery in the realm of ideas does not suffer from diminishing returns.

S&B: One of the differences? Are there other differences as well?

Paul Romer: Yes. Let's take a particular piece of knowledge, such as a piece of software, and think about the costs of production that a supplier faces. If we do that, we see that this piece of knowledge is very unusual from a traditional economic point of view.

To make the first copy of Windows NT, for example, Microsoft invested hundreds of millions of dollars in research, development, testing and so forth. But once Microsoft got the underlying bit string right, it could produce the second copy of Windows NT for about 50 cents – the cost of copying the program coded in this string of bits onto a floppy disk. Since then, all subsequent copies of the program have the same cost or even lower costs. For example, if Windows NT is distributed over the Internet, the cost of every additional copy is basically nil. So the first copy costs you hundreds of millions of dollars, but all other copies are free, no matter how many you produce.

This kind of falling cost per unit is a different manifestation of increasing returns. This is very different from the physical economy, where an important part of the cost of each good comes from the process of making an additional copy of that good.

S&B: Paul, is this kind of increasing return the same as or different from the standing-on-the-shoulders-of-giants effect that you mentioned before?

Paul Romer: These two kinds of increasing returns are logically distinct. For example, we could have falling costs of production for copies of a specific piece of software even if the standing-on-shoulders effect were not operating.

Suppose, for a moment, that Windows NT were the last piece of useful software that could ever be written. Once it is finished, it will be impossible to develop any new pieces of software. I know this sounds crazy, but bear with me. This would be an extreme case that is the opposite of the shoulders-of-giants effect. But even if this were true, the production costs for NT would still have the unusual character of huge costs up front and very, very low costs for each subsequent copy. That feature is very important for understanding what we call the industrial organization of the economy, because it means that you are going to see a great deal of monopoly power in the new economy.

S&B: How does knowledge lead to monopolies?

Paul Romer: Traditionally, in economics, you would assume that there would be a couple of leaders in a field, that their success would make it attractive for other people to come in, that there would be rivalry among all the firms and that the industry segment as a whole would grow and benefit as competition intensified.

For example, in the physical economy, suppose you've got a firm that owns a big ore deposit somewhere in the world, and there are other firms that own other ore deposits in other parts of the world. Each of these firms will operate under conditions of increasing costs and diminishing returns. One of those firms may be able to produce 100,000 tons of refined ore per year. But it can't easily scale up to 200,000 or 300,000 tons because of the nature of its physical resources. There's only one way to mine the ore and it gets more expensive as you do it faster. The physical structure of your assets means that there's a limit on how fast you can exploit it.

So you might ask: Will one company take over the whole world's supply of ore and become a monopolist in world copper? The answer is no, because the firm that wants to do that would produce up to a point where it would become more and more expensive. Other firms would be drawn into the market and might produce and sell their ore more cheaply. When firms face increasing costs and diminishing returns, no single firm can supply the whole worldwide market. If it tries, it faces increasing cost disadvantages relative to its competitors.

S&B: So there are limits to monopoly power in the physical world?

Paul Romer: Yes. In the physical economy, there is a natural equilibrating process. If one firm tries to take over the whole market, other firms would gain an advantage and will enter. When this whole process settles down, there will be many firms and a competitive market.

S&B: How does this differ in the knowledge economy?

Paul Romer: Let's think about operating systems and the world of computers for a moment. Let's say you have one firm, like Microsoft, which is going to produce Windows NT. Once it produces its first copy, it then faces no cost disadvantage. It can produce millions or billions of copies of NT at little additional cost. It truly can supply the entire worldwide market for operating systems. If anything, it probably gets even easier for Microsoft because the larger its market size gets, the more attractive it is to adopt its software because of what we call bandwagon effects. If everybody else is using a particular piece of software, it usually makes it advantageous for you to use it, too.

Now this difference between diminishing-returns industries and increasing-returns industries completely changes the dynamic of competition. Under conditions of increasing returns, competition is driven by various firms trying to capture as much market share as possible as quickly as possible and by being the first to develop a product and to flood the market with it, even – at least initially – at a loss. To see how different this is, think again about mining. If you discover a large deposit of copper ore, do you think you would want to give lots of it away for free to increase your market share? Of course not.

S&B: What does this mean in a business sense?

Paul Romer: First of all, it means that the kind of strategies you see in the knowledge economy are those like Netscape's. In that strategy, a new company comes into a new market and gives away its browser and tries to move very rapidly to supply a large part of the market. Netscape did this and it ended up with a large percentage of the total market for browsers. It is now trying to leverage that advantage into a larger advantage in the more lucrative market for server software. That kind of competition is driven by falling costs and increasing returns in the information economy. That is the way competition unfolds in the information economy.

So we are talking about two extremes: One is software, the other is resource extraction. A lot of traditional business fits somewhere in between.

S&B: How are monopolies sustained in the knowledge economy? Don't new companies come along with new products that replace the old ones?

Paul Romer: Yes, that is true and it brings us back to the two notions of increasing returns that we were discussing a minute ago. Recall the thought experiment where we shut down the increasing returns associated with the shoulders-of-giants effect but assumed that the increasing returns associated with cheap copies were still present. This leads to a rather pessimistic implication. A firm like Microsoft would become the monopoly supplier of operating systems software. It would remain a monopolist forever because no entrant could compete with it with a similar product and, according to our assumptions, there was nothing better that was left for someone else to discover.

Fortunately, we don't get this pessimistic result because the two kinds of increasing returns go together. This means that even though one firm may control a large fraction of the market at any point in time, there is another way for new firms to compete. Instead of trying to enter the market by providing exactly the same product as the incumbents at a lower price, they can enter and compete by selling something that is new and better. This is precisely what Microsoft and Intel did when they displaced I.B.M. as the dominant force in the computer market. It is what firms like Netscape, Sun and Oracle are trying to do now by leveraging the emerging power of the Internet. Economists call this monopolistic competition. It's a form of competition between different firms, each of which sells a different kind of product and can behave like a monopolist at least temporarily.

Of course, it takes various kinds of institutional infrastructure to make this system work. For example, the Government has to grant property rights over intangible assets like ideas.

S&B: The property rights you are referring to are patents, copyrights and so on?

Paul Romer: Yes, and these differ from the property rights we are familiar with for physical objects. You can give dispersed ownership to something like timber or ore. Many different people can own different pieces of the same kind of asset, so they can all compete to supply ore. But if you consider, for example, a pharmaceutical product, you see that once the Government gives a firm a patent on a new drug, this firm becomes a monopolist with regard to that piece of knowledge, that recipe for how to make that drug. We give this company a legal right to keep everyone else from using its knowledge, and this means that the company can gain the dominant position in the market. So it is the combination of low replication costs to the producer and the protection of intellectual property rights that creates the monopoly position.

S&B: This means that competition tends to take place via the introduction of new goods rather than by competing on price in existing goods?

Paul Romer: Yes, that is right. It is a very different vision of how competition works and why markets are so successful in generating high standards of living. You see, the traditional intellectual justification for laissez-faire comes from dealing with a hypothetical world filled only with scarce objects. In effect, you're just trying to figure out which mine should produce how much copper and how much total copper should be produced. In such a world, the classical notion of perfect competition is feasible and it works well. Competing firms will end up charging the right price for copper in a precise sense. The market price will determine the total amount of copper that should be produced. It will also determine how much of the total each mine will produce. Classical economists were able to show that under competition, these production and allocation decisions are efficient.

In this kind of world, it is important for policymakers and the Government to step in and break up any monopoly or cartel. By keeping the cartels at bay, the price will adjust to the efficient level and the right quantities will be produced and sold.

Now let's go to this new world, where the key challenge is to produce and distribute knowledge or ideas. The first thing to notice is that you lose the classical notion of the right price. For example, with the concept of a vaccine, the best thing to do might be to give any firm the right to use this concept for free and let everybody in the world use it to make serums so that people in general can benefit. To do this, you want the price for using the concept of a vaccine to be zero after it has been discovered. Thus, for example, we could have granted a perpetual patent on the basic concept of a vaccine to Edward Jenner, who discovered the concept in the 1700's. In fact, he and his heirs have no intellectual property rights over this idea. They collect no income when researchers and doctors all over the world use vaccines and the concept of immunity to protect us from disease. After the fact, this is efficient.

But let's back up for a moment. If you want to get people to discover extremely valuable concepts like vaccines, you would like to offer them really high prices for their discovery. This creates an incentive to do the work necessary to make the discovery. So, in this world of knowledge and recipes, there is always an unavoidable tension between wanting to have low prices after the fact, so a knowledge-good can be distributed widely, and wanting to promise strong property rights and monopoly protections in advance, as an incentive and a motivation for discovery.

S&B: How do you resolve the problem, Paul?

Paul Romer: What we have to do is work out a balance between tolerating some monopolies and monopoly profits – since that's how we motivate people to discover new recipes – with competition to keep prices low and distribute products widely. We encourage this competition by granting property rights that are partial or incomplete. In practice, what this means is that while in the physical economy, with diminishing returns, there are perfect prices, in the knowledge economy, with its increasing returns, there are no perfect prices.

S&B: Are you suggesting that we must simply tolerate monopoly prices?

Paul Romer: Yes. I'm also suggesting that we have to establish property rights that are incomplete. In the world of objects, you don't have to make these kinds of compromises. We use Government policy to limit monopoly. We also establish very strong property rights. For example, it would be very wasteful for property rights on land to expire after a certain period of time and then for everyone to be able to use it freely. But this is precisely what we do with patents. One key difference is that in the world of ideas, you cannot have both strong property rights and competition. The other is that you don't get congestion over the use of ideas.

When we look back on systems where a group of people did have free access to a physical resource like land, we speak of a "tragedy of the commons." But there is no similar tragedy of the intellectual commons.

Now, as I suggested above, if there were not all these additional things to discover, we would be pessimistic about this new world of ideas because of all the monopoly power we are creating with patents and copyrights. In fact, if there were nothing left to discover, we would treat all knowledge the same way we treat the knowledge behind the principle of vaccination. It would be common property and everybody would be free to use it.

But fortunately, in the knowledge economy, there are always new things to discover. We grant property rights over knowledge, and this leads to a leapfrogging process whereby the potential of future monopoly profits induces new discoveries. As a result, a new entity will emerge and come into a market at some point and leapfrog all the existing entities. When that happens, you'll get a big jump in terms of productivity and economic value, and the old monopolists will typically be displaced. Remember, this is a different dynamic from the one we described in the classical economy, where all competition was to produce existing goods at lower prices.

So over in this idea part of the economy, we worry much less about having the Government actively intervene to strike down any hint of monopoly power and keep all firms small. We rely much more on the process of what Schumpeter called "creative destruction," where you have a sequence of temporary monopolies that are superseded by new monopolists selling new products and services.

3   Knowledge Policy

S&B: What are the policy implications of the knowledge economy?

Paul Romer: There are big implications stemming from the recognition of the difference between the classical world of objects and the idea-based world. With objects, we have a good idea of what the right institutional arrangements are. We just establish infinite-lived property rights, make sure that there is no monopoly control and then let the market operate. This will lead to efficient allocations of physical objects.

That is the lesson of laissez-faire, and it is still a very powerful lesson, one that too many politicians still do not understand.

S&B: And the aim of laissez-faire in that respect is greater economic efficiency?

Paul Romer: Yes. But more importantly, I would say the aim in both of these worlds is to generate or create more value. The kinds of problems you've got to solve in the classical realm are relatively simple. You just have to allocate scarce commodities among alternative users and between alternative producers.

S&B: It would seem that the aim of regulation in the commodity-producer world is to foster efficient production, while the aim in the knowledge world is to bolster future discovery. These are different roles for the Government, aren't they?

Paul Romer: Yes, they are. There is something inherently static about the classical vision – that if there were nothing changing, nothing new being discovered, the price systems would be a good way to decide which mine should produce the next unit of copper. It also works well to decide which power plant should generate the extra megawatts of electricity and so on.

But over here, in the knowledge economy, there are these other imperatives. We have to worry not just about getting efficient usage from what we've got right now, but to figure out ways to discover all the new things we might need or be able to use. That is not a set of static problems. It is very dynamic.

S&B: Do the right institutions exist to make those policy choices?

Paul Romer: What's interesting about the knowledge economy is that we haven't figured out what the optimal institutions are. That's still a wide-open question. What is the best way to structure our economic world? This is true not only at the level of policy formation for a nation, but also for firms. Firms are really struggling with how they should organize themselves internally.

S&B: What are some of the policy issues within firms?

Paul Romer: The traditional logic within companies was like that in government. In the Government, people might look at medical discovery, for example, and say, "Gee, this is a market failure, we can't make the market work perfectly here." So the Government would then step in. It would collect taxes, use the revenue to pay for research taking place at universities and use that research to develop discoveries, like the principles behind vaccines. It would then give this knowledge away for free. We invented non-market institutions like universities to aid us in the production and distribution of ideas.

Firms, to a certain extent, have mimicked that solution. They say, "O.K., we need to generate new knowledge. We have different divisions that we can treat as profit centers. So, what we will do is tax those profit centers to create something that looks like a mini-internal university – the R.&D. department." They then gave the funds to the R.&D. department and told it to do good work, just like the national Government does with the universities.

Over time, when the R.&D. department produces something, it gives that something away for free – gives this knowledge away – to any of the operating divisions that needs it.

S&B: That's the classical, pre-breakup AT&T-Bell Labs model.

Paul Romer: Yes, but you also saw it at I.B.M. and at G.M. and on smaller scales in many firms. A number of firms mimicked the institutions and economic policies of government when they realized that knowledge-creation and discovery was central to their growth.

S&B: What came next?

Paul Romer: The firms found that these institutions did not work so well, so now they are trying to come up with modified institutional arrangements. They are recognizing that the simple solution that recreates the Government's command-and-control and tax-and-subsidy mechanisms is not the perfect solution. What they are finding is that while there are a billion haystacks in which there will be some very valuable needles, it is an enormously expensive proposition to go about looking underneath every one. So what they are asking themselves is, how do you allocate the resources that you devote to research most effectively? They are realizing that they cannot just give scientists lots of money and let them follow their curiosity. If they do, this form of tax-and-subsidy system runs the risk of dissipating efforts by looking in too many different directions that don't necessarily lead to the highest returns for shareholders. One way to think about the problem here is that a tax-and-subsidy system does not have the built-in checks on wasteful activities that are present in a market system.

As a result, firms are beginning to create market-like mechanisms that impose market tests on things like R.&D. departments. In some instances, this goes all the way to the extreme of the profit-center model. In these instances, they have set up R.&D. units as profit centers and they charge different divisions for any of the results they produce that other divisions use.

S&B: Does that work?

Paul Romer: Well, it gets back to one of the problems with knowledge, which is, if you charge high prices for knowledge, you don't end up with the efficient distribution of that knowledge.

Let me provide you with an anecdote. Someone at a company I know told me that he had taken over the market research division. The company used to be operated on the tax-and-subsidy model. The corporation used to give the marketing division lots of money and it went out and worked on anything that it wanted to. That system meant that the department was not really working on the right problems. So this manager took the market research budget and allocated it to all the different business units and told the units that they could buy whatever they wanted from the researchers. This of course made the market research folks focus more on the actual marketing problems that the different divisions were facing. But then he ran into a problem. One division would pay the market researchers to work on problem

X. Another division in the corporation would then come in and want the group to do a study on a very similar problem. It was inefficient for the market researchers to go out and redo the study, but the first division had property rights over the existing study. The market researchers could not just give it to the second division without getting permission from the first, and complicated negotiations would sometimes ensue over what the second division should pay the first. This sometimes led to restrictions on flows of information that would have helped other divisions, and this is clearly bad from the point of view of shareholders.

The lesson is that as soon as you start to price knowledge, you get into awkward situations where your knowledge is not being as widely used as it could be. This is just a fact of life.

S&B: So how do you price knowledge? What is the model?

Paul Romer: There is nothing so far that is perfectly neat and clean. My guess, however, is that the answer lies between the two extremes of the market system and the tax-and-subsidy system. My guess is that we're going to start to find much richer institutional arrangements to control the flow of information.

For example, firms are doing things like making people in the R.&D. units go out and spend time with the divisions, just so that they communicate more closely with people in the divisions. Firms are even making R.&D. people go out on sales calls to talk to the customers, to see what they are really interested in. This is one way to get people in the R.&d. unit focused on their markets, their market opportunities and their final customers. It's a weak, but apparently effective, way to impose a kind of market discipline on what the researchers do.

But it is an institutional arrangement, not an explicit price system. Firms could eventually augment an institutional arrangement like this with things like promotion and compensation systems, which reward being attentive to customers, as opposed to more traditional systems, which just give rewards for the number of scholarly publications, or the number of patents, whether they are useful or not. So what I expect is that there will be a lot more experimentation with arrangements that are neither pure market systems nor pure tax-and-subsidy systems.

S&B: Another model is to view the R.&D. department as the center of the firm and the rest of the company as the channel for getting the discoveries of the R.&D. department to market.

Paul Romer: Imbedded in your question is what people call the linear model of science and discovery. It was one in which the people in the research lab said, "Look, the whole game is to create knowledge. That's where value comes from. We're the center of that process. We're going to create the knowledge. Once we've created that knowledge, we'll give it to you, so you can market it and make a profit for us." In practice, that turned out to be a very bad way to structure corporations and a very bad way to think about economic activity. The problem is that it is not well guided. There are many different kinds of knowledge that researchers can produce. Some of these will be more valuable than others, and researchers may not be in the best position to tell which ones are the most valuable ones. So what's happened is that we've kind of turned this process around.

The new perspective says, "Look, the most valuable things we could do will be things we learn about from the problems we are facing in the field." In terms of information flows, that means it goes from the customer to the operating people to the R.&D. people.

The point I am making is that the problem-solving agenda should not be determined by the R.&D. unit, but by somebody else. So even though we now recognize that knowledge creation is really central to the business process, we don't think of it as being a kind of pyramid model, where the R.&D. unit is at the top and everybody else is kind of subservient to it.

It is very important to realize that the immense potential for new discovery brings with it an even more immense potential for wasted effort. Discovery is therefore associated with really hard choices. For example, what's the set of all possible software programs that could be written? If you just do a simple mathematical calculation about how many bit strings could fit on a CD-ROM, it is an unbelievably large number, far larger than the total number of particles in the universe. It's larger than any physical quantity that we can understand. Most of these possible bit strings would be useless junk. A few of them will be the "killer apps" of the future.

What's the significance of this? At the same time that we know there are good things out there to discover – new pieces of software – it would be very easy for an organization to produce a lot of software that isn't very useful. As a result, we need market-like mechanisms to focus the research efforts.

S&B: What is the Government's role in the knowledge economy?

Paul Romer: What we have done very effectively in the United States is tried to encourage the process of discovery by subsidizing the inputs that go into the discovery process. What I mean is that ever since the Civil War and the creation of the land-grant universities, we have heavily subsidized higher education. We have also subsidized training scientists and engineers, who are the key input into the research process.

In addition, the United States has maintained a regulatory and financial system that makes it easy to create new companies, raise capital and start new businesses. We also tolerate failure in the United States.

That combination seems to have worked very well. And it's very different from, say, the European perspective, where national policy – especially since World War II – has focused on what they call national champions," which they identify as a few big firms whose monopoly positions they try to protect. That really goes in all the wrong directions. What the Europeans really should be doing is thinking about the process that brings new entrants into the market. How do you get people out there working on interesting new questions to start new enterprises?

The real success of American economic policy has been to have moderately strong property rights with lots of subsidies for inputs – like research and education – that are used in the innovation process. Then we hold the Government back and let firms fight it out in the marketplace.

S&B: Should the Government do anything different?

Paul Romer: Many people think the Government should have a much more direct role over outputs, by actually contracting for research in specific areas. They feel that the Government should go out and decide which areas are most promising for technological development – synthetic fuels or hypersonic planes, for example. Then, these people argue, the Government should play an active role in leading the direction of technology development. The evidence these people cite for this argument is that the Government has been successful in the past in bringing new technologies into existence.

But this was really only the case in specialized instances when the Government happened to be the lead customer. It was the lead user with regard to a number of different military technologies. So it gave the academic and the corporate R.&D. sectors very specific problems to solve, as a user. In effect, what the Government said was that it wanted to solve a particular problem, as a customer. It did not know how to solve the problem in detail, but it did know the capability it required. This arrangement took advantage of the reverse information flow that we talked about before, the one that corporations are now trying to create, back from users to the research department.

But the problem these days is different. Most of the key technologies that need to be developed are those things for which the Government is not a lead user. In these new areas, no one in the Government has any special knowledge about what should be done. This means that unlike military applications, where the Government was a well-informed customer, in many areas of technological development the Government is likely to fail if it gets into the business of picking which technologies to develop.

4 Suggestions for Improvement

S&B: So how would you make the present system better?

Paul Romer: I would focus much more on the input side and I would subsidize those inputs. At the moment, in the United States, we are not training as many scientists and engineers as we could and should. We're not training people in areas where they would be the most valuable.

The Federal Government in the United States and governments in every country in the world are going to be extremely constrained by entitlements in the next several decades – actually, for the rest of our lives. This is a result of the baby boom and the commitments made in entitlement programs and pensions.

What this means is that the Government won't have as much in the way of resources for R.&D. as it used to have. My argument is that we should concentrate those Government resources as investments in the people. At the same time, generally speaking, you'll probably have to strengthen property rights a little bit, and let the market handle a little bit more of the discovery process than it has handled in the past.

S&B: What would you do differently with regard to the inputs like training?

Paul Romer: The problem – in my opinion – is that the university system is not producing the kinds of scientists and engineers that the private sector needs. It is still locked in the academic model and it is producing scientists and engineers who are copies of what their professors are. As a consequence, there are many areas in the private sector where there is a big demand for scientists that is not being met.

At the moment, we produce Ph.D.'s in our university system for two reasons. One is that we give research money to professors, including money for assistants, so they can use them as inputs in their research. As a result, we produce Ph.D.'s in areas where we're doing research, whether or not there's a private sector demand for people with these skills. We also produce Ph.D.'s where the universities need them as teaching assistants – as inputs in the teaching process for undergraduates.

This means that universities are responding to incentives that are dictated by research funding priorities, a good deal of which come from the Federal Government. They are also responding to their own teaching priorities, which come from university administrations and state governments. But they are not responding to the market's demands for particular types of scientists and engineers.

Now, in this system, students – who are arguably worried about their ultimate job prospects – do not control any of the resources, since most Ph.D. training is subsidized. In my view, what we really need to do is to redirect the system toward the market while, at the same time, we give people bigger incentives to go into scientific fields.

When it comes to how you redirect it, the approach I prefer is one where you give students more control over their own funds. Instead of giving the money for student fellowship positions to the research professor in the department, why not give it to the student? That way a student could take the fellowship and say, "I've seen the numbers. I know I can't get a job if I get a math Ph.D. But if I go into bio-informatics, there is this huge demand for people right now." If students could control the funds, the universities would start to cater to their demands, which would be in line with the market and the private sector's needs.

S&B: What would happen if that kind of plan were put into place?

Paul Romer: If students controlled the funds, you would start to see programs that are more practical, more like high-tech apprenticeships. You would see arrangements where graduate students spend time with firms and work on problems that come up within firms and you would see more movement back and forth between the universities and the private sector. What is interesting here is that we saw a great deal of this in the American system before World War II, before the Federal Government stepped in and began to play such a big role in funding decisions. When the Federal Government came in, it broke the links between universities and the private sector.

There is another way to go as well. I think if you gave an industry some control over research funds that are allocated to universities, the companies would focus much more on training people along the lines I was describing. In a sense, I think the students who are looking for employment and the firms who are looking for employees have interests that are very much in common.

So if you give either piece some control over the system, we will get back to where we want to be.

CHAPTER 6
A Knowledge Management Ontology[*]

Clyde W. Holsapple[1] and K.D. Joshi[2]

[1] School of Management, Gatton College of Business and Economics, University of Kentucky, Lexington, KY, USA

[2] School of Accounting, Information Systems, and Business Law, Washington State University, Pullman, WA, USA

Knowledge-based organizations are hosts for multitudes of knowledge management episodes. Each episode is triggered by a knowledge need (or opportunity) and culminates with the satisfaction of that need (or its abandonment). Within an episode, one or more of the organization's processors (human and/or computer-based) manipulate knowledge resources in various ways and subject to various influences in an effort to meet the need or take advantage of the opportunity. This chapter presents an extensive ontology of knowledge management. The ontology identifies and characterizes basic components of knowledge management episodes, the knowledge resources an organization uses in these episodes, a generic set of elemental knowledge manipulation activities that manifest within knowledge management episodes, and categories of influences on the conduct and outcomes of these episodes. This ontology was developed using conceptual synthesis and a collaborative methodology involving an international panel of researchers and practitioners in the knowledge management field. The ontology can serve as a common language for discourse about knowledge management. For researchers, it suggests issues that deserve investigation and concepts that must be considered in explorations of knowledge management episodes. For practitioners, the ontology provides a perspective on factors that need to be considered in the implementation of an organization's knowledge management initiatives.
Keywords: Conduct of Knowledge Management; Knowledge Management Episode; Knowledge Management Influences; Knowledge Manipulation Activities; Knowledge Resources; Ontology

1 Introduction

An ontology is an explicit specification of a simplified, abstract view of some domain that we want to describe, discuss, and study (Gruber, 1995). It characterizes the concepts involved in that view and tells us how they are related to each other. An ontology is important as a common language for the sharing and reuse of knowledge about a domain, providing a foundation for structuring explorations of that domain and enabling advances in our understanding of it. Many organizations have adopted ontology development as a part of their knowledge management

---

[*] This chapter is adapted with permission from articles published in *Decision Support Systems, Information and Management,* and the *Journal of Strategic Information Systems.*

(KM) initiatives. In such cases, the domain of interest could be the organization's set of knowledge assets and its ways of using those assets; a view of this domain is constructed or identified; this view is explicitly specified as an ontology of concepts and relationships. The ontology is intended to serve as a common language for discussing and thinking about knowledge assets and their usage within the organization.

Here, we focus on a different domain of interest, namely, the domain of knowledge management itself. Rather, than devising an ontology for a particular organization, we construct and present an ontology for knowledge-based organizations in general. The result is a common language for discourse about the conduct of knowledge management in organizations. The ontology can be used in asking questions about KM phenomena, in answering those questions, in making assertions or proposing hypotheses about organizations' approaches to KM, and in describing practices, sharing insights, or discussing investigations concerned with the conduct of knowledge management in organizations.

It is important to understand that there is a distinction between an ontology, on the one hand, and empirical observations on the other hand (Holsapple and Joshi, 2002a). An ontology specifies the concepts used in a domain. These concepts and their relationships are accepted by definition or convention. In contrast, there are observable facts pertaining to these concepts and relationships; these are subject to contextual variations, testing, assessment, and revision. Similarly, there are also unobservable prescriptions stated in terms of the ontology's concepts and relationships. These, too, can vary with context, be evaluated, and be modified. Thus, an ontology is not comprised of observations or prescriptions. But, an ontology can be used to frame or structure a consideration of them.

In a domain that lacks commitment to a particular ontology, it is hard to share and reuse knowledge. When this commitment is absent, those who work in and study the domain do not have a common language; this impedes advances and progress. Thus, when developing an ontology, efforts should be made to ensure that its prospective users will find the characterization of the domain to be adequate in terms of completeness, correctness, clarity, and conciseness (the 4Cs). With this in mind, we undertook a collaborative approach to ontology design.

As described in more detail elsewhere (Holsapple and Joshi, 2002a), this approach employed a Delphi process as a consensus-building mechanism among participants on an international panel of contributors. The panel was evenly divided between researchers and practitioners of KM (see the Acknowledgements section of this chapter). The Delphi process (Lindstone and Turoff, 1975) was anchored by an initial ontology synthesized from the KM literature. Panelists critiqued this anchor in terms of the 4Cs and offered suggestions about how to improve it. Based on these comments, the anchor ontology was revised in an effort to relieve panelist concerns and accommodate panelist recommendations. The resultant ontology was distributed to panelists for another round of critique and comment, resulting in another revision to the ontology. The iterations halted when no panelist expressed major reservations about the current rendition and all indicated at least moderate satisfaction with it in terms of the 4Cs (i.e., when there was appreciable panel commitment to the quality of the result).

The remainder of this chapter presents the KM ontology that was engineered via the collaborative process described above. The description is organized into four main parts. First, we consider major components of the ontology and how they relate to each other via the concept of knowledge management episodes. Second, we examine the ontology's knowledge resource component. Third, basic activities for manipulating these resources are presented. Fourth, we describe the classes of factors that can influence how manipulation activities and knowledge resources are organized for the conduct of KM in an organization.

2   Knowledge Management Episodes and the Conduct of KM

A hallmark of the emerging knowledge economy is the rise of knowledge-based organizations (Holsapple and Whinston, 1987). In these organizations, knowledge is regarded as a crucial resource processed by a joint human-computer system in changing the organization's state of knowledge and producing outputs. Individually, each human or automated processor is a knowledge worker that has a particular set of skills for manipulating knowledge. Collectively, an organization's knowledge processors are arranged into a system that amplifies the knowledge work to be accomplished.

An operational objective of KM is to ensure that the right knowledge is available to the right processors, in the right representations and at the right times, for performing their knowledge activities (and to accomplish this for the right cost). The pursuit of this objective yields a panorama, unfolding over time, of knowledge processors performing various activities and connecting with each other via knowledge flows. One way to try to understand and analyze this rich panorama of knowledge work is in terms of knowledge management episodes.

We shall term what happens between the time a knowledge need (or opportunity) is recognized and the time that it is satisfied (or abandoned) as a knowledge management episode. Such an episode may be independent of, or interdependent with, other episodes active at any given time in an organization. As depicted in Figure 1, a KME involves the execution of some configuration of knowledge manipulation activities by some assortment of processors operating on available knowledge resources to develop the needed knowledge. KM within and across episodes is both facilitated and constrained by various factors. At a micro-level, the factors influencing KM affect how knowledge activities are configured within an episode: which processors perform them, how well they are performed, which knowledge they operate on, and the sequence in which they are performed. At a macro-level, they affect the patterns of episodes that unfold in the management of knowledge.

The concept of a knowledge management episode (KME) comes from the communications literature, referring to a pattern of activities performed by multiple processors with the objective of meeting some knowledge need (Holsapple et al., 1996). Examples of KM episodes include making a decision, solving a problem, conducting an experiment, designing a product or process, brainstorming, evaluating a proposal, performing a scenario analysis, collaborating on a project, engaging in a workflow (Ganapathy, 1996), and so forth. Consider the case of a

decision-making KME. Triggered by a recognition of the need for a decision, the
episode involves one or more decision-making participants (i.e., humans, and possibly decision support systems) who carry out some knowledge manipulation activities, drawing on some portion of a knowledge-resource portfolio, and culminating in new knowledge (i.e, a decision) committing the organization to some course
of action. Decision-making episodes can spawn problem-solving episodes, special
cases of KMEs at a more micro level, where the knowledge needed is the solution
to some problem of interest to the decision maker. Another special case of the
KME concept is the notion of a knowledge acquisition episode (Holsapple and
Wagner, 1996).

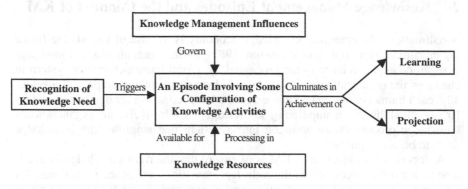

Figure 1. Architecture of a Knowledge Management Episode

By satisfying knowledge needs, KMEs create value for the organization in the
form of learning and projection. Learning is a change in the state of an organization's knowledge resources. Projecting is the embedding of knowledge in an organization's product and service outputs. Together, learning and projecting are the
basis of an organization's innovations. The management of knowledge is inseparable from "the innovation process – defined as bringing ideas to market" (Amidon, 1997). Indeed, in a top-line finding of an Ernst and Young (1997) survey, executives see innovation as the greatest payoff from knowledge management, even
though KM efforts have so far tended to concentrate on achieving productivity
gains. It is important to appreciate how organizations do, can, or should perform
knowledge management as they endeavor to innovate, learn, and project. Such an
appreciation can benefit from an ontology that characterizes

- major influences on KM episodes,
- basic knowledge manipulation activities that occur within those episodes,
  and
- the nature of knowledge resources on which they operate.

The sections that follow address these three topics, beginning with knowledge resources and culminating with KME influences.

3   Knowledge Resources

From a resource-based perspective, organizations are studied in terms of how their resources can predict their performances in a dynamic, competitive environment (Collis and Montgomery, 1994). An organization's competitive advantage stems from the uniqueness of its resource mix and the inability of competitors to replicate that mix (Mata et al., 1995). The value of a particular resource to a firm can be magnified by the presence of other resources and its interplay with them (Teece, 1986; Collis and Montgomery, 1994). According to Amit and Schoemaker (1993), resources are "stocks of available factors that are owned or controlled by the firm" and an organization's capabilities refer to its "capacity to deploy resources." Traditionally, the focus has been on stocks of monetary, human, and material factors.

From a knowledge-based perspective of organizations, the focus is on managing knowledge resources, and the associated aspects of human and material (i.e., computer) resources having capabilities for governing, operating on, and otherwise deploying knowledge (Holsapple and Whinston, 1987; Paradice and Courtney, 1989). The deployment of other organizational resources is seen as secondary, being driven by the combined effects of the organization's processors (human and computer) operating on its knowledge resources – as epitomized in an ongoing panorama of KMEs. This is in accord with the contention of Penrose (1959) that connections between an organization's tangible resources and the services they provide are mediated by managerial knowledge, an intangible organizational resource subject to continuing growth. An organization can be viewed as an institution for integrating knowledge (Grant, 1996). Heading in the direction of a knowledge-based theory of the firm, Spender (1996) views as an organization as a dynamic, knowledge-based activity system, maintaining that it is an organization's knowledge and ability to generate knowledge that form the core of such a theory. In addition to the ability of knowledge processors to generate knowledge, other activities that operate on knowledge resources are important to consider (e.g., acquisition, internalization, selection, externalization as discussed in section 4 below).

Our focus for the moment is on identifying the basic classes of knowledge resources that belong to an organization. These classes define the structure of an organization's portfolio of knowledge assets. An organization's specific assets in each resource category are used by its processors in the conduct of knowledge management and contributing to (if not determining) its competitive standing. Varying the specific knowledge assets within categories and allocations across categories affect organization performance, as do variations in the usage of these resources.

What, then, are the major classes of organizational knowledge resources that are available for KMEs, that should be considered in devising and implementing an organization's KM initiatives, that should be considered in research about the nature of knowledge-based organizations? A comparative analysis of KM frameworks reveals that the knowledge resource portfolio has received relatively little attention (Holsapple and Joshi, 1999a). Three KM frameworks that explicitly identify different kinds of knowledge resources are summarized in Table 1.

Leonard-Barton (1995) identifies two types of organizational knowledge resources: employee knowledge and physical systems (e.g., machinery, databases). Interestingly, she also differentiates between an employee's knowledge and the skills an employee has (e.g., for manipulating knowledge). The Petrash (1996) framework identifies additional knowledge resources. It recognizes employees' knowledge as human capital, but adds four other kinds of knowledge resources: customers (referred to as customer capital), organizational processes, organizational structures, and organizational culture. The latter three are referred to as organizational capital. Sveiby's framework is similar (1997). However, it incorporates customer capital within the notion of external knowledge resources, which includes knowledge resources other than customers (e.g., suppliers). Most other frameworks posited in the literature assume that knowledge resources exist, in that knowledge manipulation activities must operate on something. However, they have little to say about resource differentiation. Some researchers concentrate on one or another attribute of knowledge such as modality of human knowledge resources (i.e., tacit vs. explicit) (Nonaka, 1991). While the study of this and other knowledge-attribute dimensions is interesting and important, it does not tell us about the portfolio of knowledge resources on which KMEs are built.

Table 1. Types of Knowledge Resources Identified in KM Frameworks

Author	Knowledge Resources
Leonard-Barton, 1995	1. Employee knowledge 2. Knowledge embedded in physical systems
Petrash, 1996	Human capital 1. Organizational capital 2. Customer capital
Sveiby, 1997	External structures 1. Internal structures 2. Employee competencies

Which of the classification approaches summarized in Table 1 is preferable? Can the approaches be combined in some organized way? Are there classes of knowledge resources not covered in Table 1? In the quest for a relatively comprehensive, clear, accurate, and concise ontology of organizational knowledge resources, we used the methodology noted in section 1. Interestingly, this collaborative exercise was itself a KME, triggered by the recognition of a need for answers to the above questions and culminating in the learning of a new perspective on organizational knowledge resources plus its projection embodied in this chapter.

3.1   The Ontology's Knowledge Resource Component

The ontology recognizes four main kinds of organizational resources: financial, material, human, and knowledge resources. We focus on the latter. Knowledge manipulation activities (e.g., performed by human resources) operate on knowledge resources (KR) to create value for an organization. On one hand, the value generation depends on the availability and quality of the knowledge resources. On the other hand, productive use of KR depends on the application of knowledge manipulation skills (e.g., exercising a kind of human resource or a material resource such as a decision support system) to execute knowledge manipulation activities. The KR ontology involves a hierarchic taxonomy for classifying an organization's knowledge resources.

The taxonomy structure stems from a simple observation about an organization's knowledge resources: some can exist independent of the organization to which they happen to belong, while others depend on the organization for their existence. We refer to the latter as schematic resources and the former as content resources. The schema knowledge resources shape the working of an organization. Collectively, they establish an organization's ongoing identity. They are the basis for attracting, organizing, and deploying content resources. The content knowledge resources that exist at a given time qualify, condition, and color an organization's identity. They populate, instantiate, and enrich the frame of reference furnished by schematic resources.

As illustrated in Figure 2, the taxonomy identifies four schematic resources: culture, infrastructure, purpose, and strategy. Each is a source of revenue or wealth for an organization. Each denotes an organizational knowledge resource whose existence depends on the organization's existence. Each may change over time, but is invariably present as a knowledge resource. This taxonomy of schematic knowledge resources is consistent with traditionally studied topics in the management literature, although they are not typically viewed as being knowledge resources. This consistency provides KM researchers a base on which to build. Practitioners' familiarity with these topics should enhance the usability of this classification in managing the conduct of KM.

Content resources are comprised of participants and artifacts. A participant's (e.g., employee's) knowledge or the knowledge represented in an artifact (e.g., policy manual) can have an existence apart from the organization that happens to host it at any given time. Each is not only subject to change over time, but is also subject to elimination. The existence and use of content resources in the conduct of KM is both enabled and constrained by the schematic knowledge resources.

Both schema and content are essential portions of an organization's knowledge resources. If schema resources are eliminated from the KR classification, then would artifacts and participants' knowledge be sufficient to define an organization's knowledge resources? We suggest not. Participants and artifacts may come and go, but an organization's knowledge resources have a more enduring aspect that gives the organization continuity in the face of these comings and goings. Beyond the scope of participants and artifacts, knowledge is ingrained in an organization itself by way of its infrastructure, culture, strategy, and purpose. Schematic knowledge resources depend on the existence of the organization rather than on the existence of any particular participants and/or artifacts. However, representations of each can be embedded in artifacts and/or participants' knowledge.

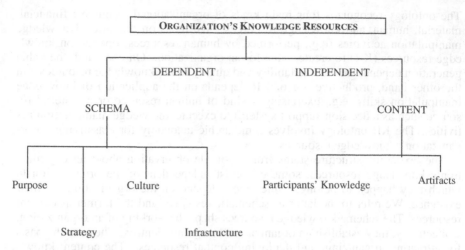

Figure 2. The Ontology's Knowledge Resource Hierarchy

The six types of knowledge resources identified in Figure 2 are both distinct and interrelated. For instance, strategy is distinct from purpose (i.e., alternative strategies are possible for a given purpose), yet strategy should conform to purpose; culture is distinct from infrastructure yet culture can constrain infrastructure and vice versa; each schematic resource is distinct from content resources, yet it may be represented in a participant's knowledge or as an artifact.

Aside from knowledge resources identified above, an organization has access to knowledge existing in its environment via its knowledge acquisition activity. The environment's knowledge resources are a crucial source for replenishing and augmenting an organization's knowledge resources.

3.1.1 Content Knowledge Resources

Content knowledge is embodied in usable representations (Newell, 1982). The primary distinction between participants' knowledge and artifacts lies in the presence or absence of knowledge processing abilities. Participants have knowledge manipulation skills that allow them to process their own repositories of knowledge; artifacts have no such skills. A participant's knowledge is made available to an organization by means of that participant's knowledge manipulation skills. In contrast, an artifact is not accompanied by a processor and does not depend on a participant for its existence.

Participants' Knowledge: An organization's participants include employees (Leonard-Barton, 1995; Stewart, 1997; Sveiby, 1997), customers (Stewart, 1997; Sveiby, 1997), suppliers, partners, consultants, and computer systems (Wiig, 1993; Leonard-Barton, 1995; Sveiby, 1997). An organization's participant knowledge resource is affected by arrival and departure of participants, participant learning, the portion of each participant's knowledge that is brought to bear on organizational work, and interrelationships allowed by schematic knowledge. One way to classify such participants is based on differences in composition. A participant can be an individual, an organization of individuals, a computer system with knowledge manipulation skills (e.g., a decision support system) or a combined computer and human system. Thus, participants can be human resources and/or material resources, but the knowledge possessed by each is a knowledge resource. Participants can also be classified as core participants or those that are ancillary to an organization. Core and ancillary examples for each composition class are exhibited in Table 2.

Table 2. A Classification of Participants

LOCUS COMPOSITION	CORE	ANCILLARY
Human – Individual	e.g., Employee	e.g., Individual customer/supplier
Human – Social	e.g., Community of practice	e.g., Organization that is a customer/supplier
Computer-based	e.g., Decision support systems	e.g., Softbots
Hybrid (Human-Computer)	e.g., Group of persons working with a group support system	e.g., Strategic Business Networks (Amidon, 1997), Ernie (Ernst &Young, 1997)

Even though the ancillary participants do not belong to an organization's collection of human and material resources, some portion of their knowledge may be regarded as virtual knowledge resources employed for the purposes of learning and projection. This is consistent with the network organization view, with core participants' knowledge being a resource of the network's core firm, ancillary participants' knowledge being resources of the network organization's partner firms, and both being a resource of the network organization (Ching et al., 1996; Favela, 1997).

Human participant knowledge is knowledge that a person or a collection of persons (e.g., group, team, or other social entity) is willing to manipulate or make available in the execution of the organization's knowledge manipulation activities. The extent to which such participants make their knowledge available as an organizational resource depends heavily on managerial influences (e.g., leadership, reward systems, evaluation systems) (Holsapple and Joshi, 2000), as well as alignment with schematic knowledge resources such as culture and purpose.

Computer-based participant knowledge is knowledge stored in a computer system that can perform one or more of the knowledge manipulation activities. Examples include decision support systems, performance support systems, and expert systems. For example, General Electric's answer center has collected customers' complaints in a database. This knowledge is part of a system that aids operators in handling customer complaints and concerns for 1.5 M potential problems (Sveiby, 1997). A computer system can preserve, formalize, and consolidate knowledge from various sources (Crowley, 1997).

Hybrid participants' knowledge is knowledge made available or used by joint human-computer entities. An example of a hybrid participant is Buckman Labs' K'Netix coupled with its human experts (Rifkin, 1997). For instance, a managing director of Asian facilities requested knowledge about pitch-control strategies in that part of the world. Within a few hours, he received 11 suggestions addressing his request and enabling him to secure a $6 million order.

Knowledge Artifacts: A knowledge artifact is an object that conveys or holds usable representations of knowledge. However, it does not have any innate knowledge processing capability. Knowledge embodiment in an artifact can be explicit, tacit, or implicit in nature. Common examples of knowledge artifacts are video training tapes, books, memos, business plans in print, manuals, patent documents, filing cabinet contents, facilities, layouts, and products (e.g., knowledge embedded in a manufactured car). An artifact belongs to an organization, but it may be under the control of (or accessible to) only some of its participants.

Knowledge embedded in artifacts can also be represented in other knowledge resources. Representing knowledge as an artifact involves embodiment of that knowledge in an object, thus positively affecting its ability to be transferred, shared, and preserved. For example, Chaparral Steel's near-net-shape casting process, in which both mold and process are patented (Leonard-Barton, 1995), is represented as two knowledge artifacts: the physical system and a document describing a patented process (thereby preserving and protecting it). It is conceivable that this process knowledge also resides with participants; however, it is the representation as a patent document that furnishes legal protection and preservation.

Organizational knowledge can be expressed in the form of products (Wiig, 1993). Products are not simply a result of material, capital, and labor resources, but also of knowledge resources. Knowledge resources guide the transformation of material, labor, and capital resources into a product. In other words, products in an organization's inventory are artifacts. They are representations of the knowledge used to build them. Once a product is released into the environment, it is no longer an organizational resource. However, these products can be exchanged for other kinds of resources (e.g., financial). A product's exchange value is influenced by what a customer is willing to pay for the knowledge it represents. For example, the value of a can of Coke to a consumer derives largely from the marketing, packaging, and recipe knowledge embodied in it, rather than from the costs of assembling certain ingredients and distributing them in containers. A subtle acknowledgment that knowledge is represented in products can be seen in competitors' attempts at reverse engineering.

3.1.2 Schematic Knowledge Resources

Schema knowledge is represented or conveyed in the working of an organization. It manifests in the organization's behaviors. Perceptions of schematic knowledge can be captured and embedded in artifacts or participants' memories, but it exists independent of any one participant and artifact. For instance, we may represent culture, infrastructure, purpose, or strategy in an artifact (e.g., documentation), but its existence does not depend on the creation of an artifact. Knowledge about these resources when embedded in artifacts can be subject to rapid selection and formalized internalization. However, aspects of schematic knowledge embodied in an artifact can be different from an organization's actual schema.

Although the four schematic knowledge resources identified in Figure 2 are interrelated, and good fits among them are important, none can be identified in terms of the others. For instance, a particular culture does not restrict an organization to a particular infrastructure, and vice versa; a given purpose does not define a single potential organization strategy, and vice versa. The schematic resources impact each other and modify each other. For example, a change in purpose could result in a revised strategy, strategies can cause infrastructure revisions, and a particular infrastructure may foster certain cultural characteristics.

Culture: Culture is defined by Schein (1985) as the "... *basic assumptions* and *beliefs* that are shared by members of an organization, that operate unconsciously, and that define in a basic taken-for-granted fashion an organization's view of itself and its environment." An organization's values, principles, norms, unwritten rules, and procedures comprise its cultural knowledge resource. This resource exists independently of the presence of any particular participant's knowledge, yet it influences each participant's use of knowledge as well as the interactions among participants' knowledge. The cultural resource is comprised of basic assumptions and beliefs that govern participants' activities. It is important for KM researchers and practitioners to appreciate this knowledge resource and the mechanisms whereby it persists and can be altered.

The perspective of culture as a knowledge resource can be recognized by observing participants' behaviors. For instance, a mill superintendent at Chaparral Steel "championed the ultimately disastrous installation of a $1.5 million arc saw for cutting finished beams. He was not penalized, but promoted" (Leonard-Barton, 1995). This encouraged the values of high tolerance for risk taking and failure. Slowly, the knowledge that a positive attitude towards risk taking is crucial to the organization's success became ingrained in its culture. This knowledge is manifested in the form of frequent experimentation performed by employees to solve problems that allows Chaparral to be innovative and creative.

An organization's cultural knowledge resource impacts participants' behaviors (e.g., knowledge sharing vs. knowledge hoarding). It affects what knowledge is acquired and internalized. Leonard-Barton (1995) points out that "Values serve as a knowledge-screening and -control mechanism." That is, the cultural knowledge resource can function as a kind of meta knowledge. It also impacts and is impacted by the other schematic knowledge resources: infrastructure, strategy, and purpose.

Infrastructure: Infrastructure is a formal counterpart to an organization's cultural knowledge resource. It is the knowledge that structures an organization's participants in terms of "the roles that have been defined for participants to fill, the relationships among those roles, and regulations that govern the use of roles and relationships" (Holsapple and Luo, 1996). The roles, relationships, and regulations in force for an organization are knowledge governing the formal structuring of work that is to be performed by its participants. Although it can change over time, this schematic knowledge resource persists even as participants come and go. The infrastructure knowledge resource governs not only ordinary organizational operations, but also the designing, enabling, monitoring, evaluating, enforcing, and modifying of organizational infrastructure itself Holsapple and Luo, 1996).

Representing knowledge as infrastructure is a means of formalizing existing organizational knowledge that can be used to generate new knowledge (Marshall et al., 1996). Role definitions are knowledge about what needs to be done by participants, about expectations for the participants assigned to the roles (e.g., what knowledge each is expected to handle or generate). That is, relationships can be implemented technologically, as well as interpersonally. Relationship definitions are knowledge about what interactions are available among participant-filled roles. The interactions that occur for one relationship pattern may generate different knowledge from those that occur for a different pattern. Technology in the guise of communication networks can facilitate particular relationship patterns. Regulation definitions are knowledge about formal rules and procedures that participants are expected to observe in filling their roles and in engaging in relationships. Examples include manufacturing and service processes, hiring processes, performance appraisal, and reward processes.

Purpose: Purpose is the schematic knowledge resource that defines an organization's reason for existence. It indicates an organization's mission, vision, objectives, and goals. It strongly influences the other knowledge resources that an organization has or needs to have. The purpose resource guides strategy formulation, the result of which then drives knowledge manipulation activities. If this knowledge is unclear, inadequate, and not carefully evaluated, then an organization may formulate and implement strategies that are detrimental to organizational performance. For example, Sears whose purpose is to sell consumer goods, bought the investment firm Dean Witter. This turned out to be a failure because consumers did not consider their financial needs to be satisfiable by a "consumer product" (Drucker, 1994). In this case, the purpose knowledge resource was inadequate or unused.

Strategy: Strategy is the schematic knowledge resource that defines what to do in order to achieve organizational purpose in an effective manner. It is comprised of plans for using an organization's infrastructure, culture, knowledge artifacts, and participants' knowledge (as well as other organizational resources). For instance, these can be plans for promoting a product or achieving effective resource allocation. A purpose of Pepsi and Chaparral Steel is to sustain their leadership positions in their respective markets. However, strategies needed to achieve the same purpose are very different for each firm. Pepsi's strategies focus mainly on gaining competencies in the areas of marketing and sales, whereas Chaparral Steel strategies focus primarily on competencies that allow it to continually improve and innovate its production processes (Leonard-Barton, 1995). In this example, Pepsi and Chaparral Steel have very different sets of strategic knowledge on how to sustain market leadership. Thus, activities for acquiring and cultivating such knowledge would be different for Pepsi and Chaparral Steel.

3.1.3   Environment Sources

Aside from its own knowledge resources, an organization's environment holds potential sources of knowledge. Through contacts with its environment, an organization can augment and replenish its knowledge resources. The environment sources do not actually belong to an organization (e.g., in the sense of core participants), nor is it controlled by the organization (e.g., in the sense of ancillary participants). When knowledge is acquired from an environment source, it becomes an organizational resource. This may or may not be difficult or expensive. The World Wide Web is an environment source of knowledge that is relatively easy and inexpensive to tap, albeit of variable quality. Other environment sources include government, media, and university entities whose knowledge is typically available for acquisition by multiple organizations. The Johns Hopkins networked database for genetic research is the "one and only one official record of every gene and piece of DNA that's mapped in the world … It [also] captures and reflects the ongoing wisdom" of experts from all over the world (Anthes, 1991). Knowledge is acquired from this environment source by thousands of medical researchers and practitioners.

3.2 Assessment of the Ontology's Resource Component

The KM ontology's resource component was assessed by panelists both qualitatively and in terms of scaled evaluations for the 4Cs criteria (Holsapple and Joshi, 2001). Evaluation of their qualitative responses detected no major or crippling reservations. Each panelist was asked to rate his/her view of the success of the ontology's resource component with respect to each of the four main criteria: completeness, accuracy, clarity, and conciseness. A seven-point Likert scale was used, ranging from "not at all successful" to "extremely successful," with a midpoint of "moderately successful." Analysis of panelists' quantitative responses showed that a *majority of respondents gauged the ontology's completeness, accuracy, clarity, and conciseness for knowledge resources as being in the successful to extremely successful range.*

3.3 Applications and Questions

At the intersection of the resource-based view of organizations and the knowledge-based view of organizations, lies the proposition that knowledge is a key organizational resource and that it can be used for competitive advantage. Research has identified a knowledge chain, comprised of nine KM activities that can be implemented in ways that give organizations competitive advantages in terms of enhanced productivity, agility, innovation, and reputation (Holsapple and Singh,

2000; Singh, 2000). But aside from KM activities performed by an organization's processors, the classes of knowledge resources identified here are potential sources of competitive advantage. This contention can be investigated from the standpoints of which individual knowledge resource classes can be devised in a way that contributes to an organization's competitiveness (and how so), what portfolio mixes across the classes tend to yield competitive advantages, and what specific practices for KM activities combine with what specific knowledge resource portfolios to enhance competitiveness.

Successful decision making is essential for competitiveness. The organizational knowledge resources discussed in section 3 identify the classes of knowledge assets that deserve consideration in efforts to make an organization's decision making more successful. The participant knowledge embodied in DSSs certainly fits within this big picture. Similarly, human participants' knowledge also comes into play. This is consistent with the notion of human decision support systems (HDSSs) (Holsapple and Whinston, 1996). The taxonomy portrayed in Figure 2 suggests several interesting research questions. For a given set of schematic knowledge resources, what mix of DSSs and HDSSs is desirable? What tradeoffs exist between representing knowledge in a DSS versus an HDSS? What kinds of DSSs work best in the context of a particular set of cultural, infrastructure, strategy, and purpose knowledge resources? Where does the knowledge system of a DSS fall on various knowledge attribute dimensions? How does a DSS knowledge resource interact with other kinds of organizational knowledge resources and how should it do so?

Efforts at measuring an organization's knowledge resources should cover each of the taxonomy's classes and may proceed along multiple attribute dimensions. Different measures may be required across, or even within, different classes. Similarly, efforts at controlling the validity and utility of knowledge may depend on the KR class in which that knowledge exists. The taxonomy identifies KR classes that are candidates for organizing or inclusion in comprehensive knowledge maps. Researchers need to study and practitioners need to understand the implementation of each knowledge manipulation activity (as discussed in section 4: acquisition, selection, internalization, generation, and externalization) as it operates on each KR class.

Each of the knowledge resources identified in this taxonomy is a concept that can be analyzed further, perhaps yielding another layer at the bottom of the hierarchy in Figure 2. For instance, culture may be further decomposed into norms, shared beliefs, values, traditions, and so on. Artifacts might be further categorized as products, buildings, documents, books, audio tapes, video tapes, patent documents, and so forth.

4   Knowledge Manipulation Activities

This component of the ontology furnishes a relatively comprehensive, unified perspective on the kinds of knowledge manipulation activities that can occur in a KM episode. As such, it forms part of a common language for discussing an organization's KM episodes. It gives a foundation for suggesting how each of the knowledge manipulation activities should be accomplished and how they should be configured within episodes. Its characterization of each manipulation activity is suggestive of functionalities that would be useful to include in the design of computer-based processors for performing or supporting the activity.

A comparative analysis of KM frameworks in the literature indicates that they identify various knowledge management activities (Holsapple and Joshi, 1999a). These are summarized in Table 3. Some frameworks treat these activities at an elemental level, while others deal with higher-level knowledge activities. For instance, the activities identified by Arthur Andersen and APQC (1996), Wiig (1993), van der Spek and Spijkervet (1997), Alavi (1997), and Szulanski (1996) appear to be more elemental than those identified by Leonard-Barton (1995), and Choo (1996). The higher-level activities seem to be groupings of more elemental activities. For example, decision making is an activity that may involve a composite of the more elemental activities identified by Arthur Andersen and APQC.

Table 3. Summary of Knowledge Management Activities Identified in the Literature

Author	Knowledge Management Activities
Alavi, 1997	1. Acquisition (knowledge creation and content development); 2. Indexing; 3. Filtering; 4. Linking involves screening, classification, cataloging, integrating, and interconnecting internal and external sources); 5. Distributing (packaging and delivery of knowledge in the form of Web pages); 6. Application (using knowledge).
Arthur Anderson and APOC, 1996	1. Share; 2. Create; 3. Identify; 4. Collect; 5. Adapt; 6. Organize; 7. Apply.
Choo, 1996	1. Sensemaking (includes "information interpretation"); 2. Knowledge creation (includes "information transformation"); 3. Decision making (includes "information processing").
Holsapple and Whinston, 1987	1. Procure; 2. Organize; 3. Store; 4. Maintain; 5. Analyze; 6. Create; 7. Present; 8. Distribute; 9. Apply.
Leonard-Barton, 1995	1. Shared and creative problem solving; 2. Importing and absorbing technological knowledge from the outside of the firm; 3. Experimenting prototyping; 4. Implementing and integrating new methodologies and tools.
Nonaka, 1996	1. Socialize (convert tacit knowledge to tacit knowledge); 2. Internalize (convert explicit knowledge to tacit knowledge); 3. Combine (convert explicit knowledge to explicit knowledge); 4. Externalize (convert tacit knowledge to explicit knowledge).

Szulanski, 1996	1. Initiation (recognize knowledge need and satisfy that need); 2. Implementation (knowledge transfer takes place); 3. Ramp-up (use the transferred knowledge); 4. Integration (internalize the knowledge).
van der Spek and Spijkervet, 1997	In the Act Process 1. Develop; 2. Distribute; 3. Combine; 4. Hold.
Wiig, 1993	1. Creation; 2. Manifestation; 3. Use; 4. Transfer.

An examination of the activities reveals considerable variation. No one view subsumes the others. This suggests there is a need for a generic ontology that describes knowledge manipulation activities clearly and completely, and also identifies their possible interrelationships.

Here, the focus is on elemental activities (and their subactivities) rather than higher-level, composite ones. The focus is on activities that directly manipulate knowledge and produce knowledge flows within a KM episode, rather than activities that start or control the episode. The latter managerial influences on KM episodes are addressed in section 5 below. The manipulation activities in this ontology are not dependent on any particular view of what knowledge is; nor do they stem from a focus on any particular attribute of knowledge such as its mode (tacit versus explicit), its type (descriptive versus procedural versus reasoning), or its orientation or domain.

4.1 The Ontology's Knowledge Manipulation Component

In a KM episode, processors use their knowledge handling skills to manipulate knowledge resources. That is, the mechanisms and results of knowledge manipulation activities are expressions of processors' knowledge manipulation skills. *Skill* is the ability to apply one's *knowledge* effectively and readily to *execution* and *performance* (Merriam-Webster, 1995).

Participants' knowledge manipulation skills differ widely, but we do not attempt to classify the diversity that differentiates them. Instead, we focus on the activities that are executed and performed using those skills. The ontology identifies a set of interrelated knowledge manipulation activities that appear to be common across diverse organizations. Identification of these activities forms a starting point for understanding how knowledge is processed in organizations and how this changes over time. The ontology highlight major activities with which a chief knowledge officer (CKO) needs to be concerned. Participants' knowledge manipulation skills need to be cultivated, harnessed, and organized in the performance of these activities.

Figure 3 identifies the major activities of **acquiring, selecting, internalizing**, and **using** knowledge. The latter refers to the activities of **externalizing** and **generating** knowledge. Arrows indicate major knowledge flows. For instance, execution and performance of the acquisition activity entails a knowledge flow into that activity from the environment and a consequent flow to the internalizing or using activity. The internalizing activity produces a knowledge flow that impacts the state of the organization's knowledge resources; externalizing impacts the environment; these are learning and projection, respectively.

Aside from the main knowledge flows, activities can send and receive ancillary messages. (For simplicity, these messages are not represented in the figure.) An example is a request from one activity to another (e.g., the generating activity requests a knowledge flow from the selection activity). Requests can range from procedural (specifying how the activity should be carried out) to nonprocedural (merely indicating what is needed). They can range from explicit (e.g., a command) to implicit (e.g., involving recognition of a need). Some may require fast responses; others tolerate performance of an activity in the background. They can range from one-time requests to standing requests that require continual monitoring. Another example of an ancillary message is a feedback message, where an activity acknowledges receipt of a knowledge flow or comments on the value the flow that is received.

Each instance of knowledge manipulation can be performed by one participant or by some configuration of multiple participants. Conversely, a participant may

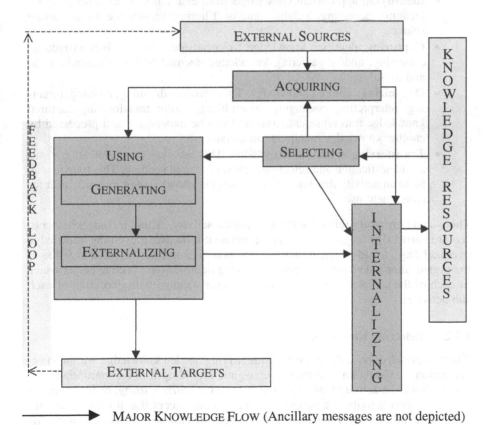

Figure 3. Major Knowledge Manipulation Activities

exercise knowledge manipulation skills to perform multiple activities within a KM episode. For instance, a person (or a computer system) may participate in both acquiring and generating knowledge within a single KM episode.

Managerial, resource, and environmental factors affect how the knowledge manipulation skills of an organization's participants are deployed to accomplish the activities. These factors (discussed in section 5) also influence the pattern of activities that occur within a specific KM episode: which are performed and by whom, how many instances are performed, which one is first, which is last, and so forth. For all cases, the ontology furnishes the following characterization of the activities.

4.1.1   Acquiring Knowledge

Knowledge acquisition refers to the activity of identifying knowledge in the environment and transforming it into a representation that can be internalized, and/or used. Its subactivities include:

- **Identifying** appropriate knowledge from external sources. This includes locating, accessing, valuing, and/or filtering knowledge from outside sources.
- **Capturing** identified knowledge from outside. This involves extracting, collecting, and/or gathering knowledge deemed to be sufficiently valid and useful.
- **Organizing** captured knowledge. This involves distilling, refining, orienting, interpreting, packaging, assembling, and/or transforming captured knowledge into representations that can be understood and processed by another knowledge manipulation activity.
- **Transferring** organized knowledge. This involves communication channel identification and selection, scheduling, and sending. This transfer can be to an activity that immediately uses the knowledge or internalizes it for subsequent use.

There are many issues related to the acquisition activity. These include whether to acquire knowledge (e.g., outsource) or generate it in-house; preventing knowledge overload (e.g., avoid acquiring knowledge that does not add significant value to the organization); developing procedures and guidelines for effective performance of each of the sub-activities (e.g., reduce costs associated with execution of each sub-activity).

4.1.2   Selecting Knowledge

Knowledge selection is the activity of identifying needed knowledge within an organization's existing knowledge resources and providing it in an appropriate representation to an activity that needs it (i.e., to an *acquiring, using,* or *internalizing* activity). This activity is analogous to acquisition, except that it manipulates resources already in the organization. However, the two activities can require different skills, levels of effort, and costs. Sub-activities include:

- **Identifying** appropriate knowledge within the organization's existing resources. This includes locating, accessing, valuing, and/or filtering knowledge.
- **Capturing** identified knowledge, which involves retrieving, collecting and/or gathering it from the organization's knowledge resources.
- **Organizing** captured knowledge. This involves distilling, refining, orienting, interpreting, packaging, assembling, and/or transforming captured knowledge into representations appropriate for subsequent manipulation.
- **Transferring** organized knowledge to an appropriate activity (e.g., the one that requested it). This involves determining the medium through which knowledge is transferred (identification and choice), scheduling, and sending it. This flow can support the acquiring, internalizing, or using activities.

Issues concerned with knowledge selection include how to adapt skills at acquiring to the activity of selecting and vice versa; how to perform the selection activity on knowledge resources that embody implicit/tacit knowledge; what techniques/tools to employ to make the selection activity effective and efficient for each of the main types of knowledge resources; ensuring that the needed knowledge reaches participants that need it and does so when it is needed.

4.1.3   Internalizing Knowledge

This involves incorporating or making the knowledge a part of the organization. The ontology views internalizing as an activity that alters an organization's knowledge resources with the results of acquiring, selecting, or generating the knowledge. It receives knowledge flows from these activities and produces flows that impact the organization's state of knowledge. Internalizing knowledge is a culminating activity in organizational learning. Sub-activities include:

- **Assessing** and valuing knowledge to be internalized. This involves determining the suitability of the knowledge, which depends on its degree of assessed utility and validity.
- **Targeting** knowledge resources. This identifies knowledge resources that are to be impacted by the knowledge flow produced by internalization.
- **Structuring** knowledge. This represents knowledge to be conveyed in the appropriate forms for the targets.
- **Delivering** the knowledge representations as targeted. This involves modifying existing knowledge resources (adding to them, deleting from them, increasing their organizational density, or perhaps fundamentally altering a knowledge resource). It involves depositing, storing, updating, disseminating, distributing, and sharing knowledge with respect to targeted knowledge resources. This also involves channel identification and choice, scheduling, and sending.

The term "internalizing" has equivalently been called assimilating to distinguish this concept from Nonaka's notion of internalizing (Holsapple and Jones, 2003).

4.1.4   Using Knowledge

The phrase "using knowledge" is an umbrella phrase that is used to cover the activities of applying existing knowledge to generate new knowledge and/or produce an externalization of knowledge. Where the activity of using knowledge exists, there is the possibility that organizational learning is innovative and adds value.

Generating knowledge: This is an activity that produces knowledge by processing existing knowledge, which has resulted from selection, acquisition, and/or prior generation. The knowledge generated may be new to the organization. This is crucial because "new knowledge provides the basis for organization renewal and sustainable competitive advantage" (Quinn, 1992). Alternatively, it may currently exist or have previously existed in the organization. Generation of knowledge that is not "new" can occur for economic reasons (e.g., it is cheaper to generate than to select), for training reasons, for validity checking, due to a lack of awareness about its existence, or due to not having been internalized when previously acquired or generated. Sub-activities for generation include:

- **Monitoring** the organization's knowledge resources and the external environment by invoking selection and/or acquisition activities as needed.
- **Evaluating** selected or acquired knowledge in terms of its utility and validity for the production of knowledge.
- **Producing** knowledge from a previously existing base. This can involve creating, synthesizing, analyzing, and constructing knowledge.
- **Transferring** the produced knowledge for externalization and/or internalization. This involves channel identification and choice, scheduling, and sending.

Broadly, there are two types of generation: **derivation** and **discovery**. *Derivation* involves the use of process knowledge (e.g., procedures, rules) and descriptive knowledge (e.g., data, information) to generate process and/or descriptive knowledge. It employs knowledge management skills that are of an analytical, logical, and constructive nature. In contrast, *discovery* generates knowledge in less structured ways, via skills involving creativity, imagination, and synthesis. The exact path from the initial to the discovered knowledge cannot always be preconceived or traced. Herman Helmholtz, a German physiologist and physicist, described his scientific discoveries as progressing through three stages: saturation (finding out everything he could learn on a subject), incubation (reflecting on what has been absorbed, by thinking about and mulling over what he has learned through the research), and illumination (arriving at a sudden solution). French mathematician, Henry Poincare, added a fourth stage to this – verification (Carson, 1992).

Issues related to generation include what methods or techniques facilitate production of knowledge; how to effectively interface with selection and acquisition activities for efficient monitoring and to minimize evaluation required during generation; how to coordinate related instances of generation; means of learning not only in the sense of generating knowledge but also in the introspective sense of how to better generate knowledge in the future, learning about generation itself and internalizing the result (e.g., as process knowledge) for subsequent selection;

guidelines for governing whether needed knowledge should be acquired, selected, or generated.

Externalizing knowledge: The activity of making something available outside the organization is termed externalization (or, equivalently, emitting (Holsapple and Jones, 2003)). Applying this to an organization's conduct of knowledge management, the ontology views externalizing knowledge as the activity that uses existing knowledge to produce organizational outputs for release into the environment. It yields projections (i.e., embodiment of knowledge in outward forms) for external consumption, in contrast to internalization which may also yield projections, but which are retained as knowledge resources. Externalization is only partially a knowledge manipulation activity because it can involve physical activities, such as the act of producing a product through transformation of raw materials. However, the flow of material can be seen as secondary to the flow of knowledge that enables, facilitates, and guides it (Cook et al., 1995). Sub-activities include:

- **Targeting** the output. This involves determining what needs to be produced for targeted elements of the environment.
- **Producing** the output. This involves applying, embodying, controlling, and leveraging existing knowledge to produce output for the target. The output is a representation of the knowledge used to produce it.
- **Transferring** the output. This is concerned with packaging and delivering the projections that have been produced for targets in the environment. This involves channel (medium through which knowledge is transferred) identification and choice, scheduling, and sending.

Externalization results in projections. When an organization transfers an output (e.g., in the form of products, services, knowledge artifacts), it is projecting. The process of effective projection adds value to an organization in forms such as profits, image, customer loyalty, and visibility. Once externalization occurs, its impact (e.g., in the forms of sales, etc.) can be captured through the knowledge acquiring activity. This environment interaction results in a feedback loop.

Externalization issues include how to innovatively apply generated knowledge for the purpose of external projections; how to mesh or intersperse instances of generation into an instance of externalization; means of identifying appropriate targets and the nature of knowledge acquisition effort with respect to them; understanding the differences and commonalties between externalization and internalization.

4.2 Assessment of the Ontology's Manipulation Component

In examining panelist reactions to knowledge manipulation component of the ontology, no major or crippling reservations were detected. Concerns related primarily to pushing beyond ontology boundaries were expressed (Holsapple and Joshi, 2002b). Panelists quantitatively evaluated the ontology's manipulation component in terms of the 4Cs criteria. All respondents rate the ontology's knowledge manipulation component as at least somewhat successful on all criteria. *A majority of panelists gauged its completeness and conciseness as being in the successful to extremely successful range. A majority of panelists gauged its accuracy and clarity as being in the moderately successful to extremely successful range.*

4.3 Implications

Identification and explanation of knowledge manipulation activities and their inter-relationships allows for better understanding of the nature and the dynamics of processing an organization's knowledge resources within and across knowledge management episodes. Each of the knowledge manipulation activities and any of their sub-activities can be characterized an analyzed in greater detail. For instance, such an analysis has been performed for the knowledge selection activity (Holsapple and Joshi, 1999b). It fleshes out concepts of selection functionalities in greater detail. Based on these, it identifies issues related to knowledge selection, uses the ontology's concepts to organize a characterization of current technological offerings for knowledge selection, and describes the interaction of all the other activities with the selection activity. Similar analysis can be carried out for each of the other activities.

Alteration of knowledge resources through knowledge valuing (i.e., what knowledge should be attained, retained, and replenished) is a very serious issue faced by organizations (Liebowitz and Wright, 1998). This is an aspect of the ontology's internalization activity. However, types of alteration, criteria for alteration, and mechanisms to execute alteration are not detailed within the internalization activity.

The ontology's activities are not confined to manipulation of explicit knowledge, but can also be performed on tacit/implicit knowledge. The manipulation skills and mechanisms needed to carry out a particular activity on one mode or type of resource can substantially differ from those useful for another type of knowledge resource.

This ontology can be used to systematically generate, study, and discuss KM-related issues. It provides a platform for communication and sharing of ideas related to knowledge manipulation activities among practitioners. The common language can aid practitioners in administering KM initiatives by addressing issues in a systematic fashion (e.g., the types of activities that need more attention; types of skills/competencies, tools, and techniques that need to be cultivated and developed to execute these activities).

The ontology's characterization of knowledge manipulation activities is descriptive, aiming to identify relevant activities and their knowledge-flow relationships. It does not advocate any particular methodology or process for coordinating these activities. They can be combined in various configurations in order to define a process or methodology.

5   Influences on the Conduct of Knowledge Management

The final component of the ontology considers factors that influence the success of knowledge management initiatives in an organization. It identifies three main classes of influencing factors (managerial, resource, and environmental) and characterizes the individual factors in each class. Understanding these factors can aid explicit, deliberate efforts at managing knowledge in organizations. It is necessary, but not sufficient, to appreciate what the knowledge resources are and what activities can be used to manipulate them.

By delineating factors that influence the management of knowledge in an organization, the ontology furnishes a check-list of considerations to keep in mind when designing or evaluating an organization's practices. Prescriptions for how to successfully accomplish KM should be cognizant of the influence factors identified in the ontology. For KM researchers, the ontology can stimulate the formulation of issues and hypotheses for investigation. Moreover, the ontology lays a foundation for systematic development and evaluation of technologies intended to aid a chief knowledge officer's efforts.

5.1 The Ontology's Influence Component

In reviewing the literature, one encounters a very broad range of factors that possibly influence the success of KM initiatives (Holsapple and Joshi, 1999a). These include: culture (Leonard-Barton, 1995; Arthur Andersen and APQC, 1996; Szulanski, 1996; van der Spek and Spijkervet, 1997), leadership (Arthur Andersen and APQC, 1996), technology (Arthur Andersen and APQC, 1996; van der Spek and Spijkervet, 1997), organizational adjustments (Szulanski, 1996; van der Spek and Spijkervet, 1997), evaluation of knowledge management activities and/or knowledge resources (Wiig, 1993; Anderson and APQC, 1996; van der Spek and Spijkervet, 1997), governing/administering knowledge activities and/or knowledge resources (Wiig, 1993; Leonard-Barton, 1995; Szulanski, 1996, van der Spek and Spijkervet, 1997), employee motivation (Szulanski, 1996; van der Spek and Spijkervet, 1997), and external factors (van der Spek and Spijkervet, 1997).

Figure 4 illustrates three major kinds of forces that conspire to influence the knowledge management episodes that ultimately unfold in an organization. It identifies the main factors involved in each influence category, and the inner core represents essential results of KM episodes (i.e., projection and learning). Relating this to Figure 1, it identifies what specific factors influence performance of knowledge manipulation activities acting on knowledge resources within and across KM episodes. In considering the three classes of KM influences, we focus on managerial influences as they are most apt to be under the control of persons responsible for KM initiatives.

5.1.1 Managerial Influences

Managerial influences emanate from organizational participants responsible for administering the management of knowledge. The ontology partitions these influences into four main factors: exhibiting leadership in the management of knowledge, coordinating the management of knowledge, controlling the management of knowledge, and measuring the management of knowledge. The notions of leadership, coordination, control, and measurement are not unique to KM. However, their impacts on KM are not widely known and their execution with respect to KM may require special techniques.

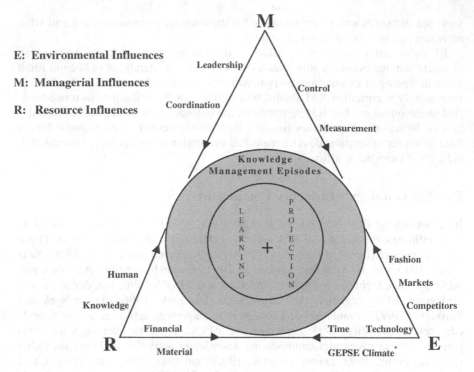

* **GEPSE Climate**: Government., Economic, Political, Social, and Educational Climate

Figure 4. Influences on the Management of Knowledge

Coordination: Knowledge development (e.g., to propel innovation) is a primary driver of KM. It can be left to serendipity or be planned and structured. The planned approach requires coordination within and across KMEs, involving the determination of what knowledge activities to perform in what sequence, which participants will perform them, and what knowledge resources will be operated on by each.

Coordination refers to managing dependencies among activities (Malone & Crowston, 1994). It aims to harmonize activities in an organization by ensuring that proper resources are brought to bear at appropriate times and that they adequately relate to each other as activities unfold (Holsapple & Whinston, 1996). In the management of knowledge, dependencies that need to be managed include those among knowledge resources (e.g., alignment of participants' knowledge with strategy, diffusion of knowledge among participants), those among knowledge activities (e.g., which activities are undertaken under varying circumstances), those between knowledge resources and other resources (e.g., what financial resources are to be allocated for knowledge activities), and those between resources and knowledge activities (e.g., use of knowledge activities to improve knowledge resources, knowledge resources among competing knowledge activities). The management of knowledge in an organization is strongly influenced by how such dependencies are managed.

Coordination involves not only managing dependencies, but also marshaling sufficient skills for executing various activities, arrangement of those activities in time (within and across KM episodes), and integrating knowledge processing with an organization's operations (e.g., What knowledge activities are involved and necessary for managing inventory operations?). Coordination approaches suggested and used to manage dependencies in a knowledge-based organization include linking reward structures to knowledge sharing, establishing communications for knowledge sharing, and constructing programs to encourage learning (Crowley, 1995; Rifkin, 1997; Marshall et al., 1996).

Control: Control is concerned with ensuring that needed knowledge resources and processors are available in sufficient quality and quantity, subject to required security. Two critical issues here are protection of and quality of knowledge resources. Protecting knowledge resources from loss, obsolescence, unauthorized exposure, unauthorized modification, and erroneous assimilation is crucial for the effective management of knowledge. Approaches include legal protection (e.g., patents, copyrights), social protection (e.g., hiring people who can blend with the current culture and help sustain current values and norms), and technological protection (e.g., security safeguards). In establishing sufficient controls to govern the quality of knowledge used in an organization, management needs to consider two dimensions: knowledge validity and knowledge utility (Holsapple & Whinston, 1996). Validity is concerned with accuracy, consistency, and certainty; utility is concerned with clarity, meaning, relevance, and importance.

Measurement: In its most basic sense, measurement involves the valuation of knowledge resources and processors. It is also a basis for evaluation of leadership, coordination, and control; for identifying and recognizing value-adding activities and resources; for assessing and comparing the execution of knowledge activities; and for evaluating the impacts of an organization's KM (i.e., learning and projection) on bottom-line performance.

Although it is an under-implemented area (Hiebeler, 1996), measuring knowledge resources or activities and linking them to financial results is feasible (Lev, 1997; Malone, 1997; Stewart, 1997). The ontology contends that KM initiatives are impacted by whether an organization attempts to measure its knowledge resources and/or performance of its knowledge activities, how it goes about measuring these, and how effective the measures are. Some organizations have already developed and applied indicators of knowledge resources of knowledge activity (e.g., Celemi (Sveiby, 1997)). Measurement indicators need not be hard and financial, but can be soft and non-financial (Webber, 1997).

Leadership: A study conducted by Andersen and APQC revealed that one crucial reason why organizations are unable to effectively leverage knowledge is because of a "lack of commitment of top leadership to sharing organizational knowledge or there are too few role models who exhibit the desired behavior" (Hiebeler, 1996).

Of the four managerial influences, leadership is primary. In alignment with the organization's purpose and strategy, it establishes enabling conditions for fruitful

KM. Coordination, control, and measurement are contributors to establishing these conditions, but there is an additional aspect to fulfilling the leadership mission. This distinguishing characteristic of leadership is that of being a catalyst through such traits as inspiring, mentoring, setting examples, engendering trust and respect, instilling a cohesive and creative culture, listening, learning, teaching (e.g., through storytelling), and knowledge sharing.

The core competencies for effective leaders of knowledge-intensive organizations are being a catalyst, being a coordinator, exercising control, and being an evaluator. The KM leader creates conditions that allow participants to readily exercise and cultivate their knowledge manipulation skills, to contribute their own individual knowledge resources to the organization's pool of knowledge, and to have easy access to relevant knowledge resources. For ongoing success of KM initiatives, it is necessary to develop leaders at all levels of functionality or accountability. The execution and cultivation of leadership depends on an appreciation of knowledge resources, of knowledge activities, and of the other KM influences.

5.1.2   Resource Influences

Financial resources put a ceiling on what can be expended on knowledge activities. Increasing the financial resources available for a knowledge activity (e.g., acquiring some needed knowledge) may affect the efficiency of that activity or the quality of its results (positively or negatively). Moreover, financial resource availability may affect the execution of leadership, coordination, control, and measurement. Knowledge manipulation skills of an organization's participants both constrain and facilitate KM. These skills are the essential mechanism for performing the knowledge activities that make up KM episodes. In the case of human participants, these skills are human resources. In case of computer-based participants, these skills are material resources. Human resources also influence KM by enabling or restricting the managerial influences.

Knowledge resources strongly influence KM in an organization. As the raw materials for knowledge activities, knowledge resources available in an organization necessarily influence its KM and the resultant learning, projection, and innovation. Some knowledge resources also affect KM by serving as the basis for coordination, control, measurement, and leadership. Major types of organizational knowledge resources include participants' knowledge (both human and computer-based), artifacts, culture, and strategy. Each can be examined along various attribute dimensions (e.g., tacit vs. explicit, descriptive vs. procedural vs. reasoning) and studied from the standpoint of its influence on KM.

5.1.3   Environmental Influences

Managerial and resource influences on KM are internal to an organization. Factors external to an organization also affect its KM. The environment influences what knowledge resources should or can be acquired in the course of KM. It influences what knowledge manipulation skills (e.g., human or technological) are available. As Figure 4 illustrates, environmental influences on KM are competition, fashion, markets, technology, time, and the GEPSE (governmental, economic, political, social, and educational) climate. Examples of these are many and varied. Organizations have little control over environmental influences. As such, they pose constraints on an organization's KM. However, the confluence of environmental influences can also present opportunities for improving KM.

5.2 Assessment of the Ontology's Influence Component

While many possible KM influences have been proposed by various authors, the ontology component outlined in Figure 4 is the result of a systematic, collaborative research effort to identify and characterize the influencing factors in a comprehensive, unified, organized way. Panelists involved in this collaborative effort evaluated the results. No major or crippling reservations within the research boundaries. Their qualitative suggestions mainly involved extending the scope of this research by adding more detail (especially for the environmental influences), by considering non-business organizations, and by prescribing what an organization should do with respect to dealing with the identified influences. A *majority of panelists gauged the ontology's completeness, accuracy, clarity and conciseness for the influence component as being in the successful to extremely successful range.*

5.3 Applications

The ontology provides a relatively comprehensive description of influence elements to consider in studies, investigations, and prescriptions of KM. It serves as a basis for thinking about extensions and refinements that could yield an improved and/or more detailed ontology of KM influences. It furnishes a language (i.e., a system of terms and concepts) for discourse about and study of KM influences, a basis for generating varied research issues to explore, a means for identifying factors with which KM practitioners should deal (i.e., a checklist of considerations), and a frame of reference for benchmarking KM practices as they relate to influences. Here, we briefly highlight some of these ontology applications.

Planning for KM initiatives in an organization needs to be grounded on an ontology that identifies the elements of interest for conducting knowledge management. Figure 1 suggests that an organization's KM ontology might include elements pertaining to knowledge management episodes, knowledge resources, knowledge activities, and influences on knowledge management. More specifically, the KM influence ontology can be applied to develop a checklist of influence considerations to address in planning a KM initiative. Table 4 presents such a checklist for the managerial influences. The factors listed for each of these influences are extracted from the final ontology description evaluated by panelists. The rightmost columns in the checklist are meant to indicate that each factor can be addressed within and/or across KMEs, depending on the scope of the initiative.

Table 4. A CKO Checklist for KM Initiatives

Managerial Influence	Factors to Consider	Episode Scope	
		Within KME	Across KMEs
Leadership	Is there top-level commitment to KM initiatives? How does it manifest? Does it align with the organization's purpose and strategy?		
	How is KM leadership cultivated at lower levels?		
	How are conditions created that allow processors to do their best individual and collaborative knowledge work?		
	How is a culture appropriate to knowledge work established?		
	Is there technological support for KM leadership?		
	How are best KM leadership practices recognized/ preserved/applied?		
Coordination	What knowledge activities are performed?		
	How are they organized to accommodate dependencies?		
	Which processors perform them?		
	What knowledge resources are used and/or changed?		
	Is the knowledge processing self-directed, guided, or dictated?		
	What incentive structures are in place to secure efforts?		
	How is the knowledge processing integrated with other operations?		
	How are best KM coordination practices recognized/ preserved/applied?		
	Is there technological support for KM coordination?		
Control	What regulations are in place to ensure quantity, quality, and security of knowledge resources and processors?		
	How are knowledge resources protected from loss, obsolesence, improper exposure/modification, and erroneous assimilation? Via legal, social, technical means?		

	What validation controls are used to ensure sufficient accuracy, consistency, and certainty of knowledge resources?		
	What utility controls are used to ensure sufficient clarity, meaning, relevance, and importance of knowledge resources?		
	How are best KM control practices recognized/ preserved/applied?		
	Is there technological support for KM control?		
Measurement	How are knowledge resources valued?		
	How are processors evaluated?		
	In what ways are effectiveness of knowledge activities, coordination approaches, knowledge controls, and knowledge management leadership assessed?		
	What are the impacts of an organization's KM on its competitiveness and bottom-line performance?		
	How is effectiveness of these measurement practices gauged?		
	How are best KM measurement practices recognized/ preserved/applied?		
	Is there technological support for KM measurement?		

Each of the factors identified in Table 4 is not only a consideration for KM practitioners, but it is also a question of potential interest for KM researchers. The subjects suggested in these questions may be investigated individually, in relation to each other, or in relation to the constraints of resource and environmental influences. The ontology can also be applied to help identify KM-related issues by juxtaposing influences with other concepts such as ethics, outsourcing, sharing, and competitiveness. Each leads to a host of specific issues, examples of which are shown in Table 5. Such a matrix can be further developed by selecting one concept and examining it in greater depth with respect to more detailed ontology elements. This is illustrated in Table 6, by extending and elaborating on knowledge sharing issues using the KM influence components. Another example is the knowledge chain model which develops the connection between managerial influences and competitiveness (Holsapple and Singh, 2000).

Table 5. Some Sample Research Issues

Influence Class	Concept for Investigation			
	Ethics	**Outsourcing**	**Sharing**	**Competitiveness**
Managerial Influences	What are the ethical boundaries for implementing controls?	How are coordination and control performed when a knowledge management episode or knowledge manipulation activity is outsourced?	What managerial leadership, coordination, control, or measurement actions can promote knowledge sharing?	Are there particular approaches to KM leadership, coordination, control, and measurement that yield competitive advantages?
Resource Influences	Where does ownership of an individual's knowledge (attained in the organization or outside of it) reside? With the individual and/or organization?	What resource conditions trigger a need for KM outsourcing?	How widely shared should a particular knowledge resource be?	To what degree is competitiveness based on knowledge resources versus the ability of processors to operate on them?
Environment Influences	To what extent should ethical values in handling knowledge within an organization be aligned with ethical norms of the GEPSE climate?	What environment factors (e.g., time, markets, technology, competitors) lead to the outsourcing of KM efforts (as enablers or drivers)?	Are there GEPSE impediments to knowledge sharing within an organization? Can these constraints be relaxed? Should they be relaxed?	Are there technologies for performing or supporting the activities and flows that occur in an organization's KM that can make the organization more competitive? Which ones? How so?

Table 6 shows an example of an exploration matrix to identify and organize issues related to knowledge sharing, an often-mentioned notion in the KM literature. For each influence class, we can consider its connection to knowledge sharing. This matrix can be used by CKOs as a guide to help ensure coverage of major factors in developing or evaluating knowledge sharing strategies and initiatives in their organizations. It can help researchers systematically identify constructs that may impact knowledge sharing. Such a matrix can help in designing research models by identifying research variables whose relationships are to be modeled. It can stimulate the identification of unexplored propositions and hypotheses related to organizational knowledge sharing (e.g., certain kinds of coordination, technology, or infrastructure to foster greater knowledge sharing).

Table 6. Examples of Knowledge Sharing Issues Suggested by the Ontology's Influence Classes

Influence Class	Issues of Knowledge Sharing in Managing Knowledge
Managerial Influences	*Leadership* is concerned with building a trusting environment conducive to sharing knowledge. *Coordination* is concerned with developing and integrating reward and incentive systems that encourage knowledge sharing, as well as scheduling knowledge flows. *Control* is concerned with governing the content and channels of sharing (e.g., what can and cannot be shared and with whom it can be shared), ensuring that knowledge that is shared is of adequate quality and that sharing is not counterproductive (e.g., sharing of knowledge that may sabotage new initiatives). *Measurement* can aim at assessing and evaluating the knowledge sharing process. If sharing is linked to reward systems, how can sufficient credit be given to individuals/teams for sharing? What type of knowledge sharing is entitled for reward? How can we measure what and how much is shared, and its impacts on organizational performance?
Resource Influences	Human participants' personal beliefs and experiences may affect their approaches to sharing. How can computer systems be employed to facilitate sharing? An organization's cultural knowledge resource will have a major impact on creating and maintaining a knowledge sharing environment. Infrastructure may dictate the channels of communications and sharing. Artifacts (such as office facilities and libraries) may affect knowledge sharing.
Environment Influences	Technology advances may affect the modes and channels of sharing. It can create means to break knowledge-sharing barriers such as geographically dispersed locations. Government regulation can inhibit knowledge sharing. Actions of a competitor (e.g., to lure away employees) can dampen knowledge sharing.

6   Conclusion

Knowledge management is concerned with application of knowledge manipulation skills to perform certain activities that operate on organizational knowledge resources. KM is guided, facilitated, and constrained by certain influences. This chapter has identified and characterized these resources, activities, and influences in a relatively comprehensive ontology constructed via a collaborative Delphi-oriented methodology. This study improved on an initial anchor ontology synthesized from the literature (Holsapple and Joshi, 2002c) by integrating insights and perspectives drawn from participants in diverse disciplines, having diverse backgrounds, and representing diverse connections to the KM field. As one of the participants pointed out, *"The only way we will be able to arrive at a 'successful' (workable, sharable) definition is via a collaborative effort that draws from many disciplines, using principles of knowledge organization that have demonstrated their effectiveness. Then we can disagree and grow effectively through resolution of disagreements."*

The participants' responses to the open-ended and scaled items indicate a favorable view of the ontology's completeness, accuracy, clarity, and conciseness. This relatively comprehensive, collaboratively-engineered ontology gives a foundation on which systematic knowledge management research and practice can develop. In the absence of a comprehensive ontology, a field's "progress is but a fortunate combination of circumstances, research is fumbling in the dark, and dissemination of knowledge is a cumbersome process" (Vatter, 1947). This assertion is reinforced by a the remark of a panelist indicating that, *"The experience I have with my clients is that until they have a coherent vision (the perspective based on an overall framework model), they cannot focus on priorities, identify how to coordinate cross-organizational efforts, or identify overall benefits."*

Even though, panelists' iterative critiques expanded and refined an initial anchor ontology to yield the one described here, the analysis of their responses and subsequent ontology modifications were subject to the authors' perceptions, interpretations, and insights about how to accommodate these critiques and suggestions. Nevertheless, at the minimum, this ontology provides a platform for organizing and discussing varying perspectives. As observed by one panelist, *"Even if one disagrees, your framework provides a basis for discussions and improvements."* In this spirit, ensuing parts of this book are organized on the basis of the ontology. Part II examines issues pertaining to knowledge resources. Part III is concerned with the manipulation of these resources. Part IV considers influences (especially the four kinds of managerial influences) on what happens within and across KM episodes. In Part V, technological support for KM episodes is covered. Part VI explores outcomes of an organization's conduct of knowledge management. Part VII ties many aspects of the ontology together in various examples of knowledge management in action. There are many possibilities for follow-up research that may extend and/or revise the KM ontology and apply it in addressing a variety of KM issues such as those indicated in this and other chapters.

Acknowledgements

Funding for this research was provided by Kentucky Initiative for Knowledge Management (established in 1988 at the University of Kentucky). We are indebted to the following persons for their participation as Delphi panelists. Those who participated in every round are indicated by an asterisk. Debra Amidon* (ENTOVATION International, Ltd., USA); Sulin Ba (University of Southern California, USA); Thomas J. Beckman* (George Washington University & IRS, USA); Kesper Deboer (Andersen Consulting, USA); Marc Demarest (The Sales Consultancy , USA); Alain Godbout* (Godbout Martin Godbout & Associates, Canada); Valerie Cliff (ICL Enterprise Consultancy , UK); Ming Ivory* (James Madison University, USA); Linda Johnson* (Western Kentucky University, USA); Mark A. Jones (Andersen Consulting, USA); Sam Khoury (The Dow Chemical Company, USA); Kai Larsen (Center for Technology in Government,

USA); Dirk Mahling (University of Pittsburgh, USA); Eunika Mercier-Laurent* (EML Conseil – Knowledge Management, France); Philip C. Murray (Knowledge Management Associates , USA); Brian Newman (The Newman Group & The KM Forum, USA); David Paradice* (Texas A&M University, USA); Gordon Petrash* (The Dow Chemical Company , USA); Dave Pollard* (Ernst & Young, Canada); Larry Prusak* (IBM Corporation , USA); David Skyrme* (David Skyme Associates Limited , England); Charles Snyder* (Auburn University, USA); Kathy Stewart* (Georgia State University, USA); Karl Sveiby (Sveiby Knowledge Management, Australia); Robert Taylor* (KPMG Management Consulting, UK); Karl Wiig (Knowledge Research Institute, Inc., USA); Andrew Whinston* (University of Texas, Austin, USA); Fons Wijnhoven* (University of Twente, The Netherlands); Dennis Yablonsky (Carnegie Group, Inc., USA); Michael Zack (Northeastern University, USA). One participant* preferred to remain anonymous.

References

Alavi, M. "KPMG Peat Marwick U.S.: One Giant Brain," Harvard Business School Case, 9-397-108, Rev. July 11, 1997.

Amidon, D., *Innovation Strategy for the Knowledge Economy: The Ken Awakening*, Boston: Butterworth-Heinemann, Boston, 1997.

Amit, R. and P. Schoemaker, "Strategic Assets and Organizational Rent," *Strategic Management Journal* 14, 1, 1993.

Anthes, G., "A Step Beyond a Database," *Computerworld*, 28, March, 1991.

Arthur Andersen and American Productivity and Quality Center, *The Knowledge Management Tool: External Benchmarking Version*, Winter, 1996.

Carson, B., *Think Big – Unleashing Your Potential for Excellence*, New York: Harper-Paperbacks, 1992.

Ching, C., C. Holsapple and A. Whinston, "Toward IT Support for Coordination in Network Organizations," *Information and Management* 30, 4, 1996.

Choo, C., *An Integrated Information Model of the Organization: The Knowing Organization*, 1996,
URL=http://www.fis.utoronto.ca/people/faculty/choo/FIS/KO/KO.html1#contents.

Collis, D. and C. Montgomery, "Competing on Resources: Strategy in the 1990s," *Harvard Business Review*, July-August, 1994, 118-128.

Cook, D., C. Chung, and C. Holsapple, "Information Flow First, Material Flow Next!" *APICS – The Performance Advantage*, 38-39, January 1995.

Crowley, A., "Memory Bank," *PC Week,* January, 1997.

Drucker, P., "The Theory of Business," *Harvard Business Review,* September-October, 1994.

Ernst & Young, "Innovation in Action – Selling Knowledge on the Net," *Perspectives on Business Innovation – Managing Organizational Knowledge*, 1997, URL=http://www.businessinnovation.ey.com/journal/features/whykno/body.html.

Favela, J., "Capture and Dissemination of Specialized Knowledge in Network Organizations," *Journal of Organizational Computing and Electronic Commerce* 7, 2/3, 1997.

Ganapathy, B.K. "The Representation of Organizational Workflows as Knowledge Management Episodes," Ph.D. dissertation, University of Kentucky, 1996.

Grant, R., "Toward a Knowledge-Based Theory of the Firm," *Strategic Management Journal*, 17, Winter Special Issue, 1996.

Gruber, T. R., "Toward Principles for the Design of Ontologies Used for Knowledge Sharing," *International Journal of Human and Computer Studies*, 43, 5/6, 1995, 907-928.

Hiebeler, R., "Benchmarking Knowledge Management," *Strategy and Leadership*, 24, 2, March/April, 1996.

Holsapple, C., L. Johnson, and V. Waldron, "A Formal Model for the Study of Communication Support Systems," *Human Communication Research*, 22,3, 1996, 421-446.

Holsapple, C. and K. Jones, "Toward an Elaboration of the Knowledge Chain Model," *Proceedings of the Americas Conference on Information Systems*, Tampa, August, 2003.

Holsapple, C. and K. Joshi, "Comparative Analysis of KM Frameworks," *Proceedings of the Hawaiian International Conference on Systems Sciences*, Maui, January, 1999a.

Holsapple, C. and K. Joshi, "Knowledge Selection: Concepts, Issues, and Technology," in Liebowitz, J. (ed.), *Handbook of Knowledge Management*, Boca Raton, FL: CRC Press, 1999b.

Holsapple, C. and K. Joshi, "An Investigation of Factors that Influence the Management of Knowledge in Organizations," *Journal of Strategic Information Systems*, 9, 2/3, 2000, 237-263.

Holsapple, C. and K. Joshi, "Organizational Knowledge Resources," *Decision Support Systems*, 31, 1, 39-54.

Holsapple, C. and K. Joshi, "A Collaborative Approach to Ontology Design," *Communications of the ACM*, 45, 2, 2002a, 42-47.

Holsapple, C. and K. Joshi, "Knowledge Manipulation Activities: Results of a Delphi Study," *Information and Management*, 39, 6, 2002b, 477-490.

Holsapple, C. and K. Joshi, "Knowledge Management: A Three-Fold Framework," *The Information Society*, 18,1, 2002c, 47-64.

Holsapple, C. and W. Luo, "A Framework for Studying Computer Support of Organizational Infrastructure," *Information and Management*, 31, 1, 1996, 13-24.

Holsapple, C. and M. Singh, "The Knowledge Chain," *Proceedings of the Annual Conference of the Southern Association on Information Systems*, Atlanta, March-April, 2000.

Holsapple, C. and W. Wagner, "Process Factors in Knowledge Acquisition," *Expert Systems*, 13, 1, 1996, 55-62.

Holsapple, C. and A. Whinston, "Knowledge-Based Organizations," *The Information Society* 5, 2, 1987, 77-90.

Holsapple, C. and A. Whinston, *Decision Support Systems – A Knowledge-Based Approach*, St. Paul, MN: West Publishing Company, 1996.

Leonard-Barton, D., *Wellsprings of Knowledge,* Boston: Harvard Business School Press, 1995.

Liebowitz, J. and K. Wright, "Valuation of Human Capital as a Component of Knowledge Assets," *Proceedings of the Association of Information Systems Conference*, Baltimore, Maryland, August, 1998.

Lev, B. "The Old Rules No Longer Apply," *Forbes ASAP*, April 7, 1997, 35-36.

Lindstone, H. and M. Turoff, *The Delphi Method: Technology and Applications*, Reading, MA: Addison-Wesley, Reading, Mass., 1975.

Malone, M., "New Metrics for New Age," *Forbes ASAP*, April 7, 1997, 40-41.

Malone, T., and Crowston, K., "The Interdisciplinary Study of Coordination," *ACM Computing Surveys*, 26, 1, 1994, 87-119,.

Marshall, C., L. Prusak, and D. Shpilberg, "Financial Risk and the Need for Superior Knowledge Management," *California Management Review*, 38, 3, 1996.

Mata, F., W. Fuerst, and J. Barney, "Information Technology and Sustained Competitive Advantage: A Resource-Based Analysis, *MIS Quarterly*, 19, 4, 1995.

Merriam-Webster, *Merriam Webster's Collegiate Dictionary*, 10th edition, Springfield, MA: Merriam-Webster Inc, 1995.

Newell, A., "The Knowledge Level," *Artificial Intelligence*, 18, 1, 1982.

Nonaka, I., "The Knowledge Creating Company," *Harvard Business Review*, November-December, 1991.

Paradice, D. and J. Courtney, "Organizational Knowledge Management," *Information Resource Management Journal*, 2, 3, 1989.

Penrose, E., *The Theory of the Growth of the Firm,* New York, NY: Wiley, 1959.

Petrash, G., "Dow's Journey to a Knowledge Value Management Culture," *European Management Journal*, 14, 4, 1996.

Quinn, J. B., *The Intelligent Enterprise*, New York: Free Press, 1992.

Rifkin, G., Buckman Labs Is Nothing But Net, *Fast Company,* April 9 1997.

Schein, E., *Organizational Culture and Leadership*, Washington: Jossey-Bass Publishers, 1985.

Singh, M., "Toward a Knowledge Management View of Electronic Business: Introduction and Investigation of the Knowledge Chain Model for Competitive Advantage," Ph.D. Dissertation, University of Kentucky, 2000.

Spender, J., "Making Knowledge the Basis of a Dynamic Theory of the Firm," *Strategic Management Journal*, 17, Winter Special Issue, 1996.

Stewart, T., *Intellectual Capital,* New York: Doubleday/Currency ,1997.

Stewart, T. "Is This Job Really Necessary?" *Fortune,* Jan. 12, 1998, 154-155.

Sveiby, K., "What Is Knowledge Management?" March 4, 1997, URL=http://www.svieby.com.au/KnowledgeManagement.html.

Szulanski, G., "Exploring Internal Stickiness: Impediments to the Transfer of Best Practice within the Firm," *Strategic Management Journal,* 17,Winter Special Issue, 1996, 27-43.

Teece, D., "Firm Boundaries, Technological Innovation, and Strategic Management," in Thomas, L. (ed.), *Economics of Strategic Planning* , Lexington, MA: Lexington Books, 1986.

van der Spek, R., and A. Spijkervet, "Knowledge Management: Dealing Intelligently with Knowledge," in: Liebowitz, J. and Wilcox, L *(eds.), Knowledge Management and Its Integrative Elements,* New York: CRC Press, 1997.

Vatter, W., *The Fund Theory of Accounting and Its Implications for Financial Reports.* Chicago: University of Chicago Press, 1947.

Webber, A., "XBS Learns to Grow," *Fast Company,* Special Collector's Edition, May, 1997, 44-51.

Wiig, K., *Knowledge Management Foundations,* Arlington, TX: Schema Press, 1993.

Knowledge: A Key Organizational Resource

The chapters in Part II deal with various aspects of the theme that knowledge is a key resource of organizations. This theme, advanced in Part I as one of the knowledge management foundations, is treated with considerable depth in Chapters 7-14. Together, these chapters prepare the reader for a consideration of an organization's knowledge processes and processors in Part III.

In "Knowledge and Competences as Strategic Assets," David Teece develops a knowledge perspective of the firm in which competitive advantage is attributed to ownership of knowledge assets, ownership of other assets complementary to them, and the firm's ability to combine knowledge and complementary assets in ways that create value. He explains that knowledge assets underpin competences and these, in turn, underpin an organization's product and service offerings in the marketplace. The substantial implications for management are discussed, including an analysis of the special properties of knowledge products. The chapter concludes that knowledge and competence are key drivers of competitive advantage in developed nations.

In Chapter 8, Leif Edvinsson takes this conclusion to a higher level in linking the wealth of nations to their respective knowledge-intensive activities. In the "Intellectual Capital of Nations," he outlines issues related to understanding and reporting a nation's intellectual capital. These are illustrated by the efforts of several nations along these lines. The major contention is that leaders of nations must recognize and cultivate the intellectual capital potentials of their countries, just as managers of firms need to do for their organizations.

Granted that knowledge resources are significant for firms and nations, "Knowledge and Its Attributes" pauses to more fully consider the nature of knowledge. This chapter outlines several perspectives on what knowledge is: systems, states, stocks and flows, and knowledge-versus-information perspectives. It then discusses the relationship between knowledge and technology, contrasting opposing views and advocating a middle path in which computer-based technology is seen as the servant of knowledge management. This chapter closes with descriptions of over twenty attribute dimensions that can be used to characterize and investigate a knowledge resource: its mode, type, domain, orientation, and so forth.

In Chapter 10, Martin Eppler explores the notion of knowledge maps as ways for making an organization's knowledge resources visible. After explaining the rationale for knowledge mapping, he presents five types of maps that an organization can use in managing its knowledge resources: source, asset, structure, application, and development maps. These are illustrated and analyzed through a series of examples. The chapter concludes by advancing a set of criteria for assessing map quality and a five-step approach for implementing maps of knowledge resources on an organization's intranet.

In Chapter 11, Murray Jennex and Lorne Olfman characterize organizational memory as knowledge captured by an organization in accessible repositories such as documents, people, computers, and culture. They discuss the forms and functions of organizational memory (OM) and how it relates to organizational learning. This chapter also explains what an organizational memory system is, gives guidelines for designing such systems, describes two models for gauging their effectiveness, and considers how to manage OM. These aspects of OM systems are illustrated in the context of a nuclear power plant case.

"Organization Culture as a Knowledge Resource" advances the realization that culture is a significant knowledge resource by virtue of its potential to facilitate knowledge creation, storage, transfer, and use. Here, Timothy Kayworth and Dorothy Leidner provide a compact summary of the organizational culture literature, including the value perspective and the behavioral perspective. Against this background, they proceed to discuss ways in which organizational culture serves as a knowledge resource, proposing several research hypotheses along the way. The chapter closes with some implications that stem from the recognition of culture as an organizational knowledge resource.

For a long time, the field of accounting has been interested in valuation and tracking of organizational resources, and changes in those resources. However, this has not traditionally included knowledge as a major organizational resource. In *"Does Accounting Account for Knowledge?"* the relatively new arena of accounting for knowledge resources is examined. Here, Dan Stone and Sony Warsono describe the economic and institutional forces that shape current knowledge accounting efforts. They then outline and compare six alternative approaches to knowledge accounting: total value creation, accounting for the future, balanced scorecard, Skandia Navigator, intangible asset monitor, and value chain scoreboard. This chapter concludes with the authors' insights on the future of and prospects for knowledge accounting.

In the final chapter of Part II, Jacky Swan points out the remarkable degree of convergence across academic disciplines and areas of industrial practice around the idea that knowledge is perhaps the most valuable resource that organizations and societies have. However, she goes on to point out that it is not so valuable in and of itself, but rather when linked to specific activities, tasks, and purposes. The chapter proceeds to develop this perspective, highlighting the importance of integrating distributed knowledge and addressing relational and action concerns such as social identity, power, conflict, and motivation. Knowledge integration refers not merely to using technology to link distributed knowledge resources, but also to the importance of building a sense of shared context and purpose for knowledge workers' actions. Distribution, sensemaking, and other aspects of processing knowledge resources are examined in Part III.

CHAPTER 7

Knowledge and Competence as Strategic Assets[*]

David J. Teece

Institute of Management, Innovation, and Organization, Haas School of Business, University of California, Berkeley, CA, USA

The firm is a repository for knowledge—the knowledge being embedded in business routines and processes. Distinctive processes undergird firm-specific assets and competences (defined as integrated clusters of firm-specific assets). The firm's knowledge base includes its technological competences as well as its knowledge of customer needs and supplier capabilities. These competences reflect both individual skills and experiences as well as distinctive ways of doing things inside firms. The essence of the firm is its ability to create, transfer, assemble, integrate, and exploit knowledge assets. Knowledge assets underpin competences, and competences in turn underpin the firm's product and service offerings to the market. Competitive advantage can be attributed not only to the ownership of knowledge assets and other assets complementary to them, but also to the ability to combine knowledge assets with other assets needed to create value.

Keywords: Competences; Competitive Advantage; Intellectual Property; Strategic Assets; Technology; Theory of the Firm

1 Introduction

Management is always confronting new challenges. Sometimes these are simply yesterday's challenges presented anew in a slightly different context. But from time to time, new challenges emerge that have no close precedent. Managing intellectual capital in the information age is possibly one such challenge, as advanced industrial economies have entered a new epoch. Many sectors are animated by new economics, where the payoff to managing knowledge astutely has been dramatically amplified, in part because of the phenomena of increasing returns, in part because of new information technology, and in part because of the changing role of intellectual property. Moreover, the context in which knowledge assets are created and exploited is today truly global.

2   Knowledge and Competitive Advantage

It has long been recognized that "economic prosperity rests upon knowledge and it useful application." (Teece, 1981). Indeed, "the increase in the stock of useful knowledge and the extension of its application are the essence of modern economic growth" (Kuznets, 1966). Enlightened economic historians have long emphasized the role of technology and organization in economic development.

Accordingly, one must inquire about the present cacophony on knowledge management. At least two classes of explanations appear to be valid. One class is simply that policy and strategy analysts have worn intellectual blinders, so that what has been obvious to some—namely, that knowledge and its applications are at the very roots of modern economic growth and prosperity—has not been transparent to all. Competing theories that stressed the role of the capital stock and natural resources would appear to have received unwarranted extended play in textbooks and policy pronouncements. Meanwhile, the study of innovation and knowledge transfer has been, until quite recently, relegated to a backwater in mainstream economics as well as in the other social sciences.

However, a small cadre of dedicated economists has long emphasized the role of technological innovation, often with few accolades. These include the late Edwin Mansfield, Richard Nelson, Chris Freeman, Sidney Winter, Paul David, Nathan Rosenberg, Giovanni Dosi, and David Mowery. Now the mainstream economic theorists (Romer, 1989) and mainstream business have begun to recognize the importance of this literature. Moreover, the ideas have become established and disseminated to a wider audience through the efforts of insightful protagonists like Ikujiro Nonaka and Hirotaka Takeuchi (1995).

The second class of factors relates to structural changes that have occurred in the economies of advanced developed countries. These have modified the nature of what is strategic and have served to highlight the importance of knowledge and its management.

2.1   Liberalization of Markets

Since the Kennedy round of trade negotiations in the 1960s, markets for goods and services have become increasingly liberalized. Tariff and non-tariff barriers have been lowered. While the world is far from being properly characterized as having adopted free trade, significant progress has been made. Final goods, intermediate goods, and factors of production flow globally with far more freedom than in earlier times. Restrictions on knowledge transfers by both importers and exporters have also been relaxed.

Accordingly, firms cannot so rapidly earn supra-competitive returns by locating behind trade barriers. Transportation costs have also fallen, and information about market opportunities often diffuses instantaneously. Together, these developments have reduced the shelter previously afforded to privileged positions in domestic markets. Competition has been sharpened.

2.2 Expansion of What's Tradable

Markets have not only liberalized, but also have been created for many types of "intermediate" products where markets hitherto didn't exist. This has been most amplified in securities markets where swaps and swaptions, index futures, program trading, butterfly spreads, puttable bonds, eurobonds, collateralized mortgage bonds, zero-coupon bonds, portfolio insurance, and synthetic cash are now commonplace (Miller, 1997). This sudden burst of financial innovation began but 20 years ago, propelled by the move to floating exchange rates and the need to protect transactions from uncertainty. It has been aided by developments in computer and information technology, which have enabled the design of new financial products and the execution of complex transactions. Also contributing has been the desire to circumvent taxation and regulation.

In addition, firms have shown greater affection for outsourcing as suppliers take advantage of the growth in the number of potential suppliers at home and abroad. In the petroleum industry, for instance, markets exist not only for many grades of crude oil and refined products, but also for a range of intermediate products (e.g., MTB) which were rarely traded, if at all, a mere decade ago. Moreover, certain forms of intellectual property are "exchanged" (cross-licensed) or sold with far greater frequency than was hitherto experienced (Grindley and Teece, 1997).

Whenever a market exists that is open to all qualified comers, including newcomers, then competitive advantage for firms cannot flow from participation in that market. That is not to say that these are not opportunities to take bets against the market, but such bets represent asset plays by investors which ought not be thought of as a foundation for competitive advantage, as gains need not require involvement in operations of any kind. Except in rare instances where one or a few firms can "corner the market," having a market-based exchange relationship cannot yield competitive advantage because it can be so easily replicated by others, who can simply enter the same (efficient) market and secure access to the same inputs or dispose of the same outputs. In short, efficient markets are a great leveler.

2.3 Strengthening of Intellectual Property Regimes

Intellectual property is an aspect of property rights which augments the importance of know-how assets. Knowledge assets are often inherently difficult to copy; moreover, like physical assets, some knowledge assets enjoy protection against theft under the intellectual property laws of individual nation states. In advanced nations, these laws typically embrace patents, trademarks, trade secrets, and copyright.

Intellectual property systems have been strengthened since the 1980s, both in the U.S. and abroad. Moreover, intellectual property is not just important in the new industries—such as microelectronics and biotechnology—it remains important in pharmaceuticals and chemicals and is receiving renewed interest in more mature industries such as petroleum and steel.

The growth of information technology has also amplified the importance of intellectual property and has injected intellectual property into new contexts. For example, it is not uncommon to discover the foundations of corporate success for wholesalers and retailers buried in copyrighted software and in information technology supporting order entry and logistics.

2.4 The Growing Importance of Increasing Returns

Contemporary textbook understandings of how markets operate and how firms compete has been derived from the work of economists such as Marshall and Chamberlain. These views assume diminishing returns and assign industry participants identical production functions (implying the use of identical technologies by all competitors) where marginal costs increase. Industry equilibrium with numerous participants arises because marginal-cost curves slope upwards, thereby exhausting scale advantages at the level of the firm, making room for multiple industry participants. This theory was useful for understanding 18th century English farms and 19th century Scottish factories and even some 20th century American manufacturers. However, major deficiencies in this view of the world have been apparent for some time—it is a caricature of the firm. Moreover, knowledge is certainly not shared ubiquitously and passed around at zero cost (Teece, 1981).

In this century, developed economies have undergone a transformation from largely raw material processing and manufacturing activities to the processing of information and the development, application, and transfer of new knowledge. As a consequence, diminishing returns activities have been replaced by activities characterized by increasing returns. The phenomena of increasing returns is usually paramount in knowledge-based industries. With increasing returns, that which is ahead tends to stay ahead. Mechanisms of positive feedback reinforce the winners and challenge the losers. Whatever the reason one gets ahead—acumen, chance, clever strategy—increasing returns amplify the advantage. With increasing returns, the market at least for a while tilts in favor of the provider that gets out in front. Such a firm need not be the pioneer and need not have the best product.

The increasing returns phenomenon is itself driven by several factors. Consider, first, standards and network externalities. To establish networks and interoperability, compatibility standards are usually critical. If such standards are proprietary, ownership of a dominant standard can yield significant "rents." The more a protocol gains acceptance, the greater the consumer benefits (network externalities), and the better the chance the standard has of becoming dominant.

Second, consider customer lock-in. Customer learning and customer investment in high-technology products amplify switching costs. This pushes competition "forward" in the sense that providers will compete especially hard for the original sale, knowing that sales of follow-along equipment and other services will be easier. While such "lock-in" is rarely long lived, it need not be momentary.

Third, consider large up-front costs. Once a high-tech industry is established, large up-front research, development, and design engineering costs are typical. This is most amplified with software products where the first copy costs perhaps hundreds of millions, and the original cost of the second copy is zero, or very nearly so.

Fourth, consider producer learning. In certain cases, producers become more efficient as experience is gained. If the underlying knowledge base is tacit, so that it resists transfer to other producers, competitors with less experience are at a comparative disadvantage. Producer learning is important where complex processors and complex assembly is involved.

The economics of increasing returns suggest different corporate strategies. In winner-take-all or winner-take-the-lion's-share contexts, there is heightened payoff associated with getting the timing right (one can be too early or too late) and with organizing sufficient resources once opportunity opens up. Very often, competition is like a high-stakes game of musical chairs. Being well positioned when standards gel is essential. The associated styles of competition are, as Brian Arthur (1988) points out, much like casino gambling. Strategy involves choosing what games to play, as well as playing with skill. Multimedia, web services, voice recognition, mobile (software) agents, and electronic commerce are all technological/market plays where the rules are not set, the identity of the players poorly appreciated, and the payoffs matrix murky at best. Rewards go to those good at sensing and seizing opportunities.

Seizing opportunities frequently involves identifying and combining the relevant complementary assets needed to support the business. Superior technology alone is rarely enough upon which to build competitive advantage. The winners are the entrepreneurs with the cognitive and managerial skills to discern the shape of the play, and then act upon it. Recognizing strategic errors and adjusting accordingly is a critical part of becoming and remaining successful.

In this environment, there is little payoff to penny pinching, and high payoff to rapidly sensing and then seizing opportunities. This is what is referred to here and elsewhere (Teece et al., 1997) as dynamic capabilities. Dynamic capabilities are most likely to be resident in firms that are highly entrepreneurial, with flat hierarchies, a clear vision, high-powered incentives, and high autonomy (to ensure responsiveness). The firm must be able to effectively navigate quick turns, as Microsoft did once Gates recognized the importance of the Internet. Cost minimization and static optimization provide only minor advantages. Plans are often made and junked with alacrity. Companies must constantly transform and retransform. A "mission critical" orientation is essential.

2.5 Decoupling of Information Flows from the Flow of Goods and Services

New information technology and the adoption of standards are greatly assisting connectivity. Once every person and every business is connected electronically through networks, information can flow more readily. The traditional nexus between the economics of goods and services and the economics of information can be broken, and information can be unbundled.

The traditional trade-off between reach (connectivity) and richness - (customization, bandwidth) is also being transformed, or at least modified. An insurance salesman is no longer needed to sell term life policies. Sufficient information can be collected by mail or on the Internet to enable customers to engage in comparative shopping, and for underwriters to do sufficient assessment of policyholders. As a result, traditional distribution channels are no longer needed for simple life or auto insurance products.

Historically, the transfer/communication of rich information has required proximity and specialized channels to customers, suppliers, and distributors. New developments are undermining traditional value chains and business models. In some cases, more "virtual" structures are viable, or shortly will be viable, especially in certain sectors like financial services. New information technology is facilitating specialization. Bargaining power will be reduced by an erosion in the ability to control information, and customer switching costs will decline, changing industry economics.

The new information technology is also dramatically assisting in the sharing of information. Learning and experience can be much more readily captured and shared. Knowledge learned in the organization can be catalogued and transferred to other applications within and across organizations and geographies. Rich exchange can take place inside the organization, obviating some of the need for formal structures.

2.6 Ramifications of New Information and Communications Technologies

Linked information and communications systems in production, distribution, logistics, accounting, marketing, and new product development have the potential to bring together previously fragmented flows of data, thereby permitting the real time monitoring of markets, products, and competitors. The requisite data can then be fed to multifunctional teams working on new product development. Networked computers using rapid communications systems thus enable major advances in corporate and intercorporate monitoring and control systems. Within organizations, computer networks can strengthen links between strategic and operations management, while also assisting linkages externally to discrete and geographically dispersed providers of complementary services.

Network computing, supported by an advanced communications infrastructure, can thus facilitate collaborative entrepreneuralism by stripping out barriers to communication. It challenges existing organization boundaries, divisions, and hierarchies and permits formal organization to be more specialized and responsive. Interorganizationally, networked organizations have blurred and shifting boundaries, and they function in conjunction with other organizations. The networked organization may be highly "virtual," integrating a temporary network of suppliers and customers that emerge around specific opportunities in fast-changing markets. Recurrent reorganization becomes the norm, not the exception.

Service firms, such as lawyers, accountants, management consultants, and information technology consultants—pose interesting issues. If knowledge and experience remain personal and are not somehow shared (either by transfer to other organization members or by being embedded in product) then the firm can at best expect to achieve constant return to scale. Larger organizations will have no advantage over boutiques and will possibly suffer bureaucratic burdens that will sap productivity.

Formalization, the sharing of personal knowledge, and the development of structural approaches as a mechanism to transfer learning throughout the firm may on the other hand sap creativity and impede learning. Ideally, one would like to develop approaches or models which have a common essential logic, but which enable customization of particular features. This is but one of the many challenges to service firms in the new economy where knowledge sharing itself can often be the basis of competitive advantage.

2.7 Product Architecture and Technology "Fusion"

With complexity becoming increasingly common, new products are rarely stand-alone items. Rather, they are components of broader systems or architectures. Innovation at the architectural level is more demanding and takes place with less frequency than at the component level, but it has greater impact.

The development of system-level integration [SLI] of ASICs—so-called systems on a chip—illustrates the point. Following Dataquest, we define SLI as an integrated circuit that contains a compute engine, memory, and logic on a single chip and has more than 100,000 utilized gates. Two types of SLI devises can be recognized: ASICs (application-specific integrated circuits) that are sold to a single user, and ASSPs (application-specific standard product) that are sold to more than one user. New manufacturing processes and improved design tools have fostered SLI. Because million-gate ASICs are now possible, they can support entire systems on a single piece of silicon. If Dataquest is right, and if industry will be able to place 40 million gates on a single chip, it will be technically possible to place multiple systems on a single chip.

SLI ASICs have already been designed into high-volume applications such as set-top boxes, multimedia, and wireless telephony. Dataquest estimates that SLI ASICs will pass $15 billion in revenues by the year 2000. However, what is even more significant is the ability of SLI ASICs to fuel further growth "of consumer electronics through dramatic reductions in size and power usage, enhanced differentiation and functionally, quicker product development, and still lower cost. This is what the technology can deliver.

Whether the technology does in fact yield its potential depends, however, on certain organizational and managerial changes. Design reuse is of paramount importance when designing high-complexity ASICs or SLI devices. System designers must design on the block level and be able to reuse and alter intellectual property in a number of subsequent designs. As Dataquest (1995) notes, "design methodology, design reuse, and intellectual property will play vital roles in determining the winners among both suppliers and users."

The organization of firms and industries and the architecture of products are interrelated. Because the relevant intellectual property needed to effectuate SLI is almost never owned by a single firm but is widely distributed throughout the industry, new arrangements are needed to support rapid diffusion and expansion of SLI architecture. Indeed, harnessing the full potential of the technology necessarily involves cooperation amongst industry participants, many of whom might also be competitors.

A related development is the increase in convergence or integration of previously disparate technologies. One thinks not just of the convergence of computers and communications, but of mechanical industries and electronics — "mechatronics" (Kodama, 1991) — or of "robochemistry," the science of applying computerization to drug molecule research, which according to some accounts is leading to "a new age in medicine" (Forbes, 1996). This by no means occurs automatically and requires internal structures that are flexible and permeable.

2.8 Implications

These developments suggest a different dynamic to competition and competitive advantage. The expansion of markets illustrates the point. Because markets are a great leveler, competitive advantage at the level of the firm can flow only from the ownership and successful deployment of non-tradable assets. If the asset or its services are traded or tradable in a market or markets, the assets in question can be accessed by all; so, the domains in which competitive advantage can be built narrows as markets expand. Not even human resources can provide the basis for competitive advantage if the skills at issue can be accessed by all in an open labor market.

One class of assets that is especially difficult, although not impossible, to trade involves knowledge assets and, more generally, competences. The market for know-how is riddled with imperfections and "unassisted markets are seriously faulted as institutional devices for facilitating trading in many levels of technological and managerial know-how" (Teece, 1981). Hence, the development of many types of new markets has made know-how increasingly salient as a differentiator, and therefore as a source of the competitive advantage of firms. This can be expected to remain so until know-how becomes more commodity-like; and this may happen soon for some components of intellectual property.

The strengthening of intellectual property is an important counterforce to the growing ease of imitation. As the diffusion of knowledge and information accelerates, intellectual property becomes more salient. While intellectual property can be traded, and can sometimes be invented around, it can no longer be infringed with impunity and without penalty.

Increasing returns frequently sharpens the payoff to strategic behavior and amplifies the importance of timing and responsiveness. Meanwhile, the decoupling of information flows from the flow of goods and services is transforming traditional value analysis, and it is suggesting the benefits of more virtual structures and obviating some of the need for hierarchy. Simultaneously, the march of technologies such as integrated circuits is transforming the linkage between intellectual property and products. Technological innovation is requiring the unbundling of the two and the formation of more robust markets for intellectual property. It is in this new environment that a critical dimension of knowledge management has emerged: capturing value from innovative activity.

3   Capturing Value from Knowledge and Competence

The proper structures, incentives, and management can help firms generate innovation and build knowledge assets. The focus here is not, however, on the creation of knowledge assets, but on their deployment and use (for an analysis of the sources of innovation, see Teece (1996)). While knowledge assets are grounded in the experience and expertise of individuals, firms provide the physical, social, and resource allocation structure so that knowledge can be shaped into competences. How these competences and knowledge assets are configured and deployed will dramatically shape competitive outcomes and the commercial success of the enterprise. Indeed, the competitive advantage of firms in today's economy stems not from market position, but from difficult-to-replicate knowledge assets and the manner in which they are deployed. The deployment dimension—involving as it does both entrepreneurial and strategic elements—is where dynamic capabilities are especially important.

It is always useful to distinguish between the creation of new knowledge and its commercialization. The creation of new knowledge through autonomous (specialized) innovation is a critical function. It can be the domain of the individual, or of the research laboratory, or of autonomous business units. It need not require complex organization. Indeed, one can argue that such knowledge creation is increasingly well suited to smaller organizational units.

However, the commercialization of new technology is increasingly the domain of complex organization. The new challenges require new organizational forms and the development and astute exercise of dynamic capabilities. They also require an understanding of the nature of knowledge and competence as strategic assets. The nature of knowledge and the manner in which it can or cannot be bought and sold is critical to the strategic nature of knowledge and competence.

3.1 The Nature of Knowledge

Knowledge can be thought of in many ways. In a business context, the following taxonomies are useful.

3.1.1   Codified/Tacit Taxonomy (Teece, 1981)

Tacit knowledge is that which is difficult to articulate in a way that is meaningful and complete. The fact that we know more than we can tell speaks to the tacit dimension. Stand-alone codified knowledge—such as blueprints, formulas, or computer code—need not convey much meaning.

There appears to be a simple but powerful relationship between codification of knowledge and the costs of its transfer. Simply stated, the more a given item of knowledge or experience has been codified, the more economically it can be transferred. This is a purely technical property that depends on the ready availability of channels of communication suitable for the transmission of well-codified information—for example, printing, radio, telegraph, and data networks. Whether information so transferred will be considered meaningful by those who receive it will depend on whether they are familiar with the code selected as well as the different contexts in which it is used. These ideas are developed further by C.E. Shannon and W. Weaver (1949); I am grateful to Max Boisot for drawing them to my attention.

Uncodified or tacit knowledge, on the other hand, is slow and costly to transmit. Ambiguities abound and can be overcome only when communications take place in face-to-face situations. Errors of interpretation can be corrected by a prompt use of personal feedback. Consider the apprenticeship system as an example. First, a master craftsman can cope with only a limited number of pupils at a time. Second, his teaching has to be dispensed mostly through examples rather than by precept—he cannot easily put the intangible elements of his skill into words. Third, the examples he offers will be initially confusing and ambiguous for his pupils so that learning has to take place through extensive and time-consuming repetition, and mystery will occur gradually on the basis of "feel." Finally, the pupil's eventual mastery of a craft or skill will remain idiosyncratic and will never be a carbon copy of the master's. It is the scope provided for the development of a personal style that defines a craft as something that goes beyond the routine and hence programmable application of a skill.

The transmission of codified knowledge, on the other hand, does not necessarily require face-to-face contact and can often be carried out largely by impersonal means, such as when one computer "talks" to another, or when a technical manual is passed from one individual to another. Messages are better structured and less ambiguous if they can be transferred in codified form.

3.1.2   Observable/Non-observable in Use Taxonomy

Much technology is (publicly) observable once sold. A new CT scanner, laser printer, or microprocessor is available for conceptual imitation and reverse engineering once it has been introduced into the market. New products are typically of this kind. Process technology, however, is often different. While in some cases the "signature" of a process may be embedded in a product and is therefore ascertainable through reverse engineering, this is generally not the case. While clues about a manufacturing process may sometimes be gleaned by closely observing the product, much about process technology can be protected if the owners of process technology are diligent in protecting their trade secrets in the factory. Thus, process technology is inherently more protectable than product technology, the patent system put to one side.

3.1.3   Positive/Negative Knowledge Taxonomy

Innovation involves considerable uncertainty. Research efforts frequently go down what turns out to be a blind alley. It is well recognized that a discovery (positive knowledge) can focus research on promising areas of inquiry, thereby avoiding blind alleys. However, it is frequently forgotten that knowledge of failures ("this approach doesn't work") is also valuable as it can help steer resource allocation into more promising avenues. For this reason, firms often find it necessary to keep their failures as well as their successes secret, even holding aside issues of embarrassment.

3.1.4 Autonomous/Systematic Knowledge Taxonomy

Autonomous knowledge is that which yields value without major modifications of systems in which it might be embedded. Fuel injection, the self-starter, and power steering were innovations that did not require major modifications to the automobile, although the latter did enable manufactures to put more weight on the front axle and to more readily fit cars with radial tires. Systematic innovation, on the other hand, requires modification to other sub-systems. For instance, the tungsten filament light bulb would not have found such wide application without the development of a system for generating and distributing electricity.

3.1.5 Intellectual Property Regime

There are many other dimensions along which knowledge could be defined or along which innovations could be classified. For instance, we can identify innovations that were architectural or non-architectural, competency enhancing or competency destroying, and so forth. However, the only other key dimension to be identified here is whether or not the knowledge in question enjoys protection under the intellectual property laws.

Patents, trade secrets, trademarks provide protection for different mediums in different ways. The strongest form of intellectual property is the patent. A valid patent provides rights for exclusive use by the owner, although depending on the scope of the patent it may be possible to invent around it, albeit at some cost. Trade secrets do not provide rights of exclusion over any knowledge domain, they do protect covered secrets in perpetuity. Trade secrets can well enhance the value of a patent position. Different knowledge mediums qualify for different types of intellectual property protection. The degree that intellectual property keeps imitators at bay may depend also on other external factors, such as regulations, which may block or limit the scope for invent-around alternatives.

3.2 Replicability, Imitability, and Appropriability

This section is adapted from (Teece et al., 1997) and the chapter on "The Dynamic Capabilities of Firms" which appears in Part VI of this book.

Replication involves transferring or redeploying competences from one concrete economic setting to another. Because productive knowledge is typically embodied, this cannot be accomplished by simply transmitting information. Only in those instances where all relevant knowledge is fully codified and understood can replication be collapsed into a simple problem of information transfer. Too often, the contextual dependence of original performance is poorly appreciated, so unless firms have replicated their systems of productive knowledge on many prior occasions, the act of replication is likely to be difficult (Teece, 1977). Indeed, replication and transfer are often impossible absent the transfer of people, although this can be minimized if investments are made to convert tacit knowledge to codified knowledge. Often, however, this is simply not possible.

In short, knowledge assets are normally rather difficult to replicate. Even understanding what all the relevant routines are that support a particular competence may not be transparent. Indeed, Lippman and Rumelt (1992) have argued that some sources of competitive advantage are so complex that the firm itself, let alone its competitors, does not understand them. As Nelson and Winter (1982) and Teece (1982) have explained, many organizational routines are quite tacit in nature. Imitation can also be hindered by the fact that few routines are stand-alone. Imitating a part of what a competitor does may not enhance performance at all. Understanding the overall logic of organization and superior performance is often critical to successful imitation.

Some routines and competences seem to be attributable to local or regional forces that shape a firm's capabilities. Porter (1990), for example, shows that differences in local product markets, local factor markets, and institutions play an important role in shaping competitive capabilities. Replication in a different geographical context may thus be rather difficult. However, differences also exist within populations of firms from the same country. Various studies of the automobile industry, for example, show that not all Japanese automobile companies are top performers in terms of quality, productivity, or product development (Clark and Fujimoto, 1991). The role of firm-specific history is a critical factor in such firm-level (as opposed to regional- or national-level) differences (Nelson and Winter, 1982).

At least two types of strategic value flow from replication. One is simply the ability to support geographic and product line expansion. To the extent that the capabilities in question are relevant to customer needs elsewhere, replication can confer value. Another is that the ability to replicate indicates that the firm has the foundations in place for learning and improvement. Understanding processes, both in production and in management, is the key to process improvement, so that an organization cannot improve that which it does not understand. Deep process understanding is often required to accomplish codification and replication. Indeed, if knowledge is highly tacit, it indicates that underlying structures are not well understood, which limits learning because scientific and engineering principles cannot be as systematically applied. Instead, learning is confined to proceeding through trial-and-error, and the leverage that might otherwise come from the application of modern science is denied.

Imitation is simply replication performed by a competitor. If self-replication is difficult, imitation is likely to be even harder. In competitive markets, it is the ease of imitation that determines the sustainability of competitive advantage. Easy imitation implies the rapid dissipation of rents.

Factors that make replication difficult also make imitation difficult. Thus, the more tacit the firm's productive knowledge, the harder it is to replicate by the firm itself or its competitors. When the tacit component is high, imitation may well be impossible, absent the hiring away of key individuals and the transfer of key organizational processes.

Intellectual property rights impede imitation of certain capabilities in advanced industrial countries and present a formidable imitation barrier in certain particular contexts. Several other factors, in addition to the patent system, cause there to be a difference between replication costs and imitation costs. The observability of the technology of the organization is one such important factor. As mentioned earlier, vistas into product technology can be obtained through strategies such as reverse engineering, but this is not the case for process technology, as a firm need not expose its process technology to the outside in order to benefit from it. Firms with product technology, on the other hand, confront the unfortunate circumstances that they must expose what they have got in order to profit from the technology. Secrets are thus more protectable if there is no need to expose them in contexts where competitors can learn about them.

The term "appropriability regimes" describes the ease of imitation. Appropriability is a function both of the ease of replication and the efficacy of intellectual property rights as a barrier to imitation. Appropriability is strong when a technology is both inherently difficult to replicate and the intellectual property system provides legal barriers to imitation. When it is inherently easy to replicate and intellectual property protection is either unavailable or ineffectual, then appropriability is weak. Intermediate conditions also exist (see Figure 1).

		Inherent Replicability	
		Easy	Hard
Intellectual Property Rights	Loose	Weak	Moderate
	Tight	Moderate	Strong

Figure 1. Appropriate Regimes for Knowledge Assets

3.3 Appropriability and Markets for Know-How and Competence

Assets can be the source of competitive advantage only if they are supported by a regime of strong appropriability or are non-tradable or "sticky." As discussed earlier, once an asset is readily tradable in a competitive market, it can no longer be a source of firm-level competitive advantage. Financial assets today are of that kind.

The main classes of assets that are not tradable today are locational assets, knowledge assets, and competences. Competences may, in turn, be embedded in other corporate assets, including assets complementary to knowledge assets. Were a perfect market for know-how to someday emerge, knowledge would no longer be the source of competitive advantage. This is unlikely to happen anytime soon, but understanding the limits on the market for know-how is important to understanding how firms can capture value from knowledge assets.

Like the market for pollution rights, or the market for art, buying and selling know-how and intellectual property has special challenges. These complicate exchange, and may limit in some fundamental sense the level of sophistication to which the market can ever evolve. They also explain why the market today is rather primitive.

By way of foundation, it is well recognized that markets work well when:

- there are informed buyers and sellers aware of trading opportunities,
- the objective performance properties or subjective utility of products can be readily ascertained,
- there are large numbers of buyers and sellers, and
- contracts can be written, executed, and enforced at low cost.

Thus the market for (standard) commodities like wheat, coal, stocks, bonds, and sports utility vehicles works well because these properties are largely satisfied.

However, know-how and intellectual property are "products" of an entirely different kind. These products have properties that complicate purchase and sale (see Figure 2). These include:

- *Recognition of Trading Opportunities*—Parties typically don't know who owns what, and who might be interested in trading. This is less so for patents because they are published. But software (particularly source code) protected by copyright and trade secrets is frequently a matter of great secrecy. There are obvious reasons why even knowledge about the existence of such intellectual property is held very close. Accordingly, out of ignorance, software is often "reinvented" despite the fact that potentially advantageous trades could be consummated.
- *Disclosure of Performance Features*—Buyers must be well informed as to the availability of intellectual property but sellers may be reluctant to negotiate because their intellectual property rights are problematic. Sellers might be reluctant to negotiate because of fear that disclosure, even if pursuant to a nondisclosure agreement, might inadvertently lead intellectual property rights to be jeopardized.
- *Uncertain Legal Rights*—When property rights are uncertain, and confidence in nondisclosure agreements or the law of confidences less than complete, beneficial transactions may be eschewed because of perceived risks. In addition to the disclosure issues identified above, sellers may be uncertain about factors such as the enforceability of use restrictions and sublicensing rights or simply about the ability to measure and collect - royalties.
- *Item of Sale*—The "item of sale" may be know-how, or intellectual property rights, complete or partial. When intellectual property is bought and sold, what is transacted is simply a bundle of rights. While rights are frequently bought and sold (e.g., view rights, pollution rights, airspace rights, mineral rights, rights to use the electromagnetic spectrum, queuing rights), such rights are not a pure commodity. Moreover, ownership requires special policing powers for value preservation. Physical barriers to theft (e.g., locks and keys) don't suffice to protect owners; confidence in contracting and the legal system is necessary to support value.

- *Variety*—While there may be multiple transactions for a given piece of intellectual property (e.g., identical nonexclusive patent license), intellectual property is itself highly variegated. This complicates exchange by making valuation difficult and by rendering markets thin. Thin markets are likely to be less robust than thick markets. Moreover, both buyers and sellers are likely to wish to customize transactions. To the extent to which this occurs, transaction costs increase, and the difficulties of setting up an exchange increase.
- *Unit of Consumption*—Intellectual property is rarely sold lock, stock, and barrel. Hence, metering arrangements of some kind must be devised. These are by no means readily identifiable, particularly for software. Is it a component and if so, should the royalty be a function of the value of the component or the system in which it is embedded? Clearly, the value is a function of other intellectual property located alongside the intellectual property at issue. Questions of the royalty/sales base are by no means straightforward.

Characteristics	Know-How/IP	Physical Commodities
1. Recognition of trading opportunities	Inherent difficulty	Posting frequent
2. Disclosure of attributes	Relatively difficult	Relatively easy
3. Property Rights	Limited [patents, trade secrets, Copyright, etc.]	Broad
4. Item of Sale	License	Measurable units
5. Variety	Heterogeneous	Homogeneous
6. Unit of consumption	Often Unclear	Weight, volume, etc.
Inherent tradeability	Low	High

Figure 2. Inherent Tradeability of Different Assets

3.4 Some Sectoral Differences in the Market for Know-How

The inherent difficulties just identified vary according to the type of know-how/intellectual property at issue. It is instructive to compare chemicals and pharmaceuticals with electronics. Indeed, even a cursory examination would suggest that in chemicals and pharmaceuticals, the inherent difficulties associated with licensing are less than in other sectors, like electronics. Figure 3 summarizes some of these difficulties.

Challenge	Chemical/Pharmaceuticals	Electronics
Recognition	Manageable	Extremely complex, often impossible
Disclosure	Handled by NDA, patents common	More difficult
Interface issues	Compatibility generally not an issue	Compatibility generally critical
Royalty stacking, royalty base dilemmas	Infrequent	Frequent
Value context dependent	Strongly so	Very strongly so
Patent strength	Generally high	Sometimes limited
Development cycle	Often long	Generally short
Know-How Market Works:	Generally Well	Often Poorly

Figure 3. Some Sectoral Differences in the Market for Know-How

There are a number of reasons why the market for know-how generally works better for chemicals and pharmaceuticals. In chemicals and pharmaceuticals, patents work especially well and are ubiquitous. A survey of the efficiency of patents conducted by researchers at Yale University showed high scores for patent effectiveness in this sector (Winter, 1987). Patents are in one sense the strongest form of intellectual property because they grant the ability to exclude, whereas copyright and trade secrets do not prevent firms that make independent but duplicative discoveries from practicing their inventions/innovations. Accordingly, problems of recognition and disclosure disappear when patents are at issue. Also, regulation often bolsters intellectual property because "me too" misappropriators may sometimes face additional hurdles (in the U.S., FDA approval) before being able to launch a product in the market.

Compatibility/interface issues are also less severe in this sector than in some others. While technologies often must work together in chemicals and pharmaceuticals, the close coupling of the kind that characterizes electronics is usually not an absolute prerequisite. Also, the number of individual items of external intellectual property that must be brought together to design a new product is often rather limited. Indeed, the items used may all come from inside the firm, although alliances and licenses are increasingly common. Because there are less complementarities necessary to make a particular product, intellectual property is often less context dependent, and the same royalty rate is appropriate in a multitude of contexts e.g., the float glass process was licensed for the same amount (i.e., 6% of sales) to multiple jurisdictions around the world. Finally, the product life cycle is defined not in months, but often in decades. Hence, requirements for speedy execution of transactions are less severe, and the opportunity to amortize set-up costs over enormous volumes of business is often possible.

The situation in the electronics industry is different. For software, patent protection is uncommon. Hence, if purchasers receive components in source code, they can read and modify programs, thereby possibly skirting intellectual property protection. Put differently, source code can be more readily converted to new programs that don't leave fingerprints. Object code, on the other hand, must first be reverse engineered into a reasonable approximation of source code before it can be advantageously modified. Thus, disseminating software components (in source code) for external use creates misappropriation hazards. While encryption creates barriers to reverse engineering (decryption), it does not compensate for weak intellectual property. The problem of disclosure (necessary to inform buyers about what they are being offered) has clear hazards in this sector. Furthermore, interface issues are critical, as integration is paramount. Because multiple sources of intellectual property must be combined for systems on silicon, intellectual property rights must be amalgamated. This is not necessary for broad level integration of physical components, where the bundling of intellectual property in products simplifies intellectual property transactions.

The market for know-how in electronics thus creates considerable challenges and is unlikely, therefore, to be completely efficient. Accordingly, new innovations (such as system-level integration in silicon) involve new organizational challenges, orders of magnitude greater than previously encountered, and perhaps orders of magnitude greater than the technological challenges. Royalty stacking situations—where intellectual property owners fail in their pricing proposals to take into account the need for the buyer to combine other intellectual property to create value—are likely to be frequent, at least until a new business model is firmly established. Also, the tremendous premium on speed and time to market puts enormous pressure to accomplish intellectual property transactions quickly. This is impossible if intellectual property agreements are customized. However, there is at present almost no standardization in intellectual property agreements, so the market can readily become bogged down by transactional complexity.

Because of these difficulties, there is at present little if any market for software components. Estimates of the annual aggregate costs in the U.S. for "reinvention" are put at between $2 and $100 billion. These estimates, if correct, speak to the value of a properly functioning market for software intellectual property. Absent such a market, certain new product architectures (e.g., systems on Silicon) may just not happen, or may not realize but a fraction of their potential.

What was just described for know-how assets also applies to competences, which can be thought of as clusters of know-how assets. Competences include discrete business-level organizational processes fundamental to running the business (e.g., order entry, customer service, product design, quality control). But they also include generalized organizational skills such as "miniaturization," "tight tolerance engineering," and "micromotors."

Competences are tangible, and can be quite durable. They are typically supported by routines, not dependent on a single individual, and generally reside inside the business functions. Like know-how assets, they cannot be readily bought and sold, absent a transaction for the entire business.

Profiting from innovation is more readily assured when high-performance business processes and/or world-class competences support a product or process offering. This is because the asset/competences cannot be traded, and the forces of imitation are muted. Not only are such assets/competences inherently difficult to imitate because they are likely to be built on a high tacit component, but there may be opaqueness to the underlying processes and uncertainty, even within the firm, as to the organizational foundations of the competence.

3.5 Complementary Assets

The asset structure of the firm is perhaps the most relevant aspect of its positioning when the commercialization of knowledge in tangible products and processes is at issue. Such (upstream) positioning may be more important than the downstream positioning in the product markets for yesterday's product. In many cases there may be a high correlation between a firm's upstream position in an asset and its downstream market position.

Complementary assets matter because knowledge assets are typically an intermediate good and need to be packaged into products or services to yield value. There are notable exceptions, of course. Software is a classic exception as it does not need to be manufactured, and with the Internet, distribution becomes instantaneous and almost costless.

However, when the services of complementary assets are required, they can play an important role in the competitive advantage equation. For instance, the design for a new automobile is of little value absent access to manufacturing and distribution facilities on competitive terms.

The effort to embed knowledge in products and to bring the new product to market must confront the whole question of access to complementary assets. If already owned by the knowledge owner, there is no issue. If not, then one must build, or buy if one can. Because the market for complementary assets is itself riddled with imperfections, competitive advantage can be gained or lost on how expertly the strategy for gaining access is executed.

Circumstances of such co-specialization can benefit the asset owner, as demand for the innovation will increase demand for the co-specialized asset. If difficult to replicate or work around, the complementary asset may itself become the "choke point" in the value chain, enabling it to earn supernormal rents. Thus, ownership of difficult to replicate complementary assets can represent a second line of defense against imitators and an important source of competitive advantage.

3.6 Dynamic Capabilities

In many sectors in today's global market, competitive advantage also requires dynamic capabilities (see Figure 4). This is the ability to sense and then to seize new opportunities, and to reconfigure and protect knowledge assets, competencies, and complementary assets and technologies to achieve sustainable competitive advantage.

It is relatively easy to define dynamic capabilities, but quite another matter to explain how they are built. Part of the answer lies with the environmental and technological sensing apparatus that the firm has established, and part lies with the choice of organizational form, and part lies with the ability to strategize.

3.6.1   External Sensing

In order for an organization to exhibit dynamic capabilities, it must sense the opportunity and the need for change, properly calibrate responsive actions and investments, and move to implement a new regime with skill and efficiency. During "sensemaking," the organization receives and interprets messages about new markets, new technologies, and competitive threats. This information is necessarily evaluated in the light of the individuals' and the organization's experience and knowledge. In formulating an action plan, the organization is necessarily guided to some extent by rules and routines, which structure inquiries and responses.

Sensemaking, or interpretation, is a critical function. Well performed, it can enable the organization to connect with its environment and invest its resources wisely, thereby generating superior returns. The fundamental challenge to sensemaking is bounded rationality; one cannot learn all there is to learn about a situation or an opportunity, and action must proceed based on hunches and informed guesses about the true state of the world. In essence, business organizations and their management must interpret the world about them. Interpretative activity is basically a form of theorizing about market and firm behavior.

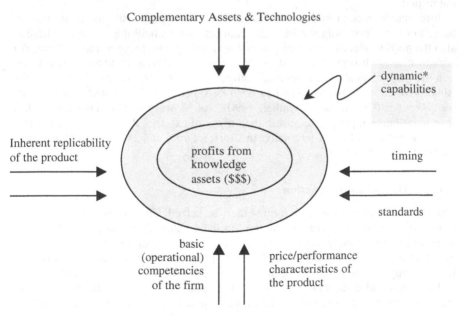

* Dynamic Capabilities are the capacity to sense opportunities and to reconfigure knowledge assets, competencies, and complementary assets and technologies to achieve sustainable competitive advantage.

Figure 4. Capturing Value from Knowledge Assets

Sensemaking can be assisted by sensemaking tools, like scenario planning, as well as the insights of brilliant outsiders—like a Peter Druker or Gordon Moore. Scenario planning can help managers develop mental maps of possible complex future realities. Such mental maps assist in the interpretation of new data and information from the market and help chart courses of action. Shell Oil is well known for its effective use of scenario planning, and its investment in this activity is widely recognized inside and outside the company to have enabled planners and managers to have extended conversations resulting in shared visions of possible futures. The object of the exercise has never been to predict the future, but to understand the fundamental drivers of change and to quickly chart action plans once key uncertainties are resolved.

When the organization has figured out what is going on, and calibrated the opportunity, it must choose among available action plans. These are not infinite in number, but may be restricted to one or two or maybe a handful of viable alternatives that are satisfactory. Actions are likely to be similar to those used in the past. Organizational routines—distinct ways of doing things—come into play. Actions and decision routines are part of the organization's procedural memory. Procedures and policies enable internal competition to be fair, objective, and legitimate. Organizational rationality can exist, despite individuals' bounded rationality, if rules, routines, and procedures guide individual decision making.

The openness of markets, stronger intellectual property protection, increasing returns, the unbundling of artifacts and information, and the possibilities for "integration" using new information technology are necessarily a part of the sensemaking milieu.

Information receipt and interpretation is by no means restricted in its importance to the understanding of business, market, and technological trends. There is also the need to identify relevant external technology and bring it into the firm. An organization's absorptive capacity with respect to external technology is a function of "the technical and managerial competence of the transferee" (Teece, 1976). Absorptive capacity is greatest when what is to be learned is related to what is already known (Cohen and Levinthal, 1990). As Mowery (1984) has explained, a firm is far better equipped to absorb the output of external R&D if one is performing some amount of R&D internally. In short, internal and external R&D are complements, not substitutes.

3.6.2   Organizational Action

Once an opportunity is sensed, it must then be seized. This is where the organization's ability to quickly contract up the requisite external resources and direct the relevant internal resources comes into play. Schumpeter referred to the importance of effectuating "new combinations." This is precisely what management must do. It increasingly involves forming alliances to access the requisite complementary technologies and complementary assets. The alliance structure is favored because markets simply don't exist for much of what must be accessed, and the alliance is a (hybrid) way to do so that shares risks and rewards but achieves a coalignment of strategy.

However, it also requires an organizational structure where decision making is immediate and action is swift. This typically implies high-powered incentives and decision making that is anything but bureaucratic. Smaller entrepreneurial companies appear to excel in many such environments, although dynamic capabilities are certainly not restricted to small companies. Larger enterprises can also deliver much of what is required if they are tuned to changes in their external environments, and if they have adopted decision-making processes that both enable and require quick response.

4   Implications for the Theory of the Firm

The firm is a repository for knowledge—the knowledge being embedded in business routines and processes. Distinctive processes undergird firm-specific assets and competences (defined as integrated clusters of firm-specific assets). The firm's knowledge base includes its technological competences as well as its knowledge of customer needs and supplier capabilities. These competences reflect both individual skills and experiences as well as distinctive ways of doing things inside firms. To the extent that such competences are difficult to imitate and are effectively deployed and redeployed in the marketplace (reflecting dynamic capabilities), they can provide the foundations for competitive advantage.

The essence of the firm is its ability to create, transfer, assemble, integrate, and exploit knowledge assets. Knowledge assets underpin competences, and competences in turn underpin the firm's product and service offerings to the market. The firm's capacity to sense and seize opportunities, to reconfigure its knowledge assets, competencies, and complementary assets, to select appropriate organization forms, and to allocate resources astutely and price strategically all constitute its dynamic capabilities.

The knowledge perspective presented here requires us to stress the entrepreneurial rather than the administrative side of corporate governance. In high-technology industries, firms are not so much organizations designed to minimize transactions costs—although this they do—but organizational structures capable of shaping and reshaping clusters of assets in the distinct and unique combinations needed to serve ever-changing customer needs. Accordingly, boundary issues (such as vertical integration) are not determined by transactions cost—considerations alone. Rather, they are strongly influenced by tacit knowledge and imitability/ replicability considerations. Even setting aside strategic and transaction cost issues, the tacit component of knowledge cannot frequently be transferred absent the transfer of personnel and organizational systems/routines. Tacit knowledge and its transfer properties help determine the boundaries of the firm and may well swamp transaction costs considerations.

Competitive advantage can be attributed not only to the ownership of knowledge assets and other assets complementary to them, but also to the ability to combine knowledge assets with other assets needed to create value. Knowing what assets to develop, and what to abandon, is a critical element in the success equation. Dynamic capabilities are critical if knowledge assets are to support sustainable competitive advantage.

The astute management of the value in a firm's competence/knowledge base is a central issue in strategic management (Teece, 1986). The firm must therefore be understood not just in terms of its competences, but also in terms of its dynamic capabilities and the ability to orchestrate internal and external assets so as to capture value. Dynamic capabilities reflect the entrepreneurial side of management. Incentives as well as the formal and informal structure of the firm are all elements of governance affecting dynamic capabilities. These elements together help define the firm as we know it. Accordingly, competitive advantage flows from both management and structure.

Thus, the competences/capabilities view of the firm sees the proper boundaries of the firm and governance structure being determined not only with reference to transactions costs, but also with reference to technological and knowledge concerns. The boundaries of the firm, and future integration and outsourcing opportunities, must clearly be made with reference to learning and knowledge issues as well as transaction cost economics.

The emphasis on the development and exploitation of knowledge assets shifts the focus of attention from cost minimization to value maximization. Governance decisions involve both questions of what assets to build inside the firm versus accessing externally, as well as how to organize internally. This perspective thus complements transaction cost economics.

5   Conclusion

Knowledge, competence and related intangibles have emerged as the key drivers of competitive advantage in developed nations. This is not just because of the importance of knowledge itself, but because of the rapid expansion of goods and factor markets, leaving intangible assets as the main basis of competitive differentiation in many sectors. There is implicit recognition of this with the growing emphasis being placed on the importance of intangible assets, reputation, customer loyalty, and technological know-how.

While there is some recognition of these changes, there is perhaps a failure to recognize just how deep these issues go. The value-enhancing challenges facing management are gravitating away from the administrative and towards the entrepreneurial. This is not to denigrate the importance of administration, but merely to indicate that better administration is unlikely to be where the economic "rents" (superior profits) reside. Indeed, if one looks at the sources of wealth creation today, they are markedly different from what they were barely two decades ago. The key sources of wealth creation at the dawn of the new millennium lie with new enterprise formation; the renewal of incumbents; the exploitation of technological know-how, intellectual property, and brands; and the successful development and commercialization of new products and services.

The implications for management are clearly quite considerable. New forms of business organization—and new management styles that enable intangibles to be developed and dynamic capabilities to be practiced—are clearly critical. There is now sufficient experience with new network organizations and with alliances to sensitize management to the richness of the organizational menu that is now available. Moreover, modern information technology clearly enables a greater variety of transactional structures than was hitherto thought possible. What is apparent is the need to focus on developing a deeper understanding of imitability and replicability issues with respect to intangibles and the role of markets in undermining traditional forms of competitive advantage.

The extension of markets and the growth of competition is a great benefit to the consumer and society. However, the post-war evolution of markets has powerful strategic implications for how and where firms position themselves to build competitive advantage. This does not appear to be well appreciated. It is no longer in product markets but in intangibles assets where advantage is built and defended. There is no such thing as a privileged product market position—unless it rests on some upstream intangible asset. The focus of strategy analysis must change, and is changing, as indicated by the burgeoning literature in strategic management on the resource-based theory of the firm (for an excellent compendium, see Foss (1997)). Managers who figure this out are likely to be well positioned to build and maintain competitive advantage in the next millennium. They must recognize that in open unregulated markets, the domains in which value can be built are likely to be more and more confined. Perhaps Andy Grove is right after all when he warns that "only the paranoid survive."

References

Arthur, B. "Competing Technologies: An Overview," in Dosi, G.; et al. (eds.), *Technical Change and Economic Theory,* London: Frances Pinter, 1988.

Clark, K. and T. Fujimoto, *Product Development Performance: Strategy, Organization, and Management in the World Auto Industries,* Cambridge, MA: Harvard Business School Press, 1991.

Cohen, W. M. and D.A. Levinthal, "Absorption Capacity: A New Perspective on Learning and Innovation," *Administrative Sciences Quarterly,* 35, 1990, 128-152.

Dataquest, *ASIC's Worldwide,* December 18, 1995.

Forbes, "A Dynamic Mix of Chips and Biotech," *Forbes,* January 26, 1996, 76-81.

Foss, N. (ed.), *Resources, Firms and Strategies: A Reader in the Resource-Based Perspective,* New York, Oxford University Press, 1997.

Grindley, P. and D .J. Teece, "Managing Intellectual Capital: Licensing and Cross-Licensing in Semiconductors and Electronics," *California Management Review,* 39, 2, 1997, 8-41.

Kodama, F., *Analyzing Japanese High Technologies,* London: Pinter, 1991.

Kuznets, S., *Modern Economic Growth: Rate, Structure, Spread,* New Haven, CT: Yale University Press, 1966.

Lippman, S. A. and R.P. Rumelt, "Demand Uncertainty and Investment in Industry-Specific Capital," *Industrial and Corporate Change,* 1, 1, 1992, 235-262.

Miller, M., *Merton Miller on Derivatives,* London: John Wiley & Sons, 1997.

Mowery, D., "Firm Structure, Government Policy, and the Organization of Industrial Research," *Business History Review,* 58, 1984, 504-531.

Nelson, R. and S. Winter, *An Evolutionary Theory of Economic Change,* Cambridge, MA: Harvard University Press, 1982.

Nonaka, I. and T. Takeuchi, *The Knowledge Creating Company,* New York: Oxford University Press, 1995.

Porter, M. E., *The Competitive Advantage of Nations,* New York: Free Press, 1990.

Romer, P., "What Determines the Rate of Growth and Technological Change," World Bank Working Papers, WPS 279, World Bank, 1989.

Shannon, C.E. and W. Weaver, *The Mathematical Theory of Communication,* Chicago: University of Illinois Press, 1949.

Teece, D. J., *The Multinational Corporation and the Resource Cost of International Technology Transfer,* Cambridge, MA: Ballinger, 1976.

Teece, D. J. "Technology Transfer by Multinational Firms: The Resource Cost of Transferring Technological Know-How," *The Economic Journal,* 87, 1977, 242-261.

Teece, D. J., "The Market for Know-How and the Efficient International Transfer of Technology," *Annuals of the American Association of Political and Social Sciences,* November, 1981, 81-86.

Teece, D. J. "Towards an Economic Theory of the Multiproduct Firm," *Journal of Economic Behavior and Organization,* 3, 1982: 39-63.

Teece, D.J., "Profiting from Technological Innovation," *Research Policy,* 15, 6, 1986, 285-305.

Teece, D.J., "Firm Organization, Industrial Structure, and Technological Innovation," *Journal of Economic Behavior and Organization,* 31, 1996, 193-224

Teece, D. J., G. Pisano, and A. Shuen, "Dynamic Capabilities and Strategic Management," *Strategic Management Journal,* 18, 7, 1997, 509-533.

Winter, S. "Knowledge and Competence as Strategic Assets," in Teece, D. (ed.), *The Competitive Challenge: Strategies for Industrial Innovation and Renewal,* New York: Harper & Row, Ballinger Division, 1987.

CHAPTER 8

The Intellectual Capital of Nations

Leif Edvinsson

Universal Networking Intellectual Capital (www.unic.net) and University of Lund, Sweden

Just as an organization's value is a function of its intellectual capital, the wealth of a nation – present and potential – is linked to its intellectual capital (IC). This chapter argues that it is imperative for leaders to recognize and address the IC potentials of their nations. Issues pertaining to consideration and reporting of a nation's IC are outlined. Activities along these lines in several nations are described.

Keywords: Financial Capital; Intellectual Capital; Longitude; Nations; Navigator;

1 Introduction

This chapter builds on what has been accomplished in understanding the intellectual capital (IC) of organizations to develop an appreciation of the IC of nations. Such an appreciation is important in addressing such questions as:

- What is the knowledge capital of your nation?
- What is the GDP per capita of your nation?
- What is the potential GDP per capita of your nation?
- What is the gap as a percentage?
- Which leader is in charge of bridging this gap of potential future wealth?

A seminal characterization of intellectual capital for organizations is as follows: it is what an organization's participants know that gives the organization a competitive advantage relative to others in its marketplace (Stewart, 1991). In a similar vein, IC is knowledge that can be applied to yield value (Edvinsson and Sullivan, 1996). IC can be seen as roughly accounting for the difference between an organization's market value and its book value. Understanding, guaging, and cultivating this difference is a major issue for leaders of organizations (and of nations). One approach to doing so is found in the IC Navigator I developed at Skandia.

The Navigator is a management and reporting approach that furnishes a perspective encompassing both the financial capital and intellectual capital of an organization (Edvinsson and Malone, 1997; Edvinsson and Grafstrom, 1998). It is a model that structures, packages, and measures IC as a guide for management and knowledge worker activity. It sees IC as including human capital and structural capital. The former involves the knowledge and skills of an organization's participants. The latter concerns all other organizational capabilities and traits that support the work of these participants. As a structure for IC management, Navigator helps orient the setting of objectives and guide the performance of knowledge workers in terms of five focus areas: financial, customer, human, process, and renewal/development. To these, it also adds global context.

The remainder of this chapter concentrates on the intellectual capital of nations and adapts the Navigator model in doing so.

2   The New Wealth of Nations

"Only knowledge will give us the opportunity to create a better world with a global economy in which we all will be able to share our limited resources in the best ways," says Lars Larsson of Ericsson. Former Oticon chief Lars Kolind poses a simple challenge: "Find out how nations may develop their countries into competence countries." Still another challenge is to develop a map of regional intellectual capital, instead of the old agricultural and industrial maps of societies, often found in regional planning offices. The key mapping dimension should be situated around the quest for finding *Where is wealth created in our region/country?*

A new political leadership agenda is evolving around the IC of nations with the focus on:

- how to visualize IC of nations
- how to cultivate IC of nations
- how to capitalize into wealth of nations

According to the Organization for Economic Co-operation and Development (OECD, 2001), the countries with knowledge-intensive activities will be the winners of future wealth. In the OECD report, the 30 member countries are scored according to IC investments such as R&D, education, patents, ICT, and so forth. As summarized by the Financial Times and Dagens Industri, the list of top potentials for future wealth looks like this:

1. Switzerland
2. Sweden
3. USA
4. Ireland
5. Netherlands
6. Hungary
7. Canada
8. Belgium
9. UK
10. South Korea

In the knowledge economy, the value of corporations, organizations, and individuals is directly related to their intellectual capital. But spread the net little wider and you begin to understand the possibilities. Think of nations. If intangibles are important to organizations, they are also important to the productivity and competitiveness of individual nations. How can we understand the dynamics of intangibles at work on a national scale? Can corporate longitude be translated into a new perspective on national performance?

3   Corporate Longitude

The logic of corporate longitude is based on a little story from early 1700s (Edvinsson, 2002). Then, the British Navy could not navigate with precision east-west, but only north-south. Consequently, the 18th century ships were lost in the fog, like today's analysts of only financial capital. So today, we are facing the problem of accounting in much the same way, as for example in the case of Enron.

The problem of the longitude found its solution, not by the professionals in the Navy, not by the academics at universities, but by a knowledge outsider – a watchmaker by the name of John Harrison. He innovated the east-west measurement approach that solved the longitude problem. To get a deeper understanding of wealth creation, it is essential to have such a lateral perspective. The latitude of stapling assets into a balance sheet, with a traditional bottom line is too narrow. A lateral accounting is necessary to include the intangibles and the non-financial assets of knowledge creation, networks, and relationships. The longitude logic is focused on sustainability, lateral, outside, and interactive value-creating dimensions of intangibles. The new space of wealth of organizations, as well as nations, is in the interaction space of human capital and structural capital resulting in financial prosperity (see Figure 1). So, a nation's wealth can be visualized in a map of both financial wealth as well as intellectual capital. Furthermore, the elements of IC form the enablers and drivers for financial wealth. So, from a leadership perspective, the strategic development focus should be on the IC components of a nation (as illustrated in Figure 2 and described in section 4).

Currently, organizations as well as societies are like 18th century ships charting their positions with only north-south navigation tools. Plotting a course solely from historical financial wealth reference points leaves them blind to the lateral horizon's opportunities and novel perspectives. Lost on a turbulent sea of change, without a lateral navigation tool to guide them, they cannot navigate the uncharted expanse of a networked world where value is derived primarily from intangible rather than tangible assets.

Profit measurement and reporting systems emphasize efficiency and cost control, using money as the basis of decision making. This ongoing obsession with planning and charting progress against tangible indicators of wealth will ultimately impoverish society and devalue the wealth of nations, because they overlook the contribution of intangibles. For example, public service sector activities are automatically undervalued because there is no way to measure their contribution, so we lose talent from the system, because they search for more lucrative openings elsewhere.

Adding value in the knowledge economy is inextricably linked to radical change in both societal assumptions and business models. Capitalism may not create value if it is obsessed with competition to the detriment of collaboration. Social values must be re-considered in the light their value generation potential. For example, allocating resources to education, health and social services, and communication infrastructure should not be based on cost, but on the potential for value creation through knowledge. If employment in private industry is only about

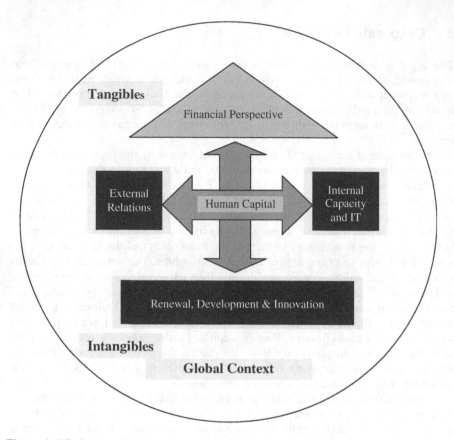

Figure 1. IC Navigator for Nations

25% of total potential mind value of the society, leveraging the rest of it more effectively depends on education and opportunity.   Research suggests that educational systems have a high degree of explanatory value in national wealth rankings, so efficient resource allocation would mean they should receive much larger elements of funding than currently they do.

Infrastructure is extremely essential too. Think about which cities and countries are truly poised for value creation? It won't be those that isolate themselves, or those with a poor communication infrastructure. Primarily, they will be ones that are well connected, with an infrastructure designed to encourage access to the knowledge and human resources that create new value. Arab countries traditionally have relied on oil as the source of wealth, so intellectual capital represents only 20% of their wealth. If they don't start navigating for the future in terms of renewal through education, making relationships with other countries, and infrastructure for networking, then their wealth is set to decline.

4   IC Reporting of Nations

The evolution is in progress. IC reporting of nations is already happening. Indeed, it was as long ago as 1986 that a voluntary pilot study was launched in Sweden to look at intangible assets. National statistics now increasingly cover intangibles, but they are mostly related to manufacturing companies with over 500 employees (OECD, 2001).

Then, in 1987, a group met to discuss the area of intangibles. They met on Konrad Day, 12 November, and became known as the Konrad Group. This group included Karl-Erik Sveiby who soon went on to do pioneering research for his Ph.D. and to write about customer capital, structural capital, and human capital as the three categories of knowledge capital. From the Konrad Group emerged the prototyping work on intellectual capital at a corporate level at Skandia. At the same time, another parallel cluster of IC pioneers emerged in the U.S.A. including, among others, Debra Amidon, Tom Stewart, Larry Prusak, and Juanita Brown. In 1991, Skandia appointed me as the world's first Director of IC to develop another logic for the renewal of Skandia. Results of this work included a refined taxonomy, measurement and accounting systems for IC, as well as innovation systems for IC.

In 1996, Sweden announced the "Year of Innovation" and the Skandia Future Center was established. As leader of that Future Center, I invited Caroline Stenfelt from the University of Stockholm and some student colleagues to prototype how our work on IC at Skandia could be translated to a national stage (Edvinsson and Stenfelt,, 1998; Rembe and ISA, 1999). The first IC of nations was born due to her pioneering work, labelled as "Welfare and Security." Later, she organized the Vaxholm Summit – the First International Meeting on Visualizing and Measuring the IC of nations, held in August 1998. As a result, the Swedish government adapted Skandia's Navigator to visualize its national intellectual capital. Later, countries such as Israel, Holland and, in particular, Denmark, began to visualize their respective intellectual capitals.

Sweden was an interesting nation on which to prototype this thinking. "Sweden appears to be a showplace for the theory of intellectual entrepreneurship," says the country's Invest in Sweden Agency, ISA.

The ISA was the first national investment organization to apply the latest knowledge of intellectual capital to assess and compare national competitiveness and performance. "Intellectual capital forms the root of a corporation – and of a nation – that supplies the nourishment for future strength and growth. A new analytical method enables these previously unevaluated resources to be assessed and compared. This can be an important tool for selecting an international location for knowledge-based companies. Sweden offers highly attractive and competitive intellectual capital assets – assets of superior value for leading edge companies," said ISA's 1999 Annual Report.

In fact, the Skandia Navigator was easily translated from the corporate to national environment, yielding the structure shown in Figure 2. Its focuses remained intact, but it covered a range of different issues:

- *Financial Focus* including per capita GDP, national debt, the mean value of the US dollar
- *Market Focus* including tourism statistics, standards of honesty, balance of services, balance of trade, balance of trade in intellectual property
- *Human Focus* including quality of life, average age expectancy, infant survival rate, health levels, education, level of education for immigrants, crime rate, age statistics
- *Process Focus* including service-producing organizations, public consumption as a percentage of GDP, business leadership, information technology such as personal computers connected by LAN's, survivors in traffic accidents, employment
- *Renewal and Development Focus* including R&D expenses as a percentage of GDP, number of genuine business start-ups, trademarks, factors important to high school students.

As all the statistics on the country's capital show, Sweden has embraced technology with enthusiasm. According to one survey, Sweden is the leading IT country in the world. This has not happened overnight. There has been long-term government support for technology – tax-breaks for employees buying a computer, following on from initiatives such as free Internet access for students and earlier programs to give children access to PCs. It has shaped an infrastructure and structural capital for future wealth.

One of the most striking IC elements in Swedish management is its international networking perspective. When it comes to producing global companies, Scandinavia is remarkably successful – the only worthwhile European comparisons are with Switzerland and, perhaps, the Netherlands. Its companies transcend boundaries in ways few others can manage. Internationalization is in the Swedish genes. We are modern knowledge Vikings. Exports account for 40 percent of Sweden's GDP. In addition, Sweden has a positive trade balance in intellectual property – indeed the value generated by music royalties is equivalent to the incomes generated by Saab. Sweden also has the highest rate of musical literacy. Investments in intangibles constitute around 20 percent of GDP. According to the above-mentioned OECD report in October 2001 Sweden is among the leading nations in the knowledge-based economy. Sweden also has one of the highest R&D per capita investments in the world.

Very interesting research in the area is being done by Nick Bontis. Based on the above mentioned model and sponsored by the United Nations Development Program, he and his colleagues have studied ten Arab States. In this study, he quantifies the state of IC for these nations and launches an "IC Index for Nations" that can be used for ranking as well as benchmarking learning between nations.

It is only by looking at such statistics through a holistic knowledge lens, like the IC Navigator for nations, that they can make overall sense. Otherwise, they appear to be idiosyncrasies. By looking at the IC wealth of nations rather than standard measures of national competitiveness, we gain new insights into where a country's strengths and weaknesses might lie. We can then nourish social innovation, society entrepreneurship, and social innovations (McElroy, 2000, 2002a, 2002b, 2002c).

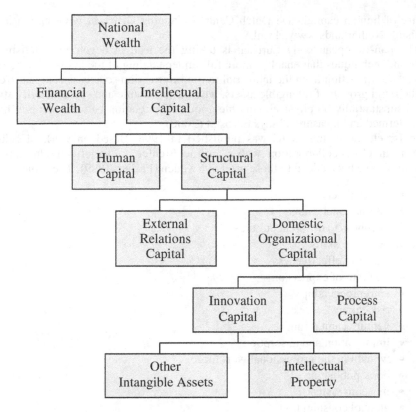

Figure 2. IC Value Scheme

In the Bontis research case, it can so far be concluded that the following ingredients, in the stated order, are key areas for the political agenda to shape the IC of nations:

1. National agenda for Renewal, Research and Development (i.e., Innovation Capital)
2. National agenda for Education (i.e., Human Capital)
3. National agenda for Foreign Trade (i.e., Relationship Capital)
4. National agenda for Industrial Productivity (i.e., Process Capital)

5   IC in the World

Sweden is not alone. At national levels, there is a great deal of activity in coming to terms with the power of intangible assets and the rise of intellectual capital.

The Dutch Central Planning Office now has a Knowledge Economy Unit. Dutch initiatives include long-term analysis of the role of knowledge in the Dutch economy as well as other work on knowledge creation in networks and the availability of human capital. See Dutch Central Planning Office at www.cpb.nl and Statistics Netherlands www.cbs.nl.

The pan-European body Eurostat is taking the lead in developing statistical tools and techniques that enable a more full understanding of the knowledge economy. "The transition from the industrial to the information society is characterized by the rapid growth of intangible assets, whereas economic and social activity still relies substantially on physical, tangible goods. The relation between the two has to be defined and measured," says Eurostat (2000).

In Israel, the country's IC was published in 1998. Based on work of Edna Pasher, in close collaboration with Caroline Stenfelt, a variety of alternative measures have been added to those used in Sweden (Pasher, 1999). These include:

- external debt
- international events
- openness to different cultures
- language skills
- teaching effectiveness
- freedom of expression
- entrepreneurship
- risk-taking
- venture capital funds
- immigration and absorption
- women in the professional workforce,
- book publishing
- museum visits
- alcohol consumption
- scientific publications.

In Denmark progress is also being rapidly made. The country has long been at the forefront in examining the role of intangibles. Copenhagen Business School's Jan Mouritsen has been working in the area for a number of years and has carried out several surveys and literature studies (Mouritson et al., 2001).

At the beginning of 1998, Denmark launched a project looking at intellectual accounting under the umbrella of its broader initiative "Ledelse, Organization og Kompetence – LOK" which aimed to help transform Denmark from an industrial to a knowledge economy. A special Competence Council was organized with Lars Kolind as chairman. This has produced interesting work on Denmark's position in the new global knowledge competition. In 2000, the Danish government also published guidelines for Intellectual Capital Statements – akin to those produced by Skandia (Danish Ministry of Industry, 2001). A Danish law is now in progress to support these various initiatives. In 2002, the Danish Ministry of Industry also inaugurated a Future Centre called Mind Lab.

Intellectual capital is also making an impact in the Netherlands. Its Minister of Economic Affairs recently observed: "The Netherlands is rapidly developing into a knowledge-intensive economy... It is therefore strange that financial accounts are dominated by information on buildings and machinery, in other words the 'classical' or physical production factors. The value of knowledge – the R&D work, training, intellectual property, etc. – is not easy to identify in accounts. And that is in fact the reason why young knowledge-intensive businesses in particular have very great difficulty in finding external financiers."

The Dutch government's shift has been one from having an emphasis on technology to emphasizing innovation. In 1998, it published a report, "The Immeasurable Wealth of Knowledge," which found that in excess of 35 percent of Dutch national investments were of an intangible nature.

Another nation strongly transforming itself into the knowledge economy is Singapore. It has renamed its Ministry of Labour the Ministry of Manpower as well as spending decades building an impressive system of structural capital, especially for IT and telecommunications. The effect on wealth is highly visible.

Examining the intellectual wealth of nations is a major advancement. But further challenges exist on a number of other fronts as the true impact of the knowledge economy is beginning to be understood as *a New Deal for New Wealth of Nations*. These are summarized in the remainder of this chapter.

5.1 Knowledge Communities and Societies

"Today we're a society awash in networks, yet starved for community," says Peter Katz, author of The New Urbanism. True communities built around knowledge are now emerging. Many of these are Web-based. In them, knowledge is free-flowing, restlessly criss-crossing the globe all day long. Furthermore, it is these infrastructures that can give leverage to human capital of societies. Unless we innovate and prototype such new structures and delivery systems for health, work places, urban areas, and so forth, we might erode the important human capital and get an increasing society cost for burn outs and brain stress.

5.2 Society Entrepreneurship

Society entrepreneurship is a new, interesting concept emerging in Norway, among others (Nordisk Industrifond, 2002). It highlights a role for society renewal that is in the space between business community and society. It is a space for collaborative prototyping based on the structural capital from each partner, but leveraged by the individual human capital and innovative talent. The challenge is to get a turbo-charge on the existing IC of societies, or in other words increasing the turbo or productivity on existing knowledge investments . A kind of IC in waiting to be tapped by challenging society entrepreneurs. Whom would you like to nominate as one among the top ten society entrepreneurs of today – for shaping tomorrow?

5.3 Knowledge Cities and Harbours

Intellectual capital can also have an impact on city planning. Planners must now create the context in which knowledge workers can be their most productive. This may bring about radical changes in the way our urban environments are conceived. Think of a harbour. Traditionally, harbours used to be for the flow of goods. But as the value of logistics has declined, we have to look at the flow of knowledge. We need to create knowledge harbours. After all, closeness to water is important for knowledge workers. It is calming – all Japanese gardens have a water feature for this very reason.

5.4 Knowledge Universities

These, you may think, already exist. But, in many ways, people are now effectively "dis-educated" for the future: they are not prepared for the challenges that will arise. Universities need to be re-configured to fit changing times. At the moment, future learning is not taking place in universities; it is mostly taking place outside in industry. It still takes four years to receive a Ph.D. Why? Learning needs to be accelerated. Otherwise, there is a tremendous inefficiency and opportunity cost for knowledge workers.

6 Key Message

The wave of IC is increasing. It has gathered within it universities, accounting standards groups, political and business communities. The message is that we need to surf the wave of knowledge economics or drown. It is a leadership liability not to address the potential or IC in waiting.

The opportunity is great (Amidon, 2002). There are a great many people who are lost at sea, lost in the fog of the labour market, the stock market, or confused by the political world. They need to understand corporate longitude; otherwise, they will continue to go around in befuddled circles. Knowledge navigation will continue on the quest for the new wealth of nations.

Links for further reading related to intellectual capital include the following:

www.corporatelongitude.com
www.isa.se
www.oecd.org/publications
www.entovation.com
www.kmcluster.com
www.bontis.com
www.minez.nl
www.ll-a.fr/intangibles/
www.cbs.nl
www.efs.dk/icaccounts
www.monday.dk

References

Amidon, D., *Entovation 100: Worldwide Knowledge Leadership*, 2002, URL=http://www.entovation.com/momentum/entovation-100.htm.

Danish Ministry of Industry, *Guidelines for Knowledge Accounts*, 2001, URL=www.efs.dk

Edvinsson, L., *Corporate Longitude*, Stockholm: Bookhouse, 2002.

Edvinsson, L. and G. Grafstrom, *Accounting for Minds,* Stockholm: Skandia, 1998.

Edvinsson, L. and M.S. Malone, *Intellectual Capital: The Proven Way to Establish Your Company's Real Value by Measuring Its Hidden Brainpower,* New York: Harper, 1997.

Edvinsson, L. and C. Stenfelt, "IC at the National Level," University of Stockholm, 1998.

Edvinsson, L and P. Sullivan, "Developing A Model for Managing Intellectual Capital," *European Management Journal,* 14, 4, 1996, 356-364.

Eurostat, "Statistical Indicators for the New Economy," 2000, URL=http://europa.eu.int/en/comm/eurostat/research/retd/sine.pdf

McElroy, M.W., "Second-Generation Knowledge Management," 2002a, URL=http://www.macroinnovation.com/papers.htm

McElroy, M.W., "Social Innovation Capital," 2002b, URL=http://www.macroinnovation.com/papers.htm

McElroy, M.W., "The Principle of Sustainable Innovation," 2002c, URL=http://www.macroinnovation.com/papers.htm

McElroy, M.W., "The New Knowledge Management," 2000, URL=http://www.macroinnovation.com/papers.htm

Mouritsen, J., H.T. Larsen, and P.D.N. Bukh, "Intellectual Capital and the Capable Firm: Narrating, Visualising and Numbering for Managing Knowledge," *Accounting, Organizations and Society,* 26, 2001.

Nirdisk Industrifond, Oslo, 2002, URL=www.nordicinnovation.net

OECD, *OECD Science, Technology and Industry Scoreboard: Towards a Knowledge-Based Economy,* 2001, URL= http://www1.oecd.org/publications/e-book/92-2001-04-1-2987/

Pasher E., "A Look to the Future: The Hidden Values of the Desert," Tel Aviv: Pasher & Associates, 1999.

Rembe, A. and ISA, *Invest In Sweden Agency Annual Report,* 1999, URL= www.isa.se/pdf/SocwareDesignCluster_2001.pdf

Stewart, T.A., "Brain Power: How Intellectual Capital Is Becoming America's Most Valuable Asset," *Fortune,* June 3, 1991.

CHAPTER 9

Knowledge and Its Attributes

Clyde W. Holsapple

School of Management, Gatton College of Business and Economics, University of Kentucky, Lexington, KY, USA

This chapter examines several perspectives on answering the question "What is knowledge?" including the usable representations view, the states view, the production view, and the knowledge-versus-information view. The relationship between knowledge and technology is considered, concluding that technology is a major enabler of knowledge-based organizations. Regardless of the view of knowledge that one adopts and the degree of technology adoption, it is valuable to be aware of various attribute dimensions that qualify the nature of knowledge.

Keywords: Knowledge; Knowledge Attributes; Knowledge States; Knowledge Types; Representation; Usability

1 Introduction

Granted that knowledge is a key asset of modern enterprises, a focal point for knowledge-based organizations, and a resource that may lead to competitive advantage, it is useful to consider the nature of knowledge. This has, of course, occupied philosophers for thousands of years. The consideration of knowledge presented here is comparatively modest in scope, yet covers basic ideas about knowledge and its attributes. It presents multiple perspectives for the reader to ponder, adopt, or adapt as desired.

From the outset, it is important to recognize that there are different views about what knowledge is, each of which can be useful in developing a well-rounded picture. Also, various attributes of knowledge have been advanced. For instance, there is the mode of knowledge, ranging from tacit to explicit. Another attribute is the type of knowledge: descriptive, procedural, or reasoning. An appreciation of these and other knowledge attributes enriches our picture of knowledge.

We begin with an examination of several perspectives about what knowledge is. A discussion of various attributes follows, each of which is applicable to any of the perspectives.

2 What Is Knowledge?

According to Webster's New Collegiate Dictionary, knowledge is the "range of one's information or understanding." Information, in turn, is said to be "knowledge obtained from investigation, study, or instruction." The dictionary also defines information as "facts, data" and defines data as "factual information used as a basis for discussion,...calculation." So, the dictionary says that knowledge is a range of information, information is knowledge, information is data, and data is information. But, this does not get us very far in appreciating the nature of knowledge. Instead, let's take a look at several perspectives on knowledge that have been advanced from various quarters.

2.1 Usable Representations

In the systems perspective advocated by Allen Newell, when a system has and can use a representation of "something (an object, a procedure,...whatever), then the system itself can also be said to have knowledge, namely, the knowledge embedded in that representation about that thing" (Newell, 1982). This perspective sees knowledge as being that which is embodied in usable representations. There are two key notions in this perspective on knowledge: representation and usability.

First, consider representation. Note that there is a distinction between knowledge conveyed by a representation and the representation itself. A representation is some arrangement in time/space. There are many kinds of representations: words in a conversation or on the printed page, diagrams, photographs, mental patterns or images, physical movements, individual or collective behavioral displays, digital patterns, and so forth. Thus, some representations are objects (i.e., static symbols), whereas others are processes (i.e., dynamic symbols). Some are overt and publicly accessible, whereas other representations are covert and privately held.

Now consider the notion of usability. Newell (1982) contends that "knowledge cannot so easily be seen, only imagined as the result of interpretive processes operating on symbolic expressions." This suggests that knowledge does not exist apart from a processor that perceives or possesses a representation that it finds to be usable. One way to think about usability is in terms of Sveiby's (1997) sense of the capacity to take action (i.e., knowledge is embodied in a representation to the extent that possessing that representation gives a processor the capacity to take action). The degree of usability might be gauged in terms of the processor's speed, accuracy, and/or satisfaction with the action taken (Fang and Holsapple, in press).

The usability of a particular representation by a particular processor is influenced by the fit between representation and processor, by the action/task being attempted by the processor, and by the environment within which the action is to take place. At the minimum, a god fit requires that the processor be able to correctly interpret the representation in a timely manner. Fit may also be affected by interaction with other knowledge available to the processor (e.g., consistency, novelty, complementarity). A representation may convey beneficial knowledge for one task, but be irrelevant for other tasks facing the processor. Similarly, the environing context may affect the relevance or importance of knowledge conveyed by the representation for the task at hand.

Processors differ. A representation that conveys knowledge for one processor may be unusable or even incomprehensible to another processor. Broadly, proces-

sors can be classified along two dimensions. One dimension distinguishes between human and computer-based processors. Each kind is able to interpret certain types of representations and take actions accordingly. In some cases (e.g., an
expert system and a human expert), the action results (e.g., advice given) may be
identical (substitiable), even though the processors belong to different classes and
work with different representations of the same knowledge. A second dimension
distinguishes between individual and collective processors. The latter range from
simple dyads, to groups, to project teams, to hierarchies, to complex enterprises
and inter-organizational processors.

Figure 1 depicts the systems perspective of knowledge as embodied in usable
representations, recognizing different kinds of representations and varying degrees
of usability for a given processor at some movement in time.

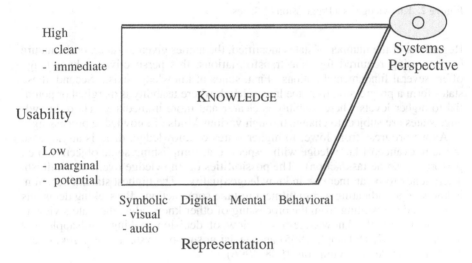

Figure 1. Knowledge as Usable Representations

2.2 Knowledge States

Variations in the usability of a representation (depending on processor, task, environment, etc.) suggest a continuum knowledge states reflecting variations in the
value of conveyed knowledge to a processor. This dove-tails with the perspective
that regards knowledge as encompassing a "complete set of knowledge states"
(van Lohuizen, 1986). Van Lohuizen identifies a progression of six states of
knowledge which he calls data, information, structured information, insight,
judgment, and decision. See Figure 2. From the knowledge states perspective,
various operations can be undertaken to progress from one state to another. For
instance, by selecting from data, a processor obtains the next higher knowledge
state (i.e., information). Aside from selecting, other operations include analyzing,
synthesizing, weighing, and evaluating.

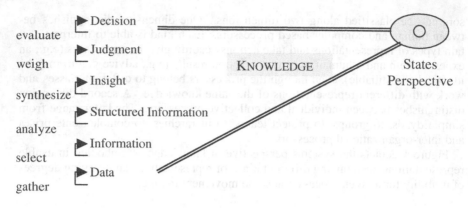

Figure 2. Knowledge as a Progression of States

Regardless of the number of states identified, the names given to states, or the nature of processing required for state transformations, this perspective on knowledge offers several fundamental notions. First, states of knowledge exist. Second, these states form a progression from the lowest level, where usability is marginal or potential to higher levels where usability is clearer and more immediate. Third, knowledge states are subject to change through various kinds of knowledge processing.

As we progress from lower to higher states of knowledge, there is an increase in the relevance of knowledge with respect to accomplishing some objective (i.e., performing some task/action). The possibilities of knowledge overload diminish. There tends to be an increase in knowledge quality. The highest state, a decision, is knowledge indicating a commitment to take some action. By seeking decisions as knowledge resulting from the processing of other knowledge, the state's view is consistent with the knowledge-based view of decision making (Holsapple and Whinston, 1987; Holsapple 1995) and decision support systems (Bonczek, et al., 1981; Holsapple and Whinston, 1988, 1996).

2.3 Stocks and Flows

The production perspective illustrated in Figure 3 views knowledge as existing in stocks and flows (Machlup, 1980). A stock is an inventory of knowledge available to one or more processors. The way knowledge is represented in a particular stock could include any of the representations noted in section 2.1 (symbolic, mental, behavioral, digital, etc.). Many of the issues pertinent to physical inventories also come into play for stocks of knowledge (e.g., replenishment, perishability, holding costs, design, quality assurance, tracking, planning).

In the production view, there are two main kinds of flows: knowledge transferal from one stock to another and knowledge flow from a stock into itself. The latter involves a processor using knowledge existing in a stock to produce new knowledge for that stock. This knowledge production is equated to learning. Learning may also be said to occur when a stock receives knowledge from another stock.

Consistent with the states view, Machlup (1980) contends that all information is knowledge, but not all knowledge is information.

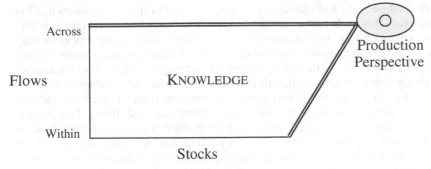

Figure 3. Knowledge as Stocks and Flows

2.4 Knowledge Versus Information

In contrast to seeing knowledge as encompassing a series of states, there is another perspective that basically views knowledge as a state in its own right, as something beyond information. For convenience, we shall refer to this as the kvi (knowledge versus information) perspective. It aims to define knowledge by differentiating it from information or data (see Figure 4). Rather than viewing data and information as aspects of a knowledge continuum, they are regarded as precursors of knowledge: data is turned into information and information is turned into knowledge (Davenport, 1998).

There are variations in how dividing lines between data, information, and knowledge are specified in a kvi perspective. Nevertheless, the basic ideas are that data are isolated observations or assertions (e.g., "the balance is $500"); information results from relating/structuring/qualifying data in meaningful ways (e.g., "John Doe opened a checking account with an initial balance of $500."); knowledge results from assembling some collection of information that is relevant to or applied to a task at hand (e.g., "based on John Doe's account activity over the past year, he is likely to be a strong candidate for a new promotional program or he will be targeted by such a program").

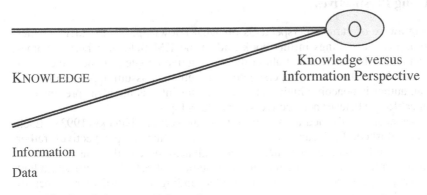

Figure 4. Knowledge versus Information

Observe that meaning and relevance are keys in trying to specify divisions in a kvi perspective. This leads to the questions: meaningful to whom? relevant to whom and for what task? What is meaningful (i.e., information) to one processor may not be to another that regards it as just data. What is relevant (i.e., knowledge) for a task presently being confronted by one processor may not be relevant for another task, another processor, or another time for which it is just information or data.

Thus, the kvi perspective is very dependent on context and its dividing lines are relative to such factors as the processor, the current task, and timing. One processor's knowledge in the kvi perspective can be another processor's information, or what is knowledge to a given processor in dealing with a certain task at a certain time may be only information for that same processor when focused on a different task or even on the same task, but at a different time (i.e., under different circumstances).

This relativism in defining what knowledge is does not arise in the previously noted perspectives on knowledge. For them, knowledge is a more all-encompassing notion, which, nevertheless, can be analyzed into various degrees of usability, various states of refinement and pertinence, or various kinds of stocks and flows. The kvi perspective can be related to the systems perspective of usable representations as follows: kvi imposes some threshold of usability, above which we have knowledge and below which we have information or data; in contrast, the systems perspective does not impose such a threshold on its definition or consideration of knowledge.

Davenport and Prusak (1998) point out that "Data, information, and knowledge are not interchangeable concepts." This view is shared by both the states and kvi perspectives. Moreover, both share the notions that data can be turned into information and that information can be turned into something more valuable. Where they differ is in naming conventions. In the kvi perspective, only the "something more valuable" than information is referred to as knowledge; in the states perspective, this "something more valuable" belongs to one of several higher states, all of which are regarded as knowledge, as are the lower states of data and information. Compare Figures 2 and 4. Also, see the related KM-Forum (1996) discussion thread for a wide range of ideas on the issue of knowledge versus information.

2.5 Using Perspectives

By being aware of various perspectives on what knowledge is, a reader is better able to appreciate writings in this book and in the KM field in general. Sometimes, an author is quite explicit about the perspective adopted. Other times, it is left to a reader to discern what perspective an author is assuming. In still other cases, an author is noncommittal; that is, the author intends the ideas presented to be applicable to whatever perspective(s) a reader adopts.

The perspectives outlined above are not exhaustive; see Nitecki (1993). Each can be embellished. Each can have variants. Because they are perspectives, rather than theories or hypotheses, they need to be evaluated more in the sense of usefulness than correctness. That is, readers and authors of KM literature can adopt whichever perspective(s) is helpful in understanding any particular aspect of knowledge handling in organizations.

Any of the perspectives can be considerably enriched by an appreciation of knowledge attributes. A representative sampling of these is examined in section 4. But first, pause to consider the relationship between knowledge and technology.

3   Knowledge and Technology

Interestingly, the 1990s rise of knowledge management as a prominent field of practice, research, and study coincided with tremendous advances in computing and communication technology. Thus, the relationship between knowledge and technology deserves some attention. Indeed, this relationship is the source of some disagreement within the broad KM community. At one extreme is the position that KM has nothing (or very little) to do with technology. At the opposite extreme is the proposition that KM is all (or mostly) about technology.

"Knowledge management today has a decidedly schizophrenic character. It caroms from the hard-edged bits and bytes of information technology to the softly shaped contours of interpersonal dynamics. People naturally gravitate toward one pole or the other. It's hard to tell that they are talking about the same thing. It's even harder for them to see that they are. Peering through a knowledge lens at the brave new organization, we will see the social anthropologist join hands with the software application analyst. The knowledge lens is a useful addition for organizations as they strive to make sense of the business world in which we live today" (Bukowitz and Williams, 1999).

3.1 Technology Is Incidental

The position that technology is incidental to progress and practice of knowledge management rests on a particular perspective of what knowledge is: knowledge is defined as uniquely human, only existing in the context of human interpretation and processing. All else is called data or information. So, that which can be represented and processed by either humans or computers is called data or information. But, if it can be represented and processed only by humans, then it is called "knowledge." Thus, by definition, this stance precludes computer-based technology from any key role in the KM field, relegating it to deal with "data and information" that, upon human interpretation, is called "knowledge."

Advocates of this position contend that breakthrough developments in KM will be human-based, not technology-based. They contend that focusing on technologies will result in overlooking the great potential of knowledge-based organizations.

However, if technology is eliminated from consideration, then KM loses a great deal:

- Classic KM success stories such as Buckman Labs (K'Netix) and Ernst & Young (Ernie) would vanish.
- Knowledge would flow via face-to-face meetings, physical bulletin boards, hardcopy reports and memos, surface mail, fax, telephone conversations, and so forth; but groupware, email, electronic forums, computer-

mediated communications, workflow systems, and computer-supported cooperative work would be of little relevance to knowledge work.
- Knowledge repositories would include pieces of paper, briefing books, filing cabinets, traditional libraries, and human memories; but digital documents, databases, Web pages, and software libraries would not have a role in KM.
- Knowledge generation would be performed by human mindpower, with the aid of pencil and paper; but solvers or spreadsheets for deriving forecasts, expectations, and analyses would be out-of-bounds; rule sets, case bases, and inference engines for deriving advice would be out-of-bounds; data mining, text mining, and automated pattern recognition for knowledge discovery would be out-of-bounds.
- Technological means for acquiring and selecting knowledge – search engines, Web crawlers, intelligent agents (aka softbots, knowbots) – would be of little importance to knowledge workers.

3.2 Technology Is Everything

In marked contrast, there is the position that KM is all about technology, that an appreciation of technology and continuing technological advances are cornerstones of knowledge management. Its proponents adopt a broader perspective on knowledge, either viewing it as encompassing the lower states of information and/or data (as in the states view), or seeing computer-based processors as capable of interpretation and processing of usable representations in the performance of their tasks (as in the systems view). They contend that breakthroughs in KM will be technological, and organizations that ignore or minimize technology in their conduct of KM are in peril of being left in the dust of competitors.

By itself, however, technology is not KM. If people and organizations are eliminated from consideration then the chance of KM success evaporates rapidly:

- Knowledge management could not have predated the advent of computer-based technology, but this would ignore the long history of organizations struggling to achieve value from knowledge assets.
- Technology would become an end in and of itself, without attention to its consequences.
- Technology vendors would become the primary sources for KM solutions.
- Technology would become the starting point and driver of KM initiatives, instead of basing KM efforts on human traits and capabilities, coupled with organizational objectives.
- KM initiatives would concentrate on explicit knowledge, leaving the tacit mode of knowledge largely unattended.
- The user of the technology would be of secondary interest, instead of letting user requirements dictate or shape the technology (if any) that is deployed.

- People would be seen as supporting the technology, instead of the technology enabling, supplementing, complementing, or amplifying human knowledge processing abilities.

3.3 The Middle Path

Rather than taking either an all or nothing position about the connection between knowledge and technology, there is, of course, a middle path. On this path, knowledge management is concerned with people, technology, organizations, and the fits among them. Within this relatively inclusive 'big tent' position, there is room to focus on any of several topics while still realizing the existence and importance of other topics.

One can focus on the representations that human processors find to be usable and methods/practices for effectively managing these representations and processors to maximize usability and improve outcomes in the context of organizational and technological environs. One can focus on representations that computer-based processors can utilize in accomplishing various tasks, the specific natures of such processors, and how they can be devised, improved, and managed to support and facilitate the human dimension of KM. The focus could be on the enterprise as a processor, custodian, and user of knowledge, realizing that it is comprised of some configuration of human and computer-based processors operating on an assortment of representations. The focus could be on alignment, synergy, and coordination of the various knowledge-related elements in the context of implementing strategies.

All of these foci are encountered, considered, and represented on the middle path taken by this book.

3.4 Computer-Based Technology: A Servant of KM

The study of computer-based technology in organizations (CBT) proceeds under a variety of names such as information systems, information technology, information and communication technology, computer information systems, management information systems, information management, business computing systems, and so forth. These labels have varying nuances and all are related to reference disciplines of computer science and management. Regardless of the preferred label, CBT researchers have an interest in what they can contribute to the KM field. This section offers a few ideas in this direction.

Over the past fifty years, computer-based technology has transformed lives and organizations. One way it has done so has been to transform how knowledge work is done. CBT is fundamentally concerned with digital means for representing and processing knowledge of several types (see section 4.2) including:

- Descriptive knowledge, in its various gradations from data and information at the low end to problem solutions, designs, and decisions at the high end
- Procedural knowledge, specifying the steps for performing some task
- Reasoning knowledge, specifying what conclusion is valid when a particular situation exists

As such, CBT has transformed the ways in which both individuals and organizations accomplish knowledge work. It has done so by amplifying, complementing, leveraging, and in some cases improving on innate human knowledge handling capabilities. It has relaxed some of the temporal, cognitive, economic, and geographic limits on human knowledge work (Holsapple and Whinston, 1996).

Tracing the evolution of CBT, we see a progression from data processing systems to management information systems to decision support systems to organizational computing systems to ubiquitous computing. These are summarized in Table 1. The trajectory of the first three phases is into increasing value, relevance, and importance for knowledge workers (adherents of the kvi perspective on knowledge would dismiss the first two of these phases). The next phase builds on the first three, adding the dimension of intra- and inter-organizational knowledge flows and knowledge reuse.

The ubiquitous computing phase builds on all that precede it and is driven by such forces as Moore's Law, Metcalf's Law, and advances in content technologies that allow computers to better represent and process. In the world of ubiquitous computing, the hallmarks are 24 x 7 operations, global connectivity, and everyday objects with embedded computers. Such objects (e.g., vending machines, appliances, drums of chemicals, running shoes, garments, vehicles, houses) will increasingly have the abilities to observe, record experiences, communicate, solve problems, and take actions. They can be constantly on, active, "aware" – interacting with their environment, other computers, and people.

Bukowitz and Williams (1999) point out that "from a knowledge perspective, technology triumphs in its ability to connect more people in more ways than ever before. E-mail, intranets, discussion forums, chat rooms – they all make the truly networked organization possible…Advantage comes from conversation, the back and forth questioning, the easier access to expertise and the broadened sense of membership in different communities…" On the horizon, Bieber et al. (2002) describe how a digital library can be augmented with computer-mediated communications, community process support technology, decision support technology, advanced hypermedia features, and conceptual knowledge structures for constructing a collaborative knowledge evolution support system.

In analyzing chess master Gary Kasparov's defeat at IBM's Deep Blue supercomputer, Huang (1998) observes that Deep Blue's collectively constructed knowledge from many individuals was explicit knowledge that overcame the master's tacit knowledge. "The embodiment of Deep Blue clearly departs from the traditional perspective on knowledge. Deep Blue…was able to calculate more than 200 million potential chess moves each second, then tap into a vast knowledge bank of how past chess games were played to evaluate and choose the most promising option. It demonstrated the power of applying today's advanced…technology to assist in collaborative efforts and knowledge sharing to generate winning results." Huang contends that a lesson learned from this exercise is that with the use of CBT "firms can capture and reproduce the tacit knowledge of their workers, to be reused at different times and in different locations, through different media to create solutions more efficiently. In turn, this allows more time for individuals to use their intuitive strengths, defining and solving problems more creatively."

Table 1. Evolution of CBT

Computer-Based Technology	Emerged	Emphasis
Data processing systems	1950s-1960s	Representation of low grade descriptive knowledge Recording transactions Producing transactions
Management information systems	1960s-1970s	Representation of low to middle grade descriptive knowledge Record keeping based on transactions Producing predefined types of reports that organize data into more usable chunks of information
Decision support systems	1970s-1990s	Representation of descriptive, procedural, and/or reasoning knowledge Use of knowledge to solve (or find) problems Delivery of knowledge needed by a decision maker • in a desired format • possibly, on the spur-of-the-moment • possibly, in response to unanticipated or novel knowledge needs Includes modeling systems, expert systems, online analytical processing, business intelligence systems
Organizational computing systems	1980s-1990s	Facilitates knowledge flows and reuse among multiple participants in some organizational form May involve descriptive, procedural and/or reasoning knowledge Includes groupware, collaboration systems, workflow systems, enterprise systems, inter-organizational systems, adaptive systems
Ubiquitous computing	1990s-	Universal, non-stop availability of knowledge and knowledge processors Includes Web-based, mobile, and embedded computing systems

CBT for connecting intelligent knowledge processors (human and computer) and for collective construction of reusable knowledge bases furnishes a foundation for implementing knowledge-based organizations (Holsapple and Whinston, 1987). This technology is evident in the e-business boom, including the notions of e-commerce, collaborative commerce, and mobile commerce. Indeed, e-business can be viewed as a major arena of KM: e-business is concerned with approaches to achieving business goals in which technological means for representing and processing knowledge are used to implement and facilitate activities within and across value chains, as well as supporting decisions that underlie those activities (Holsapple and Singh, 2000).

So, the idea is that modern knowledge management is inseparable from a consideration of computer-based technology, of CBT users, and of CBT impacts. This can't help but be the case in the emerging era of ubiquitous, pervasive computing. The assertion (discussed in section 3.2) that "KM is all about technology" is actually upside-down; that is, CBT is increasingly becoming all about KM. There are messages and opportunities in this for CBT researchers, including IS researchers, MIS researchers, IT researchers, and so on.

First, CBT researchers are (or should be) KM researchers, whether they recognize it or not. It is better to recognize this than ignore it. We do not develop and deploy technology for its own sake, but because it helps us to better deal with knowledge of various types and in various gradations enroute to better individual and organizational performance. In this effort, it is important to appreciate the KM context to which CBT research adds value, or has the potential to do so. The signs are encouraging. After decades with only a handful of CBT researchers actively and directly investigating KM issues, the last few years have seen a dramatic increase. All leading journals in the business computing field now publish KM research, many having devoted special issues to the topic over the last two years. Major conferences in the field now have full KM tracks for research presentations, and KM topics are finding their ways into university-level CBT courses.

Second, there are opportunities for research that improves on current CBT for:

- enabling and facilitating knowledge flows among knowledge processors (human and computer-based),
- supporting and performing knowledge manipulation tasks such as those identified in the KM ontology described in Part I of this book (i.e., acquisition, selection, internalization (storage/dissemination), generation (derivation/discovery), and externalization) – many of these technology issues are examined in Part V of this book,
- assisting in the measurement, control, coordination, and leadership of knowledge and knowledge processors,
- helping ensure that the right knowledge (e.g., descriptive, procedural, reasoning) gets to the right processors (human and computer-based) in the right formats at the right times and at the right cost.

Third, to advance the field of business computing, we need to better understand the users and usage of CBT in knowledge management.

- What works and under what conditions does it work?
- What does not work, and why?
- What CBT advances and breakthroughs are needed?
- How do we cultivate "good" fits between technological infrastructure on one hand and organizational infrastructure and culture on the other hand in knowledge-based organizations?

Fourth, to advance the business computing field, we need to study outcomes of using CBT in knowledge management

- What are its competitive impacts?
- How can CBT be used to implement a knowledge chain activity (Holsapple and Singh, 2001)?
- Or, in a more targeted vein, how can CBT be used to enhance productivity, agility, innovation, or reputation as a means for competitive advantage (Holsapple and Singh, 2001)?

Technology has been changing the nature of knowledge creation, publication, and sharing for decades. Ongoing CBT development will continue to have profound social and managerial implications. However, we must remember that knowledge is, first and foremost, a business issue. KM is central to business operation and strategy, and is evolving into an integral part of running a business. In this context, development and adoption of computer-based technologies needs to be oriented toward enhancing knowledge work.

4 Knowledge Attributes

Regardless of what definition of knowledge one adopts and regardless of which knowledge resource is being considered, it is useful to appreciate various attributes of knowledge. An attribute is a dimension along which different instances of knowledge can vary. An attribute dimension may comprise a range of values (e.g., knowledge age) or may be categorical (e.g., tacit vs. explicit). The categories may take the form of multilevel taxonomies. Taken together, several attributes of interest form the axes of an attribute space. A particular instance of knowledge will have some location in that space at any given time, and may assume new locations over time. Its location will determine what kind of processor(s) can operate on it and the kind(s) of processing to which it can be subjected.

An appreciation of multiple knowledge attributes enriches one's understanding of knowledge resources and their processing. Several attribute dimensions for knowledge are described in the ensuing sections. These are summarized in Table 2. The list is not necessarily exhaustive, but does give a sense of the characteristics a knowledge worker may want to consider in dealing with a knowledge portfolio. These attributes are suggestive of variables that a KM researcher may want to investigate (Holsapple and Joshi, 2001). They also highlight facets of knowledge that a manager might consider in designing and overseeing a KM initiative.

Table 2. Representative Knowledge Attributes

Attribute	Nature of Dimension	References
Mode	*Tacit* vs. *explicit* knowledge	Teece, 1981; Nonaka, 1991; Nonaka and Takeuchi, 1995
Type	*Descriptive* vs. *procedural* vs. *reasoning* knowledge	Bonczek et al., 1981; Holsapple and Whinston, 1987, 1988; Holsapple, 1995; Holsapple and Whinston, 1996
Domain	*Subject area* or *problem domain* where knowledge is used (e.g., marketing, engineering, policy, manufacturing)	van der Spek and Spijkervet, 1997
Orientation	*Domain* vs. *relational* vs. *self* knowledge	Dos Santos and Holsapple, 1989; Holsapple and Whinston, 1996
Applicability	Range from *local* to *global*	Novins and Armstrong, 1997
Management level	*Operational* vs. *control* vs. *strategic*	Anthony, 1965
Usage	*Practical* vs. *intellectual* vs. *recreational* vs. *spiritual* vs. *unwanted*	Machlup, 1982
Accessibility	Range from *public* to *private*	Holsapple and Whinston, 1996
Utility	Progression of levels from a *clear* representation to one that is *meaningful* to one that is *relevant* to one that is *important*	Holsapple and Whinston, 1996
Validity	Degree of *accuracy* or *certainty* about knowledge	Holsapple and Whinston, 1996
Proficiency	Degree *expertise* embodied in knowledge	Wiig, 1993
Source	*Origin* of knowledge	Novins and Armstrong, 1997
Immediacy	*Latent* versus *currently actionable*	Stewart, 2002
Age	Range from *new* to *established* to *old* knowledge	van der Spek and Spijkervet, 1997
Perishability	*Shelf-life* of knowledge	Holsapple and Whinston, 1987

Volatility	Degree to which knowledge is *subject to change*	Pritchard, 1999
Location	*Position* of knowledge (e.g., ontological, organizational, geographic locus)	van der Spek and Spijkervet, 1997
Abstraction	Range from *concrete* to *abstract*	Boland et al., 2001
Conceptual level	*Automatic* vs. *pragmatic* vs. *systematic* vs. *idealistic*	Wiig, 1993
Resolution	Range from *superficial* to *deep*	Wiig, 1993
Programma-bility	Degree to which knowledge *is transferable* and *easy to use*	Novins and Armstrong, 1997
Measur-ability	Degree to which knowledge or its processing can be *measured*	Holsapple and Whinston, 1987; Edvinsson and Malone, 1997; Lev, 2001
Recursion	*Knowledge* vs. *meta-knowledge* vs. *meta-meta-knowledge*	Bonczek et al., 1981

4.1 Knowledge Mode

A commonly employed attribute dimension when discussing knowledge is its mode. Following Polanyi (1962), a distinction is made between knowledge that is tacit and knowledge that is explicit. In the former case, the knowledge is inconvenient or difficult to formalize and communicate. It is not articulated, at least not yet. Typical examples include a person's mental models, perspectives, intuitions, experiences, and know-how (Nonaka, 1991). Explicit knowledge is conveyed in formal, systematic representations that are readily communicated. It is articulated, as in knowledge artifacts such as reports, books, and speech; or, it is codified (Teece, 1981) as in a database, software library, or set of rules that can be used by a computer-based processor.

Considerable research has been performed on the mode attribute of knowledge. For instance, Nonaka (1994) and Nonaka and Takeuchi (1995) have studied processes for conversion of tacit knowledge to explicit knowledge and vice versa, as well as tacit-to-tacit and explicit-to-explicit conversions.

4.2 Knowledge Type

Three primary knowledge types are the categories of descriptive, procedural, and reasoning knowledge (Holsapple and Whinston, 1988, 1996; Holsapple, 1995). Categories of secondary, derivative types of knowledge have also been identified; these include linguistic, assimilative, and presentation knowledge (Holsapple and Whinston, 1996). Knowledge belonging to any of the primary types can be tacit.

Knowledge of any of these types can be explicit, to the point of being computerized (Holsapple, 1995; Zack, 1999).

Descriptive knowledge characterizes the state of some world, be it actual, predicted, or speculative. This type of knowledge includes descriptions of objects, of concepts, of past, present, future, and hypothetical situations. Data and information are descriptive in nature. Thus, they can be regarded as descriptive knowledge that is of limited utility; or, from a kvi perspective, they are precursors of descriptive knowledge. In either case, they can lead to or be interpreted in light of other descriptive knowledge such as forecasts, expectations, problems, solutions, insights, judgments, blueprints, goals, decisions, definitions, schemas, taxonomies, and so forth.

Descriptive knowledge can be acquired from external sources (e.g., by observation, by purchase). It can be selected from internal repositories (e.g., extraction, assembly). It may be generated by derivation (e.g., results of analyses) or discovery (e.g., recognizing a pattern, creative intuition). Descriptive knowledge can be internalized (e.g., stored or disseminated internally) or externalized.

Descriptive knowledge is sometimes called declarative knowledge (Zack, 1999). That is, a description can be thought of as a declaration about some world. Descriptive knowledge has also been called environmental knowledge (Bonczek et al., 1981); the world being described is an environment for the processor of that knowledge.

Philosophers have long recognized a type of knowledge that is fundamentally different from descriptive knowledge. Russell (1948) explains that "there is knowledge which may be described as 'mirroring,' and knowledge which consists in capacity to handle." In mirroring the state of some world of interest, the former is descriptive knowledge. Very different from this is knowledge about how to do something (Ryle, 1949) or how something occurs (Zack, 1999). This knowledge, consisting of step-by-step procedures for handling various tasks or explaining various happenings, is called procedural knowledge (Scheffler, 1965).

Examples of procedural knowledge include algorithms, strategies, action plans, programs, and methods. Like descriptive knowledge, procedural knowledge can be in a tacit mode (e.g., a mental representation) or an explicit mode (e.g., a written or digital representation). Also, like descriptive knowledge, it can be acquired, selected, generated, internalized, and externalized. However, the means for performing these manipulations and the skills required for doing so may be very different for procedural versus descriptive knowledge. For instance, generating a forecast, blueprint, or goal may well require different skills and processing than generating an action plan or program. Interestingly, procedural knowledge can be applied to descriptive knowledge to derive new descriptive knowledge (Bonczek et al., 1981).

A third major type of knowledge is for reasoning (Holsapple and Whinston, 1988, 1996). An instance of reasoning knowledge specifies what conclusion is valid or what action can be taken when a particular situation exists. The connection between the situation and the conclusion/action could be based on logic, correlation, analogy, or causality. This type of knowledge is quite distinct from the description of a situation or the specification of a procedure. Examples include a rule, policy, code of conduct, regulation, principle, and case.

Reasoning knowledge can be tacit or explicit. It can be acquired, selected, generated, internalized, or externalized by an organization's knowledge processors; however, the processor capabilities needed to do so can differ from those that work for descriptive or procedural knowledge. Like procedural knowledge, reasoning knowledge can be applied to generate new knowledge. For example, for a given description of a situation and a goal, instances of reasoning knowledge may be put together to reach logical conclusions. These conclusions may take the form of procedural knowledge indicating how to reach that goal. Or, they may take the form of descriptive knowledge (e.g., characterizing a diagnosis or expectation). The use of reasoning knowledge to reach such conclusions is referred to as inference.

Instances of the three types of knowledge can be applied in the generation of new knowledge. Descriptive knowledge, in the sense of data and information, does not by itself yield new knowledge, aside from rearranging (i.e., assembling, relating, packaging it in novel ways). This may be why some observers are inclined to exclude it from being called "knowledge," reserving that term for procedural and reasoning knowledge. It is when a processor is able to manipulate procedural and/or reasoning knowledge in the processing of descriptive knowledge that its "hidden" potential is released in the guise of generating new knowledge. The value of an interplay among the three primary knowledge types has long been recognized in the building of decision support systems (Bonczek et al., 1981).

4.3 Knowledge Domain and Orientation

Some attribute dimensions are concerned with the subject of the knowledge. One such classification distinguishes among alternative subject domains (van der Spek and Spijkervet, 1997). These can be broad domains such as marketing, public policy, chemistry, or production management. Or, they may be more narrow partitions such as inventory control, scheduling, quality assurance, and facilities planning within production management. Thus, the domain attribute can form a multilevel taxonomy. A given instance of knowledge belongs to some category within such a taxonomy. Knowledge belonging to a particular domain category can be in a tacit and/or explicit mode. It can be of descriptive, procedural, and/or reasoning types.

The knowledge orientation dimension subsumes the domain attribute. It distinguishes between knowledge oriented toward domains, knowledge oriented toward relationships with other processors, and knowledge that a processor has about itself (Dos Santos and Holsapple, 1989; Holsapple et al., 1994; Holsapple and Whinston, 1996). The orientation attribute dimension recognizes that, in performing a task (e.g., solving a problem), a processor may need more than knowledge about the task domain. The processor may need to interact with other processors and, therefore, use knowledge about them in doing so – relational or relative knowledge. This relational knowledge includes an appreciation of their preferences, attitudes, skills, expertise, backgrounds, and so forth. A processor also needs knowledge of its own traits, capabilities, and resources – self-knowledge.

4.4 Knowledge Applicability, Management Level, and Usage

Any instance of knowledge is positioned somewhere on a dimension that ranges from very localized in its applicability to globally applicable. For instance, it may be usable by only a single processor and only in special circumstances; or, it may be universally usable by any of an organization's processors in dealing with ordinary, frequent situations.

A related attribute dimension is concerned with the management level at which knowledge is applicable: operational control, management control, or strategic planning (Anthony, 1965). Knowledge used to ensure that particular operational tasks are executed effectively and efficiently belongs to the operational control category. If it is used to ensure that resources are available and deployed to meet goals within policy guidelines, then it belongs to the management control level. Strategic planning knowledge is used to establish such goals and policies.

Knowledge used at any of the three management levels is an example of what Machlup (1982) calls practical knowledge. He distinguishes between this and other classes of knowledge (intellectual, recreational, etc.) based on the realm in which an instance of knowledge is used. In a similar vein, Batalden and Stolz (1993) distinguish between knowledge used professionally and that which is used for improvement. Professional knowledge is knowledge of a discipline, craft, or profession; it can be of either mode and of any of the three types. Improvement knowledge is used to enhance the quality or outcome of work.

4.5 Knowledge Accessibility and Utility

On the accessibility dimension, an instance of knowledge is somewhere in the continuum from entirely private (accessible to a single processor) to entirely public (accessible to any processor). This distinction is important in building multi-participant decision support systems (Holsapple and Whinston, 1996) where knowledge of any type or orientation can be public, semi-private, or private.

The utility attribute is concerned with how useful an instance of knowledge is. One way to gauge this dimension is in terms of four major levels, each yielding greater utility than the level below it (Holsapple and Whinston, 1996). From lowest to highest, these levels are:

- clarity – comprehensible representation
- meaning – processable interpretation
- relevance – pertinent to a problem or issue at hand
- importance – crucial for the task to be accomplished.

There are gradations within each level and the utility of a specific instance of knowledge can be assessed only relative to a knower and a context for that knower. For example, what is meaningful or important to one processor facing a particular challenge, requirement, or opportunity may not be so for a different processor (or for the same processor in a different context).

Clarity is inversely related to the degree of effort a processor expends in interpreting a knowledge representation; little effort goes with high clarity, but high effort indicates low clarity. Once a representation is comprehended, it will be more or less meaningful. This is a function of the extent to which it can be further processed. For instance, someone may comprehend that the relative strength of a particular stock is 65, but is unable to do anything with that knowledge (i.e., it is a clear statement, but not particularly meaningful). Someone else, however, is able to factor this knowledge (along with other knowledge) into making a decision about whether to liquidate a position in this stock.

An instance of knowledge may be clear and meaningful to a processor, but not pertinent to the context at hand. Within the accessible pool of meaningful knowledge, a processor faces the necessity of identifying and focusing attention on that which is relevant to the issue or problem at hand. There may be so much relevant knowledge available that a processor needs to determine what subset is most important or crucial in order to avoid overload, unnecessary complexity, delays, or higher costs.

In the case of descriptive knowledge, the progression through the four utility levels parallels the often cited progression from data to information to higher-utility descriptive knowledge. However, the gradations in utility are also evident for procedural knowledge and reasoning knowledge, for explicit and tacit modes of knowledge, for any of the three knowledge orientations, and so on.

4.6 Knowledge Validity, Proficiency, and Source

The validity attribute is concerned with the accuracy, consistency, and/or confidence in an instance of knowledge (Holsapple and Whinston, 1996). Ideally, it would be nice if all knowledge available to a processor could be scientifically validated as being accurate and consistent, or philosophically certified as consistent and trustworthy. This ideal is not generally realistic when confronted by the cognitive limits of processors, time constraints on their knowledge processing tasks, and economic limits. Nevertheless, knowledge work must proceed. It should do so with the realization that knowledge being used can include some degree of error, inconsistency, belief, bias, risk, and fuzziness. Management scientists have long grappled with formal ways to accommodate and deal with these factors.

Eckhardt (1981) contends that knowledge validity is relative to the knower and the world being known. What was valid yesterday may be less so today. What is valid in one locale (e.g., an accounting principle) may not be appropriate elsewhere. What is valid in one hypothetical world (e.g., a scenario) may not be valid in another. Because a processor may need knowledge of multiple worlds, some capacity for coping with conflicting knowledge can be helpful.

Wiig (1993) identifies the proficiency attribute, referring to the degree of expertise inherent in an instance of knowledge. Like validity, this attribute is concerned with gauging the "goodness" of knowledge. So, too, is the source attribute (Holsapple and Whinston, 1996; Novins and Armstrong, 1997). The origin of an instance of knowledge is inextricably linked to the validity, proficiency, or "goodness" attributed to that knowledge, as well as impacting its cost.

4.7 Temporal Attributes

Several knowledge attributes are directly rooted in time. These include immediacy, age, pershability, and volatility. Several of the attributes already discussed are also related to time. For instance, utility and validity of knowledge can vary with time; the temporal attributes are concerned with the kinds of variations.

The attribute of knowledge immediacy distinguishes between representations that are currently usable and those that are potentially usable. In the latter case, knowledge is said to be latent (Stewart, 2002). A processor may or may not be aware of latent knowledge. Interesting issues along this attribute dimension include how to suspect or detect latent knowledge, how to assess its potential usability or applicability, and how to minimize the cost or effort of making it current. One important approach to uncovering latent knowledge is by connecting knowledge resources that were previously insulated from each other (Ching et al., 1992)

Knowledge age is a dimension that ranges from new to established to old. As an instance of knowledge ages, its applicability, accessibility, utility, and validity can fluctuate. It may improve on these other dimensions because positive experience with using it could have grown, additional new knowledge that complements it has become available, some constraint on its use (e.g., cultural, legal, security) may have been reduced, or the world has changed (e.g., "caught up" with it). As knowledge matures it may be refined or extended in various ways that increase its value.

On the other hand, as an instance of knowledge ages, its value on other dimensions can diminish, even to the point of being spoiled or obsolete. This phenomenon is depicted in the perishability attribute, which recognizes that it may be necessary to depreciate or dispose of an instance of knowledge (Holsapple and Whinston, 1987). There may be some salvage value and disposal costs associated with perishable knowledge. In any event, realization of this attribute is important for managing (and perhaps exploiting) knowledge assets that are perishable.

The volatility attribute is concerned with the rate of change in an instance of knowledge. Does it mature rapidly? Is it frequently revised or very stable? Does it have a short "shelf-life" or is it very durable? What can be done to alter knowledge volatility or to insulate an organization from knowledge volatility? The degree of volatility can impact the locus of knowledge storage (Pritchard, 1999); for example, should it be stored in human or computer-based memory, or in some kind of artifact? Oriani and Sobrero (2001) point out that there is volatility in both an organization's stock of knowledge for a given domain and in the domain's state of knowledge as well.

4.8 Other Knowledge Attributes

Location is a multifaceted attribute of knowledge (van der Spek and Spijkervet, 1997). This refers to the position of knowledge in an organization, and this position can affect its utility. Aside from the ordinary facet of geographic position, there is the location of knowledge in an organization. Who or what holds the knowledge? An artifact, a person, an infrastructure, a culture, a computer system?

Another locational facet is the position of an instance of knowledge in an organization's ontology.

On the abstraction dimension, knowledge ranges from concrete to abstract (Boland et al., 2001). The related resolution attribute is concerned with how deep, detailed, and thorough an instance of knowledge is (Wiig, 1993). The conceptual level of knowledge can be classified as automatic, pragmatic, systematic, or idealistic (Wiig, 1993). Programmability is an attribute that characterizes the extent to which knowledge is readily transferable and easy to use (Novins and Armstrong, 1997). As such, it is related to other attribute dimensions such as mode, accessibility, and immediacy.

Knowledge measurability is an attribute whose importance has been recognized for quite some time (Holsapple and Whinston, 1987) and for which various specific approaches have been devised (Edvinsson and Malone, 1997; Lev, 2001). It is concerned with assessing the value of an instance of knowledge and/or the value of processing that knowledge. Several chapters in this book deal with knowledge measurement issues and methods.

The recursion attribute distinguishes between knowledge and meta-knowledge, the latter referring to knowledge about knowledge (e.g., the structure, features, uses, and attributes of knowledge). For instance, an organization's ontology is a kind of meta-knowledge. Reasoning knowledge that tells us about uses of descriptive knowledge is at the meta-knowledge level of recursion (Bonczek et al., 1981). Knowledge about utility, validity, source, perishability, value, etc. for a given instance of knowledge is meta-knowledge; knowledge about these same attributes for the meta-knowledge itself is at the next level of recursion: meta-meta-knowledge.

5   Conclusion

Investigation of the nature of knowledge has occupied mankind for thousands of years and will likely continue to do so for thousands more. Over the past fifty years, there has been a crescendo in how numerous, widespread, and prominent these investigations have become. In just the past decade, this has reached a sufficient critical mass for knowledge management to be recognized as a multidisciplinary field of study and practice. Yet the KM field is still emergent and formative. It is a field with rich and challenging subject matter and with considerable diversity of viewpoints and positions. It is a field of great opportunity for fostering better individual, organizational, and societal performance.

This chapter has presented some of the diverse viewpoints on what knowledge is. Appreciating these multiple perspectives is important for examining the correspondingly diverse literature of the KM field. It can also help in crafting one's own perspective on knowledge, as a basis for personally doing and researching knowledge work. However, care should be taken to avoid being overly dogmatic in adhering to one particular view on what knowledge is. Dismissing the ideas, findings, and writings of those who do not conform to that view may well overlook much that could be usefully adopted or adapted. Thus, this chapter has considered several perspectives, without necessarily advocating or championing any one of them. What it does advocate is an understanding of multiple viewpoints as a basis for understanding what is happening in the KM field and as a prelude to settling on a personal (or organizational) perspective from which knowledge work will be approached.

This chapter has also outlined differing positions on the relationship between knowledge and technology. In doing so, it has advocated a balanced position that regards both people and CBT as important elements of an organization's knowledge management equation. On this middle path, neither is excluded from consideration in designing, researching, or operating a knowledge-based organization (Holsapple and Whinston, 1987).

Finally, the chapter has assembled a partial collection of knowledge attributes. These give a foundation for studying commonalities and contrasts across distinct instances of knowledge. In a sense, they can serve as an addendum to an ontology of knowledge resources. Attributes do not tell us what knowledge is or what knowledge resources exist in an organization. They do, however, help us understand the many qualities of knowledge. Every attribute dimension is a potential variable for investigation by KM researchers and a potential lever for practitioners to wield in their KM efforts.

References

Anthony, R.N., "Planning and Control Systems: A Framework for Analysis," Boston: Harvard University Graduate School of Business Administration, 1965.

Batalden, P. B. and P. K. Stoltz, "A Framework for the Continual Improvement of Health Care: Building and Applying Professional and Improvement Knowledge to Test Changes in Daily Work," *Journal of Quality Improvement*, 19, 10, 1993.

Bieber, M., D. Engelbart, R. Furuta, S. Hiltz, J. Noll, J. Preece, E. Stohr, M. Turof, and B. van de Walle, "Toward Virtual Community Knowledge Evolution," *Journal of Management Information Systems*, 18, 4, 2002, 11-35.

Boland, R, J. Singh, P. Salipante, J. Aram, S.Y. Fay, and P. Kanawattanachai, "Knowledge Representations and Knowledge Transfer," *Academy of Management Journal*, April, 2001.

Bonczek, R., C. Holsapple, and A. Whinston, *Foundations of Decision Support Systems*, New York: Academic Press, 1981.

Bukowitz, W. R. and R. L. Williams, *Knowledge Management Fieldbook*, London: Financial Times/Prentice Hall, 1999.

Chang, A., C. Holsapple, and A. Whinston, "A Hyperknowledge Framework for Decision Support Systems," *Information Processing and Management*, 30, 4, 1994, 473-498.

Ching, C., C. Holsapple, and A. Whinston, "Reputation, Learning, and Organizational Coordination," *Organization Science*, 3, 2, 1992, 275-297.

Davenport, T., "From Data to Knowledge," *Oracle Magazine*, May, 1998
    URL = http://www.oracle.com/oramag/oracle/98-May/ind2.html.

Davenport, T. and L. Prusak, *Working Knowledge: How Organizations Manage What They Know*, Boston: Harvard Business School Press, 1998.

Dos Santos, B. and C. W. Holsapple, "A Framework for Designing Adaptive DSS Interfaces," *Decision Support Systems*, 5, 1, 1989, 1-11.

Eckhardt, W., "Limits to Knowledge," *Knowledge: Creation, Diffusion, Utilization*, 3, 1, 1981.

Edvinsson, L. and M. S. Malone, *Intellectual Capital: The Proven Way to Establish Your Company's Real Value by Measuring Its Hidden Brainpower*, New York: Harper, 1997.

Fang, X. and C. Holsapple, "The Usability of Web Sites for Knowledge Acquisition: A Taxonomy of Influences," *International Journal of Electronic Business*, 1,2,2003, 211-224.

Holsapple, C., "Knowledge Management in Decision Making and Decision Support," *Knowledge and Policy*, 8, 1, 1995, 5-22.

Holsapple, C., L. Johnson, and V. Waldron, "A Formal Model for the Study of Communication Support Systems," *Human Communication Research*, 22, 3, 1996, 421-446.

Holsapple, C. W. and K. D. Joshi, "Organizational Knowledge Resources," *Decision Support Systems*, 31, 1, 2001, 39-54.

Holsapple, C. and M. Singh, "Toward a Unified View of Electronic Commerce, Electronic Business, and Collaborative Commerce: A Knowledge Management Approach," *Knowledge and Process Management*, 7, 3, 2000, 151-164.

Holsapple, C. and M. Singh, "The Knowledge Chain Model: Activities for Competitiveness," *Expert Systems with Applications*, 20, 1, 2001, 77-98.

Holsapple, C. and A. Whinston, "Knowledge-Based Organizations," *The Information Society*, 5, 2, 1987, 77-90.

Holsapple, C. and A. Whinston, *The Information Jungle: A Quasi-Novel Approach to Managing Corporate Knowledge*, Homewood, IL: Dow Jones-Irwin, 1988.

Holsapple, C. and A. Whinston, *Decision Support Systems: A Knowledge-Based Approach*, St. Paul, MN: West, 1996.

Huang, K.-T., "Capitalizing on Intellectual Assets," *IBM Systems Journal*, 37, 4, 1998.

KM-Forum, "Knowledge vs. Information," 1996, URL=http//www.km-forum.org/t000008.htm

Lev, B., *Intangibles – Management, Measurement and Reporting*, Washington, D.C.: Brookings Institution, 2001.

Machlup, F., *Knowledge: Its Creation, Distribution, and Economic Significance*, Volume 1, Princeton, NJ: Princeton University Press, 1980.

Machlup, F., *Knowledge: Its Creation, Distribution, and Economic Significance – The Branches of Learning*, Volume II, Princeton, JN: Princeton University Press, 1982.

Newell, A., "The Knowledge Level," *Artificial Intelligence*, 18, 1, 1982.

Nitecki, J.Z., *Metalibrarianship*, 1993,
    URL= http://www.du.edu/LIS/collab/library/nitecki/metalibrarianship/ch-10.htm

Nonaka, I., "The Knowledge Creating Company," *Harvard Business Review*, November-December, 1991, 96-104.

Nonaka, I., "A Dynamic Theory of Organizational Knowledge Creation," *Organization Science*, 5, 1, 1994, 14-37.

Nonaka, I., and T. Takeuchi, *The Knowledge Creating Company*, New York: Oxford University Press, 1995.

Novins, P. and R. Armstrong, "Choosing Your Spots for Knowledge Management – A Blueprint for Change," *Perspectives on Business Innovation – Managing Organizational Knowledge*, Issue 1, 1997.
    URL = http://www.businessinnovation.ey.com/journal/features/toc.

Oriani, R. and M. Sobrero, "Market Valuation of Firms' Technological Knowledge: A Real Options Perspective," *International Conference of the Strategic Management Society*, San Francisco, October, 2001.

Polanyi, M., *Personal Knowledge: Towards a Post-Critical Philosophy*, New York: Harper Torchbooks, 1962.

Prahalad, C. and G. Hamel, "The Core Competence of the Company," *Harvard Business Review*, May/July, 1990, 79-91.

Pritchard, P., "The Three Kinds of Knowledge in the Context of Evidence-Based Medicine and Decision Support," *Proceedings of the Annual Conference of the Primary Health Care Specialist Group of the British Computer Society*, Cambridge, 1999.

Stewart, T.A., *The Wealth of Knowledge: Intellectual Capital and the 21st Century Organization*, New York: Currency Doubleday, 2002..

Sveiby, K. E., *The New Organizational Wealth: Managing and Measuring Knowledge-Based Assets*, San Francisco: Berrett-Koehler Publishers, 1997.

Teece, D., "The Market for Know-How and the Efficient International Transfer of Technology," *Annals of the American Association of Political and Social Sciences*, November, 1981, 81-86.

van der Spek, R. and A. Spijkervet, "Knowledge Management: Dealing Intelligently with Knowledge," in Liebowitz, J. and Wilcox, L. (eds.) *Knowledge Management and Its Elements*, New York: CRC Press, 1997.

Van Lohuizen, C. W. W., "Knowledge Management and Policymaking," *Knowledge: Creation, Diffusion, Utilization*, 8, 1, 1986.

Wiig, K., *Knowledge Management Foundations*, Arlington, TX: Schema Press, 1993.

Zack, M., "Managing Explicated Knowledge," *Sloan Management Review*, Spring, 1999.

CHAPTER 10

Making Knowledge Visible through Knowledge Maps: Concepts, Elements, Cases

Martin J. Eppler

Institute for Media and Communications Management, University of St. Gallen, Switzerland

This chapter seeks to establish the conceptual basis for an innovative instrument of corporate knowledge management: the knowledge map. It begins by briefly outlining the rationale for knowledge mapping, i.e., providing a common context to access expertise and experience in large companies. It then conceptualizes five types of knowledge maps that can be used in managing organizational knowledge. They are knowledge-sources, -assets, -structures, -applications, and -development maps. In order to illustrate these five types of maps, a series of examples is presented (from a multimedia agency, a consulting group, a market research firm, and a medium-sized services company) and the advantages and disadvantages of the knowledge mapping technique for knowledge management are discussed. The chapter concludes with a series of quality criteria for knowledge maps and proposes a five step procedure to implement knowledge maps in a corporate intranet.

Keywords: Knowledge Management; Knowledge Maps; Mapping Techniques; Intranet

1 The Rationale for Knowledge Mapping

A major weakness of the knowledge management domain, as it is discussed today in the business and research communities, is the apparent lack of genuinely new and effective instruments and methods for improving the way individuals, teams, and organizations create, share and apply knowledge (in the sense of the know-how, know-what, know-who, and know-why that individuals use to solve problems; for this distinction see also Quinn et al., 1996). In 1996, Davenport, Jarven-paa, and Beers argued that knowledge work processes often lack adequate support by information technology tools. This analysis still holds true to a large degree today (Davenport et al., 1996). In contrast, this chapter views knowledge management, not only as a new perspective on information management problems, but as a field that can provide new ways of improving knowledge-intensive processes (such as market research, consulting, or product development). It can do so by going beyond the mere administration of electronic information and help individuals make information actionable in new contexts, connect it with previous experiences, identify relevant experts, and enable organization-wide learning processes. Knowledge maps, as is shown below, serve exactly this purpose.

Having said that this chapter discusses a new, genuine type of knowledge management tool, one must admit that the terms knowledge map, knowledge cartography, or knowledge landscape are relatively new labels for an idea that is rather old. This idea consists of representing our vital environment in a graphic way to improve our actions within this territory. The environment or territory in the context of knowledge management is not geographic, however, but intellectual. By constructing a visual knowledge architecture, it should become possible to examine the knowledge we depend upon on a global scale and from different perspectives. Thus, a knowledge map should assist an individual employee, a team, or an organizational unit in understanding and using the knowledge available in an organizational setting. The intellectual environment that is mapped through this tool is mostly made up of referenced expertise, documented experiences, and extracted and formalized processes or procedures. It contains heuristic knowledge (know-how) in the form of people (experts), processes (e.g., complex workflows), and applications; rationales or experiences (know-why) in the form of lessons learned or project debriefings; and factual knowledge (know-what) in the form of documents or database entries which in turn can be linked to authors who can be asked for advice, assistance, or a clarification of their documented findings.

While the basic idea behind a knowledge map – to construct a global architecture of a knowledge domain – might be quite old, the application context (e.g., the corporation) and the format, as an intranet hypertext clickable map, are quite new. The reasons why knowledge maps are now viewed as a necessary tool in a corporate context are mainly the global scope of expertise that resides within larger companies and the difficulty of accessing this expertise through informal communication.

Today, these problems can be effectively resolved with the help of knowledge maps. They not only make expertise accessible through visual interfaces, but also provide a common framework or context to which the employees of a company can relate to in their search for (or contribution of) relevant knowledge. As Fahey and Prusak (1998) stress in their analysis of common mistakes in knowledge management projects, a prime goal of any knowledge management initiative should be to create a common context for the employees. Knowledge maps provide this common context in an explicit common visual model.

The technology that enables this kind of tool are intranet-based software solutions such as Lotus Development's Raven, Autonomy's Knowledge Visualizer (this tool can be used to generate ad-hoc knowledge source maps, see www.autonomy.com.), Microsoft's Visio, or IBM's KnowledgeX. All of these software tools combine powerful visualization techniques with database functionalities. Yet, while the technological implementation of a knowledge map with the help of one of these tools (or with simpler means such as DHTML/JavaScript or XML) leads, as shown below, to useful knowledge artifacts, the process of creating a knowledge map is almost as important as the final product itself.

We shall see that the technological implementation is only half of the challenge of developing and using knowledge maps in organizational knowledge management. The other even more challenging task consists of gathering the right reference information and combining it in a framework to which everybody can relate. Thus, the mapping process itself can already provide a number of insights into the knowledge assets of a company and its problems in allocating knowledge effectively. A knowledge asset in this context is any explicitly qualified source of knowledge that provides potential benefits for the solution of problems relevant to a company's success.

In our work with an intranet-based knowledge map for a market research company, for example, we conducted 35 interviews to gather the relevant knowledge we needed to create a knowledge map of the company's methodological skills. These interviews not only provided the necessary background information for the knowledge map, but also revealed a great deal about the structural improvement areas of the company. Thus, Galloway (1994, p. vii) is right in concluding the following about mapping: "Mapping is merely an enabler – a means to a more important end. It is a vehicle for expressing and releasing the knowledge, creativity, and energy that lies within every group, regardless of its position or level within an organization." For a similar conclusion see the mapping examples provided by Huff (1990) or the argumentation offered by Rhodes (1994).

In this chapter, we give examples of various types of such knowledge enablers and describe the process we followed to produce them. We do so by first outlining the five types of knowledge maps we have found useful in a corporate context. We then provide examples of such maps and assess their advantages and disadvantages (if used on a corporate intranet). Based on these insights, we outline a five-step procedure to generate a high-quality knowledge map.

2   The Concept of a Knowledge Map

A knowledge map, as it is understood in this chapter, generally consists of two parts: a ground layer that represents the context for the mapping, and the individual elements that are mapped within this context. The ground layer typically consists of the mutual context that all employees can understand and relate to. Such a context might be the visualized business model of a company (e.g., the lending business model of a bank), the actual product (e.g., a vehicle model in the case of a truck company), the competency areas of a company (as in the example of the multimedia company in section 3 below), the value chain of a firm (as in the example of the market research group below), or a simple geographic map. The elements that are mapped onto such a shared context range from experts, project teams, or communities of practice to more explicit and codified forms of knowledge such as white papers or articles, patents, lessons learned (e.g., after action reviews or project debriefings), events (i.e., meeting protocols), databases or similar applications, such as expert systems or simulations. Knowledge maps group these elements to show their relationships, locations, and qualities.

In this paper, we refer to knowledge maps as graphic directories of knowledge-sources (i.e., experts), -assets (i.e., core competencies), -structures (i.e., skill domains), -applications (i.e. specific contexts in which knowledge has to be applied, such as a process), or -development stages (phases of knowledge development or learning paths). We focus on these five types of maps as they answer the questions that came up most frequently in our action research with six companies over the course of two years. These questions were: how do I find relevant knowledge, how can I judge its quality, how can I make sense of its structure, and how do I go about applying or developing it myself?

A different, more abstract set of map categories is used by Huff in her anthology on the topic of mapping strategic thought. Her mapping typology focuses on cognitive maps and distinguishes the following map types: text and language analysis maps, classification maps, network maps, conclusive maps, and schematic maps of cognitive structures (Huff, 1990).

Many definitions of knowledge maps that we have found in the descriptions of company projects or in academic papers are similar, but less specific. Vail (1999, p. 10), for example, defines a knowledge map as follows:

"A knowledge map is a visual display of captured information and relationships, which enables the efficient communication and learning of knowledge by observers with differing backgrounds at multiple levels of detail. The individual items of knowledge included in such a map can be text, stories, graphics, models, or numbers ... Knowledge mapping is defined as the process of associating items of information or knowledge (preferably visually) in such a way that the mapping itself also creates additional knowledge."

While this definition adequately describes the purpose of knowledge mapping, it does not distinguish the various types of knowledge maps that can be used in a corporate context. Below we provide such a distinction with the aforementioned five types of knowledge maps:

1. **Knowledge source maps**: These maps structure a population of company experts along relevant search criteria, such as their domains of expertise, proximity (for an example of such a knowledge map, without hypertext links behind the map however, see Morrs et al. (1996)), seniority, or regional distribution. Knowledge source maps answer questions such as "where can I find somebody who knows how to calculate a company valuation" or "do we have people who have run large e-commerce projects?"

2. **Knowledge asset maps**: This type of map visually qualifies the existing stock of knowledge of an individual, a team, a unit, or a whole organization. It provides a simplified, graphic 'balance sheet' of a company's intellectual capital. Knowledge asset maps answer questions such as "how many SAP-consultants do we have, and how many SAP-projects have we completed?" or "how many of our software engineers have been with the company for more than five years?"

3. **Knowledge structure maps**: These maps outline the global architecture of a knowledge domain and how its parts relate to one another (for examples of this type of map, see Mok (1996) or Horn (1989)). This type of knowledge map assists the manager in comprehending and interpreting an expert domain. Typical questions that can be answered by such a map are "which are the skills needed to run a project, how do they relate to one another, and what are the available courses for every such skill?"

4. **Knowledge application maps**: These maps show which type of knowledge has to be applied at a certain process stage or in a specific business situation. Usually, these maps also provide pointers to locate that specific knowledge (documents, specialists, databases). Knowledge application

maps answer questions of people who are involved in a knowledge-intensive process, such as auditing, consulting, research, or product development. They provide answers to questions such as "who do I talk to if the market tests are inconclusive?" or "what are our experiences in moving from a prototype to mass-production?"

5. **Knowledge development maps**: These diagrams can be used to depict the necessary stages to develop a certain competence, either individually, as a team, or as an organizational entity. These maps can serve as visualized learning or development roadmaps that provide a common corporate vision for organizational learning. They answer questions such as "how do we achieve business excellence for our unit?" or "how can we prepare our unit (intellectually) for the entry into a new market?" We have also used this type of map to visualize the necessary steps to develop e-commerce competence (from mere web designing skills, to community development skills, to secure electronic contracting skills, to inter-business networking skills).

Besides these five types of maps, one can also imagine maps that combine some of the above types into a single map. Typically, a knowledge application map and a (partial) knowledge source map are combined into a single image. In this way, one can not only show what knowledge is relevant at what project stage, but also how to locate that knowledge.

There are numerous visualization techniques that can be used to design such knowledge maps. They include, but are not limited to, the methods identified in Table 1.

Table 1. Mapping Techniques for the Knowledge Map Context

Simple Mapping Techniques	Complex Mapping Techniques
Mind mapping	Concept maps
Clustering	Cause maps
Matrices or portfolio diagrams	Concentric circles or Venn diagrams
Fishbone graphs	Metaphoric maps (e.g., a house, a balance, a compass, or a park)
Cartesian and polar co-ordinate systems	Process charts or flow charts
Pyramids	Spider web graphs
Hierarchic trees	Decision trees
Geographic maps	3D-environments (e.g., globes, landscapes)

The choice of one of these techniques depends upon two factors. First, there are requirements of the conceptual framework that provides the base layer for the knowledge map (flow charts are feasible techniques for knowledge application maps, while concept maps are more apt for knowledge structure maps). Second, there are the technological infrastructure and software available to implement a clickable map. There are numerous software packages that support hypertext mind-maps, concept maps, or interactive flow charts, yet very few products that support more complex forms of knowledge maps such as metaphoric maps or 3D-environments.

The following section examines a number of examples of how these visualization techniques can be used to design knowledge maps of the five mentioned types.

3   Intranet Knowledge Map Examples

The following series of knowledge maps is a result of our action research with six partner companies over the course of three years (1998-2001). All examples represent manually generated and designed maps. Automatically generated maps also exist, but are not discussed in this context.

3.1 Knowledge Source Map

In principle, a knowledge map can be implemented on any technological platform that allows us to combine visualization engines with hypertext capability (i.e., linking sensitive, visual zones to other data points) and database technology. Nevertheless, we have found the intranet to be the most accessible medium to host knowledge map applications. This is especially true because many intranet users are familiar with clickable maps or touch-sensitive visual zones from the Internet. Hence, the user-acceptance of a knowledge map in a browser interface is likely to be higher than in a proprietary application. The first example of an intranet-based knowledge map is taken from a multimedia company that mainly works in the development of web-sites, CD-ROMs, and stand-alone multimedia terminals. One of the company's problems is the adequate staffing of such projects with the right experts.

Thus, a knowledge map was designed to help project leaders and human resources professionals to assess the current state of experts available within the company at its three main locations (New York, Berlin, Basel).

The map divides the company's competence into five areas, namely graphic design, animation (i.e., shockwave programming), database design, project management, and technology know-how (i.e. server administration). The people within the company apply these skills to the aforementioned three areas of CD-ROM production, stand-alone systems, and Web site development (the concentric circles in Figure 1).

The partial view of the actual map below reveals that the most expertise resides in the company's headquarter in Berlin (color-coded accordingly), especially for the domain of web-site development. It also reveals that there are very few project management or animation specialists within the company. The map reflects the shift in activities away from CD-ROM production to Web development where most experts in the map below apply their skills.

The technology behind this map is quite simple and consists of three elements: the actual knowledge map which is drawn in Microsoft Visio and linked to an Access database that holds the expert profiles (expert area, application area, location, phone number, etc.) and a CGI-script that provides a browser interface for the map. The experts update their profiles via a form that they can access through their browser. This form is directly linked to the Access database (which in turn is referenced in the Visio chart).

While this particular map is still in the testing phase, an identical application with the same architecture and map design has already been used for several months in a semiconductor company where it is also used to map specialized communities of practice.

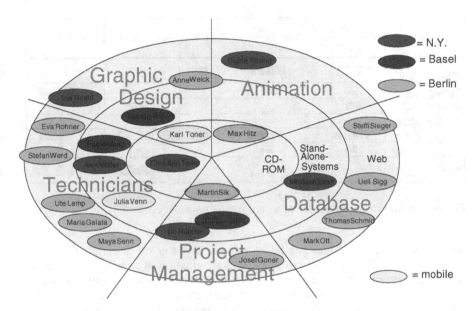

Figure 1. A Knowledge Source Map for a Multimedia Company (excerpt)

3.2   Knowledge Asset Map

Knowledge asset maps provide a visual balance sheet of a company's capabilities. These capabilities can be represented in the form of a core competency tree or as a visual directory of individual or aggregated skills of the work force. For a depiction of a core competence tree see (Prahalad and Hamel, 1990). Based on such a map, a company can outline its capability profile bottom-up instead of top-down (as in a core competence tree). The following simple map provides an overview of a consulting team in terms of the competencies of its members. Large blocks represent expert knowledge on the particular topic, small blocks refer to basic knowledge in a particular domain. The domains in which these consultants work are IT (information technology), strategy, mergers and acquisitions (M&A), accounting and marketing.

The knowledge asset map in Figure 2 illustrates various properties of the know-how constellation of the consulting staff. The map reveals, for example, that Andi Ehrler is a central asset for the company in terms of his skills (he is also the practice leader for accounting as the shaded block in that column indicates). He has substantial experience in all five sectors of the consulting activities. The map also reveals that there is a general lack of specialized knowledge in the domain of mergers and acquisitions. Thus, it might be advantageous to drop this consulting service in the future. The map furthermore reveals training and personnel development needs. It shows clearly that Carl Brenner has not yet been able to gather an expert status in any of the five domains. The future staffing decisions need to take this fact into account.

Consultants	IT	Strategy	M&A	Accounting	Marketing
Tinner, Jeff	▬	▬	▪		
Borer, André		▪			▬
Brenner, Carl	▪			▬	
Deller, Max					▬
Ehrler, Andi	▬	▬	▪	▬	▬
Gross, Peter	▪	▪			▪
. . .				▬	▬

Figure 2. A Knowledge Asset Map of a Consulting Company (excerpt)

Such a knowledge asset map can be valuable to plan the allocation of staff members or their training needs or assess the overall situation of a company's intellectual assets. By clicking on a name, further information on the consultant is provided (such as e-mail, location, special interests, etc.). By clicking on a block, the map reveals the projects and courses that the consultant has completed in the particular field.

A similar version of this map has been implemented two years ago in a telecom consulting company. According to the head of operations, it has proved especially useful for the planning of training activities and for emergency cases where experts have to be identified quickly.

3.3   Knowledge Structure Map

As mentioned earlier, knowledge structure maps divide a skill domain into logical blocks. The map in Figure 3 shows that a Web publisher requires three levels of know-how. First, basic editing knowledge is needed, which consists of layout and sequencing skills, as well as the content selection for an Internet site, plus an adequate vocabulary and writing style for its communication. Secondly, the publisher or editor requires knowledge on how to design the interactive environment for the pages he or she generated. Lastly, the Web site designer needs to know the relevant HTML or Java codes (Web programming languages) to make the site look attractive and implement adequate security measures.

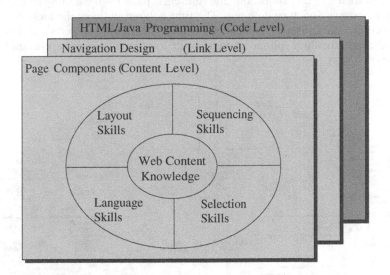

Figure 3. A Knowledge Structure Map for the Internet Authoring Context

Other examples of knowledge structure maps can be found in product development (where the various engineering, marketing, and management capabilities are mapped around a product or process), project management (where the various skills that are required to manage a project are mapped in a framework that shows which skills serve what purpose in the course of a project), or financial engineering (where the inter-relationship of insurance skills and banking skills are mapped out).

3.4 Knowledge Application Map

The knowledge application map is probably the most frequently used knowledge mapping format today. It outlines which knowledge is required at a certain process step, e.g., in the value chain of a company. In the example below, the value chain of market research company is divided into four processes: acquiring or generating data, transforming it into information by analyzing it, administrating and archiving this information, and transforming it into knowledge by educating its clients about its findings.

In every process step, various IT-based tools and conceptual methods can be applied. If an employee is interested in one of these (approx. seventy) instruments, he can simply click at the name of a tool or method and a short description of the tool, its application context, functioning and contact person (as well as a rating of the tool or method by the corresponding specialist) will appear on the screen.

Figure 4 shows the actual map (with the exception of the terms translated into English) that is currently installed in the knowledge portal of the company's intranet. Underlined methods or tools are also sold as products to clients. Every term in the map is linked to an explication- and reference-page for the corresponding tool. This page consists of three columns. The first column outlines the tools title, the second column describes its application context, functioning, experts and their rating of the tool, the third column provides links to related tools or to relevant Internet sites.

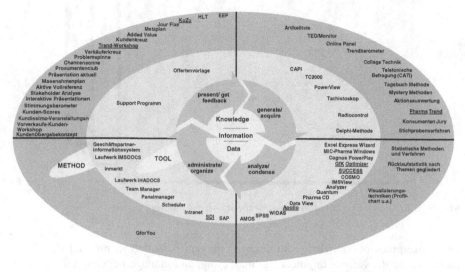

Figure 4. A Knowledge Application Map of a Market Research Company

3.5 Knowledge Development Map

The last type of knowledge map can be used to visualize the necessary steps to develop a certain type of competence. The relevant knowledge is mapped at various (sequential) levels. By clicking on a certain level of knowledge, the map reveals further details and describes the necessary activities to acquire or develop that competence. The example shown in Figure 5 is taken from an e-business context.

The map can be used to illustrate the necessary steps to develop competence in e-commerce passing through various stages from a mere web-presence that only provides on-line information, to more complex sites that offer community functionalities (e.g., forums, mailing lists, polls, etc.) or full scale e-business sites that include payment services. The map in its current form is not yet hypertext-based. Hence, the mapped steps cannot be "zoomed in" on the corporate intranet.

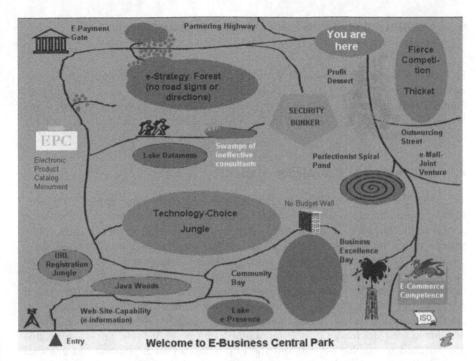

Figure 5. A Knowledge Development Map for E-Business Competence

3.6 Purposes of the Maps

In summary, these examples illustrate that knowledge maps can serve the following five purposes:

1. They increase the visibility of knowledge sources and hence facilitate and accelerate the process of locating relevant expertise or experience.
2. They improve the evaluation of intellectual assets (and liabilities) in a corporation.
3. They assist employees in interpreting and evaluating knowledge domains.
4. They connect processes with knowledge sources (and thus go beyond the mere documentation of a process as found in most quality manuals).
5. They sketch the necessary steps for knowledge development in a certain area.

Having outlined the various functions of knowledge maps, we will now examine their possible disadvantages and advantages in more detail, before outlining a five-step procedure to implement a knowledge map.

4   Evaluation of Knowledge Mapping: Advantages and Disadvantages

Knowledge maps are one possible way to improve the knowledge transfer and utilization in a company (other ways include yellow pages type expert directories, communities of practice, or knowledge fairs). Associated with this way are various advantages and disadvantages that one has to take into account in a knowledge mapping project.

4.1   Advantages of Knowledge Maps

The general advantages of knowledge maps should have become apparent by now. First, they render corporate knowledge assets visible for all employees that have access to the Intranet. Thus, they provide a systematic context for the retrieval of reference information. Second, they can connect experts with each other or help novices or rookies identify experts quickly. As a consequence, knowledge maps can speed up the information seeking process and facilitate systematic knowledge development since they connect insights with tasks and problems. Another central advantage of knowledge maps is their potential to make implicit knowledge explicit through the use of visual metaphors and symbols. For illustrations of this advantage see (Sparrow, 1998). From a marketing point of view, knowledge maps can be used to emphasize and sell the competencies of a company to external groups (e.g., potential clients, potential employees, shareholders, analysts etc.).

In summary one can say that knowledge maps can help employees and clients remember, comprehend, and relate knowledge domains through the insightful visualization and aggregation of information about the company's experiences, skills, or intellectual resources in general. To clarify this advantage, which is a direct result of the visualization techniques used in knowledge mapping, we can rely on the following explanation by hypertext cartography expert Michael P. Peterson (1995, p. 34):

"Firstly, a diagram offers a synoptic, global representation of structure or a process and this contributes to the globality and the immediacy of understanding. Secondly, a diagram is an ideal tool for bridging between a conceptual interpretation and the practical expression of a certain reality. A diagram is a synthesis between these two apparently opposed types of representations – the symbolic and the iconic. Diagrams are not, generally, the direct image of a certain reality. It is the figural expression of an already elaborated conceptual structure, like any other symbolic system."

Although a knowledge map uses these two features of a diagram – global understanding and conceptual representation of reality – it is more than just a diagrammatic representation. A knowledge map is more than a simple diagram because it offers more dimensions and richer semantics than a diagram. Specifically it offers more elements that are relevant to solve a problem than a diagram, such as time, location, quality levels, relationships, and time aspects. Unlike a diagram it is not inert and finished, but interactive and expandable.

In addition knowledge maps make extensive use of metaphors (such as mountains, layers, routes, or buildings). Finally, a map also shows pathways and options and can relate to other maps (e.g., via embedded hypertext links).

A knowledge map is therefore more similar to a geographic map than a diagram. It answers the same basic four questions that a geographic map seeks to answer, namely:

1. Where am I, what is my context (environment)?
2. Where can I go, what are my options?
3. How do I get there quickly, and in the most direct way possible?
4. What does it take to get there; what are the required resources?

In consequence, a knowledge map provides systematic orientation in the intellectual territory of a company and helps to find directions, assess situations, or plan resources. For further advantages, see (Wexler, 2001, p. 260).

4.2 Disadvantages of Knowledge Maps

As with geographic maps, which still many people find difficult to comprehend or use, knowledge maps also have certain disadvantages. The disadvantages associated with this method of conveying knowledge are summarized in Table 2. It shows that there are several potential drawbacks from knowledge maps for map users and for map designers. The dangers of using a knowledge map may result from the direct legitimate use of a low-quality map, such as misinterpreting it or using an outdated or overloaded map. They may also result from an illegitimate use of the map by headhunters, competitors or competitive intelligence professionals who abuse the map for purposes that were not intended by management. The drawbacks for map designers are mainly the costs of creation, design and maintenance.

Table 2. Disadvantages of Knowledge Maps

Disadvantages for Map Users	Disadvantages for Map Designers
• the potential harmful effects if the map is seen by illegitimate users (such as head hunters or competitors) • the danger of misinterpretation • the fixation or 'reification' of one frame of reference (i.e., the layout of the knowledge map) • the danger of information overload if the map represents too many elements or dimensions of a knowledge area • the danger of using an outdated map	• the commitment to one scheme of order and neglect of other perspectives • the difficult depiction of dynamic processes • the relatively high costs for production and updating • the missing quantification of inter-dependencies • the reduction of complex structures to graphic symbols • the difficult and time-consuming task of ergonomic visualization

These numerous potential disadvantages have to be weighed against the benefits that result from establishing a knowledge map. In the following section, we propose an implementation process and accompanying quality criteria to avoid this extensive list of disadvantages.

5   Implementation and Quality Control

To construct and design a knowledge map that avoids the aforementioned disadvantages, the following five steps need to be sequentially completed:

1. Identify knowledge intensive processes, problems, or issues within the organization. The resulting map should focus on improving such knowledge intensive areas. This step typically involves a screening of a company's value chain or main processes and various interviews with key employees (involved in knowledge-intensive business activities).
2. Deduce the relevant knowledge sources, assets, or elements from the above process or problem. The question which needs be answered at this point is: "In order to manage the process or area well, what expertise and what experience is needed or helpful, and where and how can one access that knowledge?"
3. Codify these elements in a way that makes them more accessible to the organization as a whole. Build categories of expertise that are relevant to the process or area identified in step one. If the process is, for example, project management, possible categories might be experts on project planning, controlling, project documentation, or experts in IT-support for project management.
4. Integrate this codified reference information (i.e., the different types of project management specialists or resources) on expertise or documents into a visual interface that allows the user to navigate or search visually. Connect this navigation system to the process or working environment itself (integrate it into the workflow of the process or the homepage of an organizational unit). This step involves the actual design and implementation of the knowledge map. Here, a specific visualization technique has to be chosen that best fits the objective of the map. Knowledge application maps, for example, are usually best visualized with process flow maps or decision trees.
5. Provide means of updating the knowledge map. A knowledge map is only as good as the links it provides. If these links are outdated or obsolete, the map is useless. Therefore, a map needs to be continuously updated by the 'map maker' or the people who are represented in it. This step may involve designing an automatic workflow that regularly asks experts to update their position in a knowledge map.

These five steps provide a generic sequence of activities to establish a knowledge map. In all of these steps, one has to be aware of the quality of the final map. In our experience in implementing three such maps, the last step is often the most difficult and crucial one in order to assure the quality of a knowledge map. Hence, it makes sense to define a set of quality criteria for the resulting map at the very beginning of the mapping process in order to prevent quality issues in step five. Vail (1999, p.14) distinguishes the following quality criteria for knowledge maps:

- participative: the mapping team creates the map interactively and involves as many employees as possible,
- shared: the map represents a truly shared model that all knowledge workers can relate to,
- synergistic: the experts all contribute their different expertise to the map, in order to generate one logical and comprehensive picture,
- systemic: the map's elements can be combined logically to an integrated whole,
- simple: the map can be overlooked at one glance,
- visual: the map uses a visual framework that is made up of iconic elements,
- information rich: the map is informative in the sense that it aggregates a great amount of noteworthy references that help in the problem solving process.

Table 3. Knowledge Map Quality Criteria

Knowledge Map Quality Dimensions	Review Questions
1. Functional map quality	• Does the map serve an explicit purpose for a specific target user group? • Is there an implemented process to update and review the knowledge map periodically? • Is there a feedback mechanism through which users can suggest improvements to the map?
2. Cognitive map quality	• Can the map be grasped at one glance (not overloaded)? • Does it offer various levels of detail? • Does it allow to compare elements visually? • Are all elements clearly discernible?
3. Technical map quality	• Is the access time sufficient (no time lags)? • Can the map be used with a browser-interface? • Does the map appear legibly on various screen resolutions? • Is the map securely protected against unauthorized access?
4. Aesthetic map quality	• Is the map pleasing to the eye (adequate color and geometric form combinations)? • Can the map's visual identity be kept when new elements are added (map scalability)?

These criteria already provide some guidance in gathering the elements and designing the framework for a knowledge map. When completed, we suggest that the map be again reviewed in terms of the quality criteria identified in Table 3, which furnishes a concise checklist that can be further elaborated according to an organization's standards and policies.

If these criteria are met, an intranet knowledge map may well become one of the killer-applications of a corporate intranet, because it provides a quick and comprehensive overview of a company's intellectual assets.

6   Conclusion

Knowledge maps provide a visual orientation for managers or specialists who wish to locate, evaluate or develop knowledge in an organizational context. They condense information about knowledge sources, assets, structures, applications, or development needs in an accessible way. As Wurman (1990) points out, the creative organization of such information can create new information and insights. Each way that one organizes information can create new knowledge and understanding. This new understanding results from the organizational context that knowledge maps can provide. Nevertheless, knowledge maps have not yet lived up to their potential in the corporate world.

Management literature on the topic has still only a few success stories to illustrate the potential of such maps, such as the Swiss pharmaceutical company Hoffmann-La Roche where a comprehensive knowledge map was used to improve the (knowledge-intensive) new drug approval process and hence improve the time-to-market of new products. For a depiction of this map, see (Wurman, 1996, p.172). However, with the rapid development of intranet technology and its potential to combine appealing visual interfaces with database applications, knowledge maps may soon prove to be a standard element in any company's knowledge management repertoire.

References

Davenport, T.H, S. L. Jarvenpaa, and M.C. Beers, "Improving Knowledge Work Processes", *Sloan Management Review*, 37, 4, 1996, 53-65.

Fahey, L. and L. Prusak, "The Eleven Deadliest Sins of Knowledge Management", *California Management Review*, 40, 3, 1998, 265-276.

Galloway, D., *Mapping Work Processes*, Milwaukee: ASQC Quality Press, 1994.

Horn, R., *Mapping Hypertext, Analysis, Linkage, and Display of Knowledge for the Next Generation of On-Line Text and Graphics*, Waltham: The Lexington Institute, 1989.

Huff, A.(Ed.), *Mapping Strategic Thought*, New York: Wiley. 1990.

Morris, S., J. Meed, and N. Svensen, *The Intelligent Manager, Adding Value in The Information Age*, London: Pitman Publishing, 1996.

Mok, C., *Designing Business, Multiple Media, Multiple Disciplines*, San Jose: Adobe Press, 1996.

Prahalad, C.K. and G. Hamel, "The Core Competence of the Corporation", *Harvard Business Review*, 68: 3, 1990, 79-91.

Peterson, M.P., *Interactive and Animated Cartography*, New Jersey: Prentice Hall, 1995.

Quinn, J.B., P. Anderson, and S. Finkelstein, "Managing Professional Intellect: Making the Most of the Best," *Harvard Business Review*, March-April, 1996, 71-80.

Rhodes, J., *Conceptual Toolmaking, Expert Systems of the Mind*, Oxford: Blackwell Publishers, 1994.

Sparrow, H., *Knowledge in Organizations*, Thousand Oakes: Sage, 1998.

Vail, E.F., "Mapping Organizational Knowledge," *Knowledge Management Review*, Issue 8, May/June, 1999, 10-15.

Wexler, M.N., "The Who, What and Why of Knowledge Mapping," *Journal of Knowledge Management*, 5, 3, 2001, 249-263.

Wurman, R.S., *Information Architects*, Zurich: Graphis, 1996.

Wurman, R.S., *Information Anxiety, What to Do When Information Doesn't Tell You What You Need to Know*, New York: Bantam Books, 1990.

CHAPTER 11

Organizational Memory

Murray E. Jennex[1] and Lorne Olfman[2]

[1] Information Decision Science Department, College of Business Administration, San Diego State University, San Diego, CA, USA

[2] School of Information Science, Claremont Graduate University, Claremont, CA, USA

Organizations create and use knowledge and information. To facilitate the use of knowledge and information, organizations are building and using organizational memory systems. These systems provide processes for capturing, searching, and retrieving knowledge and information. This chapter discusses what organizational memory is, how it relates to organizational learning and knowledge, what an organizational memory system is, how to design these systems, and how to manage organizational memory.

Keywords: Organizational Memory; Organizational Learning; Knowledge; Knowledge Management

1 Introduction

An engineer receives a problem report that a pump is making more noise than usual. While searching the pump's maintenance history a problem investigation analysis is found for a similar situation. The analysis states that under certain loads, alignments, and plant conditions, the pump will exhibit a change in its noise profile but suffers no change in its performance. The engineer verifies that the conditions mentioned in the analysis currently exist and notifies the plant operators that this is a known phenomenon and no corrective action is needed.

The above scenario describes an engineer acting within the norms and standard procedures of the organization and using information from a previous activity to solve a current problem. It demonstrates the benefit and promise of Organizational Memory (OM). However, not all work practices are as simple, as the following scenario illustrates:

Engineer A receives a problem report that there are leaking tubes in a heat exchanger. The leaks are not large so the engineer has them plugged per standard operating procedures for small leaks. A couple of months later the plugged tubes rupture, severely damaging several adjacent tubes and resulting in costly repairs and down time. During subsequent investigation it is found that a similar heat exchanger experienced tube failures in the same region of the tube bundle as the failed heat exchanger. In that case, the tube failures were attributed to flow induced vibration and were fixed by rodding and plugging the tubes susceptible to this failure mechanism. When the current heat exchanger was analyzed, it was found that the ruptured tube also was caused by flow induced vibration. Because the heat exchangers were of different manufacture, a computer-based search on problem reports done by Engineer A failed to relate the current event to the earlier one. Engineer B, who identified the original flow induced vibration failure, sat in the cubicle adjacent to Engineer A. However, he was not informed of the current problem so he offered no advice or experience to his colleague. The subsequent investigation also found that if Engineer A had not followed standard practice he would have been more likely to identify the actual problem.

This scenario illustrates problems with OM. Three issues stand out. First, Engineer A acted within the norms of his organization's culture by following standard procedures and actions for a routine problem when actually a non-routine problem had been found. Second, the engineer was unable to locate and use related information. Third, there was a failure of communication between coworkers that could have uncovered relevant information.

Both scenarios illustrate why there is interest in OM, and some of the problems with regard to managing and using OM. When used well, as illustrated by the first example, OM has the capability to improve organizational performance. When used poorly, as illustrated by the second example where a routine solution was applied to a non-routine problem, OM has the capability of damaging organizational performance far worse than if OM had not been used at all.

This chapter explores managing and using Organizational Memory. The first section defines OM and discusses its relationship to Organizational Learning and Organizational Knowledge. The second section outlines how and where OM is stored. This is followed by a description of an organizational memory system (OMS) and a discussion of how such a system can be effective. These discussions form the foundation for a section on managing OM and OMS. The chapter concludes with a mini-case study on the OMS at a nuclear plant.

2   Definition of Organizational Memory

2.1   What Is Organizational Memory?

No single accepted definition of OM exists. Huber, Davenport, and King (1998) summarize OM as being the set of repositories of information and knowledge that the organization has acquired and retains. Stein and Zwass (1995) define OM as the means whereby knowledge from the past is brought to bear on present activities resulting in higher or lower levels of organizational effectiveness. Walsh and Ungson (1991) define OM as stored information from an organization's history that can be brought to bear on present decisions. This chapter uses the Stein and Zwass definition with the repositories from Huber, Davenport, and King. OM is seen to have two principle goals: to integrate information across organizational boundaries and to control current activities and thus avoid past mistakes. Basic functions of OM are perception, acquisition, abstraction, recording, storage, retrieval, interpretation, and transmission of organizational knowledge (Stein and Zwass 1995). Walsh and Ungson (1991) propose that organizational memory consists of five retention facilities: individuals, culture, transformations, structures, and ecology.

OM can be viewed as abstract or concrete. It is comprised of unstructured concepts and information that exist in the organization's culture and the minds of its members, and can be partially represented by concrete/physical memory aids such as databases. It is also comprised of structured concepts and information that can be exactly represented by computerized records and files. Sandoe and Olfman (1992) and Morrison (1997) describe these two forms of OM as having two functions, representation and interpretation, as shown in Table 1. Representation presents just the facts (or knowledge or expertise) for a given context or situation. Interpretation promotes adaptation and learning by providing frames of reference, procedures, guidelines, or a means to synthesize past information for application to new situations.

Table 1. Forms and Functions of Organizational Memory

	REPRESENTATION FUNCTION	INTERPRETATION FUNCTION
CONCRETE FORM	data documents and hypertext formalized knowledge formalized expertise frameworks information	organizational device policies standard operating procedures
ABSTRACT FORM	cognitive maps conceptual lenses frameworks	culture ecology language social structures

This discussion suggests that learning and knowledge are associated with OM. They also provide insight into the content and repository perspectives of OM. The content perspective focuses on the information and knowledge that is captured and the context in which it is used. The repository perspective focuses on where and how information and knowledge is stored and retrieved. Both perspectives are relevant to this chapter. As such, we further define organizational learning and knowledge in the following sections.

2.2 Organizational Learning

Malhotra (1996) defines Organizational Learning (OL) as the process of detection and correction of errors. In this view, organizations learn through individuals acting as agents for them. Individual learning activities are seen as being facilitated or inhibited by an ecological system of factors that may be called an organizational learning system. Learning in this perspective is based on Kolb's (1984) model of experiential learning where individuals learn by doing.

Huber, Davenport, and King (1998) believe an organization learns if, through its processing of information, its potential behaviors are changed. Huysman, Fischer, and Heng (1994) as well as Walsh and Ungson (1991) believe organizational learning has OM as a component. In this view, OL is the process whereby experience is used to modify current and future actions. Huber (1991) considers four constructs as integrally linked to OL: knowledge acquisition, information distribution, information interpretation, and organizational memory. In this case, OM is the repository of knowledge and information acquired by the organization. Organizational Learning uses OM as its knowledge base.

A different perspective on organizational learning from Sandoe, et. al. (1998) is that organizations do not learn, rather only individuals learn. During work, people gain experience, observe, and reflect in making sense of what they are doing. As they analyze these experiences into general abstractions, their perceptions on how work should be done changes. As these individuals influence their co-workers, the "organization" learns and the process is gradually changed. Learning in this perspective is also based on Kolb's (1984) model of experiential learning.

To summarize, Organizational Learning is the process whereby an organization assimilates experiences of its members and uses that experience to modify the organization's potential actions. Whether the actual organization learns or only its members learn and then share their learning with other members is not important. In both cases, OM is necessary to facilitate the processing and retention of information and knowledge needed for learning to take place.

2.3 Organizational Knowledge

Davenport and Prusak (1998) view knowledge as an evolving mix of framed experience, values, contextual information, and expert insight that provides a framework for evaluating and incorporating new experiences and information. They found that in organizations, knowledge often becomes embedded in documents or repositories and in organizational routines, processes, practices, and norms. Nonaka (1994) expands this view by stating that knowledge is about meaning in the sense that it is context-specific. This implies that users of knowledge must understand the context in which it is generated and used for it to have meaning to them. This also implies that for a knowledge repository to be useful it must also store the context in which the knowledge was generated. That knowledge is context specific argues against the idea that knowledge can be applied universally, however it does not argue against the concept of organizational knowledge. This chapter considers organizational knowledge to be an integral component of what organizational members remember and use. Comparing to the definition of OM, it is obvious that knowledge and OM are related through experience and learning. This chapter also considers knowledge to be a subset of OM. This implies that the processes of knowledge management are also a subset of OM processes.

2.4 Summary

OM is characterized as the data, information, and knowledge captured by an organization in accessible repositories. These repositories consist of people, culture, documents, and computers. The use of captured data, information, and knowledge results in learning that may take place by individuals and/or an organization. It is generally expected that learning will improve organizational effectiveness but it is possible that organizations can learn incorrect behaviors. When this happens, use of OM can result in incorrect actions being performed, such as in the second scenario at the start of this chapter.

3   Repositories of Organizational Memory

3.1 Functions of Repositories

The function of OM repositories is to store captured OM in forms that can be retrieved and applied. OM is created as a result of individual and/or organizational activities and learning. As individuals and organizations learn they modify their potential actions through capturing and applying experience. Capturing experience involves two types of information and knowledge. The first is the capturing of structured, concrete information and knowledge in databases, documents, and artifacts. Individuals do this through the filing of reports, updating of records, changing of procedures, modification of work processes, and/or learning. The second involves capturing unstructured, abstract information and knowledge. This is more difficult because records, files, and databases can only capture representations of this information and knowledge. For this type individuals act as the method of capturing the information and knowledge as they can synthesize it into their internal base knowledge and apply it to actions such as changing procedures and work processes.

OM can be applied to situations, leading to modifying the actions that would have been taken. Application of structured, concrete information and knowledge involves implementing modified procedures and work practices and utilizing OM to solve or resolve applicable problems or situations. Application of unstructured, abstract information and knowledge involves the individuals retaining the information and knowledge with respect to applicable situations and/or problems and applying them to similar situations or problems. In both cases, as the information and knowledge are applied over time, the organization's culture changes to reflect its use. In short, change takes time because organizational members need to reach a consensus that the changed organizational actions, norms, or values are appropriate and acceptable to the organization. Consensus making is time consuming. Sandoe, et. al. (1998) discuss this aspect of change in detail.

3.2   Types of OM Repositories

It is proposed that ultimately there are three types of OM repositories: paper documents, computer-based documents/databases, and self-memories.

Paper documents incorporate all hard copy documents and are organization-wide and group-wide references that reside in central repositories such as a corporate library. Examples include reports, procedures, pictures, video tapes, audio cassettes, and technical standards. An important part of this memory is in the chronological histories of changes and revisions to these paper documents as they reflect the evolution of the organization's culture and decision-making processes. However, most organizations do not keep a separate history of changes, but do keep versions of these documents.

Computer-based documents/databases include all computer-based information that is maintained at the work group level or beyond. These may be made available through downloads to individual workstations, or may reside in central databases or file systems. Additionally, computer documents include the processes and protocols built into the information systems. These are reflected in the interface between the system and the user, by who has access to the data, and by the formats of structured system inputs and outputs. New aspects of this type of repository are digital images and audio recordings. These forms of OM provide rich detail but require expanded storage and transmission capacities.

Self-memory includes all paper and computer documents that are maintained by an individual as well as the individual's memories and experiences. Typical artifacts include files, notebooks, written and un-written recollections, and other archives. These typically do not have an official basis or format. Self-memory is determined by what is important to each person and reflects his or her experience with the organization.

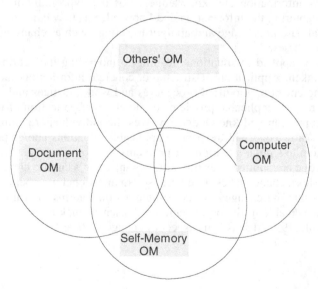

Figure 1. Organizational Memory Repositories

Repositories have overlapping information and knowledge as shown in Figure 1. Paper documents are indexed or copied into computer databases or files, self-memory uses paper and computer-based documents/databases, computer databases or files are printed and filed. Spheres for self-memory and others' memory reflect that organizations consist of many individuals, and that the OM base contains multiple self-memories. Finally, the relative size of each sphere depends on the nature of the organization. Organizations that are highly automated and/or computerized would be expected to have a greater dependence on computer-based repositories while other organizations may rely more on paper or self-memory-based repositories.

Sandoe and Olfman (1992) suggest that the increasing transience of organizational workers will lead to a shift in the location of OM. They state that organizations will have to capture and store OM in more concrete forms such as paper or computer-based repositories. They also suggest that stronger attempts should be made to capture the unstructured, abstract information and knowledge in concrete forms. On the other extreme, Jennex and Olfman (2002) found that new workers in an organization have trouble using the document and computer-based repositories and rely on the self-memories of longer-term members. This continues until the new member gains sufficient context to understand and use the information and knowledge stored in the concrete paper and computer-based repositories. While these guidelines are contradictory because transient organizations will tend to have more new members, they do emphasize that organizations should minimize reliance on self-memories for the retention of concrete, structured OM while using self-memories as the mechanism for teaching organizational culture and passing on unstructured, abstract OM.

This explains the role of organizational culture as a repository of OM. Organizational culture provides the context for using OM, and guides members in how to interpret and use it. Organizational culture uses the three types of repositories to reflect the culture as represented in procedures, guidelines, and work processes; the unstructured, abstract OM that includes reflexive (e.g., habits and norms) knowledge, anecdotes, stories, and histories that are passed on by organizational members, provides new members with the context for using the OM.

4   Organizational Memory Systems

4.1   What is an Organizational Memory System?

An Organizational Memory System, OMS, consists of processes for identifying and capturing OM, OM repositories, processes for storing, searching, retrieving, and displaying OM, and users (see Figure 2). It is not required that the OMS be computer-based, however, two capture processes are shown. The first represents manual capture by individuals who identify OM to be retained and then take the necessary steps to place the OM in a repository. The second is a capture process integrated into automated processes. An automated capture process requires that someone identify OM products of the process up front so that system designers can build databases and automated processes into the system to capture the OM.

Figure 2 is a high-level process diagram for an OMS. The spheres or "bubbles" represent OMS processes. Regular squares represent actions or needs from the OMS users. The heavy lined square represents OMS repositories. The figure is representative of an OMS designed to support a single work process or one designed to support an entire organization for OM associated activities.

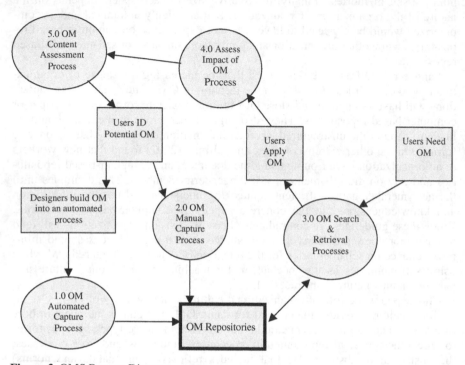

Figure 2. OMS Process Diagram

Figure 2 indicates that an OMS includes a feedback loop. As OM is used its impact should be monitored and assessed. OM found to improve organizational effectiveness should be retained and possibly expanded. OM that is not improving effectiveness should be analyzed to determine what data, information, and/or knowledge is needed and the OM capture process modified to include the new data, information, and/or knowledge. Users are emphasized since they are the ones using OM. IS personnel may be users but in general they should not be the ones identifying OM needs.

4.2   Types of Organizational Memory Systems

There are two approaches to building an OMS. A process/task-based approach and an infrastructure/generic system-based approach. The process/task-based approach focuses on the use of OM by participants in a process, task or project in order to improve the effectiveness of that process, task or project. This approach identifies the information and knowledge needs of the process, where they are located, and who needs them. The OMS is designed to capture OM unobtrusively and to make OM available when needed to whomever needs it.

The infrastructure/generic system-based approach focuses on building a base system to capture and distribute OM for use throughout the organization. Concern is with the technical details needed to provide good mnemonic functions associated with the identification, retrieval, and use of OM. The approach focuses on network capacity, database structure and organization, and information and knowledge classification. The key difference is that the process/task-based approach has known users and OM requirements while the infrastructure/generic system approach does not. The process/task approach is user centered while the infrastructure/generic system approach is IT centered. Also, the process/task approach tends to more immediate payoffs and visible success while the infrastructure/generic system approach tends to long term payoff with little quick visible success.

Both approaches may be used to create a complete organization-wide OM. The process/task-based approach supports specific processes and projects, getting users involved and motivated quicker, while the infrastructure/generic system approach integrates all OM into a single system, leading to bigger dividends when successful because the OM can be leveraged over the total organization instead of just a process or project. The process/task-based approach is preferred for identifying localized OM needs and meeting them, and for smaller organizations with well-defined OM goals. The infrastructure/generic system approach is preferred when OM needs are not known, but the organization knows OM is necessary. It gives the system developers time to determine needs while building the OM infrastructure. Morrison and Weiser (1996) support the dual approach concept by suggesting that an OMS be designed to combine an organization's various task/process-based OMSs into a single environment and integrated system.

4.3 Examples of OMS

Several examples of OMS exist. One of the earliest is Answer Garden (Ackerman, 1990). Answer Garden is an organization-wide OMS that could "grow" memory when users could not get an answer from the existing memory. Ackerman (1994) studied six organizations that had implemented Answer Garden as a generic, organization wide system and found one successful implementation. These findings threw doubt on the viability of the organization wide OMS. Ackerman and Mandel (1996) looked at organizations that implemented Answer Garden within work groups. They found successful implementations and proposed the concept of "memory in the small". In this approach OMS designers break OM into manageable pieces that correspond to specific processes or tasks. These smaller pieces form the overall organizational OMS. Croasdell and Paradice (2002) used this concept in the development of the Task Oriented Organizational Memory System (TOOMS). TOOMS is designed as a generic framework for task-based OMS.

Jennex (2000) describes a task-based OMS used to support a virtual project team and an infrastructure-based OMS used to support an industry wide effort.

The task-based OMS was very successful. The infrastructure-based OMS was technically good but not effective. The success and lack of success for these systems was determined to be due to context. The task-based OMS served the direct needs of the project team who had a shared context. The infrastructure-based OMS contained excellent information and knowledge but did not have the context necessary for many users to fully utilize the information and knowledge. Additionally, the search and retrieval functions were insufficient because the OMS designers did not know how the users needed to find and retrieve information and knowledge.

Cross (2000) discusses the system used by Anderson Consulting to store and retrieve knowledge related to projects and methodologies. This system has been developed over several years and is an example of a successful infrastructure or generic-based OMS as it is designed for the total organization and no one special task or process. Jennex and Olfman (2002) describe the OMS for an engineering organization. This OMS is a generic OMS serving a variety of needs. What makes it interesting is that it is comprised of both task and process-based OMS. The infrastructure-based OMS is successful because the task and process-based OMS are successful and effective, however, the infrastructure-based OMS is not as effective as it could be. This OMS is described in detail near the end of the chapter.

4.4 Designing an OMS

Figure 2 illustrates the basic process components of an OMS. These are capturing, storing, searching, retrieving, using, and assessing OM. A successful OMS should perform these functions well. However, other factors can influence OMS success. Mandviwalla, et. al. (1998) describe several issues affecting the design of the OMS:

- Focus of the OMS – designers need to reconcile perspectives on OM from different organizational groups
- Quantity – designers need to decide how much OM should be captured and in what formats; decisions need to be made to ensure information overload does not occur and that storage repositories are not overloaded with video or other images or with documents
- Filters – who decides what becomes OM
- Role of self-memory – what reliance and/or limitations are placed on the use of individual memories in the OMS
- Storage – what devices, locations, and amounts are needed; at what cost
- Retrieval – how is information and knowledge organized and stored so that it can be searched and linked to appropriate events and use
- Integration/Re-integration – since OM can be stored in various formats and repositories, designers must create processes for integrating the various repositories and for re-integrating information and knowledge extracted from specific events

Mandviwalla, et. al. (1998) proposed some generic OMS design requirements to address these issues. These requirements are based on the key informational elements of work – data, time, space, and activities.

Data requirements include types of data, representation of information and knowledge, and capture of data, information and knowledge. OM repositories need to be designed to accommodate several different data types.

- Metadata defines associations between work activities, processes, and context. Metadata can include email, organizational charts, procedures, and guidelines.
- Structured data are formal records from activities and processes. Structured data can include completed forms, procedures, notifications, and listings.
- Semi-structured data are typically paper documents used in work, but they can also be digital documents.
- Unstructured data include videos, audio, and digital images. This data is used for recording events and activities, training, and meetings.
- Temporal data are for work over a period of time. Temporal data includes all the previous forms of data stored over the period of an activity or event.

Representation is the key to the use of data, information and knowledge. Two issues define it: how the previous forms of data are organized and stored, and how this data is represented in the user interface. The traditional database relational structure is sufficient for much of this data, but is difficult to use with digital documents, metadata, and unstructured data. Hobbs and Pigott (2001) provide a methodology for conceptually modeling and designing multimedia databases. Hyperlinks and other approaches can be used to link data within digital documents. Numbering systems and database reference links can be used to represent links between paper documents and activities. However, representation through the user interface is always difficult. Users need to be able to visualize data in a way that will enhance their cognitive processes. For example, Eppler (2001) provides various knowledge maps supporting different contextual uses of data, information and knowledge. Ultimately designers will need to analyze the needs of the OMS users to see what user interface representations work best. Finally, capture refers to how the data, information and knowledge are placed into OM repositories. Methods vary from automatic capture to updating OM repositories by designated personnel. OMS designers need to select the methodology that fits the culture, politics, and work processes of the organization.

Time and space requirements are related to where the OM is used and how long it is useful. All OM has a life cycle. As OM ages it needs to be purged once it is no longer useful. Designers need to consider retention times and methods for identifying outdated OM. Space depends on the architecture of the OMS. Users rarely access OM from a single location. Designers need to provide networks and methods for accessing OM remotely or from distributed work locations.

Activities indicate where OM is used. Designers need to be aware of the work activities and processes that utilize OM so that they can ensure it is available to support those activities. This requires designers to coordinate users, OM, and work activities and to establish boundaries on use. Boundaries are necessary to establish security and protect the OM.

Table 2. OMS Enabling Recommendations

Factor	Recommendation
System Quality	SQ1. Use a common network structure, such as an intranet and/or the Internet.
	SQ2. Add OM skills to the technology support skill set.
	SQ3. Use high end PCs.
	SQ4. Standardize hardware and software across the organization.
System and Information Quality	SIQ1. Incorporate the OMS into everyday processes and IS.
	SIQ2. Use an enterprise wide data dictionary to design the knowledge base.
	SIQ3. Add multimedia databases to the organizational infrastructure.
	SIQ4. Allocate maintenance resources for OMS.
	SIQ5. Train users on use and content of the OMS.
Information Quality	IQ1. Create and implement a KM Strategy/Process for identifying/maintaining the knowledge base.
	IQ2. Expand system models/life cycles to include the knowledge process.
	IQ3. Assess system/process changes for impact on the OMS.
	IQ4. Automate data capture.
	IQ5. Design security into the knowledge base.
Use	U1. Incorporate OM into personnel evaluation processes.
	U2. Implement OMS use/satisfaction metrics.
	U3. Identify organizational culture concerns that could inhibit OMS usage.

Jennex and Olfman (2000) studied successful OMSs and proposed a set of design recommendations based on applying Delone and McLean's (1992) IS Success Model. As shown in Figure 3, this model has three constructs that were used to assess design considerations: system quality, information quality, and use/user satisfaction. Table 2 summarizes these design recommendations, which are very similar to the generic recommendations outlined above, but tend to be more focused on specific tactics that OMS designers should use. The main additions are with respect to doing system maintenance and getting users to access the OMS when use is optional. Maintenance recommendations evolved from the observation that many organizations looked at the development of the OMS as a one time activity and failed to allocate resources to maintain the system or the data, information and knowledge. Organizations also failed to recognize the need for expertise in these systems and failed to add OMS experts to their technical and organizational staffs. Recommendations for improving OMS use came from the need to identify the impact of using the OMS and applying feedback from use to improving or adjusting the OM and OMS. This is essential for encouraging voluntary use.

Ultimately the above suggests that OMS designers studying an organization's memory should include a review of the nature of the organization's work force, the activities they perform, and how they apply OM. This will allow for a determination of what forms and representations of memory can best serve the particular organization.

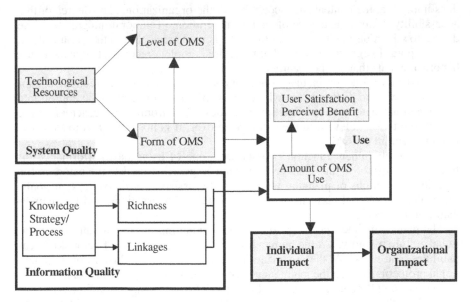

Figure 3. The OMS Modified IS Success Model

5   Effectiveness of Organizational Memory Systems

Once an organization has implemented an OMS how will effectiveness be measured and should the organization wait until the OMS is implemented to determine
effectiveness? The second part of the question is easiest to answer; the organization should have a good idea that the OMS will be effective prior to implementing
it. The hard part of the question is how to measure OMS effectiveness. This section looks at two models for measuring and predicting effectiveness, the Competing Values Model from Stein and Zwass (1995) and the Jennex and Olfman
(2002) OM modification of DeLone and McLean's (1992) IS Success Model.

5.1   Competing Values Model

Stein and Zwass (1995) propose that organizational effectiveness can be described
using the competing values model proposed by Quinn and Rohrbaugh (1983). An
implicit assumption of this model is that organizational effectiveness is partly derived from the Organizational Memory System, OMS. The model uses four organizational effectiveness criteria that have been found to be consistent with effectiveness functions for systems of action. OMS have been found to be directly relevant to four functional clusters of effectiveness.

The integrative function is the IT capability for providing local and instantaneous access to OM. Integration in total involves sharing across both space and
time. Spatially integrated organizational memories are completely connected.
This does not imply centralization; the contents of memory can be distributed. It
does imply that the contents are accessible to the organization. The degree of this
accessibility defines the degree of spatial integration. Temporal integration is the
degree to which past and present knowledge is made available to the organization.
Full temporal integration implies that there are complete records of organizational
historical events that can be readily retrieved.

The adaptive function includes boundary-spanning activities to recognize, capture, organize, and distribute knowledge about the environment to the appropriate
organizational actors. This function provides links from specific actors to the
knowledge that is relevant to the actor. Moreover, it is not restrained to information only within the OM.

The goal attainment function is essentially one of using past performance information to establish and manage performance goals. It assists the actors in the
traditional functions of planning and control by assisting in the storage of goals,
the evaluation of goal performance, identification of alternatives, and the maintenance of goal histories.

The pattern maintenance function is for maintaining the human and organizational culture memory. At the human level it provides histories of actor skills, capabilities, and work. At the organizational level it provides a history of organizational protocols through the maintenance of procedures and procedure changes.

Jennex and Olfman (2002) applied this model to assessing the effectiveness of
an OMS. While it showed the subject OMS to be effective and provides insight
for designing an OMS, it does not predict if the OMS will be used, especially if
use of the OMS is voluntary. This led to exploring the use of DeLone and
McLean's IS Success Model (1992).

5.2   IS Success Model

Jennex and Olfman (2002) generalized assessment of OMS success by adapting
DeLone and McLean's (1992) IS Success Model as shown in Figure 3. The
DeLone and McLean model is based on a review and integration of 180 research
studies that used some form of system success as a dependent variable. A description of the modified IS Success model follows. The modified model provides
guidance to designing the OMS through the System and Information Quality
blocks. Use is predicted through an adaptation of the Perceived Benefit Model.
The Perceived Benefit Model is used to predict use of a system when use is voluntary. The modification concludes by looking at the impact the OMS has on users
and the organization. This model was found to be very useful and provides a
widely accepted theoretical basis for assessing OMS success and effectiveness.

5.2.1   System quality

The "System Quality" block defines system quality in terms of the technological
characteristics of the OMS as described by three constructs: the technological resources of the organization, the form of the OMS, and the level of the OMS.
Technological resources define the capability of an organization to develop and
maintain an OMS. These include aspects such as amount of experience already
gained in developing and maintaining an OMS, the amount of expertise that is
used to develop and maintain the system, the type of hardware used to run the system, and the competence of the users.

The form of OMS refers to the extent to which it is computerized and integrated, that is, how much of the accessible information/knowledge is on line and
available through a single interface. The key aspect is the coherence of the logical
knowledge base structure. The technological resources of the system influence
form.

The level of the OMS refers to its ability to bring past information to bear upon
current activities. This refers explicitly to the search and retrieval functions of the
system and is influenced by the technological resources and form of the system.

Given the effectiveness of information technology to provide timely information, it is expected that a more fully computerized system utilizing network and
data warehouse technologies will result in the highest levels of system quality.

5.2.2   Information quality

The "Information Quality" block model defines information quality in terms of
three constructs: the knowledge/strategy process, information richness, and linkages between knowledge components. Davenport and Prusak (1998) discuss two
primary types of knowledge: links to experts who serve as sources of knowledge
and rich, detailed knowledge. Jennex and Olfman (2002) found that OMS users
new to an organization utilized knowledge linkages more than any other aspect of
the OMS. More experienced members of the organization relied on retrieving detailed, accurate, and timely information from the OMS. A successful OMS should

be able to support both new and experienced users so both are included in the model.

Knowledge management strategy and process reflects that the knowledge needs of the OMS users change over time. Jennex and Olfman (2002) integrated KM and OM and used KM to represent end user or knowledge worker actions. For consistency in this chapter knowledge is considered to be a part of OM whereas the original source used KM. Strategy is needed to determine what information and knowledge should be in the OM, where it is located, and how it is to be acquired. The process is necessary to ensure that knowledge requirements are reviewed on an ongoing basis.

5.2.3   Use

The "Use" block includes both actual use and user satisfaction. Actual use refers to the utilization of the outputs of the system. This construct is most applicable as a success measure when the use of a system is required. User satisfaction is a construct that measures perceptions of the system by users. It is considered a good surrogate for measuring system success when use of the system is voluntary, and amount of use would depend on meeting user expectations. However, it is evident that both of these constructs provide feedback to each other, especially where use is voluntary. Use will influence user satisfaction either positively or negatively, and user satisfaction will influence continued use. A more satisfied user might be expected to increase usage. Jennex and Olfman (2002) used a perceived benefit model adapted from Thompson, Higgins, and Howell (1991) to measure user satisfaction and predict continued use of the OMS. Thompson, Higgins, and Howell's (1991) perceived benefit measure utilizes Triandis' (1980) theory that perceptions on future consequences predict future actions. The instrument was adapted to measure the relationships between social factors concerning OM use, perceived OMS complexity, perceived OM job fit, perceived long-term benefits of OM use, and fear of job loss with respect to willingness to contribute to the OM.

5.2.4   Individual and organizational impact

An individual's use of a system will produce an impact on that person's performance in the workplace. In addition, DeLone and McLean (1992) note that an individual 'impact' could also be an indication that an information system has given the user a better understanding of the decision context, has improved his or her decision-making productivity, has produced a change in user activity, or has changed the decision maker's perception of the importance or usefulness of the information system. Each individual impact will in turn have an effect on the performance of the whole organization. Organizational impacts are typically not the summation of individual impacts, so the association between individual and organizational impacts is often difficult to draw.

6   Managing Organizational Memory and OM Systems

6.1   Why Manage OM?

It is usually expected that an organization will benefit from using OM. However, as shown in the second scenario in the introduction, this does not always happen. Walsh and Ungson (1991) define the outcome of the use of OM through seven propositions. The first three of these propositions deal with the general use of OM, the second three deal with its misuse, and the last with the abuse of OM. The seven propositions are:

1. Decisions that are critically considered in terms of an organization's history as they bear on the present are likely to be more effective than those made in a historical vacuum.
2. Decision choices framed within the context of an organization's history are less likely to meet with resistance than those not so framed.
3. Change efforts that fail to consider the inertial force of automatic retrieval processes are more likely to fail than those that do.
4. The automatic retrieval of past decision information that fails to meet the requirements of more novel situations is likely to promote deleterious decision making.
5. In inertial situations that call for routine solutions, the critical consideration of purposefully retrieved past decision information consumes a manager's time and energy and, thus, creates wasteful opportunity costs.
6. The controlled retrieval of decision information that is not examined in the context of novel situations is likely to promote deleterious decision making.
7. The self-serving manipulation of OM's acquisition, retention, and retrieval processes by an organization's members will enable their autocratic entrenchment and, thus, compromise the organization's sustained viability.

There are three contexts of misuse contained within the above propositions. These are:

1. The automatic retrieval of information may be allowed to shape a routine decision response when a non-routine response is called for.
2. The controlled retrieval of information may contribute to a non-routine response when a routine decision would have been appropriate.
3. A controlled retrieval process may be appropriately activated in an attempt to elicit a non-routine response, but it may be employed poorly.

Understanding these contexts of use and misuse of OM is important as they can be used to interpret the effectiveness findings of the OMS. Finding a less than effective OMS may be traced back to these contexts, conversely, finding an effective OMS should find also that the OMS implements these contexts of use. The scenarios at the start of this chapter illustrate these outcomes. The first scenario reflects appropriate use of the OM as shown in the first outcome above. The second scenario reflects inappropriate use of the OM as shown in the fourth outcome above and the first context of OM misuse. Because OM and the OMS can be misused or abused, managers need to manage the use of OM and the OMS by assessing the impact from use of the OMS and using the information to adjust the contents of the OM. To accomplish this outcome, management needs to establish performance measures for the OMS. Figure 2 shows this process in "bubbles" 4.0 and 5.0.

There are additional reasons for managing OM. Table 2 lists OMS design recommendations from Jennex and Olfman (2000) that are focused on successfully enabling OM and an OMS. All of these recommendations require management action for creation and implementation of policies and/or procedures.

Several of these recommendations require special management attention. SQ1, SQ2, SQ4, and SIQ2 require IT management to commit to organizational wide standards and processes. SIQ1, SIQ4, SIQ5, AND IQ1 require IT/IS and line organization management to work together to ensure the OMS has adequate resources to maintain the value of the OM and to ensure the OMS is used appropriately. Stein and Zwass (1995) found that OMS users with more computer experience and more positive computer attitudes will have better outcomes than OMS users with less experience and poorer attitudes. Jennex (1997) found that for users to successfully use the OMS, they needed training regarding the OMS (interface), organization of data, information, and knowledge in the OM, and the processes for using the OMS. U1 and U3 require line organization management to take actions that will encourage use of the OMS. These recommendations influence management to monitor and adapt organizational culture to encourage and support the use of the OMS.

6.2 Managing Organizational Culture

Stein and Zwass (1995), Walsh and Ungson (1991), and Jennex and Olfman (2002) found that use of OM could improve the effectiveness of the organization. However, for effectiveness to improve, the OMS must be used. The use of the OMS depends upon the culture of the organization.

Jennex (1997) studied an organization's use of OM. As noted earlier, Thompson, Higgins, and Howell's (1991) perceived benefit model can be used to assess the organization members' willingness to voluntarily use the OMS. One aspect of the model is environmental factors. This measure looks at organizational traits such as management, process, and peer support for using the OMS. The model was found to work well for predicting continued OMS use. Additionally, the findings suggest that willingness to contribute to OM is determined by an organizational culture that promotes sharing between organizational members. Sharing can be promoted through management support and by the reward system used by the organization to assess individual performance. A complementary finding was that a fear of job loss due to use of the OMS was not observed in the organization that promoted sharing and use of the OMS. Sandoe and Olfman (1992) support this assertion that organizational structure impacts the use of organizational memory. Walsh and Ungson's (1991) conclusion that an organization must be designed to take advantage of OM for it to be effective and Schatz's (1992) finding that willingness to contribute to the OM is determined by the reward system used by the organization and competitiveness within the organizational culture also support this assertion.

Prior to implementing an OMS management needs to assess organizational culture to determine if the organization can fully utilize the system. Not all organizations will have cultures that support the structured use of OM. Organizations that find less than the desired level of support for using OM in this way need to manage expectations from the use of an OMS to give the organization time to change. These organizations need to ensure that senior management is not oversold on the immediate benefits of OM. Concurrently they need to implement actions to change the culture. It is beyond the scope of this chapter to address the topic of how to change organizational culture. However, it is recommended that a top down approach be adapted to changing the culture. Organizational management needs to build awareness and support for an OMS from the top. Creating an effective OMS strategy, incorporating OM into personnel evaluations, and designing work processes to utilize and capture OM takes time and support. Only management can allocate the resources necessary to make these activities happen. Since changing an organizational culture takes time, senior management expectations need to be managed to recognize that the time and resources needed to make the change happen need to be made available.

7 Summary

Organizational Memory is the retention of experience, knowledge, information, and data about events in an organization that are then applied to future events to support decision-making. Organizational Memory Systems are the systems organizations build to support the capture and application of OM. It is anticipated that applying OM will result in improved organizational performance. This may or may not happen. Organizations need to have a strategy for determining what goes into the OMS and how OM should be applied. Organizations then need to monitor the application of OM and assess its impact to the organization. They then need to adjust their OMS strategy to ensure that the appropriate OM is captured and then used correctly.

8 Mini-Case: Organizational Memory in a Nuclear Plant

8.1 Introduction

Jennex and Olfman (2002) report a longitudinal study of OM in the engineering department at a nuclear power plant. An engineering organization was selected because engineers are knowledge workers and make decisions as a part of their job function; engineers use OM to make decisions; and engineer productivity is improved by increasing the speed and/or quality of the decisions they make. This specific organization was selected because it was accessible and the use of OM within the nuclear industry was known to occur. This organization resolves equipment and operational problems within the nuclear facility. The engineers utilize performance and maintenance histories, lessons learned, and previous problem resolutions to arrive at new solutions or courses of action. How well they do this is reflected in how well the facility operates. The organization has approximately 100 engineers organized into groups that support specific facility systems or programs.

8.2 OMS Structure

The basic OMS structure was identified using Stein and Zwass' (1995) framework. A list of potential OMS tools and repositories was developed using document research. A survey was used to gather data on the frequency of use for these tools and repositories. Interviews were done to refine the OMS components. The outcome was a listing of task/process-based repositories and systems that comprise the overall infrastructure/generic OMS. Table 3 lists these OMS components.

Table 3. OMS Repositories/Components (Note that acronyms used in this table refer to site-specific names of systems)

Type	System	Contents
Document	CDM	Documents: memos, correspondence, drawings, procedures, vendor info, Records: procedures, tests, surveillances, Maintenance Orders, Reports
	Engineer Library	Licensing Documents, Codes, Standards, NUREGS, Reg Guides, Design Basis Docs, EPRI Documents, Reports, Correspondence, Vendor Info
	Training Master File	Qualification Guides, Qualification Guide Answer Keys, Event evaluations, Lesson Plans, Task Analyses, Various Training Materials
	Operator Logs	Chronological record of events in the plant, kept in the control room
Computer	MOSAIC	Operability Assessments, Engineering Evaluations, Event Reports, Maintenance Orders, Nonconformances, Priorities, Problem Histories
	NCDB	Drawing Revision History, Base Engineering Info., Program (such as IST) History and Info., Document History, Calculations
	TOPIC	Hypertext files of Licensing Documents, ISEG Evaluations, Reports, Correspondence

	NDMS	Drawing/Document Revision History
	Internet	Vendor/Utility/NRC Info.
	NATS	Short term assignments, etc.
	Vision	Vibration history, corrective action history, audio information
Self Other	Self	Email archives, pictures, files, notebooks, in head memory, etc.
	Coworker	Email archives, pictures, files, notebooks, in head memory, etc.
	External various	Various, includes INPO and NPRDS, EPRI, NRC, Vendors, User's Groups, Trade Groups

The OMS used all three forms of OM repositories. As expected, information and knowledge stored in the repositories overlapped each other. This was due to process automation and reengineering replacing many documents and processes with IT substitutes. The OMS model remained relatively constant over the five years of the study with the only significant changes being that the Maintenance Order (MO) Work Done Sections were moved from MOSAIC to CDM and Email dropped in importance. The MO change was due to resource limitations in the Maintenance group. The drop in importance of Email was due to changing the Email system from CCMail to Lotus Notes. The Email change was performed without converting Email archives with the effect that Email-based OM was lost. This experience taught the organization not to rely on Email as a repository.

One form of OM grew extensively during the study, digital image files. Digital cameras were very limited in availability and use at the start of the study, but as camera prices dropped and the value of digital pictures was discovered, their use proliferated. Digital images are very useful for recording material conditions following events and special equipment alignments and for recording special events and evolutions. Engineers found they could reduce radiation exposure by having one person take an image then distribute it via email. They also found problem resolutions and root cause evaluations were easier to document with digital images embedded into reports or files. Additionally, digital images were easier to store and retrieve. Standard image formats, additional bandwidth for broadcasting large numbers of files, and disk storage space all became issues that had not been resolved as of the fall of 2001 (Jennex, et. al., 2000).

8.3   OMS Effectiveness

Effectiveness was evaluated using the OM Modified IS Success Model. The findings for each block are explained in the following subsections.

8.3.1   System and information quality

This was assessed using two methods. The first method used a model based on
Stein and Zwass's (1995) proposed use of Quinn and Rohrbaugh's (1983) Competing Values Model of organizational effectiveness. Table 4 summarizes these functions and findings. Scores were developed based on a 5-point Likert scale with 1
being Strongly Agree. Data for this model was collected during interviews. This
model supported an effective OMS throughout the longitudinal study.

The second method used qualitative analysis of interviews of several subjects.
Interviewees were asked to state their opinions and give examples on the effectiveness of the OMS. A consensus was found that the OMS made the subject audience more effective. Nearly all agreed that most past decision information
needed could be retrieved within a couple of hours and usually within minutes.
Also, nearly all agreed that the OMS could be better. Elements of these interviews
were used in each of the follow on studies with the same results. Examples of
comments include:

- It (the OMS) helps us to keep from reinventing the wheel. Every deci-
  sion we make is not a new decision. Our systems help us to do this.
- We have much more capability now than we did. As a Shift Technical
  Advisor (STA) we can do so much more than we could ten years ago.
  There is almost too much data.
- The information is there but the tools are slow, systems crash, and the in-
  formation and tools are unreliable.

Table 4. Results of Effectiveness Functions

Factor	Score	Result
Integration	2	Good time/spatial integration, support effective OMS
Adaptation	2	Boundary spanning done, outside information brought in, support effective OMS
Goal Attainment	1	Goals/ performance tracked, support effective OMS
Pattern Maintenance	1.5	Procedures/revisions, individual skills tracked, supports effective OMS

While the OMS is considered effective, it was found wanting in the areas of hardware and overall integration. Users with a PC with less than a Pentium processor
(early in the initial study) or a lower level Pentium (later in the study) found the
systems slow and cumbersome. Lack of adequate RAM was a common issue (initially 32 Mbytes were needed, expanding to 128 Mbytes by the end of the study
with over half the subjects having PCs with half [or less] of the necessary RAM).
Also, users noted that there were many tools and sources but no observed inten-

tional cohesion between them. Users liked the fact that all the systems are on Windows so that data could be copied/cut and pasted, thus providing a basic level of integration. However, no master plan for developing or maintaining the OMS was developed during the study period and no evidence was found suggesting this would ever be done. This suggests that the OMS will continue to lack cohesion and will not improve in effectiveness. The two observed changes in the OMS actually reduced effectiveness. Movement of the MO Work Done Section increased access times for this memory source. Reducing dependence on Email, while better from reliability, accuracy, and security standpoints, reduced individual effectiveness by removing an easy to use, readily accessible repository.

8.3.2   Use

A survey was used to measure OMS usage and the OMS perceived benefit based on Thompson, Higgins, and Howell's (1991) Perceived Benefit Model. Usage averaged 2.9 hours per day per engineer. Table 5 summarizes findings for the perceived benefit factors and supports that the OMS is effective because it is and will be used.   Scores were based on a 5-point Likert scale with 5 being Strongly Agree.

Table 5. Perceptions Affecting Usage

Perceived Benefit Factor	Score	Result
Social factors	4.08	environmental support for using OMS found
Complexity (inverse scored)	2.38	not complex, support for using OMS found
Job fit, near term consequences	4.56	fit job well, support for using OMS found
Job fit, long term consequences	3.36	Neutral
Fear of Job Loss	2.32	no support, no fear found

8.3.3   Individual impact

Effectiveness was used as a measure of engineer productivity and individual impact. Interviews were used to determine what measures the managers used to evaluate their engineers and what the engineers thought should be used. While no one set of measures was identified, several factors were found that when combined could be used for this measure:

- Timeliness in completing assignments
- Number of assignments completed
- Identifying and completing high priority assignments
- Completeness of solutions (all the bases are covered)

- Quality of solutions (well written with complete documentation)
- Solving problems right the first time
- Amount of work that has to be repeated
- Complexity of work that can be assigned to a worker
- Amount of backlog

This is a mix of qualitative and quantitative measures, most of which are influenced by the effectiveness and use of the OMS. However, these factors provide an indication that there is an individual impact on users of the OMS. An interesting finding was that the ability to use the OMS is a basic skill required of all engineers.

8.3.4   Organizational impact

Identifying productivity measures for the organization was more difficult than for individuals. Three approaches were used. The first looked at performance assessments done by external organizations. The second looked at performance relative to the business plan goals. The third looked at performance relative to preset key performance indicators.

The first measure used the SALP, Systematic Assessment of Licensee Performance, Reports issued by the Nuclear Regulatory Commission, NRC. Review of scores issued since 1988 showed an increase from a rating of 2 to a rating of 1 in 1996. This rating was maintained through the five years of the study. The other external evaluation process is the site evaluation performed by the Institute of Nuclear Power Operations, INPO. An evaluation was conducted during the spring of 1996 and resulted in a 1 rating. This rating was also maintained throughout the five years of the study. External assessments identified several strengths directly related to engineer productivity. These include decision-making, root cause analysis, problem resolution, timeliness, and Operability Assessment documentation. This demonstrates a direct link between engineer productivity and organization productivity. Also, since organization productivity is rated highly, it can be inferred that engineer productivity is high.

The second method looked at performance relative to the business plan. Very few goals related to the subject organization and few performance indicators and goals could be used to determine productivity. Two indicators were linked to OM: unit capacity and unplanned automatic shutdowns. Unit capacity and unplanned shutdowns are influenced by how well the engineers evaluate and correct problems. Both factors improved over time. These two factors plus unplanned outages and duration of outages became the standard measure during the study. Reporting and monitoring these factors significantly improved during the study. Originally, information on site performance was distributed infrequently with little attention paid to it. During the last two years management became more aware of how OM could be used to measure their effectiveness, and the process was changed. Currently, performance information is available on the site's intranet. Also a quarterly report is produced that discusses site performance, paying particular attention to lessons learned, what is working well, what is not working well, and where there are problems. Originally, this method was not considered a good measure of effectiveness. However, it is now considered to be a very effective measure and has replaced the first method as the method of choice for assessing organizational effectiveness.

The third productivity measure used performance indicators selected by the subject organization. These indicators are monitored monthly and graphs illustrating performance are printed and posted. This method provided less than useful results. It does tie in well with the organization's overall goals as defined in the second method (above), but only addresses the quantifiable measures of engineer productivity. Because OM primarily affects the qualitative and competency skills aspects of engineer productivity, this method does not provide any insight into whether OM improves productivity. However, this method was rolled into the second method and is now used to report quantifiable results as well as to report on qualitative measures such as lessons learned.

8.4 Management of OM and the OMS

This was quite weak. No management was applied to the OM and OMS until near the end of the study. As a result the OMS lacked integration and there were examples where OM was misused. Both examples used to start this chapter came from this OMS and illustrate that the OMS was not always used properly. Other management issues identified included a lack of resource support, user training, or an OM strategy. However, organizational culture strongly supported using OM and the OMS and that tended to minimize the impact of lack of management.

8.5 Summary

This was a successful OMS. Its success is due to it consisting of a series of task/process-based OMS that support their associated work processes well. It rated average as an infrastructure/generic system OMS. However, as the organization grew to understand OM and its benefits, the infrastructure/generic system OMS began to improve. It is expected that this form of the OMS will ultimately be as successful as its task/process-based components.

Acknowledgements

We wish to thank Henry Linger and Joline Morrison for feedback and comments on this chapter that helped improve it from the original draft. We also wish to thank Clyde Holsapple for asking us to write this chapter.

References

Ackerman, M. "Definitional and Contextual Issues in Organizational and Group Memories," *Proceedings of the Twenty-Seventh Annual Hawaii International Conference on System Sciences*, IEEE Computer Society Press, 1994, pp. 191-200.

Ackerman, M. and E. Mandel, "Memory In the Small: An Application to Provide Task-Based Organizational Memory for a Scientific Community," *Proceedings of the Twenty-Ninth Annual Hawaii International Conference on System Sciences*, IEEE Computer Society Press, 1996, pp. 323-332.

Coliter, P. and R. Dixon, "The Evaluation and Audit of Management Information Systems," *Managerial Auditing Journal*, 10, 7, 1995, 25-32.

Croasdell, D.T. and D. B. Paradice, "TOOMS: In Pursuit of Designing an Organizational Memory System for Category Managers," *Proceedings of the 35th Annual Hawaii International Conference on System Sciences*, IEEE Computer Society, January 2002.

Cross, R., "Technology Is Not Enough: Improving Performance by Building Organizational Memory," *Sloan Management Review*, 41, 3, 2000.

Davenport, T.H. and L. Prusak, *Working Knowledge*, Harvard Business School Press, 1998.

DeLone, W.H. and E. R. McLean, "Information Systems Success: The Quest for the Dependent Variable," *Information Systems Research*, 3, 1992, 60-95.

Eppler, M. J., "Making Knowledge Visible Through Intranet Knowledge Maps: Concepts, Elements, Cases," *Proceedings of the Thirty-Fourth Hawaii International Conference on System Sciences, HICSS34*, January, 2001.

Hobbs, V. and D. Pigott, "Entity-Media Modeling: Conceptual Modeling for Multimedia Database Design," *Information Systems Development Conference 2001, ISD2001*, September, 2001.

Hobbs, V. and D. Pigott, "A Methodology for Multimedia Database Design," *Information Systems Development Conference 2001, ISD2001*, September, 2001.

Huber, G.P. "Organizational Learning: The Contributing Processes and the Literatures," *Organization Science*, 2, 1991, 88-115.

Huber, G.P., T. H. Davenport, and D. King, "Some Perspectives on Organizational Memory, "*Unpublished Working Paper for the Task Force on Organizational Memory*, in Burstein, F.; Huber, G.; Mandviwalla, M.; Morrison, J. and Olfman, L. (eds.), presented at the 31st Annual Hawaii International Conference on System Sciences. Hawaii, HI, January, 1998.

Huysman, M.H., S. J. Fischer, and M. S. H. Heng, "An Organizational Learning Perspective on Information Systems Planning," *Journal of Strategic Information Systems*, 3, 3, 1994, 165-177.

Jennex, M.E., "Organizational Memory Effects on Productivity," Unpublished doctoral dissertation, UMI Number 9724343, Claremont Graduate School, Claremont, CA, 1997.

Jennex, M.E., "Using an Intranet to Manage Knowledge for a Virtual Project Team," in Schwartz, D; Divitini,M. and Brasethvik, T. (eds), *Internet-Based Organizational Memory and Knowledge Management*, Hershey, PA: Idea Group Publishing, 2000.

Jennex, M.E. and L. Olfman, "Development Recommendations for Knowledge Management/ Organizational Memory Systems" *Information Systems Development Conference 2000, ISD2000,* August, 2000.

Jennex, M.E. and L. Olfman, "Organizational Memory/Knowledge Effects on Productivity, A Longitudinal Study," *Proceedings of the 35th Annual Hawaii International Conference on System Sciences*, IEEE Computer Society, January 2002.

Jennex, M. E., L. Olfman, P. Pituma, and P. Yong-Tae, "An Organizational Memory Information Systems Success Model: An Extension of DeLone and McLean's I/S Success Model" *Proceedings of the 31st Annual Hawaii International Conference on System Sciences*, January, 1998.

Jennex, M., P. Franz, M. Duong, R. Haverkamp, R. Beveridge, D. Barney, J. Redmond, L. Pentecost, J. Gisi, J. Walderhaug, R. Sieg, R. Chang, "Project Report: Assessment of IT Usage in the Engineering Organizations", July 2000

Malhotra, Y., "Organizational Learning and Learning Organizations: An Overview," URL=www.brint.com/papers/orglrng.htm, 1996.

Malhotra, Y., "Knowledge Management for the New World of Business," URL=www.brint.com/km/whatis.htm, 1998.

Mandviwalla, M., S. Eulgem, C. Mould, and S. V. Rao, "Organizational Memory Systems Design," *Unpublished Working Paper for the Task Force on Organizational Memory*, F. Burstein, G. Huber, M. Mandviwalla, J. Morrison, and L. Olfman, (eds.) Presented at the 31st Annual Hawaii International Conference on System Sciences. Hawaii, HI, January, 1998.

Morrison, J., "Organizational Memory Information Systems : Characteristics and Development Strategies," *Proceedings of the Thirtieth Annual Hawaii International Conference on System Sciences*, IEEE Computer Society Press, January 1997.

Morrison, J. and M. Weiser, "A Research Framework for Empirical Studies in Organizational Memory" *Proceedings of the Twenty-Ninth Annual Hawaii International Conference on System Sciences*, IEEE Computer Society Press, 1996.

Nonaka, I., "A Dynamic Theory of Organizational Knowledge Creation", *Organization Science*, Vol. 5, No. 1, 1994.

Quinn, R. E. and J. Rhorbaugh, "A Spatial Model of Effectiveness Criteria: Towards a Competing Values Approach to Organizational Analysis" *Management Science*, Volume 29, Number 3, 1983, pp. 363-377.

Sandoe, K. and L. Olfman, "Anticipating the Mnemonic Shift: Organizational Remembering and Forgetting in 2001" *Proceedings of the Thirteenth International Conference on Information Systems*, ACM Press, 1992, pp. 127-137.

Sandoe, K., D. T. Croasdell, J. Courtney, D. Paradice, J. Brooks, and L. Olfman, "Additional Perspectives on Organizational Memory," *Unpublished Working Paper for the Task Force on Organizational Memory* in Burstein, F.; Huber, G.; Mandviwalla, M.; Morrison, J. and Olfman, L. (eds.), presented at the 31st Annual Hawaii International Conference on System Sciences. Hawaii, HI, January, 1998.

Schatz, B.R. "Building an Electronic Community System," *Journal of Management Information Systems*, 8, 3, 1992, 87-107.

Stein, E.W. and V. Zwass, "Actualizing Organizational Memory with Information Systems" *Information Systems Research*, 6, 2, 1995, 85-117.

Swanson, E. B. "The New Organizational Knowledge and its Systems Foundations" *Proceedings of the Twenty-Ninth Annual Hawaii International Conference on System Sciences*, IEEE Computer Society Press, 1996.

Triandis, H.C. "Beliefs, Attitudes, and Values," Lincoln, NB: University of Nebraska Press, 1980, 195-259.

Thompson, R.L., C. A. Higgins, and J. M. Howell, "Personal Computing: Toward a Conceptual Model of Utilization," *MIS Quarterly*, March 1991, 125-143.

Walsh, J.P. and G. R. Ungson, "Organizational Memory," *Academy of Management Review*, 16, 1, 1991, 57-91.

CHAPTER 12

Organizational Culture as a Knowledge Resource

Timothy Kayworth[1] and Dorothy Leidner[2]

[1] Department of Information Systems, Hankamer School of Business, Baylor University, Waco, Texas, USA

[2] M.J. Neeley School of Business, Texas Christian University, Ft. Worth, Texas, USA

Organizational culture has long been recognized as the underlying set of values systems that determines how firms perceive and react to their environments. While there is widespread agreement over the relevance of culture and its impact on organizations, many believe that culture exists as a concept than can be neither measured nor controlled. This chapter considers an alternate view in characterizing culture as an important knowledge resource that facilitates the management of a firm's intellectual (knowledge) assets. We first present a brief overview of organizational culture and then examine culture as an organizational resource that facilitates four key knowledge management activities. As part of this analysis, a series of research hypotheses is offered to provide a link between certain cultural sub-types and effective knowledge management practice in each of four areas: knowledge creation, storage, transfer, and application. A key implication of this chapter is that firms must increasingly view their culture as a competitive resource that must be managed in order to become a learning organization. As part of this management process, senior executives must be able to manage the various sub-cultures found within their organizations and to foster those sub-cultures consistent with knowledge management objectives. The chapter concludes by considering knowledge management initiatives as an opportunity to change corporate cultures.

Keywords: Communities of Practice; Learning Organizations; Knowledge Management; Knowledge Sharing; Organizational Culture; Resource-Based Perspective; Tacit Knowledge

---

1 Introduction

The knowledge-based theory of the firm suggests that intellectual resources are a key organizational asset that enables sustainable competitive advantage (Hansen and Oetinger, 2001; Wenger and Schneider, 2000). Under this perspective, those firms able to effectively leverage their knowledge resources can expect to reap a wide range of benefits related to; improved customer service, reduced costs in people and infrastructure, innovation, improved corporate agility, the rapid development of new product lines, quick and efficient problem resolution, and efficient transfer of best practices (Davenport and Klahr, 1998; Hansen and Oetinger, 2001; Skyrme, 1998). In fact, some have come to view corporate knowledge as the dominant, and perhaps the only source of competitive advantage (Drucker, 1998; Ruggles, 1998). Hansen and Oetinger (2001, p. 107) comment on this knowledge-based perspective:

> "Despite their best efforts, most companies continue to squander what may be their greatest asset in today's knowledge economy: the wealth of expertise, ideas, and latent insights that lie scattered across or deeply embedded in their organizations."

Given the growing perception of importance of intellectual resources, it is not surprising that firms have begun to engage in a wide range of strategies to create, store, transfer, and apply knowledge within their organizational contexts. These strategies (broadly referred to as knowledge management) generally fall into one of two categories: codification or personalization (Hansen, Nohria, and Tierney, 1999). Codification has a technology-based focus where knowledge management systems are developed and implemented in attempts to increase the quality and speed of knowledge creation and distribution in organizations. Systems aimed at codification might include such technologies as intranets, data warehousing, knowledge repositories, decision support tools, and groupware (Ruggles, 1998). In contrast, the focus on the personalization strategy is to build social networks or communities of practice to facilitate the transfer of tacit knowledge among individuals and groups (Brown and Duguid, 2000; Hansen et al, 1999; Wenger and Schneider, 2000).

Regardless of the approach taken, knowledge management efforts are often seen to clash with corporate culture and, as a result, have limited impact (Delong and Fahey, 2000; O'Dell and Grayson, 1998). An Ernst and Young study, as reported in *ComputerWorld* (January 26, 1998) identified culture as the biggest impediment to knowledge transfer citing the inability to change people's behaviors as the biggest hindrance to managing knowledge (Watson, 1998). In another study of 453 firms, over half indicated that organizational culture was a major barrier to success in their knowledge management initiatives (Ruggles, 1998). The importance of culture is also evident from consulting firms such as Ernst and Young, which report that a major aspect of knowledge management initiatives involves working to shape organizational cultures that hinder their knowledge management programs (KPMG, 1998). The resulting solutions by these firms typically lead to incentives that attempt to promote behaviors, even if they do little to change values.

Consequently, much of the literature proposes that a fundamental managerial role in knowledge management initiatives is to foster the underlying cultures necessary to help support these efforts (Verespej, 1999; Hargadon, 1998; Davenport, DeLong, and Beers, 1998; Greengard, 1998). Regarding the importance of culture, Fahey and Prusak (2001. P. 109) comment: "Obviously, there is a set of tools such as Lotus Notes, intranets, etc. which you need to be knowledge based. But technology is only 20% of the picture. The remaining 80% is people. You have to get the culture right."

Knowledge management initiatives may clash with existing organization culture for a variety of reasons. First, these initiatives often require behaviors that run counter to firm member's values. Effective knowledge management practice requires a culture that fosters and rewards the creation and use of knowledge as well as it's sharing among individual members and groups (Davenport et al, 1998; O'Dell and Grayson, 1998; Leonard and Sensiper, 1998). However, in reality, companies may foster environments where individual expertise is highly rewarded, but mentoring and assisting are not (Leonard and Sensiper, 1998). In such environments, there may be active discouragement or self-censoring from participation in knowledge sharing activities and individuals may actually be rewarded for information hoarding practices. DeLong and Fahey (2000, p. 118) point to the example of one of their case sites where senior management placed very high emphasis on individual expectations by the firm's engineers. While this management strategy (whether intentional or otherwise) motivated individual accomplishment, it had a de-motivating effect on individual propensity to share knowledge and expertise. One engineer's comments help illustrate this situation: "In divisional reviews, the senior manager says, show me something I've never seen before. So the whole goal is to blow their socks off. Nobody ever says, show me where you've worked together with another business unit."

In another example, Kidder Peabody's highly publicized $350 million securities scandal was attributed to its knowledge hoarding culture that insulated senior management from what was taking place (Marshall, et al., 1996).

Second, effective knowledge management practices may be inhibited by a lack of trust across organizational sub-units as well as differences across sub-cultures (DeLong and Fahey, 2000; Bloor and Dawson, 1994). In one firm, certain functional areas (e.g., R&D and marketing) were more highly valued than others (e.g., manufacturing and information systems) that "reinforced a silo mentality and encouraged employees to spend unproductive time defending their units' perspective. In another study, hospital staff were found to be extremely reluctant to share critical insights with physicians who were perceived to be members of a dominant sub-culture (Bloor and Dawson, 1994).

Third, knowledge management practice may be hindered by organizational cultures that are highly formalized and depend heavily on standard operating procedures (SOPs), rules, and regulations as templates for decision-making (Hargadon, 1998; Huber, 1991; von Krogh, 1998; Newman, 1985). These rules may stifle the creation of new knowledge as members attempt to address novel problems with fixed patterns of thinking that may no longer be appropriate.

These examples and others (Hasan and Gould, 2001; Schultze and Boland, 2000) help demonstrate the profound impact that culture may have on knowledge management practice and the crucial role of senior management in fostering cultures conducive to these practices (Brown and Duguid, 2000; Davenport et al, 1998; Gupta and Govindarajan, 2000; Hargadon, 1998; von Krogh, 1998; DeLong and Fahey, 2000). Furthermore, they suggest that culture in some companies may be a "core rigidity" that actually constrains innovation (Leonard-Barton, 1998). While this view is reasonable, we suggest an alternative perspective that regards organizational culture as a significant knowledge resource through its ability to facilitate the creation, storage, transfer, and use of knowledge.

Few authors have examined the positive contribution of organizational culture to knowledge management or considered culture as a knowledge resource. This paper will take such a stance, and attempt to demonstrate that culture is an important knowledge resource. In doing so, we draw heavily from the Holsapple and

Joshi (2001) framework that explicitly identifies culture as one of four key types of organizational knowledge resources (termed schematic resources) dependent upon the organization for existence. These resources are: organizational purpose, strategy, infrastructure, and culture. Under this framework, the cultural resource is composed of organizational values, norms, unwritten rules and procedures. Culture exists independently of the presence of any particular knowledge worker, yet it influences each member's use of knowledge as well as the interactions among participants. Furthermore, culture affects what knowledge is acquired and internalized, and it impacts and is impacted by infrastructure, strategy, and purpose.

We begin this analysis with a brief overview of organizational culture and then examine culture as a resource that facilitates the creation, storage, transfer, and application of knowledge. We conclude by considering knowledge management initiatives as an opportunity to change corporate cultures.

2   Overview of Organizational Culture

Culture is a multi-faceted dimension that includes artifacts, behaviors, values, emotions, and motivational roots (Hawkins, 1997). At the deepest level, culture consists of values, which are embedded tacit preferences about what the organization should strive to attain and how it should do it. (Delong and Fahey, 2000). At a more observable level, culture also consists of norms and practices that are derived from underlying values (Delong and Fahey, 2000). Culture may be manifested in rituals and routines, stories and myths, symbols, power structures, organizational structures, and control systems (Bloor and Dawson, 1994; Johnson, 1992). Schein (1985) defines organizational culture as "the set of shared, taken-for-granted implicit assumptions that a group holds and that determine how it perceives, thinks about, and reacts to its various environments." Burack (1991) defines culture as the "organization's customary way of doing things and the philosophies and assumptions underlying these," and Johnson (1992), as "the core set of beliefs and assumptions which fashion an organization's view of itself." These are similar to Hofstede's (1980, 1991) definition of national culture as the "collective programming of the mind that distinguishes one group of people from another." Culture is hence viewed as a shared mental model that influences how individuals interpret behaviors and behave themselves. Members are often unaware of the underlying assumptions of their culture and may not become aware of their culture until they encounter a different one (Schein, 1985).

Whereas a wealth of inconclusive contingency research examines the appropriate structure and technology in various environments to maximize organizational effectiveness, we are only now beginning to see research aimed at determining the contribution of organizational culture to organizational effectiveness. Part of the reason for this has been the difficulty of categorizing and measuring organizational cultures. Furthermore, there may have been an unstated view that cultures evolve and are beyond the control of organizational decision makers; hence, research focused on more malleable constructs such as structure, technology and decision making processes.

In the organizational culture literature, culture is usually examined either as a set of assumptions or as a set of behaviors. Behaviors, or norms, are a fairly visible manifestation of the mental assumptions, although some argue that the behaviors should be considered "organizational climate" and the norms, as comprising organizational culture. We now present a brief discussion of both the values and behavioral perspectives of culture.

2.1 The Value Perspective of Organizational Culture

In their interpretive study of five firms, Denison and Mishra (1995) identified four underlying sub-types of organizational culture (involvement, consistency, adaptability, and mission) and examined their relationships to organizational effectiveness. High involvement cultures are those that foster a high sense of psychological ownership and voluntary commitment to the firm's goals. This will engender a strong sense of ownership and responsibility among the firm's members. Highly consistent cultures are those that value behaviors, systems, and meanings that foster internal coordination and control. While consistent cultures may achieve high levels of internal integration (through coordination and control) they may be among the most resistant to change and adaptation. Furthermore, highly consistent cultures tend to achieve member commitment not through voluntary participation (e.g., high involvement cultures), but through stressing individual conformity through an implicit control system of internalized values. Adaptable cultures are ones that have a high capacity to change internally in response to external conditions. Finally, cultures high in mission are those that emphasize centrality of purpose of meaning for the organizations existence. In contrast to adaptable cultures, high mission cultures emphasize the stability of an organization's central purpose and de-emphasize its capacity for situational adaptability and change (Denison and Mishra, 1995: 216).

Drawing from Quinn and Rohrbaugh's (1983) value set framework, Denison and Mishra argue that organizations focus to various degrees either internally or externally, and, in terms of structure preferences, have tradeoffs in stability and control versus flexibility and change. Thus, a given company might exhibit an organizational culture with either a high external orientation (high adaptability and strong sense of mission) or a high internal orientation (high involvement and consistent work practices and regulations) or one that values change and flexibility (high involvement and adaptability) over stability and direction (sense of mission and consistent work practices). This work is significant since it is one of relatively few empirical studies that link culture to organizational effectiveness. Table 1 illustrates these relationships.

Table 1. Denison and Mishra (1995) Classification of Organizational Culture Sub-Types

	Change&Flexibility	Stability & Direction
External Orientation	Adaptability	Mission
Internal Orientation	Involvement	Consistency

Hofstede et al (1990) examined culture both in terms of values and behaviors. In terms of value, they found that organizational culture was tied to the national culture dimensions identified by Hofstede (1980) and reflected preferences for centralized versus decentralized decision making (power distance), preferences for the degree of formalization of routines (uncertainty avoidance), degree of concern over money and career versus family and cooperation (masculinity/femininity dimension), and degree of identification with the company and preference for individual versus group reward systems (collectivistic/individualistic dimension). When the authors eliminated the effects due to nationality, the value differences between organizations were primarily dependent upon subunit characteristics rather than overall membership in the organization. Hence, the authors concluded that organizational subunits were the more appropriate level of analysis for organizational culture study. Moreover, they found that behaviors were a better means of distinguishing subunit cultures than were value systems.

Others have expressed organizational culture in terms of the differing orientations (value sets) among individual sub-units. In Hofstede's (1998) study of a large Danish Insurance firm, he identified distinct professional, administrative and customer interface sub-cultures all within the same firm. Similar work by Duncan (1989) has classified organizational sub-cultures into the categories of: enhancing cultures, counter-cultures, or orthogonal cultures. Consequently, a crucial role of senior managers is to identify the firms various sub-cultures and effectively manage their differences (Hofstede, 1998).

2.2   The Behavioral Perspective of Organizational Culture

In contrast to a focus on underlying assumptions, the behavioral perspective focuses on culture as defined by actual work practices. In one prominent work, empirical data showed shared perceptions of daily practices formed the core of organizational subunit culture (Hofstede et al, 1990). The behavioral dimensions isolated by the authors were:

1. *Process Versus Results Oriented*: This dimension refers to a focus on improving the means by which organizational goals are achieved (process) as opposed to a focus on the attainment of goals. Individuals in process-oriented sub-cultures tend to be risk averse while those in results oriented cultures are comfortable in unfamiliar situations and look forward to challenging situations.

2. *Employee Vs. Job Oriented:* Employee orientation suggests a concern for people whereas a job orientation refers to a concern over performing tasks effectively. Thus, in employee-oriented cultures, important decisions tend to be made by committees with high concern for individual welfare. In contrast, job-oriented cultures tend to foster strong pressure for "getting the job done" with limited concern over employee personal or family welfare. Important decisions in this type of environment tend to be made by individuals.

3. *Parochial Vs. Professional:* A parochial orientation suggests that individuals are loyal to their organization whereas a professional orientation suggests that individuals are loyal to their profession. In parochial subcultures, individuals get their identity from the company they work for whose social values and norms are similar to their own. In contrast, in professionally driven cultures, individuals obtain their sense of identify from the type of work they are involved in and whose values may not necessarily coincide with the organization they work for. Typically, organizations with parochial cultures tend to hire the "whole person" taking into consideration social and family background. In contrast, professionally dominated cultures tend to hire individuals based solely on the basis of job competence.

4. *Open Vs. Closed System:* This dimension describes the communication climate in the subunit. In open cultures, the organization considers itself open to outsiders and new employees with little time needed for new employees to feel at home. In contrast, closed cultures are typically secretive and very wary of outsiders as well as insiders. Only a select few people may be part of the "inner circle" and new employees may require a significant amount of time (up to a year) to feel at home.

5. *Loose Vs. Tight Control:* The control dimension reflects the degree of internal structuring, with loose organizations having few written or unwritten codes of behavior and tight organizations having strict unwritten and written policies. In loose control cultures, members may display a casual attitude towards such things as deadlines and cost constraints and may often make fun of the unit they are a part of. In contrast, tightly controlled cultures tend to place more importance on cost-consciousness and punctuality and rarely joke about their company or job.

6. *Normative Vs. Pragmatic:* Pragmatic units are market driven and customer oriented whereas normative units are product oriented. Thus, in normative cultures great emphasis is placed on following procedures as opposed to the achievement of results. In pragmatic units, members place great emphasis on meeting customer needs with less regard for how results are achieved. In normative cultures, members tend to have higher standards in issues related to business ethics. Interestingly, some units were found to be pragmatic but not results oriented (i.e., a goal of improving customer service might not imply a goal of improving the bottom line).

The process/results, parochial/professional, loose/tight, and normative/pragmatic dimensions were found to relate partly to the industry, confirming Chatman and Jehn's (1994) conclusion that industry or environmental factors affect organizational cultures, whereas the employee/job orientation and open/closed system were more determined by the philosophy of the founders and senior managers. These latter dimensions might therefore be more malleable.

3   Effects of Culture on Knowledge Management Processes

This section discusses the ways that culture may act as a resource that facilitates knowledge management processes. We consider knowledge management processes as consisting of knowledge creation, storage, transfer, and use.

3.1   Cultures That Influence Knowledge Creation

Organizational knowledge creation involves developing new content or replacing existing content within the organization's tacit and explicit knowledge (Pentland, 1995). Through social and collaborative processes as well as individuals' cognitive processes (e.g.,, reflection), knowledge is created, shared, amplified, enlarged, and justified in organizational settings (Nonaka, 1994). While a great deal of explicit knowledge is created through formalized mechanisms (e.g., surveys, R&D, performance reviews, competitive analysis), others suggest that the unarticulated knowledge—consisting of expertise, ideas, and latent insights—"is the very basis of creativity, and is not easily captured or codified" (Leonard and Sensiper, 1998, p. 2). Thus, at its very core, the creation of new knowledge is not a formal process; rather, it is a socially constructed process that occurs over time largely through informal human networks (Brown and Duguid, 2000; Fahey and Prusak, 1998; Wenger and Snyder, 2000).

Indeed, some authors argue that formalization may actually stifle knowledge creation activities (Von Krogh, 1998; Hargadon, 1998; Hansen et al, 1999). Huber (1991, p. 95) supports this idea noting "units capable of learning may not have access to knowledge because of existing routines for message routing or organizational politics." In this same vein, Hargadon (1998) draws a distinction between the use of formalized versus cultural control as means for fostering knowledge brokering activities. He argues (p. 209) against the use of formalized routines (controls) stating that cultural controls are much more effective means for promoting knowledge creation practices particularly in "non-routine situations that require initiative, flexibility, and innovation."

Thus, the ability to mold or shape organizational culture is of paramount importance in fostering learning environments. Leonard (1995) gives the example of Chapparel Steel, a company whose norms and values supported the growth of knowledge. The learning culture at Chapparel was cited as part of the reason for Chapparel's consistently excellent performance (Leonard, 1995). Tracey, et al (1995) provide some insights into some of these fundamental aspects of culture that typify learning organizations. Firstly, such organizations create an environment in which the acquisition of skills and knowledge is viewed as a key responsibility of each employee. Secondly, in such organizations, skills and knowledge acquisition are supported by the interaction and encouragement of organizational members. Thirdly, employees are provided with opportunities for personal development and are encouraged to apply job-related knowledge. And finally, there is a shared belief that innovative ideas are a valuable aspect of staying competitive in the marketplace (Tracey et al. 1995).

These arguments suggest that it would be difficult for organizational cultures characterized by stability and control (see Table 1) to create the conditions favorable to becoming a continuous learning organization. Contrarily, change and flexibility organizations might be readily able to introduce knowledge creation strategies and become continuous organizational learning communities. This leads to our first research hypothesis:

Hypothesis 1: Organizational cultures characterized by high degrees of change and flexibility will have a more positive effect on knowledge creation (learning) than will cultures characterized by high degrees of stability and control

3.2 Cultures That Foster Knowledge Storage

Organizational memory is the means by which knowledge is stored for future use (Huber, 1991). It includes knowledge residing in various component forms, such as written documentation, structured information stored in electronic databases, codified human knowledge stored in expert systems, documented organizational procedures and processes and tacit knowledge acquired by individuals and networks of individuals (Tan, et al., 1999). Significant problems with organizational memory are that organizational members are often unaware of the existence of organizational memory and that organizations may fail to anticipate future needs for information causing such information not to be stored (Huber, 1991).

Typically, efforts at overcoming these problems are geared toward either expanding the networks of organizational members (personalization) or toward codifying and storing knowledge (codification) (Hanson et al, 1999). However, neither approach consciously attempts to embed the knowledge into organizational behaviors or practices. Regarding this problem, Cole (1998) notes that much of the use of new information technologies to codify knowledge storage has been oriented to moving information from one organizational member to another rather than embedding the knowledge into organizational routines.

Huber (1991) and others (Feldman, 1989; Gioia and Poole, 1984; Nelson and Winter, 1982) argue that a significant amount of organizational knowledge is stored in standard operating procedures, rules, and scripts. Thus, effective knowledge storage practices should not only seek to codify knowledge and expand human networks; they should also try to embed knowledge into the formalized rules, standard operating procedures, and organizational practices that constitute part of the organizational culture. Brown and Duguid's (2000) distinction between culture and process echo these sentiments. They argue that while culture is most important in knowledge generation (e.g., creation), the role of process (e.g., formalization) becomes paramount in activities related to organizational memory. Thus, we would expect greater difficulties embedding new knowledge into organizational routines where organizations have flexibility and change cultures, because such cultures anticipate continuously adapting routines. Contrarily, the stability and control organizations that are slower to learn, might be quicker to embed new knowledge into routines, so that the organization returns to a state of stability following change. This leads to our second hypothesis:

Hypothesis 2: Organizational cultures characterized by high degrees of stability and direction will have a more positive effect on knowledge storage capabilities than will cultures characterized by high degrees of change and flexibility.

3.3 Cultures That Foster Knowledge Transfer

Considering the distributed nature of organizational cognition, an important process of knowledge management in organizational settings is the transfer of knowledge to locations where it is needed and can be used. Transfer occurs at various levels: between individuals, from individuals to explicit sources, from individuals to groups, between groups, across groups, and from the group to the organization.

An important aspect of transfer is that of knowledge sharing. Knowledge sharing involves organizational members willingly contributing their knowledge to organizational memory. Organizational values and norms will influence what knowledge is considered important (Delong and Fahey, 2000). It will also influence whether individuals view their knowledge as a personal possession or as an organizational asset (Leidner, 2000) and will hence, influence the quality of knowledge that is committed to organizational memory. Thus, culture is an important resource in encouraging individuals to share and as Hargadon (1998) notes, this resource can either encourage or discourage innovative knowledge management practices.

Many companies attempt to force sharing by instigating reward mechanisms. For example, Price Waterhouse has implemented explicit reward mechanisms where managers must produce evidence of knowledge sharing activities (e.g., training, mentoring, publications) as part of their performance evaluations (O'Dell and Grayson, 1998). While this may be considered good knowledge management practice, some companies (e.g., Sun Microsystems) have been able to successfully initiate knowledge sharing efforts in spite of having little or no external reward systems in place. While Sun Microsystems has no formal knowledge sharing strategy, they have become pace-setters in knowledge management practice simply by maintaining a culture open to knowledge sharing among groups and individuals (Verespej, 1999). This may be due in part to the belief that much of the knowledge sharing that occurs in organizations is tacit in nature and is best transmitted through informal "open" environments as opposed to formal control systems (Wenger and Snyder, 2000; Brown and Duguid, 2000). In such open cultures, the communications climate is one that fosters the free flow of information both vertically and horizontally throughout the organization where individual information hoarding or secrecy is discouraged. In contrast, closed cultures can be expected to foster communications climates that limit the free flow of ideas, expertise, and latent insights throughout the organization to a few insiders considered to be "experts" (Hofstede, 1990). This leads to our third research hypothesis:

Hypothesis 3A: Organizational cultures characterized as "open" will have a greater tendency to transfer (share) knowledge among members than will firms with "closed" cultures.

One of the problems with knowledge sharing is that organizational members may be unable to ascertain the long-term benefits to both themselves as well as to the organization. As a result, employees may be hard pressed to see the benefits to be achieved from sharing their personal insights, expertise, and ideas with other organizational members and outsiders. Also, organizational members may lack the motivation to share their knowledge particularly in the absence of motivational systems designed to reward these practices. Thus, a critical management task in knowledge sharing efforts is to convince members that what is beneficial to the overall organization will ultimately benefit them personally. This may easier to accomplish in parochial cultures whose members tend to personally identify with the organization and to exhibit high degrees of loyalty (Hofstede, 1990). Thus, in parochial cultures, employees may share knowledge simply because it is "good for the company". In contrast, it may be much more difficult to accomplish this in professional cultures where members tend to identify with their profession as opposed to the organization and where company loyalty may be very limited. This suggests the following research hypothesis:

Hypothesis 3B: Organizational cultures characterized as "parochial" will have a greater tendency to transfer (share) knowledge among members than will firms with "professional" cultures.

A common theme in the knowledge sharing literature is the need to establish a shared context between both sources and recipients of knowledge (Fahey and Prusak, 1998; O'Dell and Grayson, 1998; Huber, 1991; Leonard and Sensiper, 1998). The basic idea behind shared contexts is that there must be some source of relationship or intimacy for knowledge to flow freely among individuals or groups (Leonard and Sensiper, 1998). In the absence of a shared context, groups with different cognitive maps may have different interpretations that may lead to learning "disabilities" and dysfunctional decision-making (Huber, 1991). In one striking example of this, GM (Detroit) was unable to effectively transfer best practices (e.g., knowledge) from its Toyota (California) partner in spite of literally hundreds of fact-finding visits from GM managers to the Toyota plant (O'Dell and Grayson, 1998). This failure was attributed, to a great extent, to the lack of shared context or "personal tie" between individuals at both plants. In a similar vein of research, von Krogh (1998) shows how caring relationships (characterized by high levels of trust, empathy, and sense of justice towards others) among organizational members cultivates higher levels knowledge sharing activities. These findings suggest that those sub-cultures that foster intimacy, caring and concern among employees (e.g., employee-oriented cultures) will generally experience a greater ability to share knowledge and information. This leads to the following research hypothesis:

Hypothesis 3C: Organizational cultures characterized as "employee-oriented" will have a greater tendency to transfer (share) knowledge among members than will firms with "job-oriented" cultures.

3.4 Cultures That Foster Knowledge Application

While much research has focused on the issue of knowledge transfer, far less has considered the issue of individuals seeking out existing knowledge. The ability to do this may be constrained by the simple fact that those seeking knowledge may not be aware of those who have it (Huber, 1991; O'Dell and Grayson, 1998). However, in other situations members may be fully aware of knowledge in other units yet still be reluctant to draw from and apply this existing knowledge to their benefit. In one example, a frustrated CEO of a commercial-services firm commented: "We provide pretty much the same service in every location. But my regional managers would rather die than learn from each other" (Gupta and Govindarajnan, 2000, p. 71). This suggests that culture may have a strong influence in motivating individuals to pursue knowledge application practices. Through norms and practices, culture influences the lengths to which employees will go to seek and build upon existing knowledge (Delong and Fahey, 2000). Organizational efforts to foster knowledge application through rewards and other incentives will ultimately fail unless the underlying cultural climate exists that rewards, celebrates, and values knowledge application (O'Dell and Grayson, 1998).

Knowledge application is closely related to knowledge sharing, with the key difference being that organizational members are seeking to access and apply existing knowledge. In either case you have organizational members reaching out to others either to contribute what they know (knowledge sharing) or to appropriate that which they don't know (knowledge application). Thus, it is reasonable to assume that similar organizational climates will foster knowledge sharing as well as knowledge application (seeking) activities. We could expect that cultures characterized as being open, parochial, and employee-oriented will be those that most favor knowledge application practices. This leads to the following three hypotheses:

Hypothesis 4A: Organizational cultures characterized as "open" will have a greater tendency to apply (seek) knowledge among members than will firms with "closed" cultures.

Hypothesis 4B: Organizational cultures characterized as "parochial" will have a greater tendency to transfer (share) knowledge among members than will firms with "professional" cultures.

Hypothesis 4C: Organizational cultures characterized as "employee-oriented" will have a greater tendency to transfer (share) knowledge among members than will firms with "job-oriented" cultures.

A second important aspect of knowledge application is that of interpretation, which Daft and Weick (1984) define as "the process through which information is given meaning" (cited in Huber, 1991, p. 102). The significance of this is that varying interpretations may lead to applications and use of knowledge that are fundamentally different from the original contributors. Knowledge interpretation may be shaped by the uniformity of prior cognitive maps possessed by organizational units (Huber, 1991) or the degree of shared context among stakeholders (Alavi and Leidner, 2001). Thus, individuals will be more readily able to apply and use knowledge from within their communities of practice than from an outside community due to similar cognitive maps. In more densely linked or centralized areas of a network, there should be a greater sharing of beliefs and a greater ability to interpret knowledge should exist (Abrahamson and Fombrum, 1994).

The role of culture in all this is that it creates the context for social interaction (through values, norms and practices) that shapes and molds individual interpretations and ultimately determines how effective the organization will apply knowledge (Delong and Fahey, 2000). In organizations composed of multiple subcultures, incompatible knowledge interpretations may lead to organizational conflict and the inability to effectively apply knowledge. Denison and Mishra (1995) note examples of competing sub-cultures at both People's Express (customer service management and pilots) and at Detroit Edison (politicians and engineers). In both cases, inherently different subcultures had much different interpretations of knowledge, which led to dysfunction in their application, and use of that knowledge. In contrast, more homogenous or unitary cultures will tend to foster environments with similar cognitive maps through similar shared assumptions, beliefs, and practices. The result of this will be higher degrees of shared interpretation across the organization in member's application and use of knowledge. Denison and Mishra's (1995) dimension of consistency characterizes these "strong" cultures that engender similar shared meanings and place high emphasis on individual conformity. This leads to our final research hypothesis:

Hypothesis 5: Organizational cultures characterized as being highly consistent (e.g., strong cultures) will tend to generate high levels of shared meaning that will lead to more effective knowledge application.

4   Culture-Changing KM Initiatives

While some may recommend that knowledge management should be built around existing organizational culture and while it is argued that organizational culture has an important influence on knowledge management processes, for many organizations, knowledge management highlights a need to change organizational culture. For example, the CEO of Buckman, recognizing that investing in IT would not change culture itself, embarked on a three-year campaign to reshape norms and practices that defined the relationships between individual knowledge and the organization (Delong and Fahey, 2000). While the intent of the KM initiative at Buckman was to create a global knowledge-sharing environment, the concept of a global knowledge forum was ill received by non-American employees. The underlying problem appeared to be lack of shared language and understanding across the communities of practice that had created dysfunction and divisions in communication. A philosophy of "anything was discussible and anyone could participate in the community of practice" was introduced and made known to everyone. Top management took time to explain to the employees that the company is made up of individuals – each of whom had different capabilities and potentials – all of which are necessary to the success of the company.

Despite the relatively popular reaction to the new philosophy as a flexible guideline to global transfer behavior, many of employees were still not very comfortable without specific outlines on participating in global knowledge transfer. In essence, establishing new values without explaining appropriate behaviors, was unsuccessful in shifting the existing culture. Subsequently, top management sought to proactively change the organizational culture. One method used was the introduction of the "Buckman Code of Ethics" to provide precise guidelines to employees on how to behave in global knowledge sharing (which were printed on a wallet-sized laminated card and given to every employee) stipulating a new operating philosophy, embracing a common language and understanding to facilitate

participation in global knowledge sharing. A metaphor (waterline) was introduced. Buckman employees were encouraged to think about the company as a
ship, with the Code of Ethics as the waterline. According to the Chairman of the
organization:"You do not shoot below the waterline, because you can sink the
ship. However, you are free to be as innovative as you wish in changing the super-
structure of the ship to meet the needs of the customer."

In making sure that employees understood the metaphor, great effort went into
explaining the meaning and the practicalities involved. Top management, as well
as some middle management was encouraged to participate in promoting the
metaphor on-line (Pan and Leidner, 2001). Buckman's experience demonstrates
that even with top management backing, changing culture is a long and arduous
process. It also demonstrates that culture itself is a valuable resource that needs
careful attention.

5   Conclusion

In our analysis, we have built the case that organizational culture is a knowledge
resource. By definition, culture consists of certain underlying values, norms, and
practices (Delong and Fahey, 2000) that are manifested through various symbols,
languages, ideologies, myths and rituals within organizational contexts (Pettigrew,
1979). This characterization is consistent with prevailing definitions of knowledge
as relevant, high value information that is dependent on context, that is linked to
meaningful behavior, and is embodied in language, stories, concepts, rules, and
tools (Leonard and Sensiper, 1998; Fahey and Prusak, 1998). Secondly, we have
demonstrated the role of culture as a knowledge resource by nature of its ability to
facilitate knowledge creation, storage, transfer, and application. This view is supported by a wealth of knowledge management literature that consistently argues
that firms need to foster the right cultures in order to successfully leverage their
intellectual resources.

There are several implications for viewing culture as an organizational knowledge resource. First, organizations need to increasingly view their culture as a
competitive resource that may lead to some degree of sustainable advantage. This
resource-based view suggests that internal firm resources (e.g., culture) that cannot be easily created, bought, substituted or imitated by competitors may lead to
significant advantages over rivals (Barney, 1991). One significant example of this
is Southwest Airlines whose informal "people friendly" culture has become legendary in the airline industry.

Second, viewing culture as a knowledge resource suggests a crucial role for
senior management in shaping this asset. Given the difficulty in changing culture
as well as the far reaching impacts it may have on the organization, senior management must take the lead in shaping the values, norms, and practices of the firm
to enhance the competitive positioning of the firm (Davenport et al, 1998; Gupta,
2000). Furthermore, our research suggests that a key aspect of this leadership role
will be to manage relationships among multiple sub-cultures each with potentially
diverging interests and objectives. One area ripe for research is to look at how

firms can manage to pursue common corporate goals in environments composed of disparate sub-cultures (e.g., MIS and corporate management).

Finally, our research suggests that a "one size fits all" approach to culture may be an inadequate perspective since different cultural styles (e.g., internal vs. external focus) may be more or less appropriate depending on a variety of external as well as internal company factors. Thus, what works for Southwest Airlines in the rapidly changing transportation industry may not be the type of culture needed for M&M Mars in a much more stable industry. Different types of organizational cultures will thrive in different environments. A fruitful area of research might be to look at what types of organizational cultures are suitable under different contingencies.

References

Abrahamson, E. and C. Fombrun, "Macrocultures: Determinants and Consequences," *Academy of Management Review*, 19, 4, 1994, 728-755.

Alavi, M. and D. Leidner, "Knowledge Management and Knowledge Management Systems: Conceptual Foundation and An Agenda for Research," *MIS Quarterly*, March 2001, 107-136.

Barney, J., "Firm Resources And Sustained Competitive Advantage," *Journal of Management*, 17, 1, 1991, 99-120.

Bloor, G. and P. Dawson, "Understanding Professional Culture in Organizational Context," *Organization Studies*, 15, 2, 1994, 275-295.

Brown, S.J. and P. Duguid, "Balancing Act: How To Capture Knowledge Without Killing It," *Harvard Business Review*, May-June 2000, 73-80.

Burack, E., "Changing the Company Culture–the Role of Human Resource Development," *Long Range Planning*, 24, 1, 1991, 88-95.

Chatman, J. and K. Jehn, "Assessing the Relationship Between Industry Characteristics and Organizational Culture: How Different Can You Be?" *Academy of Management Journal*, 37, 3, 1994, 522-553.

Cole, R.E., "Introduction," *California Management Review*, 45, 3, 1998, 15-21.

Daft, R.L. and K.E. Weick, "Toward A Model of Organizations as Interpretation Systems," *Academy of Management Review*, 9, 1984, 284-295.

Davenport, T.H. and P. Klahr, "Managing Customer Support Knowledge," *California Management Review*, 40, 3, 1998, 195-208.

Davenport, T. H., D.W. De Long, and M.C. Beers, "Successful Knowledge Management," *Sloan Management Review*, 39, 2, 1998, 43-57.

DeLong, D.W. and L. Fahey, "Diagnosing Cultural Barriers To Knowledge Management, *Academy of Management Executive*, 14, 4, 2000, 113-127.

Denison, D.R. and A.K. Mishra, "Organizational Culture and Effectiveness," *Organization Science*, 6, 2, 1995, 204-223.

Drucker, P. *Managing In A Time of Great Change*, New York: Dutton/Plume, 1998.

Duncan, W.J., "Organizational Culture: "Getting A Fix On An Elusive Concept," *Academy of Management Executive*, 3, 3, 1989, 229-236.

Fahey, L. and L. Prusak, "The Eleven Deadliest Sins Of Knowledge Management," *California Management Review*, 40, 3, 1998, 265-276.

Feldman, M., *Order Without Design: Information Production and Policy Making*, Stanford: CA, Stanford University Press, 1989.

Gioia, D.A. and P.P. Poole, "Scripts In Organizational Behavior," *Academy of Management Review*, 9, 1984, 449-459.

Greengard, S., "Storing, Shaping And Sharing Collective Wisdom," *Workforce*, 77, 10, 1998, 82-88.

Gupta, A.K. and V. Govindarajan, "Knowledge Management's Social Dimension: Lessons From Nucor Steel," *Sloan Management Review*, 42, 1, 2000, 71-80.

Hansen, M.T., N. Nohria, and T. Tierney, "What's Your Strategy For Managing Knowledge?" *Harvard Business Review*, March-April, 1999, 106-115.

Hansen, M.T. and B.V. Oetinger, "Introducing T-Shaped Managers: Knowledge Management's Next Generation," *Harvard Business Review*, March 2001, 107-116.

Hargadon, A.B., "Firms As Knowledge Brokers: Lessons In Pursuing Continuous Innovation," *California Management Review*, 40, 3, 1998, 209-227.

Hasan, H. and E. Gould, "Support for the Sense-Making Activity of Managers," *Decision Support Systems*, 31, 1, 2001, 71-86.

Hawkins, P., "Organizational Culture: Sailing between Evangelism and Complexity," *Human Relations*, 50, 4, 1997, 417-440.

Hofstede, G., Culture's Consequences: International Differences In Work-Related Values, Beverly Hills: CA, Sage Publications, 1980.

Hofstede, G., *Cultures and Organizations: Software of The Mind*, London: UK, McGraw Hill, 1991.

Hofstede, G., "Identifying Organizational Subcultures: An Empirical Approach," *Journal of Management Studies*, 35, 1, 1998, 1-12.

Hofstede, G., B. Neuijen, D.D. Ohayv, and G. Sanders, "Measuring Organizational Cultures: A Qualitative and Quantitative Study Across Twenty Cases," *Administrative Science Quarterly*, 35, 1990, 286-316.

Holsapple. C. and K.D. Joshi, "Organizational Knowledge Resources," *Decision Support Systems*, 31, 1, 2001, 39-54.

Huber, G., "Organizational Learning: The Contributing Processes and the Literatures," *Organization Science*, 2, 1,1991, 88-115.

Johnson, G., "Managing Strategic Change–Strategy, Culture and Action," *Long Range Planning*, 25, 1, 1992, 28-36.

KPMG Management Consulting, *Knowledge Management: Research Report*, 1998.

Leidner, D. E., "Understanding Information Culture: Integrating Knowledge Management Systems into Organizations," in Galliers, R.; Leidner, D. and Baker, B. (eds.) *Strategic Information Management.* Oxford: Butterworth Heinemann, 1999, 523-550.

Leonard, D. and S. Sensiper, "The Role Of Tacit Knowledge In Group Innovation," *California Management Review*, 40,3, 1998, 112-132.

Leonard, D. *Wellsprings of Knowledge*, Harvard Business School Press, Boston, 1995.

Marshall, C., L. Prusak, and D. Shpilberg, "Financial Risk and the Need For Superior Knowledge," *California Management Review*, 38, 3, 1996, 77-101.

Nelson, R. and S. Winter, *An Evolutionary Theory of Economic Change*, Cambridge: MA, The Bellhop Press of Harvard University Press, 1982.

Newman, M., "Managerial Access To Information: Strategies For Prevention and Promotion," *Journal of Management Studies*, 22, 1985, 193-212.

Nonaka, I., "A Dynamic Theory of Organizational Knowledge Creation," *Organization Science*, 5, 1, Feb. 1994, 14-37.

O'Dell, C. and C.J. Grayson, "If Only We Knew What We Know: Identification And Transfer Of Best Practices," *California Management Review*, 40, 3, 1998, 154-174.

Pan, S and D. Leidner, "Bridging Communities of Practice: The Pursuit of Global Knowledge Sharing," working paper, National University of Singapore, 2001.

Pentland, B. T., "Information Systems and Organizational Learning: The Social Epistemology of Organizational Knowledge Systems," *Accounting, Management and Information Technologies*, 5, 1, 1995, 1-21.

Pettigrew, A.M., "On Studying Organizational Cultures," *Administrative Science Quarterly*, 24, 1979, 570-581.

Quinn, R.E., and J. Rohrbaugh,, "A Spatial Model Of Effectiveness Criteria: Towards A Competing Values Approach To Organizational Analysis," *Management Science*, 29, 3, 1983, 363-377.

Ruggles, R., "The State Of The Notion: Knowledge Management In Practice," *California Management Review*, 40, 3, 1998, 80-89.

Schein, E.H., *Organizational Culture and Leadership*. San Francisco, CA: Jossey-Bass, 1985.

Schultze. U. and R. Boland, "Knowledge Management Technology And The Reproduction Of Knowledge Work Practices," *Journal of Strategic Information Systems*, 9, 2-3, 2000, p. 193-213.

Skyrme, D. J. and D.M. Amidon, "New Measures Of Success," *Journal of Business Strategy*, 19, 1, 1998, 20-24.

Tan, S., H. Teo, B.C.Y. Tan, and K. Wi, "Developing a Preliminary Framework for Knowledge Management in Organizations," Proceedings of the Americas Conference of Information Systems (AIS), Baltimore, Maryland, 1999, 629-631.

Tracey, J.B., S.I. Tannenbaum, and M.J. Kavanagh,, "Applying Trained Skills on the Job: The Importance of the Work Environment," *Journal of Applied Psychology*, 20, 3, 1995, 239-252.

Von Krogh, G., "Care in Knowledge Creation," *California Management Review*, 40, 3, 1998, 133-153.

Verespej, M., "Knowledge Management: System Or Culture?" *Industry Week*, 284, 15, August 16, 1999, 20.

Watson, S., "Getting To 'Aha!' Companies Use Intranets To Turn Information And Experience Into Knowledge – And Gain A Competitive Edge, *Computer-World*, January 26, 1998.

Wenger, E.C. and W.M. Snyder, "Communities Of Practice: The Organizational Frontier," *Harvard Business Review*, January-February 2000, 139-145.

CHAPTER 13

Does Accounting Account for Knowledge?

Dan N. Stone[1] *and Sony Warsono*[2]

[1] Department of Accounting, Gatton College of Business and Economics, University of Kentucky, Lexington KY, USA

[2] Accounting Department, Gadjah Mada University, Yogyakarta, Indonesia

How can organizations best account for knowledge management? In this chapter, we explore two dimensions of this problem: (1) determinants of the value of accounting information and the economic and institutional forces that shape existing knowledge accounting (KA) efforts, and (2) a discussion of six proposed alternative methods of knowledge accounting. We conclude by arguing that KA is problematic due to the economic characteristics of knowledge.

Keywords: Financial Reporting; Knowledge Accounting; Measurement

1 Introduction

Assertions that financial and managerial accounting fail to account for knowledge management (KM) activities are ubiquitous in the KM literature and popular press. For example, Edvinsson and Malone (1997, p. 1) argue that, "the traditional model of 'accounting' which so beautifully described the operations of companies for a half-millennium, is now failing to keep up with the revolution taking place in business." Such criticisms generally center on two points: (1) the engine of economic productivity in the "new" economy is knowledge, not physical capital and (2) financial and managerial accounting are trapped in an industrial and organizational model in which physical capital is the primary productivity enabler (Upton, 2001).

Is it accurate to assert that accounting has failed the knowledge management revolution? What forces determine how publicly held companies report knowledge management initiatives? In this chapter, we explore two dimensions of this problem. First, we examine determinants of the value of accounting information and the economic and institutional forces that shape existing knowledge accounting efforts. Second, we discuss six proposed alternative methods of knowledge accounting.

2 Accounting for Knowledge Accounting: Information Theory & Accounting Institutions

2.1 Existing Knowledge Accounting

Existing financial accounting standards sharply distinguish between physical and intangible assets (Lev, 2001). Physical assets (e.g., property, plant, and equipment) are valued on the balance sheet at the price paid to obtain them, less accumulated depreciation. In contrast, intangible "assets" are expensed as incurred. Consequently, investments in knowledge management that are purchased from others (e.g., computer hardware and software) are accounted for as assets that are charged to the income statement as expenses over their useful lives. In contrast, the costs of internally developed knowledge management initiatives (e.g., human resource programs, creating knowledge repositories) are expensed as incurred. Critics argue that this approach is capricious, and leads to undervaluing companies with large investments in intangible assets (Blair and Wallman, 2001). Proponents argue that the reliability of information is at least as important as its relevance, and that the value of intangible assets is realized, if at all, only long after their creation.

The essence of the knowledge accounting (KA) issue is when (not if) knowledge-creating activities should be recognized. Successful knowledge management efforts eventually improve financial performance by increasing sales, decreasing expenses, or both, while unsuccessful knowledge management efforts increase expenses more than they increase sales. However, the time lag between knowledge management (KM) investments and the realization of their financial benefits (if any) can be lengthy. Initial investments in physical assets increase assets and produce small depreciation expenses on the income statement. In contrast, initial investments in intangible assets produce potentially large, immediate expenses. Consequently, in the short term, the earnings of companies investing in intangible assets will be lower than the earnings of companies investing in physical assets.

2.2 What Determines the Value of Accounting Information?

Understanding the determinants of the value of accounting information is a prerequisite to understanding existing and proposed KA. The Financial Accounting Standard Board's (FASB) Statement #2 argues that accounting information derives its value from its relevance and reliability (FASB, 1980). Relevant information affects decisions because it is timely, and has feedback and predictive value. Reliable information is unbiased, complete, and verifiable. In addition, it corresponds to that which it purports to measure. At a gross level of analysis, relevance and reliability positively co-vary. For example, highly unreliable information is irrelevant. However, a more subtle analysis suggests that any accounting system must trade off relevance against reliability. For example, management's earnings projections from a KM initiative are relevant to investors, but are such projections reliable (i.e., unbiased)? Similarly, audited annual financial statements are reliable, but the time required for their production leads some critics to question their relevance (i.e., timeliness).

The trade-off between relevance and reliability is fundamental to KA. Implicitly, KA critics argue that financial and managerial accounting over-emphasize reliability and under-emphasize relevance. However, important, non-obvious reasons exist for accounting's attention to information reliability. Exploring the reason for accounting's emphasis on reliability, even at the expense of relevance, helps to illuminate the economic, social, and institutional factors that shape KA. These factors include accounting issues, such as the definition of an asset and the objectives of financial statements, and business issues, such as a corporate manager's incentives and the U. S. legal environment.

2.3 Why Does Accounting Prefer Reliable to Relevant Information?

2.3.1   Accounting Issues: What Is an Asset?

Accounting defines an asset as owned property that: (1) was obtained in an arm's length transaction and (2) provides probable future economic benefits (FASB 1985). This definition is often criticized because it excludes much of what KA critics argue fuels the economic prosperity of organizations. For example, people are not assets since (with the exception of slaves) companies do not own their employees. Consequently, employees (who are central to most KM initiatives) are not assets and are excluded from the balance sheet. Accounting for human resources has long been recognized as problematic for the existing accounting model (e.g., see (Scott, 1925)). Academic accountants and others have proposed a variety of models and methods to account for human resources; see Sackmann et al. (1989) for a review.

As a second issue in defining an asset, consider assets that are purchased versus internally constructed. To KA critics, it is irrelevant whether a company purchases or constructs an asset. But the purchase versus construction distinction is critical to the reliability of "asset" information. Purchased assets are acquired in verifiable market transactions. In contrast, valuing (and in some cases even identifying) internally constructed assets is problematic. For example, should Dow Chemical's innovative KM process for identifying and valuing its patents (Petrash, 1998) be recognized as an asset? And if so, what value should be placed on this "asset"?

The definition of an asset is among the most critical and controversial issues for KA. The most effective knowledge management strategies are often internal efforts to create and develop knowledge (Hansen et al., 1999). That the resulting knowledge is difficult to value is integral to an optimal knowledge management strategy, i.e., of internally growing (rather than purchasing) organizational knowledge. But identifying and valuing the resulting "asset" is inherently problematic. For internally grown knowledge systems, valuing knowledge assets can become like Justice Stewart Potter's attempt to distinguish art from pornography.... "I shall not today attempt further to define [pornography] ... but I know it when I see it" (Simpson's Contemporary Quotations, 1988).

2.3.2   Accounting Issues: The Objectives of Financial Statements

Financial statements provide information that is useful to business and economic decisions. For financial statements to be comparable across companies and countries, information must be quantified in monetary terms (e.g., in dollars) (FASB, 1978). The choice to include only monetary information in financial statements is neither capricious nor arbitrary but is instead motivated by the desire to provide reliable, objective, comparable information.

It is possible to include non-financial information as supplemental information to the financial statements. Existing financial statements and annual reports do include considerable supplemental information in footnotes, letters from CEOs, and reports of company plans. But ultimately, the existing model of financial reporting precludes directly including non-financial information in the financial statements of an organization.

The exclusion of non-monetary information from financial statements is an important limitation on KA. Most existing calls for the reform of KA give prominence to non-monetary measures of knowledge activities (e.g., the number of new employees with Ph.D.s – (Skandia AFS, 1998)). But such information can only appear in the body of the financial statements in monetary form (i.e., by creating an asset, liability, income, or expense). Consequently, financial statements themselves must play a limited role in KA, because KM activities only become evident in the financial statements after their activities have created significant monetary (i.e., financial) effects.

2.3.3   Business Issues: Manager's Incentives

It is a basic assumption of economics that financial incentives motivate behavior (Baker et al., 1988). Therefore, it is no surprise that stock options and bonuses based on financial performance provide strong incentives for managers to systematically bias (i.e., lie about or exaggerate) performance measures. For example, MicroStrategy's management systematically inflated company earnings by reporting revenue when contracts were signed instead of when the revenue from the contracts was earned. MicroStrategy's per share stock price fell from $140 to $86.75 after the SEC forced company management to appropriately recognize revenue (Saylor, 2000). The company restated its 1999 revenue to $150 million, approximately $55 million less than originally reported.

Good auditors are aware of management's incentives and biases, and are appropriately skeptical of management's assertions about financial performance. Because of this, investors value audited financial statements (e.g., see Dopuch et al. (1986), Melumad and Ziv (1997)). But would management's assertions about the extent to which employees were "empowered" by a KM initiative (e.g., see Liebowitz & Suen, (2000)) be sufficiently reliable to be auditable? Any effort to increase the relevance of KA must address managers' incentives to systematically misreport the measures on which they are evaluated.

2.3.4   Business Issues: Liability from Shareholder litigation

Financial statement auditors opine as to whether a company's financial statements fairly represent its financial position. Auditors are often sued by investors who lose money when a company's stock price declines. The plaintiffs in such suits generally allege that audited financial statements misrepresent the financial position of the company. The agency relationships between investors, managers, and auditors demand more reliable (and necessarily less relevant) measures of management performance. For example, a company's management may assert that a KM initiative will result in a 50% return over the next three years. Such information is certainly relevant to investors interested in the company. But only a foolish auditor would accept an audit engagement to attest to the accuracy of this management assertion. The auditor is generally among the first parties named in a lawsuit if the assertion failed to materialize. The U.S. legal environment demands KA measures that are verifiable because auditors must have a basis in law for defending themselves against investor allegations of auditors' failure to exercise due diligence in evaluating management's assertions in the financial statements (cf. Erickson et al., 2000).

Legal threats also exist to management for making non-mandatory disclosures of financial information. For example, the Security and Exchange Commission's recently adopted Regulation FD prevents corporate managers from selectively disclosing information to financial analysts or other company outsiders (RR Donnelley & Sons, 2001). Therefore, it is unsurprising that the most innovative KM reporting initiatives have occurred in non-U.S. companies (e.g., in Scandinavian) where shareholder litigation is comparatively infrequent.

3   Measuring Knowledge – Alternatives to the Status Quo

Considerable effort has been devoted to alternative accounting models that capture the value-creating activities of KM before their financial realization. These efforts began with the recognition that financial statements focus on value realization, not value creation. For example, a Wharton School symposium on financial reporting and standard setting concluded that "continuing on the present course, we believe, will lead to the growing irrelevance of conventional financial reporting in the new age of information" (AICPA 2000). Here, we briefly describe six alternative approaches to KA (Upton, 2000). These alternatives are summarized in Table 1. Following this, we compare the alternative approaches to KA and consider the future of KA.

3.1 Total Value Creation (TVC)

Total Value Creation (TVC), designed by a consortium headed by the Canadian Institute of Chartered Accountants (CICA), attempts to capture an organization's value-creating activities, instead of the value-realizing activities that are the focus of existing financial accounting efforts (CICA, 2000). Traditional financial reporting focuses on realized economic transactions. In contrast, TVC provides a porting focuses on realized economic transactions. In contrast, TVC provides a means for reporting value-creating activities before they are realized through transactions. The basic TVC model is a discounted cash flow framework within which managers can disclose their planned value-creating activities and the antici- pated consequences of these activities. TVC's authors argue that it is a supple- ment to, not a replacement of, existing financial reporting approaches. Currently, the consortium of developers provides two case studies that illustrate reporting us- ing the TVC model. Proponents argue that TVC may initially be most valuable as an internal reporting system for management to assess plans for value-creating ac- tivities. After extensive testing as an internal reporting system, the CICA argues that TVC may also be a useful supplement to existing financial reports.

3.2 Accounting for the Future (AFTF)

Nash (2000) uses the discounted cash flow approach advocated by the TVC to propose a replacement for existing financial reporting. Accounting for the Future (AFTF) redefines assets, liability, and equities using present values instead of pur- chase costs. For example, consider a company that purchases a $200,000 com- puter system to use in constructing a knowledge system that has an expected pre- sent value of future cash flows of $1,000,000. Using traditional financial report- ing, the computer system would be valued as a $200,000 asset. Using AFTF, the computer system would be a $1,000,000 asset. In AFTF, physical and intangible assets, as well as acquired and internally developed assets are all valued at the pre- sent value of their expected future cash flows.

Table 1. Summary of Proposed Knowledge Accounting Approaches

Approach	Source	Characteristics
Total Value Creation (TVC®)	Canadian Institute of Chartered Accountants (CICA) (2000)	• Discounted Cash Model of Value Creating Activities • Financial and Non-Financial Information • Supplements Existing Financial Reporting Systems
Accounting For The Future (AFTF)	Nash (2000)	• Discounted Cash Model of Value Creating Activities • Physical & Intangible Assets Valued at Present Value of Fu- ture Cash Flows • Replaces Existing Financial Reporting System • Financial but no Non-financial Information

Balanced Scorecard	Kaplan & Norton (1992, 1996, 2000)	• Customized: Measures Derive from Management's Strategic Objectives • Supplements Existing Financial Reporting Systems • Focuses on Performance in Four Areas: Financial, Customer, Internal Processes, and Innovation and Learning • Financial and Non-Financial Information
Skandia Navigator	Skandia AFS (1998)	• Very Similar to the Balanced Scorecard Approach • Focuses on Performance in Five Areas: Financial, Customer, Human, Process, and Renewal and Development • Supplements Existing Financial Reporting Systems • Customized: Measures Derive from Management's Strategic Objectives • Financial and Non-Financial Information
Intangible Asset Monitor	Sveiby (1997, 1999a, 1999b)	• Builds upon Skandia AFS Approach • Very Similar to the Balanced Scorecard Model • Supplements Existing Financial Reporting Systems • Financial and Non-Financial Information
Value Chain Scoreboard	Lev (2001)	• Ten Step Model of the Process by Which Innovation Creates Value • Criteria for Choosing among Measures • Supplements Existing Financial Reporting Systems • Financial and Non-Financial Information

3.3 Kaplan's Balanced Scorecard

Kaplan & co-authors (Kaplan and Norton 1992, 1996, 2000) propose the Balanced Scorecard as a method for better capturing the value-creating activities that derive from intangible assets. Managers establish balanced scorecards that reflect the specific measurable objectives that derive from their corporate strategy. Typically, managers identify measures in each of four strategic areas: financial performance, customers, internal processes and, learning and growth. Since no single measure or area completely captures a company's value-creating activities, companies and managers should be evaluated across all four areas of strategic focus.

Kaplan proposes the balanced scorecard as an internal supplement to existing reporting systems. Consequently, using the balanced scorecard approach would not affect existing financial statement reporting. Instead, a balanced scorecard reporting approach would provide supplemental information about intangible assets that would otherwise go unreported. In addition, because balanced scorecard measures derive from corporate strategies, such measures are unique to individual companies. As a result, knowledge management initiatives reported under a balanced score would be incomparable across companies.

3.4 Skandia Navigator

Skandia AFS, a Swedish insurance and banking company is an innovator in financial reporting on intellectual capital (Skandia AFS, 1998). Skandia's Navigator is a business-planning model that is strikingly similar to the balanced scorecard approach of identifying critical business areas and developing related measures. Navigator includes five focus areas: financial, customer, human, process, and renewal and development. Skandia's subdivisions report 18 to 20 measures across each of the five Navigator categories. Skandia AFS currently uses the model for both internal and external reporting.

Consistent with concerns about the comparability of balanced scorecard style reporting approaches, existing Skandia financial reports suggest that comparability across units is not present in Skandia's own application of the Navigator model (Upton, 2000). For example, The American Skandia Variable Annuities group uses the number of contracts as its measure of customer success, while the SkandiaBanken Distance Banking group has chosen the number of customers as its key customer success measure.

3.5 Intangible Assets Monitor Model

In 1988, a small group of Swedish service companies and accountants (called the Konrad Group) published "The Invisible Balance Sheet", which called for supplementing annual reports with information about organizational intangible assets (Sveiby, 1997, 1999a). Parts of this report, such as its distinction between individual capital, structural capital, and customer capital, are now well integrated into the KM literature (e.g., included in Skandia's intellectual capital reporting initiatives). The report defined key indicators of each type of capital, and discussed the annual reports of Swedish company innovators in reporting on intangible assets.

Karl-Erik Sveiby has continued the development of the model by proposing an "intangible assets monitor" (Sveiby, 1997) – a reporting system that is quite similar to a business scorecard approach. The similarities between the business scorecard and intangible assets monitor approaches are sufficiently similar that Sveiby has a Web site devoted to discussing their similarities and differences (Sveiby, 1999b).

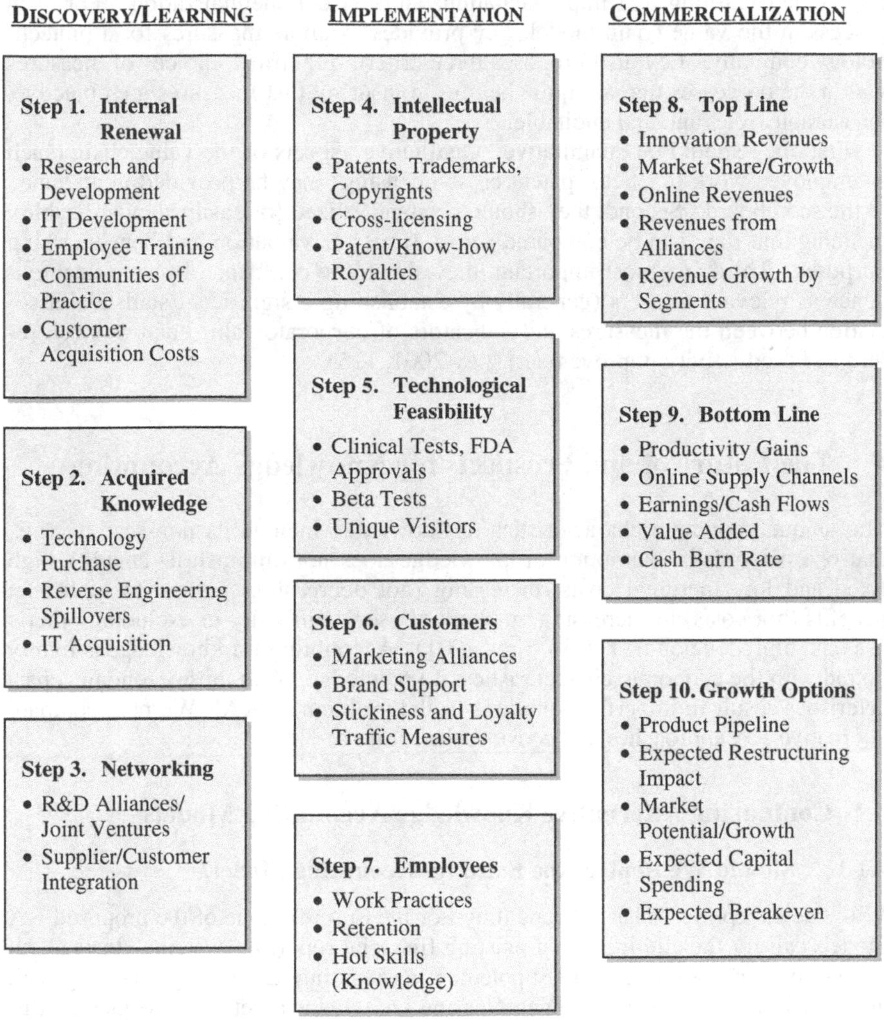

DISCOVERY/LEARNING	IMPLEMENTATION	COMMERCIALIZATION

Step 1. Internal Renewal
- Research and Development
- IT Development
- Employee Training
- Communities of Practice
- Customer Acquisition Costs

Step 2. Acquired Knowledge
- Technology Purchase
- Reverse Engineering Spillovers
- IT Acquisition

Step 3. Networking
- R&D Alliances/ Joint Ventures
- Supplier/Customer Integration

Step 4. Intellectual Property
- Patents, Trademarks, Copyrights
- Cross-licensing
- Patent/Know-how Royalties

Step 5. Technological Feasibility
- Clinical Tests, FDA Approvals
- Beta Tests
- Unique Visitors

Step 6. Customers
- Marketing Alliances
- Brand Support
- Stickiness and Loyalty Traffic Measures

Step 7. Employees
- Work Practices
- Retention
- Hot Skills (Knowledge)

Step 8. Top Line
- Innovation Revenues
- Market Share/Growth
- Online Revenues
- Revenues from Alliances
- Revenue Growth by Segments

Step 9. Bottom Line
- Productivity Gains
- Online Supply Channels
- Earnings/Cash Flows
- Value Added
- Cash Burn Rate

Step 10. Growth Options
- Product Pipeline
- Expected Restructuring Impact
- Market Potential/Growth
- Expected Capital Spending
- Expected Breakeven

Figure 1. The Value Chain Scoreboard (from Lev (2001))

3.6 Value Chain Scorecard

Lev (2001) has recently proposed the Value Chain Scorecard in an attempt to capture the economic processes by which intangible assets create company financial
value. The Value Chain Scoreboard model consists of ten economic processes that
attempt a comprehensive representation of the innovation process (See Figure 1).
Lev categorizes these ten processes into the three broader categories of: (1) discovery and learning, (2) implementation, and (3) commercialization. For each
process in the value chain model, Lev provides example measures for a biotechnology company. Lev also proposes three criteria for firms' choices of measures
within the processes that are quite helpful in insuring that measures are objective,
measurable, relevant, and auditable:

First, they should be quantitative. Qualitative aspects of the value chain (such
as employee work practices, patent cross-licensing) may be provided in an annex
to the scoreboard. Second, they should be standardized (or easily standardizable),
meaning that they can be compared across firms for valuation and benchmarking
purposes. Third and most important, they should be confirmed by empirical evidence as relevant to users (generally by establishing a significant statistical association between the measures and indicators of corporate value such as stock return and productivity improvement) (Lev 2001, 115).

4   The Future of and Prospects for Knowledge Accounting

The unique economic characteristics of knowledge include its non-scarcity (i.e.,
that one person's consumption of knowledge does not diminish its supply), high
fixed and low marginal costs, increasing (not decreasing) returns to scale, net
benefits (not costs) to increasing numbers of users, difficulty in excluding other's
use, and high development risks (Lev, 2001). Accounting for knowledge is tightly
bound with the economic characteristics of knowledge. And these economic characteristics result in imperfect solutions to the problem of KA. We next compare
alternative KA approaches and consider the future of KA.

4.1 Comparing Alternative Knowledge Accounting Models

4.1.1   Should We Replace the Existing Accounting Model?

With one exception (Nash's Accounting For the Future), none of the proposed KA
models call for the elimination of existing financial reporting systems. Instead, all
(except one) proposals call for supplementing existing accounting reporting with
additional information about intangibles and knowledge assets. Consequently, the
proposed KA approaches sharply contrast with criticisms of existing KA that assert the fundamental irrelevance of the economic model of existing financial reporting. As previously noted, the fundamental KA issue is the timing of the recognition of KM initiatives, not to economic substance. Successful KM efforts
eventually improve financial performance. The alternative accounting approaches
proposed would recognize and report KM initiatives earlier than existing account-

ing approaches. However, with the exception of Nash's proposal, no proposed KA method would replace the existing accounting model of organizational financial performance.

4.1.2   Comparing Knowledge Accounting Methods

Two of the proposed KA approaches, TVC and AFTF are based on discounted present value models of management's organizational plans. While these models may hold value as internal reporting systems that are used to evaluate divisions and managers, it is difficult to reconcile their inherent subjectivity with the economic demand for reliable, objective information in external financial reports. The CICA's proposal that TVC disclosures be a supplement to, rather than a replacement for, existing financial statements would seem to be feasible. In contrast, Nash's proposal that AFTF data replace existing financial statements would seemingly fail to consider the economic and institutional characteristics that give rise to the demand for existing financial reports.

Three of the proposed KA approaches, the Balanced Scorecard, Skandia Navigator, and the Intangible Assets Monitor are strikingly similar. All identify focal areas of organizational concern and propose that organizations individually choose measures within each focal area that are consistent with management's objectives. Such an approach has obvious and important advantages for linking organizational strategies with measurable goals (Kaplan and Norton, 2000). However, such an approach is inconsistent with the normative principle of information comparability. That is, information should be comparable across industries and companies when possible (FASB, 1980). In addition, these approaches provide little guidance for choosing measures. Consequently, the current versions of these three approaches may best serve as internal indicators of a company's value-creating activities, and may be of less use in creating KA reports for use by external stakeholders who hope to compare the knowledge activities of multiple companies, or, to compare the divisions of a single company (Upton 2001).

Of the existing approaches, Lev's appears most feasible as a supplemental financial reporting approach that captures KM value-creating activities. Lev's proposal appropriately includes the economic characteristics of innovation as an integral part of accounting for innovations. At the same time, Lev's proposal is preliminary with many of the actual characteristics of financial reporting unresolved. In addition, Lev's approach has the potential to create a non-comparable reporting system if companies and standard-setters ignore his proposed criteria of standardization in the choices of innovation metrics.

4.1.3   Should Knowledge Management Reports Supplement Financial Statements?

A commonly advocated KA approach is to supplement existing financial reports with any one of the six alternative reporting approaches described herein. However, a variant of Occam's razor suggests that simpler explanations are preferred to complex ones. Restating Occam's razor in economic terms suggests that the benefits of KA must exceed its disclosure costs. This criterion is a nontrivial obstacle to the proposed KA methods, given the considerable cost of implementing some of the proposed alternatives. For example, organizations are likely to require considerable resources to implement the TVC or AFTF models, which require financial statements that include discounted cash flow analyses of all company assets and liabilities. In addition, it seems unlikely that financial statement auditors would be willing to attest to the veracity of (highly subjective) reports prepared using the TVC or AFTF models.

Despite the ubiquitous assertions that accounting has failed the new economy, few U.S. companies have experimented with voluntary disclosures of supplemental information regarding intellectual capital and knowledge management (Blair and Wallman, 2001). Further, there is only limited evidence that the market punishes companies for failing to disclose such information (e.g., Lev 2001). Ultimately, calls for the reform of accounting must meet a market test as to whether KA information provides sufficient value to justify its considerable cost.

Further, it is not enough to observe whether markets "use" supplemental knowledge disclosure information about intellectual capital and KM (Chatterjee et al., 2001). Product and information use can be functional or dysfunctional. For example, surveys would likely indicate that heroin users enthusiastically intend to continue using heroin. Similarly, some investors rely on psychics for investment advice (e.g., Psychic Investor (2001)). Yet, few would argue that heroin use or psychic investment advice is rational or wise. Consequently, a research finding that the "market" "uses" KA information is insufficient to justify its production and dissemination. Instead, research findings of market "use" of information provide a starting point for deeper investigations of whether the market's use of such information is functional or dysfunctional.

4.2 Prospects and Possibilities for Knowledge Accounting

The primary virtue of existing KA is reliability. The primary deficiency of existing KA is its irrelevance and inconsistency in accounting for intangible and physical assets. The primary virtue of the alternatives to existing KA is relevance. The primary deficiency of these alternatives is a lack of reliability. Hence, all existing and proposed solutions to KA are imperfect. None meet the goals of a perfectly objective, reliable, relevant system of KA.

KA is closely bound with the economics of knowledge, and with the institutions, social forces, and political realities of financial reporting. These forces are neither arbitrary nor capricious. Instead, they attempt to balance the conflicting and competing needs of investors, managers, and society. These forces have led to a strong preference for objective, verifiable, monetary measures, and a lower preference for relevant measures with low reliability. Critics of existing KA practices have generated useful KA methods that hold promise for improving the relevance of organizational financial reports. At the same time, claims that the basic accounting model is irrelevant in the face of changing economic conditions are unsupported by an examination of the alternative methods for KA. We look forward to a future that better integrates the economics of knowledge into KA, and better reconciles the conflicting demands of relevance and reliability in KA.

References

American Institute of Certified Public Accountants (AICPA), "Improving Business Reporting – A Customer Focus (the Jenkins Report)," February 21, 2000, URL=http://www.aicpa.org/members/div/accstd/iber/appiv.htm.

American Institute of Certified Public Accountants, "Improving Business Reporting – A Customer Focus," 1994, URL=http://accounting.rutgers.edu/raw/aicpa/business/chap1.htm.

Arthur Andersen & Co., *The Valuation of Intangible Assets.* London: The Economist Intelligence Unit, 1992.

Baker, G. P., M. C. Jensen, and K. J. Murphy, "Compensation and Incentives: Practice vs. Theory," *The Journal of Finance*, 43, 3, 1988, 593-616.

Barth, M. E., R. Kasnik, and M. F. McNichols, "Analyst Coverage and Intangible Assets," *Stanford University Research Paper,* No. 1575R3, August, 1999.

Baum, G., C.Ittner, D. Larcher, J. Low, T.Siesfeld, and M.S. Malone, "Introducing the New Value Creation Index," *Forbes ASAP*, April 4, 2000. URL=http://www.forbes.com/asap/2000/0403/140.html

Blair, M. M. and S.M.H. Wallman, *Unseen Wealth: Report of the Brookings task Force on Understanding Intangible Sources of Value.* Washington: Brookings Institution, 2001.

Brown, B. and S. Perry, "Removing the Financial Performance Halo from Fortune's Most Admired Companies," *Academy of Management Journal*, 37, 5, 1994, 1347-1359.

Brown, J.S. and P. Duguid, "Organizing Knowledge," *California Management Review*, 40, 3, 1998, 90-111.

Bryant, L., "Value-Relevance of Capitalizing Successful Exploration Activities: Implications for R&D Accounting," Working Paper, Ohio State University, October, 2000.

Brynjolfsson, E., and L. Hitt, "Breaking Boundaries," *Information Week*, Special Issue, September 22, 1997, 34-36.

Canadian Institute of Chartered Accountants, Total Value Creation®, 2000, URL=http://www.totalvaluecreation.com/index.html.

The Canadian Performance Reporting Initiative, *Intellectual Capital Management: Challenge and Response,* URL=http://cpri.matrixlinks.ca/icm/IcmReport.html.

Cash, J. I., W.F. McFarlan, J.L. McKenney, and L.M. Applegate, *Corporate Information Systems Management.* Burr Ridge, IL: Irwin, 1992.

Chatterjee, K., V. Richardson, and R. Zmud, "Examining the Shareholder Wealth Effects of Announcements of Newly Created CIO Positions," *MIS Quarterly*, 25, 1, 2001, 43-70.

Clemons, E.K., "Corporate Strategies for Information Technology: A Resource-Based Approach," *Computer*, 24, 11, 1991, 131-136.

Danish Trade and Industry Development Council., *Intellectual Capital Accounts – Reporting and Managing Intellectual Capital*, Copenhagen, September, 1997.

Desjardins, J., *The Measurement of Shareholder Value Creation*, Toronto: Canadian Institute of Chartered Accountants, 1998.

Dopuch, N., R. Holthausen, and R. Leftwich, "Abnormal Stock Returns Associated with Media Disclosures of 'Subject To' Qualified Audit Opinions," *Journal of Accounting and Economics* 8, 1986, 93-119.

Dos Santos, B. L., G. K. Peffers, and D.C. Mauer, "The Impact of Information Investment Announcements on the Market Value of the Firm," *Information Systems Research*, 4, 1, 1993, 1-23.

Eccles, R. G., and H. D. Kahn, *Pursuing Value: The Information Reporting Gap in the U.S. Capital Markets*, New York: PricewaterhouseCoopers LLP, 1998.

Edvinsson, L. and M. S. Malone, *Intellectual Capital: Realizing Your Company's True Value by Finding Its Hidden Brainpowe,*. New York: HarperBusiness, 1997.

Erickson, M. M., B. W. Mayhew, et al., "Why Do Audits Fail? Evidence for Lincoln Savings and Loan," *Journal of Accounting Research*, 38, 1, 2000, 165-194

Ernst & Young Center for Business Innovation, *Enterprise Value in the Knowledge Economy*. Boston, MA: Ernst & Young Center for Business Innovation, 1997.

Financial Accounting Standards Board, "Objectives of Financial Reporting by Business Enterprises," *Statement of Financial Accounting Concepts No. 1.* Stamford, CT: FASB, 1978.

Financial Accounting Standards Board, "Qualitative Characteristics of Accounting Information," *Statement of Financial Accounting Concepts No. 2.* Stamford, CT: FASB, 1980.

Financial Accounting Standards Board, "Elements of Financial Statements," *Statement of Financial Accounting Concepts No. 6.* Stamford, CT: FASB, 1985.

Grant, R.M., "Toward a Knowledge-Based Theory of the Firm," *Academy of Management Executive*, 17, 1996, 109-122.

Hall, R., "The Strategic Analysis of Intangible Resources," *The Strategic Management Journal*, 13, 1992, 135-144.

Hansen, M., N. Norhria, and T. Tierney, "What's Your Strategy for Knowledge Management?" *Harvard Business Review*, March-April, 1999, 106-116.

Ives, B., S.L. Jarvenpaa, and R. O. Mason, "Global Business Drivers: Aligning Information Technology to Global Business Strategy," *IBM Systems Journal*, 32, 1, 1993, 143-162.

Kaplan, R.S. and D.P. Norton, *The Balanced Scorecard: Translating Strategy into Action*. Boston, MA: Harvard Business School Press, 1996.

Kaplan, R.S. and D.P. Norton, "The Balanced Scorecard – Measures that Drive Performance," *Harvard Business Review*, January-February, 1992, 71-79.

Kaplan, R.S. and D.P. Norton, "Having Trouble With Your Strategy? Then Map It," *Harvard Business Review*, September-October, 2000, 3-11.

Keen, P. G. W., *Shaping the Future: Business Design Through Information Technology*. Cambridge, MA: Harvard Business Press, 1991.

Knivsflå, K.H. and N.E. Joachim Høegh-Krhon, "Accounting for Intangible Assets in Scandinavia, the UK, the US, and by the IASC: Challenges and a Solution," *The International Journal of Accounting*, 35, 2, 2000.

Knivsflå, K.H., *Accounting for Intangible Assets: The Informational Relevance of Deferred Charges*, Working Paper, Foundation for Research in Economics and Business Administration, December, 1999.

Konrad Group, *The Invisible Balance Sheet*. Stockholm: Arbetsgruppen Konrad (Orginal published in Swedish asn Den Osynliga Balansräkningen), 1990.

Leadbeater, C., *New Measures for the New Economy*. London: Institute of Chartered Accountants in England & Wales, March, 2000.

Lev, B. and D. Aboody, "Information Asymmetry, R&D, and Insider Gains," *The Journal of Finance*, December, 2000.

Lev, B. and P. Zarowin, *The Boundaries of Financial Reporting and How to Extend Them*. Working Paper, Stern School, New York University, February, 1999.

Lev, B., *Intangibles: Management, Measurement, and Reporting*. Washington: Brookings Institution, June, 2001.

Liebowitz, J. and C. Y. Sven, "Developing Knowledge Management Metrics for Measuring Intellectual Capital," *Journal of Intellectual Capital*, 1, 1, 2000, 54-67.

Litan, R.E. and P. Wallison, *The GAAP Gap: Corporate Disclosure in the Internet Age*. Washington: AEI-Brookings Joint Center for Regulatory Studies, 2000.

Lucas, H.C., "The Business Value of Information Technology: A Perspective and Thoughts for Future Research," in Banker R.; Kauffmann, R.; and Mahmood M.A. (eds.), *Strategic Information Technology Management: Perspectives on Organizational Growth and Competitive Advantage*, Harrisburg, PA: Idea Group Publishing, 1993, 375-403.

Marshall, C., L. Prusak, and D. Shpilberg, "Financial Risk and the Need for Superior Knowledge Management," *California Management Review*, 38, 3, 1996, 77-101.

McKenney, J. L., *Waves of Change: Business Evolution Through Information Technology*. Cambridge, MA: Harvard Business School Press, 1995.

McLean, R.I.G., *Performance Measures in the New Economy*. Toronto: Canadian Institute of Chartered Accountants, 1995.

Melumad, N. D. and A. Ziv, "A Theoretical Examination of the Market Reaction to Auditors' Qualifications," *Journal of Accounting Research*, Autumn, 1997, 239-256.

Nash, H., "Accounting for the Future: A Disciplined Approach to Value-Added Accounting," 2000, URL=http://home.sprintmail.com/~humphreynash/Draft_Proposal.htm.

Netherlands Ministry of Economic Affairs, *Intangible Assets, Balancing Accounts with Knowledge,* The Hague: Ministry of Economic Affairs, October, 1999.

Nolan, R. *Note on Estimating the Value of the IT Asset.* Harvard Business School Note #9-195-197, 1994.

Nonaka, I. and N. Konno, "The Concept of 'Ba': Building a Foundation for Knowledge Creation," *California Management Review*, 40, 3, 1998, 40-54.

Nonaka, I. and Tekeuchi, H., *The Knowledge-Creating Company,* New York: Oxford University Press, 1995.

Nonaka, I., "A Dynamic Theory of Organizational Knowledge Creation," *Organization Science*, 5, 1994, 14-37.

Norton, D.P. "Should Balanced Scorecards Be Required?" *Balanced Scorecard Report*, July-August, 2000, 14-15.

Pavitt, K., "What We Know About the Strategic Management of Technology," *California Management Review*, Spring. 1990.

Petrash, G., "Intellectual Asset Management at Dow Chemical," in Sullivan, P.H. (ed.), *Profiting from Intellectual Capital: Extracting Value From Innovation*, New York: Wiley, 1998, 205-220.

Psychic Investor, 2001, URL=http://www.marcusgoodwin.com/, see also M. Goodwin, *The Psychic Investor*, 2000, Adams Media.

RR Donnelley & Sons, *Regulation FD*, 2001, URL=http://www.realcorporatelawyer.com/regulationFD.html#whatis.

Sackmann, S.A., E. Flamholtz, and M. Bullen, "Human Resource Accounting: A State-Of-The-Art Review," *Journal of Accounting Literature*, 8, 1989, 235-264.

Sambamurthy, V. and R.W. Zmud, "At the Heart of Success: Organizationwide Management Competencies," in Sauer, C. and Yetton, P.W. (eds.) *Steps to the Future: Fresh Thinking on the Management of IT-Based Organizational Transformation,* San Fransisco: Jossey-Bass, 1997, 143-163.

Saylor, M., "MicroStrategy Falls on Earnings Cut," *Bloomberg News, 2000*, URL=http://news.cnet.com/news/0-1007-200-1577065.html.

Scott, D.R., *Theory of Accounts*. New York: Henry Holt Co., 1925.

Simpson's Contemporary Quotations, compiled by James B. Simpson. 1988, http://www.bartleby.com/63/.

Skandia AFS., *Human Capital in Transformation, Intellectual Capital Prototype Report*. 1998 URL=http://wwwl.skanida-afs.com/.

Storey, R.K. and S. Storey, *The Framework of Financial Accounting Standards and Concepts,* Norwalk, Conn.: FASB, January, 1998.

Strassman, P.A., *The Squandered Computer,* New Haven, CT: Information Economics Press, 1997.

Strassman, P.A. *The Business Value of Computer.* New Haven, CT: The Information Economics Press, 1990.

Sveiby, K., "The Intangible Assets Monitor," 1997, URL=http://www.sveiby.com.au/intangass/companymonitor.html.

Sveiby, K., *The Intangible Assets Monitor.* 1999a, URL=http://www.sveiby.com.au/IntangAss/CompayMonitor.html..

Sveiby, K., "The Balanced Score Card (BSC) and the Intangible Assets Monitor," 1999b, URL=http://www.sveiby.com.au/BSCandIAM.html.

Teece, D.K., "Capturing Value from Technological Innovation: Integration, Strategic Partnering and Licensing Decisions," in Tushman, M. and Anderson, P. (eds.) *Managing Strategic Innovation and Change,* Oxford: Oxford University Press, 1986, 287-308.

Upton, W.S., *Special Report: Business and Financial Reporting, Challenges from the New Economy.* Norwalk CT: FASB, April, 2001.

Waterhouse, John, and A. Svendsen, *Strategic Performance Monitoring and Management: Using Non-Financial Measures to Improve Corporate Governance.* Toronto: Canadian Institute of Chartered Accountants, 1998.

CHAPTER 14

Knowledge Management in Action?

Jacky Swan
Warwick Business School, University of Warwick, Coventry, UK

This chapter is structured in two main parts. The first part offers a brief, and self-admittedly stylized, overview and critique of dominant approaches to knowledge management and its links with innovation. Adopting a view of knowledge as socially constructed, it concludes from this that, where the specific purpose is innovation, then action concerns need to be as critical to knowledge management as cognitive or decision concerns. The second part draws upon a case study example to begin to draw out some key issues from a more action-oriented approach to knowledge management. This suggests, first, that innovation is often, by nature, a highly interactive process requiring knowledge and expertise from different functions and layers across the organization. In such cases critical problems concern the integration of knowledge across disparate, sometimes loosely formed, social groups and communities, rather than the accumulation of knowledge within communities. Second that if knowledge integration is to develop, then a more action-oriented perspective on knowledge management and the development of associated tools and technologies may be needed.

Keywords: Knowledge Management; Innovation; Action; Knowledge Integration; Community

1 Introduction

One of the first things to be said about knowledge management is that definitions abound. This is likely (even desirable) because knowledge itself is defined in many different ways and approached from many different angles and levels of analysis. Whereas some focus on knowledge as an individual phenomenon – for example Nonaka's (1994) acceptance of knowledge as 'justified true belief' – others, highlight its collective nature. Spender (1995), for example, argues for a pluralistic epistemology of knowledge based on the extent to which knowledge is individually or socially located, and the extent to which it is implicit or explicit. Importantly knowledge is seen as comprising "both meaning (i.e., cognitive, affective, symbolic and cultural) *and* praxis (i.e., behaviours, rituals, and organizational routines)" (p:73). This chapter accepts that knowledge, and therefore knowledge management, are complex, multilayered, and multifaceted phenomena (Blackler, 1995). Knowledge management is therefore scoped out very broadly as any process or practice of creating, acquiring, capturing, sharing and using knowledge, wherever it resides, to enhance learning and performance in organizations (Quintas et al., 1996).

This chapter also argues that approaches to knowledge management have, thus far, tended to privilege an individual view of knowledge and a single dimension – that of meaning. Hence there has been a strong emphasis on the conversion of (individual) tacit knowledge into explicit (Nonaka, 1994). The individual and cognitive aspects of knowledge – in particular the tacit-explicit dichotomy, often attributed to Polanyi (falsely, since Polanyi was only concerned with tacit knowledge) – have thus tended to subsume its social and praxis-based components. This risks divorcing knowledge from social context and action. In contrast this chapter seeks, not to discard the cognitive, but merely to redress the balance of debate in knowledge management by stressing the essentially social nature of knowledge (Lave and Wenger, 1988).

Knowledge, then, even individual knowledge, thus is seen as socially constructed – produced and negotiated through social action – action that is anchored in a social context and connected to specific (if not articulated) purposes. Thus, borrowing from Tsoukas and Vladimirou (2001), a working definition of knowledge can be taken as "the individual capability to draw distinctions, within a domain of action, based on an appreciation of context or theory, or both. Organizational knowledge is the capability members of an organization have developed to draw distinctions in the process of carrying out their work, in particular concrete contexts, by enacting sets of generalizations whose application depends on historically evolved collective understandings" (p.973). According to this view, knowledge lacks meaning if divorced from the context of action in which it has been produced and accepted.

The notion that 'knowledge' is an asset that needs to be nurtured and protected in order to sustain the survival or organisms and organizations is not new. The development of American patenting systems of the 18th Century, and Tayloristic attempts to manage (identify, codify, control and apply) the tacit craft-based knowledge of workers at the turn of the last century, cast a familiar shadow behind the current knowledge management 'revolution' (Chumer et al., 2000). Yet, recent decades have seen an explosive growth in the attention and status afforded to knowledge in relation to economic growth. Studies tracking the emergence of the term 'knowledge management', for example, demonstrate exponential growth since it first appeared in the mid 1990s (Scarbrough and Swan, 2001). Web searches on knowledge management also result in an astonishing number of 'hits', albeit many are marketing devices for consultants and software vendors (Chumer et al., 2000).

The explosion of interest in knowledge management no doubt reflects, to a large extent, its fashionable tendencies – with management 'pop stars' and consultants such as Drucker, Sveiby, and Senge, turning up the volume. In this hyped environment, it is easy to dismiss knowledge management as just another management fad, not worthy of any further serious attention. Yet, if we look behind the hype, what is interesting is the remarkable degree of convergence across academic disciplines and areas of industrial practice around the notion that knowledge is a – if not *the* – most valuable asset and resource that organizations and societies currently have. Discussions and debates around post-industrialism, knowledge work, intellectual and social capital, the knowledge economy, knowledge intensive firms, and so forth, are undoubtedly wide ranging and diverse in their particular histories, perspectives, and approach. Yet all tend to be underpinned by one central assumption – knowledge is a critical resource and the more there is of it, the better off we will all be. Despite some early warning signs (e.g., see Blackler et al.'s introduction to the 1993 special issue of *Journal of Management Studies* on Knowledge Work), and a few critical studies (e.g., Chumer et al., 2000), few writers in the field (broadly defined) of knowledge management attempt to distance themselves from this assumption.

As 'knowledge' has come to be viewed as such a critical organizational resource, there has also been a corresponding tendency towards what might be termed a 'quantity approach' to knowledge management in much of the literature. According to this, knowledge (however difficult to define) is assumed to have a direct and positive relation to innovative capability and organizational performance. The role of knowledge management is therefore to enhance the production, circulation and exploitation of knowledge. By capturing, stockpiling and transferring greater quantities of knowledge the organization's performance will be automatically improved. A message seems to be "we don't know what knowledge is but it seems to solve problems in a functional way so let's use it anyway" (Alvesson and Karreman, 2001). This quantitative approach has led to numerous general and prescriptive models aimed at increasing the quantity and circulation of knowledge available within the firm (Prusak, 1997).

A problem, however, with such quantitative approaches is that, whilst they assume a positive relationship between the accumulation of knowledge and improvement in innovative capability and organizational performance, this relationship is rarely examined. More often than not, knowledge is treated as valuable in its own right – divorced from the social action and tasks that actually generate changes in performance – the assumption being that the more knowledge an organization has, the more innovative and therefore more successful it will become. Yet knowledge can only generate changes in performance if it is linked to concrete actions, tasks and purposes (McDermott, 1999). Dorothy Leonard Barton likens 'purposeless' knowledge to the misfortunes of Sisyphus in the Greek fable: *"For all eternity, Sisyphus was sentenced to haul an immense boulder painfully to the top of a hill only to see it repeatedly crash back down to the bottom. Too often, the researchers and engineers on development projects harness their mental and physical creative powers to achieve the almost impossible – often at considerable personal cost – only to wonder, at the project's end, whether and why the corporation needed that particular boulder moved, or to speculate that they were climbing the wrong hill and the work was in vain".* Leonard-Barton, (1995; pp. 88-89).

More recently a 'new wave' of research on knowledge management has underlined a critical reaction to this quantity approach to knowledge. Drawing, typically, from earlier work on communities of practice and situated learning (Lave and Wenger, 1988, Lave 1991), a number of writers observe that too great an emphasis on knowledge as a resource, per se, risks divorcing it from concrete actions, practices, and outcomes (McDermott, 1999). This may lead to excessive stockpiling of knowledge (or, perhaps more accurately, information) at the expense of important organizational tasks, as well as to problems such as information overload (Schultze and Vandenbosch, 1998). These writers argue that knowledge should not be seen as valuable in itself, but as adding value only where it is created and applied for specific activities, tasks and purposes (McDermott, 1999; Seely Brown and Duguid, 2001). Yet, despite these observations, there are relatively few empirically grounded examples that actually link the deployment and management of knowledge to tasks and action (with notable exceptions – e.g., Orr, 1996, Hansen, 1999). Fewer still question or explore the role of knowledge as it connects with action.

The remainder of this chapter develops this alternative perspective by linking knowledge and its management to action directed at specific tasks and purposes, in a specific context – that of the development of new technology in a particular case firm. Whereas quantity approaches see a direct and linear relationship between knowledge stocks and flows and innovative outcomes (Amidon, 1998), this analysis suggests a need to understand the relation between knowledge deployment and action as nonlinear and essentially socially and contextually embedded. In particular, the chapter highlights the ways in which the deployment of knowledge in organizations is *driven by* action that is connected to a specific purpose – in this case technological innovation

The remainder of the chapter is structured as follows: first a brief overview of dominant perspectives in the literature on knowledge management is offered. This highlights the need to question some of the dominant orthodoxy of knowledge management in order to connect, more closely, knowledge and knowledge management to tasks and action. Moving from this rather abstract discussion, the chapter then uses a case study example of innovation in order to provide a closer (more tangible?) analysis of the tasks and activities associated with managing knowledge in the context of an innovation project. This demonstrates, first, that in many cases innovation is an interactive process requiring knowledge and expertise that is widely dispersed across multiple functions and layers across the organization. In such cases – and agreeing with authors such as Grant (2001) – critical problems concern the integration and synthesis of knowledge across disparate social groups rather than, simply, the accumulation or transfer of ever greater quantities of knowledge. Second, that if knowledge integration is to develop, then a more action-oriented perspective on knowledge management and the corresponding development of knowledge management tools and approaches is needed. Finally, based on this case example of innovation, the chapter hints at some directions that an action-oriented perspective might take.

2   Perspectives on Knowledge Management

Although early writings on knowledge management were dominated by an emphasis on tools and techniques, now the 'field' – referring here to the, now large, literature on the subject – appears to have diverged. Currently, and broadly speaking, at least two main perspectives and approaches seem to dominate behind the meaning of 'knowledge management' with the latter strengthening and gathering ground largely as a result of a critique of the former.

Consciously polarizing these perspectives in order to highlight their different orientations, the first can be described as 'knowledge management as technology' camp (Alvesson and Karreman, 2001). This has been labeled, variously, as the

Engineering perspective (Markus, 1999, Shadbolt and Milton, 1999), the *Cognitive* perspective (Swan et al., 1999) or the *Codification* strategy (Hansen, et al., 1999). This perspective is grounded in seminal work from library and information studies – that informed the development of internet search engine technologies (e.g., Salton, 1968) – as well as in a strong tradition of knowledge engineering research among artificial intelligence and computer science experts – that has informed the development of knowledge-based systems development (e.g., Schreiber et al., 2000). It has also informed attempts among Information Systems experts to develop IT-based tools (e.g., intranets, data warehouses, data exchange tools) aimed at the capture, storage, retrieval and sharing of knowledge.

Proponents of the engineering school often comment that knowledge management is *not* simply about developing computer systems (Shadbolt and Milton, 1999). However, following this initial caveat and some hints of discomfort with the technologically deterministic view, the focus frequently then narrows to an emphasis on using IT-based systems and methodologies to capture, codify and store knowledge so that it can be exploited more effectively in the organization (Chumer et al., 2000). Thus, comments as: "*some might say that cultural problems are insurmountable using knowledge technology. We disagree. We believe that with further modification and adaptation our techniques and tools can be used to capture the ways in which behavioural, cultural and organizational change takes place, and how it can be managed best*" (Shadbolt and Milton, 1999). Such beliefs in the power of technology are rarely as honestly or openly stated, but nonetheless appear to underpin much of what is written in the 'knowledge management as technology' perspective.

This approach, then, emphasizes the *cognitive* aspects of knowledge – knowledge is seen as something (that resides predominantly in peoples' heads) that can be extracted, codified, stored, and transferred in order to improve the information processing capability of the organization. As with information processors, the main problems associated with knowledge management are to do with the capacity and heuristic capabilities of the tools and systems involved – including the human systems' limited capacity to use knowledge management tools. The basic assumptions of this perspective, then, are:

- knowledge can be codified, stored and distributed
- knowledge management is about managing/fitting together pieces of intellectual capital
- knowledge is as an objective 'stock' or entity, with characteristics in its own right (i.e., knowledge is reified)
- the purpose of knowledge management is the explification of knowledge – the conversion of tacit to explicit and explicit to explicit (or, in the terms of Nonaka, 1994, externalization and combination)
- knowledge can be captured and transferred via IT systems. 'Weak ties' are also important (Hansen, 1999).
- the outcomes of knowledge management are reuse (or, in the terms of Levinthal and March, 1993, exploitation)

Its conclusions are, then, that knowledge is able to be abstracted from context and transferred from place to place and therefore using IT systems is essential for knowledge management. The main strategy for knowledge management could be described as codification (Hansen et al., 1999).

More recently an alternative perspective on knowledge management has emerged in the literature. This can be described broadly as the 'knowledge management as people camp' and has been labeled variously as the 'cultivation' perspective (Markus, 1999), the 'community' perspective (Swan et al., 1999) and the 'personalization' strategy (Hansen et al., 1999). This perspective dominates in the fields of organization studies (in particular organizational learning) and strategic management, and has emerged in part as a backlash to the failure of knowledge management systems and the obvious limits of technology in codifying relevant organizational knowledge (Newell et al., 2000). Hence comments such as: *"There is much more to KM than technology alone: KM is a business process ...KM is not seen as a matter of building a large electronic library but as one of connecting people so they can think together"* (Sarvary, 1999). This approach, then, emphasizes the cognitive but also the social and relational nature of knowledge (Nonaka, et al. 2001). For example, knowledge is seen as developing through and within social relationships and 'learning communities' or 'communities of practice' (Nonaka, et al., 2001, Seely Brown and Duguid, 2001). Moreover, the exploitation of intellectual capital is seen as developing through the development of social capital and networks (Nahapiet and Goshal, 1998). Here, technology is seen as possibly enabling the development of such communities, but not an essential component of knowledge management. The major assumptions of this perspective, then, are:

- the development of knowledge is closely linked to the development of social relationships, networks and communities of practice
- sharing tacit knowledge is critical but much valuable knowledge remains tacit – hence there are limits of codification
- knowledge is seen as (i) in peoples' heads but also (ii) situated in social communities. the purpose of knowledge management is the sharing of tacit knowledge (or, in Nonaka's 1994 terms, socialization and internalization)
- knowledge flows through networks and communities that connect people. 'Strong ties' are important for sharing tacit knowledge (Hansen, 1999).
- the outcomes of knowledge management are to exploit and create new knowledge (or, in Levinthal's terms the emphasis is on exploration as well as exploitation)

Its conclusions are, then, knowledge is social in nature – inextricable from the communities that create it. Thus, while IT may enable knowledge management by linking people, it is secondary (if needed at all). The strategy for knowledge management could be described as personalization (Hansen et al., 1999).

This latter wave of debate in knowledge management stresses that knowledge is social in nature and that social relationships are dependent on context (e.g., organizational, institutional), there is a need to understand knowledge as contextually embedded and situated in practice and action (Lave and Wenger, 1988). As noted, the perspectives outlined above are consciously stylized in order to demonstrate the different waves of thinking in relation to knowledge management. Of course, the distinction between the two 'camps' is not clean cut. For example, whilst the community perspective may pay closer attention to socialization and internalization processes, it would not dismiss combination and externalization as important for the creation of knowledge. The difference is one of emphasis rather than type. Moreover, some common assumptions – and underlying critiques – can be noted in connection with both perspectives, especially in terms of their treatment of social relations and action. These are outlined next.

3   Some Points of Critique of Dominant Perspectives

This section offers some points of critique that could be made in relation to both cognitive and community approaches. These concern, specifically: their assumptions about information technology and people, their assumptions about the nature and impacts of knowledge (particularly in terms of the functionality of knowledge for innovation) and the different – possibly conflicting – rationalities underpinning knowledge management and action.

3.1   Assumptions about IT and People

The first note of caution concerns the obvious danger of creating an artificial divide between technology and people – with the first 'camp' driven by the interests of those wishing to sell KM tools and systems, and the second driven by those wishing to privilege the role of people in organizations. More recently, there have been attempts to bridge these two perspectives so that both technology (and IT strategy) *and* people (and Human Resources strategy) are addressed (e.g., Quintas, 1997). These developments are, interestingly enough, reminiscent of other waves of debate in Organization Studies and Information Technology. For example, the development of socio-technical systems was an attempt to redress earlier claims of technological determinism. The notion of Business Process Reengineering also led to a wave of critique as being the 'fad that forgot people' (Davenport, 1996). And debates about IT and decentralization have swung between a technological imperative, an organizational imperative, and a managerial one (George and King, 1991). Arguably, these debates are now being resurfaced in discussions around knowledge management. Because the nature of IT is always changing, the cycling of management fashions around its application may be more rapid. It is easy, then, to fall into the trap of reworking old debates under new guises (Mumford, 1994)[1].

One consequence of debates around technological or social imperatives is the generation of more task-contingent views that link the relative emphasis on either people or technology to the task at hand (Hansen, 1999). However, contingency views continue to 'blackbox' technology, downplaying the socially constructed

---

[1] I am indebted to one of the anonymous reviewers for making this point.

nature of technology itself – i.e., the 'knowledge' embedded in technology (McLoughlin, 1999). Others adopt the view that technology is socially constructed and, therefore, most technologies are fundamentally equivocal (Weick, 1990; McLoughlin, 1999), being subject to multiple interpretations, negotiation and meanings. This is more in line with the broader definition of knowledge used here. According to this perspective, technical artifacts act as important channels for social relations and power (Scarbrough and Corbett, 1992; McLoughlin, 1999). Therefore, the use of knowledge management tools and methods cannot be separated from their social and political context. Arguments concerning the interplay between technology and organization are well made elsewhere (e.g., Orlikowski, 1996; De Sanctis and Poole, 1994). In terms of knowledge management, it means that the introduction of knowledge management tools may therefore have enabling effects in one context but disabling effects others (Cohen, 1998). As Cohen (1998) notes: *"an intranet is a powerful tool that, when used correctly can enhance communication and collaboration, streamline procedures, and provide just-in-time information to a globally dispersed workforce. Misused, however, an intranet can intensify mistrust, increase misinformation, and exacerbate turf wars."*

Thus the interplay between the technological artifacts and the organizational context in which artifacts are developed may lead to rather different outcomes to those intended. Ciborra and Jelassi (1994) refer to such emergent outcomes as 'drifting', as they occur because of "the matching between plasticity of the artifact and the multiform practices of the actors involved' (p. 9). Such drifting was clearly seen in Newell et al.'s (2000) study of the introduction of Intranet technology in a global retail bank as a vehicle for knowledge management across its highly decentralized divisions. Instead of facilitating, as intended, global knowledge sharing, in this case Intranet technology merely reinforced the social and cultural boundaries that already existed across the divisions. The launch of Intranet technology, for example, resulted in around 150 entirely different 'look and feel' intranet sites that did not connect with one another and, in many cases, repeated the same information and mistakes.

In relation to cognitive and community perspectives, a socially constructionist view means that it does not make sense to talk about knowledge management tools and technologies as either central (hence people relatively less important) or peripheral (hence people are relatively more important). Rather, knowledge management tools are themselves socially constructed – people and social relations are *always* important. Therefore, although it may be helpful to privilege technology or organization/people in order to get some focus on the subject of knowledge management, we might remind ourselves occasionally they do not exist as separate, or indeed separable, entities – the distinction is somewhat arbitrary. This means that endless arguments about the relative importance of technology or people in knowledge management are rather fruitless – it is merely a matter of taste.

3.2 Assumptions about the Objective Nature of Knowledge

Underpinning discussions about knowledge management, there is often an implicit assumption that at least some knowledge is objectifiable – as such it can be separated from the people and context in which it is deployed. Knowledge thus tends to be reified as 'thing like' with its own objectifiable parameters. This is implied by definitions of knowledge, for example, as "justified *true* belief" (Nonaka, et al. 2001). Much of the discourse treats knowledge like a building block – reflected in terms like stockpiling knowledge (Cole-Gomolski, 1997), or 'mass of knowledge' (Wikstrom and Normann, 1993), or 'storing' knowledge (Starbuck, 1992). The idea of knowledge as a stock to be piled (using IT systems) or as a thing to be transferred (by connecting people through communities) still pervades the literature. The metaphor is jigsaw-like with the critical thing being to amass pieces of knowledge (through codification) and join them together (through connecting people).

The implicit wish to objectify organizational knowledge arguably underpins many attempts to categorize and describe 'it' according to types. Thus "the management literature is replete with attempts to establish mutually exclusive and definitive typologies of knowledge" (Alvesson and Karreman, 2001) – taxonomies typically employing dichotomies, such as tacit-explicit, collective-individuals, embodied-embrained, and so on. For example, the widely held distinction between tacit and explicit knowledge is prevalent in both engineering and community perspectives, with community perspectives focusing on the sharing of tacit knowledge and engineering perspectives focusing on the sharing of explicit knowledge. This dichotomy also underpins some of the most widely cited writings on knowledge creation (e.g., Nonaka, 1994). It also implies that at least some knowledge can be separated from its social context – made explicit – making knowledge a more portable commodity.

Critiquing this notion, others note that all knowledge is contextual, subjective/intersubjective and constructed through social relationships in particular contexts (Tsoukas, 1996). What is meaningful in one context may be meaningless in another. Taxonomies and dichotomies may be useful but, if taken too far, may obscure more than they reveal. For example, explicit knowledge is always underpinned by tacit understandings. In short: "knowledge is not developed in splendid isolation from social context and culture" (Tsoukas, 1996). This is why some authors prefer to talk about claims to knowledge (e.g., Alvesson and Karreman, 2001) and about processes of knowing (e.g., Blackler, 1995), thus highlighting the highly situated nature of knowledge.

While many accounts of knowledge management note the social nature of knowledge creation (e.g., the importance for knowledge sharing of connecting people), they regularly stop short (even those in the community 'camp') of pursuing the socially constructed nature of knowledge itself (Alvesson and Karreman, 2001). With exceptions, for example, cognitive accounts tend to freeze knowledge and social relations in time and space, focusing on form and structure rather than on process and context. However, knowledge management is more than just stockpiling information or connecting people – it is also about understanding how meanings and interpretations are negotiated and established through particular social actions taking place within particular contexts and mediated by particular artifacts (Blackler, 1995). One implication, then, is a stronger need to address the processes underlying 'activities of knowing' and the ways in which these are shaped by social context (Blackler, 1995). Notwithstanding Polanyi's insightful exposition of the links between knowledge (knowing) and action, there is still work to be done here in the context of knowledge management in organizations. For example, research could seek to address how social networking relations, power relations, and technical artifacts play out in relation to attempts to manage knowledge in particular organizational contexts thus linking knowledge more closely to action (Orlikowski et al., 1995). The case of BT later attempts a (small) step in this direction.

3.3   The Functionality of Knowledge and Knowledge Management

As noted earlier, both engineering and community perspectives start from the assumption that knowledge is a critical resource and essential for innovation (Seely-Brown and Duguid, 2001; Grant, 2001). The primary concern for developers of knowledge management strategies and systems is therefore to facilitate greater knowledge creation and transfer either (or both) through the linking/connecting of people (i.e., the community approach) or the codification and transfer of knowledge (i.e., the engineering approach). More recently, research has started to look at the need to match these different strategies to the purpose of the task at hand. Thus Hansen (1999), drawing on social network analysis, and a detailed study of product innovation in a large electronics firm, developed a contingent view of knowledge management. This argues that the relative emphasis on knowledge management strategies (personalization or codification) and associated network links (strong or weak) need to vary according to (i) the purpose of the task at hand (exploration versus exploitation) and (ii) the kind of knowledge that is important to achieve it (tacit or explicit). Similarly, our own work has suggested that different strategies (networking, community or cognitive) may be more or less relevant for managing knowledge across different episodes of the innovation process (Swan and Scarbrough, 2001).

These contingent views are still driven by the assumption that knowledge (however poorly defined) is functional and so managing knowledge – albeit in ways that are perhaps complex and contingent – is fundamentally a good thing. A corollary is that developing IT systems or close-knit communities of practice, so that more knowledge can be shared, is a primary goal. This message is supported by evidence (mostly anecdotal) of organizations that have been able to achieve great performance improvements through the introduction of knowledge management. It also resonates with gurus that herald the criticality of knowledge and knowledge work in the information age (Drucker, 1988).

However there are a few problems with this claim. First, there is a possible tautology in terms of the evidence presented. Claims in the literature of performance improvement through knowledge management suggest that these are due to the companies' concerned abilities to exploit their superior (mostly tacit) knowledge, but evidence of this superior knowledge is also implied by performance (Davenport et al., 1996). Second, the assumed importance of knowledge for wealth production in society at large and associated reforms in organizational design (e.g., Drucker, 1988) should be treated with some caution. The importance of knowledge is supposedly increased by the potential for IT to change work practices in ways that exploits knowledge more effectively. However, it is not apparent that such generalist claims about the future are warranted (Seely Brown and Duguid,

2001). For example, at the same time that Drucker was talking about the importance of knowledge work and knowledge workers, Ritzer was providing evidence for the 'McDonaldisation of society'; firms were rationalizing on a mass scale through, for example, the reduction and outsourcing of managers with specialist expertise and the use of IT to automate previously skilled work; and mergers among large powerful corporations were signifying "dinosaurs herding together in the face of likely distinction" (Seely Brown and Duguid 2001). It may be dangerous, then, to generalize about the degree of organizational reform, the declining role of institutions, and the supposed rosy future of communities of knowledge workers and their value for economic performance, at least in some sectors (Seely Brown and Duguid, 2001).

Such caution should be reinforced when we remember that 'knowledge' has a strong symbolic value (Alvesson and Karreman, 2001). It helps consultancies sell services, helps academics raise the profile of their work, and helps managers initiate change, but it does not necessarily map, in any direct way, onto actual value in terms of performance improvement. There are other things than knowledge (defined simply in cognitive terms) that are important for organizational performance – such as action, motivation and emotional commitment. This has been emphasized by earlier work on organizational learning (Argyris and Schon, 1978).

3.4 Knowledge Management and Action

This leads to a final concern around the connection (or lack thereof) in the knowledge management literature between knowledge and action. Leaving aside epistemological debates about the nature (i.e., objectified or socially constructed) and importance (i.e., functionality) of knowledge, studies of knowledge typically take a working definition of knowledge as "justified personal belief that increases an individual's capacity to take effective action" (Alavi and Leidner, 1999; Nonaka, 1994). This emphasizes knowledge as primarily concerned with individual cognitive belief structures: "Information becomes knowledge once it is processed in the mind of an individual. This knowledge then becomes information again once it is articulated or communicated to others in the form of text, computer output, spoken or written words or other means. The recipient can then cognitively process and internalize the information so that it is converted back to tacit knowledge" (Alavi and Leidner, 1999). Knowledge management, then, tends to be about making individual cognitive knowledge accessible so that others may make use of it.

A problem is that this view essentially knowledge with cognition, thought and decision-making, the assumption being that if valid and appropriate knowledge can be supplied in optimal amounts then decisions can be taken that will then lead to effective action. In other words, 'if we know then we can do'. This view of knowledge divorces it from action and treats it as something independent of social context. Knowledge is viewed as something that is necessary in order to make a decision and the decision is a precursor to action. Yet, as seen, action (embedded in social context) is part of and not apart from, knowledge.

Moreover there is more to action than just knowledge. Actions are about doing things and so motivational, emotional and commitment concerns are just as important as knowledge (Brunsson, 1982; Agryris and Schon, 1978). The notion that

knowledge (seen in cognitive terms) and decisions are necessarily useful to encourage action is also questionable, even as far as individuals are concerned, and
highly dubious when it comes to organization of collective action (Argyris and
Schon, 1978). Importantly, Brunsson observes, that what is needed making decisions is not necessarily the same as what is needed for taking action, especially in
the context of organizational action. For example, decisions are about knowing
what to do and how to go about doing it. Therefore having tightly specified
knowledge about the problem and the pros and cons of alternative solutions is important for making the right decision. Perversely, in organizational settings, sharing tightly specified knowledge about problems and alternative solutions may be
bad for action because knowledge can generate conflict and uncertainty over
which solution to follow. Thus Brunsson argues that, in contrast to what is needed
for decisionmaking, what may be needed for action is a broad, clear, but suitably
ambiguous, ideology that helps to generate a context in which people can act.

If knowledge management is really to make performance improvement possible
through innovation, then action (doing things) is just as important as choosing
what to do and how to do it. Hence Alavi and Leidner's (1999) observations that
"*to make information resources productive they should be converted into actionable knowledge.*" Engaging in actions (whatever they happen to be) can also create opportunities for learning. This doesn't mean that decision is controllable and
action is somehow anarchic, wayward or uncontrollable. Action can also be purposeful but is much more situated – based on the here and now, on intuition and
instinct albeit within a context of plans and decisions (Ciborra, 1999). As a case in
point, innovation involves knowledge but also people doing things, sometimes in
the absence of much knowledge. Ciborra (1999), for example, refers to the importance of 'improvisation' – working 'in situ' to develop ad hoc ways of solving
problems, or "*situated performance where thinking and action occur simultaneously and at the spur of the moment*". To encourage innovation – an oft-cited reason for knowledge management – knowledge management systems and strategies
may need to prioritize action as much as thinking, considering both the requirements for each, and the possible tensions between.

4   The Case of BT Industries

The remainder of the chapter focuses on the various ways that knowledge was
'managed' during a particular innovation project (the Sales Support Project) in a
particular company (BT Industries). This is done in order to provide a concrete
example of the links between knowledge management and innovation. The analysis of BT Industries adopts the view, outlined at the start, that knowledge is produced and negotiated through social action – action that is anchored in a social
context and connected to specific purposes. Thus the focus is on illustrating the
various ways that knowledge was 'managed' through new combinations of actors,
actions and social practices within this specific context, where the purpose of the
action was innovation. The aim here is not to come up with a new set of (overly)
generalized prescriptions about knowledge management – this would not be possible from a single case. Rather, the aims is merely to draw out some key issues

that could inform understanding and practice from a more action-oriented perspective on knowledge management. The case example, then, focuses on knowledge, and knowledge management, in the context of action.

The purpose of this innovation project was to achieve organizational integration in a geographically dispersed company through the introduction of a large scale IT system. BT Industries is the third largest manufacturer and service provider of specialized materials handling (forklift trucks and hand trucks) equipment. It has its headquarters in Sweden and divisions are spread across Europe, Asia and the USA. At the time of the research, BT had around 3400 employees, 4.9 billion Swedish Kroner turnover and was increasing its market share by around 1% per year. Around half the business was in manufacturing and half in sales/after-sales service, the latter including short and long-term truck rental agreements. The SSP was aimed at multi-site, multi-national and cross-functional strategic co-ordination of the European service side of the business, prompted by a need to provide common services to global customers. A significant part was to improve the sharing of information across the disparate business units through the implementation of a standard IT system that would integrate information used for parts and service delivery across BT companies in the different countries in Europe.

Until this point, each of the BT companies had operated more or less autonomously and each had gone its own way in terms of systems development for business applications. BT's structure was largely de-centralized and its culture could be described as one of 'responsible autonomy' (Friedman, 1977). The implementation of this new standardized IT system would, therefore, involve significant changes in core work practices (Swanson, 1996). Moreover, there was no "off-the-shelf" package available that met BT's multi-site, multi-functional and complex leasing requirements. Therefore a new system would need to be designed and developed. The SSP was to achieve the design and implementation of an integrated management information and planning system for all the European businesses through the introduction of common, integrated IT platforms and information systems – essentially Enterprise Resources Planning (ERP) technology. It was launched in 1996, with overall responsibility resting with the small corporate IT function in Sweden. The vision of implementing a common and standardized software platform represented a major cultural change for BT in the way people thought about, and managed, IT. Nonetheless, owing to perceived millennium problems with existing systems, this was to be completed within an ambitious, 2-year time schedule.

Although he did not specifically use the term, the SSP Project Leader recognized early on that knowledge management would be a critical issue. There were three main reasons for this. First, reflecting BT's decentralized structure, IT support for software development was effectively 'insourced' to a small group at the Centre, while hardware and network infrastructure provision was outsourced. There were very limited resources available in the Central IT Group (only 14 people worked there) so they would be unable to support a project of this scale and scope single-handedly. Second, the Project leader recognized that he and his small team did not have sufficient knowledge of the working practices across the different businesses and functional areas, that would be needed to design the new system. The knowledge and skills of end users across far-flung sites in Europe would therefore be required. Third, given BT's overall culture, in particular the core value placed on local autonomy, changes that were seen as imposed by the Swedish Centre would likely be met with local resistance (this had happened in the past). The SSP Leader was therefore keen for local BT firms to provide necessary expertise and resources, and to 'own' the project themselves, by managing their own implementation. The role of the SSP team was to 'kick start' the changes and to then provide ongoing support where needed (hence the label 'Sales Support'). However, given differences in IT skills and local variation in systems, this could prove very difficult. A key knowledge management issue, then, was to identify people locally with relevant expertise as well as with the interest and motivation to manage each implementation. Managing knowledge, as well as expectations and motivational concerns, was therefore critical in order to get others to act in relation to the innovation.

The SSP began by bringing together a small group of senior managers representing different functional areas and different countries to review and evaluate systems available on the market. They concluded that none could handle BT's core business portfolio. Following negotiations with various external suppliers, BT contracted a Swedish software supplier, Intsoft, to design and develop a new version of their software, jointly with BT personnel. Intsoft was chosen because, even though their software had less requisite functionality than a competitor bid, managers in BT trusted that the relationship with Intsoft would be a close, mutually beneficial partnership. BT would have an ERP system that fitted their business requirements, and Intsoft would have a new version of their system that they could market more widely to other similar businesses using BT as a reference site. Prior informal, personal contacts among some BT and Intsoft personnel, and the fact that Intsoft was also a Swedish company, helped to establish this initial trust.

The Project Leader recognized early on that selection, recruitment and commitment would be a critical in developing a project team with the necessary knowledge of IT and business. The Human Resources Director was therefore called upon to help in designing the project management procedures to be used prior to the work formally starting, and continued to have informal contact with the Project Leader throughout. The project team was selected through informal consultation with senior managers from the different European divisions, who suggested those divisional staff who had the most knowledge of the local systems they were currently using. These were often people with detailed knowledge of operating procedures (e.g., from finance functions) rather than IT specialists.

The design and development phase was intensive, with Intsoft consultants working alongside BT managers representing different functional areas (e.g., from sales, finance, operations), and different European divisions, brought together on one site in Sweden for approximately three days a week, over a twelve week period. In addition, two (later 4) graduates in Business and IT were employed on the SSP. These were employed by Intsoft but, usually, were offered the option of employment either with Intsoft or BT when the project ended. These graduates worked partly on site at BT and partly in Intsoft and proved to be important 'knowledge brokers' in the relationship between BT and Intsoft, bringing valuable expertise, and acquiring detailed knowledge of both Intsoft's product and BT's operating context.

Following this design and development work, implementation of the ERP system was managed by three co-ordinated project teams, each of which were responsible for two to four different European sites. Each team comprised representatives from Intsoft, the corporate IT function, and divisional business managers who (where possible) were those that had been involved during the design phase. The teams were thus multiskilled and, importantly, involved representatives from most of the different social communities that would be affected by the system and who, therefore, had important knowledge of the local operating contexts. They were selected (on an informal basis) to comprise different 'personality types'. For example, where it was known informally that a team leader was less 'dynamic' (but suitably senior) they would be complemented by one of the more proactive BT or Intsoft staff.

These teams traveled to the sites to deliver initial training in the software. However, it was continuously stressed that implementation itself had to be owned locally. Therefore local divisions provided their own project managers who were seconded to the SSP during implementation. Importantly, the activities of the three implementation teams were coordinated so that they traveled two weeks in three and, where possible, returned to the Swedish corporate centre on the same third week. This was specifically to encourage knowledge sharing across the teams, and hence across the European Divisions they were responsible for.

There was little formal project documentation, although email was used extensively for communication both within and across teams and across divisions. For example, an email site, which emerged informally, for 'frequently asked questions', began to provide an important network for users in different countries to learn from one another about implementation problems in other sites. Noticing this, the Project Leader arranged for the site to be supported more formally by his group. Further every local user was provided with the 'ring binder' – a book on the related subject of network implementation. Importantly this IT-based communication of written information was supported by a high degree of verbal communication, either face-to-face or by telephone (every team member was provided with a mobile phone). Knowledge sharing in the innovation project was characterized, then, by a high degree of informal networking, which emerged as different social groups began to practice with the new system and to experience common problems.

Our research tracked the innovation project over its lifecycle and found that, despite its ambitious nature and the significant knowledge management challenges faced, it was largely successful. Indicators of this were: the project met most of its initial expectations; the overall project was completed within 1 month of target; with a few exceptions the new software delivered the functionality needed; the project team developed a relatively good long-term relationship with their software supplier; there was high reported satisfaction and low turnover of project team staff and key users. The next section highlights those practices relevant to the management of knowledge that appeared to be important in this case.

5   Key Findings – Knowledge Management in Action

The case of BT illustrates some of the mechanisms used, more or less effectively, to mobilize different kinds of knowledge and expertise in order to enable a particular innovation. These are discussed next and suggest a need to apply knowledge management strategies and practices to action concerns.

5.1   Limits of the Cognitive and Community Approaches

As seen a cognitive/engineering approach to knowledge management would suggest the importance of developing knowledge transformation processes (i.e., from tacit to explicit) so that relevant knowledge can be distributed. Conversely, the community approach would stress the development and linking social communities so that tacit knowledge can be shared. While not denying the importance of these, we had some difficulty in seeing these distinct approaches being played out. For example, and perhaps predictably, it was very difficult to distinguish tacit from explicit knowledge. In this case codified material (e.g., summary reports with bulleted headings) was always tied in with implicit understandings.

Moreover, it was difficult to actually identify at the outset the different social groups that would get involved in the innovation process. This meant that it would have been very difficult to adopt an approach to knowledge management that sought to connect different social communities. This was linked to the nature of the innovation process studied, i.e., multi-site, multi-functional. The nature of this innovation process meant that it cut across preexisting roles and structures within the organization – cast in functional or business division terms. The 'communities' involved in this case, then, were not defined in advance but became defined through their involvement with the innovation process itself. They were not tightly bounded and were much more fluid and shifting than the literature on 'communities of practice' might suggest, with the innovation process itself opening up new possibilities for networking and social interaction. For example, intensive network building occurred as those who became involved in the different BT firms sought to mobilize the knowledge and political support they needed for their particular aspect of the project.

An example of this was the emergence of the largely informal, but ultimately identifiable, community of 'key users' comprising members of different BT companies. These individuals were not necessarily those with formal IT responsibilities, but were merely those that had been the main point of contact for the local implementation of the system. Membership of this community emerged as people across BT firms worked with the new technology and to began to encounter similar problems. Initially email-based, eventually this group established a more formal 'frequently asked questions' database and developed their own 'trouble shooting' forums. These dealt with ERP but also branched into other areas. This community of 'key users' formed, therefore, around shared activities. Their common experience with working with the SSP meant that, despite operating in very different local business units, they shared some 'context' (i.e., around the innovation) and developed a framework and language for discussion. These 'key users' began to be seen as a group of 'knowledgeable experts' in the system. As such, and by being associated with what was seen a 'success story', they also acquired status in the wider organization.

Whilst a community perspective emphasizes the importance of identifying and linking definable social communities, the relevant communities in this case would have been difficult to locate, build or connect at the outset in any formal of planned way. Innovation is characteristically uncertain – it is often difficult to know what you might need to know, or who has relevant knowledge, until actions have been taken – definitions of problems often chase solutions (Swan and Clark, 1992). Here, it was only by participating 'in-situ' in highly uncertain practices of innovation that a community began to define itself and formal systems were developed to support it (Cibbora, 1999). This is not to pit chaos and informal social practices against order and formal planning. In terms of knowledge management, there were significant strategic actions that encouraged this 'loose' community, around the SSP, to consolidate itself. The Project leader, for example, was proactive in both initiating and supporting the community of 'key users'. For example, he deliberately targeted individuals at the outset to get involved who were likely to be enthusiastic about (but not necessarily formally responsible for) the ERP system. He also provided technical support necessary for them to communicate and to develop their own database. In this case, then, the development of formal systems for managing knowledge (i.e., a cognitive approach) was interwoven with the development of an informal social community mobilized around a set of shared problems and interests (a community approach). More formal knowledge management systems were, in effect, 'socialized' around those who needed to use them.

In this example, then, it was not a case of either adopting a cognitive approach (emphasizing technology) or a community approach (emphasizing people) to managing knowledge. Nor was it a case of switching from one to the other. Rather, the broad approaches were mutually constituted, with an emphasis on the former being supported (cognitive) by, and supporting, a continued focus on the latter (community). This supports earlier points regarding the dangers of maintaining a false dichotomy within cognitive and community approaches (or more broadly between technology and people). It suggests instead – in line with the view of knowledge taken in this chapter – that both are always relevant to knowledge management, but that the relative emphasis should depend on specific action concerns. In this case, then, the strong emphasis on building and maintaining a community was relevant to the action requirements of the innovation task at hand.

5.2 The Importance of Knowledge Integration

What seemed to be crucial in BT was, less the ability to accumulate 'stocks' of knowledge, and more the ability to integrate knowledge across social communities that were constantly shifting. This integration involved more than just connecting or linking social groups or making tacit knowledge explicit. It also involved finding ways of creating a 'shared context for knowing' across social communities – defined in terms of preexisting roles and structures – that had previously had relatively little in common (Blackler, 1995). Such shared context was important for allowing knowledge created in one context to be 'located in' another (Tsoukas,

1996). This meant providing support so that people involved could locate their own ideas and experiences in the context of others. In BT, then, the actions involved in implementing a system meant that the key users shared some context for understanding even though they operated in very different local conditions. As Boland and Tenkasi (1995) put it: "the problem of integration of knowledge ...is not a problem of simply combining, sharing or making data commonly available. It is a problem of perspective taking in which the unique thought worlds of different communities of knowing are made visible and accessible to others". In this case it was not essential, then, for those involved to develop the same 'world view' or common understanding but, rather, simply to have some experience in common that allowed them to appreciate, at some level, the worldviews of others.

If knowledge integration is the key issue then this suggests limitations to a 'connectionist' approach to knowledge management where IT is used simply to connect people across social communities. Studies on technologies such as Lotus Notes, for example, suggest organizational members who communicated frequently or infrequently without Lotus Notes continued to communicate on the same basis with it (Vandenbosch and Ginzberg, 1996). Similarly, Newell et al. (2000) found that the introduction of an intranet where the aim was knowledge management merely served to reinforce social groupings and boundaries and/or expose conflict around pre-existing groups in a large, geographically distributed bank. This had the paradoxical effect of reducing, rather than creating, opportunities for knowledge sharing (Newell et al., 2000). This concurs with Alavi and Leidner's (1999) observation that *"in the absence of an explicit strategy to better create and integrate knowledge in the organization, computer systems which facilitate information sharing have only a random effect at best"*. Knowledge integration, then, implies more than just using IT to link people – it highlights the importance of developing, to some degree, a sense of shared context and purpose to peoples' actions (e.g., surrounding implementation problems) so that they can appreciate the possibilities for sharing knowledge.

5.3 Developing a Rationality for Action

BT Industries addressed their problems of knowledge integration through a particular approach to 'orchestrating' its different and emerging knowledge-communities (Ciborra, 1999). This was not primarily concerned with accumulating or sharing as much 'knowledge' relevant to the SSP project as possible – i.e., a quantitative view. The project leader was aware, for example, that if the UK and French sites (recognized in business terms as the largest) were brought into the project in any significant way at the start then there would be so much argument about tailoring the system to their needs that nothing would get done. The knowledge management 'strategy' was more concerned, then, with generating a rationality for taking action (Brunsson, 1982). In this case, this was not a top-down strategy with high degrees of formal planning but, rather, an emergent set of loosely co-ordinated practices. However these did have some critical features.

5.3.1 Developing a Broad Ideology

Brunsson (1982) argues that a broad but clearly defined ideology is important in order to generate, what he terms, a rationality for action. This should be broad enough to engage the interests of heterogeneous groups but not so woolly so that acting on it can be avoided. Interestingly, this could be one reason why 'knowledge management' itself has such wide appeal – as with other fashionable management ideas, it couples ambiguity and breadth with simplicity and a clear imperative for action (i.e., to improve performance in order to survive (Clark and Salaman, 1995)). This provides a high degree of 'interpretative flexibility' which, arguably, gives the concept of knowledge management wide appeal (Bijker et al., 1987). In BT a significant aspect of the ideology of the SSP was the 'cut-off' date to meet Y2K requirements. This was broad but clearly defined (in that the end date was both fixed and widely communicated) but the process of getting there was only very loosely defined. This helped to generate a 'must do' imperative among those that needed to be involved but without aggravating the conflict that would very likely have occurred if knowledge about specifics of the design and implementation of the system was shared freely among all (especially the English and French sites).

5.3.2 Dealing with Power and Conflict

Conflict refers here not necessarily to outright fighting across different social groups but to tensions between the different imperatives or 'logics of action' of those involved (Scarbrough, 1999). In other words individuals and groups within (or across) organizations may fail to engage in activities aimed at sharing knowledge, not because they are being defensive, but merely because they are concerned with different activities, agendas and priorities. For example, in this case the software suppliers were interested in designing standard software they could sell widely, whereas BT's main interest was in developing software they could use in their particular context. These different interests may have precluded opportunities for creating new knowledge. However, BT's approach to managing knowledge found interesting ways of redressing these possible tensions. These were centred on developing a close partnership with 'Intsoft'. For example, BT and Intsoft agreed on a long term partnering agreement where Intsoft would dedicate the amount of time required to undertake the desired modifications for a fixed (cheap) fee – very much to BT's advantage – whilst being able to develop a new standard (multisite, multifunctional) version of their software and using BT as a reference site. This agreement was reinforced by the innovative joint employment contract for the graduates employed in the project. These new 'hybrid' employees played a critical role in limiting 'insider-outsider' tensions and in integrating knowledge by embodying both BT business and Intsoft systems expertise (Blackler, 1995).

A critical feature of knowledge management here, then, could be usefully characterized as introducing mechanisms for the "quasi resolution of conflict" (Cyert and March, 1963) – that is mechanisms for uniting, temporarily (in this case for a period of about 18 months) divergent sets of practices. The literature on communities of practice tends to see communities as tightly bounded by shared interests and common practices – shared practice "enables participants over time to develop a common outlook on, and understanding of, their work and how it fits into the world" (Seely Brown and Duguid, 2001). This does not entirely reflect the situation here. Here it was perhaps more important that members of organizations or sub-units with different, and possibly conflicting, agendas and outlooks could accommodate one anothers' interests on a temporary basis.

5.3.3   Creating Redundancy

Knowledge management is frequently driven by a perceived need to avoid reinvention and redundancy. However, this case suggests that, sometimes, actually building in redundancy and reinvention (so that those concerned share the experience of doing something similar even if they get it a bit 'wrong') can be extremely valuable in action terms. At BT, for example, there was significant reinvention across the three mobile implementation teams, as they worked in parallel and each tackled similar problems. However, their work schedules were also coordinated – allowing them to meet face-to-face on average every third week, with interim communication on a regular basis via specially provided mobile phones. That they had worked through at some level through similar problems, meant they were better able to synthesize their knowledge and ideas during the periods when they did meet – soon developing a common code of language and a shared sense of identity as 'Mobile sales support teams'.

5.3.4   Establishing Social Identity

Integrating knowledge during innovation projects takes effort, especially where such projects co-exist with other line responsibilities. Creating a shared social identity can be a powerful means for generating effort among individuals, for example, through normative control mechanisms. This works from the basis that your own sense of self worth and positive self esteem (e.g., as a 'good colleague' or as 'an expert') is linked with your identification as a member of a particular social group (Tajfel, 1978). As Kogut and Zander (1996) note, the flow of knowledge in organizations is closely linked to the formation of identity. Others argue, similarly, that a critical feature of knowledge intensive work is the motivational aspects of developing, at some level, a social identity – e.g., as 'knowledge workers' – even if individuals themselves may very diverse (Alvesson, 1994). Thus social identity can be a mechanism for establishing new communities and for balancing diversity with co-ordinated action. A critical question, then, is the level at which identity is established. If it is accepted, as is argued elsewhere, that organizational identities are unlikely to be unitary (e.g., Tsoukas, 1996) and that identity forms through social practice, then, by extension, identity is formed at the level where practice is interdependent (Seely Brown and Duguid, 2001). This implies that in organizations of multiple practices, multiple social identities are formed. As Seely Brown and Duguid argue, these may become critical subdivisions that prevent knowledge from being shared across the organization.

A critical feature of the type of highly interactive innovation project observed here is that, by definition, it cuts across existing occupational roles and work practices and, therefore, social identities associated with these (Brewer, 1991). This poses significant challenges in terms of knowledge integration. Similarly, the problem with many knowledge management initiatives (e.g., intranets for global KM) is precisely that they are often introduced to deal with the problems of linking heterogeneous communities. Individual members of these communities may have few incentives for getting actively involved. A key feature of knowledge management in this case, then, was to mobilize the development of an identity, however loosely defined, around the innovation project itself. For example, identity as an "SSP project team member" appeared to be an important mechanism for knowledge integration, helping to motivate individual members and address tensions and conflicts among individual experts who primarily identified with their local business, their function or their role as manager, software programmer and so forth. At the same time, this had to be supported through structural means. For example, individuals in local businesses with other line management responsibilities were actually seconded onto the SSP project for considerable amounts of time. This provided important resources and at the same time symbolized to others the significance and legitimacy of the project.

The issue of social identity is not one that receives close attention by designers of knowledge management systems and strategies. Yet, as seen, simply developing infrastructures aimed at stockpiling or communicating ever more quantities of 'knowledge' can result in disappointingly low levels of use. Similarly, simply providing forums whereby people may be able to share their tacit knowledge begs the question, why? Where the purpose of managing knowledge is to achieve innovation and change, there may need to be a stronger motivational element and sense of purpose underlying the particular knowledge management system or strategy adopted. This might be derived from its ability to develop or reinforce a social identity that has status attached and, by extension, the positive sense of self worth of those that engage with it. For example, arguably one of the best examples of knowledge sharing is the 'Open Sourcing' movement. It could be argued that this is mobilized by the interests of those involved in developing their identities as an elite breed of software designers. With open sourcing it is *only* by sharing your ideas openly with the rest of the community that you can remain part of it, and that your own expertise can be recognized by others. Thus there are strong payoffs for the individual to share what they know. Looking more closely it seems that open sourcing is not a completely anarchistic and open sharing of ideas. Rather, there are strong normative pressures, 'rules' and social practices (such as 'flaming' – a form of public flogging if the ideas are deemed poor by the group) that act as powerful normative control mechanisms and help to sustain the identity of community members as the 'software elite' (Lindquist, 2000).

6 Conclusions

This chapter has touched on some areas that could be core concerns for those interested in generating knowledge management approaches focusing more closely on action concerns. These could clearly be extended to incorporate issues such as trust, legitimacy, status, and so forth. From the analysis presented here, a few broad conclusions can be underlined. First, knowledge is created and deployed through action and interaction as individuals from different backgrounds and disciplines come to understand other perspectives and frameworks. Knowledge, even individual knowledge, can be understood as fundamentally dialectic – that is embedded in, and constructed through, relationships with others (Tsoukas and Vladimirou, 2001). Knowledge management initiatives need, then, to address not just information processing and decision concerns (e.g., accumulation of stocks of information, or the conversion of tacit to explicit knowledge) but also relational and action concerns (such as social identity, power, conflict, motivation). Whilst there is much attention to the former of these concerns in the literature on knowledge management, it is rare to see the latter addressed in any serious way. This chapter has sought to redress this balance.

Designers of knowledge management initiatives could think, then, in terms what is necessary for action (for example, motivation, emotional commitment) not just decision (e.g., providing ever more of information or mechanisms for knowledge transfer). However, engineering and, to a lesser extent, community approaches to knowledge management have still not seriously tackled the problem of action or the socially constructed nature of knowledge. For example, most 'knowledge management systems' still tend to be underpinned by 'quantitative' assumptions – assuming the accumulation of knowledge (treated in cognitive terms) is necessarily a good thing. This has been driven by a view of knowledge, couched in a scientific, decision rationality, that sees 'it' as an objectifiable (functional) entity. This is despite efforts by some to encompass assumptions other than decision rationality into system design (Ciborra, 1999). Innovation processes, at least of the particular kind presented here, often rely on knowledge being created spontaneously, at the point of action, as the innovation process itself allows dispersed groups to engage in new, often unanticipated, forms of social interaction. In such cases then, a model of knowledge management based on scientific rationality may have limited relevance.

Second, if action is to be taken seriously, then a critical problem for knowledge management – and for the building or bridging of communities that engage in action – may be not so much to do with the transfer or flow of knowledge but to do with the integration of distributed knowledge. Knowledge integration is based in being able to share context. Our research suggests, however, that context is created not so much through harmonizing or sharing views, opinions and stories but through addressing conflict and diversity (Scarbrough, 1999). The roles of knowledge management systems and strategies could be recast, then, in terms of building a 'shared context for knowing' (Blackler, 1995), rather than providing a facility for the storage and transfer of knowledge. For example, systems aimed at framing or generating common experience (either direct or vicarious), or for building in (rather than necessarily avoiding) redundancy and reinvention, could be extremely valuable in action terms because they help to create a shared context for negotiation and interpretation that may allow heterogeneous and disparate social groups to share practice.

References

Alavi, M. and D. Leidner, "Knowledge Management Systems: Issues, Challenges and Benefits," *Communications of the Association for Information Systems*, 1, Article 7, 1999.

Alvesson, M. "Talking in Organizations: Managing Identity and Impressions in an Advertising Agency," *Organization Studies*, 15, 4, 1994, 535-563.

Alvesson, M. and D. Karreman, "Odd Couple: The Contradictions of Knowledge Management," *Journal of Management Studies*, 38, 7, 2001, 995-1018.

Amidon, D.M., "The Evolving Community of Knowledge Practice: The Ken Awakening," *International Journal of Technology Management*, 16, 1998, 45-63.

Argyris, C. and D. A. Schon, *Organizational Learning: A Theory of Action Perspective*. Reading, MA: Addison-Wesley, 1978.

Bijker, W.E., T. Hughes, and T.J. Pinch (eds), *The Social Construction of Technological Systems*, London: MIT Press, 1987.

Blackler, F., "Knowledge, Knowledge Work and Organizations: An Overview and Interpretation," *Organization Studies*, 16, 6) 1995, 16-36.

Blackler, F., M. Reed, and A. Whitaker, "Editorial Introduction: Knowledge Workers and Contemporary Organizations," *Journal of Management Studies*, 30, 6, 1993, 851-861.

Boland, R.J. and R.V. Tenkasi, "Perspective Making and Perspective Taking in Communities of Knowing," *Organization Science*, 6, 4, 1995, 350-363.

Brewer, M.B., "The Social Self: On Being the Same and Different at the Same Time," *Personality and Psychology Bulletin*, 17, 1991, 475-482.

Brunsson, N., "The Irrationality of Action and Action Rationality: Decisions, Ideologies and Organizational Actions," *Journal of Management Studies*, 19, 8, 1982, 29-44.

Chumer, M., R. Hull, and C. Prichard, "Situating Discussions about 'Knowledge'," in Prichard, C.; Hull, R.; Chumer, M. and Wilmott, H. (eds), *Managing Knowledge*, London: Macmillan, 2000, 1-19.

Ciborra, C. and T. Jelassi, *Strategic Information Systems: A European Perspective*, Chichester: John Wiley, 1994.

Ciborra, C., "A Theory of Information Systems Based on Improvisation," in Currie, W. and Galliers, R. (eds.), *Rethinking Management Information Systems*. Oxford: OUP, 1999.

Clark, T. and G. Salaman, "The Management Guru as Organizational Witch Doctor," *Organization*, 3, 1996, 85-108.

Cohen, S., "Knowledge Management's Killer Applications," *Training and Development*, 52, 1, 1998, 50-53.

Cole-Gomolski, B., "Users Loathe to Share Their Know-How," *Computerworld*, 31, 46, 1997, 6.

Cyert, R.M. and J.G. March, *Behavioural Theory of the Firm*. Englewood Cliffs, NJ: Prentice-Hall, 1963..

Davenport, T.H., S.L. Jarvenpaa, and M.C. Beers, "Improving Knowledge Work Processes," *Sloan Management Review*, Summer, 1996, 53-65.

De Sanctis, G. and M.S. Poole, "Capturing the Complexity in Advanced Technology Use: Adaptive Structuration Theory," *Organization Science*, 5, 2, 1994, 121-147

Drucker, P. "The Coming of the New Organization," *Harvard Business Review*, January-February, 1988.

George, J.F. and J. King, "Examining the Computing Centralization Debate," *Communications of the ACM*, 34, 1991, 63-72.

Grant, R., "Toward a Knowledge Based Theory of the Firm," *Strategic Management Journal*, 17, 1996, 109-122.

Grant, R., "Knowledge and Organization," in Nonaka, I. and Teece, D. (eds.), *Managing Industrial Knowledge: Creation, Transfer and Utlization*, London: Sage, 2001, 145-169.

Hansen, M.T., "The Search Transfer Problem: The role of Weak Ties in Sharing Knowledge across Organizational Sub-Units," *Administrative Science Quarterly*, 44, 1999, 82-111.

Hansen, M.T., N. Nohria, and T. Tierney, "What's Your Strategy for Managing Knowledge?" *Harvard Business Review*, March-April, 1999, 106-116.

Kogut, B. and U. Zander, "What Firms Do?: Co-ordination, Identity and Learning," *Organization Science*, 7, 1996, 502-518.

Lave, J., *Cognition in Practice: Mind, Mathematics and Culture in Everyday Life*. Cambridge, UK: Cambridge University Press, 1988.

Lave, J. and E. Wenger, *Situated Learning: Legitimate Peripheral Participation*. Cambridge, UK: Cambridge University Press, 1991.

Leonard, D., *Wellsprings of Knowledge*, Cambridge, MA: Harvard Business School Press, 1995.

Levinthal, D. and J. March, J., "The Myopia of Learning," *Strategic Management Journal*, 14, 1993, 95-112.

Lindquist, J., "Open Sourcing," *European Conference on Information Systems*, Vienna, July, 2000..

Markus. L., "Knowledge Management," *Warwick Business School Seminar Series*, University of Warwick, August, 2000.

McDermott, R., "Why Information Technology Inspired but Cannot Deliver Knowledge Management," *California Management Review*, 41, 1999, 103-117.

McLoughlin, I., *Creative Technological Change*. London: Routledge, 1999.

Mumford, E., "New Treatments or Old Remedies: Is Business Process Reengineering Really Socio-Technical Design?" *Journal of Strategic Information Systems*, 3, 4, 1994, 313-326.

Nahapiet, J. and S. Ghoshal, "Social Capital, Intellectual Capital and the Organizational Advantage," *Academy of Management Review*, 23, 2, 1998, 242-266.

Newell, S., H. Scarbrough, J. Swan, and D. Hislop, "Intranets and Knowledge Management: De-Centred Technologies and the Limits of Technological Discourse," in Prichard, C.; Hull, R.; Chumer, M. and Wilmott, H. (eds.), *Managing Knowledge*, London: Macmillan, 2000, 88-106.

Nonaka, I., "A Dynamic Theory of Organizational Knowledge Creation," Organization Science, 5, 1994, 14-37.

Nonaka, I., R. Toyama, and N. Konnon, "Ba and Leadership: A Unified Model of Dynamic Knowledge Creation," in Nonaka, I. and Teece, D. (eds.), Managing Industrial Knowledge: Creation, Transfer and Utlization, London: Sage, 2001, 13-43.

Orlikowski, W.J., J. Yates, K. Okamura,M. Fujimoto, "Shaping Electronic Communication: The Metastructuring of Technology in the Context of Use," *Organization Science*, 6, 4, 1995, 423-444.

Orlokowski, W.J., "Improvising Organizational Transformation over Time: A Situated Change Perspective," *Information Systems Research*, 7, 1, 1996, 63-92.

Orr. J., *Talking about Machines: An Ethnography of a Modern Job*, Ithaca, NY: IRL Press, 1996.

Prusak, L., *Knowledge in Organizations*, Oxford: Butterworth-Heinemann, 1997.

Quintas, P., "Knowledge Management: A Strategic Agenda," *Long Range Planning*, 30, 1997, 385-391.

Ritzer, *The McDonaldization of Society*, Thousand Oaks, CA: Pine Forge Press, 1993.

Salton, G., *Automatic Information Organization and Retrieval*, New York: McGraw-Hill, 1968.

Sarvary, M., "Knowledge Management and Competition in the Consulting Industry," *California Management Review*, 41, 1999, 95-107.

Scarbrough, H., "The Management of Knowledge Workers," in Currie, W. and Galliers, R. (eds.), *Rethinking Management Information Systems*, Oxford: OUP, 1999.

Scarbrough, H. and J.M. Corbett, *Technology and Organization: Power, Meaning and Design*, London: Routledge, 1992.

Scarbrough, H. and J. Swan, "Explaining the Diffusion of Knowledge Management." *British Journal of Management*, 12, 2001, 3-12.

Schreiber, G., H. Akkermans, A. Anjewierden, R. de Hoog, N. Shadbolt, W. Van de Veide, and B. Wielinga, *Knowledge Engineering and Management*, Cambridge, MA: MIT Press, 2000.

Schultze, U. and B. Vandenbosch, "Information Overload in a Groupware Environment: Now You See It, Now You Don't," *Journal of Organizational Computing and Electronic Commerce*, 8, 2, 1998, 127-148.

Seely Brown, J. and P. Duguid, "Structure and Sponteneity: Knowledge and Organization," in Nonaka, I. and Teece, D. (eds.), *Managing Industrial Knowledge: Creation, Transfer and Utlization*, London: Sage, 2000, 44-67.

Shadbolt, N. and N. Milton, "From Knowledge Engineering to Knowledge Management," *British Journal of Management,* 10, 1999, 309-322.

Starburck, W., "Learning by Knowledge-Intensive Firms," *Journal of Management Studies*, 34, 1992, 389-414.

Swan, J. and P. Clark, "Organizational Decision-Making in the Appropriation of Technological Innovation: Cognitive and Political Dimensions," *European Work and Organizational Psychologist*, 2,1992, 103-127.

Swan, J. and H. Scarbrough, "Knowledge, Purpose and Process: Linking Knowledge Management and Innovation," *HICSS Conference*, Maui, 2001.

Swan, J., S. Newell, H. Scarbrough, and D. Hislop, "Knowledge Management and Innovation: Networks and Networking," *Journal of Knowledge Management*, 3, 1999, 262-275.

Swanson E.B., "Information Systems Innovation Among Organizations," *Management Science*, 40, 9, 1996, 1069-1092.

Tajfel, H., "Social Categorization, Social Identity and Social Comparison," in Tajfel, H. (ed.), *Differentiation Between Social Groups: Studies in the Social Psychology of Intergroup Behaviour*. London: Academic Press, 1978.

Tsoukas, H. "The Firm as a Distributed Knowledge System: A Constructionist Perspective," *Strategic Management Journal,* 17, 1996, 11-25.

Tsoukas, H. and E. Vladimirou, "What Is Organizational Knowledge," *Journal of Management Studies,* 38, 7, 2001, 973-994.

Vandenbosch, B. and M. Ginzberg, "Lotus Notes and Collaboration: Plus CA Change," *Journal of Management Information Systems*, 13, 1996, 65-82.

Weick, K.E., "Technology as Equivoque: Sensemaking in New Technologies," in P.S. Goodman, L.S. Sproull and Associates (ed.), *Technology and Organisations*, Oxford: Jossey-Bass, 1990.

Wikstrom, S., and R. Normann, *Knowledge and Value*. London: Routledge, 1993.

Knowledge Processors and Processing

The chapters in Part III consider ways in which an organization operates on its knowledge resources. In concentrating on the processing of knowledge, these chapters necessarily deal with the processors as well.

As foreshadowed by the central theme in Chapter 14, the first chapter of Part III builds on the basic axiom that knowledge resources enable decisions and actions. In it, Bo Newman presents an ontology for understanding knowledge flows among an organization's processing agents. These flows link the knowledge transformations performed by agents into sequences that support specific organizational decisions or actions. Distinctions among agents are noted, including individual, automated, and collective knowledge processors. Distinctions among the kinds of knowledge they operate on are also noted, including both cognitive and physical knowledge representations. Such distinctions affect the knowledge flows associated with creating, retaining, transferring, and utilizing an organization's knowledge resources.

In Chapter 16, Brian Gaines develops a model of organizational knowledge acquisition. He begins with a collaborative exercise in which practicing managers reach a consensus that identifies the kinds of knowledge acquisition routinely encountered in an organization's operations. The similarities and differences among these types of knowledge acquisition activities are examined in terms of two dimensions. Drawing on personal construct psychology, structuration theory, and theory of worlds, the chapter advances a model of organizational knowledge acquisition that integrates three levels of human agents (and their supporting infrastructures) with four worlds of operation. The chapter discusses the interfaces of knowledge processing agents to these worlds, suggests ways in which the modeled knowledge acquisition process can be managed, and reviews tools that support organizational knowledge acquisition.

The next two chapters explore knowledge generation processes. In "Problem Solving: A Knowledge Management Process," Tom Whalen and Sub Samaddar characterize decision making as a knowledge-intensive process that recognizes and solves problems (i.e., derives or discovers knowledge) in the course of reaching a decision. The decision itself is knowledge generated to indicate what is to be done. They proceed to look at the roles and value of computing and management science in problem solving. In particular, they contend that knowledge management can exploit the emerging arena of soft computing and postmodern management science to support problem solving efforts involving inexact environments.

Suzie Allard's "Knowledge Creation" chapter stresses the importance of organizational processes for creating knowledge in a turbulent global environment. This chapter examines the symbiotic relationships between the activity of generating knowledge and other activities such as knowledge acquisition and selection. It describes the maturation process involved in knowledge creation, the connections between knowledge creation and knowledge sharing processes (at both individual and collective levels), and the roles of sensemaking and organizational learning as drivers of knowledge creation.

Chapter 19 focuses on the relationship between knowledge management and sensemaking. Here, Dick Boland and Youngjin Yoo review the process of sensemaking and discuss how it gives a unique way of understanding the nature of organizational knowledge. They illustrate this in a case study of a global consulting firm and identify implications for the design of knowledge management systems.

In "Creating and Facilitating Communities of Practice," Heather Smith and Jim McKeen underscore the importance of communities of practice as knowledge processors and outline their major characteristics as means for creating and sharing knowledge. To help answer questions about how management can and should develop and facilitate communities of practice, the authors convened a focus group of practitioners from a variety of industries. The chapter integrates the focus group's comments with published material to furnish a practical guide for appreciating, implementing, and fostering the success of an organization's communities of practice.

Processes of sharing knowledge are considered at a cultural level in Chapter 21. Here, Jay Liebowitz and Yan Chen argue that knowledge sharing proficiency is a critical element of knowledge management effectiveness and point out that organizations are developing such proficiencies as parts of their reward and recognition systems. To assist such efforts, the authors introduce a knowledge sharing effectiveness inventory whose elements reveal factors to be considered in designing knowledge sharing processes and in devising incentive systems to promote knowledge sharing proficiencies. A case study is provided to illustrate how the inventory can be applied.

In "Business Process as Nexus of Knowledge," Omar El Sawy and Robert Josefek explore the interplay between knowledge management activity and business processes, seeing the latter as inseparable from the former. They outline a set of knowledge management strategies for business process redesign oriented toward increasing knowledge creating capacity, improving value creating capacity, and fostering organizational learning. These are illustrated in the context of three case studies. This chapter examines linkages of structural, human, and relationship capital to business processes before concluding with a discussion of emerging issues and directions related to the conception of business processes as a nexus of knowledge.

Part III closes with a look at the overarching phenomenon of organizational learning -- an intricate, knowledge-intensive process that enriches an organization's knowledge resource base through an assortment of knowledge manipulation activities. In this chapter, Alex and Dave Bennet explore the intersection between learning and knowledge management (KM) including such areas as individual learning and KM programs, learning approaches and communities of practice, learning and a systems thinking perspective, and learning and core knowledge flows. The chapter presents a learning continuum model to understand and study relationships between learning and the environment as change drives the need for new knowledge, triggering a panorama of knowledge management episodes. Part IV focuses on various influences on the conduct of knowledge management within and across such episodes.

CHAPTER 15

Agents, Artifacts, and Transformations: The Foundations of Knowledge Flows

Brian (Bo) Newman
The Knowledge Management Forum

This chapter presents the foundations for a basic understanding of knowledge flows, agents, artifacts, and transformations critical to any examination of knowledge processing. In doing so, it attempts to bridge the gap between a conceptual understanding of how knowledge contributes to corporate objectives, and the practical issues of knowledge management and knowledge engineering. The base ontology presented builds on elements ranging from epistemology to traditional information design and communications engineering to develop an approach that is both domain neutral and fully scaleable. Expanding on the basic axiom that *knowledge enables actions and decisions,* it examines knowledge flows as sequences of transformations performed by agents on knowledge artifacts in support of specific actions or decisions. It points out the significant differences between the individual, automated, and collective agent, and how these differences factor into knowledge flows; the concept of knowledge artifacts comprised of both cognitive and physical elements; and the primary behaviors associated with knowledge flows including knowledge creation, retention, transfer, and utilization. Through an examination of how knowledge enables actions and decisions and the supporting knowledge flow behaviors, it examines the role played by ontologies, the importance of semantic analysis, and the functions knowledge performs in knowledge utilization.

Keywords: Agents; Artifacts; Knowledge Creation; Knowledge Engineering; Knowledge Flows; Knowledge Management; Knowledge Retention; Knowledge Transfer; Knowledge Utilization; Transformations

1 Introduction

This chapter presents a base ontology and modeling language for modeling knowledge flows and the major behaviors through which knowledge is developed, discovered, retained, recalled, translated, transferred, and applied. It bridges the gap between our conceptual understanding of how knowledge contributes to corporate goals and objectives, and the practical issues of how to engineer knowledge-based solutions that meet the needs of the enterprise.

Why are knowledge flows important? Within business, there are two major classes of behaviors. First, there are those directly associated with the over-all business process. Second, and the reason for the growing interest in knowledge flows, there are those behaviors that support the flow of knowledge which *enables* those business processes.

For the Knowledge Manager facing decisions effecting the knowledge needed to satisfy the knowledge needs of the enterprise, knowledge flows are the heart of the issue. For the Knowledge Engineer, an understanding of knowledge flows provides the foundation for a comprehensive methodology, supporting both the analysis and design of holistic knowledge-based systems (Newman, 1996).

While an understanding of knowledge flows is important to today's business environment, its relevance does not stop there. The critical distinction between specific business behaviors and the supporting knowledge flow behaviors makes knowledge-flow-based analysis truly domain independent. Whether the concern is international business, the practice of medicine, economic analysis, research and development, or any other domain where actions and decisions are enabled by knowledge, the fundamental aspects of knowledge flows are the same.

Effective management of knowledge flows not only requires a thorough understanding of how they impact business processes, but also the effect corporate policies, values, and management directions can have on internal and external knowledge flows. This chapter provides the foundations necessary for understanding knowledge flows and a window into some of the key issues facing the knowledge engineer.

The improvements gained by understanding and modeling knowledge flows overcome some of the limitations of previous and current approaches in two primary ways; domain independence and scalability. Knowledge flows are scaleable because they are nested. Any given knowledge flow is part of a larger one, and each knowledge flow can be decomposed into smaller ones. By approaching the subject in this way, researchers, practitioners and students of Knowledge Management and Knowledge Engineering, have an improved and comprehensive framework for examining the roles played by the agents, artifacts, and transformations that enable mission critical enterprise decisions and actions.

To establish the base ontology needed for understanding knowledge flows, this chapter focuses on the three major elements found in all knowledge flows. It:

- Re-visits and reinforces the practical concept of the *knowledge artifact* and contrasts it with the more theoretical concept of "knowledge,"
- Examines what it means to be an agent within a knowledge flow and establishes a workable framework for modeling the differences between major classes of agents,
- Describes a set of basic *transformations* that are endemic to all knowledge flows and form the behavioral component of knowledge flow models.

In the section on Optimizing Knowledge Flows, these three components are reintegrated during an examination of a number of issues normally associated with knowledge flow analysis.

2   Deconstructing Knowledge Flows

The fundamental premise underlying a comprehensive examination of knowledge flows is *knowledge enables actions and decisions*. All knowledge flows consist of the actions of agents on artifacts. However, not all knowledge flows are the same. Knowledge flows differ in many ways, and when we study their characteristics, we can understand their dynamics and can take the steps necessary to promote those knowledge flows critical to the success of the enterprise.

Critical to any discussion of knowledge flows are three basic concepts; agents, artifacts, and transformations. These are related by the fact that *agents perform transformations on artifacts.* Knowledge flows are simply a collection of such behaviors directed toward some meaningful end.

The concept of being an agent (agency) is one that occurs frequently in the existing literature on knowledge management, information technology, organizational dynamics, and other related fields. Within these domains, two general definitions seem to predominate: agents as specialized objects, and agents as specific roles played by people, organizations, societies, automata, and so forth. More specifically, within Knowledge Management literature, the dominate theme seems to revolve around computer systems (as a specialized object) acting as agents. (Bradshaw et al., 1997; Baek et al., 1997; Lacher and Koch, 2000).

The discussions surrounding the general concept of agency, especially those dealing with causality (Chisholm 1976; O'Shaughnessy, 1980), are both interesting and relevant in forming our foundations for the practice of Knowledge Management. However, from a practical viewpoint, what the Knowledge Manager and the Knowledge Engineer need is an easily understood framework to discuss, understand, and model requirements and characteristics of knowledge-based systems.

In most discussions of this nature, the roles within knowledge-based systems fall into one of three groups: the people, the technology, or the organization. This grouping captures a number of meaningful distinctions that characterize the strengths and limitations of agents within knowledge-based systems.

Within this chapter, I refer to these groups as *individual agents, automated agents, and collective agents.* Individual agents are human, automated agents are non-human, and collective agents are a specific collection of individual and/or automated agents.

The second of the three major concepts associated with knowledge flows is the knowledge flow artifact, or simply, the knowledge artifact. These are the documents, memories, norms, values, and other things that represent the inputs to, and products of, the knowledge-enabled activities of agents.

Art Bardige, in his 1995 epistemological work, "Unique Artifacts," makes the argument that as "artifact" is the word we use to describe what we as humans construct, then it should be equally valid as a description of our mental or conceptual constructions (Bardige, 1995). Bardige seized the idea of artifacts resulting from mental or conceptual constructions as the foundation for his theories on the growth and evolution of knowledge. However, to those concerned with knowledge flows, the concept fills a more important role.

In many circles, references to the abstract nature of a given knowledge artifact are made by the use of the terms data, information, knowledge, understanding, and wisdom. While these distinctions may still prove helpful in some cases, problems in definition and interpretation often arise from any attempt to maintain rigid lines of demarcation. This, in turn, impacts both their usefulness and scalability when it comes to understanding knowledge flows. These problems can be avoided through the use of the collective term *artifact* (knowledge artifact) without any significant loss in the effectiveness or validity of the framework. As important as the concept of the artifact was to Bardige's work, so it is to our understanding of knowledge flows.

The third essential knowledge flow concept is *transformation*. Transformations are the behaviors that agents perform on artifacts. If we were to address every possible way in which an agent could act upon a knowledge artifact, the list of possible transformations would be too large to support effective modeling (the full range would include such behaviors as inference, logical and deductive reasoning, abstraction, translation, transliteration, assumption, and goal seeking, summation, integration, ordination, aggregation, selection, conversion, separation, confrontation, realization, looking at consequences, introspection, denial, transference, acceptance, faith, trust, belief, awareness of potential, exposure, education, mutation, evolution, compartmentalization). Therefore, we have chosen instead to focus on four major categories of activities that are common to all knowledge-based systems. These are knowledge creation, knowledge retention, knowledge transfer, and knowledge utilization. Each of these is addressed in more detail later in this chapter. These four categories have been chosen because each represents a fundamental difference in both policy and process.

Knowledge creation includes all those behaviors through which new knowledge enters a knowledge-based system. Knowledge can enter a system in one of two ways. It can either be created within the system or captured from external sources. Knowledge transfer covers those behaviors through which agents share knowledge and knowledge artifacts. Knowledge retention includes all the ways in which we store, maintain, and retrieve previously developed knowledge. The final category, knowledge utilization, actually forms the cornerstone of knowledge-based behaviors. Knowledge utilization addresses the ways in which we use knowledge to further the goals and aims of the enterprise.

Together, the three basic concepts, agents, artifacts, and transformations, form the building blocks of knowledge flows. Precisely stated,

> *knowledge flows are sequences of transformations performed by agents on knowledge artifacts in support of specific actions or decisions.*

Knowledge flows focus on the *enablers* for business process tasks rather than on the sequence by which the tasks are associated. One should not confuse the concept of a knowledge flow with the related concepts of business processes and workflows. In general, the idea of a "workflow" relates to the creation of explicit representations of process logic. Methodologies and tools, focus on workflow mapping and analysis, have their greatest application in the computerized control, monitoring, optimizing, and support of business processes. In contrast, knowledge flow analysis and mapping has its greatest application in the engineering of holistic systems that encompass the full spectrum of knowledge-based activities.

The concepts of data and information flows, as used in the practice of software engineering or business process engineering, relate almost exclusively to explicit, well codified, and structured artifacts. In comparison, knowledge flows address the full range of knowledge artifacts regardless of how, or how well, the knowledge artifacts may be codified. Knowledge flow modeling extends more traditional information management modeling approaches by factoring in the knowledge utilization event, thus providing a firm anchor to the fundamental business process.

To better understand the ramifications and characteristics of knowledge flows, it is important that we expand our understanding to include their three key elements; agents, artifacts, and transformations. We continue our examination of the elements within knowledge flows with a closer look at knowledge artifacts.

3   Knowledge Artifacts

For most, exposure to knowledge flows comes through various knowledge artifacts. Knowledge artifacts are what we deal with every day. We write reports, send e-mail, read books, remember bits and pieces of old thoughts, engage in conversations, and follow procedures. The use of the term "knowledge artifact" does more than just provide us with an effective collective. It also points to the fact that, as with other artifacts, we need to be mindful of the processes associated with retention, establishing provenance, and enabling reusability.

When we speak of a knowledge flow artifact, we are actually making a simultaneous reference to two important entities. First, we are referring to *the cognitive knowledge artifact*, which makes up our awareness and understanding of a particular aspect of our real or meta-physical world. This is commonly referred to simply as "knowledge." Second, we are referring to the *physical knowledge artifact*, which serves as a representation of the associated cognitive knowledge artifact. Understanding both the cognitive and physical characteristics of a knowledge artifact, and how they relate to the unique behavioral characteristics of the individual, automated, and collective agents, is a critical aspect in modeling how knowledge is applied in making decisions and enabling actions. Understanding the critical aspect improves our ability to engineer knowledge artifacts and knowledge flows that support critical business processes and decisions. All knowledge artifacts contain aspects of the cognitive and the physical and fall somewhere between fully cognitive (tacit) and fully physical (explicit). The degree to which they are predominantly one or the other will have a significant impact on how it relates to other elements of the knowledge flow.

Knowledge artifacts differ one from another in other ways as well. These variations include the way they are codified, the way they are rendered, and their degree of abstraction. Knowledge artifacts also vary in their structure, their content, their intended context, and in how well they are articulated. Individually, knowledge artifacts can be explicit, implicit or tacit. However, most artifacts, depending on how they are used, occur in complex forms that contain a combination of explicit, implicit, and tacit components.

The term "knowledge artifact" has not always been used in the way I have just described. Denham Grey[2], Tom Finneran (Finneran, 1999), and Robert Seiner (Seiner, 2000) are among those who, while agreeing that knowledge artifacts are human constructs (i.e., cognitive) to which we have attributed a degree of reality, would argue that they occupy a much more specific and limited position within a knowledge architecture. Grey views knowledge artifacts as an important new genre of object closely tied to the knowledge economy (see http://www.voght. com/cgi-bin/pywiki?KnowledgeArtifacts). He sees knowledge artifacts as one level above what John Seely Brown terms "boundary objects"[3] with greater levels of "invested energy, support rituals, and greater reach." Boundary objects are classifications, conventions, and processes that carry meaning between communities allowing effective exchange and transitions to take place. Boundary objects represent a special group of knowledge objects because they cross organizational boundaries and carry meaning, they serve as both containers and carriers. Boundary objects are also a highly abstract and generalized form of knowledge organization to which we have attributed a degree of reality (reification.) If you place people, activities, and relationships in the context of boundary objects with which they are associated, you have a powerful way to portray, arrange and monitor knowledge flows.

Finneran invests knowledge artifacts with a degree of reality that exists independent of any agent. He also seems to agree that knowledge artifacts can be retained, transferred, and enable actions and decisions. Finneran, however, limits the overall role and scope of knowledge artifacts when he associates them with an instance of a "knowledge asset."

Grey (1998) and Finneran typify those who would limit knowledge artifacts to instances of explicit codification, as is the case when the term is used in association with the field of Artificial Intelligence – and in contrast with the processes associated with human decision making. The limitations imposed by restricting the term to the just the explicit and codified have resulted in the implied exclusion of all knowledge artifacts that cannot be made explicit. To address the full range of artifacts associated with knowledge flows, it is important that we include those artifacts that exist across the full spectrum of articulation, including the explicit, implicit, and tacit.

Whether a knowledge artifact is explicit, implicit, or tacit can have a significant effect on how different types of agents are able to interact with them. All agents are not equally qualified to deal with differing forms of codification. Therefore, significant insights can be gained by examining the characteristics of the knowledge artifacts that form the inputs and outputs of agent behaviors.

By far, explicit knowledge artifacts are the most familiar to us. Explicit artifacts are those that have been codified in a way that makes it possible to touch, see, hear, feel and/or manipulate them (e.g., books, reports, data files, newsreels, audio cassettes and other physical forms). Explicit knowledge artifacts can be transferred from one person (or agent) to another. However, regardless of how well a report is written, or how complete and comprehensive it might be, if it is written (i.e., codified) in a language not understood by the agent who will use the report, it will have little value in supporting the associated knowledge flow. For a moment, consider the case of highly detailed listings of computer programs or rule bases that serve to codify complex procedural knowledge. When transformed by a compiler or other suitable automated agent, they can prove to be a highly effective aspect of a larger automated knowledge-based system. However, they may not be nearly as effective if used as an input to the activities of a Board of Directors (a collective agent). Recognition of this fact is one of the primary motivators behind why web site authors offer different "views" and personalization.

Not as well articulated, but just as effective in the right situation, are the implicit knowledge artifacts. These are knowledge artifacts whose meanings are not explicitly captured, but can be inferred. In effect, the codification process is incomplete. Whereas explicit artifacts can be interpreted based on their content, interpreters of implicit artifacts must rely on knowledge from other sources. Even those knowledge artifacts that are well structured and highly codified (i.e., explicit) will also contain some element of the implicit. For example, in a highly detailed computer program listing, there could be inferences as to the type of computer on which the program would run, to knowledge of mathematical theorems, to logical proofs, or to natural limits or conditions in the physical world – such as the implied knowledge that programs written in the early days of business applications need not be concerned with events taking place after 1999.

The potential for ambiguity is one of the characteristics of implied knowledge artifacts. Most readers of the statement, "Ann put on her heavy coat and locked up her classroom," would infer that it is winter and Ann is a teacher. However, there are other inferences that could be made as well. For consistent interpretation, the person making the statement, as well as the person interpreting it, must share some common frame of reference to understand when heavy coats are worn and who locks up classrooms.

The underlying knowledge embedded in processes or process descriptions can also be considered as an implicit artifact. For example, a manual detailing the safe way to handle corrosive materials might include statements such as, "this material should not be used on polished or anodized aluminum surfaces," or, "if swallowed, immediately rinse mouth and drink a glass of milk or water. Do not induce vomiting." The implicit knowledge contained within these warnings, combined with what the reader might recall from high school chemistry, tells the reader that the material is likely to be caustic.

Implicit knowledge artifacts can also be found in process-specific software. In developing the software, the designers had to conceptualize the processes that the software would be supporting. That knowledge will become apparent in the way the software is intended to be used and in the range of behaviors it directly supports. Even if not explicitly apparent, the implicit decisions made by the software designer, such as, which function to implement and how to implement it, can significantly constrain users' actions. This is often referred to as, "implicit policy making by technologists" (Conrad, 1995).

When we look to the far end of the scale, we find those artifacts that seem to defy codification. These tacit artifacts may be the most insidious and powerful of the three. The problem of tacit knowledge, its acquisition, and epistemic status has been the focus of considerable philosophical investigation by such people as Ludwig Wittgenstein, Edmund Husserl, Hilary Putnam and, most significantly, Michael Polanyi. Polanyi referred to tacit knowledge as "knowing more than we can say" (Polanyi 1966). Tacit artifacts are those that defy expression and codification. However, this is not to say that tacit knowledge artifacts are without influence. In fact, they may be the more prevalent and influential of the three.

4   Agents

Agents are the active components of knowledge flows. Knowledge artifacts do not perform actions or make decisions. Actions and decisions are performed by agents; people, organizations, societies and/or, technology. Agents carry out all the actions and exhibit all the behaviors within a knowledge flow. While individual agents are an essential element of any knowledge flow, in today's enterprise, they rarely, if ever, operate alone. Computers and other forms of *automated agents* have clearly established that non-human agents have their place in knowledge flows as well. Besides the individual and automated agents, most knowledge flows involve one or more *collective agents*. Groups, organizations, companies, societies, and trade unions are all examples of *collective agents*. As a class of agents, collective agents are not limited to just aggregations of individual agents. They can just as well include automated agents and other collective agents. Collective agents can range from the purely organic to the well-engineered, from one with a general social orientation to one geared to a specific organizational need.

By categorizing agents in this way, we strengthen our understanding of knowledge flows. By focusing attention on the significant differences in the capabilities of each of these three types of agents, we can better understand how they interact with various types of artifacts. For instance: the individual agent can deal with tacit artifacts, whereas the automated agent cannot. The collective agent can retain knowledge beyond the life of individual agents. Automated agents can perform many types of transformations on explicit artifact much faster and with a greater degree of repeatability than can individual agents.

Individual agents sit at the center of every knowledge flow. For most analysts, the individual (human) serves as the prototypical active force for affecting change. By referring to this category of agents as "individuals," we do not mean to imply that every *specific* individual is capable of the full range of behaviors attributed to this class of agent, rather, that as a class of agents, we share some general behaviors and capabilities.

As individual agents, we are capable of working with knowledge and knowledge artifacts in all degrees of abstract articulation. We are limited, however, in our ability to deal with artifacts that are codified in ways that fall outside the range of human perception (i.e., radio waves). As individual agents, we are unique in that we are the one agent type capable of performing all aspects of knowledge development, retention, transfer, and utilization without the need for intervention by either of the other two agent types. However, with their help, there are things we can do better.

Automated agents include any human construct that is capable of retaining, transferring, or transforming knowledge artifacts. They are not exclusively computerized processes. For example, a conventional camera that encodes a representation of the visual world through chemical changes to the surface of a film acts as an automated agent, supporting both knowledge creation and capture.

The third category of agents is the collective agent. As with all agent types, problems can arise from ascribing a single behavioral model to all collective agents. Nevertheless, there are some basic characteristics that do apply to all collective agents. For instance, collective agents are not homogeneous. The agents that make up the collective agent will differ in their abilities to create, retain, transfer, and make use of knowledge, and to interact with different forms of knowledge artifacts. The collective agent will also manifest characteristics that may not be exhibited by any particular agent within the collective.

One important characteristic that collective agents exhibit is the ability to transcend ontological differences between constituent agents through the formation of shared values and world views.

Much has been written about the ability of organizations and communities to establish value systems that outlive the involvement of specific individuals and the power that these value systems have to influence the behavior of individuals and groups (von Krogh and Roos, 1995; Kuhn, 1996; Hofstede, 1991; Covey, 1994). However, the principles and practices that make up these value systems are often not codified. In fact, when individuals within the organization attempt to describe an organization's value system, their descriptions are usually incomplete, reflecting either their interpretation of the organization's values or a blending of organizational and individual values. The common use of terms, such as "unwritten rules" and "organizational culture," is a clear reflection of the difficulties involved, and further evidence that collective agents can, and do, act as repositories of tacit knowledge.

The idea that collective agents can retain and act upon tacit knowledge may appear to be entirely logical, but for some, it may also be problematic because it does not offer one specific place where such tacit knowledge would reside. In actuality, this inexpressible knowledge is codified, in part, as a component of the relationships between the members of the collective. Foundations for this position can be traced to work performed in the fields of individual human cognition and individualized knowledge (von Krogh and Roos, 1995) which is consistent with our views of knowledge held by individual and automated agents.

Because of the myriad of knowledge flows occurring within a collective agent, you may be tempted to simplify our model of agents and concentrate on just the individual and automated agents. However, evidence clearly points to the dangers of such a position, and the reader is strongly cautioned against such shortcuts. To eliminate the collective agent from our analysis and understanding is to ignore the effects of cultural norms, organizational paradigms, shared values systems, and almost the entirety of societal impacts. The collective agent, and the knowledge embedded therein, is a source of highly important structural couplings between member agents. These structural couplings are critical factors in agent-to-agent alignments and the availability of much of the content and context within knowledge flows.

5   Transformations

We now come to the third of the three fundamental elements of knowledge flows, transformations. Knowledge flows are the medium through which knowledge is made available to enable the actions and decisions that, in turn, enable individuals and organizations to achieve their goals. As we have seen, agents are responsible for the actions that transform knowledge artifacts from one form to another in the process of creating, retaining, transferring, and using knowledge. Now, it is time to look at those behaviors through which agents create, change, remove, and otherwise transform knowledge artifacts within knowledge flows.

Knowledge creation includes those behaviors (transformations) associated with the entry of new knowledge into the system in question. Knowledge creation includes development, discovery, capture, and elicitation. Knowledge creation is also closely linked to the broader set of behaviors we label innovation. In most cases, knowledge enters the organization through a wide range of mechanisms, many of which may not be easily recognized. For instance, when we hire a new employee, we are in effect acquiring access to some portion of that person's knowledge. When we implement a new customer relationship management software program, we are acquiring access to the knowledge artifacts embedded within that software or methodology. When companies form alliances, some of the knowledge held by each becomes available to the other.

Note, we have not said anything about who *owns* the knowledge. Ownership of knowledge and the rights to use it are topics that have been, and will continue to be, debated for some time. To the analyst trying to understand a specific organizational knowledge flow, legal and/or economic issues might well be important. In that case, related decisions and actions could be, and should be, included in the supporting analyses. However, for simplicity, we will make the assumption that any rules for ownership and rights-to-use have been satisfied as part of the knowledge acquisition process. The important point is that the knowledge has become available to agents working within the knowledge-based system. Knowledge, of course, can also be created within the system. Knowledge creation can come from research and development, experience, examination of lessons learned, data mining and analysis, and various other ways.

Once we understand how knowledge is acquired by a system, one of the next questions we need to address is how it is retained. This is true whether the knowledge is to be applied in the near term, or sometime in the future. Like acquisition, knowledge retention can take many forms. The behaviors and transformations associated with knowledge retention include all activities that preserve knowledge and allow it to remain in the system once introduced. Knowledge retention also includes those activities that maintain the viability of knowledge within the system. To properly understand the dynamics of knowledge retention within knowledge flows, it is necessary to address such issues as:

- How the selection of retention transformations are constrained by agent capabilities
- The role of meta-knowledge in knowledge retention
- The role of context in knowledge retention

- The role of classification schemes and methodologies
- The effects of previously retained knowledge on future knowledge retention processes
- The ramifications of various codification schemes on long-term knowledge viability.

Any time a knowledge flow involves more than a single agent, there will be a need for some type of knowledge transfer behavior. For this reason, knowledge transfer behaviors are one of the most prevalent types of behaviors within knowledge flows. This includes, but is not limited to, communication, translation, conversion, filtering, and rendering.

A comprehensive analysis of knowledge transfer behaviors would create a sizable list of influencing factors. While a full treatment of these factors is beyond the scope of this chapter, two warrant mention because of how easily they can go unnoticed. The first factor pertains to the impacts of rendering methods, and the second, to the effects of differing agent ontologies.

When we decide how to render a knowledge artifact for transfer between agents, we are, in fact, choosing how we will interpret the meta-physical content of the artifact and represent that interpretation in some explicit form. Each of these two transformations, interpretation and representation, involve selecting certain elements of the artifact and ignoring others. What makes it through the rendering process, and what doesn't, can have a significant impact on how well the resulting artifact supports down-stream transformations, behaviors, and ultimately, the ability to enable the action or decision in question.

A similar problem surfaces when we consider the role of agent-specific ontologies. An agent's ontology is their way of viewing and understanding the world. As such, it comprises such elements as concepts held, taxonomies, syntax (terminology), semantics (meaning), rules, relationships, and constraints. How agents view the world effect what they consider important and significant when it comes to knowledge transfers. The ontology of a sales organization may cause it to place a different importance on product customization than would the accounting department or the production manager. These differences could have significant impacts on the nature of the knowledge artifacts created, retained, and transferred by, and between, these collective agents as they work to achieve the goal, "maintain target gross profit per unit."

This brings us to our fourth class of transformations and behaviors, the use of knowledge contained within the system to enable those actions and decisions through which we achieve our goals and objectives. When we speak *of knowledge utilization behaviors*, we are referring to all those behaviors, transformations, and actions directly related to applying knowledge to enable decisions and actions.

It is important to remember that in modeling knowledge flows, two major categories of behaviors are recognized. First there are those directly associated with the overall business process. Performance-focused behaviors are what we refer to when we speak of a *knowledge utilization event* (KU). The second includes all of the behaviors that *support* the knowledge flows that enable the KU.

For many years, researchers and practitioners in disciplines such as psychology, sociology, and education, have established a substantial body of work on just *how* people, either individually or in concert with one another, apply what they know to make decisions or perform certain types of actions. In the same fashion, those working in computer science and related fields continue to provide us with important understandings of the application of knowledge by the automated agent. In our analysis of knowledge flows, our view of knowledge utilization often starts at the point where the knowledge has been made available to the agent responsible for the given action or decision. At this point, our challenge is to understand those behaviors directly associated with how knowledge, once it is available to the agent, enables a decision or an action. To meet this challenge, we need to focus on the contribution knowledge makes to the process (i.e., what function does knowledge play as agents make decisions and perform actions). A partial list of these functions would include:

- An enabler that satisfies the questions
  - Am I allowed to make this decision?
  - Do I have all the facts?
- A constraint that tells us
  - Limits imposed on our actions
  - Bounds within which we can make a decision
- Criteria that tells us
  - What standards apply to this decision
  - What precedence applies in this situation

The fact that, within knowledge utilization behaviors, a given knowledge artifact can be applied in one or more ways leads directly to the issue of semantics and meaning.

In examining how knowledge is created, retained, and transferred, we have addressed the knowledge artifact as both our understanding of a particular aspect of our real or meta-physical world (the conceptual artifact), and the representation of that understanding (the physical artifact). As we look at the part knowledge plays in knowledge utilization, we need to understand how the conceptual aspects of the knowledge artifact, as part of an integrated set of contextual elements, contributes to the satisfaction of the specific action or decision.

The keys to this semantic analysis are the evaluation of both content of the knowledge artifact and context within which that content is applied. This evaluation establishes the starting point for the semantic interpretation of the content represented, or conveyed by, the knowledge artifact. This basic starting point needs to address:

- Are dealing with a decision or an action?
- What type of agent (or agents) is responsible for the KU?
- What other knowledge is available at that time?

The first two of these question are relatively straightforward. The differentiation between an action or decision can be determined through process analysis, and in determining the type of agent, we define it's basic capabilities. The third, the evaluation of the total conceptual context, requires the identification of the knowledge artifacts that will be used to satisfy the KU. This includes previously retained knowledge from internal and external sources and event-specific knowledge developed just for this particular action or decision. With the basic framework in place, the final task is to establish the contribution made by the content of each knowledge artifact toward satisfying the KU.

When you examine this critical alignment of context and content, ask yourself the following questions. If knowledge is to be usable in a given situation, is it appropriate, available, recognized, and understood? If it is to be used, can the user trust the knowledge and/or its source? If the KU is to be satisfied, is there appropriate knowledge available to satisfy all of the enabling functions? Is the knowledge to be applied to each of the specific enabling functions sufficient for that purpose?

6 Optimizing Knowledge Flows

The value of a knowledge-flow-based analysis is demonstrated in how it enables the Knowledge Manager or the Knowledge Engineer to better understand the ways in which knowledge flows impact critical business tasks and processes. While a full description of the Knowledge Flow Analysis Methodology is beyond the scope of this chapter, certain highlights of the methodology are worth mentioning. To place these in perspective, this section uses based on an approach that starts at the point where knowledge enables a specific action or decision. For those involved in the engineering of solutions to real-world business problems, this perspective has significant relevance. We start with the management position that there is a specific business task that needs to be accomplished. It is not, however, the only analytical perspective that can be taken. Knowledge-flow-based analysis works equally well if you start from the perspective of the knowledge seeker or from the perspective of the knowledge provider. The knowledge-flow-centric approach is also a natural complement for more traditional function-centric requirements analysis methods.

One of the most telling characteristics of a knowledge flow is its purpose. What is the specific decision or action enabled by this knowledge flow? In other words, what is the KU? The selection of the KU is one of the most important steps in any examination of a specific knowledge flow. Through the selection of the KU, we control the *scope* of any examination. If the KU in question is an enterprise level objective, such as "expand market penetration by 100%," then our examination of the knowledge flows that enable this objective will address such agents as "the marketing department" or "alliance partners." However, if the KU is a low-level objective such as, "should this tool bit be replaced now or later," then clearly our perspective changes. The key to maintaining the appropriate level of focus is a clear and consistent understanding of the KU in question.

When you understand the KU, you also gain considerable insight into the temporal drivers associated with the knowledge flow. By understanding how the required knowledge is made available, we gain insight into the component artifacts that feed the knowledge flow and the agents that will be involved in the transformations. To complete our high-level characterization, we also need to determine the geographical setting. By identifying who, what, where, when, why, and how, we have all of the basic elements to characterize our knowledge utilization event.

A more detailed analysis of knowledge flows can include stability, agent-to-agent interactions, density, and criticality. The issue of knowledge flow stability needs to be examined from several aspects. We need to ask whether this flow is one that has existed unchanged for some time and will most likely continue to do so, or does it seem to be reinvented each time the KU occurs? Stability, or lack thereof, is neither a "must have" nor a undesirable characteristic, but it is a characteristic which can be very important when it comes to identifying and solving problems in knowledge-based systems. One important question that can be addressed through an examination of stability is whether or not the specific knowledge flow is a suitable candidate for an engineering-based mediation, or whether it would be better addressed through management-based approaches, such as changes in policy or objectives.

We need to examine the characteristics of the agent-to-agent interactions that occur in association with the knowledge flow. Are these interactions planned or spontaneous? Do artifacts flow in just one direction or both ways? How many agents are involved, and are the interactions synchronous or asynchronous? Is there just one dominant chain of interactions, or are there multiple concurrent paths? Many of these are questions already asked in the process of information systems design. In knowledge flow analysis, these patterns of agent interactions can be an indicator of potential problems caused by misalignments, due to specific agents capabilities, ontologies, and motivations.

On the surface, it might seem logical to keep the number of agent-to-agent interactions to a minimum to improve reaction time, decrease communication losses, or reduce cost. However, closer examination may well show that by adding a "translator" between two agents speaking different languages, or coming from differing backgrounds (for example, production departments and the sales force), may actually improve the flow of knowledge, and how well customer orders (the KU) are filled.

Elements of communications engineering can also play an important part in analyzing knowledge flows. For instance, it pays to understand the density of our knowledge flows. Are we trying to cram too much through too small a pathway? Can the agents involved deal with the intricate complexities and nuances and, at the same time, support all of the other knowledge flows in which they are involved? Are we wasting bandwidth? Are we using overly skilled agents to support simple repetitive knowledge flows? Are the codification methods we are using actually causing us to loose contextual elements in an attempt to force more and more "facts" into each transaction? These and similar questions can tell us much about how we are using our knowledge flow resources.

Perhaps the criticality of the situation is such that no matter how routine the transaction, we need to take every precaution to insure only the highest quality knowledge is applied. This might be the case in medicine, or maintaining the chain of custody for evidence collected during a criminal investigation. Perhaps there are opportunities to reallocate some of that capability to support more problematic knowledge flows? Careful examination of the content of our knowledge flows, both in terms of complexity and amount, can prove very helpful in balancing resource requirements and identifying potential choke points in our knowledge flows.

7 Summary

Armed with an understanding of knowledge flows and the agents, artifacts, and transformations from which they are formed, both the knowledge manager and the knowledge engineer are better equipped to address the critical problem of enabling the activities that make up our business process.

Expanding on the basic axiom that knowledge enables actions and decisions, we saw how we can bridge the crucial gap between our conceptual understanding of the way knowledge contributes to corporate objectives, and the practical issues facing knowledge managers and knowledge engineers. We saw that the key to crossing this chasm was an understanding of knowledge flows – sequences of transformations performed by agents on knowledge artifacts in support of specific actions or decisions.

The base ontology presented in this chapter is far from being all encompassing. In its fifteen-year growth and evolution, it has drawn from elements of epistemology, traditional information design, communications engineering, systems engineering, and many other fields. In use, this base ontology it has proven to be both domain neutral and fully scaleable, and has served as the foundation for the development of practical methods ranging from improved requirements analysis to fiscal and strategic planning, content analysis, project management, and enterprise-wide collaborative management.

In closing, I would like to offer a few words to the wise. In your pursuit of managing and engineering solutions to knowledge enabled systems, do not fall into the trap of thinking of knowledge flows as simple linear patterns of behaviors where small changes have small effects and larger changes have larger effects. Instead, remember that knowledge flows are truly complex systems and that, when conditions are "right," they can easily exhibit unforeseen emergent properties and behaviors. Moreover, be heedful of the ramifications that can result from attempting to "manage" such systems without first understanding them.

Acknowledgements

I would like to thank Kurt Conrad, Art Murray, Joe Beck, members of the Knowledge Management Forum, members of the larger knowledge management community, and those I have had the pleasure of serving in both the public and private sector over the last 15 years, in helping me to formulate and articulate the concepts, theories, and practical implications expressed in this chapter.

References

Baek, S., J. Liebowitz, S. Prasad, M. Granger and M. Lewis. "An Intelligent Agent-Based Framework for Knowledge Management on the Web," *Proceedings of AIS Conference* 1997, 146-48.

Bardige, A., "The Invention of Knowledge; The Unique Artifacts Theory," July, 1995, URL=http://www.artifacts.com.

Bradshaw, J., et al, "Roles for Agent Technology in Knowledge Management: Examples from Applications in Aerospace and Medicine," *Proceedings of the AAAI Spring Symposium, Artificial Intelligence in Knowledge Management,* 1997.

Chisholm, R., *Person and Object: a Metaphysical Study,* LaSalle, IL: Open Court, 1976.

Conrad, K. W., "SGML, HyTime, and Organic Information Management Models," *Second International Conference on the Application of HyTime,* August 1995, URL=http://www.sagebrushgroup.com/organic.htm.

Covey, S., "Principles of Quality," *The Community Quality Forum,* Special 1994, 1-3.

Finneran, T., "A Component Based Knowledge Management System," *The Data Administration Newsletter (TDAN.COM),* TDAN Issue 9, June 1999, URL=http://www.tdan.com/i009hy04.htm.

Grey, D., Knowledge Management and Information Management: The Differences, 1998, URL=http://www.smithweaversmith.com/km-im.htm.

Hofstede, G., *Cultures and Organization: Software of the Mind,* London: McGraw-Hill, 1991.

Kuhn, T., *The Structure of Scientific Revolutions,* Chicago: The University of Chicago Press, 1996.

Lacher, M. S., and M. Koch, "An Agent Based Knowledge Management Framework," *Proceedings of AAAI Spring Symposium,* 2000.

Newman, B. D., "Knowledge Management vs. Knowledge Engineering," *The Knowledge Management Theory Papers,* 1996, URL=http://www.km-forum.org

Newman, B.D. and K. Conrad, "A Framework for Characterizing Knowledge Management Methods, Practices, and Technologies," *The Data Administration Newsletter (TDAN.COM),* TDAN Issue 12, 2000, URL= http://www.tdan.com/i012fe04.htm.

O'Shaughnessy, B., *The Will: A Dual-Aspect Theory,* Cambridge: Cambridge University Press, 1980.

Polanyi, M., "The Logic of Tacit Inference," *Philosophy,* 40, 1996, 369-86.

Seiner, R., "Meta Data as a Knowledge Management Enabler," *The Data Administration Newsletter (TDAN.Com),* Issue 15, January, 2001, URL=http://www.tdan.com/i015fe01.htm.

von Krogh, G. and J. Roos, *Organizational Epistemology,* New York: St. Martin's Press, 1995.

CHAPTER 16

Organizational Knowledge Acquisition

Brian R. Gaines
Knowledge Science Institute, University of Calgary, Calgary, AB, Canada

This article develops a model of organizational knowledge acquisition in terms of modern psychological, sociological, economic and management theories by deconstructing the terms involved: an *organization* as a collective agent having goals and capabilities to achieve them; *knowledge* as the hidden state variables imputed to an agent as the basis of its capabilities; and *acquisition* as the reproduction of dispositions. This form of model enables one to relate the knowledge processes involved to existing models of organizational processes, and to understand such phenomena as knowledge economics and knowledge management. The breadth of the notion of organization encompasses markets, firms and societies; the operational definition of knowledge clarifies its role and the utility of the notion; and the focus on reproduction of dispositions in knowledge acquisition enables the management of knowledge acquisition to be analyzed.

Keywords: Concept Mapping; Expertise; Habitus; Knowledge Acquisition; Organization; Personal Construct Psychology; Repertory Grid; Structuration Theory; Theory of Worlds

1 Introduction

The phrase, *organizational knowledge acquisition*, is deceptively simple if interpreted colloquially. We probably all believe that organizations acquire knowledge, and would be quite happy to explain or speculate about how they do so. However, if we attempt to do this in a professional context and to sustain our position through well-structured arguments we encounter many problems.

The notion of *organization* is a loose one that encompasses firms, markets, hierarchies, networks, territories and their infrastructure, governments, societies, and many other forms of collectivity and infrastructure. The notion of an *organization in general* needs careful delineation (Scott, 1992; Thompson, 1967), and it is not clear that there is meaning to the phrase *knowledge acquisition in organizations in general*.

The notion of *knowledge* is at least as problematic, another compendium term denoting a natural kind defined by our usage and not subject to precise definition (Gadamer, 1972; Goodman and Fisher, 1995). The recognition of knowledge as critical in distinguishing rational arguments from emotional ones was a major innovation of the Athenian enlightenment (Solmsen, 1975). Havelock (1963) has argued that knowledge as an abstraction became possible through the transition from an oral to a literary culture, and Sullivan (1997; 1999; 2000) has traced the developing use of terms relating to human thought processes such as *phren*, *nous* and *psyche*, in the early Greek literature of Aeschylus, Sophocles and Euripides. Plato has Socrates ask *What is knowledge?* in *Theaetetus* (Plato and Cornford, 1935) and note that *Herein lies the difficulty which I can never solve to my satisfaction.* Developing an answer to this question was a major topic for philosophers in the seventeenth century enlightenment. In particular, Bacon's (1960) answer that knowledge must be based on empirical observation was major feature of the ideology inspiring the scientific revolution.

The notion of *acquisition* is normally easier to define in terms of the transfer of property rights (Alchian, 1977; Barzel, 1997), but not so easy when the property being acquired is as ill-defined as knowledge and the acquirer as ill-defined as an organization. As research in knowledge acquisition has developed it has been recognized that knowledge is not readily transferable both because it exhibits *stickiness* (Hippel, 1994) at its source and and also because there is a need for *absorptive capacity* (Cohen and Levinthal, 1990) in its intended recipient.

Thus, modeling knowledge acquisition by an organization presents some conceptual and terminological problems, and it is important to have operational definitions of the notions involved. However, it is also important not to define away the rich complexity of knowledge acquisition phenomena in the real world, and hence the next section will present the results of an empirical study of how managers approach knowledge acquisition in practice.

2   Mapping Concepts of Organizational Knowledge Acquisition

Managers involved in an ongoing project on knowledge modeling of manufacturing processes in small companies were asked to take a day away from the primary project and focus instead on the routine acquisition of knowledge that took place in their normal businesses. How did their organizations acquire knowledge? Seven of us brainstormed to develop a scenario in which key people might be leaving, new requirements were arising, new processes and materials had become available, and so on, and asked how the new knowledge necessary to cope with these changes would normally be acquired. Most of the possibilities had immediate referents in the experience of members of the group, including recollections of the most valuable sources of relevant knowledge.

The tool used to collect and organize the data, *KMap*, is a scriptable, multi-user concept mapping system (Gaines and Shaw, 1995b) that we had previously used to model various manufacturing processes (Gaines and Shaw, 1994b). For this application it was scripted to provide the supportive environment recommended by the Arizona University team (Nunamaker et al., 1991) in which possible topics can be proposed anonymously by several people simultaneously, freely discussed by the group, and accepted on a consensual basis or edited/put-on-hold if such acceptance proves difficult (Gallupe and Cooper, 1993). Each user, or group, interacted with a large, central, shared screen through a local workstation that allows the user or group to develop and assess their ideas before posting them to the entire community. Figure 1 shows the central, shared screen listing the knowledge acquisition activities that had been elicited towards the end of the session. We discussed and refined them, editing the text where it was awkward or ambiguous, eventually reaching a consensus represented by Figure 1.

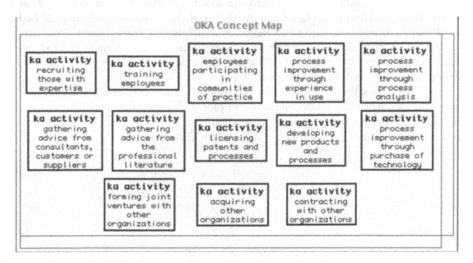

Figure 1. KMap Showing Consensus Reached on Routine Knowledge Acquisition Activities

As usual there was a debate about the comprehensiveness of the list—did all our new knowledge come routinely through one of the routes shown? However, it was eventually agreed that the list covered most practical possibilities that we could exemplify, and that it would not be problematic to add to it later if appropriate. Experience in using the knowledge acquisition tools for knowledge modeling had left everyone comfortable with the notion that all knowledge is *provisional*—what had been elicited could be changed and edited. It was interesting to note how many of the knowledge acquisition activities involved human resources—knowledge management is as much a matter of people as of technology.

We now had a reasonably comprehensive list of knowledge acquisition activities that the organization used routinely in its operation, and wanted to model these in terms of their properties, similarities and differences. The tool we had used to model manufacturing processes in these terms was *WebGrid* (Gaines and Shaw, 1997), an implementation of Kelly's (1955) *repertory grid* technique for eliciting the critical dimensions along which a related set of elements may be characterized. Kelly called these dimensions the *constructs* that enabled us to characterize the similarities and differences between the elements. He emphasized that these dimensions were not necessarily 'objective' features, but would often be idiosyncratic to individuals or communities, representing the cultural frameworks in which they operated.

From the early years of personal construct psychology, techniques have been developed to support the elicitation of the construct systems being used by indi-

viduals or groups and, since the 1970's, many of these have been embodied in interactive computer programs that elicit the elements and constructs, and represent
logically and graphically the relations between them (Shaw, 1980). WebGrid is
the latest in a series of such programs (Mancuso and Shaw, 1988). It operates
through the World Wide Web to support distributed communities in collaborative
knowledge acquisition activities. It had the advantage that our managers were already familiar with it in application to modeling their business processes, and had
no difficulty transferring their experience to a different domain. Seven constructs
were elicited from the group: *internal—external; same size—expand; process improvement—process development; coded—tacit; active—passive; transmitted—
experiential;* and *technology—people.*

Figure 2 shows the *Map* facility in WebGrid used to perform a principal components analysis of the grid developed and plot it in two dimensions to show the
relationships between the elements, in this case the knowledge acquisition activities of Figure 1, and the constructs or dimensions distinguishing them.

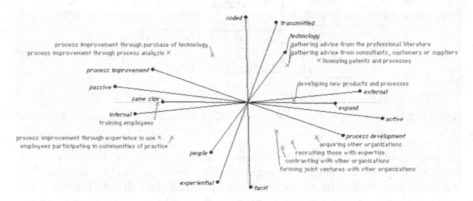

Figure 2. Map of Repertory Grid of Constructs Distinguishing Knowledge Acquisition
        Activities

Two major constellations of dimensions are apparent in Figure 2: a horizontal one
characterized by process improvement, passive knowledge acquisition, internal
processes and keeping the organization the same size at one end and by process
development, active knowledge acquisition, expanding the organization and external processes at the other; and a vertical one characterized by people, experiential
knowledge acquisition and tacit knowledge at one end and by technology, transmitted knowledge acquisition and overt knowledge at the other.

3   Deconstructing Organizational Knowledge Acquisition

As noted in Section 1, the notion of knowledge has been subject to analysis since
the fifth century B.C., and that analysis has had substantial impact on progress in
science and technology. Beninger (1986) has documented the growth in industry

since the industrial revolution that necessitated what he terms the *control revolution* leading to an *information society*, and Chandler (1977) has noted how it also lead to a *managerial revolution* imposing a *visible hand* on industry. Drucker (1993) has characterized the managerial revolution as one in which knowledge is being *applied to itself*, and this has stimulated developments in *scientific management* and *knowledge-based* or *expert systems*, and a focus on *knowledge management*.

3.1 Knowledge and Capabilities

Recognition of the role of knowledge in the managerial revolution has drawn attention to the need to understand the nature of knowledge and knowledge processes in society with an emphasis on a pragmatic stance reminiscent of Peirce, James, Dewey, *et al*, that characterizes knowledge in terms of its *utility*. For example, in the artificial intelligence literature, Allen Newell (1982) has analyzed what he terms the *knowledge level* and has situated knowledge in the epistemological processes of an observer attempting to model the behavior of another agent:

> *The observer treats the agent as a system at the knowledge level, i.e. ascribes knowledge and goals to it.*

emphasizing that:

> *The knowledge level permits predicting and understanding behavior without having an operational model of the processing that is actually being done by the agent.*

He defines knowledge as:

> *Whatever can be ascribed to an agent such that its behavior can be computed according to the principle of rationality.*

noting that:

> *Knowledge is that which makes the principle of rationality work as a law of behavior.*

and defining rationality in terms of the principle that:

> *If an agent has knowledge that one of its actions will lead to one of its goals, then the agent will select that action.*

That is, for Newell, knowledge is ascribed to an agent to explain its capabilities, and there is no knowledge without capabilities. However, note that knowledge as defined above need not be *communicable*. It can be *tacit* (Polanyi, 1958) and not encoded as information that can be transmitted to another agent. Also, note that Newell's definition applies equally whether the *agent* is an individual or an organization—indeed, it suggests a *collective stance* (Gaines 1994a) in which organizations are modeled as compound individuals.

Newell's definition has been formalized, in the educational literature by Doignon and Falmagne (1999) who provide a set-theoretic model of *knowledge space* for a given topic and procedures to determine a student's position in the space, and in the artificial intelligence literature by Gaines (1997) who shows that the natural axioms of knowledge space define a *system of logic*. He also shows that knowledge/capabilities acquisition may be expedited by a process that increases the difficulty of a task as the performance of the learner improves and requires no other knowledge of the learner's processes or the knowledge necessary to perform the task.

Newell's analysis of the knowledge level is important in providing a close link between knowledge and capabilities and demonstrating that knowledge management is a matter of *capabilities management*. Ultimately, the objective of knowledge acquisition is capabilities acquisition (Sanchez and Heene, 1997). Bacon emphasized this aspect of knowledge also in his famous aphorism:

> *Human knowledge and human power meet in one; for where the cause is not known the effect cannot be produced. Nature to be commanded must be obeyed; and that which in contemplation is as the cause is in operation as the rule.* (Bacon, 1960)

Similarly, Penrose (1959) in her analysis of the growth of the firm modeled it as a *bundle of resources* but emphasized that:

> *Strictly speaking, it is never resources themselves that are the 'inputs' in the production process, but only the services that the resources can render.*

3.2   Classification of Capabilities

There is a natural dependency structure among capabilities, that possessing one capability, or a combination of capabilities, normally entails possessing another. There are also differences in the value of various capabilities to an organization. Pralahad and Hamel (1990) have analyzed capabilities in terms of their roles in securing competitive advantage, and distinguished *core capabilities* as those which both give competitive advantage and are also difficult to acquire. Leonard-Barton (1995) has extended the classification:

> *Supplemental capabilities are those that add value to core capabilities but could be imitated...Enabling capabilities are necessary but not sufficient in themselves to competitively distinguish a company*

It is tempting to extend this classification to the knowledge underlying the capabilities but this would be misleading since there is not a one-to-one relationship between knowledge and capabilities—usually, many different sets of knowledge can lead to the same capability.

There are a number of critical constructs that apply to knowledge and capabilities. The two that underlie the Pralahad/Hamel and Leonard-Barton analysis are: *easy to acquire—difficult to acquire; provides competitive advantage—does not provide competitive advantage*. Note that these are properties relative to an organization—what is easy to acquire for one organization may be difficult for another, and what provides competitive advantage for one may not for another, even in the same market sector.

Other critical constructs are: *abstract—concrete* capturing generality; *direct—meta* capturing level of operation; *individual—organizational* capturing location; *widely diffused—narrowly diffused* capturing accessibility; *tacit—coded* capturing communicability; *passive—active* capturing utility. Boisot (1995) has analyzed such constructs in depth, characterizing *information space* and modeling *knowledge assets* (1998) in terms of them.

Figure 3 uses a cross-plot of the *tacit—coded* and *passive—active* dimensions corresponding to the principal axes in Figure 2 in order to highlight important aspects of knowledge acquisition. Passive knowledge that is acquired but not used is *data* that just represents *experience* if it is tacit but becomes *information* if it is coded. Active knowledge that is used as a problem-solving capability supports a *skill* if it is tacit but becomes *know-how* (Kogut and Zander, 1992) if it is coded.

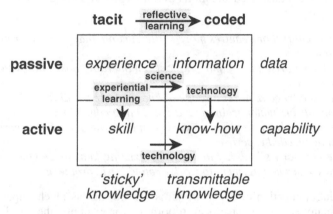

Figure 3. Constructs of Knowledge

Bacon's prescription for science based on observation corresponds to reflective learning from experience to information. His 'knowledge is power' aphorism corresponds to the transition from information to know-how. This transition and that from skill to know-how underlie the development of *technology* and of human *technical culture* (Hall, 1959). The latter transition is that emphasized by Nonaka and Takeuchi (1995) as underlying the *knowledge-creating company*, by Hall (1959) as underlying success in training civilian clerks in technical skills in World War II and by Gibbons et al (1994) as being a *Mode 2* method of knowledge acquisition underlying the *new production of knowledge*.

3.3   Expert Systems Technology—Automating Declarative-Procedural Transformation

Advances in knowledge representation tools supporting the transition from information to know-how and acquisition tools and techniques supporting the transition from tacit knowledge to coded knowledge triggered off a boom in industrial interest in *expert systems* in the 1980s:

For the past 15 years, applied work in artificial intelligence has focused increasingly on the use of knowledge to build 'expert systems.' These systems achieve levels of performance in complex tasks that equal or even exceed that of human experts. Because they incorporate much human knowledge, these systems are called knowledge-based expert systems or, simply, knowledge systems...The industrialization of knowledge engineering began in 1981 with the formation of two commercial spin-offs from the Stanford university Heuristic Programming Project...Teknowledge focuses on industrial and commercial uses of knowledge engineering. Sales this year will be $3 million to $6 million. Hayes-Roth (1984)

Hayes-Roth also characterized situations that instigate knowledge engineering initiatives:

1. *The organization requires more skilled people than it can recruit or retain.*
2. *Problems arise that require almost innumerable possibilities to be considered.*
3. *Job excellence requires a scope of knowledge exceeding reasonable demands on human training and continuing education.*
4. *Problem solving requires several people because no single person has the needed expertise.*
5. *The company's inability to apply its existing knowledge effectively now causes management to work around basic problems.*

The industrial application of expert systems has not has as much impact as first hoped, but many successes have been reported—for example, the April and July 2000 issues of *InTech Magazine* published by the Instrumentation, Systems and Automation Society, has a paper from Eli Lilly on the deployment in its fermentation plant of an expert system programmed in Gensym's G2:

Within a few weeks, Phil was satisfied that the expert system reliably came to the same conclusions he would have by looking at the same data (i.e., the system did what it was purported to do, which was an application and validation objective). The expert system then took over this part of Phil's job, freeing up 40 hours per month of his time for other work. Of course, whenever G2 detected a problem fermentor, or one it was unsure of, Phil, or an assistant, would be immediately paged. This application became affectionately known as "Phil in a box." Phil retired from Lilly in 1993 when the company offered an early retirement program. In fact, many of the experienced fermentation personnel at this plant, as well as several at other Lilly plants, also retired. (Alford et al., 2000)

The importance of such projects is that the knowledge of a human expert has been successfully encoded as information in a declarative structure of *production rules* that automatically reproduced the human expertise when interpreted by the G2 expert system shell.

The commercial potential of expert systems technology was over-stated in the 1980s (Feigenbaum et al., 1988) and they are not fashionable currently and do not have a significant role in the knowledge management literature. Figure 4 characterizes the growth of the literature in artificial intelligence (AI), expert systems (ES), knowledge acquisition (KA), and knowledge management (KM) through 2001 by plotting the number of books in the library catalog of a world-class university with strong AI and KM research areas.

The number of books with *expert system(s)* in the title shows a standard sigmoidal learning curve (Crane, 1972), with the peak growth during the 1986 to 1992 period and publication waning thereafter. The number of books with *artificial intelligence* in the title is still growing and it is difficult to characterize accurately the peak growth period but the data so far is consistent with that being from 1986 through to 1998. The number of books with *knowledge acquisition* in the title follows the same pattern as for 'expert systems' and that for *knowledge management* appears to be at an early stage of take off, much as was artificial intelligence in the early 1980s.

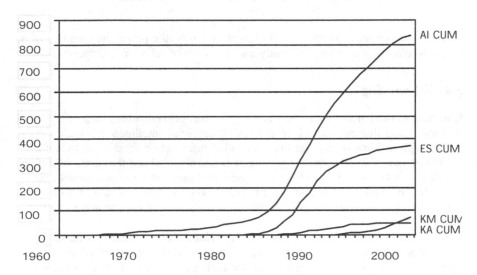

Figure 4. Growth in Number of AI, ES, KA and KM Books Held in a Library

Expert system concepts and technology are appearing in organizations in other guises. *Neuron Data*, one of the most innovative and successful of the original expert system companies, was taken over and now trades as *Blaze Software* (http://www.blazesoft.com/). It supports the *business rules* layer in the IBM/Microsoft multi-layer client server enterprise model through use of the powerful knowledge modeling tools that were developed for Neuron Data's expert system shell, *NEXPERT*. Seiler (1999), the founder of *Rule Machines Corporation*, shows the role of business rules within an enterprise architecture (Figure 5) and emphasizes that they are not *expert systems* or *database triggers* but rather a way in which end-user management can specify activities in terms of what he

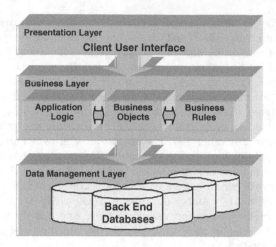

Figure 5. Business Rules within N-Tier Application Architecture (Seiler, 1999)

terms *business speak*. Kremer (1991) has shown how the procedures manual of a major oil company translates naturally into a system of rules and exceptions.

3.4 E-Learning

It is the *automation of human intelligence* that has proved slower to develop than predicted, and that part of the objectives of artificial intelligence research concerned with making knowledge overt as coded information remains of fundamental importance in knowledge management. It has always been the prime objective of science and technology, and if, in the short and medium term, computers cannot make the knowledge active and use it to solve problems then there is still the possibility that human learners, people and organizations, can use the more overt expression of knowledge do so.

Hayes-Roth's list of applications in the previous section overlaps with those of knowledge management initiatives, and much of what has been learned and developed in knowledge acquisition studies for both education and expert systems is relevant to knowledge management. For example, he emphasizes the role of expert systems *when an organization requires more skilled people than it can recruit or retain*, and a standard corporate approach to such labor shortages is through *training. E-learning*, on-line computer-based education and training, has developed extensively during the same period as expert systems and there is now a major industry supporting *corporate universities* (Meister, 1998), and providing *on-the-job training* and *just-in-time learning* (Wills, 1998). For example, the Learn4life division of SAIC, a $10B/year company, provides modules targeted on the full range of emergency services, law enforcement, fire service and search and rescue (http://www.Train4life.com/), and Motorola University offers courses in a wide range of core skills areas where recruitment is problematic such as software engineering (http://mu.motorola.com/).

There is much to be learned from the education and training literature that is relevant to organizational knowledge acquisition and knowledge management. For example, the analysis of *educational objectives* (Hauenstein, 1998) that is used to structure e-learning provides taxonomies that may also be used to characterize organizational knowledge. Metfessel, Michael, and Kirsner (1969) provide tables that allow well-formed objectives to be generated in different domains through a 'buzz-word' process that is simple to implement with a computer and use to generate required organizational capabilities in statements of knowledge management objectives.

4 The Nature of Human Expertise

One outcome of the research effort directed at knowledge acquisition for expert systems has been to develop cognitive models of people and organizations based on empirical data and the application of psycho-social theory. In the early days of artificial intelligence, Dreyfus (1972) argued that human intelligent behavior could not be reproduced by information in a computer, and Dreyfus and Dreyfus (1986) have argued that:

> *logic machines will always be inferior to people—whether teachers, managers, physicians, or professionals of any kind—as sources of insight, reflection, and real-world expertise.*

Their arguments against the possibility of artificial intelligence are based on Wittgenstein's (1953) analysis that suggests that the notion of human behavior *following a rule* is paradoxical:

> *This was our paradox: no course of action could be determined by a rule, because every course of action could be made to accord with the rule ... 'obeying a rule' is a practice ... If I have exhausted the justifications I have reached bedrock, and my spade is turned. Then I am inclined to say: "This is simply what I do."* (Wittgenstein, 1953)

However, Kelly's (1955) *personal construct psychology* provides a constructivist model of *anticipation*, prediction and action, in human experience in which rules are *supervenient* on the process of construing experience, and there is no explicit representation or use of rules in human expertise. Wittgenstein's statement above is correct in personal construct psychology because the agent is not *obeying a rule* but rather making a choice based on past experience, usually attempting to maximize the probability of correct anticipation but, possibly, doing something entirely different (such as win an argument or confound an observer). Continuing construction of experience will change the apparent *rules and procedures* being followed without those rules and procedures having actuality or being subject to reflection; much as modeled by the *evolutionary theory* of economic systems of Nelson and Winter (1982) and the *behavioral theory of the firm* of Cyert and March (1963).

Personal construct psychology has been cited in the knowledge management literature by Loasby (1999) and Lant & Mezias (1996), and in the sociological literature by Luhman (1995) who notes:

> *Everything that can be imagined is possible in reference to something else, and only thus can information be acquired and processed. A psychological theory adequate to this has been worked out by George A. Kelly.* (1995)

It has also been used to model knowledge acquisition and inference processes, and to develop tools to elicit knowledge and model it in operational form through *ontologies* represented in *semantic networks* (Gaines and Shaw, 1993a).

It is salutary to examine the quality of judgement of experts and wonder whether it is as good as the attempts to emulate it through *expert systems* suggests. In a survey of studies of the accuracy of human subjective probability judgements, Tversky and Koehler conclude:

> *The evidence reported here and elsewhere indicates that both qualitative and quantitative assessments of uncertainty are not carried out in a logically coherent fashion, and one might be tempted to conclude that they should not be carried out at all. However, this is not a viable option because, in general, there are no alternative procedures for assessing uncertainty.* (Tversky and Koehler, 1994)

In the domain of expertise in scientific research, Feyerabend (1975) has argued that there is no evidence of a rational methodology, and Fortun and Bernstein (1998) have provided a compelling account of scientific progress as *muddling through*. In *Voltaire's Bastards*, Saul argues:

> *Among the illusions which have invested our civilization is an absolute belief that the solution to our problems must be a more determined application of rationally structured expertise. The reality is that our problems are largely the product of that application.* (Saul, 1993)

Gadamer has cast doubt upon the role of knowledge in expertise:

> *The nature of experience is conceived in terms of that which goes beyond it; for experience can never be science. It is in absolute antithesis to knowledge and to that kind of instruction that follows from general or theoretical knowledge. The truth of experience always contains an orientation towards new experience. That is why a person who is called 'expert' has become such not only through experiences, but is also open to new experiences. The perfection of his experience, the perfect form of what we call 'expert', does not consist in the fact that someone already knows everything and knows better than anyone else. Rather, the expert person proves to be, on the contrary, someone who is radically undogmatic; who, because of the many experiences he has had and the knowledge he draws from them is particularly equipped to have new experiences and learn from them.* (Gadamer, 1972)

and, in the artificial intelligence literature, Clancey has criticized approaches to expert system development based the assumption that expertise can be captured in overt knowledge, and comes to similar conclusions:

> *The new perspective, often called situated cognition, claims that all processes of behaving, including speech, problem-solving, and physical skills, are generated on the spot, not by mechanical application of scripts or rules previously stored in the brain. Knowledge can be represented, but it cannot be exhaustively inventoried by statements of belief or scripts for behaving. Knowledge is a capacity to behave adaptively within an environment; it cannot be reduced to representations of behavior or the environment.* (Clancey, 1989)

Bourdieu, the French philosopher and sociologist, has generated a major literature on human psychology, culture and sociology, that stemmed from consideration of Wittgenstein's discussion of the status of rules of human behavior:

> *I can say that all my thinking started from this point: how can behaviour be regulated without being the product of obedience to rules?* (Bourdieu, 1990)

Bourdieu's answer to this question is a constructivist one, that all human behavior is *generated* within a rich *background* (to use Searle's (1992) terminology) that is implicit and not consciously represented, and is constituted through acculturation processes that internalize the historic development of a particular society or institution.

Bourdieu builds on the previous analyses of Aristotle, Hegel, Nietzsche, Husserl, Schutz, Wiggenstein, Heidegger and Merleau-Ponty, to provide a very detailed analysis of socially-embedded human behavior in terms of three major constructs: *habitus* which is a system of *dispositions* extending Aristotle's (2000) analysis of *hexis*; *field* which is a network of influences and power relations extending Lewin's (1936) analysis of behavior within a social field; and *symbolic capital* abstracting and generalizing Marx's (1973) analysis of capital formation and Weber's (1968) extension of it to cultural domains. Bourdieu's output in books and papers is prolific, ranging from detailed ethnographic and statistical studies through sociological models of a wide range of institutions to deep theoretical analyses; a good starting point is the interviews and essay in Bourdieu (1990).

Bourdieu's model of *habitus* is particularly important to the modeling of human expertise:

> *I am talking about dispositions acquired through experience, thus variable from place to place and time to time. This 'feel for the game', as we call it, is what enables an infinite number of 'moves' to be made, adapted to the infinite number of possible situations which no rule, however complex, can foresee. Action guided by a 'feel for the game' has all the appearances of the rational action that an impartial observer, endowed with all the necessary information and capable of mastering it rationally, would deduce. And yet it is not based on reason.* (Bourdieu, 1990)

5   The Dynamics of Expertise Formation

How is it that imperfect human capabilities are construed as expertise and that muddling through is effective? One answer is that human expertise arises in the context of human action as a pragmatic process of dealing with present contingencies knowing that there will be further opportunities to deal with the consequences of our actions at a later stage. The decision to treat a customer in a certain way is an *experiment* that entails monitoring the consequences with a view to planning future interaction. Human action takes place in a control loop with imperfect information at each decision point, and with the unfolding process continually changing the state of play.

In many situations it is more important to act in a way that is not wildly wrong rather than to compute the optimum action, particularly when available information is inadequate, inaccurate, expensive to obtain, and so on. It is generally important to know who has the authority to act and who is accountable for monitoring the consequences, taking follow-up action, and so on. The giving, or taking, of the authority to be in control in a particular domain demarcates the abstract role of an *expert* in that domain relative to the social norms of the institution that accepts ownership of the domain.

A simple analysis of the phenomenon of such assignment of authority in a society of learning agents shows that actual expertise, in the sense of greater capabilities, arises naturally through the positive feedback processes involved in proto-experts having greater access to learning experiences (Gaines, 1988).

Figure 6 is a diagram of the processes of expertise formation through a variety of feedback processes (Gaines, 1989). The central loop showing the client-expert dialog derives from studies by Hawkins (1983) of industrial experts in mineral exploration, and emphasizes that the generation of advice is a feedback process of discourse and modeling. The upper and lower ovals showing the expert's interaction with his or her professional and client communities is what I would now want to describe in terms of the development of the expert's *habitus*, using Bourdieu's term deliberately to avoid any implication of the development within the expert of explicit knowledge.

The dynamics of the professional community are ones of effective expertise development and transmission, of access through apprenticeship, case reports, evaluation of procedures, rationalization through links to existing models, related literatures and so on. Discourse is at the level of managing the formation of expertise and this may involve reflective processes raising *why* questions and addressing foundations, but note that the objective of these is to develop expertise, a coaching function, rather than to discover *truth* or uncover *reality*. Rationalizations are valid to the extent that they help the development of expertise, and that development does not necessarily leave any residue of the rationalization in the expert's mind. It is possible to have an effective knowledge-level approach to expertise development without basing it on a knowledge-level approach to expert performance (Vickers, 1990).

Bourdieu's other dimensions of *field* and *social capital* may also be exemplified in terms of Figure 6. The expert acts in a specific situation within a social network of power relations with clients, colleagues, regulatory agencies, and so

Figure 6. Expertise Formation through Expert-Community Interaction (Gaines, 1989)

on, and competes within that field for symbolic capital that will affect his or her ongoing and future status within such fields. That is, the decisions and recommendations made are not just an outcome of the problem situation and the expert's dispositions through his or her habitus, but also reflect the interaction of habitus and field, in particular, the impact upon the expert's symbolic capital of the possible outcomes. The solution of any particular problem is situated within the processes of developing the overall competence of the community as a social network. Shapin (1994) has documented the importance of the power relations and symbolic capital in the development of science.

6   A Unified Model of Organizational Knowledge Acquisition

The preceding discussion emphasizes how important it is to be able to model social processes in expertise formation and organizational knowledge acquisition. The individual never acts alone but always in the context of what Wertsch (1991), following Bakhtin's (1981) discussion of the *dialogic imagination*, terms *voices of the mind*, the memories of past social discourse. We are agents in a distributed cognizant system, whether organization, group, person, role, module or neural complex. Simmel made this inter-relation of wholes and parts the central theme of his sociology:

> *Society strives to be a whole, an organic unit of which the individuals must be mere members. Society asks of the individual that he employ all his strength in the service of the special functions which he has to exercise as a member of it; that he so modify himself as to become the most suitable vehicle for this function....man has the capacity to decompose himself into parts and to feel any one of these as his proper self.* (Simmel, 1950)

Simmel's insight that the group member is always a fragment of a person, a role created precisely to enable the person to enter the group has been developed by Wolff with his notions of *surrender* and *catch*:

> *From the standpoint of the world of everyday life, the mathematician, as we often put it, lives in the 'world of mathematics', dealing with 'nonreal' elements, notably numbers, whose relation to 'real' things, to 'reality', is not part of his concern. Analogously for the logician. What makes our subject-object approach to this attitude misleading is the fact that the subject, the student of mathematics or logic—his or her individuality, including motives and attitudes—is irrelevant for our understanding; the only thing that counts is the pursuit, with its results and questions.* (Wolff, 1976)

He makes the key point that not only does the real world, the object, disappear to be replaced by the world of mathematics, but also that in entering into this world the person doing mathematics, the subject, also disappears to be replaced by a new entity, the mathematician.

In terms of Wolff's *object* Popper's concept of a *third world* of *statements in themselves* (Popper, 1968) is a useful representation of that which we *catch*, emphasizing the distinct ontological status of *knowledge*:

> *I regard the third world as being essentially the product of the human mind. It is we who create third-world objects. That these objects have their own inherent or autonomous laws which create unintended and unforeseeable consequences is only one instance (although a very interesting one) of a more general rule, the rule that all our actions have such consequences.* (Popper, 1974)

Popper terms the physical world, *World 1*, and the mental world, *World 2*, separating the objective knowledge of World 3 from the world represented and the agents doing the representation. Shaw (1985) has developed these notions to show how personal construct psychology accounts for the psychological processes not only of individuals but also for those of functional groups such as a product executive.

Figure 7 brings all these notions together to provide a conceptual framework for human psychology, sociology, action and knowledge. The central region presents a three-layer model of human agents and their supporting infrastructures, whether roles, people, groups, organizations or societies. At the bottom are the processes of interaction with the environment, of percepts, acts, reflexes, sensa-

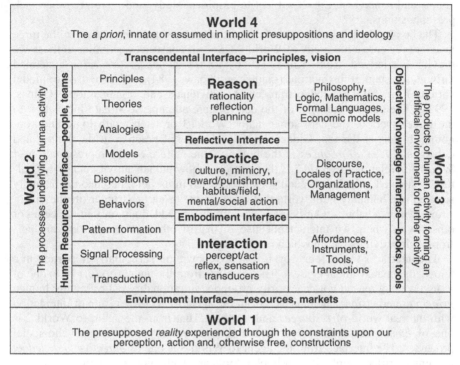

Figure 7. An Integrated Model of Levels and Worlds of Being in Organizational Knowledge Acquisition

tion, transducers, and so on. This is the level that is being emulated through neural networks (Elman et al., 1999). At the top are the processes of reason, of rationality, reflection, planning and so on. This is the level that is being emulated through digital computation. In the middle are the processes of practice, of culture, habitus and field characterizing the mental and the social, action, mimicry, reward and punishment. This is the level where neither neural networks nor digital computation have so far provided adequate emulation, and lack of such emulation of habitus is the greatest impediment to the development of expert systems.

The four surrounding boxes set human agents within the context of Popper's (1968) *three worlds*, but adding a fourth world at the top to balance the presupposed World 1 of physical reality with an equally presupposed World 4 of transcendental *a priori* presuppositions and ideology. Popper would probably have placed this World 4 in his World 3, as a human artifact, but it is separated here to emphasize its psychological and cultural status as something presupposed not constructed. Friedman (1999) has presented a reconstruction of the work of the logical positivists, particularly Carnap, suggesting that their contribution is best understood as offering a new conception of *a priori* knowledge and its role in empirical knowledge, the link between our Worlds 4 and 1. Searle (1998) has argued that realism is based on a presupposition of a real world underlying all our further discourse and hence is not itself subject to empirical study, and there are other such presuppositions.

The box on the left of the central core attempts to situate in relation to the three layers of the core a hierarchy of World 2 levels of construction similar to those we previously derived from Klir's (1976) *epistemological hierarchy* generated through a system of distinctions (Gaines and Shaw, 1984), and have used to model various forms of knowledge transfer in individuals and organizations (Gaines, 1994a). The box on the right of the central core attempts to situate in relation to the three layers of the core some major World 3 products, with logic and economic models at the top, Giddens' (1986) *locales* of practice in the center, and Gibson's (1979) *affordances* at the bottom. One feature of this representation of World 3 in relation to World 2 is that it stresses how human activity is not just culturally situated in its habitus and socially situated in its field, but also artifactually situated in a humanly built world that exists in major part to trigger off the dispositions within a habitus. Our being is essentially embedded not only in the being of others with whom we interact but also in that of others who have left artifacts from their activities within which ours take place.

The interfaces to the four worlds that are shown are particularly important in a knowledge management context. The interface from the agent to World 4 is one of transcendental reason not necessarily grounded in rationality but reflecting human *principles* and *vision*. The interface from the agent to World 1 is one of interaction with the real world of *resources* and *markets*. That from the agent to World 2 is one of *human resources*, of people and organizations and their psycho-social processes. The interface from the agent to World 3 is one of *objective knowledge*, of human artifacts embodied in books, tools and technologies. There are also internal interfaces in the three-layer agent model: a *reflective* interface mediating between practice and reason; and an *embodiment* interface mediating between practice and interaction with the world.

From a collective stance perspective the architecture of Figure 7 models any coherent cross-section of a society, a nation, an ethnic culture, an organization, a firm, a market, a team, an individual, or a role. Each level involves the processes represented in Figure 7, with some of the processes linking up in level, e.g. from individual to firm, and others linking down in level, e.g. from firm to individual. The *routines* and *procedures* studied by Nelson and Winter (1982) and by Cyert and March (1963) arise out of the *habitus* of the firm and structure those of its employees. Equally, through the process that Giddens (1986) terms *structuration*, the reciprocal process occurs in which the habitus of the firm is structured by those of its employees. The firm and the employees acquires *knowledge* through all processes that make that structuring effective including the internalization of principles, reinforcement learning and mimicry.

7   Managing Habitus

Managing organizational knowledge acquisition involves managing the entire infrastructure shown in Figure 7 with particular emphasis on the processes shown in Figure 3. There is not as yet an integrative theory of all the processes shown in Figure 7. It is probable that one will eventually be developed based on personal construct psychology used to model the way in which individuals, organizations and their artifacts interact with one another and the external world(s). In the central three-layer model, the top-level domain of reason is best understood, and the management of reflection and planning processes has a powerful literature ranging from the formality of Porter's (1980; 1985; 1986; 1990) analyses of the processes leading to competitive advantage to Schön's (1983; 1987; 1991) humanistic studies of the *reflective practitioner*. Argyris has also collaborated with Schön to develop an *action science* (Argyris, et al., 1985) framework for organizational learning (Argyris and Schön, 1978; Argyris and Schön, 1996). The bottom-level domain of interaction is also comparatively well understood, and the management of manufacturing, market research and sales processes also has an extensive literature.

However, the management of the central region of *practice,* based on an organizational habitus of dispositions acquired through experience, is not well-understood except as a system that is extraordinarily difficult to manage but critical to sustainable competitive advantage. Human resource management has always had concerns with this level (Fombrun et al., 1984; Mabey et al., 1998; Sofo, 1999; Ulrich, 1997). Competence-based (Nordhaug, 1993) and economic (Becker, 1993) models of human capital have modeled the importance of skilled people to organizations. There are also models of organizations (Foss and Knudsen, 1996; Foss et al., 1998; Foss and Mahnke, 2000; Loasby, 1999; Nooteboom, 2000) being developed in terms of *transaction cost economics* (Williamson and Masten, 1995) that could eventually provide a framework encompassing the management of an organization's habitus. There has also been increasing attention to modeling *organizational culture* (Harris, 1994; Jones, 1983; Leydesdorff, 2000) and managing it for competitive advantage (Fiol, 1991).

Polanyi's (1958) original book and literature deriving from it (Gill, 2000) provide one important source of material on the tacit knowledge embedded in habitus. Bourdieu's (1977; 1989; 1990; 1993; 1998; 1992) massive collection of books and derivative literature (Calhoun et al., 1993; Swartz, 1997) provides a foundational resource. Baumard's (1999) *Tacit Knowledge in Organizations* and Wenger's (1998) *Communities of Practice* are currently the definitive source of management models and case histories relating to tacit knowledge in organizations. Nonaka, who first argued for the role of converting tacit to coded knowledge in the success of Japanese companies (Nonaka and Takeuchi, 1995), has since published collections of related material (Nonaka and Nishiguchi, 2001; Nonaka and Teece, 2001). One very promising development has been that of *actor-network theory* (ANT) originally stemming from Latour and Woolgar's (1987; 1986) ethnographic studies of *Laboratory Life* and *Science in Action* but being extended by Law, Callon, *et al* (Law and Hassard, 1999) to the phenomena of habitus in many other domains. An important feature of ANT is that it treats non-human entities, including technological artifacts, as first class members of social networks and examines, for example, their perspectives on events.

The primary dynamics of habitus within an organization depend on the constructs of those constituting the organization and its value chain, the extent to which these are generally shared, and the extent to which they correspond to the critical constructs of management at all levels. Management of the injection and diffusion of constructs within an organization is the main mechanism available with which to manage its habitus. Mimicry of role models, experiential learning, and learning through examples are the primary mechanisms for the injection of tacit constructs, together with descriptions of case histories for coded constructs. The management of personnel relationships and situations is the primary resource for influencing these processes. Managers play a key role in in this: through leadership they provides constructs that structure the meanings of experience for all employees and hence also for customers and suppliers (Smircich and Morgan, 1982; Witt, 1998); through personnel practices they influences the composition of the agents that constitute the organization and produce and reproduce its habitus; and through the situations they create they provide opportunities for experiential learning.

8   Tools to Support Organizational Knowledge Acquisition

The knowledge acquisition research community has developed a range of techniques and supporting tools to use for knowledge elicitation from experts and end users (Boose and Gaines, 1988) that are also well-suited to organizational knowledge acquisition. Most of the tools have been derived from other domains such as education and psychology. Section 2 illustrated two such tools: *concept maps* deriving from education (Novak, 1998; Novak and Gowin, 1984) and *repertory grids* (Kelly, 1955; Shaw, 1980; Shaw, 1981) deriving from clinical psychology. Concept maps represent mental models in terms of concepts and the relations between them. Repertory grids represent mental models in terms of construct systems, the distinctions made between entities in the domain being modeled.

Semantic networks (Lehmann, 1992; Sowa, 1991) are concept maps with strictly defined operational semantics that are used for the formal representation of knowledge as facts and theories. Tools have been developed for ease of development of both concept maps (Gaines et al., 1995; Gaines and Shaw, 1994a; Gaines and Shaw, 1995b) and semantic networks, some operating in groupware mode to support multiple users at different sites (Gaines and Shaw, 1995a; Kremer and Gaines, 1994) particularly on the World Wide Web (Gaines and Shaw, 1995c; Kremer and Gaines, 1996). Tools have also been developed for ease of development of semantic networks including inference from them (Gaines, 1993a; Gaines, 1993b; Gaines, 1994b; Gaines and Shaw, 1999). Similarly tools have been developed for the elicitation of personal construct systems (Gaines and Shaw, 1993a; Gaines and Shaw, 1993b) some of which operate on the World Wide Web to collect and compare mental models from multiple, distributed users (Gaines and Shaw, 1996; Shaw and Gaines, 1999).

One important feature of repertory grids is that techniques and tools have been developed to compare mental models in the same domain by comparing the distinctions made by constructs from different individuals. This allows pairs of constructs, one from each individual, to be allocated to the four quadrants shown in Figure 8, indicating consensus, conflict, correspondence and contrast (Gaines and Shaw, 1989; Shaw and Gaines, 1989).

Constructs

Same	Different
Consensus	**Conflict**
Individuals use terminology and constructs in the same way	Individuals use same terminology for different constructs
Correspondence	**Contrast**
Individuals use different terminology for the same constructs	Individuals differ in terminology and constructs

Figure 8. Consensus, Conflict, Correspondence, and Contrast in Construct Systems

It is also possible to compare complete grids in the same domain to determine the best matches for constructs in one grid in another, and *vice versa*. This results in asymmetric links between grids corresponding to one person being able to understand the constructs of another, and a *socionet* may be plotted based on such understanding (Shaw, 1980).In a study of quality control at a garment factory where grids were elicited from plant operators and all levels of management, it was found that the socionet exactly reproduced the management hierarchy (Shaw and Gaines, 1983)—each level of management could understand the constructs of the level below even if the knowledge involved was tacit.

9   Conclusions

As a socio-economic system approaches its optimum performance its system dynamics become increasingly unstable and subject to wild fluctuations (Anderson et al., 1988; Arthur et al., 1997). As evidence has mounted that the global economic system is entering this state (D'Aveni and Gunther, 1994; Doeringer, 1991; Drucker, 1978; Frank, 1998; Ilinitch et al., 1998), it has become increasingly important to those responsible for major organizations that they understand and manage organizational processes more effectively. This has led to interest in knowledge management, the nature of expertise, and the management of knowledge acquisition so as to enhance the capabilities of the organization.

This chapter has presented a unified model of organizational knowledge acquisition, linking it to a wide range of relevant literature and to management practices. The discussion draws on research in knowledge acquisition for expert systems, and the article recounts the background to such systems and the issues which limited their development. The model draws on personal construct psychology to provide a constructivist account of human agents and organizations, on Bourdieu's analysis of dispositions internalizing the history of experience to account for the construct systems underlying practice, on Giddens' structuration theory to account for the way in which organizational habitus is both structured by those of the individual in the organization and is in turn structured by them, and on Popper's theory of worlds to separate the physical, mental, objective knowledge and transcendental worlds.

The model is used to suggests ways in which the knowledge acquisition process can be managed, particularly that for the tacit knowledge which constitutes Bourdieu's habitus. It is suggested that concept mapping and repertory grid tools that were developed for knowledge acquisition for expert systems development will also prove useful in organizational knowledge acquisition.

Acknowledgment

Financial assistance for this work has been made available by the Natural Sciences and Engineering Research Council of Canada. I am grateful to Mildred Shaw and to colleagues in the GNOSIS international Intelligent Manufacturing Systems consortium for many stimulating discussions and for access to their data. Further reports may be accessed at http://repgrid.com/reports/, WebGrid at http://repgrid. com/ WebGrid/, and the author at mailto:gaines@ucalgary.ca

References

Alchian, A. A., *Economic Forces at Work,* Indianapolis: Liberty Press, 1977.

Alford, J., C. Cairney, R. Higgs, M. Honsowetz, V. Huynh, A. Jines, D. Keates and C. Skelton, "Real Rewards from Artificial Intelligence," *InTech*, April, 2000, 52-55.

Anderson, P. W., K. J. Arrow and D. Pines, *The Economy as an Evolving Complex System*, Reading, MA: Addison-Wesley, 1988.

Argyris, C., R. Putnam and D. M. Smith, *Action Science*, San Francisco: Jossey-Bass, 1985.

Argyris, C. and D. A. Schön, *Organizational Learning*, Reading, MA: Addison-Wesley, 1978.

Argyris, C. and D. A. Schön, *Organizational Learning II,* Reading, MA: Addison-Wesley, 1996.

Aristotle, *Nicomachean Ethic,*. Cambridge: Cambridge University Press, 2000.

Arthur, W. B., S. N. Durlauf and D. A. Lane, *The Economy as an Evolving Complex System II*, Reading, MA: Addison-Wesley, 1997.

Bacon, F., *The New Organon, and Related Writings,* Liberal Arts Press, 1960.

Bakhtin, M., *The Dialogic Imagination: Four Essays by Michael Bakhtin,* Austin: University of Texas Press, 1981.

Barzel, Y., *Economic Analysis of Property Rights,* Cambridge: Cambridge University Press, 1997.

Baumard, P., *Tacit Knowledge in Organizations*, Thousand Oaks, CA: SAGE Publications, 1999.

Becker, G. S., *Human Capital (3rd Edition),* Chicago: University of Chicago Press, 1993.

Beniger, J. R., *The Control Revolution: Technological and Economic Origins of the Information Society*, Cambridge, MA: Harvard University Press, 1986.

Boisot, M., *Information Space: A Framework for Learning in Organizations, Institutions, and Culture,* New York: Routledge, 1995.

Boisot, M., *Knowledge Assets: Securing Competitive Advantage in the Information Economy,* Oxford: Oxford University Press, 1998.

Boose, J. H. and B. R. Gaines, Eds, *Knowledge Acquisition Tools for Expert Systems,* London: Academic Press, 1988.

Bourdieu, P., *Outline of a Theory of Practice,* Cambridge: Cambridge University Press, 1977.

Bourdieu, P., *The Logic of Practice,* Cambridge: Polity, 1989.

Bourdieu, P., *In Other Words: Essays Toward a Reflexive Sociology,* Oxford: Polity, 1990.

Bourdieu, P., *Sociology in Question,* London: Sage, 1993.

Bourdieu, P., *Practical Reason: On the Theory of Action*, Stanford: Stanford University Press, 1998.

Bourdieu, P. and L. J. D. Wacquant, *An Invitation to Reflexive Sociology,* Chicago: University of Chicago Press, 1992.

Calhoun, C. J., E. LiPuma and M. Postone, *Bourdieu: Critical Perspectives,* Cambridge: Polity Press, 1993.

Chandler, A. D., *The Visible Hand: The Managerial Revolution in American Business,* Cambridge: Belknap Press, 1977.

Clancey, W. J., "Viewing Knowledge Bases as Qualitative Models," *IEEE Expert,* 4,2, 1989, 9-23.

Cohen, W. M. and D. A. Levinthal, "Absorptive Capacity: A New Perspective on Learning and Innovation," *Administrative Science Quarterly*, 35, 1990, 128-152.

Crane, D., *Invisible Colleges: Diffusion of Knowledge in Scientific Communities*, Chicago: University of Chicago Press, 1972.

Cyert, R. M. and J. G. March, *A Behavioral Theory of the Firm*, Englewood Cliffs, N.J.: Prentice-Hall, 1963.

D'Aveni, R. A. and R. E. Gunther, *Hypercompetition: Managing the Dynamics of Strategic Maneuvering*, New York: The Free Press, 1994.

Doeringer, P. B., *Turbulence in the American Workplace*, Oxford: Oxford University Press, 1991.

Doignon, J.-P. and J.-C. Falmagne, *Knowledge Spaces*, Berlin: Springer, 1999.

Dreyfus, H. L., *What Computers Can't Do: A Critique of Artificial Reason*, New York: Harper & Row, 1972.

Dreyfus, H. L. and S. E. Dreyfus, *Mind over Machine: The Power of Human Intuition and Expertise in the Era of the Computer*, New York: Free Press, 1986.

Drucker, P. F., *The Age of Discontinuity*, New York: Harper & Row, 1978.

Drucker, P. F., "From Capitalism to Knowledge Society," in *Post Capitalist Society*, New York: HarperBusiness, 1993, 19-47.

Elman, J. L., E. A. Bates, M. H. Johnson, A. Karmiloff-Smith, D. Parisi and K. Plunkett, *Rethinking Innateness: A Connectionist Perspective on Development*, Cambridge, MA: MIT Press, 1999.

Feigenbaum, E., P. McCorduck, and H. P. Nii, *The Rise of the Expert Company*, New York: Times Books, 1988.

Feyerabend, P. (ed.), *Against Method*, London: NLB, 1975.

Fiol, C. M., "Managing Culture as a Competitive Resource: An Identity-Based View of Sustainable Competitive Advantage," *Journal of Management*, 17,1, 1991, 191-211.

Fombrun, C. J., N. M. Tichy, and M. A. Devanna, *Strategic Human Resource Management*, New York: Wiley, 1984.

Fortun, M. and H. J. Bernstein, *Muddling Through: Pursuing Science and Truths in the 21st Century*, Washington: Counterpoint, 1998.

Foss, N. J. and C. Knudsen, *Towards a Competence Theory of the Firm*, London: Routledge, 1996.

Foss, N. J., B. J. Loasby, and G. B. Richardson, *Economic Organization, Capabilities and Coordination: Essays in Honour of G.B. Richardson*, London: Routledge, 1998.

Foss, N. J. and V. Mahnke, *Competence, Governance, and Entrepreneurship: Advances in Economic Strategy Research*, Oxford: Oxford University Press, 2000.

Frank, A. G., *ReOrient: Global Economy in the Asian Age,* Berkeley: University of California Press, 1998.

Friedman, M., *Reconsidering Logical Positivism,* Cambridge: Cambridge University Press, 1999.

Gadamer, H. G., *Wahrheit und Methode,* Tübingen: Mohr, 1972.

Gaines, B. R., "Positive Feedback Processes Underlying the Formation of Expertise," *IEEE Transactions on Systems, Man & Cybernetics,* SMC-18, 6, 1988, 1016-1020.

Gaines, B. R., "Social and Cognitive Processes in Knowledge Acquisition," *Knowledge Acquisition,* 1,1, 1989, 251-280.

Gaines, B. R., "A Class Library Implementation of a Principled Open Architecture Knowledge Representation Server with Plug-In Data Types," *IJCAI'93: Proceedings of the Thirteenth International Joint Conference on Artificial Intelligence,* San Mateo, California: Morgan Kaufmann, 1993a, 504-509.

Gaines, B. R., "Experience with a Class Library for Organizational Modeling and Problem Solving," *Integrated Computer-Aided Engineering,* 1,2, 1993b, 93-107.

Gaines, B. R., "The Collective Stance in Modeling Expertise in Individuals and Organizations," *International Journal of Expert Systems,* 7,1, 1994a, 21-51.

Gaines, B. R., "A Situated Classification Solution of a Resource Allocation Task Represented in a Visual Language," *International Journal Human-Computer Studies,* 40,2, 1994b, 243-271.

Gaines, B. R., "Knowledge Management in Societies of Intelligent Adaptive Agents," *Journal for Intelligent Information Systems,* 9,3, 1997, 277-298.

Gaines, B. R., D. H. Norrie, and A. Z. Lapsley, "Mediator: An Intelligent Information System Supporting the Virtual Manufacturing Enterprise," *Proceedings of 1995 IEEE International Conference on Systems, Man and Cybernetics,* New York: IEEE, 95CH3576-7, 1995, 964-969.

Gaines, B. R. and M. L. G. Shaw, "Hierarchies of Distinctions as Generators of System Theories," *Proceedings of the Society for General Systems Research International Conference.* A. W. Smith, Louisville, Kentucky: Society for General Systems Research, 1984, 559-566.

Gaines, B. R. and M. L. G. Shaw, "Comparing the Conceptual Systems of Experts," *Proceedings of the Eleventh International Joint Conference on Artificial Intelligence,* San Mateo, California: Morgan Kaufmann, 1989, 633-638.

Gaines, B. R. and M. L. G. Shaw, "Basing Knowledge Acquisition Tools in Personal Construct Psychology," *Knowledge Engineering Review,* 8,1, 1993a, 49-85.

Gaines, B. R. and M. L. G. Shaw, "Eliciting Knowledge and Transferring It Effectively to a Knowledge-Based System," *IEEE Transactions on Knowledge and Data Engineering,* 5,1, 1993b, 4-14.

Gaines, B. R. and M. L. G. Shaw, "Concept Maps Indexing Multimedia Knowledge Bases," *AAAI-94 Workshop: Indexing and Reuse in Multimedia Systems*, Menlo Park, California: AAAI, 1994a, 36-45.

Gaines, B. R. and M. L. G. Shaw, "Using Knowledge Acquisition and Representation Tools to Support Scientific Communities," *AAAI'94: Proceedings of the Twelfth National Conference on Artificial Intelligence*, Menlo Park, California: AAAI Press/MIT Press, 1994b, 707-714.

Gaines, B. R. and M. L. G. Shaw, "Collaboration through Concept Maps," *Proceedings of CSCL95: Computer Support for Collaborative Learning.* J. L. Schnase and E. L. Cunnius, Mahwah, New Jersey: Lawrence Erlbaum, 1995a, 135-138.

Gaines, B. R. and M. L. G. Shaw, "Concept Maps as Hypermedia Components," *International Journal Human-Computer Studies,* 43,3, 1995b, 323-361.

Gaines, B. R. and M. L. G. Shaw, "WebMap: Concept Mapping on the Web," *World Wide Web Journal,* 1,1, 1995c, 171-183.

Gaines, B. R. and M. L. G. Shaw, "WebGrid: Knowledge Modeling and Inference through the World Wide Web," *Proceedings of Tenth Knowledge Acquisition Workshop.* B. R. Gaines and M. A. Musen, 65-1-65-14 (http://ksi.cpsc.ucalgary.ca/KAW/KAW96/gaines/KMD.html), 1996.

Gaines, B. R. and M. L. G. Shaw, "Knowledge Acquisition, Modeling and Inference through the World Wide Web," *International Journal of Human-Computer Studies,* 46,6, 1997, 729-759.

Gaines, B. R. and M. L. G. Shaw, "Embedding Formal Knowledge Models in Active Documents," *Communications of the ACM,* 42,1, 1999, 57-63.

Gallupe, R. B. and W. H. Cooper, "Brainstorming Electronically," *Sloan Management Review*, 1993, 27-36.

Gibbons, M., C. Limoges, H. Nowotny, S. Schwartzman, P. Scott and M. Trow, *The New Production of Knowledge: The Dynamics of Science and Research in Contemporary Societies,* Thousand Oaks, CA: SAGE Publications, 1994.

Gibson, J. J., *The Ecological Approach to Perception,* Boston: Houghton Mifflin, 1979.

Giddens, A., *The Constitution of Society: Outline of the Theory of Structuration,* California: University of California Press, 1986.

Gill, J. H., *The Tacit Mode: Michael Polanyi's Postmodern Philosophy,* Albany: State University of New York Press, 2000.

Goodman, R. F. and W. R. Fisher (eds.), *Rethinking Knowledge: Reflections across the Disciplines,* Albany: State University of New York Press, 1995.

Hall, E. T., *The Silent Language,* New York: Doubleday, 1959.

Harris, S. G., "Organizational Culture and Individual Sensemaking: A Schema-Based Perspective," *Organization Science,* 5,3, 1994, 309-321.

Hauenstein, A. D., *A Conceptual Framework for Educational Objectives: A Holistic Approach to Traditional Taxonomies,* Lanham, MD: University Press of America, 1998.

Havelock, E. A., *Preface to Plato,* Cambridge: Harvard University Press, 1963.

Hawkins, D., "An Analysis of Expert Thinking," *International Journal of Man-Machine Studies,* 18,1, 1983, 1-47.

Hayes-Roth, F., "The Industrialization of Knowledge Engineering," in Reitman, W. (ed.), *Artificial Intelligence Applications for Business,* Norwood, New Jersey: Ablex, 1984, 159-177.

Hippel, E. V., ""Sticky Information"and the Locus of Problem Solving: Implications for Invention," *Management Science,* 44,4, 1994, 429-439.

Ilinitch, A. Y., A. Y. Lewin, and R. A. D'Aveni, *Managing in Times of Disorder: Hypercompetitive Organizational Responses,* Thousand Oaks: Sage, 1998.

Jones, G. R., "Transaction Costs, Property Rights, and Organizational Culture: An Exchange Perspective," *Adminstrative Science Quarterly,* 28, 1983, 454-467.

Kelly, G. Λ., *The Psychology of Personal Constructs,* New York: Norton, 1955.

Klir, G. J., "Identification of Generative Structures in Empirical Data," *International Journal of General Systems,* 3, 1976, 89-104.

Kogut, B. and U. Zander, "Knowledge of the Firm, Combinative Capabilities, and the Replication of Technology," *Organization Science,* 3,3, 1992, 383-397.

Kremer, R. and B. R. Gaines, "Groupware Concept Mapping Techniques," *Proceedings SIGDOC'94: ACM 12th Annual International Conference on Systems Documentation,* New York: ACM, 1994, 156-165.

Kremer, R. A. and B. R. Gaines, "Embedded Interactive Concept Maps in Web Documents," *Proceedings of WebNet96,* Charlottesville, VA: Association for the Advancement of Computing in Education, 1996, 273-280.

Kremer, R. C., "Experience in Applying KRS to an Actual Business Problem," *Proceedings of the Sixth AAAI Knowledge Acquisition for Knowledge-Based Systems Worksho,* Calgary, Canada: University of Calgary, 1991, 11-1-11-12.

Lant, T. K. and S. J. Mezias, "An Organizational Learning Model of Convergence and Reorientation," in Cohen, M.D. and Sproull, L. (eds.), *Organizational Learning,,* Thousand Oaks: Sage, 1996.

Latour, B., *Science in Action: How to Follow Scientists and Engineers Through Society,* Cambridge, MA: Harvard University Press, 1987.

Latour, B. and S. Woolgar, *Laboratory Life: The Construction of Scientific Facts,* Princeton, N.J.: Princeton University Press, 1986.

Law, J. and J. Hassard, *Actor Network Theory and After,* Oxford: Blackwell, 1999.

Lehmann, F. (ed.), *Semantic Networks in Artificial Intelligence,* Oxford: Pergamon Press, 1992.

Leonard-Barton, D., *Wellsprings of Knowledge: Building and Sustaining the Sources of Innovation,* Boston, MA.: Harvard Business School Press, 1995.

Lewin, K., *Principles of Topological Psychology,* New York: McGraw-Hill, 1936.

Leydesdorff, L., "A Model Engine for the Simulation of "Lock-In," "Break-Out," and the Dissemination of Technological Culture," *Proceedings of the 44th Annual Conference of the International Society for the System Sciences,* Toronto, ISSS, 2000.

Loasby, B. J., *Knowledge, Institutions, and Evolution in Economics,* London: Routledge, 1999.

Luhmann, N., *Social Systems,* Stanford, CA: Stanford University Press, 1995.

Mabey, C., G. Salaman, and J. Storey (eds.), *Strategic Human Resource Management,* London: Sage and Open University, 1998.

Mancuso, J. C. and M. L. G. Shaw (eds.), *Cognition and Personal structure: Computer Access and Analysis,* New York: Praeger, 1988.

Marx, K., *On Society and Social Change. With Selections by Friedrich Engels,* Chicago,: University of Chicago Press, 1973.

Meister, J. C., *Corporate Universities: Lessons in Building a World-class Work Force,* New York: McGraw-Hill, 1998.

Metfessel, N. S., W. B. Michael, and D. A. Kirsner, "Instrumentation of Bloom's and Krathwohl's Taxonomies for the Writing of Educational Objectives," *Psychology in the Schools,* 6, 1969, 227-231.

Nelson, R. R. and S. G. Winter, *An Evolutionary Theory of Economic Change,* Cambridge, Massachusetts: Belknap Press, 1982.

Newell, A., "The knowledge Level," *Artificial Intelligence,* 18,1, 1982, 87-127.

Nonaka, I. and T. Nishiguchi, *Knowledge Emergence: Social, Technical, and Evolutionary Dimensions of Knowledge Creation,* Oxford: Oxford University Press, 2001.

Nonaka, I. and H. Takeuchi, *The Knowledge-Creating Company,* Oxford: Oxford University Press, 1995.

Nonaka, I. and D. J. Teece, *Managing Industrial Knowledge: Creation, Transfer and Utilization,* Thousand Oaks, CA: Sage, 2001.

Nooteboom, B., *Learning and Innovation in Organizations and Economies,* Oxford: Oxford University Press, 2000.

Nordhaug, O., *Human Capital in Organizations: Competence, Training and Learning,* Oslo: Scadinavian University Press, 1993.

Novak, J. D., *Learning, Creating, and Using Knowledge: Concept Maps as Facilitative Tools in Schools and Corporations,* Mahwah, NJ: Lawrence Erlbaum, 1998.

Novak, J. D. and D. B. Gowin, *Learning How to Learn,* Cambridge: Cambridge University Press, 1984.

Nunamaker, J. F., A. R. Dennis, J. S. Valacich, D. R. Vogel and J. F. George, "Electronic Meetings to Support Group Work," *Communications of the ACM,* 34,7, 1991, 40-61.

Penrose, E. T., *The Theory of the Growth of the Firm*, New York: Wiley, 1959.

Plato and F. M. Cornford, *Plato's Theory of Knowledge: the Theaetetus and the Sophist of Plato,* London: K. Paul Trench Trubner, 1935.

Polanyi, M., *Personal Knowledge: Towards a Post-critical Philosophy,* Chicago: University of Chicago Press, 1958.

Popper, K. R., "Epistemology without a Knowing Subject," in Rootselaar, B.V. (eds.), *Logic, Methodology and Philosophy of Science III*, Amsterdam: North-Holland, 1968, 333-373.

Popper, K. R., "Autobiography of Karl Popper," in Schilpp, P.A. (ed.), *The Philosophy of Karl Popper,*La Salle, Illinois: Open Court, 1974, 3-181.

Porter, M. E., *Competitive Strategy: Techniques for Analyzing Industries and Competitors,* New York: Free Press, 1980.

Porter, M. E., *Competitive Advantage: Creating and Sustaining Superior Performance,* New York: Free Press, 1985.

Porter, M. E., *Competition in Global Industries,* Boston: Harvard Business School Press, 1986.

Porter, M. E., *The Competetive Advantage of Nations*, New York: Free Press, 1990.

Pralahad, D. and G. Hamel, "The Core Competence of the Corporation," *Harvard Business Review*, May-June, 1990, 79-91.

Sanchez, R. and A. Heene, *Strategic Learning and Knowledge Management*, New York: Wiley, 1997.

Saul, J. R., *Voltaire's Bastards: The Dictatorship of Reason in the West*, Toronto: Penguin, 1993.

Schön, D. A., *The Reflective Practitioner,* New York: Basic Books, 1983.

Schön, D. A., *Educating the Reflective Practitioner: Toward a New Design for Teaching and Learning in the Professions,* San Francisco: Jossey-Bass, 1987.

Schön, D. A., *The Reflective Turn: Case Studies in and on Educational Practice,* New York, 1991.

Scott, W. R., *Organizations: Rational, Natural and Open Systems (3rd Edition).* Englewood Cliffs, New Jersey: Prentice-Hall, 1992.

Searle, J. R., *The Rediscovery of the Mind*, Cambridge, MA: MIT Press, 1992.

Searle, J. R., *Mind, Language and Society: Philosophy in the Real World*, New York, NY: Basic Books, 1998.

Seiler, H. (1999). *Managing Business Rules: A Repository-Based Approach*, Indialantic, FL: Rule Machines Corporation.

Shapin, S., *A Social History of Truth: Civility and Science in Seventeenth-Century England*, Chicago: University of Chicago Press, 1994.

Shaw, M. L. G., *On Becoming A Personal Scientist: Interactive Computer Elicitation of Personal Models Of The World*, London: Academic Press, 1980.

Shaw, M. L. G. (ed.), *Recent Advances in Personal Construct Technolog,*. London: Academic Press, 1981.

Shaw, M. L. G., "Communities of Knowledge," in Epting, F. and Landfield, A.W. (eds.), *Anticipating Personal Construct Psychology,* Lincoln, Nebraska: University of Nebraska Press, 1985, 25-35.

Shaw, M. L. G. and B. R. Gaines, "Eliciting the Real Problem," in Wedde, H. (ed.), *Adequate Modeling of Systems*, Berlin: Springer, 1983, 100-111.

Shaw, M. L. G. and B. R. Gaines, "A Methodology for Recognizing Conflict, Correspondence, Consensus and Contrast in a Knowledge Acquisition System," *Knowledge Acquisition,* 1,4, 1989, 341-363.

Shaw, M. L. G. and B. R. Gaines, "Modeling the Social Practices of Users in Internet Communities," *UM99: User Modeling: Proceedings of the Seventh International Conference,* New York: Springer, 77-86, 1999.

Simmel, G., *The Sociology of Georg Simmel,* New York: Free Press, 1950.

Smircich, L. and G. Morgan, "Leadership: The Management of Meaning," *Journal of Applied Behavioral Science,* 18,3, 1982, 257-273.

Sofo, F., *Human Resource Development,* Business and Professional Publishing: Australia, 1999.

Solmsen, F., *Intellectual Experiments of the Greek Enlightenment,* Princeton, N.J.: Princeton University Press, 1975.

Sowa, J. F. (ed.), *Principles of Semantic Networks: Explorations in the Representation of Knowledge*, San Mateo, California: Morgan-Kaufman, 1991.

Sullivan, S. D., *Aeschylus' use of Psychological Terminology,* Montreal: McGill-Queen's University Press, 1997.

Sullivan, S. D., *Sophocles' use of Psychological Terminology*, Ottawa: Carleton University Press, 1999.

Sullivan, S. D., *Euripides' use of Psychological Terminology,* Montreal: McGill-Queen's University Press, 2000.

Swartz, D., *Culture & Power: The Sociology of Pierre Bourdieu,* Chicago: University of Chicago Press, 1997.

Thompson, J. D., *Organizations in Action: Social Science Bases of Administrative Theory,* New York: McGraw-Hill, 1967.

Tversky, A. and D. J. Koehler, "Support Theory: A Nonextensional Representation of Subjective Probability," *Psychological Review,* 101,4, 1994, 547-567.

Ulrich, D., *Human Resource Champions: The Next Agenda for Adding Value and Delivering Results,* Boston: Harvard Business School Press, 1997.

Vickers, J. N., *Instructional Design for Teaching Physical Activities: A Knowledge Structures Approach,* Champaign, Illinois: Human Kinetics, 1990.

Weber, M., *Economy and Society: An Outline of Interpretive Sociology,* New York: Bedminster Press, 1968.

Wenger, E., *Communities of Practice: Learning, Meaning, and Identity*, Cambridge: Cambridge University Press, 1998.

Wertsch, J. V. (ed.), *Voices of the Mind: A Sociocultural Approach to Mediated Action*, Cambridge, MA: Harvard University Press, 1991.

Williamson, O. E. and S. E. Masten, *Transaction Cost Economics*, Aldershot, Hants, England: Edward Elgar, 1995.

Wills, G., *The Knowledge Game: The Revolution in Learning and Communication in the Workplace*, London: Cassell, 1998.

Witt, U., "Imagination and Leadership—The Neglected Dimension of an Evolutionary Theory of the Firm," *Journal of Economic Behavior and Organization*, 35, 1998, 161-177.

Wittgenstein, L., *Philosophical Investigations*, Oxford: Blackwell, 1953.

Wolff, K. H., *Surrender and Catch: Experience and Enquiry Today*, Dordrecht, Holland: Reidel, 1976.

CHAPTER 17

Problem Solving: A Knowledge Management Process

Thomas Whalen and Subhashish Samaddar

Department of Management, J. Mack Robinson College of Business, Georgia State University, Atlanta, GA, USA

Organizations manage their knowledge resources to provide an environment for their members to make well-informed decisions and to take problem-solving actions. A decision-making process is a knowledge intensive process that both recognizes and solves problems along the way to the objective of producing a decision. During such a process knowledge is continually created, stored and retrieved, shared, used, and modified to create new knowledge. In this chapter we present the evolving trend in which soft computing and an emerging "post-modern" management science will provide an environment that will stimulate, shape, and challenge the discipline of knowledge management in creating new opportunities and capabilities for organizational problem solving. We posit that the discipline of knowledge management must accept a new mission: bringing the power of soft computing and post-modern management science into the mainstream of business problem solving. We show how this mission can be achieved.

Keywords: Education; Fuzzy Logic; Knowledge Management; Post-Modern Management Science; Problem Solving; Soft Computing

1 Introduction

It is the nature of knowledge to increase and bear fruit. Wise organizations manage and husband their knowledge resources in order to provide an environment for their members to make well-informed decisions and to take problem-solving actions. A decision-making process is one of both recognizing and solving problems along the way to the objective of producing a decision. Any problem solving process traverses through three decision-making phases, known as intelligence, design, and choice (Simon, 1959). Within each phase of a decision-making process, the decision maker carries out various subactivities. Each of these activities is intended to solve some problem (Holsapple and Whinston, 1996). Each such problem-solving process is a knowledge-intensive one. During such a process, knowledge is continually created, stored and retrieved, shared, used, and modified to create new knowledge. Thus, in the decision support literature a decision-making process has been described as a knowledge-manufacturing process (Holsapple, 1995; IBM Research, 1995). Furthermore, identification of a problem and the consequent problem-solving process can be viewed as important knowledge management processes.

The central position of this chapter is that soft computing and an emerging "post-modern" management science will provide an environment that will stimulate, shape, and challenge the discipline of knowledge management in creating new opportunities and capabilities for organizational problem solving. Pre-modern knowledge management emphasized individual wisdom acquired from experience and tradition; twentieth century knowledge management emphasized a "hard science" approach centered on facts arranged at first in filing cabinets (introduced around 1900) and later in structured electronic databases. We opine that the knowledge management of the new millennium, while never discarding individual wisdom and objective facts, will be heavily influenced by the emerging computational theory of perception based on the technologies of soft computing. The growing knowledge management emphasis on continuously creating, discovering, reshaping, and deploying corporate knowledge by converting its tacit knowledge to explicit knowledge and vice-versa exploits the other foundation for postmodern management science. We posit that the discipline of knowledge management must accept a new mission: bringing the power of soft computing and postmodern management science into the mainstream of business.

We start by discussing in section 2, the dichotomy of hard and soft computing. We describe the efficacy of soft computing in real-life problem solving over that of what hard computing can offer. In that section we introduce various soft computing methods amenable for different knowledge management functions and we make the case how these methods complement and advance traditional management science. In section 3 we discuss the essence of traditional management science

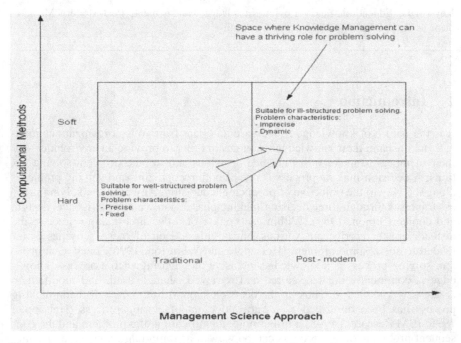

Figure 1. Evolution of Knowledge Management Problem Solving Space

as it relates to practice and education in this important field for business problem solving, and its current status in business education. We specifically note four key organizing questions that traditional management science seeks to answer by applying computational methods.

In section 4, we make the case for postmodern management science being more relevant and useful for knowledge management for contemporary business problem solving. Finally, in section 5, we conclude by making the case that knowledge management (KM) plays a key role in problem solving as indicated in Figure 1. The joint space of postmodern management science and soft computing is the new support that knowledge management can further exploit to provide support for problem solving involving inexact environments. In short, KM plays a critical role in both quadrants indicated in Figure 1, with the arrow pointing from what has been well developed to what needs to be further developed.

2 Hard and Soft Computing for Problem Solving

Real business problem solving mostly confronts imprecise data, models, and goals. However traditional hard computing is generally concerned with, and has grown to handle, precise problem-solving environments. One of the distinguishing characteristics of "postmodernism" in philosophy and the humanities generally is the de-emphasis on fixed meanings and precise structures of measurement, and the emphasis on discourses that dynamically shape and are shaped by the perceptions, concepts, and participants of which they are comprised. On one hand, Zadeh's (1998) writings on computing with words as a foundation for a computational theory of perception are one sign that the postmodern viewpoint has begun to contribute to the advancement of the problem solving. Such a foundation recognizes the imprecise nature of knowledge that is desirable to be used in problem formulation and solving. On the other hand, as discussed in section 4, Nonaka's (1995) emphasis on continuously creating, discovering, reshaping, and deploying corporate knowledge by converting its tacit knowledge to explicit knowledge and vice-versa can benefit from post-modern management science.

In contrast to the traditional computational methods, which regard precision as a *sine qua non*, soft computing tolerates, indeed welcomes, imprecision, ambiguity, and partial truth. Imprecision and ambiguity are pervasive, and precision and certainty carry a cost that often outweighs their benefits, even if achieving them (as opposed to merely assuming them) is possible at all. Soft computing exploits the tolerance for imprecision, ambiguity, and partial truth to achieve tractability, robustness, low solution cost, and creativity. Whalen (2001) summarizes six techniques for decision-making under uncertainty when the available information about probabilities is most honestly expressed by words and relations, rather than by numbers.

This view of ambiguity is fundamentally different from conventional views of uncertainty, although the two can coexist in a single model. Uncertainty assumes that every variable always has a precise value, but that we have only imperfect knowledge of this value. Soft methods assume that various values are more or less compatible with the value of a variable. While these gradations of compatibility must be represented in the computer by numeric values that look much the same as the numeric values used to represent probabilities, the interpretation is inherently much looser. Soft techniques are intentionally insensitive to small variations in representation, as opposed to conventional techniques that use sensitivity analysis to identify inputs for which a small variation will drive a major change in the output.

Lotfi Zadeh defines soft computing as a consortium or a partnership of three principal constituents: fuzzy logic, neurocomputing, and genetic algorithms. In the remainder of this section, we analyze how these three constituents help two fundamental knowledge management processes: *knowledge modeling* and *knowledge creation*. In section 4, we present and discuss three other areas needed for the exploiting post-modern management science in support of knowledge management for problem solving: *decision support systems*, *data mining and knowledge discovery*, and *data visualization and applied virtual reality*.

2.1 Knowledge Modeling with Fuzzy Logic

In the narrow sense, fuzzy logic refers to an extension of classical logic to handle imprecise concepts. This branch of fuzzy logic is highly effective when there are one or more human experts who can articulate their solutions to a class of problems in language that can be effectively translated into fuzzy if-then rules. The principal contribution of fuzzy logic is a methodology for approximate reasoning and, in particular, for computing with words (Whalen, 1984).

The term "fuzzy logic" is also widely used in a much broader way than the narrow sense of fuzzy generalizations of classical logic. The extension principle of fuzzy mathematics permits introducing quantitative linguistic variables as fuzzy sets into any mathematical structure or operation. Thus, it is very straightforward to add things like fuzzy mathematical programming, fuzzy regression, fuzzy time series, and fuzzy decision analysis to the management science toolbox (Zadeh, 1998, 1999).

"Computing with words" essentially means using a high-level language or meta-knowledge that lets the humans who develop, use, and maintain a computer program view the objects of computation in terms of quantitative linguistic variables expressed by words and propositions drawn from a natural language (e.g., small, large, far, thin, not very likely, low and declining, near San Francisco). Humans can perform a wide variety of physical and mental tasks without any measurements and any conscious computations: driving and parking a car, playing golf, riding a bicycle, understanding speech, and summarizing a story. Viewed from the perspective of knowledge management, computing with words is a powerful avenue for using problem knowledge that is otherwise not available in explicit quantifiable form. An example of computing with linguistic data is shown in Exhibit 1.

In Zadeh's view, this capability is essentially a matter of the brain's crucial ability to manipulate perceptions – perceptions of distance, size, weight, color, speed, time, direction, force, number, truth, likelihood, and other characteristics of physical and mental objects. He proposes computing with words as a foundation for a computational theory of perceptions. Knowledge theorists would argue that such

Exhibit 1. Computing with Linguistic Data for Possibilistic Decision-Making

As an example of soft computing for decision support, consider a simple abstract decision problem in which disutility is granulated to low, medium, and high, and usuality is granulated to usual, plausible, and rare.

Actions:	Usual State	Plausible State	Rare State
A1	low	medium	high
A2	low	high	medium
A3	medium	high	low
A4	high	low	medium
A5	high	medium	low

For simplicity, assume that the membership of "plausible" in the fuzzy set of possible states is less than the membership of "high" in the fuzzy set of bad outcomes but greater than the membership of "low" in the fuzzy set of bad outcomes, and that "medium" disutility is similarly between "usual" and "rare" possibilities. Then the ordinal calculations to assess the overall attractiveness of the five actions are as follows:

	Usual State	Plausible State	Rare State	Overall Risk
A1	min(low, usual) = low	min(medium, plausible) = ?	min(high, rare) = rare	max(low,min(medium, plausible), rare) = min(medium, plausible)
A2	min(low, usual) = low	min(high, plausible) = plausible	min(medium, rare) = rare	max(low, plausible, rare) = plausible
A3	min(medium, usual) = medium	min(high, plausible) = plausible	min(low, rare) = rare	max(medium, plausible, rare) = medium
A4	min(high, usual) = ?	min(low, plausible) = low	min(medium, rare) = rare	max(min(high, usual), low, rare) = min(high, usual)
A5	min(high, usual) = ?	min(medium, plausible) = ?	min(low, rare) = ?	max(min(high, usual),min(medium, plausible), min(low, rare)) = min(high, usual)

Because action A1 has disutility less than or equal to that of A2 and A3, and strictly less than A4 and A5, we select action A1. Computationally, this sort of reasoning can be automated in either of two ways: using symbol manipulation software, or by translating the ordinal relations into linear constraints in a mathematical programming environment (Whalen, 2001).

perception-based inputs mostly reside in the tacit form and may not be available for machine-based computing without the help of computing with words. Developing such a theory can lead to great advances in our ability to understand how humans make perception-based rational decisions in an environment of imprecision, uncertainty, and partial truth.

Such insight can help us to train a new generation of managers to do these things even better for their organizations. It can also form the foundation for post-modern generations of highly flexible computer-based management science "problems" that can be used to model the new century's "troubles" ever more expressively and lead to problem solutions that exploit tacit knowledge of the firm and can guide ever more successful actions.

A "computing with words" problem includes an initial state expressed in declarative sentences and a set of constraints expressed as fuzzy if-then rules. The conclusions are arrived at within the computer by the same binary operations as any other computation. However, the process is controlled and interpreted by the high-level language of quantitative linguistic variables rather than measurements expressed by numbers (though the latter can always be included as a special case of the former). If the goal is to provide insight as one element of a human decision process, the internal conclusions are translated back into a natural language; if the goal is automatic control, they are defuzzified into a specific numeric value. In terms of traditional management science, fuzzy rule-based systems permit an enormous expansion and transformation of the use of flowcharts, checklists, and menus to help humans through complex procedures. Computing with words permits an orders-of-magnitude increase in the application of computational power to these logical and qualitative procedures for decision and action.

2.2 Knowledge Creation by Neurocomputing

Neural network systems and genetic algorithms are both methods that build a model from data or experimentation. In this regard, they resemble the regression models used in forecasting as well as in other traditional management science activities. However, they proceed by a process of systematic random search rather than deterministic minimization of squared error.

In the data based learning approach, the model learns from a fixed database. Each case in the database consists of several input variables, based usually on conventional numeric, ordinal, or nominal scales, together with a criterion variable. The goal of the learning is to develop a model whose output from a particular set of inputs matches the criterion variable associated with these inputs in the database. Unlike the least-squares optimality guaranteed by regression models, determining when the training of a neural or genetic model of a database is good enough is a heuristic "perception", not a conventional optimality measurement. However, these newer approaches are able to converge to a good approximation of almost any linear or nonlinear relation embodied in the data. And they do so with considerably less need for the user or system developer to pre-specify the lineaments of the relation than earlier approaches. In an extensive review of published applications of neural networks, Sharda concluded that there is some evidence that neural networks are superior for classification problems whereas traditional forecasting models and neural models appear to be of equal strength for forecasting problems (Sharda, 1994).

In the mode of learning by experimentation, the output of the system consists of a set of choices and parameters that define an action either with respect to a real system or with respect to a simulation. When this action is carried out in the real or simulated realm, the outcome is assessed either by a programmed fitness function or by human judgment. The goal of learning is to search for an action that produces a favorable outcome. In more advanced systems, the fitness function is performed by a "critic" which itself learns to give better and better guidance, in the form of reward and punishment, to the main learning algorithm. This process has some external similarity with older mathematical programming and search algorithms in traditional management science.

From a user's standpoint, the major difference between neurocomputing and evolutionary computing is that neurocomputing uses a generalized gradient approach, while evolutionary computing is gradient-free. The implicit assumption of neurocomputing is that there is an underlying multidimensional continuum defined by the input and output variables. Some variables may be treated as discrete or even nominal, but the neural network system is actually varying a set of real-valued connection weights in order to search a space of smooth functions in which points that are nearby in terms of the input variables tend to generate program outputs that are near to one another in value and gradient. Thus, neurocomputing can even be used to augment more traditional approaches such as simulation, that are known to be suitable for rather complex problems. Mollaghasemi, LeCroy, and Georgiopolous (1998) used such a combined approach successfully for a system design problem.

Genetic algorithms, on the other hand, represent their parameters as distinct "genes" arrayed along a "chromosome". The fundamental assumption is that randomly taking some genes from one successful parent and the rest from another will result in an even more successful offspring often enough to make the method wok. (Simulated mutation also plays a role, but this is secondary to the aforementioned processes, known as selection and crossover.) Some of the genes in an evolutionary system may be coded to represent real numbers, but this is more a matter of how fitness is calculated than a fundamental property of the evolutionary system per se.

3   Management Science

The traditional discipline of management science views the application of computational methods to organizational decision making in terms of four key organizing questions: 1. "What's best?" (optimization); 2. "What's next?" (forecasting); 3. "What if ...?" (modeling and simulation); and 4. "What's my best bet?" (decision analysis).

The process of problem solving using management science tools is often presented in an idealized, linear manner: first identify the problem and then formulate it precisely. After this is completed, select the appropriate tool to solve the problem. Most authors admit that the process can be iterative and cyclical. Such as the view, adopted from Simon's Intelligence, Design, and Choice phases of problem solving, is shown in Figure 2. However, it is still not uncommon to encounter views of management science where problem solving is perceived as only goal-driven and top-down, where tools and techniques for problem solving can only be picked after formulation of the problem.

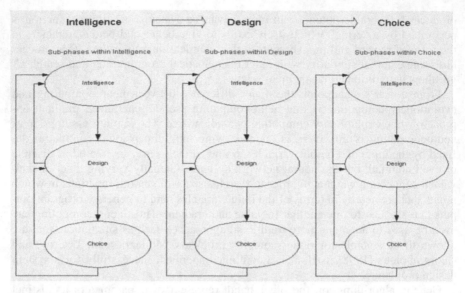

Figure 2. The Cycle and Iterative Process of Problem Solving (adapted from Simon (1962))

3.1 Problem Solving in Management Science

A more realistic view of the process recognizes that the "problems" solved by management science techniques arise from the convergence between a concern for a more-or-less amorphous sea of "troubles" on the one hand and a collection of "puzzles" that management science techniques can solve.

3.1.1 Trouble

In this more realistic view, the management science approach begins by recognizing a "trouble" in the real world. A trouble is a gap between what is perceived and what is desired. One form of trouble is a failure or disturbance, in which current performance is perceived to be below a usual or normal level. Thus, there is a drive to remove the trouble and return the performance of the system to normal.

Another kind of "trouble" is not seen in so negative a light; it is an opportunity or ambition to raise the organization's performance to new heights or to achieve improvement by exploiting new methods or new areas of operation. But the two kinds of "trouble" are really quite similar in the underlying perception that things ought to be better than they are.

3.1.2 Puzzles

The distinguishing characteristic of management science is the mating of a problem to a puzzle to form a model that can be solved. A "puzzle" is an artificial structure with a starting point (such as the pieces of a jigsaw puzzle jumbled in the box or a crossword puzzle with the squares blank), a well-defined goal point (the completed picture or crossword), and a set of allowable procedures for moving from the starting point to the goal. Someone who is skilled at solving a particular class of puzzles has a good collection of procedures for moving quickly and efficiently from the starting point to the goal of most or all puzzles in the class. These procedures range from algorithms that are deterministic and guaranteed to succeed if given enough time, to heuristics and hunches that are fallible but offer impressive savings in time and effort when they succeed.

The "puzzles" of management science are more respectably referred to as "problems". What follows are only illustrative examples of the puzzles or problems constructed to complement each of the four organizing questions:

The mathematical programming problem takes an objective function, a set of constraints as a starting point, and an optimal feasible solution as the well-defined goal point; the puzzle is solved by answering the question "What's best?" in terms of the assumptions of the problem.

The starting point of a time series forecasting problem is a series of numbers with dates, plus a set of assumptions (such as the autoregressive moving average assumptions). The goal point is a formula that comes closer to predicting the data than any other formula within the allowable class of formulas. Projecting this formula into the future answers the question "What's next?".

The very wide class of simulation problems has a formal description of a real or potential system as a starting point. The procedure is to develop the formal description into a computer program representing the system. The inputs to the program represent design and/or operation choices, and the outputs of the program represent system performance. The goal point is reached by choosing inputs to the program, which will lead it to produce outputs corresponding to ideal system performance. It's a game of "What if?" to try one alternative set of inputs after another until the puzzle is solved.

The decision analysis problem is inherently a game of chance. The starting point is a collection of allowable actions, a set of possible states of nature, and a subjective or objective utility measure for each state-action pair. The goal point is a specification of which alternative action provides the best compromise between the hope for a high utility and the fear of a low one.

3.1.3   Models

The process of management science model building involves choosing a problem or puzzle from the management scientist's bag of tricks in order to mirror a trouble that has been perceived in the real world. The puzzle is then crafted into as close a representation of the trouble as possible, inevitably with the help of some selective perceptions and simplifying assumptions about the real world trouble. The result is a management science model of the situation, with an initial state resembling what is perceived to be the current situation, a set of operations resembling what it might be possible to really do about the trouble, and a goal state that corresponds to the cure of a disturbance or the successful exploitation of an opportunity.

3.1.4   Solutions

The reason for the management science modeling exercise is that a puzzle, by definition, has a solution. Using today's powerful and plentiful computers, finding the solution to a management science problem is almost always the quickest and easiest step of the whole process, although in the early days of management science in the 1940s it consumed tremendous amounts of expensive labor over slide rules and adding machines.

3.1.5   Application

The all-important stage of application is the inverse operation to model building. Model building is a move from the real world of troubles into the world of unsolved but solvable puzzles. Application is a move from the world of solved puzzles into the world of troubles and real actions to deal with them. In some instances, application can be very simple and straightforward: the optimal output numbers of mathematical programming or the most successful input numbers of simulation become volts, hours, or dollars in the real world, the optimal choice in decision analysis becomes a signature on a contract, and the projection of a forecasting model is treated as a peek into the future. In more sophisticated applications of management science models, the responsible human managers use a process of reasoning by analogy to gain insights about the real world that go far beyond slavishly copying computer outputs. The more we take into consideration the approximations and uncertainties in the modeling process, the more insight we can gain during the application phase. Directly or indirectly, the application phase results in a plan of action, which in this imperfect world will more than likely eventuate in new troubles, so the process continues.

3.2   Current Status of Management Science in Business Education

The discipline of management science in contemporary schools of business is, to a large degree, a victim of its own success. Traditional models such as linear and nonlinear programming, time series, and causal regression models, "What if" simulation analysis, and decision trees are now available as user-friendly features or add-ins to the ubiquitous spreadsheet programs.

In past decades, all students needed a semester of management science instruction to be intelligent consumers of the services of specialists in these modeling techniques. One reason for this was that the relatively limited computational power of the computers of past decades made it necessary to formulate models in such a way as to allow computational efficiency – for example, using linear programming models to the near exclusion of integer, quadratic, and general nonlinear models. This made for difficult compromises between the expressivity and the tractability of a model. Preparing for these compromises took special training.

Another reason for the prevalence of management science coursework in the business curriculum was the fact that the best models were still relatively new. Thus, they were not yet thoroughly integrated into the substantive areas of management, accounting, finance, and other traditional fields of business education. In fact, many excellent teachers, researchers, and practitioners in the traditional fields did not have a broad grounding in management science techniques; they had only learned the subareas most relevant to their own work, after embarking on their careers.

Beyond the introductory course, it was possible to draw interested students into management science as a field of specialization because the active areas of research were relatively accessible to anyone with a broad interest and reasonable mathematical grounding. These areas included logistical models in mathematical programming, seasonality analysis in forecasting, discrete-event simulation practices, and prospect theory in decision analysis.

Today, however, the standard view of management science is in retreat as an identifiable field. The basic techniques of management science are already integrated into the various functional areas of business such as production, marketing, and finance; they do not need to be treated as a separate discipline. For example, Samaddar (1993) provides a taxonomical view of management science approaches used in the field of production and operations management.

The computer tools are powerful and user friendly, and they do not require as much clever preprocessing making them tractable. Present-day faculty in the traditional areas are now prepared to teach the standard techniques in the "natural habitat" of their own courses. On the other hand, the advanced areas of management science research have progressed to the point where one needs a thorough preparation in a sub-discipline to understand even the problem, much less the solution.

In the remainder of this chapter, we argue that the discipline of post-modern management science needs to take on a new mission: bringing the power of soft computing and knowledge management into the mainstream of business practice, in the same way that it brought in the previous generation of mathematical models like linear programming, regression, simulation, and decision trees.

4   Postmodern Management Science and Knowledge Management

As noted in section 3, one distinguishing characteristic of "postmodernism" in philosophy and the humanities generally is the de-emphasis on fixed meanings and precise structures of measurement, and the emphasis on discourses that dynamically shape and are shaped by the perceptions, concepts, and participants making them up. Such a de-emphasis on fixed meanings in problem solving can be obtained by using Zadeh's works on computing with words as a foundation for a computational theory of perception. On the other hand, for the capability to implement discourses in problem solving processes, one can use Nonaka's discourse methods of continuously creating, discovering, reshaping, and deploying corporate knowledge by converting its tacit knowledge to explicit knowledge (and vice-versa). Consequently, Zadeh's computing with words and Nonaka's knowledge discourse when put to work in tandem can create the foundation of post-modern management science. Such a foundation recognizes the dynamic nature of knowledge management that is desirable to be used in problem formulation and solving.

We argue that knowledge management can particularly be a very effective problem solving approach if it helps solve imprecise, large, messy, and ill-defined problems. A similar argument was made for management science in the mid 1970s (Ackoff, 1979). However, then management science was functionally void of soft and dynamic methods. This expectation was, and still is, in line with the real need of most organization and social problems. Similar sentiment for using soft systems methodology has been echoed in the 1980s (Checkland 1981, 1985a, 1985b; Rosenhead 1989, 1996), and it became imperative that management science should use both hard and soft approaches (Dando and Bennet, 1981). In recent years, soft approaches for management science have been used increasingly and successfully, and paved the way to implement successful use of knowledge management. For example, Ormerod (1995, 1996) successfully combined methods of cognitive mapping, soft systems methodology, and strategic choice for a complex problem at the largest UK supermarket chain. More specifically, in the area of handling imprecise problem data and assumptions, Cooper, Park, and Yu (1999) tackle imprecision in DEA modeling, and Basu and Blanning (1998) use a meta-graphic approach to tackle imprecise and uncertain requirements of assumptions for model management.

In the early 1990s, James R. Evans (1997a, 1997b) brought to the attention of the management science community the use of creativity in problem solving, which welcomes and exploits creative thinking in people. Use of creatively designed new ideas and novel insight can be viewed as another relatively new dimension to soft problem solving. Evans' earlier work treats creativity as a contingent property of an individual human. Taking a somewhat different view, Tsoukas and Papoulias (1996) examined the epistemological basis for creative practice of management science. Evans put together various creative techniques for soft problem solving. More recently, various soft techniques such as paradigm preserving, paradigm stretching, and paradigm breaking have evolved to be used for group decision-making (McFadzean, 1999). Such techniques use a varied degree of imagination, cognitive inertia, and creative stimulation, and thrive on exploiting group creativity and possible humanization of a problem.

We now present and discuss two knowledge management functional areas: knowledge deployment and discovery. We show, as an illustration, that these two areas can exploit three specific post-modern management science supports: 1. decision support systems, 2. data mining and knowledge discovery, and 3. data visualization and applied virtual reality.

4.1 Knowledge Deployment via Decision Support Systems

Ralph Stair (1997) defines a decision support system as "An organized collection of people, procedures, software, databases, and devices used to support problem-specific decision making when faced with unstructured or semi-structured business problems." What distinguishes a decision support system from other decision-making tools is the fact that the user's tacit perceptions drive a process of human-computer interaction, often on a moment-to-moment basis. The interaction is completed when the human perceives an acceptable explicit solution.

Decision support systems are a well-established area within management science. Zadeh does not list decision support systems in his usual discussions of soft computing, because his focus is on self-contained computational automation. However, decision support systems are certainly examples of computation driven and shaped by explicit knowledge and tacit human perceptions rather than hard optimization of an arithmetical quantity. Development of a coherent science of soft computing, computing with words, and computational theory of perception has the potential to move the field of decision support systems to a new level of confident artistry.

An early evidence of such a new level of artistry can be found in decision support systems that use case-based reasoning. A case-based reasoning method captures the knowledge from previously solved cases. By using such knowledge from a case repository and by using analogical reasoning, a case-based reasoning method attempts to improve both the problem solving methodology and the cognitive model of reasoning capabilities of the human mind. Gupta concludes that such methods are ideal for domains that are rich in experiential knowledge mostly available in tacit form whereas expert systems are ideal for domains that are rich in explicit knowledge (Gupta, 1994).

4.2 Knowledge Discovery by Data Mining

Data mining involves a collection of tools and techniques for finding useful patterns relating the fields of very large data bases, usually derived from records of sales or other transactions with customers or clients. Combinatorially huge numbers of potential correlations are evaluated by the computer to provide a user with a manageable collection of potentially interesting patterns. The user's human ability to perceive what makes sense and what is most likely a statistical fluke is crucial, especially as we move from the more machine-oriented world of data warehousing and data mining to the more human-centered world of knowledge discovery.

An oft-repeated anecdote rule found by mining real transactional data of a super market store indicates that the male customers who bought diapers on Thursdays also tended to buy beer; consequently, the grocery moved the beer display closer to the diaper display, and sold beer and diapers at full price on Thursdays (Berry and Gordon, 1997). Similar correlations, and insights derived from them, can also improve an enterprise's ability to work with its suppliers, turning the overhead of purchasing, receiving, and stocking into a dynamic and profitable focus on supply chain management. In a special issue of *Communications of the ACM* dedicated to the topic of data mining and knowledge discovery, business users are reported to observe that "Ad hoc techniques – no longer adequate for sifting through vast collection of data – are giving away to data mining and knowledge discovery for turning corporate data into business advantage" (Brachman et al., 1997). The National Basketball Association explored a data mining application using image recordings of basketball games. Data mining identifies play combinations with higher or lower than average success rates, with pointers to video clips of the crucial seconds of the games in question (IBM Research, 1995).

The newest form of data mining is the linguistic summarization of data, which aims at a computer-generated verbal description of the knowledge implicit in a database, often in the form of if-then rules that resemble fuzzy knowledge granules (Kacprzyk, 1999).

4.3 Knowledge Discovery by Data Visualization and Applied Virtual Reality

Visualization tools are a class of advanced graphical presentation tools that facilitate data exploration, hypothesis development, testing, and evaluation of new or existing theory and knowledge. It is difficult to decide a priori the usefulness of the visual that is being generated. Quite often the usefulness of the image can be judged only after creating the visual.

Computer-generated animation can give a direct perception of motion rates and direction, depths, heights, material surface properties, etcetera. Using appropriate computer technology, a skilled and well-motivated human user can directly visualize patterns, connections, correlations, or lack thereof, among parameters that have been measured or calculated. While these parameters can be codified in numbers, visualization brings the enormous power of human perception to bear in entirely new ways. Some forms of interaction permit the user to query images to obtain the numerical values of important parameters at different points in the image.

One of the important uses of visualizing complex relationships among several variables could be to understand the nature of empirical data in order to improve the choice of statistical techniques that should be applied for in-depth study.

Business visualization is still in its infancy and no definite rules have been established for using this methodology to make more informed decisions in business. The images in the business world almost always depict an abstract shape, while most scientific and nearly all engineering applications depict actual three-dimensional objects and processes. The business executive needs to understand the salient patterns in the data and communicate this understanding to other people within or outside the organization. Symbolic inferencing is one recent approach that can help business executives explicitly convey their understanding of formal organizational knowledge and complex reasoning processes that are difficult, if not impossible, to communicate. Gaines and Shaw (1999) present a formal visual language that presents symbolic business knowledge visually and is successfully used in a real business environment.

No technique of visualization is applicable in all situations. Different users may derive different amounts of information from representations or views of the same data. Complex visuals are difficult to understand and interpret at the first glance. Users need to define the problem that is being studied explicitly, and it helps to create a mental model of the image that is expected.

Development of virtual reality support through standardized protocols on the World Wide Web is likely to facilitate the use of business visualization in the future. The quality and complexity of visualization techniques and images is also likely to increase with wider acceptance of such standards. The ultimate goal of applied data visualization and virtual reality is to help human beings to make more "perceptive" decisions (Chaturvedi and Gupta, 1997).

5 Soft Computing and Post-Modern Management Science Support Effective Knowledge Management

In this concluding section, we make the case for how soft computing and post-modern management science go in tandem to support effective deployment of knowledge management for ill-structured business problem solving. In business decision making, the moment of decision hinges on the perception that a course of action is "good enough." When this perception can be reduced successfully to a measurement, traditional management science has a great deal to say.

However, most decisions in business and elsewhere are made by a satisficing approach (Simon, 1959). Alternatives are examined in sequence until one is found that is rated as acceptable. At this point, the acceptable alternative is selected and the decision maker moves on to the next problem rather than pursuing the theoretically optimal alternative. The criterion of acceptability is flexible and dynamic; in other words, it is a fuzzy perception of acceptability, not a precise measurement.

Soft computing seeks an output that is perceived to be acceptable; inputs may be measured or perceived. In soft computing, as in real management practice, a mathematical "proof of optimality" is nowhere to be found. It addresses the four basic questions of management science (as described in section 3 of this chapter) in ways that may be more relevant to the needs of future managers in undergraduate or MBA curricula. These are the techniques now used by "early adopters." Managers will have to decide when, where, and how to deploy the techniques.

Soft computing will also provide a rich lode of more productive opportunities for future research into the core questions of management science. Applying the new, human-oriented techniques to a host of previously-intractable business processes will produce a research environment comparable to, or even more exciting than, the days of the most rapid expansion of the old management science in the nineteen sixties and seventies.

Rather than focusing primarily on the automation of decision processes, the goal of the post-modern management science should be the humanization of decision processes, and thus, help exploit both epistemological and ontological (Nonaka, 1995) knowledge management functions. Stakeholders in an organization are best served when the managers are free to make important decisions that confidently reflect the real goals of the organization. Three broad "troubles" can impair this freedom and confidence: the press of too many trivial decisions; information pathologies such as ignorance, misperception, or overload; and the need to compromise real perceptions of the situation and goals in order to fit overly restrictive tools. Soft computing offers powerful ways to automate the decisions that ought to be delegated to a sufficiently capable machine, to manage information in support of truly perceptive human decision making, and to fit the tool to the problem rather than vice versa.

Inherent in modern organizational decisional making is the changing nature of the problem environment's knowledge content. Knowledge management methods as supported by soft computing and postmodern management science can focus on creating, deploying, and reshaping the problem, which in turn will improve the relevance and currency of problems solved and solutions found. Consequently, we envision knowledge management thriving in the space as shown in Figure 1.

References

Ackoff, R.L., "Resurrecting the Future of Operational Research," *Journal of the Operational Research Society*, 30, 3, 1979, 189-199.

Basu, A. and R.W. Blanning, "The Analysis of Assumptions in Model Bases Using Metagraphs," *Management Science*, 44, 7, 1998, 982-995.

Berry, M. J. A. and G. Linoff, *Data Mining Techniques: For Marketing, Sales and Customer Support*, New York: John Wiley and Sons, Inc., 1997.

Brachman, R.J., T. Khabaza, W. Kloesgen, G. Piatetsky-Shapiro, and E. Simoudis, "Mining Business Databases," *Communications of The ACM*, 39, 11, 1996, 42-48.

Chaturvedi, A. and S. Gupta, "Visualization of Information 3D," *INFORMS College on Artificial Intelligence Newsletter*, 1997,
URL= http://www.cba.ufl.edu/dis/caims/3dviz.html

Checkland, P.B., *Systems Thinking, Systems Practice*, Chichester, England: John Wiley and Sons, 1981.

Checkland, P.B., "From Optimization to Learning: A Development of Systems Thinking," *Journal of the Operational Research Society*, 36, 9, 1985a, 757-767.

Checkland, P.B., "Achieving 'Desirable and Feasible' Change: An Application of Soft Systems Methodology," *Journal of the Operational Research Society*, 36, 9, 1985b, 821-831.

Cooper, W.W., K.S. Park, and Y. Gang, "IDEA and AR_IDEA: Models for Dealing with Imprecise Data," *Management Science*, 45, 4, 1999, 597-607.

Dando, M. R. and P.B. Bennet, "A Kuhnian Crisis in Management Science," *Journal of the Operational Research Society*, 32, 2, 1981, 91-103.

Evans, J. R., "Creativity in OR/MS: The Creative Problem Solving Process, Part 1," *Interfaces*, 27, 5, 1997a, 78-83.

Evans, J. R., "Creativity in OR/MS: The Creative Problem Solving Process, Part 2," *Interfaces*, 27, 6, 1997b, 106-111.

Gaines, B.R. and M.L.G. Shaw, "Embedding Formal Knowledge Models in Active Documents," *Communications of The ACM*, 42, 1, 1999, 57-63.

Gupta, U.G., "How Case-Based Reasoning Solves New Problems," *Interfaces*, 24, 6, 1994, 110-119.

Holsapple, C.W., "Knowledge Management in Decision Making and Decision Support," *Knowledge and Policy*, 8, 1, 1995, 5-22.

Holsapple, C.W. and A.B. Whinston, *Decision Support Systems: A Knowledge-based Approach*, St. Paul, MN: West Publishing Company, 1996.

IBM Research, "Data Mining: Advanced Scout," 1995,
URL= http://www.research.ibm.com/scout/home.html

Kacprzyk, J., "Fuzzy Logic for Linguistic Summarization of Databases," *Proceedings of Eighth International Fuzzy Systems Association World Congress*, Taipei, 1999, 813-818.

McFadzean, E., "Creativity in MS/OR: Choosing The Appropriate Technique," *Interfaces*, 29, 5, 1999, 110-122.

Mollaghasemi, M., K. LeCroy, and M. Georgiopolous, "Application of Neural Networks and Simulation Modeling in Manufacturing System Design," *Interfaces*, 28, 5, 1998, 100-114.

Nonaka, I.and H.Takeuchi, *The Knowledge Creating Company*, New York: Oxford University Press, 1995.

Ormerod, R. J., "Putting Soft OR Methods to Work: Information Systems Strategy Developments at Sainsbury's," *Journal of the Operational Research Society*, 46, 3, 1995, 821-831.

Ormerod, R.J., "Information Systems Strategy Development at Sainsbury's Supermarkets Using 'Soft' OR," *Interfaces*, 26, 1, 1996, 102-130.

Rosenhead, J., *Rational Analysis for a Problematic Word: Problem Structuring Methods for Complexity, Uncertainty and Conflict*, Chichester, England, John Wiley and Sons, 1989.

Rosenhead, J., "What's the Problem? An Introduction to Problem Structuring Methods," *Interfaces*, 26, 6, 1996, 117-131.

Samaddar, S., "A Model for POM Curriculum: Rediscovering Taxonomical Balance," *Decision Line*, 24, 4, 1993, 17-20.

Sharda, R., "Neural Networks for the MS/OR Analyst: An Application Bibliography," *Interfaces*, 24, 2, 1994, 116-130.

Simon. H., "Theories of Decision Making in Economics and Behavioral Science," *American Economic Review*, 49, 3, 1959, 253-80.

Stair, R., *An Introduction to Information Systems*, Boston: Course Technology, 1997.

Tsoukas, H., D.B. Papoulias, "Creativity in OR/MS: From Technique to Epistemology," *Interfaces*, 26, 2, 1996, 73-79.

Whalen, T., "Fuzzy Knowledge Based Systems in Management" *Human Systems Management*, 4, 1984.

Whalen, T, "Decision Making Under Uncertainty With Ordinal Linguistic Data" in Ruan, D.; Kacprzyk, J. and Fedrizzi, M. (eds.), *Soft Computing for Risk Evaluation and Management. Applications in Technology, Environment and Finance*, pp. 3-16, Heidelberg: Physica-Verlag, 2001.

Whalen, T. and S. Samaddar, " Post-Modern Management Science : A Convergence of Soft Computing and Knowledge Management," *Human Systems Management*, 2001, in press.

Zadeh, L., "From Computing with Numbers to Computing with Words: From Manipulation of Measurements to Manipulation of Perceptions," *Proceedings of Third International Conference on Applications of Fuzzy Logic and Soft Computing*, Wiesbaden, 1998.

Zadeh, L., "A New Direction in Fuzzy Logic: Toward Automated Reasoning with Perceptions," *Proceedings of Eighth International Fuzzy Systems Association World Congress*, Taipei, 1, 1999, 1-5.

CHAPTER 18

Knowledge Creation

Suzie Allard

College of Communication and Information Studies, University of Kentucky, Lexington, KY, USA

Knowledge is becoming a primary driver of social and economic well-being as economies begin to depend less on the traditional resources of land, labor and capital (Drucker, 1993). Thus, knowledge creation is an important activity for organizations that strive to achieve greater effectiveness and responsiveness in this turbulent global environment. Knowledge creation is important not only for organizational competitiveness and survival, but can have far-reaching societal, national, and global consequences. This chapter discusses the knowledge creation process and its relationship with other knowledge activities, as well as its role in knowledge management. It examines different types of knowledge and the processes that encourage knowledge creation.

Keywords: Conduct of Knowledge Management; Innovation; Knowledge Creation; Knowledge Generation; Knowledge Mode; Knowledge Type; Maturation Cycle

1   Introduction

The goal of knowledge management (KM) initiatives is to "make the right knowledge available to the right processors (human or computer) at the right times in the right presentation for the right costs" (Holsapple and Joshi, 1999). Often times, the "right" knowledge is new knowledge; it does not exist within the organization and it is too expensive, too revealing, too unreliable, too slow, or outright impossible to acquire it from external sources. Therefore, knowledge creation is an essential part of the conduct of knowledge management within an organization. The relationship between knowledge creation and knowledge manipulation activities is evident in the collaboratively built ontology of KM conduct (Holsapple and Joshi, 2002a).

In this KM ontology, there are five basic kinds of knowledge activities; knowledge can flow among these activities, and the activities can be arranged in various configurations and can be performed by various processors. *Knowledge acquisition* occurs when knowledge in the external environment is identified, and possibly transformed (e.g., filtered, restructured), for use within the organization. *Knowledge selection* describes the identification, and possible transformation, of knowledge from among an organization's internal knowledge asset base. *Knowledge internalization* is the activity of taking knowledge that has been acquired, selected, or generated and distributing or storing it within the organization.

Knowledge externalization is the activity of embedding knowledge in outputs (e.g., products, services) for release into the external environment. *Knowledge generation* entails the production of new knowledge from existing knowledge; it can take the forms of discovery or derivation.

Although some authors include both acquisition and generation as being knowledge creation, this chapter centers on knowledge creation in the sense of generation (taking the view that acquiring something is not really creating it, in any direct sense). Nevertheless, there is an active and ongoing relationship between knowledge generation, on the one hand, and the other knowledge manipulation activities. That is, a KM episode that creates new knowledge may involve not only knowledge generation, but also acquisition, selection, and internalization that enable the generation activity to happen.

Knowledge creation plays a vital role in innovation, a process that is important because it facilitates an organization's ability to keep pace with a dynamic environment. In fact, creating new knowledge for innovation is considered one of the three reasons that organizations are motivated to use information (Choo, 1998). An innovation has been described as "an idea, practice, or object that is perceived as new" to a person or organization (Rogers, 1995). In a KM context, the act of innovation involves the generation of knowledge that is perceived to be new by the organization that does the generating. Innovation can serve many purposes. For instance, it may entail finding new ways to approach questions, solve problems, or reach decisions. It may yield new processes, products, or services. Innovation impacts not only the organization that implements it, but also other organizations within the same domain. They must respond to or cope with the innovation.

2   Attribute Dimensions for Knowledge Creation

Knowledge can be thought of as being multi-dimensional, having a variety of attributes. Two fundamental attribute dimensions are the knowledge type and the knowledge mode. The former is concerned with distinctions in the nature of the knowledge itself; each type of knowledge can be created and each type can be used in the creation of knowledge. The latter is concerned with the way the knowledge can be processed in transforming it from one mode to another; knowledge creation can occur for either mode, and perhaps during the transformations between modes.

The first attribute dimension, featuring defining characteristics, partitions knowledge into three types – descriptive knowledge, procedural knowledge, and reasoning knowledge (Holsapple and Whinston, 1988; Holsapple, 1995). Each type of knowledge is an integral part of the knowledge creation process. *Descriptive knowledge*, which can be thought of as "know what," describes the state of a domain, the items that exist in it, the context in which they exist, and the relationships that may exist between the items and different domains. *Procedural knowledge*, which can be thought of as "know how," is comprised of algorithms such as the steps needed to reach a specified goal. *Reasoning knowledge*, which can be thought of as "know why," is comprised of logic that specifies what consequences are expected, what conclusions are valid, or what actions are appropriate if a certain situation is given or assumed to exist. Newly created knowledge could be any one of these types. For example, a new forecast is descriptive knowledge, a new plan is procedural knowledge, a new heuristic is reasoning knowledge. A relationship that is particularly notable is that applying existing procedural or reasoning knowledge to existing descriptive knowledge often generates new knowledge, thus jumpstarting the knowledge creation process.

The second attribute dimension stems from the notion that knowledge is the result of a process whereby meaning is attached to it via interpretation and cognitive construction (Malhotra, 2000). This dimension recognizes knowledge as existing in two modes – tacit and explicit – with the possibility of transforming knowledge existing in one mode into the other and the possibility of transforming (e.g., creating) knowledge within a mode (Nonaka and Takeuchi, 1995). Gaining an understanding of tacit and explicit knowledge and the relationship between them is helpful in understanding the dynamic nature of knowledge creation processes.

Tacit knowledge is the implicit knowledge that people have developed. Examples of tacit knowledge can be found in formal and informal face-to-face conversations, telephone conversations, and what a person keeps in his/her own mind (Srikantaniah, 2000).

Explicit knowledge is knowledge that has been put in a form that allows its creator, acquirer, or others to access and use it. Explicit knowledge is found in many familiar forms including journals, magazines, newspapers, business records, databases, email, and Web sites.

Knowledge can become more valuable when it evolves from tacit to explicit. As knowledge loses its tacit quality it often becomes more commonly available although that varies depending on the environment it is acting within. For example, at an educational institution the dissemination of new knowledge is likely to be quite broad and include public venues. Conversely, in a corporate setting, knowledge may be distributed across departments or job sites, but will still be confined to organizational boundaries.

A third mode of knowledge that is primarily associated with organizations is *cultural knowledge* (Choo, 1998). This knowledge is held in the assumptions, beliefs, and norms of the organization, and in a corporate sense could be called corporate culture.

The two attribute dimensions provide different perspectives on the knowledge creation phenomenon, and interaction exists between the dimensions. For example, someone may hold procedural knowledge in a tacit form, which is characterized by the fact that he/she has performed the procedure repeatedly, but there is not yet a way (e.g., shared language) to formally pass this knowledge on to others. The tacit version of of some other procedural knowledge may be amenable to being recorded in a manual, thereby being converted into explicit knowledge.

Knowledge creation can result from a serendipitous event or an intentional act. For example, some new knowledge is discovered unintentionally. One example is the discovery of penicillin, which resulted from observing the antibiotic effects of some molds during an unrelated experiment. Other times, knowledge creation begins when a situation reveals a gap in the existing knowledge, and the individual or organization reacts to fill it. The gap could be filled by acquiring the desired knowledge from an external source or selecting it from an internal repository.

However, if this is not practical or possible, then new knowledge needs to be created via a generation activity that occurs in the context of – and through the use of – what is already known.

Knowledge in tacit, explicit, and cultural modes and of descriptive, procedural, and reasoning types may be utilized to generate new knowledge through two different means: knowledge discovery or knowledge derivation (Holsapple and Joshi, 2002b). *Knowledge discovery* describes finding new knowledge in relation to what is already known, perhaps through a creative insight, analogy, pattern recognition, or synthesis. *Knowledge derivation* applies procedural and/or reasoning knowledge to descriptive knowledge to reach new conclusions, often through analysis and logic.

Examples of how knowledge creation may occur include tapping the skills of the organization's own workers or acquiring knowledge from those outside the group. At the individual level, knowledge is shared through dialogue, discourse and other formal channels with analogies and metaphors being used to share intuitive knowledge. At the organizational level, the organization may view knowledge as a process rather than a product, which suggests that the knowledge creation process may be guided by gatekeepers who regulate information flow and boundary spanners who help link different areas of knowledge (Choo, 1998).

Similar to the individual level, knowledge creation at the organizational level begins when the organization serendipitously finds new knowledge or when it recognizes that new knowledge is needed. Additionally, there are subactivities associated with knowledge generation. These include monitoring the organization's external environment and its own knowledge resources, evaluating selected and acquired knowledge to determine if it will impact knowledge generation, and using an existing knowledge base to create, synthesize, analyze, and construct new knowledge (Holsapple and Joshi, 2002b).

3   The Knowledge Maturation Cycle

Because knowledge is dynamic, it may be regarded as passing through different phases of a cycle. Knowledge creation, and its ultimate role in a knowledge economy, can be examined in terms of Shukla's (1997) four-stage maturation cycle for knowledge. This cycle is heavily based on the works of Boisot (1983, 1987), who studied cultural learning and technology strategy, and Nonaka (1995) who focused on how tacit knowledge affects organizations.

Stage 1: Discovered knowledge. This stage occurs when an idea, need, or possibility leads to knowledge creation. At this stage, knowledge is tacit; it exists in the mind of the discoverer. However, a KM system can provide an important service by offering an e-workspace within which a knowledge discoverer can begin to organize these ideas. Information seeking often accompanies the process of knowledge discovery, because the discoverer is likely to research his/her ideas or at least search for confirmatory information. KM systems that allow people to easily incorporate this information-seeking into the process will enhance this stage and create greater value within the firm.

Stage 2: Codified knowledge. The discovered knowledge is translated into a physical form that helps it survive and become useful. Codification is explicit knowledge because it can be represented by skills, documents, or products. KM systems should have the capability to handle the different desired representations of codified knowledge.

Stage 3: Migratory knowledge. When knowledge is codified it gains mobility. This means that knowledge takes on its own identity and is no longer attached to its originator or owner. This is the stage when dissemination begins to take place. This is the area in which KM systems excel and can create added value in the knowledge creation process.

Migratory knowledge creates special challenges. For example, knowledge can exist in more than one place at a time, but depending on the environment it is in, it may not be identified with the same classification terms. Additionally, as knowledge migrates, it generally becomes less scarce, which means that there are more "versions" available. This could lead to the quality of the knowledge degrading, as it is subject to "wear and tear," which could make it less accurate. The challenge then becomes finding and identifying authoritative versions of the codified knowledge.

Stage 4: Invisible knowledge. As knowledge spreads, it begins to be viewed as commonplace and is viewed as a public good. This means the knowledge has lost its special character and instead has become so pervasive that it changes the social and business environment. This can happen in a proprietary situation; for example many current-day "basics" of aerodynamic designs were once carefully guarded migratory knowledge. KM systems play a role at this stage in several ways including retaining an authoritative version of the knowledge before it became "invisible" and supplying information that allows participants to ascertain the validity of "invisible" knowledge, because this type of pervasive knowledge may also be corrupted.

4   Knowledge Sharing and Knowledge Creation

Because knowledge sharing and transformation facilitate the knowledge creation process, it is important to find ways to encourage them. An example of knowledge sharing would be one department allowing another department to use its customer records to build product profiles. However, some of the knowledge about these customers may be tacit, in that a manager has insights or intuitions that are not reflected in the explicit records, but that would be important for the other department. The success of knowledge sharing also relies heavily on knowledge leadership, because sharing activities are facilitated in an environment that discourages knowledge hoarding and rewards knowledge creation.

Nonaka and Takeuchi (1995) outline four processes that explain how knowledge is shared. The first process is *socialization*, where the tacit knowledge of one person is converted through conversation or other personal means into tacit knowledge for another person. An example would be an informal conversation between coworkers in which one shares an insight about a customer with the other. The second process is *externalization,* in which tacit knowledge is converted into explicit knowledge such as when someone writes down what they have learned. An example of this would be writing a memo about a meeting, or creating a manual about a specific process that has not been previously recorded. The third process is *combination,* in which explicit knowledge is converted into another form of explicit knowledge. Some examples of combination include writing a paper that incorporates explicit knowledge or creating a Web site from some form of explicit knowledge. The final process is *internalization*, in which explicit knowledge is converted into tacit knowledge. This is demonstrated when a person reads a manual and can perform the procedure described therein.

In organizational contexts, some of these processes have been integrated into three models of knowledge creation: knowledge conversion, knowledge building, and knowledge linking (Choo, 1998, p. 119-138).

Knowledge conversion features conversion between personal, tacit knowledge of the individual and the shared, explicit knowledge of the organization. Once it has become explicit knowledge within the organization, then it is converted back into tacit knowledge as individuals learn about it and assimilate it. This model focuses on an internal knowledge cycle, and requires some special conditions within the organization (Nonaka and Takeuchi, 1995). The organization must have an "organizational intention" and this vision must be transmitted to individuals so they know what knowledge is valuable to the organization. The individuals must also be allowed to work with autonomy, so they are free to discover new knowledge.

Sharing of tacit knowledge and other ideas needs to be promoted through "information redundancy," which is the idea that it is acceptable for information to be repeated/replicated among individuals and throughout the organization. The organization can also encourage the knowledge conversion process through "fluctuation and creative chaos" which sets the stage for rethinking and reinventing routines. Finally, the organization's internal diversity must be a good match for the diversity visible in the external environment. This means that an organization must have a sufficient range of resources and processors to address the dimensions of the external environment. For example, an organization that exists in the domain of biotechnology, needs to have a sufficient array of experts and knowledge resources to address the issues that comprise this field.

Knowledge building is a process that relies on the organization creating an environment that nurtures knowledge building activities and increases the core capabilities of the individuals within the organization. These kinds of activities include shared problem solving, experimenting and prototyping, importing knowledge from outside the organization, as well as implementing and integrating new processes and tools.

Knowledge linking features learning alliances with other organizations that allow knowledge to be transferred between them. This model requires examination of and coordination of specialized relationships, work cultures, and operating styles.

Each of these three models encourages interaction between individuals and ideas, thereby raising the possibility that any given problem may be tackled from multiple perspectives. Knowledge often takes on different meaning when observed from different viewpoints. This creates the synergy that drives innovation and knowledge creation. But, this also breeds several problems in terms of system design including how to classify and organize knowledge artifacts so that they can be utilized from these multiple perspectives and subject to disparate interpretations.

These models also illustrate how knowledge creation depends on the individual's skills and expertise as well as the individual's ability to learn and to be able to use this learning to create knowledge. Other important characteristics for knowledge creation are having processes that allow individuals to share skills and knowledge, and fostering a culture that values knowledge building and sharing.

5   Focusing KM on the Process

Knowledge creation does not happen in a vacuum, but instead is a result of finding or understanding contextual relationships. As Dewey said "To grasp the meaning of a thing, an event, or a situation is to see it in its relation to other things..." (Dewey as quoted in Malhotra, 2000). Thus, knowledge creation is in some cases, the process of constructing a framework or schema that captures new perspectives on relationships. KM systems can be helpful in this task because they can be designed to capture complexity of human organizations and human thought in order to create patterns of relationships that create new knowledge.

KM can furnish a framework for integrating human intellectual processes with other aspects of knowledge and knowledge creation. A good system focuses on learning and innovating processes and also considers how people communicate both on the interpersonal and organizational level.

Some KM models describe organizations as existing in a traditional value chain, but the new economy has created the realization that the model needs to have the ability to represent greater complexity. One solution is designing KM webs that are able to reflect multiple connections across all forms of traditional barriers including institutions, countries, time, and disciplines. While each node in the web may have its own information or knowledge system, they must be tied together to facilitate knowledge creation (Duffy, 2000).

KM may be manifest in an initiative, practice, and/or system. For a moment, let us look at the added value of KM-associated systems. These may encourage knowledge creation through the use of an organization's infrastructure to integrate explicit knowledge and tacit knowledge. An organization's infrastructure includes technological infrastructure, management, social capital, employee development programs, and sufficient resources to invest in KM. The infrastructure varies based on the organization's complexion – including its complexity, resources, objectives, and goals (Srikantaiah, 2000). For example, some KM systems include specific procedures for collaborating, debating, and questioning, as well as specific methods for the recording and sharing results of these interactions (Duffy, 2000). These systems are effective because they address procedural and reasoning knowledge as well as descriptive knowledge. Therefore, KM can be thought of as the sum total of systems, intellectual capital, and social capital.

6   Knowledge and Sensemaking

Organizations use knowledge in three primary ways: to make sense of a changing environment, to create new knowledge for innovation, and to make decisions using past experience to adapt to the future (Choo, 1998). In the past, organizations prized stasis and cherished stability. However, this has changed and organizations now look at how they fit in relation to the environment, the source of information, the pool of resources, and the ecological milieu (Choo, 1995). When an organization is faced with this environment, creating new knowledge to make sense of the relationships may be the only way to understand the situation and act upon it.

The dynamic environment facing organizations forces them to attempt to make sense of the world around them. Weick (1979) points out that sensemaking begins with a change in the environment that creates a disruption in the expected experience, which encourages activities in people and organizations. Interpreting, prioritizing, and sorting these environmental messages is the first step towards building shared meaning. Often, explanations of messages are attached from past experience and frequently there is an exchange and negotiation of views to reach a common explanation. Weick's description of looking at an existing store of knowledge in order to attach meaning to new events is a form of organizational knowledge discovery, and as such is an aspect of knowledge creation.

Weick (1979) notes that the process of sensemaking includes enactment, selection, and retention. Enactment defines the environmental boundary and interprets raw data. Selection puts meanings on data from past experience. Retention stores successful sensemaking for future use.

Organizational sensemaking can be based on beliefs or actions (Weick, 1995). Sensemaking based on beliefs begins with an initial set of beliefs that is used to connect information to a larger structure of knowledge. The action approach begins by looking at the actions and growing meaning around them.

7   Organization Learning: A Beneficial Environment for Knowledge Creation

"OL (Organization Learning) is a science practiced by all of us...learning extends our capacity to create and generate" (Senge, 1990). The idea that the nature of organizations is changing is not new. Nearly four decades ago, it was noted that organizations were becoming more complex and that the change was occurring at an increasing rate (Malhotra, 2000). The environment has changed in two ways. It has become more complex in terms of the numbers, diversity, and interconnectedness of relationships. It has also become more turbulent because events and their reactions occur more quickly. Thus, learning on the organizational level is dependent, at least in part, on knowledge creation.

Organizational learning (OL) requires that the organization have the ability to access its collective knowledge base. Learning organizations are skilled at creating, acquiring, and transferring knowledge which is then used to modify the organization's behavior (Garvin, 1993). This behavior reflects new knowledge and insights.

In many circumstances, OL is a process of detection of an error, proper diagnosis of its cause, and correction of the error so that it can learn from experience and take actions that are favorable for its survival. Often this leads to identifying a need that requires new knowledge to be created to answer the need.

Learning in an organization can be considered to take place in two ways. Adaptive, or single loop learning, occurs when problems are resolved using standard operating procedures; however, there isn't attention to error reduction. Generative, or double loop learning, occurs when the organization detects, diagnoses, and corrects errors; this is the hallmark of a learning organization. A learning organization is based on five pillars: personal mastery, shared mental models, team learning, shared vision, and systems thinking. OL is essential because the organization's intelligence is greater than the sum of the knowledge of the individuals within that organization (Ching et al., 1992; UNESCO, 2000).

OL relies on an environment that encourages learning, and that has information processes and systems that promote knowledge creation and use. In this type of organization, knowledge creation is not just the responsibility of a few. Instead, it is a collaborative effort driven by a shared vision. This means that processes are integrated, often through an open network. OL is further facilitated by the dissolution of organizational boundaries that isolate groups and block the flow of knowledge.

These requirements mean that an organization must have a structure that encourages communication, interaction, and flexibility. What type of structure is needed? Historically, many organizations were structured in a pyramid-like hierarchy. However, the global communications and fast-paced decision making that are hallmarks of the knowledge economy have highlighted the pyramid structure's inability to respond quickly to change. Organizations have sought a way to create a more flexible structure that allows greater responsiveness to environmental change. These flexible structures often involve complicated network relationships and computing/communication technologies serve as the rope that binds together this vast network of teams (Johansen and Swigart, 1994; Ching et al., 1996)).

Johansen and Swigart (1994) use the metaphor that these new structures are fishnets. This reflects how the traditional hierarchy has been flattened and how the new structure is more horizontal. This new structure is composed of complex interconnections that allow soft hierarchies to develop as needed for specific tasks. In an organization of this type, teams are often the key work group. However, because teams can align into informal ad hoc networks as the task demands, they also have a tendency to encourage knowledge creation through knowledge sharing and synergy.

All this comes at a time when the need for faster decision making is in the forefront. And to make decisions people need knowledge of all three types and all modes. The change in organization structure, and the environments they exist in, has led to a need for faster knowledge processing, renewal, and creation (Malhotra, 2000). This means that knowledge is no longer centralized, but that it can emerge at any point in the environment, and that a system, and perhaps people to mediate it, must be in place to receive it.

As OL is encouraged, the organization's knowledge requirements are enlarged. Learning organizations rely not only on external sources of knowledge, but also on their own knowledge capital. Knowledge capital includes the tacit knowledge of its employees and also the knowledge that results from knowledge sharing within the organization (Ryske and Sebastian, 2000).

Four concepts from the discipline of architecture are very useful in creating effective learning organizations (Gerstein, 1992):

- Architecture's ultimate test is that it provides utility to the people who have to use it. A learning organization should be configured so that it provides utility to the individuals within the organization including facilitating knowledge creation.
- The best architecture doesn't have rigid specifications. Organizations benefit from architecture that guides, facilitates, and provides a framework for knowledge creation.
- Architecture must meet the immediate needs of the organization, but it must also be capable of reflecting the aspirations of those who use it.
- Architecture cannot be imposed, but must evolve. An organization represents a large number of people working together toward a shared vision. In a sense, the organizational architecture could be thought of as having a social dimension.

KM systems can have a vital role in a learning organization. For example, a KM system can be instrumental in helping assure that the following three components of a learning organization are implemented successfully (Shukla, 1997):

- Supporting leadership processes that facilitate the intent to learn and create.
- Supporting learning mechanisms that encourage knowledge creation and acquisition.
- Supporting structures and processes that facilitate learning activities.

Obviously, learning organizations are very different from the traditional model, and they have many characteristics that are worth noting (Shukla, 1997), including permeable boundaries versus clear boundaries, evolving design versus being pre-designed, maximizing skills versus minimizing skills, integrated processes versus segmented tasks, and open, multi-functional networks rather than functional, hierarchical groupings.

8   Conclusion

Knowledge creation is a dynamic activity that can enhance organization success and economic well-being. In addition, it is an important driver of innovation, which can increase organizational agility and improve organizational performance,

Knowledge creation is associated with knowledge generation, which is one of the five primary knowledge manipulation activities identified by the ontology for the conduct of KM. Knowledge creation also has a very symbiotic relationship with knowledge acquisition and knowledge selection, and often the three activities are closely linked.

Knowledge can be viewed as having two major attribute dimensions, The first includes the defining characteristics of knowledge and can be identified as three types: descriptive knowledge, procedural knowledge, and reasoning knowledge. The second attribute recognizes three modes of knowledge: tacit knowledge, explicit knowledge, and cultural knowledge. Knowledge can be created through serendipity or intent, but in either case it may come into being either through discovery or derivation.

Knowledge creation involves a maturation process that begins when knowledge is discovered, is then codified, becomes migratory, and finally invisible. However, this dynamic process still relies on individual processors to share knowledge and transform it. Knowledge sharing relies on strong support from leadership. Sharing can occur in four processes – socialization, externalization, combination, and internalization. On an organizational level, knowledge creation can occur through knowledge conversion, knowledge building, or knowledge linking. Additionally, organizational information seeking or sensemaking can drive knowledge creation as can organizational learning.

Knowledge management efforts can facilitate knowledge creation by helping individuals develop knowledge-compatible competencies and by designing systems that provide enabling infrastructure. The knowledge creation process is complex and is growing more interdisciplinary every day. KM provides the framework to support knowledge creation by focusing on the relationships between knowledge activities and identifying areas that are essential elements of successful knowledge creation.

References

Abell, A., "Skills for Knowledge Environments," *Information Management Journal,* 34, 3, 2000.

Boisot, M.H., "Convergence Revisited: Codification and Diffusion of Knowledge in a British and Japanese Firm," *Journal of Management Studies,* 20, 1983, 159-190.

Boisot, M.H., *Information and Organisation: The Manager as Anthropologist,* London: Collins, 1987.

Ching, C., C.W. Holsapple, and A.B. Whinston, "Reputation, Learning, and Organizational Coordination," *Organization Science,* 3, 2, 1992, 275-297.

Ching, C., C.W. Holsapple, and A.B. Whinston, "Toward IT Support for Coordination in Network Organizations," *Information and Management,* 30, 4, 1996, 179-199.

Choo, C.W., *Information Management for the Intelligent Organization: The Art of Scanning the Environment,* Medford, NJ: Information Today, 1995.

Choo, C.W., *The Knowing Organization : How Organizations Use Information to Construct Meaning, Create Knowledge, and Make Decisions*, New York: Oxford University Press, 1998.

Conciecao, P. D. Gibson, M.V. Heitor, and S. Shariq, "Towards a Research Agenda for Knowledge Policies and Management", *Journal of Knowledge Management*, 1, 2, 1997, 129-141.

Dewey, J., *How We Think*, Boston: D.C. Heath and Company, 1933.

Drucker, P., *Post-Capitalist Society*, New York: HarperCollins, 1993.

Duffy, J., "Knowledge Management : What Every Information Professional Should Know," *Information Management Journal*, 34, 3, 2000.

Garvin, D.A., "Building a Learning Organization," *Harvard Business Review*, 71, 4, 1993, 78-92.

Gerstein, M.S., "From Machine Bureaucracies to Network Organisations: An Architectual Journey," in Nadler, D.A.; Gerstein, M.S., and Shaw, R.B. (eds.), *Oranisational Architecture: Designs for Changing Organisations*, San Francisco: Jossey-Bass, 1992.

Holsapple, C.W., "Knowledge Management for Decision Making and Decision Support," *Knowledge and Policy*, 8, 1, 1995, 5-22.

Holsapple, C.W. and K.D. Joshi, "Knowledge Selection: Concepts, Issues, and Technologies," in Liebowitz, J. (ed.), *Handbook on Knowledge Management*, Boca Raton, FL: CRC Press, 1999.

Holsapple, C.W. and K.D. Joshi, "An Investigation of Factors that Influence the Management of Knowledge in Organizations," *Journal of Strategic Information Systems*, 9, 2-3, 2000, 237-263.

Holsapple, C.W. and K.D. Joshi, "Organizational Knowledge Resources," *Decision Support Systems*, 31, 1, 2001, 39-54.

Holsapple, C.W. and K.D. Joshi, "A Collaborative Approach to Ontology Design," *Communications of the ACM*, 45, 2, 2002a, 42-47.

Holsapple, C.W. and K.D. Joshi, "Knowledge Manipulation Activities: Results of a Delphi Study," *Information and Management*, 39, 6, 2002b, 477-490.

Holsapple, C. and A. Whinston, *The Information Jungle: A Quasi-Novel Approach to Managing Corporate Knowledge*, Homewood, IL: Dow Jones – Irwin, 1988.

Johansen, R. and R. Swigart, *Upsizing the Individual in the Downsized Organization: Managing in the Wake of Reengineering, Globalization, and Overwhelming Technological Change*. Reading, MA: Addison-Wesley Publishing Company, 1994.

Malhotra, Y., "From Information Management to Knowledge Management: Beyond the 'Hi-Tech Hidebound' Systems," in Srikantaiah, T.K. and Koenig, M.E.D. (eds.), *Knowledge Management for the Information Professional*, Medford, NJ: Information Today, 2000.

Nonaka, I.. "The Knowledge-Creating Company," *Harvard Business Review*, November-December, 1991, 96-104.

Nonaka, I. And H. Takeuchi, *The Knowledge-Creating Company.* New York: Oxford University Press, 1995.

Rogers, E.M., *Diffusion of Innovations*, Fourth Edition, New York: The Free Press, 1995.

Ryske, E.J and T.B. Sebastian, "From Library to Knowledge Center: The Evolution of a Technology InfoCenter," in Srikantaiah, T.K. and Koenig, M.E.D. (eds.), *Knowledge Management for the Information Professional*, Medford, NJ: Information Today, 2000.

Senge, P., *The Fifth Discipline: The Art and Practice of the Learning Organization,* New York: Currency Doubleday, 1990.

Shukla, M., *Competing through Knowledge: Building a Learning Organization,* New Delhi: Response Books, 1997.

Srikantaiah, T.K., "Knowledge Management : A Faceted Overview," in Srikantaiah, T.K. and Koenig, M.E.D. (eds.), *Knowledge Management for the Information Professional*, Medford, NJ: Information Today, 2000.

UNESCO, Knowledge Management, Organizational Intelligence and Learning and Complexity. *Encyclopedia of Life Support Systems (EOLSS),* 2000, URL= http: www.utdallas.edu/dept/socsci/Fourth.htm

Weick, K.E., *The Social Psychology of Organizing,* second edition, New York: Random House, 1979.

Weick, K.E., *Sensemaking in Organizations,* Thousand Oaks, CA: Sage, 1995.

CHAPTER 19

Sensemaking and Knowledge Management

Richard J. Boland, Jr. and Youngjin Yoo

Information Design Studio, Weatherhead School of Management, Case Western Reserve University, Cleveland, OH, USA

Sensemaking is presented as a distinctive and powerful view of what organizational knowledge *is* and what it is knowledge *of* that can usefully guide the design of knowledge management systems. Sensemaking is distinguished from the traditional, decision-making view of a manager which assumes that she faces an independently knowable environment and prospectively chooses courses of action in order to achieve certain purposes. Sensemaking, in contrast, assumes that a manager faces an equivocal situation and must retrospectively impose a sense of order on it. Sensemaking also assumes that the equivocal situations we encounter in organizational life are importantly the result of our own previous action. We present a case study of a knowledge management system in an international consulting firm showing how the behaviors of highly effective consultants reflect principles of sensemaking in their use of the system. We then develop implications for the design of knowledge management systems.

Keywords: Design; Knowledge Management; Narrative; Sensemaking

1 Introduction

It is commonplace to distinguish between explicit knowledge which can be verbalized and tacit knowledge which cannot (Nonaka and Takeuchi, 1995). Appreciating the difference between these two types of knowledge helps us to understand the limits of knowledge management systems and also gives us opportunities to design systems which can take into account the various types of knowledge we can expect to encounter in an organization (Boland and Tenkasi, 1995, Boland, et al., 1994). In this chapter, we explore the importance of understanding sensemaking by managers to the design of knowledge management systems. We believe that this distinctive sensemaking view of organizational knowledge, based on the social psychology of Karl Weick, is perhaps more important for guiding the design of knowledge management systems than the more familiar explicit / tacit distinction.

Intuitively, we understand sensemaking to be the process whereby something surprising, unexpected, or equivocal is made sense of. But as Karl Weick has developed the concept in his social psychology of organizing (Weick, 1979, 1995, 1998, 2001; Weick, 1991; Weick and Bougon, 1986; Weick and Roberts, 1993), it has far reaching implications for understanding knowledge management. Weick

has established sensemaking as an evolutionary theory of organizing that emphasizes how people impose a sensible interpretation on the steam of ambiguous
situations that they encounter in organizations. It is evolutionary in the sense that
people are seen as first engaging in a continuous stream of action which generates
the equivocal situations they experience in an organization, and then retrospectively imposing a structure or schema on the situations they face in order to make
them sensible. Schemas that seem to work in making useful sense of a situation
are retained in memory and habit for future imposition on subsequent situations.
Acting to create ambiguous situations, selecting interpretive schemes to impose on
them, and retaining the helpful schemas for future use is the essence of a sensemaking view of organization.

In this chapter we first review the process of sensemaking as developed by
Weick, and then discuss how sensemaking provides a unique way of understanding what organizational knowledge *is* and what it is knowledge *of*. Then, we present a case study of a knowledge management system in a global consulting firm
and show how sensemaking helps to explain the different uses of the system by
high versus average performing consultants. Finally, drawing on the sensemaking
view of knowledge management systems, we identify some implications for designing effective knowledge management systems.

2   An Overview of Sensemaking

Sensemaking is an evolutionary view of organizations and knowledge in that it
views the interaction of people and their unique environments as the ultimate
source of both organizations, environments and our knowledge of them. Sensemaking emphasizes that social interaction is an organizing process that continually
constructs both the organization and its environment, although we normally take
both of them for granted as being "simply out there". It is also an ecological view
of knowledge and organizations in that both the organization and its environment
are viewed as a whole dynamic system that is continually evolving as managers in
the organization act on their environment and create change in both their environment and their organization. This ever changing organization / environment system continually needs to be made sense of by its managers, and at the same time,
its evolution is shaped by the sensemaking processes of its managers.

Perhaps the best way to present an overview of sensemaking as an organizing
force is to contrast it with our traditional, decision-making way of characterizing
managerial action. The traditional decision-making view can be summarized as
starting with a picture of the manager facing a knowable environment that presents
alternative courses of action. The manager is a purposeful actor who has a set of
goals she is trying to achieve, and evaluates the future consequences of her alternative course of action in light of those goals. The manager then chooses a course
of action and carries it out. Afterward, the manger engages in learning as she receives feedback about the consequences of her actions and adjusts her knowledge
of the situation and her future action accordingly. This decision-making view is
based on a cybernetic feedback control model of the manager in which goals or
purposes lead to a decision among alternatives which leads to action that produces

outcomes. The outcomes are then used as feedback to either adjust the action or the goals being sought. Under this cybernetic view of the manager, her goals and her purposes as reflected in her decision making are the determinants of action.

The sensemaking process turns this traditional view of the manager on its head. Yes, Weick acknowledges, managers do have goals and they do make decisions that lead to purposeful action, but they only do this occasionally. Most of the time, they are confronted by an environment that they do not understand clearly enough to know the alternatives open to them, or how to decide among those alternatives. Instead, most of the time, they are engaged with an equivocal, ambiguous environment which must be made sense of. In other words, sensemaking, not decision making, is the primary way that managers spend their time. We should note that sensemaking is also based on a cybernetic model of the manager and the organization, but one that starts with an equivocal environment that the manager herself has created as its input.

Weick refers to this input as an enacted environment in order to highlight that the environment we face in an organization is one that has been and continues to be changed by the manager's own actions. This enacted environment, constantly changed by the manger's ongoing stream of actions, is the "raw material" for her sensemaking. The manager, as sensemaker, draws out certain aspects of her environment to pay attention to, and ignores others. This is a tacit process and not a conscious choice. In effect, she tacitly attends to those aspects of the enacted environment that she will make sense of. The manager also tacitly selects a frame of reference or structure of understanding to use in making sense of the selected elements of her environment. Thus, the manager is seen as spending most of her time engaged with an equivocal, enacted environment by tacitly selecting aspects of it to pay attention to, as well as the mental schemas to employ in making an interpretation of it. Interpretations that seem to work in that they make a plausible and useful sense of the situation are retained by the manager. Subsequently, through feedback and memory, these retained structures for interpretation become available to guide future tacit selection of elements and schemas in an ongoing process of sensemaking.

This cybernetic image of the manager differs from the decision-making view by putting action and the creation of the enacted environment first, rather than last. Action continuously creates equivocal outcomes that require selection and interpretation to become sensible. Selection strategies that seem to work are retained, and the next episode of engaging an enacted environment is begun.

Sensemaking also differs from the decision-making view of a manager by emphasizing that sense is always made retrospectively. First something happens, then we need to make sense of it. In the decision- making view, by contrast, purpose and analysis of alternatives comes first, with action following a deliberate planning by the manager. This difference between the retrospective versus prospective nature of knowledge in organizations is crucial to understanding the implications of sensemaking for knowledge management. The manager is seen as being much more fallible; organizational knowledge is seen as being much less certain; the store of organizational knowledge is seen as continually being refreshed through selection and retention processes; and the action of the manager herself is seen as a major source of the uncertainty the organization faces.

3   Implications of a Sensemaking View of Knowledge Management

We now turn from a brief overview of sensemaking to discuss its significance as a lens for understanding knowledge management. Two aspects of a sensemaking perspective will be explored: its implications for understanding what organizational knowledge *is*, and its implications for understanding what it is knowledge *of*.

As for the first aspect, sensemaking highlights the way in which knowledge is a retrospectively imposed structure on our organizational stream of experience. Such an ordering structure is often implicitly assumed to take the form of a cause map (also known as an influence diagram) showing the elements that are being selected out of the enacted environment that its managers face, and the causal relations among them. A classic example of such a cause map is Maruyama's (1963) account of the self-propelled dynamic by which a city grows. In his description of city growth, a series of feedback loops are overlaid leading the dynamics of city growth to unfold over time as a series of reverberating environmental changes. To point out just two of these loops, a change that increases the number of people in a city positively affects its level of modernization, which in turn increases its desirability as a migration area, leading to more people in the city. Simultaneously, however, an increase in the population of the city leads to an increase in its garbage production and associated bacteria, which increases the incidence of disease and thereby reduces the population of the city. None of these relations are the result of purposive planning, known in advance. They are, instead, proposed as a plausible, retrospective account of its autonomous growth dynamics. Once a change is set in motion, for whatever reason, it continues to stimulate further change and continuously produce newly enacted environments to be made sense of by the city's leaders.

From a sensemaking perspective, this type of causal mapping represents what the vast majority of our stock of organizational knowledge *is*. This type of retrospective knowledge structure is an imposition of order that makes plausible sense of the ecological field of organizational action. This type of retrospective knowledge structure also often takes the form of a narrative. In a narrative, the events that have been selected from the enacted environment are strung together in a sequence by the narrator. The logic of a narrative is not an if - then – else... type of logic, but is rather a sequential first - then – then... type of logic in which the sequence of events in the story implies a logic (or a plot) rather than spelling it out. Much of the careful field work on organizational knowledge shows it to be in the form of narratives which make sense of past events (Boland and Tenkasi, 1995; Brown and Duguid, 1991; Brown and Duguid, 2000; Orr, 1990). Cause maps and narratives are just two of the ordering devices employed in sensemaking, but whatever technique is used, the important point is that sensemaking is a retrospective ordering of equivocal, enacted environments and requires a constant attention to the reflexive review of the past in an effort to make it sensible in the face of continual change and surprise (Boland and Tenkasi, 1995; Boland, et al., 1994).

As for the second aspect of what organizational knowledge is *of*, sensemaking emphasizes that an adequate understanding of organizations requires an understanding of the ecological setting of the organization and its environment. This includes an appreciation of how the actions taken within the organization "leak out" and participate in creating the equivocality that their enacted environment presents to its managers. Sensemaking therefore includes an awareness of how the managers themselves are part of the dynamic and uncertain environment they face. In summary, a sensemaking perspective means that what we can know about organizations is an ecological knowledge of organization / environnent interaction, along with an evolving sense of how the actions that have been taken shape the nature of the situations we face.

4   A Case Study

In this section, we examine how sensemaking behaviors of employees of a global management consulting service firm ("the firm" hereafter) are manifest in their routine knowledge management activities. In particular, we examine how high-performers of the firm differ from average performers in their knowledge creation, sharing, and preservation.

The firm has offices in 80 different countries and employs about 65,000 consultants. To support effective process of knowledge management and knowledge sharing at a global level, the firm has developed and implemented a global knowledge management system ("the system" hereafter). Furthermore, the leadership of the firm consistently emphasizes the importance to the firm's success of effective knowledge management and knowledge sharing among individual consultants. Conceived in 1991, the system was fully implemented by 1993 and rolled out across the global enterprise. An internal strategy document, released in March, 1992 contained the following statement: "We will establish 'Knowledge Management' as a new function within [the firm]. Key responsibilities will be to ensure the leading edge currency of our knowledge capital, and to keep [the system] demand driven rather than supply driven."

The system is currently composed of 4500 Lotus Notes databases containing both internal and external information in document repositories, special applications known as practice aids, discussion databases and directories. The system and all knowledge management practices within the firm are supported by over 500 fulltime knowledge management professionals. Internal knowledge capital in the repositories consists of such things as client deliverables, white papers, evaluations, presentations, proposals, methodologies, best practices and tools. External information includes subscription databases provided by arrangement with content vendors, Internet news groups and Internet based services, news feeds and the like. The system is available for all employees to access from laptop or desktop PCs over the firm's global wide area network, by dialing in to the network remotely, through the networks at client sites where connectivity arrangements have been made, or over the local area networks in each office of the firm. The system is constantly undergoing development and revision in order that content remain current, to adapt to changing needs and to reflect changes in the firm's organization and priorities. New technologies are applied as needed.

The firm has developed an organizational culture which emphasizes that knowledge creation and sharing are core activities of its consultants. Through

training, internal marketing, and technology support, the leadership of the firm
sends unequivocal messages to the consultants that knowledge is the core asset
that their competitive advantage is built upon.

4.1 Data Collection and Analysis

We conducted in-depth interviews with 31 consultants working in two Midwest
offices of the firm. The average age was 28.3; all interviewed consultants had
been with the firm from 2 to 5 years with the average of 3.1 years; and eight of
them were female. Among 31 interviewed consultants, 14 of them were identified
as high-performers. All interviews were tape recorded and transcribed for data
analysis.

Each interview lasted about 1.5 hours. We conducted semi-structured interviews, using a critical incident method. We asked each consultant his or her most
recent and significant experiences in knowledge creation, preservation and sharing, and seeking. Thus, each interviewed consultant told us three recent critical
incidents, one for each phase of knowledge management. We probed the nature of
the incidents by asking follow-up questions. We also asked consultants about
their general perceptions of the firm's knowledge management system including
usefulness, impediments to effective use, and the perceived usage of the system.
Individual consultants' job performance data provided by the firm was used to
identify high-performers and average-performers.

The data were analyzed by two coders. Following the recommendations by
Eisenhardt (1989) and Yin (1994), each interview transcript was treated as a single
case. Each interview transcript was subjected to a within-case analysis that involved repeatedly reading the transcript and taking thorough notes. For each case,
we summarized into a few short phrases the key aspects of the interviewee's experience in knowledge creation, knowledge preservation and sharing, and knowledge seeking. After the individual interviews had been analyzed, we began cross-
case comparisons that involved listing similarities and differences between the
high- and average-performing consultants in the sample to find different patterns
between the two groups. This led to a search for patterns and finally the grouping
of related behaviors into themes or categories (Boyatzis, 1998; Strauss and Corbin, 1990).

4.2 Results

The results of the interviews with these consultants reveal some important differences between high- and average-performers in their behaviors during knowledge
creation and knowledge preservation. First, the results indicate that, in the knowledge creation process, high-performers tend to view their knowledge creation as
"integrations" or "syntheses," rather than new inventions. Over 60% of interviewed high-performers mentioned that their primary contributions to the firm's
knowledge management system were not completely new inventions, but rather
integrating parts of solutions created for other contexts. High-performers tend to
take advantage of accumulated experiences of their own and other consultants of

the firm as they try to solve new problems for their clients. For example, one high-performing consultant said:

> "As a firm, we accumulate our knowledge over time. I would say that every time I implement a system to a new client, about 20% of what I do is new to the firm. We have to invent something new... because it is new. It is a different context. The solution you can find from the system doesn't fit 100% with that client's needs. The other 80% comes from [the firm's knowledge management systems], other colleagues, or my own experiences. You modify the existing solutions, you integrate new solutions you develop into those existing methods. That's where you add values. When you do it over and over again, after awhile, it becomes completely new knowledge."

On the other hand, the majority (around 60%) of the interviewed average-performers mentioned writing new software modules, developing new procedures, or coming up with novel approaches to the problems as their primary contribution to the systems. However, most of them were not sure whether these were in fact new and novel to the firm. One consultant said: "Well, there is nothing really new in this business. But, it was new, at least for me." Such comments suggests that in the firm, despite the firm's efforts "not to re-invent the wheel", many consultants seemed to perform redundant efforts for different projects in different countries. In part, it is related to the inability of the average-performing consultants to see the "big picture". Instead, they tend to jump right in to invent new solutions for their clients.

This local-orientation of average-performers was evident again when they were asked what were the types of documents that they posted on the firm's knowledge management systems. Over 50% of the interviewed average performers mentioned that they posted their deliverables to the clients to the system without much change. On the other hand, an overwhelming 80% of the interviewed high-performers mentioned much more general types of documents, such as white papers, templates, and general-purpose software libraries, as representative contributions to the system. While these high-performers also posted deliverables to the systems, these consultants took extra time (in many cases without being asked) to extract important general knowledge that can be immediately applicable in other contexts. One consultant commented on a training manual that he was working on:

> "Actually [the tool] is currently being used to create applications for a number of clients in Europe, South America, the U.S., Japan, and Asia. So what I am really doing is trying to actually improve the existing documents which was pretty weak. For example, all of the folks that are currently using [the tool], all those projects had people from the original project team to come out and help them... So, the real goal is to try and capture the knowledge in a further documentation so that it will be easier for others who have never even heard of [the tool] and use it to create an application for a customer."

Here, the consultant emphasizes the fact that what he was doing was not a new invention, but rather a re-interpretation of what had happened to many customers in order to retrospectively generalize the lessons learned from those engagements so that other consultants can more easily use the tool in their own contexts.

In the knowledge preservation process, we found that high-performers are more likely to reflect upon and summarize the lessons-learned, skills, and know-how that they gained from various sources. Again, over 80% of the interviewed high-performers mentioned that they kept some form of personal journals, notes, or summaries of important lessons-learned. On the other hand, only about 35% of the interviewed average-performers mentioned such behaviors. More specifically, many high-performers write their own personal journal in which they recount in narrative form the important issues they faced and the way in which they resolved (or did not resolve) those issues. Similarly, many high-performers mentioned that they create their own short summary of downloaded documents from the web or the firm's knowledge management systems. On the contrary, many average-performers mentioned that they simply took "mental notes" of what happened. Many of them mentioned that they did not have enough time to reflect upon what happened in a project before they moved on to the next one. Most of the average performers simply downloaded documents for their specific needs and stored them on their personal computers, without any form of summary or organization.

In this firm, consultants are asked to share their experiences and knowledge with others primarily through the firm's knowledge management system that connects consultants all over the world. One critical challenge of such a global organization is that individuals attempt to optimize their local conditions without considering the global context. Similarly, individuals often attempt to apply solutions developed for a different local condition to pursue efficiency through standardization. In addition, the relentless tempo of modern business makes it difficult for individuals in the organization to reflect on the meanings of their actions in a larger context. In this firm, surprisingly, a large number of high-performers find a way to stop in their busy daily routine of producing solutions for the clients, reflecting on the meanings of what they do for their local customer in the firm's global context as well as other individuals of the firm in different local contexts.

The case study seems to indicate that high-performers are mindful of their relative locations in the distributed knowledge network as they perform their actions. The heedful knowledge management behaviors of high-performers are also manifested in their efforts to preserve "general" knowledge as well as local knowledge. High-performers seem to be able to move freely between the global knowledge domain with the firm and the local knowledge domain for their particular engagements. This constant dialogue between global and local knowledge domains seems to be one of the key characteristics of high-performers in the firm. This observation is consistent with that of Weick and Roberts (1993) who found heedful behaviors performed by individuals were the key for a highly reliable and vigilant systems operating in novel and uncertain situations.

Another important characteristic of high-performers was their discursive and reflective use of the knowledge acquired from their experiences and from the knowledge management system. That is, high-performers tend to create their own interpretations of the documents in the knowledge base. Given that they seldom use these summary documents for their daily work, the documents themselves do not seem to be a source of their high performance. We believe, instead, that it is the reflexive, sensemaking process of creating such documents that help them enhance their performance. Current management education tends to emphasize concrete experience and active experimentation, at the expense of abstract conceptualization and reflection, and this trend is certainly evident in the behaviors of average-performers that we observed (Kolb, 1984). Our finding suggests that both active experimentation and abstract reflection are required in a knowledge management process for one to perform at a high level.

5 Discussion

The distinctive themes of sensemaking were clearly evident in the behavior of the high-performing consultants in this case study. And, surprisingly, a variation of the decision-making view of the manager was evident in the average-performing consultants. The high performers made extensive use of retrospective reflection and they also stove to put their local experience into the larger global context of the firm and its environments. The average performers, on the other hand, saw themselves as primarily creators of new solutions, focusing on the local task at hand. The high performers were driven by an engagement with an evolving and equivocal environment about which they kept diaries to make sense of, while the average performers were driven by action and the purposeful creation of new solutions.

The high performers in this case study displayed the essential enactment, selection, and retention features of the sensemaking process. By making their own syntheses of the material in the knowledge base, the high performers took it as an equivocal environment which the organization had enacted. They made selections from it as to what aspects to attend to and then applied selected schemas and ordering structures to create their own interpretations of it. More importantly, they saw that the process of retrospectively reflecting upon the work of the firm was the principle value adding activity that it provided to its clients.

After an engagement, the high-performing consultants took special effort to add not just the work product of their consulting engagement to the knowledge base, but also their own interpretation of its significance for other consultants. Here, they again were involved in selecting from the enacted environment of the engagement those aspects to give further attention, and they also selected interpretive schemes to make sense of them in narrative form. In these retrospective interpretations of their own engagements, they took into account a sense of the global logic of the firm as well as their local logic, and also tried to anticipate the local logic of the firms' consultants in other practice areas.

Although this one case study may not generalize across all industries and uses of knowledge management systems, it does give some credence to the value of considering a sensemaking perspective when designing knowledge management systems and training managers how to use them to best advantage. The decision-making view of the manager which we have used as a foil in this presentation certainly has a continuing value for informing our thinking about knowledge creation and use. We are not arguing against it. Instead, we are proposing that the sense-making view, which in many respects is a reversal of central tenets of the deci-sion-making view, should also be taken into consideration. And this is, curiously enough, one of the larger implications of sensemaking – that we should never be-come too enamored of one way of viewing our environment. A certain degree of ambivalence as to which aspects of the enacted environment to select for attending to and which types of interpretive schemes to apply to them, is an important strat-egy for keeping our sensemaking productive and effective in knowledge manage-ment.

6   Implications for Knowledge Management

The opening theoretical discussion combined with the case study presented above provides several important implications for knowledge management practice. First, the behavioral differences between high- and average-performers related to sensemaking in knowledge creation and knowledge preservation can be used to develop knowledge management behavioral "manuals" for employees. For exam-ple, organizations can instruct employees to first search and examine what others in the organization have done in related areas that might be retrospectively adapted to their own situation before they invent new solutions for their problem. Also, organizations can encourage employees to create more introspective sum-mary notes and journals in order to share their own sensemaking of a completed project. Learning strategies based on Kolb's experiential learning model (Kolb, 1984) can be helpful here. Along with prior suggestions for individual behaviors by Nonaka and Takeuchi (1995) and Leonard-Barton (Leonard-Barton, 1995), we believe that knowledge management behaviors incorporating a reflective sense-making process will enrich the creation and preservation of knowledge in organi-zations.

Second, designers of information technology to support knowledge manage-ment in organizations can take our findings into consideration. Our study suggests that the design of knowledge management systems should encourage and support a sensemaking process, rather than replace or suppress it. The current implemen-tation of knowledge management systems based on "repository of best practice" model effectively encourages uncritical replication of global knowledge in local contexts, thus discouraging a reflective sensemaking process. When used appro-priately, information technology can provide powerful ways to encourage reflec-tive sensemaking processes (Boland and Tenkasi, 1995; Boland, et al., 1994; Kar-sten, et al., 2001). As suggested by Alavi (2000) and Yoo and Ifvarsson (2001), information technology can connect people in different learning communities and different geographic spaces, thus allowing them to see the global context as they take local actions. Just as we believe in a certain degree of ambivalence between decision-making and sensemaking views in knowledge management, we suggest that a certain degree of ambivalence between the storing and connecting roles of information technology in knowledge management is necessary.

Finally, as organizations attempt to implement knowledge management initia-tives, they must consider their organizational structures and incentive systems.

The organizational structure and the incentive systems should provide ample opportunities for sensemaking in knowledge management. For example, Hansen and Von Oetinger (2001) suggest that a human portal should connect people in different parts of the organization. Similarly, the organizational learning literature points our the importance of "boundary-spanners" in knowledge creation and sharing in organizations (Katz and Tushman, 1983; Tushman and Scanlan, 1981; Wenger, 1998). Organizations need to pay special attention to such positions and roles and provide enough incentives to make such positions effective.

References

Alavi, M., "Managing organizational knowledge" in Zmud, R. (ed.), *Framing the Domain of IT Management: Projecting the Future from the Past*, Cincinnati, OH: Pinnaflex Educational Resources, 2000.

Boland, R. J., and R. V. Tenkasi, "Perspective Making and Perspective Taking in Communities of Knowing," *Organization Science*, 6, 4, 1995, 350-372.

Boland, R. J., R. V. Tenkasi, and D. Te'eni, "Designing Information Technology to Support Distributed Cognition," *Organization Science*, 5, 3, 1994, 456-475.

Boyatzis, R., *Transforming Qualitative Information: Thematic Analysis and Code Development*, Thousand Oaks, CA: Sage, 1998.

Brown, J. S. and P. Duguid, "Organizational Learning and Communities of Practice: Toward a Unified View of Working, Learning, and Innovation" *Organization Science*, 2, 1, 1991, 40-57.

Brown, J. S. and P. Duguid, *The Social Life of Information*, Boston, MA: Harvard Business School Press, 2000.

Eisenhardt, K. M., "Building Theories from Case Study Research" *Academy of Management Review*, 14, 4, 1989, 532-550.

Hansen, M. and B. Von Oetinger, "Introducing T-Shaped Managers: Knowledge Management's Next Generation," *Harvard Business Review*, 79, 3, 2001, 106-116.

Karsten, H., K. Lyytinen, M. Hurskainen, and T. Koskelainen, "Crossing Boundaries and Conscripting Participation: Representing and Integrating Knowledge in a Paper Machinery Project," *European Journal of Information Systems*, 6, 2, 2001, 89-99.

Katz, R., and M.L. Tushman, "A Longitudinal Study of the Effects of Boundary Spanning Supervision on Turnover and Promotion in Research and Development," *Academy of Management Journal*, 26, 3, 1983, 437-456.

Kolb, D. A., *Experiential Learning: Experience as the Source of Learning and Development*. Englewood Cliffs, NJ: Prentice-Hall, 1984.

Leonard-Barton, D., *Wellsprings of Knowledge: Building and Sustaining the Sources of Innovation*. Boston, MA: Harvard Business School Press, 1995.

Maruyama, M., "The Second Cybernetics: Deviation-Amplifying Mutual Causal Processes," *America Scientist* , 51, 1963, 164-179.

Nonaka, I., and H. Takeuchi, *The Knowledge-Creating Company: How Japanese Companies Create the Dynamics of Innovation*, New York: Oxford University Press, 1995.

Orr, J., "Sharing Knowledge, Celebrating Identity: War Stories and Community Memory in a Service Culture," in Middleton, D.S. and Edwards, D. (eds.), *Collective Remembering: Memory in Society,* Beverly Hills, CA: Sage Publications, 1990.

Strauss, A. and J. Corbin, *Basics of Qualitative Research: Grounded Theory Procedure and Techniques*. Newsbury Park, CA: Sage, 1990.

Tushman, M. L. and T.J. Scanlan, "Boundary Spanning Individuals: Their Role in Information Transfer and Their Antecedents," *Academy of Management Journal,* 24, 2, 1981, 289-305.

Weick, K., *The Social Psychology of Organizing* (revised edition), Reading, MA: Addision-Wesley, 1979.

Weick, K., *Sensemaking in organizations*, Thousand Oaks, CA: Sage, 1995.

Weick, K., "Improvisation as a Mindset for Organizational Analysis," *Organization Science*, 9, 5, 1998, 543-555.

Weick, K., *Making Sense of the Organization,* Oxford: Blackwell Publishers, Ltd., 2001.

Weick, K., "The Nontraditional Quality of Organizational Learning," *Organization Science*, 2, 1, 1991, 116-124.

Weick, K. E. and M.G. Bougon, "Organizations and Cognitive Maps: Charting Ways to Success and Failure," in Sims, H. and Gioia, D. (eds.), *The Thinking Organization*, San Francisco: Jossey-Bass, 1986.

Weick, K. E. and K.H. Roberts, "Collective Mind in Organizations: Heedful Inter-relating on Flight Decks," *Administrative Science Quarterly*, 38, 1993, 357-381.

Wenger, E., *Communities of Practice: Learning, Meaning, and Identity*, Cambridge, UK: Cambridge University Press, 1998.

Yin, R. K., *Case Study Research: Design and Method,* Thousand Oaks, CA: Sage, 1994.

Yoo, Y. and C. Ifvarsson, "Knowledge Dynamics in Organizations: Toward a Theoretical Framework.," in Coakes, E.; Willis, D. and Clarke, S. (eds.), *Knowledge Management in the Sociotechnical World: The Graffiti Continues,* London, UK: Springer-Verlag, 2001.

CHAPTER 20

Creating and Facilitating Communities of Practice

Heather A. Smith and James D. McKeen

Queen's Management Research Centre for Knowledge-Based Enterprises,
School of Business, Queen's University, Kingston, Ontario, CANADA

Communities of practice (CoPs) are an emerging, unstructured organizational form that many believe will help companies to truly leverage what they know. CoPs appear to have the potential to galvanize knowledge sharing, learning, and change thereby improving a company's performance and making it more competitive. However, a major problem with them is that their organic and informal nature makes them highly resistant to management supervision and interference in their activities. CoPs are therefore controversial because there is no clear role for management in them. In fact, if management does get involved, the community often dissipates. Yet paradoxically, CoPs require specific managerial efforts to develop and support them so that their full power can be leveraged.

To discuss CoPs and their role in organizations, the authors convened a focus group of knowledge managers from a variety of industries. To help them prepare for the session, participants were given a series of questions to consider in advance on how management can and should develop and facilitate CoPs. This paper discusses the challenges and successes they have had in implementing CoPs and makes recommendations for practising knowledge managers who wish to encourage and support the development of CoPs in their organizations.

It concludes that communities of practice have the potential to dramatically change how enterprises operate and compete because they are the mechanism through which knowledge gets both created and turned into action. While they are made possible by technologies that enable people to share insights and ideas around the world, they are first and foremost a social mechanism. Over the next few years, we can expect to see CoPs evolve and new management techniques develop as we learn new ways to leverage knowledge to create value.

Keywords: Communities of Practice; Networks for Collaboration; Communities of Interest; Communities of Experts

1 Introduction

As we move deeper and deeper into a knowledge economy, many companies are discovering that they need another mechanism in their organizations to truly leverage what they know. Communities of practice (CoPs) are an emerging, unstructured organizational form that many believe may be this mechanism. CoPs appear to have the potential to galvanize knowledge sharing, learning and change thereby improving a company's performance and making it more competitive. Others are more sceptical of these claims and are not rushing to develop CoPs. They note that a major problem with them is that their organic and informal nature makes them highly resistant to management supervision and interference in their activities. CoPs are therefore controversial because there is no clear role for management in them. In fact, if management does get involved, the community often dissipates. However, it is an interesting paradox that *"CoPs require specific managerial efforts to develop them and to integrate them into the organization so that their full power can be leveraged."* (Wenger and Snyder, 2000).

To discuss CoPs and their role in organizations, the authors convened a focus group of knowledge managers from a variety of industries. To help them prepare for the session, participants were given a series of questions to consider in advance on how management can and should develop and facilitate CoPs. These questions included:

1. How do you identify potential CoPs that will enhance company capabilities?
2. What role can/should management play in defining the strategic intent, domain, and membership criteria of a CoP?
3. What role(s) can/should management play in the ongoing leadership and facilitation of a CoP?
4. What technological infrastructure and support should a company provide to a CoP?
5. What roles and structures will facilitate or inhibit the effectiveness of a CoP?
6. How can management assess the value of a CoP?
7. What makes a successful and effective CoP?
8. How can management balance the risks and benefits of sharing intellectual capital outside the organization (e.g., with partners or customers)?
9. What cultural changes should be expected where CoPs are in place? How should company management and procedures adjust to these?

Focus group participants presented what their companies were doing to develop CoPs and discussed strategies for supporting and nurturing them. This chapter integrates a variety of published material on CoPs with the focus group's comments to give the practising knowledge manager answers to the questions he or she needs to know about these new organizational forms. It first describes the characteristics of CoPs, and why they are becoming more important to organizations. It then looks at how companies can develop and facilitate CoPs. Finally, it discusses some of the factors that are critical to their success.

2   Characteristics of CoPs

2.1   What are CoPs?

A very broad definition of a CoP is that it is a group of people with a common interest who work together informally in a responsible, independent fashion to promote learning, solve problems, or develop new ideas (Storck and Hill, 2000;

Wenger and Snyder, 2000). Within a CoP, people collaborate directly; teach each other; and share experiences and knowledge in ways that foster innovation. As a result, for the corporate world, they are a force that is both social and professional which operates outside traditional organizational boundaries and hierarchies. Because they are action-oriented and knowledge-based, and uninhibited by the strictures of organization structure, CoPs have been called one of the most important elements of any organization where thinking matters (Stewart, 1996). Stewart (1996) describes CoPs as "the shop floor of human capital, the place where stuff gets made."

Interestingly, CoPs are not new. In fact, most of us belong to one or more CoPs at any particular point in time and are an integral part of our daily lives. However, "they are so informal and pervasive that they rarely come into explicit focus." (Wenger, 1998). In our homes, workplaces, hobbies, and social lives, we all participate in informal, unstructured networks that help us learn and get things done. What is new about CoPs is their name and the fact that recognition of their existence is changing how we understand and support learning in organizations.

Today, CoPs come in many different shapes and sizes, possibly because companies are still experimenting with them. Several writers have tried to identify the hallmarks of a CoP to distinguish it from a variety of other organizational groups (such as teams, networks, grapevines, and competency groups). Stewart (1996) and Wenger (1998) both point to several broad, defining characteristics. First, because a CoP must develop over *time*, it has a history of learning. Second, it has an *enterprise* – something that forms around a "value-adding something-we-are-all-doing" – but it does not have an agenda of action items as a team would. Third, *learning* is a key element of this enterprise. As a result, CoPs develop their own ways of dealing with their world. Fourth, they are *responsible* only to themselves and self-policing. There's no boss. Leaders tend to emerge on an issue-by-issue basis. In addition, because *relationships* within a CoP are ongoing and indeterminate, they tend to be characterized by mutual trust (Storck and Hill, 2000). Finally, CoPs are concerned about *content* rather than form. As a result, they are not identifiable or designable units (Wenger, 1998).

Focus group members saw CoPs as bridging mechanisms that cut across regional, divisional, and geographic boundaries within an organization. Their companies are implementing many different kinds of CoPs. Some are fairly loose groups of people who interact only occasionally; others are much more active and tightly integrated. They also recognize that other types of groups, such as special interest groups and networks, may eventually evolve *into* CoPs although they lack all the hallmarks of a true CoP. Focus group members therefore took a broad perspective on CoP definition, suggesting that more loosely coupled groups can serve many of the purposes of a CoP and are in fact, the breeding ground for new communities.

Within a CoP, there are also different, legitimate types of participation. Wenger (1998) points out that not all members of a CoP have to be equally active. While CoPs depend on a core group of committed and involved members, a community can also offer peripheral forms of participation as well. This is how these groups socialize the young and encourage newcomers. There are three stages to becoming a full member of a CoP (Sproul, 1998). The first is simply finding the community and "lurking" to see what is going on. The second is learning how to get around and participate in the community. And the third is knowing how and where to break the rules and to innovate. Signs of full membership in a CoP include shared tacit conventions, understandings, and assumptions, and a common worldview (Wenger, 1998). Focus group members disagreed on how one becomes a member of a CoP. In one organization, membership is a "badge of honour" – by invitation only and based on recognized competence. In others, membership is typically self-selected based on interest. There was general agreement however, on the importance and value of knowledgeable, active, and committed members who form the core of the community.

2.2 CoPs and Teams

Unlike other organizational groups, CoPs are organic. At present, we have little experience as to how to oversee and harness value from this type of organizational entity. What we do know is that CoPs differ from other organizational groups, especially teams. Wenger (1998) notes that there are two views of an organization:

1. **The designed organization** which defines the roles, qualifications, and distribution of authority and which establishes relations of accountability.
2. **The practice(s)** which give life to the organization and which are frequently a response *to* the designed organization.

While we are familiar with the first view and its structures and hierarchies, the second view suggests that there is a completely different form of organization that coexists within and around designed organizations. Because it is based on practice and social response, it requires a very *human* touch to make it grow and thrive (Macdermott, www.co-i-l.com). In order to learn how to integrate CoPs effectively into our organizations, it is especially important to know how they differ from other common organizational forms with which we are more familiar.

CoPs are most often confused with teams. But unlike teams, CoPs are typically voluntary and unstructured groups with membership that cuts across internal and/or external organizational boundaries. While focus group members were inclined to suggest that teams and CoPs had many areas of overlap, researchers in this area believe that it is important to understand the principal differences between the two. These have been summarized in Table 1.

Teams and CoPs compete for their members' time and create a tension in the organization. However, there is general agreement that both types of groups are necessary to the future of the modern organization.

3   CoPs and the 21st Century Organization

It is well understood that globalization and its related trends of deregulation, privatization, and increased customer sophistication, have raised the competence standards and expectations of organizations (Quinn, 1992). Other organizational trends which together are producing a "sea-change" for businesses, include: em-

Table 1. The Differences between Teams and CoPs

	Communities of Practice	Teams
Objective	To share knowledge and promote learning in a particular area	To complete specific projects
Membership	Self-selected; includes part-time and marginal members	Selected on the basis of the ability to contribute to the team's goals; ideally full-time
Organization	Informal, self-organizing, leadership varies according to the issues;	Hierarchical with a project leader/manager
Termination	Evolves; disbands only when there is no interest	When the project is completed (in some cases, a team *may* evolve into a community)
Value Proposition	Group discovers value in exchanges of knowledge and information	Group delivers value in the result it produces.
Management	Making connections between members; ensuring topics are fresh and valuable.	Coordination of many interdependent tasks.

bedding knowledge in products and services; the increasing capacity of technology; accelerating knowledge accumulation and depreciation rates; and the increasing demand for more meaningful work (Snyder, 1997). These all add up to the conclusion that competition has increasingly come to be regarded as a "learning race" (Powell, 1998).

Developing learning linkages, especially externally, has become the new way to compete. Access to knowledge is now a fundamental and pervasive concern of highly competitive industries. It is becoming ever more important as the knowledge base becomes more complex (e.g., as in the pharmaceutical industry) and when uncertainty is high. Thus, collaboration is becoming a key dimension of competition. (Powell, 1998)

Within organizations, the ability to compete is also related to "real-world" competence. Brown and Gray (1995) define this as "a sustained capacity to outperform the competition". They note that this form of competence is built as much on implicit know-how and relationships, as it is on tangible products and tools because, "you can't divorce competencies from the social fabric that creates them." Put another way, companies are discovering that there is real value in sharing ideas and insights that are not documented and hard to articulate. CoPs are the ideal vehicles for leveraging this tacit knowledge because they engage a whole group in advancing their field of practice. Thus, CoPs are increasingly being seen as the best way to develop these critical real-world competencies.

3.1 CoPs and Traditional Organizational Structures

Focus group participants and researchers are in strong agreement that if CoPs are to be developed in organizations, traditional hierarchies, business practices, and management styles will not be adequate for the job. As noted above, we know very little about how to promote and deliver value and effectiveness in the informal, social environment of CoPs. Wenger (1998) and Snyder (1997) call these communities "the organizational frontier". They note that there are three reasons why they aren't more prevalent in today's enterprises. First, we are only just becoming aware of their existence. Second, we are just beginning to recognize that CoPs must be nurtured and supported. And third, it is not particularly easy to build and sustain them or to integrate them with the rest of the organization since they are resistant to supervision and interference. To integrate CoPs effectively into our organizations, managers will have to find out how to do two things: how to collaborate, and how to learn, *as an organization*, from collaboration (Powell, 1998).

The advent of CoPs signals that organizations are becoming more fluid than they have been in the past. Whereas organizations have traditionally had clear borders, in the future these will become more and more 'fuzzy' as CoPs reach out into their members' professional communities and include the enterprise's allies, partners, vendors, and customers. Internally, organization will look more like webs of participation, again crossing traditional project and functional boundaries (Cohen, 1998). In short, focus group members suggested that enterprises are moving more towards operating within 'spheres of influence' rather than as discrete entities. As a result, it is almost inevitable that, where implemented, CoPs will somewhat undermine traditional formal organization structures and processes (Stewart, 1996)

This trend causes tension between the 'occupational principles' of the CoP and the 'administrative principles' of the traditional organization that has yet to be resolved. Focus group members did not believe that this means that CoPs are emerging as a *replacement* for more traditional work structures. Instead, they feel they are a *complement* to them adding new dimensions to work and learning. For example, CoPs may help spread a team's learnings across the organization. Thus, while traditional organizations take a vertical view of work (e.g., regions, lines of business, or projects), communities take a horizontal view, integrating learning and action across vertical boundaries (e.g., learning, practices, insights).

To manage such a two-way organization, companies will need to develop both the ability to coordinate competencies to enact recognized business processes (CoPs), *and* the ability to integrate multiple aspects of knowledge and skills to meet specific task requirements (teams) (Snyder, 1997). Enterprises which learn to successfully integrate these two *different kinds* of structures will be "double-knit" organizations because they weave tightly knit vertically-organized teams together with loosely-knit horizontal communities into a functional, yet flexible structure (McDermott, 1999b).

3.2   CoPs and Knowledge Management

> *"Today in the US, most knowledge practice focuses on collecting, distributing, re-using, and measuring existing codified knowledge and information... Most firms' efforts consist of investing in knowledge repositories, such as intranets and data warehouses... These activities treat knowledge pretty much like steel or any other resource to be gathered, shared, and distributed."*
> (Pfeffer and Sutton, 1999)

Because this approach to knowledge management captures only the most explicit forms of knowledge, it results in much knowledge management effort being divorced from the day-to-day activities of people and from how knowledge is used in practice. We now believe that knowledge is more appropriately viewed as a dynamic ecosystem that grows and develops, involving a complex web of interdependent parts (Cohen, 1998). Therefore, 'knowledge management' is really closer to 'knowledge ecology' because knowledge should include the physical and social environments in which information resides, social relations, trust, beliefs, practices, and meanings, in addition to explicit information.

Because knowledge incorporates such a wide range of items, companies are now recognizing the critical role communities play in creating, maintaining, and transferring knowledge. Indeed, some believe CoPs are the main source of knowledge creation (Cohen, 1998). Focus group members described CoPs as being the 'glue' of knowledge management. Others see them as being the building blocks of knowledge management and a critical part of social learning systems (www.KnowledgeEcology.com). They are "knowledge in action" (Snyder, 1997).

There are three principles about work in modern organizations that are shaping our understanding of the role of CoPs in knowledge management (Brown and Gray, 1995):

- *Processes don't do the work, people do.* Behind the official work processes are the real-world practices that actually get things done. "The real genius of organizations is the informal, impromptu, often inspired ways that real people solve real problems in ways that formal processes can't anticipate."
- *Learning and work are both social activities.* "The more you explore real work, the more you appreciate the power of ... tacit knowledge ... i.e., intuition, judgment and common sense." In groups, this knowledge exists in the practices and relationships that emerge from working together over time, i.e., the social fabric of the community.
- *Organizations are webs of participation.* At the core of the modern company is participation. And at the heart of participation is the heart and spirit of the knowledge worker. Only workers who choose to opt in can create a winning company. "When a company acknowledges the power of community and adopts the elegantly minimal processes that allow communities to emerge, it is taking a giant step towards the 21st century."

Today, the challenge for managers is how to translate these principles into action by facilitating CoPs.

4   Developing CoPs

Although CoPs are critical organizational assets, they are also a resource that can be easily overlooked and taken for granted simply because they do not require much in terms of institutional resources or structures. Nevertheless, they do require attention, energy and resources to make them effective. While organizations are still learning about how to develop and facilitate CoPs, it is clear that communities cannot simply be ignored or left to themselves. Organizations looking to introduce CoPs must take an active role in both identifying appropriate communities and learning how to facilitate them.

4.1   Identifying CoPs

Companies use a variety of different mechanisms to identify the communities they will support. Wenger and Snyder (2000) stress that CoPs cannot be mandated and should not be created in a vacuum. Thus, a common approach to identifying CoPs is to find the informal groups that are already operating around the organization's core competencies and help them come together as communities. However, it is important that CoPs not be confused with competencies. They are not skills groups because they are not limited to explicit knowledge (Stamps, 1997). Two focus group companies take a different approach to CoP identification. They begin with a business model and ask, *"What types of knowledge communities will enhance this model?"*

What both these approaches have in common is that they recognize that not all interest groups in an organization can or should become officially-sanctioned CoPs. For the focus group organizations, a community of practice should have a *strategic intent* that links the CoP *in some way* to organizational performance. Thus, a CoP is really a "community of purpose" from which the organization derives value. Once identified, it is management's job to shape the community's intent, help define its boundaries, and facilitate its development.

4.2   Facilitating CoPs

All CoPs benefit from cultivation. "Like gardens, they respond to attention that respects their nature ... You can't tug on a cornstalk to make it grow faster or taller ... you can however, till the soil, pull out the weeds, add water, and ensure ... proper nutrients." (Wenger and Snyder, 2000). Focus group members agreed with this analogy and pointed out that different CoPs also require different types of support. For example, CoPs that extend beyond the organization's boundaries or that are worldwide in scope will need different forms of cultivation than those that are more local in nature. Thus, management has a responsibility to identify a CoP's real needs and to support them accordingly. There are three general areas in which organizations can provide support to a CoP: management, technical infrastructure, and culture.

4.2.1   Management

What leaders do really matters in building CoPs. Pfeffer and Sutton (1999) believe their most important task is not necessarily to make strategic decisions, but to create an environment in which there are "a lot of people who both know and do." Through their *actions*, managers create environments, reinforce norms, and help set expectations. This is a new role for many managers and one for which some focus group companies feel they are still unprepared.

As a first step, managers need to recognize CoPs and their importance to the company. Then, they will feel more comfortable providing them with the resources they need, e.g., time and encouragement to participate in a CoP, and access to meeting space and technology. Most companies find that CoPs don't need a lot of money or time – in fact, some consultants advise against providing a lot of resources, "Fund them too much and you'll start to want deliverables." (Stewart, 1996).

Apart from resources, managers should focus their attention on creating a culture in which CoPs can thrive. Mintzberg (1998) suggests that this requires "covert leadership" because culture-building is not a discrete management activity but is infused in everything a leader does. Culture is based on the core values of the corporation. Although managers cannot create or change culture, they *can* enhance it and *use* it to define the uniqueness of the community and its spirit.

4.2.2   Technical Infrastructure

There is no doubt that technology is a key enabler of CoPs. "In making information more widely available, what technological advances really do ... is create wider and more complex ... communities." (Wenger, 1998). However, when considering how to facilitate CoPs, an organization's first reaction is all too often to buy and install technology and then wait for the enterprise to be transformed (Moore, 1998). In short, technology is very useful in helping a community connect but CoPs still need a very human touch (McDermott, www.co-i-l.com.)

Focus group members agreed that while use of technology alone is not enough to facilitate a CoP, a supportive technical infrastructure, with the following elements, is critical:

- *Local practitioner support,* including good communications such as, access to telephone, fax and e-mail.
- *An enterprise-wide library and Web-access,* as well as the ability to access both expertise and documents.
- *Conversational technology* (beyond e-mail) facilitating access and sharing both locally and globally.
- *Collaborative technology* to enable people to work together. Tools which organizations are finding useful are applications that allow members to represent problems, build prototypes and create solutions.
- *Tools that make it easy to connect with, contribute to, and access the community.* This might mean making use of familiar software to reduce the difficulties and 'friction' of trying to work together (McDermott, www.co-i-l.com). Some focus group members utilize tools that automatically capture, track and codify knowledge for later reuse.

Since many of these types of tools are very different from those needed in a traditional organization, companies should also consider forming a team to investigate, implement and maintain them for the enterprise.

4.2.3   Culture

Of all of the issues surrounding CoPs, the need for a culture that supports communities, learning and knowledge-sharing is considered a critical success factor by both practitioners and researchers. Moore (1998) writes, "A culture hospitable to knowledge repeatedly surfaces as the key make or break factor in [their] successful implementation." A focus group member agreed, "Having a collaborative culture where sharing is done naturally has made it easy for us to implement CoPs." As noted above, although culture is not something that can be changed overnight, it can be enhanced. Some of the areas where culture can be made more supportive of communities include:

- *Build enough background context to enable people to better understand each other.* What people consider valuable to share depends on their experience, goals, problems and mental frameworks. A mismatch between two people's contexts has been called the biggest single reason ideas and insights are rejected. Even with simple information-sharing, people need to build a shared context to understand how to use it.
- *Use multiple forums to share knowledge.* Since CoPs have many different kinds of knowledge to share, they need multiple ways to connect. Single mediums tend to get clogged with inappropriate information that can distract or repulse members. (McDermott, 1999a)
- *Give people time.* An organization that values learning and sharing will give people time to reflect and share ideas. It will also send the message that CoPs are 'okay' to participate in.
- *Provide for face-to-face meetings.* Focus group members felt strongly that electronic communication should be a complement to, but not a replacement for, face-to-face meetings. Face-to-face meetings both increase the likelihood of a CoP developing and accelerate their development. Electronic communication can then be used to sustain and deepen these relationships.

5   Making CoPs Work

Once an organization has identified its strategic communities and has taken steps to create a supportive managerial, technical and cultural environment, it is still faced with the challenge of making them work in a way which is consistent with the enterprise's needs and practices. Wenger explains that to make a CoP effective, knowledge needs to be integrated into specific business practices. "What makes information into knowledge, what makes it empowering, is the way in which it can be integrated... into practice." This is more difficult than it sounds, because while we can try to design a culture that is encouraging of knowledge-sharing and communities, it is the *response* to that design which is what is actually incorporated into practice. The challenge of changing a corporate culture is to work with this response, include it, and make it an opportunity for the organization. Thus, learning cannot be designed but it can be designed *for* and a culture evolved which can facilitate it. This section explores some practical advice for knowledge managers seeking to integrate CoPs effectively into their organizations.

5.1 Understand the Hurdles

In spite of all that can be done to support and facilitate CoPs, there are a number of significant hurdles still to be overcome in our understanding of how to make CoPs work. For example, some researchers believe it is unrealistic to expect knowledge to flow through organizations because people's time and energy are limited and they will choose to do what they believe will give them the most return on these scarce resources (Cohen, 1998). While most of our emphasis up to now has been on building the stock of knowledge under the presumption that knowledge, once possessed, will be used appropriately and efficiently. However, there is really a bigger gap between knowing and doing than between ignorance and knowledge (Pfeffer, and Sutton, 1999). Others point out that it is not easy to turn information into knowledge or to turn individual learning into organizational learning. This is particularly true in fields where information is abundant and accumulates rapidly (Powell, 1998). In short, there is still a great deal that we don't know about how to get the most out of CoPs and deliver value to the organization and knowledge managers would be wise to manage expectations during this learning process.

5.2 Make Knowledge Easy to Use

Community space needs to be familiar and easy to move around in. Therefore, it must be organized according to principles that reflect the natural way in which community members think about their practice. In addition, wherever possible, focus group members commented that they try to embed knowledge capture and sharing into work processes. One company monitors email in a proactive search for content and enables staff to email notes from conferences. All content is then fully indexed so that users are only a few clicks away from the information they need. Other companies keep track of all interactions with clients so that as much customer knowledge as possible is retained even after individuals move on. Another allows users to define their own particular knowledge interface that filters in only information they wish to learn about. These mechanisms illustrate the conclusion that many practitioners have reached which is that the best way to build knowledge-sharing into work is to lock documentation into people's work tools. Finally, Xerox's early recognition that information is more useful when it is validated has been reinforced by the focus group's experience. Most provide some means of editing and eliminating old or ineffective knowledge, while highlighting what others have found useful.

5.3   Measure Value

Every member of the focus group struggles with the need to demonstrate the value of their organization's CoPs to senior management and this is becoming more urgent with time. However, many believe that there is a different mechanism of value operating in CoPs that needs to be better understood before value can be identified. This proposition suggests that value comes not from hoarding information but from sharing it (Sproul, 1998). There are unfortunately, no absolute measures of the value of a CoP as yet and there is a great deal of debate about what kinds of measures are appropriate. Larry Prusak, for example believes that 'crude and fuzzy' measures (e.g., stories) capture knowledge value more effectively than more precise ones (Cohen, 1998). Thus, he suggests companies should be looking for non-traditional measures that recognize the value that has been added by CoPs. Others believe that CoPs must be somehow linked to traditional and widely understood business metrics so that the link between sharing and outcomes can be appreciated by senior management (Manville, 1996). One focus group member uses a balanced scorecard to do this. To date however, there is no agreement on how to assess a CoPs value or to connect it with organizational performance. Focus group members recommended that senior managers begin to acquaint themselves with this issue by periodically reviewing and assessing the work of all their CoPs. Places where companies can begin to look for value include: business problems solved; new knowledge created; existing knowledge leveraged; innovation in products, ideas or processes; and improvements in process performance metrics.

5.4   Develop Trust

CoPs thrive on trust and building this up between members is therefore an important way to improve their effectiveness. Trust is developed first and foremost through face-to-face contact, which is a key reason why technology cannot be used to completely replace physical get-togethers. One focus group member commented, "The issue of trust is big and it can't be built up virtually." Trust can also be encouraged through frank discussions of real problems, and candidness between members.

5.5   Establish Coordinating Roles

All focus group organizations have established a number of coordinating roles to ensure that their CoPs work effectively. Members identified the following roles:

- *Sponsor* – A senior manager who communicates the company's support for the CoP and helps remove any barriers that obstruct community progress.
- *Champion* – The chief organizer of events and communications for the CoP.
- *Facilitator/Coordinator* – The person who clarifies information and helps keep discussions on topic. Good coordinators help build the one-on-one relationships which are essential for a strong community.

- *Practice (or Knowledge) Leader* – The acknowledged leader of the CoP. Leadership is based on competence, not position. The practice leader person is responsible for maintaining and advancing the body of knowledge in the CoP and for getting thought leaders involved in a CoP from its inception. He/she is key to building the energy of the community.
- *"Infomediaries"*– Some organizations also use people who are not necessarily content experts to do much of the initial filtering of information. They could be librarians, knowledge managers, or researchers.

5.6 Motivate People

Participation in a CoP will not come about simply because it is 'good' to share. There must be incentives for individuals to participate. These can take several forms. For example, some focus group companies have begun to reflect contributions to knowledge, participation in a community, and use of knowledge bases in an individual's compensation. In other companies, management makes sure that people are motivated to try new things with knowledge. They do this by letting staff know that it's okay to take time to be part of the community and that it's okay to make mistakes. Without this assurance, people will likely be too fearful to take the time or the risks involved in true sharing (Pfeffer and Sutton, 1999). Finally, it is important that CoPs are used to create dialogue around issues that people really care about, rather than simply to document best practices. Getting the right people involved in a CoP can do this. These people will then energize and stimulate the whole group.

5.7 Monitor Evolution

Focus group members were aware that our understanding and practice surrounding CoPs is evolving continually. Therefore, it is essential that knowledge managers monitor both research and practice to consider what others are doing. In addition, they must also monitor their own successes and failures with CoPs and learn from them. At present, most CoPs are internal to companies, but in the future, with the increasing number of alliances and partnerships being developed, CoPs will include members of other companies and take on a different character with new benefits and risks. For example, while it is natural to develop CoPs within the networks of companies that are created by partnerships, today's partners can become tomorrow's competitors very easily. Therefore, businesses will have to continually reassess what is flowing out of the organization through its CoPs and determine where a loss of intellectual capital can lead if it goes too far. This situation will require a clear understanding on the part of CoP members of what information must be protected and what can be shared. Managers must be prepared to anticipate such potential risks and to establish guidelines within which CoPs can work.

6   Conclusion

Communities of practice are emerging organizational forms that have the potential to dramatically change how enterprises operate and compete. CoPs form the foundation of knowledge management because it is through them that knowledge gets both created and turned into action. While they have been made possible by technologies that enable people to share insights and ideas around the world, they are first and foremost a social mechanism. Over the next few years, we can expect to see CoPs evolve and new management techniques develop as we learn new ways to leverage knowledge to create value. In the meantime, knowledge managers and others must recognize and learn how to work with the social and cultural elements of CoPs to help them realize their true potential.

References

Anonymous, *"Communities of Practice,"* www.KnowledgeEcology.com.

Anonymous, "What is a 'Community of Practice'?" www.co-i-l.com.

Brown, J. and S. Gray, "The People are the Company," *Fast Company,* November, 1995.

Cohen, D., "Toward a Knowledge Contest: Report on the First Annual U.C. Berkeley Forum on Knowledge and the Firm," *California Management Review,* 40, 3, 1998.

Manville, B. and N. Foote, "Harvesting Your Worker's Knowledge," *Datamation,* July, 1996

McDermott, R., "Knowing in Community: 10 Critical Success Factors in Building Communities of Practice," www.co-i-l.com.

McDermott, R., "Learning Across Teams: The Role of Communities of Practice in Team Organizations," *Knowledge Management Review,* May-June, 1999a

McDermott, R., "Nurturing Three Dimensional Communities of Practice: How to Get the Most Out of Human Networks," *Knowledge Management Review*, Fall, 1999b.

Mintzberg, H., "Covert Leadership: Notes on Managing Professionals," *Harvard Business Review*, 76, 6, 1998.

Moore, C., "KM meets BP," *CIO Magazine*, November 15, 1998.

Pfeffer, J. and R. Sutton, "Knowing 'What' To Do is Not Enough: Turning Knowledge into Action," *California Management Review,* 42, 1, Fall, 1999.

Powell, W., "Learning From Collaboration: Knowledge and Networks in the Biotechnology and Pharmaceutical Industries," *California Management Review,* 40, 3, 1998.

Quinn, J. B., *Intelligent Enterprise,* New York, NY: The Free Press, 1992.

Snyder, William, "Communities of Practice: Combining Organizational Learning and Strategy Insights to Create a Bridge to the 21st Century," www.co-i-l.com., August 1997.

Sproul, L., "Creating and Facilitating Communities of Practice." Notes from a private meeting of the Society for Information Management Advanced Practices Council, 1998.

Stamps, D., "Communities of Practice: Learning is Social. Training is Irrelevant?" *Training Magazine,* February, 1997.

Stewart, T., "The Invisible Key to Success," *Fortune*, 134, 3. August, 1996.

Storck, J. and P. Hill, "Knowledge Diffusion Through 'Strategic Communities'," *Sloan Management Review*, 41, 2, 2000.

Wenger, E., *Communities of Practice: Learning, Meaning, and Identity.* New York, NY: Cambridge University Press, 1998.

Wenger, E. and W. Snyder, "Communities of Practice: The Organizational Frontier," *Harvard Business Review*, 78, 1, 2000.

CHAPTER 21

Knowledge Sharing Proficiencies:
The Key to Knowledge Management

Jay Liebowitz and Yan Chen

Department of Information Systems, University of Maryland-Baltimore County, Baltimore, MD, USA

A key element of knowledge management is building and nurturing a knowledge sharing culture. A number of organizations are developing knowledge sharing proficiencies as part of their recognition and reward systems. Knowledge sharing effectiveness is a critical aspect of knowledge management, and this chapter takes a look at this area in terms of developing and applying a knowledge sharing effectiveness inventory in order to rate how well an organization is performing knowledge sharing activities.

Keywords: Knowledge Management; Knowledge Sharing; Knowledge Sharing Effectiveness; Knowledge Sharing Proficiency

1 Introduction

The mantra within the knowledge management community is that 80% of knowledge management is people and culture, and 20% is technology. A key component of the people and culture factors deals with encouraging a knowledge sharing environment within the organization (Liebowitz, 1999; Davenport and Grover, 200). Kochikar (2000) has developed a knowledge management maturity model in which the highest level is "Sharing." This level involves reaching the institutionalization of a culture of sharing, whereby sharing becomes second nature to all. Organizational boundaries are rendered irrelevant, and knowledge flows frictionlessly (Kochikar, 2000).

Knowledge sharing has become a cornerstone in many top companies. Xerox's reputation has been built on a strong knowledge sharing culture. Xerox's Eureka system contains many thousands of tips to help repair technicians worldwide who repair copiers at clients' sites. At Xerox, knowledge sharing has become part of a fabric inside the company for all employees (Hickins, 1999). Dow Corning has created clubs to promote research and development interaction for knowledge sharing purposes (Easton and Parbhoo, 1998). Many organizations like American Management Systems have created Corporate Knowledge Centers in core competency areas to encourage online communities of practice for increased knowledge sharing (Preece, 2000). Lockheed-Martin applies knowledge sharing by matching the type of knowledge with the right transfer method (Dixon, 2000).

Knowledge is not always easy to share, sometimes it is inaccessible. According to The Delphi Group (Hickins, 1999), a study of more than 700 US companies showed that the majority of corporate knowledge is in employees' brains which presents a challenge in trying to share this knowledge. About 12% of the corporate knowledge was in electronic knowledge bases, 42% in employees' brains, 26% in paper documents, and 20% in electronic documents. In order to elicit and represent the knowledge in people's heads in a formal way, the knowledge acquisition bottleneck (from the days of knowledge engineering) plays a critical role (Liebowitz, 2001; Schreiber et al., 2000). The knowledge engineering paradox states that the more expert an individual, the more compiled is his/her knowledge, and the harder it is to extract this knowledge. This makes knowledge sharing a challenging task, but an organization can promote and nurture its knowledge sharing culture by instilling knowledge sharing measures within a motivate and reward structure within an organization.

Several organizations already have developed knowledge sharing proficiencies in order to further encourage the use of knowledge sharing within the organization and externally to the organization's customers (Liebowitz and Chen, 2001). The World Bank has learning and knowledge sharing criteria as part of their employees' annual job performance review. Arthur Andersen once had six levels of knowledge sharing proficiencies, and in order to be promoted, one needed to reach at least level five. American Management Systems evaluates employees partly on how well they contribute to the organization's knowledge repositories and what is the value-added benefit derived from applying the knowledge from these repositories (Andriessen and Tissen, 2000). Gemini Consulting has similar measures for knowledge sharing as part of their employee's performance review.

In order to leverage employee know-how, organizations have found that developing knowledge sharing proficiencies for the organization and incorporating these proficiencies as part of the employee's annual appraisal seems to be a necessary step in helping to build and jump-start a knowledge sharing culture. As the knowledge sharing process becomes institutionalized over time, the culture for knowledge sharing will become a natural occurrence in the organization.

2   Knowledge Sharing Proficiencies

Before creating knowledge sharing proficiencies, we must first provide a definition for a "knowledge sharing proficiency." A knowledge sharing proficiency is an attribute that allows the creation of knowledge to take place through an exchange of ideas, expressed either verbally or in some codified way. Some organizations like Johnson & Johnson and The World Bank have knowledge fairs geared to promoting an increase in knowledge sharing and generating new colleague-to-colleague relationships for better transfer of tacit knowledge. A number of organizations have already created knowledge sharing as a guiding principle for the organization. For example, the Public Service Commission in Canada has "Knowledge, Information, and Data Should Be Shared" as one of their four guiding principles. Specifically, they indicate:

- Sharing will be rewarded. We will create an environment where people feel free to contribute what they know and to seek out knowledge from colleagues.
- Performance evaluations should be linked to how well a person contributes to generating, assessing, and transferring knowledge.
- Knowledge will be available to all employees except where there is a demonstrated need for confidentiality or protection of privacy.
- Our knowledge will be shared to support collaboration with other federal government departments, other levels of government, and our other partners.
- We will establish processes and tools to enable us to capture and share our knowledge in order to support collaboration.

The World Bank, which wants to be known as the Knowledge Bank, includes learning and knowledge sharing factors as part of their annual performance evaluation. These factors include: open to new ideas and continuous learning; shares own knowledge, learns from others, and applies knowledge in daily work; builds partnerships for learning and knowledge sharing. In a university setting, Liebowitz and Chen (2001) developed knowledge sharing proficiencies within the Information Systems Department to consist as follows:

Collaboration, in the form of:

- Joint proposals/papers one has written with colleagues within and outside the department
- Co-Principal Investigators on funded research efforts
- Part of research teams with team members from faculty/students in the Department
- Consulting engagements with faculty/students in the Department
- Joint teaching or giving guest lectures to colleague's courses (e.g., Honors courses, filling in for others if colleague is out of town)
- Mentoring colleagues in the Department and providing lessons learned to colleagues
- Letting your colleagues teach courses that you normally teach, especially if it can advance their area of research (i.e., eliminating the philosophy that an individual faculty member "owns" a course)

Thinking of We, Not Me:

- Circulating articles and special issue announcements that may interest other colleagues in the Department
- Circulating announcements for conferences and RFPs (request for proposals) to colleagues, and putting together joint sessions at conferences
- Engaging in activities to help strengthen the Department versus ones to enhance individual achievement

- Offering appropriate colleagues in the Department to write invited papers if one is unable to do so
- Offering to others a chance to review papers for journals if in the colleague's area of specialization
- Being pro-active in Department and University Activities (e.g., attending IT company briefings, meeting IT-related company CEOs, attending IT-related seminars)
- Letting department faculty and students use one's lab for research appropriate to that Lab's focus (versus the attitude that this is MY lab)
- Providing leads to colleagues for possible research/consulting
- Providing leads to students for jobs and calling personal contacts to allow students to get their foot in the door

Other possible knowledge sharing proficiencies could include (Liebowitz and Suen, 2000): the number of new colleague-to-colleague relationships spawned; the reuse rate of "frequently accessed/reused" knowledge; the number of key concepts that are converted from tacit to explicit knowledge in the knowledge repositories and used by members of the organization; the dissemination of knowledge sharing (i.e., distribution of knowledge) to appropriate individuals; the number of new ideas generating innovative products or services; the number of lessons learned and best practices applied to create value-added; the number of "apprentices" that one mentors, and the success of these apprentices as they mature in the organization.

The US Department of Navy is starting to embrace knowledge management and knowledge sharing principles to transform itself into a knowledge-centric organization. As the sharing of information and knowledge becomes embedded in day-to-day activities, the flow and change of best practices should increase, providing the fluid for true process improvement. In addition, the high visibility of content areas across the organization facilitates the exchange of new ideas regarding process change.

3   A Knowledge Sharing Effectiveness Inventory

Over the years, various instruments have been advanced to assess knowledge management and organizational effectiveness. Some of these instruments include the KMAT (Knowledge Management Assessment Tool) by the American Productivity & Quality Center, Expedient Knowledge Inventory by Strategy 1st, the Organizational Effectiveness Inventory by Human Synergistics Inc., and the Learning Effectiveness Index by CapitalWorks. These instruments broadly cover elements of how well an organization is learning and applying its knowledge, but they didn't specifically look at the issues of knowledge sharing effectiveness for potentially building knowledge sharing proficiencies for an organization.

In order to fill this vacuum, Liebowitz and Chen (2001) developed a knowledge sharing effectiveness inventory that consists of 25 questions, divided into four parts. The first part deals with "Communications Flow" which tries to assess how knowledge and communication exchanges are captured and disseminated through-out the organization. The second part examines the "Knowledge Management Environment" which looks at internal cultural factors related to knowledge management within the organization. The third part deals with "Organizational Facilitation" which assesses the sophistication of the knowledge management infrastructure and knowledge sharing capability within the organization. The last part deals with the "Measurement" to assess the likelihood of knowledge sharing and knowledge management being successful within the organization.

This inventory has 25 questions in which strongly agree equals 4 points, agree is 2 points, neutral is zero points, disagree is –2 points, and strongly disagree is –4 points. The maximum score is 100, that is, if one answered strongly agree to each question. The following scale was used to determine if the organization rates an A, B, C, D, or F in terms of knowledge sharing:

A: 76-100 points (minimum is 13 questions are strongly agree and 12 questions are agree)
B: 50-75 points (minimum is 25 questions marked agree)
C: 0-49 points (minimum is 25 questions marked neutral)
D: minus 50-minus 1 (minimum is 25 questions marked disagree)
F: minus 100-minus 51 (minimum is 25 questions marked strongly disagree).

If an organization rates as an A overall, it has done very well in knowledge sharing. An integrated system strategy provides a direction for knowledge sharing. Company culture also supports the behaviors of knowledge creation, inquiry, and sharing. Supporting technologies, tools, and equipment are provided to foster communication.

A "B" knowledge sharer means that the organization does well in knowledge sharing. From the results of the four areas of the questionnaire discussed above, the specific areas for improvement can be pinpointed.

In rating as a "C" knowledge sharer, even though there is some knowledge sharing culture, there still needs to be supporting technologies, flexible guides, maps, processes, and pathways for locating and sharing knowledge. A knowledge sharing strategy needs to be further created.

It is not good to be ranked as "D" or "F" respectively. It says that the culture and environment in the organization resists knowledge sharing, and there are few, if any, strategies, technologies, and communication channels for knowledge sharing. The organization should first check the obstacles to knowledge sharing by examining the output from the questionnaire. Also, the organization can take advantage of other best practices, and develop a knowledge sharing strategy for the organization.

The instrument for guaging knowledge sharing effectiveness inventory is shown below:

Knowledge Sharing Effectiveness Inventory

This questionnaire has been developed by Dr. Jay Liebowitz and Yan Chen in the Laboratory for Knowledge Management at the University of Maryland-Baltimore County. Kindly mark a response for each statement. Thank you for your help.

	Strongly Agree	Agree	Neutral	Disagree	Strongly Disagree
ABOUT COMMUNICATION:					
1. Key expertise is often captured in an online way in my organization.					
2. I get appropriate lessons learned sent to me in areas where I can benefit.					
3. I usually have time to chat informally with my colleagues.					
4. Individualized learning is usually transformed into organizational learning through documenting this knowledge into our organization's knowledge repository.					
ABOUT KM ENVIRONMENT:					
5. There are many knowledge fairs/exchanges within my organization to spawn new colleague to colleague relationships.					
6. There are lessons learned and best practices repositories within my organization.					
7. We have a mentoring program within my organization.					
8. We have Centers of Excellence in our organization whereby you can qualify to become a member/affiliate of the Center.					
9. We typically work in teams or groups.					
10. Our main product is our knowledge.					
11. I feel that we have a knowledge sharing culture within our organization versus a knowledge hoarding one.					
12. We have a high percentage of teams with shared incentives whereby the team members share common objectives and goals.					
13. There are online communities of practice in my organization where we can exchange views & ideas.					

About Organizational Faciliation:					
14. I am promoted and rewarded based upon my ability to share my knowledge with others.					
15. There is an adequate budget for professional development and training in my organization.					
16. Success, failure, or war stories are systematically collected and used in my organization.					
17. The measurement system in my organization incorporates intellectual and customer capital, as well as the knowledge capital of our products or services.					
18. We have the technological infrastructure to promote a knowledge sharing environment within our organization.					
19. We typically have integrated assignments where the number of projects in which more than one department participates occurs.					
20. We have internal surveys on teaming which surveys employees to see if the departments are supporting and creating opportunities for one another.					
21. We track the degree to which the organization is entering team-based relationships with other business units, organizations or customers.					
22. The organization's office layout is conducive to speaking with my colleagues and meeting people.					
About Measurement:					
23. The reuse rate of "frequently accessed/reused" knowledge in my organization is high.					
24. The distribution of knowledge to appropriate individuals in my organization is done actively on a daily basis.					
25. New ideas generating innovative products or services are a frequent occurrence in my organization.					

4   Case Study: Applying the Knowledge Sharing Effectiveness Inventory

In order to apply the knowledge sharing effectiveness inventory and to create associated knowledge sharing proficiencies, a Learning Resources Group of a major government agency was used for testing this inventory. This Group was interested in knowledge management and was wondering how well they were performing in the knowledge sharing area, and what types of knowledge sharing proficiencies could be developed to possibly encourage knowledge sharing. The frequency distributions of responses for the 25 questions are shown in Tables 1-25.

Table 1. Q.1-1 Key expertise is often being captured in an online way in my organization

Question	Percentage Answered
Strongly Agree	0.0%
Agree	10.5%
Neutral	10.5%
Disagree	63.2%
Strongly Disagree	15.8%

Table 2. Q.1-2 I get appropriate lessons learned sent to me in areas where I can benefit

Question	Percentage Answered
Strongly Agree	0.0%
Agree	21.1%
Neutral	15.8%
Disagree	47.4%
Strongly Disagree	15.8%

Table 3. Q.1-3 I usually have time to chat informally with my colleagues

Question	Percentage Answered
Strongly Agree	10.5%
Agree	63.2%
Neutral	26.3%
Disagree	0.0%
Strongly Disagree	0.0%

Table 4. Q.1-4 Individualized learning is usually transformed into organizational learning through documenting this knowledge into our organization's knowledge repository

Question	Percentage Answered
Strongly Agree	0.0%
Agree	5.3%
Neutral	10.5%
Disagree	57.9%
Strongly Disagree	26.3%

Table 5. Q.2-1 There are many knowledge fairs/exchanges in my organization to spawn new colleague relationships

Question	Percentage Answered
Strongly Agree	0.0%
Agree	5.3%
Neutral	0.0%
Disagree	78.9%
Strongly Disagree	15.8%

Table 6. Q.2-2 There are lessons learned and best practices repositories within my organization

Question	Percentage Answered
Strongly Agree	0.0%
Agree	15.8%
Neutral	10.5%
Disagree	47.4%
Strongly Disagree	26.3%

Table 7. Q.2-3 We have a mentoring program within my organization

Question	Percentage Answered
Strongly Agree	15.8%
Agree	68.4%
Neutral	5.3%
Disagree	5.3%
Strongly Disagree	5.3%

Table 8. Q.2-4 We have Centers of Excellence in our organization whereby you can qualify to become a member/affiliate of the Center

Question	Percentage Answered
Strongly Agree	0.0%
Agree	5.3%
Neutral	15.8%
Disagree	47.4%
Strongly Disagree	31.6%

Table 9. Q.2-5 We typically work in teams or groups

Question	Percentage Answered
Strongly Agree	15.8%
Agree	68.4%
Neutral	5.3%
Disagree	5.3%
Strongly Disagree	5.3%

Table 10. Q.2-6 Our main product is our knowledge

Question	Percentage Answered
Strongly Agree	15.8%
Agree	31.6%
Neutral	21.1%
Disagree	26.3%
Strongly Disagree	5.3%

Table 11. Q.2-7 I feel that we have a knowledge sharing culture within our organization versus a knowledge hoarding one

Question	Percentage Answered
Strongly Agree	0.0%
Agree	15.8%
Neutral	10.5%
Disagree	47.4%
Strongly Disagree	26.3%

Table 12. Q.2-8 We have a high percentage of teams with shared incentives whereby the team members share common objectives and goals

Question	Percentage Answered
Strongly Agree	0.0%
Agree	15.8%
Neutral	42.1%
Disagree	42.1%
Strongly Disagree	0.0%

Table 13. Q.2-9 There are online communities of practice in my organization where we can exchange views and ideas in areas of common interest

Question	Percentage Answered
Strongly Agree	0.0%
Agree	10.5%
Neutral	15.8%
Disagree	47.4%
Strongly Disagree	26.3%

Table 14. Q.3-1 I am promoted and rewarded based upon my ability to share my knowledge with others

Question	Percentage Answered
Strongly Agree	0.0%
Agree	10.5%
Neutral	15.8%
Disagree	52.6%
Strongly Disagree	21.1%

Table 15. Q.3-2 There is an adequate budget for professional development and training in my organization

Question	Percentage Answered
Strongly Agree	0.0%
Agree	31.6%
Neutral	15.8%
Disagree	26.3%
Strongly Disagree	26.3%

Table 16. Q.3-3 Success, failure, or war stories are systematically collected and used in my organization

Question	Percentage Answered
Strongly Agree	0.0%
Agree	0.0%
Neutral	15.8%
Disagree	47.4%
Strongly Disagree	36.8%

Table 17. Q.3-4 The measurement system in my organization incorporates intellectual and customer capital, as well as the knowledge capital of our products or services

Question	Percentage Answered
Strongly Agree	0.0%
Agree	5.3%
Neutral	15.8%
Disagree	47.4%
Strongly Disagree	31.6%

Table 18. Q.3-5 We have the technological infrastructure to promote a knowledge sharing environment within our organization

Question	Percentage Answered
Strongly Agree	5.3%
Agree	52.6%
Neutral	10.5%
Disagree	15.8%
Strongly Disagree	15.8%

Table 19. Q.3-6 We typically have integrated engagements where the number of projects in which more than one business unit participates occur

Question	Percentage Answered
Strongly Agree	0.0%
Agree	36.8%
Neutral	21.1%
Disagree	26.3%
Strongly Disagree	15.8%

Table 20. Q.3-7 We have internal surveys on teaming which surveys employees to see if business units are supporting and creating opportunities for one another

Question	Percentage Answered
Strongly Agree	0.0%
Agree	5.3%
Neutral	15.8%
Disagree	52.6%
Strongly Disagree	26.3%

Table 21. Q.3-8 We track the degree to which the organization is entering team-based relationships with other business units, organizations or customers

Question	Percentage Answered
Strongly Agree	0.0%
Agree	5.3%
Neutral	15.8%
Disagree	36.8%
Strongly Disagree	42.1%

Table 22. Q.3-9 The organization's office layout is conducive to speaking with colleagues / meeting people

Question	Percentage Answered
Strongly Agree	5.3%
Agree	52.6%
Neutral	10.5%
Disagree	21.1%
Strongly Disagree	10.5%

Table 23. Q.4-1 The reuse rate of 'frequently accessed/reused' knowledge in my organization is high

Question	Percentage Answered
Strongly Agree	0.0%
Agree	10.5%
Neutral	21.1%
Disagree	47.4%
Strongly Disagree	21.1%

Table 24. Q.4-2 The distribution of knowledge to appropriate individuals in my organization is done actively on a daily basis

Question	Percentage Answered
Strongly Agree	0.0%
Agree	10.5%
Neutral	10.5%
Disagree	57.9%
Strongly Disagree	21.1%

Table 25. Q.4-3 New ideas generating innovative products or services are a frequent occurrence in my organization

Question	Percentage Answered
Strongly Agree	0.0%
Agree	15.8%
Neutral	31.6%
Disagree	31.6%
Strongly Disagree	21.1%

4.1 Data Analysis on Each Category

Taking "Strongly Agree" as A, "Agree" as B, "Neutral" as C, "Disagree" as D, and "Strongly Disagree" as F, the data analysis based on the survey results and question categories (number of questions per category is shown in parentheses; numbers in table represent counts) is shown in Table 26.

	A (Strongly Agree)	B (Agree)	C (Neutral)	D (Disagree)	F (Strongly Disagree)	Score	Average Score
Communications Flow (4)	2	19	12	32	11	– 62	– 15.5
Knowledge Management Environment (9)	9	45	24	66	27	– 114	– 12.7
Organizational Facilitation (9)	2	38	26	62	43	– 212	– 23.6
Measurement (3)	0	7	12	26	12	– 86	– 28.67

In calculating the score for each category, we take A as +4, B as +2, C as 0, D as –2, and F as –4. As there are four questions in the first category (i.e., communication flows), nine questions in the second category, and so forth, the average score is the smoothed score after considering the different number of questions in each category. The resultant average scores are comparable.

So, from the data in the table, it can be seen that this organization has a relatively better knowledge management environment and communications flow versus organizational facilitation and measurement. However, in all four categories, the average score is a D, which suggests that this organization is not faring well at all in terms of knowledge sharing and overall knowledge management effectiveness.

5   Concluding Observations

The government, like other not-for-profits, has some unique challenges to develop a knowledge sharing capability as compared with industry (Liebowitz, 2001). First, developing a "motivate and reward" system for encouraging knowledge management and sharing is difficult in government primarily because only limited financial awards/incentives can be provided and there is typically just a Pass-Fail system with respect to government employees' annual job performance reviews which makes it difficult to base promotions on the level of knowledge sharing proficiencies met. A second reason why knowledge management is hard to accomplish in government versus industry is that government agencies are typically hierarchical, bureaucratic organizations with still many organizational layers, even after the "Reinventing Government" initiative. This causes lengthy approval processes and stymies innovation, where knowledge management could hopefully foster. A last major hurdle in gaining knowledge management acceptance in government is the knowledge hoarding culture. In many government agencies, people keep their knowledge close to heart as they move through the ranks by this "knowledge is power" paradigm. In the author's experience in working with several major government agencies, people seem reluctant to share their knowledge internally with colleagues and others due to a self-preservation mentality. If they give away their respective expertise and resulting competitive edge, they feel that they may be less likely to be promoted and rewarded, thus creating a counter culture to knowledge sharing.

In developing knowledge management strategies at the Federal Communications Commission (FCC) and the Naval Surface Warfare Center-Carderock Division (NSWCCD), the author experienced many of the aforementioned elements which made acceptance for and institutionalization of a knowledge management strategy difficult in these organizations. With the FCC, many of the employees are attorneys and, by nature and training, seemed to be generally suspicious and reluctant to share their knowledge. They didn't seem to view knowledge management as a genuine process of improving and helping them complete their work in efficient and effective ways. They felt that knowledge management was another management fad of the day, similar to Total Quality Management, Total Quality Leadership, and Business Process Reengineering. Those with the foresight of seeing the advantages of knowledge management appreciated the need for knowledge sharing to better leverage knowledge internally and externally to all stakeholders. They viewed online communities of practice as an extension of listservs for facilitating interactions and sharing of insights and knowledge. There were some legal concerns about subpoenaing these types of emailed interactions that might be used later in the courts.

With the NSWCCD, the Strategic Planning Director fully recognized and supported the virtues of developing a knowledge management strategy and sharing culture for the organization. The Center seemed to be turning into a job-shop mentality versus its basic charter as the leading research and development laboratory for ship and submarine design. The technical workforce was graying and many of the mid-career employees were leaving the organization. Additionally, the younger scientists and engineers felt fractured by being pigeonholed in their respective branch and not aware of what was happening in other parts of their organization, even though similar work and methods were being used elsewhere in the organization. Online communities of practice, expert and knowledge retention programs, expertise locator systems, and repositories for codifying knowledge were recommended elements of the overall NSWCCD knowledge management strategy. When presented to the Board of Directors, it was felt that there were higher priorities that could produce more "tangible" benefits than knowledge management and thus knowledge management was put on hold.

These types of attitudes and events are not atypical to government agencies. Even though the government's basic mission is to better inform the general public and thus hopefully share and push knowledge externally to their stakeholders, a paradox exists whereby the sharing of knowledge internally within a government agency isn't as widely accepted as its external mission. Perhaps the annual evaluation rating system needs to be restructured to encourage and reward internal knowledge sharing practices. Additionally, government agencies need to be further streamlined to eliminate the domineering hierarchical structure so that knowledge sharing could be further facilitated. If the US government wants to attract the "best and the brightest", as is done in Japan (it's a great honor to work for the Japanese government and they therefore attract the best), government agencies will need to attract talented individuals who have the creativity and energy to "make a difference" versus "doing things the same old way." By making these individuals feel a part of the organization and allowing them to reach out to others in the organization and sister agencies, a knowledge sharing culture will start to exist and thrive.

References

Andriessen, D. and R. Tissen, *Weightless Wealth*, London: Prentice Hall Financial Times, 2000.

Davenport, T. and V. Grover (eds.), "Special Issue on Knowledge Management," *Journal of Management Information Systems*, 18, 1, 2001.

Dixon, N., "The Insight Track," *People Management*, 6, 4, February 17, 2000.

Easton, T. and B. Parbhoo, "Clubs Promote R&D Interaction at Dow Corning," *Research Technology Management*, 41, 1, 1998.

Liebowitz, J. (ed.), *The Knowledge Management Handbook*, Boca Raton, FL: CRC Press, 1999.

Liebowitz, J., *Knowledge Management: Learning From Knowledge Engineering*, Boca Raton, FL: CRC Press, 2001.

Liebowitz, J., "Lessons Learned in Developing Knowledge Management Strategies for the Government," *KM World*, January, 2001.

Liebowitz, J. and Y. Chen, "Developing Knowledge Sharing Proficiencies," *Knowledge Management Review*, January/February, 2001.

Liebowitz, J. and C. Suen (2000), "Developing Knowledge Management Metrics for Measuring Intellectual Capital," *Journal of Intellectual Capital*, 1, 1, 2000.

Hickins, M. "Xerox Shares Its Knowledge," *Management Review*, 88, 8, 1999.

Kochikar, V., "The Knowledge Management Maturity Model—A Staged Framework for Leveraging Knowledge," *Proceedings of the KMWorld 2000 Conference*, New Jersey, September, 2000.

Preece, J., *Online Communities: Designing for Sociability and Usability*, Chichester, UK: John Wiley, 2000.

Schreiber, G., H. Akkermans, A. Anjewierden, R. de Hoog, N. Shadbolt, W. van de Velde, and B. Wielinga, *Knowledge Engineering and Management: The CommonKADS Methodology*, Cambridge, MA: MIT Press, 2000.

CHAPTER 22

Business Process as Nexus of Knowledge

Omar A. El Sawy and Robert A. Josefek, Jr.

Marshall School of Business, University of Southern California, Los Angeles, CA, USA

Knowledge management is rarely thought of as a strategy for redesigning business processes. This chapter examines approaches to knowledge management within the context of business process redesign. In it, we illustrate and explain how knowledge management can be used both to support and to enhance business processes.

Keywords: Business Processes; Knowledge Management; Process Redesign

1 Introduction

Knowledge management is rarely thought of as a strategy for redesigning business processes. This chapter examines approaches to knowledge management within the context of business process redesign. In it, we illustrate and explain how knowledge management can be used both to support and to enhance business processes.

The chapter begins with an examination of the relationship between knowledge management and business processes. Next, it outlines a set of strategies for redesigning business processes to increase their knowledge creating capacity, enhance their capacity to create value, and make them more "learningful." Case study examples from a variety of settings illustrate these ideas and practices. Attention then turns to how structural, human, and relationship capital can be reconceived around business processes. The chapter ends with an examination of emerging issues and future directions in knowledge management and business process redesign.

2 Linking Knowledge Management and Business Processes

Twenty years ago, Walter Wriston, the legendary Citibank Chairman and insightful pioneer of electronic banking had a famous quote: *"The time will come when the information created from a financial transaction will be more valuable than the execution of the actual transaction itself."* While perhaps a little exaggerated, it epitomized the changes that were about to take place in the information age, and demonstrated the increased value of information. Wriston's quote was just about information rather than also knowledge, and about transactions rather than also business processes. In this age of knowledge management and e-business processes, perhaps it is time to update his famous quote to reflect the emergence of knowledge that goes beyond information, and the prominence of business processes that go beyond transactions:

> *"The time will come when the knowledge created from a business process will be more valuable than the execution of the actual business process itself"*.

Consider the following example in which knowledge management and business process are interlinked. The setting is a credit approval process for consumers who are refinancing home loans. As interest rates drop significantly, there is a flurry of activity that affects lending institutions, loan brokers, and credit reporting agencies. As the applications are processed, massive amounts of data are collected, much information is exchanged between the parties involved, and the potential for creating new knowledge exists every time the process is executed. If an organization can capture and creatively use this knowledge that is generated around the business process, it can add value for itself and its customers and suppliers in a variety of ways and along multiple dimensions. To accomplish this, the organization must have in place the means to analyze, synthesize, or otherwise create knowledge from the business process activities underway. Furthermore, if the organizations can share this knowledge, there is an opportunity to increase value along the entire value chain. For example, if the process is capable of identifying new consumer profile types, it may be possible to improve the quality of credit decisions or alter the process flow to expedite processing. The organization may also use the new knowledge to improve its process for completing credit approval by incorporating different processing methods to handle exceptions. Alternatively, a credit approval knowledge base may be augmented to include new frequently asked questions and assist the recently hired personnel who were brought onboard to handle the onslaught of applications. In this way, knowledge management can be used to develop and enhance business processes on an ongoing basis. When considered this way, the use of knowledge management practices around business processes can be thought of as an important element in the redesign and reengineering of business processes

Thus, a business process can be viewed as the nexus around which knowledge sharing and creation can thrive, and knowledge management can be thought of as a strategy of business process redesign. In order to better comprehend and leverage this relationship between knowledge management and business process redesign, it is helpful to understand the evolution of business process redesign over time. The evolution is shown in Figure 1 and is explained below.

During the past 20 years there has been a progression of methods for improving and redesigning business processes as shown in Figure 1. A business process is a coordinated and logically sequenced set of work activities and associated resources that produces something of value to the customer. In the 1980s, business processes were improved through total quality management where the focus was on ways of reducing variability and decreasing defects in process outputs. Information and knowledge about the process were already a part of these redesign efforts, but information technology was in a primitive stage and could not yet be leveraged to the extent it would be later.

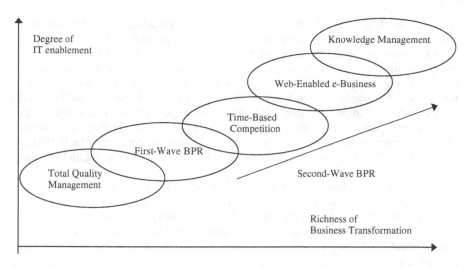

Figure 1. Waves of Business Process Improvement (El Sawy 2001)

In the early 1990s, companies engaged in what might be called "first wave" business process re-engineering (BPR) in which radically innovative cross-functional business processes replaced departmentally compartmentalized tasks. First wave BPR was facilitated by increased use of information technology that structurally changed the way that business processes were carried out. Altering the dynamics of information flows using information technologies was a critical component of this strategy. The richness of the business transformation was many orders of magnitude greater than the incremental approach of total quality management. However, the "slash and burn" downsizing and short-term performance focus taken by many BPR efforts then tainted the term to the point where its use fell out of favor.

A "second wave" of BPR began to take hold in the mid-1990s. Initially, the second wave focused on time-based competition. Cycle-time became the key diagnostic for strategic organizational change as companies transformed processes so that they were fast, focused, and flexible. This too was facilitated by information technologies that continued to augment the richness of the business transformation produced by business process designers. Then, in the late 1990s, the Internet and the World Wide Web captured the attention of companies and they began to focus on cross-enterprise processes. Business process designers considered the implications of these new technologies and realized there was considerable potential to develop or improve cross-enterprise electronic interfaces and collaborative business processes with suppliers, customers, and other partners.

Starting at the turn-of-the-century, we began to see the potential of knowledge management as a strategy for business process redesign. Knowledge management is set of activities aided by information technology infrastructures that are designed to help enterprises more effectively create, capture, synthesize, and deploy organizational knowledge. Knowledge management can also be done around business processes and be used as a strategy for BPR. The knowledge management approach to BPR enabled new ways of enriching, enhancing, and transforming business processes in ways never before practically possible. This was aided by advancements in intelligent information technologies that were capable of effectively handling knowledge management. This enabled process designers to expand the knowledge creation and capturing capacity of business processes. Knowledge management could now also be used to create more effectively the competencies for improving new processes on an ongoing basis. It also opened up new avenues for establishing competitive advantage and creating new value. Processes, process redesign, and knowledge management could now be inextricably interlinked. A business process became a rich nexus for capturing and creating knowledge.

Knowledge management has typically been evoked in the context of seemingly knowledge-intensive business processes that are focused on innovation and creativity and that are relatively unstructured. However, all types of business processes can be a nexus for capturing and creating knowledge whether they are as mundane and physical as the order fulfillment process, or as complex as the customer support process.

Altering information flows around the process changes the nature and design of a business process whether this is status information about the process, the type and frequency of information distributed to people who are exposed to the process, or information that is necessary to produce the outputs of the process. These information flows feed the growth of knowledge and the knowledge creating capacity of the process. Knowledge around a process includes the requisite collective knowledge that participants must have in order to execute the process effectively under various conditions. It can also include knowledge about trends, exceptions, frequently asked questions, improvement ideas, etc. that can be synthesized over time by those who interact with the process or by the process itself. The growth of knowledge is fuelled by the information flows around the business process, and enabled by information technology infrastructures that support the process and its participants. In other words: as information flows, so knowledge grows.

There are also varieties of different information technologies that enable knowledge management. These can perhaps be best identified by understanding the multiple conceptions of knowledge. Knowledge as *object* is a static, repository-oriented view of knowledge that is easily contextualized: it is seen as a pattern of information that produces insight. Related knowledge management technologies center on managing knowledge repositories and the effective reuse of knowledge. Examples include online frequently asked question databases, searchable knowledgebases, and the contents of interactive training applications. Knowledge as *process* is a view that centers on the creation and sharing of knowledge. Knowledge is dynamic, forever-changing, and evolving – as in learning. Related knowledge management technologies include information analysis tools such as text mining tools, search engines enhanced with advanced querying capabilities, and discussion board technologies. Knowledge as *capability* treats knowledge as a competence that is leveraged to execute processes – including execution in new situations. This knowledge can be leveraged by technologies for just-in-time training of production workers, delivery of diagnostic and repair knowledge to technicians in the field, and remote management of end user computing devices.

Information technologies that enable knowledge management and strategies for managing knowledge around a process offer a new set of BPR options. In addition to restructuring workflow for a process and changing the information flows around it, we can also redesign it by changing the knowledge management capabilities around it.

3   Knowledge Management Strategies for Redesigning Business Processes

Enterprises can now leverage knowledge management technologies to increase their capability to learn faster through processes. In an environment characterized by rapid and accelerating change, the enterprise that can learn the fastest will have the competitive advantage. For example, the enterprise that is learning faster is more quickly understanding the changes in customer requirements and competitive market conditions; it is accelerating the creation of valuable production expertise; and it is rapidly learning how to do business with new partners. The need for such capability has been identified through work on the knowledge value spiral by Housel and Bell (2001). The strategies that we address in this section are aimed at achieving this goal of learning faster by constructing knowledge management systems around processes to: a) increase their knowledge creating capacity, b) enhance their capacity to create value, and c) make them more learningful (i.e., better able to learn).

Redesigning a business process involves more than restructuring the workflow. It also involves changing the information flows around the business process and changing the knowledge management capabilities of the process. In this dynamic environment, business professionals need to learn how to describe, analyze, diagnose, and redesign business processes using robust methodologies and tools. In addition, they must learn to leverage the collected intellectual assets that surround the process. Information technologies that enable new ways of carrying out these knowledge-intensive business processes include group technologies for collaboration, search engines and data mining tools, and adaptive databases. In addition, people – both those who execute processes and customers of processes – can obviously play an important role.

Three process redesign principles and associated tactics provide insight into how an enterprise can harness the collected intellectual assets around a process using knowledge management technologies. These principles and tactics enable the knowledge creation capacity of a business process to expand and to enable faster learning. **Principle 1: Analyze and Synthesize** tells us to augment the interactive analysis and synthesis capabilities around a process to generate additional value. **Principle 2: Connect, Collect, and Create** calls for all who touch a process contribute to growing intelligently reusable knowledge around that process. **Principle 3: Personalize** recommends making the process intimate by learning and using the preferences and habits of participants. By implementing these knowledge management strategies and tactics around a process, the enterprise can take advantage of collected expertise to create, capture, deploy, share, preserve, and reuse knowledge intelligently.

The first principle, **Analyze and Synthesize**, tells us to add analysis capabilities through software and intelligent information feeds that generate knowledge. This knowledge can become a major part of the deliverable to the customer of the process. As a result, both the executors and the customers of the process can become more knowledgeable about the process and its results. Over time, this knowledge may be used to improve the process to create better or more valuable outcomes. This tactic is especially applicable in knowledge-intensive processes when the value proposition to the customers of the process is increasingly based on providing good advice or enabling customers to make intelligent decisions. This tactic is especially powerful in the provision of complex products and services. Examples of the analyze and synthesize principle in action include: *"what-if"* capabilities that enable users of a process to analyze decision options; *"slice-and-dice"* data analysis capabilities used to detect patterns; and *"intelligent-integration"* capabilities that cross and combine multiple information sources.

The airline reservation process used by customers of Travelocity, the web-based travel agency, takes advantage of the "analyze and synthesize" principle. Customers can perform what-if analysis by varying itinerary parameters to see what effect changes will have on ticket fees. Travelocity also offers information from other information providers to help travelers plan. For example, a Travelocity customer can access perform a "destination check" to determine whether a destination aligns well with the travelers personal interests. This service is available because of intelligent-integration with VacationCoach, Inc. a personalized travel planning company that offers its clients instant, expert, objective advice about vacation and weekend getaway destinations.

The second principle, **Connect, Collect, and Create**, calls for increasing the level of participation by everyone who is involved in the process. The ability to grow intelligently the knowledge around and through a process can be enhanced when both executors and customers of the process are actively engaged in identifying best practices, sharing tips, and otherwise interacting to improve subsequent executions of the process. Eventually, the learning that results can be used to change further the fundamental design of the process. Companies are experimenting with a variety of methods from the simple to the complex to achieve this. *Frequently asked questions* (FAQ) shared among those who perform a process represent a simpler approach. *Expertise maps* and *"Yellow Pages"* related to the process can also help. Some organizations are even creating *communities of practice* around processes. Building *knowledge repositories* that can be reused to enhance the performance of the process represents a more complex technical solution. *Embedded knowledge-sharing spaces* for interactive dialogues take this technology-supported approach even further.

The traveler advice section of Travelocity includes a knowledge sharing space in the form of message boards. Travelers booking tickets to a destination can post questions or read what other travelers have to say about an area. Hundreds of messages are posted for cities like London, Paris, and New Orleans. Frequently asked questions lists are abundant as well. Photo and video galleries, maps, and historical weather information are all available to the interested reservation-making customer or prospect. These value-adding services are the result of the investment in knowledge management technologies and implementation of the principle of connect, collect, and create.

The third principle, **Personalize**, recommends increasing the capabilities to learn about the preferences and habits of the executioner and customers of the process as a way to improve execution and outcomes. With a knowledgebase containing process participant profiles and preferences, subsequent process executions can be personalized with respect to task sequence and outcomes. By taking advantage of knowledge about process preferences and habits, the enterprise can add value for process participants and increased process speed on subsequent executions. Taken together, this knowledge may also be used to provide new process offerings and redesign the process. Tactics for implementing the personalization principle include *tracking personal process execution habits*, constructing *dynamic profiles*, triggering *alternate processing rules* based on prior execution patterns and dynamic profiles, and use of *automatic collaborative filtering* techniques.

Barnes&Noble.com, one of the largest web-based booksellers, uses collaborative filtering software from Firefly to generate additional sales and create more value for the customer. For example, after a customer profile is established, the software matches information from the profile with similar customer profiles using statistical association techniques and it can then make personalized book recommendations. This is accomplished by using purchasing data from multiple customers to inform a customer that others who bought book X (that the customer is inquiring about or has recently purchased) also bought books A, B, and C. The bookseller also tracks habits and preference for shipping and payment so that customers can easily pay and ship in their customary fashion; of course other options are also available but the process is dynamically configured to ease selection and processing in the fashion predicted by the customer's profile.

Advances in information technologies, and knowledge management in particular, are enabling business transformation on a scale and of a quality never before imagined. Consequently, business process re-designers are finding that they must learn new ways to build systems and processes. The new redesign heuristics include those that center on increasing the knowledge creating capacity of the process. These heuristics are useful for both the highly structured clerical and production work that has been subject to previous business process redesign and to the re-engineering of knowledge work that is less well defined, more fluid, and less likely to be repetitive. Each of the principles presented here contribute to increasing the knowledge creating capacity of a process, enhancing the capacity of the process to create value, or making the process more learningful.

4   Cases for Application of Knowledge Management to E-Business Processes

Case studies from Merrill Lynch, DaimlerChrysler, and Virgin help illustrate the three principles for knowledge management for business process. While these companies are using multiple strategies, we use each case to highlight a single principle. In this way, we illustrate the ideas in practice in a variety of settings.

4.1   Analyze and Synthesize: Merrill Lynch

Merrill Lynch, a full-service brokerage firm, provides financial advice and asset management services to 5 million brokerage account customers with more than $1 trillion in assets. The company was experiencing increasing pressure from low-cost, flat-fee discount brokerages and Internet trading upstarts such as Charles Schwab & Co. and E*Trade. Using Internet technologies, these relative newcomers were providing unprecedented customer access to transaction processing and investment information. It was clear to Merrill Lynch that in order to compete effectively against this low-cost competition, they needed to better leverage the skilled financial consultants on their staff and provide better full-service value to their customers. Merrill Lynch accomplished this by redesigning its service delivery process, dramatically improving the analysis and synthesis capabilities embedded in the processes used by its financial consultants.

Prior to the redesign, information feeds around the service delivery process were inefficient. Merrill Lynch financial consultants were spending too much time searching for information ranging from customer account data to research reports and market data. While much of this information was available online, the financial consultants often had to navigate across multiple incompatible systems; often, this required use of the several computer terminals arrayed across the consultant's desk. Consequently, financial consultants spent time collecting, synthesizing, and integrating information rather than providing financial advice to their customers. This affected everything from the analyst's ability to evaluate portfolio performance to the assessment of alternative investment options as financial consultants worked multiple individual analyses. Even results of automated analysis were not easily linked together – especially when a client had multiple accounts.

In late 1998, Merrill Lynch implemented their Trusted Global Adviser system – a new IT infrastructure and application system that provides impressive information feeds and analysis capabilities to 17,000 Merrill Lynch financial consultants around the world. The IT infrastructure enables feeds from a variety of systems and media including internal legacy mainframe databases, client/server and Web browser applications, real-time feeds from stock exchanges, e-mail, CNN live TV broadcasts, and Webcasts. Each financial consultant according to their preferences can customize the information feeds. Several information feeds may be viewed simultaneously on one screen in a logically organized, easy-to-interpret, and intuitive interface. The system also enables financial consultants to run "what-if" analysis on a client's portfolio and to see the results of multiple analyses graphically, on one screen, in an integrated fashion. This makes it much easier to know what actions are best given the clients financial goals. Now, the financial consultant is much more efficient, better informed, and better able to advise quickly their client. The redesigned knowledge management-enhanced processes allows the financial consultant to spend more time advising clients, increases the value-added proposition for full-service customers, and results in stronger relationships between Merrill Lynch and its clients.

4.2   Connect, Collect, and Create: DaimlerChrysler Corporation

Chrysler Corporation, now part of DaimlerChrysler, redesigned their automotive design and engineering process for building cars in the early 1990s. Prior to the change, they followed the traditional automotive industry practice in which work was organized around functional "stove pipes" (e.g., design, engineering, manufacturing, or marketing) and components (e.g., engine, body, or power train). After the change, engineers and automotive designers focused on a single type of car platform (e.g. small car, truck, large car, or sport utility vehicle). The reengineered product design process delivered an impressive reduction in product development cycle time. The first car produced with the new platform-oriented approach went from concept to production in 39 months, cutting nearly one year from the previous 50-month execution time.

However, the reorganization of the design and engineering process had some unintended consequences. Design errors were starting to appear more frequently and it was as though Chrysler had forgotten its own practices and procedures for designing and building cars. The company soon realized that when they reorganized into platform-oriented teams, they disintegrated core technical groups and lost the critical mass of peers who had previously shared information and knowledge. For example, people who previously worked in the engineering function on engine components were now scattered around the company in small car, large car, truck, and sport utility car platform teams. No longer did these individuals have access to the same expertise sharing opportunities that they once knew. Therefore, while the automotive design process executed much more quickly, the knowledge creating capacity of the design process suffered. Resolving this problem would require rethinking how knowledge management was integrated into the design process.

In 1996, Chrysler product development made knowledge management a vital priority and embarked on a redesign effort that would involve rethinking both the physical and virtual networks of knowledge related to the design and engineering process. The result is an even faster and higher quality process supported by a knowledge repository that encompasses best practices in the design and engineering of cars. This interactive electronic repository, the Engineering Book of Knowledge (EBOK), is accessible to engineers and automotive designers across all car platforms and enables shared knowledge creation and reuse. It is also part of the company's official design review process.

Using EBOK, an engineer can selectively find the best practice for her particular section of the automobile whether it is customer requirements or information about parts suppliers (including history and comparative performance) or competitor intelligence. In addition, the knowledgebase performs "collect" functions by drawing from various databases including product management systems, CAD/CAM systems, supply and procurement databases, and vehicle test data. Other sources of knowledge depend upon "connect" technologies: Web browser-enabled dialogue and discussion running on Grapevine Technologies as a Notes/Domino application; the use of "electronic sticky notes" for communicating among authors and users of the repository to support or refine content. This collection of resources provides a rich and fertile knowledgebase around the automotive design process. With such a volume of information, it has become essential that EBOK be integrated with the design and engineering process such that the knowledge is intelligently reusable and does not inundated engineers with undifferentiated information.

Recognizing the importance of maintaining high quality within the repository, Chrysler has institutionalized knowledge sharing and collaboration as part of the corporate culture. A set of incentives and procedures for taking best practices, refining them, and entering them into EBOK helps to support "create" aspects of the knowledge management strategy and to ensure that platform teams are working with high-quality information. Functionally organized communities are practice called Tech Clubs help reunite designers and engineers with others in the same area of functional expertise in other platform groups. These Tech Clubs have regular social gatherings for sharing ideas and mentoring. The clubs also work to ensure the quality of knowledge in the repository. They have formal responsibility for governing EBOK policies and assigned authors, editors, and reviewers for EBOK content. In all, seven Tech Clubs (body, chassis, advanced engineering, electronics, interior, power train, and vehicle developments) create, share, and maintain the set of best practices and technical expertise related to the design and engineering processes. In addition, Chrysler has been working through the cultural, liability, and security issues associated with integrating suppliers into the EBOK repository. Although supplier entries currently must be approved by the Tech Clubs before entry into the knowledge-base, they are working harder to redesign the process to make full use of the expertise of suppliers protect the process.

4.3 Personalize: Gymboree Corporation

Gymboree Corporation began as an interactive play program for parents and children. It has evolved into a specialty retailer of high-quality apparel, accessories, learning, and play products for children. Today, in addition to 400 franchised Gymboree Play Program sites in 21 countries, the company operates over 500 retail stores that sell Gymboree brand products. It was also one of the first brick-an-mortar retailers to experiment with online commerce and has clearly leveraged the personalize strategy. "This isn't simply about the Internet. This is about learning as much as we can about our customers' needs and preferences, and using that information to tailor our approach and merchandise to get the most out of those relationships," says Susan Neal, Gymboree's vice president of business development (Blue Martini Software case study).

Online (http://www.gymboree.com), prospective customers begin the personalization process when they select from gender and age group categories to describe the child and product categories like tops, bottoms, accessories, etc. This information allows the customer to begin a process of building outfits using combinations of products that work well together. The Matchmatics® technology that underlies building outfits increases sales revenue through intelligent cross selling and gives the customer an increased sense of confidence that clothing purchases represent money well spent. Gymboree describes this as "Mix, match & multiply the options...so you can create nearly two weeks of outfits from just six separate pieces."

Collected data including information from registration forms, customer account preferences, and clickstreams form a customer profile that helps set the stage for the next execution of a shopping experience. This data is used in conjunction with similar information about other customers to generate e-mail messages that are tailored to the individual purchaser. Upon return to the online store, Gymboree can match personalized marketing promotions with specific customers and the customer experience can be tailored even further. Specific results include a 25% increase in site traffic the day after e-mail messages are sent and 36% higher than average order sizes. By taking advantage of the knowledge that resides in Gymboree's systems, the company can drive repeat business, maximize up-selling and cross-selling, and construct a deeper personal relationship with each of their customers.

5   Linking Knowledge Management and Human Capital around Business Processes

Processes can be redesigned by changing the process architecture and flow, the information technologies that enable the process, the organization structure that houses the process, and the skills, incentives, and performance measures of the people who execute the process. Up to this point in the chapter, we have focused primarily on the structural aspects of knowledge management. We now turn our attention toward people.

We have seen that implementing knowledge management around process can create greater value for process executors, process recipients, and the enterprise. We have argued that the newly created value results from the design of the process and the knowledge management infrastructure around the process. In this section, we explore the role of human capital in such processes. Human capital is the knowledge, skills, and abilities embedded in individuals. Human capital can also be managed for process advantage.

We focus on three strategies for human capital management in the context of business processes and knowledge management systems: 1) the transfer of knowledge from the individual to the enterprise, 2) the transfer of knowledge from the enterprise to the individual, and 3) the exchange of knowledge among multiple individuals and the enterprise.

We can think of each execution of a process as an instance of the process. By capturing information about what triggered the process, how the process executed (e.g., the sequence and timing of tasks), and the outcome(s) of the process, a knowledge management system can obtain the raw data necessary to reconstruct the process under the same conditions. For example, a customer calls a technical support center with symptoms of a problem; the process directs the technical support representative (TSR) to enter symptoms into the knowledge management system and the trigger is captured. As troubleshooting begins, the TSR applies human capital (individual knowledge), while the process calls on the TSR to inform the knowledgebase of actions taken and results. Upon completion of the call, the process prompts the TSR to enter information about the outcome. In this way, the knowledge management system captures the raw data necessary to execute a similar instance of the process. Over time, as the enterprise obtains more data about individual instances, the knowledge of individuals involved in the process is transferred to the enterprise. By the design of the process, the knowledge management system transforms human capital into intellectual capital.

Subsequent instances of the process are opportunities to create more intellectual capital or to share existing intellectual capital stored in the knowledge management system with individuals involved with the process. For example, many call center systems now provide callers with expected wait time before a call in answered. This information – based on prior call data, the number of calls in the queue, and the nature of calls in process – can help the caller manage activities during the call wait time to more productive ends. Now suppose the call reaches a TSR who does not know how to solve the caller's problem (i.e., does not have the necessary human capital). The TSR can draw upon the enterprise's knowledgebase for assistance. This results in a transfer of knowledge from the enterprise to the individual and results in a transformation of intellectual capital to human capital. Over time, we would expect that both the level of intellectual capital and the level of human capital would grow.

The exchange of knowledge among multiple individuals and the knowledge management system offers the potential for creating new knowledge and for developing process innovations. It also offers an interesting opportunity to simultaneously protect the enterprise from the effects of turnover and increase the value of employees to other employers. The turnover protection is the result of the transfer of individual knowledge to the enterprise so that when an individual quits, their human capital does not exit the enterprise entirely (Josefek and Kauffman, 2001). Conversely, the availability of the knowledgebase to the individual represents an opportunity for the individual to gain the knowledge of the enterprise. Once learned by the individual, that knowledge, now human capital, is under the control of the individual and can exit the organization when the individual quits.

By considering human capital as well as structural aspects of knowledge management, we can further enhance the value creating potential of business processes. Using business processes as a platform creates a context within which the relationship between knowledge management and human capital can be better understood in a more concrete way.

6   Emerging Issues and Future Directions

The chapter has examined knowledge management as a strategy for redesigning business processes, and has shown through various examples and case studies how business processes can be conceived as being a nexus of knowledge. The notion of business process as nexus suggests a number of emerging issues and future directions for both practice and research:

1. Exception Processes as Knowledge Intensive Foci: Business processes are becoming increasingly complex. For example, typical day-to-day supply chain processes, such as procurement or order management in e-business that are executed repeatedly, can include hundreds of activities and contingencies, as well as associated information flows and knowledge management. Large complex processes with hundreds of repeated executions and multiple customers and suppliers are likely to generate a large number of exceptions when conditions around process execution change or cannot be handled normally. This brings to the foreground a key process redesign question: how do we best design business processes in situations where a large number of exceptions is very likely to occur while the process is being executed? Dealing effectively with exceptions in complex processes is important as they are typically extremely expensive when compared to routine processing. Consequently, they need to be minimized and prevented from occurring as much as is possible. However, they are also the source of much knowledge and provide opportunities for learning about changes in the environment, in the requirements of customers of the process, and for unearthing problems and opportunities with the process. These opportunities may be taken advantage of by having effective knowledge management around the processes. One intriguing process redesign thought that is starting to be implemented in practice suggests that the exception processing itself should be designed as a separate process. This approach results in two processes: a simple process that maps the typical way the process works under normal conditions, and a separate exception process that captures both identified and non-identified exceptions that should only occur infrequently. The logic of the separation is that the two processes are structurally and inherently different and should be treated as different. The exception process is much more knowledge-intensive, involves heavier information exchange, is generally much more costly, and may require very frequent redesign as new exceptions occur. With this approach, the exception process will become an intensive nexus for knowledge management solutions and practices.

2. Expanding the Bounds of Knowledge Management around Processes: The increase of e-business activities between enterprises is increasing the focus on inter-organizational business processes and supply chains. The idea of a business process as the nexus of knowledge extends to supply chains as well. Knowledge management across supply chains brings with it a host of issues that need to be more carefully examined. These include understanding knowledge intermediation roles around supply chain processes, understanding knowledge sharing incentives between enterprises and how they can be formed around common business processes, and the design of information systems for enhancing cross-enterprise knowledge management.

3. Managing the Half-Life of Knowledge around Business Processes: As changes occur in the business environment within which a process operates, there is a risk that the existing process will become misaligned and consequently less effective. These environmental changes occur when for example customer requirements change, related processes change, inputs to the process change, or the availability of resources around the process change. These changes can cause degradation in the usefulness of existing knowledge around the process. The greater and faster the changes, the shorter will be the half-life of knowledge around the process, and the greater will be the need to purge and unlearn knowledge that is no longer relevant. A variety of questions arise as to how to identify knowledge that reached the end of its useful life, how to remove that knowledge from repositories related to the process, as well as how to train people to unlearn. Practices that can help manage the half-life of knowledge phenomenon may include building-in early sensing mechanisms into process designs, devising real-time ways of capturing changes, and developing adaptive knowledge bases. This will become a critical issue in knowledge management for both practice and research.

7   Conclusion

Our understanding of the interplay between knowledge management and business process redesign will continue to develop as enterprises seek new ways of redesigning their business processes in a world of rapid learning and constant change. Knowledge management will increasingly be seen as an activity that can be intimately linked and grounded in the execution of business processes, and business processes will increasingly be seen as a nexus of enterprise knowledge.

References

El Sawy, O. A. and G. Bowles, "Redesigning the Customer Support Process for the Electronic Economy: Insights from Storage Dimensions," *MIS Quarterly*, December, 1997.

El Sawy, O A., *Redesigning Enterprise Processes for e-Business*, New York: McGraw-Hill Publishing, 2001.

Housel, T. and A. Bell, *Measuring and Managing Knowledge*, New York: McGraw-Hill, 2001.

Josefek, R. A. and R. J. Kauffman, "Separation Thresholds, Retention Frontiers, and Intervention Assessment: Human Capital in the Information Technology Workforce," University of Southern California Working Paper, 2001.

CHAPTER 23

The Partnership between Organizational Learning and Knowledge Management

Alex Bennet[1] and David Bennet[2]

[1] U.S. Department of Navy Deputy Chief Information Officer for Enterprise Integration
[1] Co-Chair, Federal Knowledge Management Working Group
[2] Chairman of the Board and Chief Knowledge Officer, Dynamic Systems, Inc.

This chapter examines the interdependent relationship of learning and the emerging discipline of knowledge management (KM). Following a clarification of definitions, the common ground is explored in terms of structure, strategy, technology, leadership, and environment. Specific areas of intersection addressed include individual learning and KM; learning and communities of practice; learning and systems thinking, and learning and flow. A learning continuum is presented to illuminate the relationship between learning and the environment as change drives new knowledge needs.

Keywords: Adult Learning; Communities of Practice; Double-Loop Learning; Flow; Learning; Learning Continuum; Organizational Learning; Systems Thinking

1 Introduction

Learning and knowledge go hand in hand. It took several hundred years for the most advanced nations of the world to move from agricultural to industrial to information-driven economies that continue to challenge organizations to improve performance. During the past decade the new field of knowledge management (KM) has generated excitement and achieved increased visibility for its potential to leverage the newly recognized asset we call knowledge and by doing so, bootstrap organizational effectiveness. During this same decade, the notion emerged that organizations can learn and from that learning create competencies that lead to competitive advantage and agility.

Because KM is a relatively new field, there is still a lot of trial-and-error learning taking place. Nevertheless, KM has developed a number of successful processes and demonstrated its value to many firms as they struggle to understand and respond to threats and opportunities rising from a turbulent environment. Some examples of successful KM processes are knowledge acquisition, knowledge sharing, and knowledge audits. While individual and organizational learning have long been recognized as essential in a changing environment, the concept of organizational learning in support of knowledge management is new. This paper focuses on that relationship. As in most new fields of inquiry, there is little agreement on the meaning of key concepts and terms in knowledge management. After suggesting useful working definitions for some of the basic concepts such as knowledge, knowledge management, and organizational learning, we address organizational learning in a KM context and the role that learning plays in contributing to long-term organizational performance.

2 Working Definitions

2.1 Data, Information and Knowledge

To gain insight into the relationship of organizational learning and knowledge management, it is useful to start with a careful interpretation of knowledge. We are in close agreement with Sveiby when he takes knowledge to be the capacity to act. (Sveiby, 1997) For us, knowledge is best understood as the capacity to take *effective* action, with the recognition that capacity includes both potential and actual ability. Knowledge can therefore be in a person's mind and/or in his or her implementation of the right action in a given situation. That is, the action is effective when it produces the anticipated and desired results. Many of the ideas normally considered to make up knowledge (data, information, facts, truths, concepts, theories, judgment, intuition, insight, experience, predictability, etc.) contribute to creating the understanding and ability needed to take effective action. This means that knowledge exists only in, and can be created by, the human mind. Because individuals, teams and organizations all may have the capacity to take effective action, they can all possess knowledge. Teams and organizations may have collective knowledge (both potential and actual) and therefore be capable of taking actions that an individual could not take.

While knowledge emphasizes understanding and sense making (the "why and how"), information is more awareness of something (the "who and what"). Similar to Davenport and Prusak, we consider information a message meant to inform and communicate to a receiver. Information can be stored, manipulated and shared through hard and soft networks. (Davenport and Prusak, 1998). Data can be understood as raw numbers, markers, or indicators and may provide the "where and when." Admittedly these distinctions are imperfect, albeit useful.

2.2 Knowledge Management

Knowledge management is the systematic process of creating, maintaining and nurturing an organization to make the best use of its individual and collective knowledge to achieve the corporate mission, broadly viewed as sustainable competitive advantage or achieving high performance. The goal is for an organization to become aware of its knowledge, individually and collectively, and to shape itself so that it makes the most effective and efficient use of the knowledge it has or can obtain. By management we do not mean control in the sense of strong authority and direction. This style of management fails with knowledge because no one can control another person's mind – where the knowledge is. Instead, managers must first set examples through leadership, management, and personal behavior. Then they must strive to create and nurture a culture and an infrastructure that stimulates workers to create, use, and share their knowledge and that also supports their freedom to act effectively over a broad range of situations. When an organization lives in a turbulent, unpredictable, and challenging world, it must also be a learning organization, capable of handling change, uncertainty, and complexity. That is, the culture and infrastructure must be such that individuals and groups of individuals can and will continuously question their beliefs in order to create and apply their new knowledge to achieve desired goals and objectives.

2.3   Organizational Learning

The term organizational learning may refer to individual learning within the organization, the entire organization learning as a collective body, or anywhere in between these extremes. However, most organizational learning refers to either team learning or the entire organization-level learning. Of course, individual learning, or learning in small or large groups, or as an entire organization may be needed for the firm to possess the requisite knowledge to take effective action. From a knowledge management perspective, all levels of learning are important and all must be nurtured and made a natural part of culture. To date, most of the KM emphasis has been put on locating, creating, and sharing knowledge. For this reason, we consider organizational learning to refer to the capacity of the organization to acquire or generate the knowledge necessary to survive and compete in its environment. However, there is an important distinction between individual learning and team/organizational level learning. Individual learning is a cognitive or behavioral activity between an individual and his/her environment, whereas in teams or organizations, learning is a collective process dependent upon relationships and interactions among individuals such that learning occurs primarily through the interaction of the participants.

While individual learning is achieved by study, observation, cognition, experience, practice, and developing effective mental models in the mind, organizational learning (being primarily a social versus a cognitive activity) occurs when groups learn to interact, share their knowledge, and act collectively in a manner that maximizes their combined capacity and ability to understand and take effective action.

Organizational learning requires a sharing of language, meaning, objectives, and standards that are significantly different from individual learning. When the organization learns, it generates a social synergy that creates knowledge, adding value to the firm's knowledge workers and to its overall performance. When such a capability becomes embedded within the organization's culture, the organization may have what is called a core competency. These are usually unique to each organization and can rarely be replicated by other firms. The knowledge behind a core competency is built up over time through experiences and successes. It rests as much in the relationships and spirit among the knowledge workers as in the sum of each worker's knowledge.

Because individuals create organizations, it is they who establish the standards, processes, and relationships that enable team and organizational learning. But organizational learning is more than the sum of the parts of individual learning. For example, when individuals leave, effective KM will enable the organization to retain its corporate knowledge, that is, the knowledge that comes from the experience, cooperation, and collaboration of its employees.

Some of the specific ways that organizations learn include: Single-Loop, Double-Loop, Deutero, and strategic learning. Single-loop learning (SLL) occurs when mistakes are detected and corrected, and then organizations carry on with their present policies and goals. Double-loop learning (DLL) occurs when, in addition to detection and correction of errors, the organization is involved in the questioning and modification of existing norms, procedures, policies, and objectives. DLL involves changing the organization's knowledge base or organization-specific competencies or routines (Argyris and Schon, 1978).

Deutero-learning (DL) occurs when organizations learn how to carry out single-loop and double-loop learning. DDL and DL are concerned with the why and how to change the organization, while SLL is concerned with accepting change without questioning underlying assumptions and core beliefs. SLL may prevent DLL from occurring. In order to encourage the deeper learning, organizations must move away from mechanistic structures and adopt flexible and organic structures. This requires a new philosophy of management that encourages openness, self-reflection, and the acceptance of error and uncertainty. Adopting a bottoms-up or participatory approach can encourage DLL. There is often a difference between what people say (espoused theory) and what they practice (theory in use).

Strategic learning is defined as "the process by which an organization makes sense of its environment in ways that broaden the range of objectives it can pursue or the range of resources and actions available to it for processing their objectives" (Mason, 1993).

3   The Common Ground

In an organization where understanding and the ability to take effective actions are major challenges because of the organization's environment or the nature of its work, both knowledge management and organizational learning become critical factors in its long-term survival. In fact, these two fields are so important that they must become embedded within the organizational philosophy and culture such that they are continuous, widespread, and mostly invisible; that is, such that they are found in the habits, norms, and expectations of the workforce, managers and leaders of the organization. To the extent that such an ideal can be achieved, knowledge management and organizational learning will be interdependent and inseparable, but not identical. To understand this relationship we explore a number of characteristics of organizational learning and knowledge management and see how they naturally complement and reinforce each other.

In the current and future environment of business, the major challenge relates to finding, creating, or developing *understanding and meaning* of the complex events and situations arising from an uncertain, complicated, and rapidly changing world. When major paradigm shifts occur in an organization's environment, or within its own strategy or vision, the organization may face its ultimate challenge: finding a new self-image, giving up current doctrine, and replacing strongly held beliefs with ones that more accurately represent the new reality. Thomas Kuhn, Chris Argyris, and others have noted the great difficulty organizations have when confronted with the need to rethink their basic assumptions and beliefs because of rapid shifts in their landscape. This is precisely where organizational learning is put to its greatest test and where knowledge management finds its reason for being. It is not easy to share knowledge; but it is even harder to give up old practices and beliefs that have worked well in the past. As noted above, this requires double-loop learning. KM, focusing on organizational mission, strategy, and vision, should be able to detect changes in the outside world. Organizational learning, then, has the challenge of identifying the new learning that will succeed and replacing the old knowledge with the new.

Ideally, one would like to embed organizational learning within a knowledge management program in support of KM processes. To achieve this there would need to be a knowledge network of workers, managers, and leaders supported by an infrastructure of technology and processes, with an organizational structure of collaborating teams and a culture of learning and sharing. This combination would significantly improve the organization's ability to change its learning (and unlearning) rate. This would result in the organization's ability to provide rapid internal adjustments that allow it to quickly change in response to external demands. Such an organizational agility is the result of close collaboration between knowledge management and organizational learning efforts.

Organizational memory can be made of both hard data (such as numbers, facts, figures, reports and other documents and rules) and soft information and knowledge (such as expertise, experiences, anecdotes, critical incidents, stories, artifacts, context information, details about strategic decisions, and tacit knowledge). Most firms have information systems such as inventory control, budgetary, and administrative systems that store and retrieve hard data or facts, but many do not capture the softer information. Ideas generated by employees in the course of their work are often quickly forgotten, yet they can be captured through explicit narratives stored electronically for future reference.

Firms are increasingly focusing on the concept of organizational learning to increase their competitive advantage, innovation, and effectiveness. Organizational learning is accelerated when a firm, through knowledge management, creates a common knowledge repository, identifies and codifies competencies and routines, including acquiring, storing, interpreting, and manipulating information from within and external to the organization. Knowledge management, through knowledge sharing processes, leverages both individual and organizational learning. By improving the quality and speed of communication and the understanding of problems and changes surrounding the organization, organizational learning and knowledge management jointly increase the quality of decisions of the organization and the effectiveness of their implementation.

Organizations learn to increase their adaptability and efficiency during times of change. Learning is a dynamic process that manifests itself in the continually changing nature of organizations, as exemplified by innovation, collaboration, culture shifts and high morale, especially during times of uncertainty and external challenge. Both knowledge management and organizational learning use knowledge generation and knowledge sharing as foundation elements. To be successful, these capabilities require a high level of attention to human factors: roles and responsibilities, experience, motivation, self-image, respect and trust, honesty and integrity and the quality of interpersonal relationships throughout the firm. Since much of our knowledge is tacit, existing within our memories and unconscious mind and not easily articulated, its development and sharing is very much a social process (Nonaka and Takeuchi, 1995).

In today's rapidly changing, erratic, and increasingly complex environment, knowledge creation, acquisition, and application through continuous learning are likely to be the only solution to survival and excellence. Organizational learning is contingent on a number of factors such as leadership, structure, strategy, environment, technology, and culture. Knowledge management hopes to create and nurture these same factors to make optimum use of the organization's knowledge. Looking at several of these factors will allow us to see the close relationship between knowledge management and organizational learning.

3.1 Structure

Structure represents the set of arrangements among the resources of the organization. The resources may be people, facilities, technological, financial, or conceptual. How these resources are related to each other, and especially their influence on human culture and human relationships, influences a firm's self-image, its beliefs about the external world, and its ability to learn and change. Whether a firm lives in denial of external change or embraces that change and, through learning, strives to adapt or influence those changes is heavily influenced by both structure and culture. The increasing emphasis of many firms on information management rather that classical capital management can be seen from Strassman's estimate that "corporations throughout the developed world are devoting between four and ten times the resources to information management than are deployed for industrial-age capital management."

Hierarchical, controlling structures by their very nature tend to prefer stability and minimize the learning and close collaboration needed to meet significant change or paradigm shifts. Loose structures (even hierarchical) that have a culture of sharing and collaboration can often facilitate learning and allow the freedom to change. However, they must also have clear direction and coordination, otherwise the resulting actions will be diverse and the lack of focus may make them unable to support major organizational objectives. Organizational learning can occur for all the wrong reasons, but it may be incapable of providing value to the firm. Here is where a knowledge management effort that creates and manages a structure to correlate the learning and concomitantly focus the application of that learning can pay big dividends. KM can do this by integrating corporate strategy, vision, and structure, using knowledge as the common denominator and corporate vision as the guidepost. However, too much limitation on knowledge focus can create an inability to respond to surprises and major environmental paradigm shifts.

Unless deliberately provoked, most organizational structures tend to become rigid over time. To prevent such rigor mortis, and to keep the workforce flexible and open to personal and professional change, organizational learning and knowledge management need to encourage and make use of flexible and changing structures, at the same time retaining the capacity to focus and correlate local knowledge and activities. Policies such as moving people around to broaden their experience and revitalize their challenges, continuously bringing new people into the organization at all levels, and deliberately changing organizational relationships will catalyze and perpetuate both individual and organizational learning. Encouraging open communications, getting both managers and workers to constantly challenge basic assumptions, and supporting prudent risk taking and team collaboration will encourage a culture that nourishes and updates the organization's knowledge, ergo its effectiveness. From a measurement view, the only true measure of effectiveness of organizational learning and knowledge management is how well the organization meets its current and strategic objectives — the true bottom line of the firm. This will require a line of sight from the organization's policies, decisions, and actions to its organizational learning and knowledge management efforts to its overall performance.

3.2 Strategy

Strategic applications of information systems for knowledge acquisition can take two forms: Capabilities for assimilating knowledge from the outside (such as competitive intelligence systems acquiring information about other companies in the same industry) and capabilities for creating/generating new knowledge from the reinterpretation and reformulation of existing and newly acquired information (such as executive information systems or decision-support systems). They can also be environmental scanning and notification systems and intelligent and adaptive filters.

Learning is stimulated both by environmental changes and internal factors in a complex and iterative manner. An organization's strategy influences learning by providing a limit or focus to decision-making and a framework for perceiving and interpreting the environment. In turn, the strategic options chosen will depend on the unique history, culture, and learning capacity of the organization. Such causal loops are widespread within organizations, demonstrating why it is so difficult to change organizational behavior and mindset. Knowledge management, by providing a systems-wide perspective that can affect all parts of the firm, may initiate change in the perception of knowledge and learning and in their roles in improving organizational performance. By making multiple changes throughout a firm, it is possible, but never certain, that the above-mentioned closed causal loops can be modified in such a way that employee behavior becomes redirected toward learning and knowledge application. For example, a knowledge management effort might change the technology, the communication networks, the physical spaces, the questions asked by policy makers, and the expectations of employees—all changed in a way that would encourage and facilitate learning, collaboration and the awareness and respect for knowledge and its role in the organization.

3.3 Technology

The influence of information systems, in particular, can be considered two-fold: Direct influence and indirect influence. Information systems can indirectly influence organizational learning by affecting contextual factors such as structure and environment, which in turn influence learning. They can also directly influence the organizational learning process. The introduction of information systems flattens the structure of the organization and promotes greater dissemination of information to all individuals. Through the Internet, intranets, communities of practice, communities of interest, groupware, etc. anyone in the corporation can talk to anyone else, almost at any time. These open, informal networks and multi-paths serve to partially equalize positional influence and emphasize the value of information and knowledge. These equalizers, if used effectively, will facilitate the evolution of the organization's culture toward learning and knowledge management objectives. The information technology should be low-cost, support low-friction information and knowledge transfer and, over time, become an invisible part of the infrastructure.

Through the increased availability of information and the sharing of that information, the organization becomes more informed, flexible and organic. Information systems go beyond automating to "informating." In an informated organization, the focus of control shifts from managers to workers, who are now empowered with all the information required for their effective performance. A number of current technology trends will help the organizational discernment and discrimination problem. Discernment and discrimination are elements of the organization's filtering process. Discernment is the ability to differentiate the meaning and value among multidimensional concepts; and discrimination is the ability to choose those things upon which the organization needs to focus.

Technology is moving beyond expert systems (which make logical inferences based on a fixed set of rules) to systems that combine the use of embedded textual information with human cognition and inference to maximize the decision-making and interpretation processes needed to understand and act upon messy, complex situations. Technologies such as network publishing on the Internet and the information superhighway can facilitate the creation of organizational repositories. These repositories not only capture formal documents such as training manuals, employee handbooks, training material, etc., but also informal experience such as tacit know-how, expertise, experiences, stories, etc., often ignored in organizations. The use of such information systems to support and enhance organizational memory (and learning) by improving the precision, recall, completeness, accuracy, feedback, and review of informal knowledge complements well the human contribution to decision making—creativity, rational thinking, intuition, emotion, and social synergy.

3.4 Leadership

The essential function of leadership is to provide direction, build an organization's culture, and shape its evolution. Leaders must shape the design of the organization's structure and policies to best fulfill its corporate mission. To do this, they must model desired behavior, communicate the organization's vision and strategy and insist on effective implementation of requisite policies and procedures. Organizational learning also requires commitment from executives for a long-term process with adequate budget and resources. Organizational culture (beliefs, ideologies, values, and norms) and the amount of resources (money, facilities, people, and ideas) heavily influence the quality and quantity of learning.

3.5 Environment

Learning organizations treat competition as a means of learning, because competition enables organizations to compare their own performance with others in the industry and learn from that exercise. Through knowledge sharing, learning results as the organization interacts with its environment. Knowledge management looks at the external environment as a source of knowledge and as a testing ground for its understanding and interpretation of itself and the outside world. As part of a major feedback loop, the environment presents a standard for measuring the organization's learning; unfortunately, it can also be a harsh taskmaster for organizational mistakes.

4   Points of Intersection

Having addressed the broad areas of structure, strategy, technology, and the environment, we now look at a number of specific areas where knowledge management and organizational learning intersect.

4.1 Individual Learning and KM

Organizational learning is greatly dependent upon individual learning and the competency of the workforce. If the firm has a culture and leadership conducive to organizational learning, chances are that that same environment will also support individual learning. It is not so clear that KM facilitates individual learning, as, to date, many KM efforts have emphasized technology and knowledge sharing rather than individual development. However, the culture of KM closely matches that needed for individual learning. Borrowing heavily from adult learning expert Malcolm Knowles, the main characteristics of adult learners are summarized below (Knowles, 1998).

Adults want to learn more that just data and facts, they are interested in understanding "the why and how" of their information. Because most adults are not closely supervised, they see themselves as autonomous and self-directing. This same self-image becomes particularly strong when they are in a learning environment. Feeling that only they know how best they understand something, they do not want to be told what they need to know and how to learn it in a pedagogical manner; they want to take ownership for their learning. Adults use their prior experience and their mental models to make sense of new information and knowledge. This may prove beneficial or detrimental, depending on the validity of these past experiences. Spending much of their time solving problems at work, adults tend to prefer practical, goal-oriented problem solving in a realistic context versus textbook solutions. Preferably, these problems should relate directly to their current work and interests. Comfortable with work-place conversations, they tend to prefer learning through group discussions and dialogue rather than self-study.

From these learning characteristics it is clear that a successful knowledge management program would provide many of the conditions desired by knowledge workers, and by doing so greatly leverage learning throughout the organization. For example, KM builds a culture of knowledge sharing and open communication, both leading to an environment conducive to adult learning. Communities of practice, teams, knowledge repositories, intermediaries, yellow pages, etc. all support the autonomous worker to meet his/her own learning needs. A somewhat surprising consequence of KM is the awareness and instantiation of the importance and payoff of learning and knowledge in the minds of the organization's knowledge workers.

4.2 Learning and Communities of Practice (CoP)

Communities of practice accelerate learning. The practice of COPs denotes a group with the same work focus, and therefore participants that have much in common in their every-day work lives, including a common language. The community part of COPs denotes a group that has a relationship built on trust and a focus on the open sharing of ideas and best practices. In COPs the creating, learning, sharing, and using of knowledge are almost indivisible. John Seely Brown and Paul Duguid (2000) explained this phenomena: "... talk without the work, communication without practice is if not unintelligible, at least unusable. Become a member of a community, engage in its practices, and you can acquire and make use of its knowledge and information. Remain an outsider, and these will remain indigestible."

Etienne Wenger, a thought leader in communities of practice and formerly of the Institute for Research on Learning, found that group was important to both what people learn and how they learn. Within the group setting of claims processors, Wenger discovered that knowledge, traveling on the back of practice, was readily shared (Wenger, 1998). This same pattern was found from shop floors to professional fields, where scientists, doctors, architects, or lawyers, after years of classroom training, learn their craft with professional mentors. "Here, they form learning communities capable of generating, sharing, and deploying highly esoteric knowledge" (Brown and Duguid, 2000).

Communities can facilitate both single-loop and double-loop learning. Single-loop learning occurs when problems are solved by changing actions or strategies for achieving a desired result, without changing the underlying theory or assumptions about those actions. Focusing on a particular field, communities provide a thought test-bed for creating and sharing better ways of taking actions, developing new processes, tools and methods, and the application of new management ideas. This is *single-loop learning* (Argyris, et al., 1985).

But the open exchange of ideas and interactions among members of the community may challenge the basic theory and belief about how the system works. In other words, when problems arise and never seem to be solved, the underlying theory of how the system works may be wrong. Or, when the environment changes, the system must change to continue to meet its responsibilities. When this occurs, an entirely new understanding of the system's structure and what makes it behave the way it does must be reviewed and a new theory developed. This is *double-loop learning*. It is the most difficult of all because it requires groups of people to change their understanding of their theory of success, to break through their defensive routines to accept and believe that a new theory of action is right and will work.

This is where communities have an advantage. Communities encourage the exchange of ideas, assumptions, and theories that open their members to new ways of seeing situations. The continuous, rapid feedback system of a community provides the opportunity to tie discussions and dialogues to decision results, generating new ways of understanding the system. Within the trusting framework of communities, individuals can observe other's results and rethink their assumptions and theories.

The value of learning in general, and double-loop learning in particular, will be to speed up the acceptance and application of new ideas, techniques, methods, and tools that provide themselves in the workplace. Of equal importance is the full acceptance of new ways of doing business that change roles and relationships among organizations and individuals. Relationships among manager-employee, colleague-colleague, community-community members, government-industry, headquarters-field activities, buyers-users will all change in one form or another. How effective these changes will be depends on the beliefs and actions of the individuals in each area. Learning and change are the primary forces for success because they are absolutely essential for adaptation, experimentation, and innovation. In today's world, every decade and every year we find new technologies, new rules, and new environments which demand new perspectives, new insights, and new actions.

4.3   Learning and Systems Thinking

Systems Thinking and System Dynamics facilitate both individual and organizational learning. Systems Thinking, according to Peter Senge, is an approach to understanding complex systems (such as organizations) that have many elements and relationships (Senge, 1990). Systems Dynamics is the technical side of systems thinking that provides the analytical techniques and the software for computer programming of the fundamental causal relationships within an organization that are identified by informed knowledge workers. Systems Thinking provides a conceptual process and a visual way of describing multiple causality relationships that include both positive and negative feedback loops, as well as time delays and nonlinear influences.

Systems Thinking encourages groups to have dialogues and develop a common understanding of a complex problem within the organization and thereby, learn from each other and become better able to make decisions and implement them. Systems Thinking also helps restructure views of reality by identifying and challenging prevailing mental models and fundamental assumptions and by promoting double loop learning. In the process of understanding how organizations work, Systems Thinking encourages exploration of multiple viewpoints to any problem through dialogue and discussion. It is via such knowledge sharing and creation processes that knowledge management and organizational learning benefit each other.

There is another interpretation of Systems Thinking: being aware of what systems are, what characterizes them, and their general properties. Perspective and viewpoint are often critical to solving problems and understanding situations. A systems perspective permits one to see the organization, external threats, or internal processes as systems with boundaries, elements, relationships, and networks of influence that provide insight and understanding of how the system works and how it will respond to a specific action. Learning by using the system perspective greatly facilitates the development of knowledge of both individuals and groups. It also puts each situation in its true place relative to other systems, permitting more effective priority setting and prediction of knowledge application.

The best organizational learning is distributed throughout the firm such that from a backdrop of continuous learning to meet routine challenges, teams and processes can arise to anticipate and meet fundamental threats and opportunities that challenge the organization. This means that learning must be local and distributed, and it must be both continuous and episodic. These demands may strain knowledge workers and their managers, because they require living with change and uncertainty relative to both what needs to be learned, how fast it must be learned, and how to apply such new knowledge. This highlights the difference between learning and knowledge processes. While there are generic knowledge processes such as knowledge creation, sharing, and storing that may be described in general with some assurance, successful learning processes are mostly local and depend on the history, nature, local culture, and leadership of the firm, and on the learning styles and recent experience of both its knowledge workers and the teams they comprise. Knowledge managers must be sensitive to the locality of effective learning and to the unpredictable nature of many learning situations.

A fundamental requisite to learning is the attitude and motivation of the individual knowledge worker. While knowledge managers may influence individual attitude and motivation, the amount of such influence is limited. Given this limitation, what knowledge managers can do is to support individual learning and organizational learning through the effective nurturing of culture, infrastructure, technology, policies, and personal behavior. In today's changing, uncertain and complex business environment, knowledge organizations must be learning organizations and knowledge managers must therefore recognize and accept the responsibility of building and maintaining an organization that treats learning as a key success factor that consists of the normal KM areas of concern and the individual and group needs and capabilities of knowledge workers as they relate to learning, changing, risk taking, innovation, and courage.

4.4 Learning and Flow

Organizations flourish with the flow of data, information and knowledge; the flow of people across and in and out of the organization; and flow in terms of the optimal human experience. In a learning-centric organization, learning and knowledge that is core to the business of the organization is captured and shared. The more learning is valued in the organization, the better the core knowledge flows and is built upon through innovation, mission performance, and the creation of new knowledge. While each individual is important to this process, it is the continuous flow of knowledge and learning among people that generates organizational learning. This continuous flow is facilitated through the movement of people in and out of networks, communities of practice, and workgroups as they change jobs, change their priorities and interests, and grow in new areas of thought. Even better than teams, this fluid movement of people in and out of communities of practice and networks creates diversity of perspectives and ideas, bringing together new combinations of knowledge and learning that offer ever increasing opportunities for discovering better ways of doing their jobs and achieving their organizational mission.

Considerable work is emerging on the science of knowledge flow within organizations. Nonaka considers knowledge flow through four steps. Because he states that new knowledge is created only by individuals and is necessarily tacit in nature, this flow occurs through a process of *socialization*, with members of a community sharing their experiences and perspectives (Nonaka, 1994). A second flow occurs through *externalization*, where the use of metaphors, stories and dialogue leads to the articulation of tacit knowledge, converting it to explicit knowledge. A third flow occurs through *combination*, where community members interact with other groups across the organization. A fourth flow occurs through *internalization*, where individuals throughout the organization learn by doing and perhaps even through listening to stories are able to create knowledge, usually in tacit form. When all four of these processes coexist, they produce knowledge spirals which result in accelerated organizational learning (Nonaka and Takeuchi, 1995).

Optimal flow is a psychological state identified by Csikszentmihalyi (1990) as one in which an individual, while actively performing some task, looses track of time and easily and naturally makes use of all of his/her experience and knowledge to achieve some goal. Within an organization, these three forms of flow can work together to activate and accelerate both creativity and cohesion of action. High personal productivity, useful dialogue, and knowledge sharing, when coupled with new employees having different perspectives and asking challenging questions, will create an organizational synergy that moves the knowledge-based organization to achieve its best performance.

Although flow and knowledge spirals are knowledge management concepts, one can easily appreciate their power to support and facilitate organizational learning. Although learning is inherently an individual experience, that experience can be significantly influenced to help the individual and the organization learn and create knowledge.

5   The Learning Continuum

John Seely Brown and Paul Duguid (2000) view learning as a social phenomenon. Certainly looking at "social" as of, relating to, or occupied with matters affecting interactions, discourse, and human welfare, we agree fully. The social phenomenon of learning is not only among individuals, but among any individual and the environment, whether that environment consists of people, places, processes or things; whether it is silent or active; whether it is defined in terms of the individual with a negative or positive influence.

Alex Bennet and David Bennet

We have focused on, and talked about the importance of both learning and knowledge management throughout this paper. Indeed, knowledge on the subjects of organizational learning and knowledge management has become increasingly important as a point of focus for the business world driven by the development of the Internet and virtual worldwide access to the exponentially increasing amount of data and information. Because knowledge is situationally dependent (i.e., what is understood as knowledge relates to some specific domain, situation, and context), a changing environment insinuates changing knowledge needs. Learning is the individual and organizational process for creating new knowledge to meet changing environments.

Figure 1 illustrates the learning continuum, ranging from an individual or organization that is highly interactive with its environment, in the flow state, to an individual or organization whose thinking and actions have become locked, or static, and therefore continuously diminishes in effectiveness as the environment changes. For ease of explanation, the model is discussed in terms of organizational learning. As an organization realizes the value of a product or process, it tends to freeze that process or product in time. This occurs for a number of reasons such as the need to train, limited funding, or temporary success. Perceived competitive advantage also causes a locking in as new products/processes move into a mature phase where the focus is on sales and/or implementation. If the organization has healthy feedback loops in place and these are responded to, the organization moves in and out of learning cycles to periodically develop and produce new versions of the product/process.

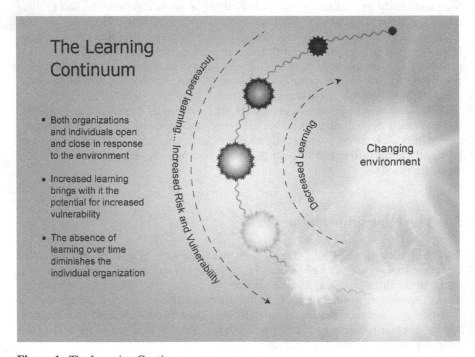

Figure 1. The Learning Continuum

The organization just described sits in the middle of the learning continuum as it markets and implements its process/product, and moves down along the continuum as it receives feedback from its environment, learns from that feedback, and creates an improved version of its product/process. The innovative development environment, discussed in case studies of Apple Computer, lays further down along the learning continuum. (Drucker, 1985) The Apple organization was highly open and interactive with its environment, with minimal locking in of products/processes. The furthest learning point along this continuum represents the state of Flow introduced by Csikszentmihalyi (1990), where there is a fluid exchange among the environment, the organization and individuals within that organization. In the Flow state, autotelic work, work whose purpose lies within the individual and is done for its own sake, is both a goal and a reality.

Moving upward along the continuum, still using an organizational scenario, the organization is achieving enough continuing success with its product/process that it does not recognize the need for change and remains locked into that product/process. In fact, in a large customer base, this success may continue for a number of years (dependent on how rapidly the organization's areas of focus is changing) as front-runners move on to new and better processes and products, followers move in behind them to continue purchasing/using the offered product/process. However, over time, the product/process will diminish in value and the market will look to new ideas and products/processes for satisfaction. When this happens it is usually too late to catch up with alert and more nimble competitors who have continued growing themselves and their products/processes.

Another way to use the learning continuum model is to reflect on the fit between individuals and the organization within which they work. If an organization is locked into a product/process and in the distribution mode, it would be difficult for an individual who operates near a state of flow to flourish. In like manner, for an individual who has locked onto a specific set of beliefs and work habits, it would be difficult to succeed in a learning organization that fluctuates and bounces in response to the environment.

Taking a systems view of relationships among organizations and the people who work within those organizations, to succeed in organizational structures built on the bureaucratic model, it is necessary to have the ability to solidify ideas and slowly work them into the system. Simultaneously, to respond to the fluctuating environment, it is necessary to have the ability to be open to interact with that environment, and learn from it. This points to the need for individuals and organizations to develop a capability to move in and out of learning modes, although that movement along the continuum will be burdened by capacity and culture. Still, the ideal condition is the ability of individuals and organizations to choose where to function on the continuum at a specific time and in a specific situation. It must be noted, however, that there is a limit to the amount of flexibility an individual or organization can achieve. The further an individual or organization moves to either end of the continuum, and the longer he/she/it remains in that mode, achieving a comfort level, the more difficult it becomes to move away from that comfort level; hence, the irony of a learner being unable to learn how to learn. In all things there is a balance, a region within which movement assures strength and stability.

On the other hand, while an organization (or individual) is in an increased learning mode, there is also increased risk and vulnerability. This is due to the large amount of interaction with the environment that provides both negative and positive data and information, and the increased need for greater discernment and discretion. In organizational terms, this may be thought of as the need for increased discrimination capability in a world with porous and permeable boundaries, where a large amount of data and information flows into the organization and much of it is irrelevant or false. *What* the organization learns may be more important than how fast it learns. In fact, an organization may become saturated with learning and fall into the trap of always trying something new without discerning the learning that is applicable to its immediate needs.

The selection and validation competency (discretion and discernment) developed by a high quality knowledge organization can focus learning in the right directions to reduce error signals, confusion, and wasted effort. Recall that knowledge is the capacity to take *effective* action. The word effective is significant because of the inundation of possibilities and the chaotic nature of events in the environment of many extant firms. To learn to take effective action means to learn all of the right things, to unlearn those things that prohibit the right actions, and not fall prey to educated incapacity. Recall that knowledge is the capacity to take effective action and learning provides the continuous creation and updating of knowledge. Taken together, knowledge management and organizational learning provide the foundation for leveraging the full value of the organization's human resources.

6   Final Thoughts

As uncertainty and complexity increase in the future and decisions become more challenging, individual, team and organizational learning, coupled with a strong knowledge management program, offers the best capability an organization can have to change, adapt, and influence its environment in a way that maximizes its performance over time. Within the organization, focused, flexible, and friendly communities will help knowledge workers continually learn and change. By combining the strengths of organizational learning and knowledge management, smart organizations will create cultures, structures, and leadership styles that enable them to scan, perceive, evaluate, anticipate, and take effective action on new, ambiguous, unexpected, and complex threats and opportunities. Achieving such an ideal is as challenging as it is productive.

References

Argyris, C., R. Putnam, and D. McLain Smith, *Action Science,* San Francisco: Jossey-Bass Publishers, 1985.

Bennet, A. and D. Bennet, "Characterizing the Next Generation Knowledge Organization", *Knowledge and Innovation: Journal of the KMCI,* 1,1, 2000, 8-42.

Bennet, D. *IPT Learning Campus: Gaining Acquisition Results through IPTs,* Alexandria, VA: Bellwether Learning Center, 1997.

Bennet, D. and A. Bennet, "Exploring Key Relationships in the Next Generation Knowledge Organization", *Knowledge and Innovation: Journal of the KMCI,* 1,2, 2001, 91-108.

Brown, J. S. and P. Duguid, *The Social Life of Information,* Boston, MA: Harvard Business School Press, 2000.

Csikszentmihalyi, M., *Flow: The Psychology of Optimal Experience,* New York, NY: Harper & Row, 1990.

Davenport, T. and L. Prusak, *Working Knowledge: How Organizations Manage What They Know,* Boston, MA: Harvard Business School Press, 1998.

Drucker, P., *Innovation and Entrepreneurship: Practice and Principles,* Special Edition for the Presidents Association, New York: Harper & Row Publishers, 1985.

Espejo, R., W. Schuhmann, M. Schwaninger, and U. Bilello, *Organizational Transformation and Learning,* New York: John Wiley and Sons, 1996.

Knowles, M., *The Adult Learner,* Houston, TX: Gulf Publishing Company, 1998.

National Research Council, *Learning, Remembering, Believing,* Washington, D.C.: National Academy Press, 1994.

Nonaka, I., "A Dynamic Theory of Organizational Knowledge Creation," *Organization Science* 5, 1, 1994, 14-37.

Nonaka, I. and H. Takeuchi, *The Knowledge Creating Company: How Japanese Companies Create the Dynamics of Innovation.* New York, NY: Oxford University Press, 1995.

Sveiby, K.E., *The New Organizational Wealth: Managing & Measuring Knowledge-based Assets.* San Francisco, CA: Berrett-Koehler Publishers, Inc., 19

Tiwana, A., *The Knowledge Management Toolkit: Practical Techniques for Building a Knowledge Management System,* Upper Saddle River, NJ: Prentice Hall, PTR, 2000.

Wenger, E., *Communities of Practice,* New York: Cambridge University Press

Influences on Knowledge Processing

A primary component of the knowledge management ontology presented in Part I involves factors that influence how knowledge management is practiced in organizations. It identified three major classes of such factors: resource influences, managerial influences, and environment influences. The opening chapters in Part IV of the Handbook on Knowledge Management concentrate specifically on the four categories of managerial influences: measurement, control, coordination, and leadership. The closing chapters deal with influences at a higher, more general, level.

In Chapter 24, Susan Conway discusses the linkage between knowledge management behaviors and performance measures. The basic proposition is that a valid measurement program influences the conduct of knowledge management by promoting productive workflow and accountability and by furnishing a feedback system for improvement. The chapter presents a framework for knowledge management value assessment. It focuses on interfaces between business drivers, work performance, and work behaviors with the intent of demonstrating flows, trends, and changes in work behaviors and recommending behaviors that enhance knowledge worker productivity. Both qualitative and quantitative analyses of work behaviors are discussed.

Just as measurement factors can influence what happens in a knowledge management initiative, so too can control factors related to knowledge quality, availability, privacy, legality, and security. Chapter 25 addresses control issues, pointing out that there are risks and consequences associated with these initiatives. How they are handled impacts the operations and outcomes of an organization's knowledge management episodes. In this chapter, Rodger Jamieson and Meliha Handzic introduce a framework and guidelines for management to contemplate in determining the nature of KM governance to exercise in an organization. A case study is provided for illustration purposes.

Coordination is a managerial influence concerned with designing structure, processes, and incentives for a knowledge management initiative. Along these lines, John Storck and John Henderson present a framework that identifies options for deciding how to leverage knowledge resources in a sustained manner over time. The framework has two dimensions: sensemaking and administration. Design issues for each are discussed and, together, the dimensions give rise to basic strategies for implementing knowledge management initiatives. The authors discuss the application of the framework and the evolution of KM initiatives across strategies.

The fourth, and perhaps penultimate, managerial influence is leadership. The next two chapters deal with connections between leadership and the conduct of knowledge management. In "The Leaders of Knowledge Initiatives," Alex Bennet and Robert Nielson describe results of workshops conducted by the U.S. government-wide Knowledge Management Working Group to define the role and duties of a Chief Knowledge Officer. This includes characterizations of competencies and skills that make these leaders of KM efforts successful, plus learning objectives for knowledge manager certification.

In the "7 C's of Knowledge Leadership," Debra Amidon and Doug Macnamara explain how leadership in the knowledge economy differs from traditional notions. They proceed to posit and discuss seven domains that deserve to be considered for knowledge leadership: context, competence, culture, communities, conversation, *communication, and coaching. The chapter closes with a knowledge leadership litmus test.*

One task of a leader is to build a culture of trust. In Chapter 29, Dianne Ford describes the various types and bases of trust. She then analyses the implications of these for each of several knowledge management processes. She argues that successful implementations of knowledge management initiatives require the promotion of several types of trust in an organization.

Yogesh Malhotra provides a wide-ranging examination of factors that enable and constrain the conduct of knowledge management in today's enterprises. This chapter covers all four categories of managerial influences on KM and considers resource and environmental influences as well. It offers guidelines and suggestions for minimizing the risk of failures in knowledge management systems by meeting challenges related to business and technology strategy, organizational control, knowledge sharing culture, enterprise infrastructure, knowledge representation, managerial command and control, and economic returns. The central contention is that both knowledge harvesting and knowledge creation need to be integrated with each other within a business model to ensure both short term and long term success in doing the right thing.

The ongoing conduct of knowledge management in an organization is greatly influenced by the recognition, sharing, and usage of its own best practices. In "Identifying and Transferring Internal Best Practices," Carla O'Dell and C. Jackson Grayson examine why organizations are interested in transferring best practices, the obstacles they face in doing so, and methods for doing so -- including benchmarking teams, best practice teams, knowledge networks, and internal audits. Each of these approaches is illustrated with examples. The chapter discusses the influence on best practice transfer of such factors as leadership, measurement, culture, and technology. Based on experiences with many organizations, the authors offer seven key lessons for managers of KM efforts.

In Chapter 32, Sven Carlsson examines the issue of how organizations can strategically manage knowledge to enhance performance and achieve sustainable competitive advantage. He develops a conceptualization of strategic knowledge managing in networks that includes both inter-organizational and environmental influences on the conduct of knowledge management. A related framework is presented that gives a process model for strategic knowledge managing. Finally, the chapter provides a discussion of roles that technology can play in the context of knowledge management networks. Part V, which opens Volume 2 of the Handbook on Knowledge Management, *examines technology support for KM in depth.*

CHAPTER 24

Valuing Knowledge Management Behaviors: Linking KM Behaviors to Strategic Performance Measures

Susan Conway

Microsoft Consulting Services, Microsoft Corporation, Redmond, WA, USA

This chapter focuses on the development of quantitative measurement methods to support management policies and practices that drive the growth and development of intangible assets. The central proposition is that a valid measurement program will promote increased productivity through better workflow and accountability. The chapter pays particular attention to the role that human capital and knowledge management data play in that picture. Growing an organization's intangible asset base necessitates resource allocation and the optimization of multiple asset categories along with a sound design and execution of specific management policies and practices. These requirements necessitate a clearly defined measurement method and model that is subscribed to by all parties.

Keywords: Human Capital; Intangible Assets; Knowledge Assets; Knowledge Management; Measurement

1 Introduction

Perhaps the most interesting attribute of knowledge management (KM) is its capability to leverage the ability of organizations to mobilize and exploit their intangible assets—the people, process, technology and the knowledge generated by them. Intangible asset leverage has become far more important and decisive in the knowledge-based economy than investing and managing physical (tangible) assets (Itami, 1987). In an extremely competitive global economy, companies see increasing pressure to cut costs, increase productivity and innovation. John W. Kendrick, George Washington University economist (as cited in Laing, 2000), in his recent study viewing economic investments from 1929 – 1990, demonstrated that business investment trends at the close of the 20th century had reversed themselves with intangible rather than tangible assets consuming the majority of the investment dollars. Kendrick noted that "brick-and-mortar" tangible asset investments are now growing by only around 31 percent whereas business investments in intangible assets are growing by nearly 63 percent.

Managing in this era requires that organizations measure the business value of the investment. "An organization's ability to leverage its content and data management issues, share knowledge to increase employee competency, and use technology to deliver content and infer relationships within data and content will be a major difference between those that thrive in 2001 and those that lag or go out of business" (Rasumus, 2001). Most organizations are acknowledging these economic facts and the realization that they have much to learn about how best to manage and optimizes their investment in human capital. Yet, management receives little, if any, systematic feedback on the economic value of these investments and even less information about how to improve the value produced by such investments. Often, an organization has only an overhead budget line item relating to KM. For KM to become a recognized contributor to business value, methods for identifying, categorizing, and measuring knowledge management behaviors must be established so as to promote accountability and increase productivity.

Knowledge management is concerned with the effect that human capital (people) creates through the utilization of other intangible and tangible assets. Measuring this effect is currently not an established management practice. In developing the framework and measures presented in this chapter, the assumption is made, as visualized in Figure 1, that value is created from the consumption, transformation, production or transmission of an organization's assets. Thus, it is critical to identify and measure the means whereby such processing of corporate assets occurs.

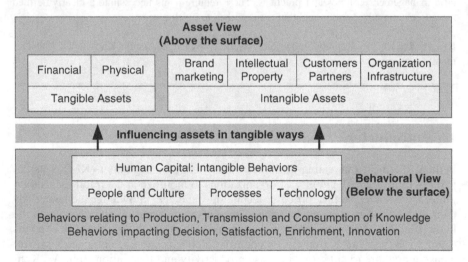

Figure 1. Visualizing Corporate Assets

Industry reviewers, such as Giga Information Group, have estimated that well over half the Fortune 1000 organizations will be involved in some form of KM project in the next three years with the goal of increasing the value of their intangible asset base (information, expertise and/or processes). "Successful organizations will seek and leverage information and knowledge that support strategic initiatives in an integrated fashion, with an emphasis on the relationships and feedback loops between systems, people and processes" (Rasumus, 2000). These knowledge management programs promote, support and enhance the active development of human capital (HC), and the related intellectual property (IP), within companies. Currently, KM measurement is in the experimental stage without solid metrics that relate to bottom line return on investment. Indeed, current accounting practices view human capital activities as an expense without direct relationship to revenue production (Lev, 2001).

Although many companies have been able to make value statements relating to intellectual property (the portion of intangible assets that are visible), they do not have a method to properly value the behaviors that create, maintain, and deploy those assets (as distinct from valuing the assets themselves). Companies ignore the measure of person-to-person (tacit-tacit) and person-to-physical (tacit-explicit) creation and evolution of knowledge within a corporate environment until it produces a tangible output.

Michael Polanyi (1974) referred to *knowledge* as static and social and the concept of *knowing* as dynamic and personal. When explicit knowledge is taken in by an individual it becomes personal *knowing* and subject to change by the mind of the person. Using this strict interpretation, it is easy to understand why companies often confuse repository or library systems (databases and/or file systems designed to electronically track and/or hold intellectual property) with knowledge management programs (that should target the support and promotion of collaboration, as well as the delivery of explicit intellectual property). When this confusion takes place, management tends to count the number of knowledge assets (documents, processes, diagrams, code samples, patents and so forth), but not the ways to create them or their resultant impact on delivered value.

Polanyi presents arguments that demonstrate why this strictly objective (explicit) view of knowledge should be considered too limiting. Some of man's most important knowledge, he might argue, is tacit and very difficult to articulate, good examples of this concept are the knowledge of how to swim or how to judge beauty. Yet, people use such knowledge and even depend on it for their survival (Polanyi, 1974). In business, if companies adhere to the strictly objective view of knowledge, then large portions of the human capital value are left uncounted, unsupported, and often drift away unrecognized.

The current evolution in technology has revealed another layer or middle ground in this discussion— the social cyberspace. This is space where we explicitly exchange tacit knowledge. By viewing intangible assets as having both explicit and tacit components, it is easier to understand why KM reflects a large, uncounted element of value. Closing the measurement loop on the human capital effect will move an organization closer to the goal of producing repeatable and sustainable accountability in this area. The strategic goal of a KM measurement program is to link the development of a clear statement of value linking the human capital component to the intangible asset picture. This chapter provides an overview of a simple and clearly aligned measurement framework designed to help organizations manage and optimize the value they create through their human capital in an online environment. This framework and the associated tools to view KM behaviors in virtual community environments were developed by Microsoft Consulting Services (MCS) and Microsoft Research (MS Research). They are based on a review and synthesis of research, best practices, and innovation in the management of knowledge through the advances in online technology. Specifically, the chapter:

1. Establishes the relationship between intangible asset value generation and human capital,
2. Develops the equation of value derived from the association of human capital (work activities-behaviors of people) to knowledge sources (people and/or intangible assets, such as intellectual property or data), and
3. Presents a measurement model and method for knowledge management initiatives.

2 Background

Organizations need to surface, expose and value intangible assets. To value intangible assets, it is necessary to first define them and then determine how to establish value. As shown in Figure 1, intangible assets are generally composed of, or are driven by people. They are the most complex of corporate assets. To measure the value of these assets, we first need to determine their relationship to other corporate assets and the proposed measurement tools or indicators of value.

Human capital activities, in our model, are seen as a supporting and contributing factor to all explicit forms of assets through the process of *knowing* (the transformation of tacit knowledge into visible assets). Using this taxonomy, a company should target its efforts in knowledge management at increasing the effectiveness of the human capital component. Through a series of related activities and behaviors, people transform, transmit and/or consume tangible/explicit corporate assets in the pursuit of profits. Thus, to determine the best way to increase profitability is to determine which behaviors are most productive when associated with specific activities.

The Knowledge Management Value Assessment (KVA) framework, shown in Figure 2, also highlights the critical insight that interdisciplinary management, demanded by the interdependence of intangible assets, requires a systematic, clearly defined approach. As discussed earlier, the process of *knowing* often involves the blending of experiences and learning with factual (visible) knowledge. This process underscores the concept that knowledge is not private but social. Socially transmitted knowledge is blended with personal experience to create a new manifestation of knowledge.

Sveiby (1997) defines knowledge as the conscious or unconscious capacity to act. Using this definition he later underscores the element of action, which is the capacity to act that can only be demonstrated through action. Through this definition, as with Polanyi's, each person through his/her *knowing*, recreates the knowledge he/she has acquired (Sveiby, 2000). Growing a firm's intangibles thus necessitates resource allocation and the optimization of multiple asset categories along with a sound design and execution of specific management policies and practices. These requirements necessitate a clearly defined vision and model to which all parties subscribe.

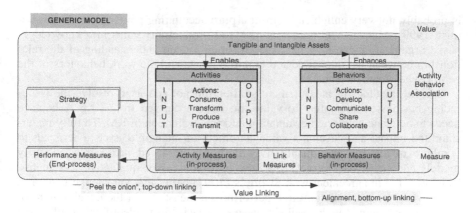

Figure 2. KM Measurement Model Overview

The KVA framework is designed to surface KM initiative results at the operational level as a management information and feedback system. Its goal is to demonstrate the flow, trends, and changes in work activities and recommend behaviors that support knowledge worker productivity. This goal requires identifying tracking metrics deep within the business unit. One cannot universally apply a traditional accounting approach that depends on discrete transactional data to this problem because there is not a simple algorithm that relates the activities performed and the KM related behaviors being measured. Essentially, this chapter develops a measurement methodology for correlating managed knowledge to the business drivers. The proposition is that a valid measurement program will promote increased productivity through productive workflow and accountability.

The KVA framework, described in this chapter, and the related work recently completed by Microsoft Research on the analysis of persistent conversations (Smith, 2001), is focused on the quantitative measurement of the knowledge related behaviors of human capital. Baruch Lev (2001) has identified human capital as the most renewable corporate resource and one of the few resources known that increases when shared. "[Such] intangible or "knowledge" assets are clearly less homogeneous than the physical sort. Although some intangible assets are highly marketable – Cadbury Schweppes, a British food and drink firm, hopes to make a wholly tangible $1.1 billion by selling some of its soft-drink brands to Coca-Cola – others, such as a company's culture, are evanescent." (Economist, 1999) There appears to be general consensus that though this resource has great value, it is one of the more elusive components of intangible assets.

Intangible assets are important not only in the market valuation of a company, but in viewing the way business value is created in a company. Sveiby (2000) notes that "people are seen as the only true agents in business; all tangible physical products, assets as well as the intangible relations, are results of human action and depend ultimately on people for their continued existence" (p.15). The *Economist* points out the need for better accounting of intangible assets when it quotes Bill Gates who states, "Our [Microsoft's] primary assets, which are our software and our software development skills, do not show up on the balance sheet at all. This is probably not very enlightening from a pure accounting point of view" (Economist, 1999). Management accountability and productivity gains in a knowledge-based organization can only be driven through a deep understanding of the relationship between the intangible and tangible assets and the work behaviors of the people who create the value.

Existing methods of measurement studied did not appear to resolve the issues facing businesses attempting to value the benefit derived from KM. A balance needs to be made between the valuation and the evaluation of KM. To fully understand the impact and develop a value statement of intangible assets, one needs to combine qualitative and quantitative methods. Balanced scorecards, maturity models and participant surveys provide good sources of qualitative statements. This model is in agreement with Sveiby's (1997) belief that knowledge generates value when related to bottom line performance measures. In the development of the KVA, we agreed with Sveiby's basic approach to the identification of a few indicators that relate to basic business drivers such as growth, renewal, and efficiency (Sveiby, 1998).

The goal of the KVA is to demonstrate a closer link for management of the specific activities and behavior trends that would, over time, drive increased productivity within their unique business. Further, we sought to develop a method to derive this information via non-intrusive methods that a company can implement in an online KM environment. Quantitative statements with regard to KM continue to be problematic. As demonstrated in the KVA framework in Figure 2, we are seeking to address the need to quantify the activity and work behaviors as they correlate to bottom-line business drivers without putting a direct monetary value on each behavior.

Earlier, we underscored the concept that businesses that neglect the holistic view of their information and knowledge will be at a competitive disadvantage. Successful organizations will seek to leverage information and knowledge that support key business drivers in an integrated fashion. Lev (2001) has called for the creation of quantitative, standardized measures associated with an intangible assets value chain. He lists the links in this chain as internal renewal (reuse); acquired assets; networking; intellectual property (and unstructured explicit knowledge assets); technology; customers; employees; revenue growth from innovation (visible intellectual property); bottom line (relationship to business drivers); and growth options (Lev, 2001).

The KVA model focuses on the interfaces between business drivers (expressed as performance measures), work performance (in terms of activities), and work behaviors (in terms of how people accomplish work). The model utilizes two major categories of knowledge indicators as its base metrics that are then correlated back to the performance measures — behaviors relating to explicit assets and tacit behaviors relating to knowledge exchange/growth. Each category has an abundance of potential indicators depending on the business structure and industry. During the course of this discussion, I use examples from the IT consulting and software industry that Microsoft has studied. The KVA framework supports the proposition that human capital behaviors, and their related operating effects, have a strong impact on the ability to deliver on identified business drivers.

3   KM Value Assessment Framework

In order to develop a quantitative statement, it will first be necessary to clearly define the components of the KVA and what a business might measure. In this section, I present some simple examples of each component of the KVA value model that will form the core of this measurement discussion.

As a business, you have a business model. Within the scope of this business model, you are driving toward certain performance targets that relate to performance measures within the business. You support each business performance measure by one or more strategies that will have deliverables and measurable targets. This performance (or end measure) goal is both the starting and ending point of the KVA. The majority of businesses will have multiple goal statements, such as to increase new patents by 10 percent or increase profit margin on services by 20 percent (see Table 1). Each goal statement will require a unique value model to support it.

Businesses support or implement a performance goal through a set of services or activities within and across groups. Each activity consumes certain input, adds new or modifies content, and produces a certain output. Work behaviors enable the actual activity itself, or performance of it. Activities are often enabled by, or related to, one or more tangible assets (such as working capital, material, machinery and tools), and/or intangible assets (such as behaviors, human capital, information technology, and organizational procedures). We can measure the performance of each activity in terms of cost of consumption, production and transmission. The activity measures are typically the amount of time, effort, and assets required to complete the activity. The quality and delivery of one activity often has a cost impact on other activities. For example, low quality and/or poorly formatted information will increase the effort required to consume the information. A searchable database, template-based documents, or documents reviewed and edited by experts can improve the quality, thus reducing the time to consume and produce information. A few sample activities that might typically be seen in relation to the performance measures listed earlier such as research, analysis, gathering needs, and delivering services (see Table 1).

In the context of knowledge management, the focus is on the behaviors that individuals, teams, or organizations perform to achieve the desired goals. As these behaviors are knowledge-centric, they are highly dependent on the quality and availability of human capital (people). Behaviors are the functions through which people add value to visible corporate assets. It is the behavior of the people in an organization that achieves the conversion from *knowing* or tacit (solely in the minds of people) to explicit (tangible enough to transfer to another worker) knowledge. Indicators, or the occurrences of a behavior, can be profiled from a number of sources. These sources can include, but are not limited to, KM systems, repositories, Web sites, portals, resource management, learning, and HR systems.

As this chapter has implied, intangible assets are more or less valuable in proportion to their ability to support the generation of business value, measured in terms of tangible revenue and/or their ability to leverage other intangible assets, which at the same time are revenue generators. Templates, for example, in a consulting organization can reduce the cost of producing a required output, which is a

Table 1. Sample Behaviors Mapped to Activities & Performance Goals

Role	Performance Measure	Activities	Activity Measures	Behaviors	Behavior Measures
Research	Growth in new patents applications	• Research • Analyze • Recommend • Implement	• Research papers written • Patent proposal written	• IP reuse • IP submission	• seminars attended • Best practices used/ submitted
Consulting	Meet or exceed profit targets for all accounts	• Gather needs • Estimate cost • Review • Develop solution	• Needs analysis • Project plan • Solution delivery	• IP reuse • Training	• Templates used • Best practices used/ submitted • Code reuse • e-Learning • Online Expert (see persistent conversations below)

revenue generator. Once people use the template, its value is buried unless the re-use (of the template) behavior is captured. The key to measuring this value is to first determine the indicators of behavior (to be measured) that would influence the generation of measurable value (work measures).

People-related intangible assets are key components of the learning and growth process of the organization. Employee learning and growth constitutes only one set of knowledge development indicators. Increased knowledge of customers, suppliers, and business partners is another knowledge development indicator in a complex knowledge-era enterprise where customers, vendors, and suppliers often act as one virtual enterprise. Human capital is commonly measured in terms of the quantity and quality of employee contributions to solve internal business issues, team participation (quantity of team assignments in which the employee has been involved), and the quantity and quality of the decisions taken by the employee without upward delegation.

In a similar way, the tacit understanding and knowledge of customers and markets are critical for creating and increasing business value. In order to measure the trends and knowledge in these areas, organizations have developed knowledge management applications to store, manage, consolidate, and share market and customer information in both structured and unstructured formats. Through related infrastructure systems (such as customer or project tracking databases) organizations can measure, customer by customer or segment by segment, how much business they are receiving. Variables such as customer retention, customer satisfaction, and customer profitability trends are good indicators of how human capital is contributing to the creation of value. Correlating the KM indicators to the performance indicators will, over time, provide a productivity model that best suits a given business.

A variety of behaviors that directly relate to the performance of work activities such as the use of templates, viewing past work done for similar clients, or seeking advice from internal experts all demonstrate KM related behaviors that affect the ability of employees to complete work activities and achieve performance goals. These types of behaviors can often be measured with electronic, noninvasive tracking methods on a routine or even continuous basis. It is possible to correlate these *in situ* measures with surveys and other invasive measures for an even more comprehensive picture of intangible assets.

4   Developing KM Indicator and Analysis

While qualitative data provides insight into the user's subjective experience, quantitative analysis provides a more objective representation of the online KM behaviors. Qualitative analysis provides an understanding based on observation and experience (such as project reports, individual or group sessions with participants). These observations can provide useful information about the content and relationships, but they come with limitations. Direct observation can miss many forms of the interactions and patterns that are difficult to observe from a first person view, it tends to reflect the biases of the observer, and often lacks broad representation due to its labor intensive nature. Thus, to recommend the appropriate behavioral indicators, it was necessary to analyze both qualitative data and quantitative analysis of user behavior.

In an online KM environment, quantitative analysis of system data files provides a useful counter balance to qualitative commentary. System data analysis of user participation can be used to produce a range of measures of the structure and types of interaction in the KM environment. Combined with qualitative data, these measures can provide a multi-dimensional picture of what goes on in the online space. On their own, or correlated with performance results, quantitative measures at least provide a possible basis for the management of future work behaviors (Smith, 2001).

In the course of our study of work-related behaviors, system data files were analyzed to generate reports and graphs that profiled KM users. These files were aggregated based on the events and explicit activity relationships to produce a range of behavioral measures. We found that the data files relating to explicit content use did not truly display the full range of KM behaviors required to fulfill the work activities of the consultants studied. Explicit content reuse is a major factor in KM systems, especially document-centric systems. Behavior patterns around this intangible asset base are a major consideration for any KM metrics process.

Reviewing nearly two years of Microsoft Consulting Services KM data relating to the knowledge asset downloads and submissions provided a partial picture of these behaviors in the improvement of the desired performance goals. We found that the data files were somewhat incomplete. To assess the value of a variety of behavioral patterns associated with the primary activities of a consultant we compared 23 participants' subjective evaluations of usage and value to behavioral metrics from the system data files. We found the repository content was often downloaded once and reused numerous times resulting in a loss of data points. Survey results indicated that people reused the most useful knowledge assets in this manner well over 50 percent of the time. Consultants often did not submit content to the repository due to technical problems (such as connectivity from remote locations) or time constraints. This content loss reduces the long-term value of the KM repository for other consultants, compounding the problems going forward. These combined events resulted in data loss and skewing of counts.

Numerous surveys were run over the course of a two year period to determine the value and usefulness of the content. This qualitative data was correlated to the download and submission patterns to validate related system data. In general, the KM project could make only a limited quantitative statement regarding the number and estimated value of the explicit content. The 2000-2001 study revealed an estimated time savings of 2.5 to 3 hours of consultant time for each knowledge asset downloaded and used. More definitive work is planned in this area over the next year as improvements in the technology and the organizational enablers evolve to support the behavior.

Because KM is about how to maximize the ability of an organization's people to create new knowledge and how to build environments that support knowledge sharing, examining the peer-to-peer and peer-to-expert exchanges within the various communities of practice would appear to be good KM behavioral indicators. Using Polanyi's views, these would most likely be considered the most significant benefits in the KM environment. The tacit-to-tacit exchange is often considered the trigger point for innovation and the real leverage vehicle for KM. Of the many online and electronic mechanisms available to us today, the persistent threaded conversation is one that is growing in value to the larger online KM environment. A well designed interface to persistent, threaded conversations could reinforce the desired KM behaviors by demonstrating the pattern of user participation. Based on the data generated by the Netscan data-mining project (Netscan), Microsoft Research has developed a set of tools for illustrating the structure of discussion threads like those found in Usenet newsgroups and the patterns of participation within these discussions (Smith, 2001).

The current difficulty that KM users have in developing a meaningful respondent profile (or image) tends to undermine their confidence in the answers received, in development of trust, and in development of common goals. Although participants can eventually develop a refined sense of the expertise about the community members (sorting out the real experts from those who would like to be seen as experts) this information does not come easily or transfer readily to other environments. "Many of the resources and practices that constrain abuse and sustain trust in social relationships are missing in social cyberspaces, thus limiting the effectiveness of established methods of encouraging and maintaining collective projects" (Kollock, 1996). This faceless nature of the virtual electronic community may be a contributing factor to the difficulty in creating measurement tools around online KM projects.

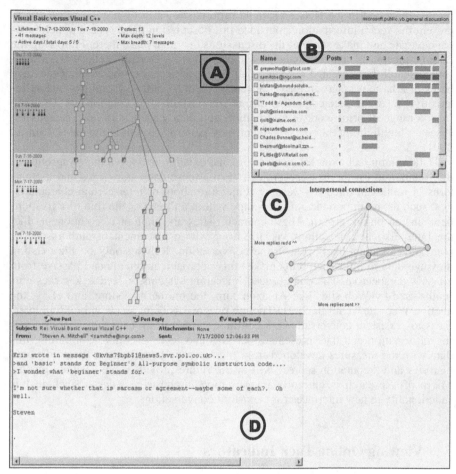

The Netscan dashboard combines the thread tree, piano roll, reply-based sociogram views, message display, and header information.

(A) The thread tree visualization presents information about the structural and temporal history of the selected thread. Selecting a message displays its contents in the message pane (D) below.

(B) The piano roll component displays a list of all posters who are present in the selected thread ordered by the number of posts they contributed. Columns for each day the thread was active contain bars if the poster posted on that day. When the user mouses over each poster the related posts are highlighted in the thread tree and the interpersonal connection component.

(C) The interpersonal connection component displays a sociogram that relates users with those they reply to and who reply to them. Posters are located based on the number of responses the send (the x axis) and the number they receive (the y axis)

(D) The message display pane presents the contents of a selected message and controls for replying via Usenet or email.

Figure 3. Netscan Dashboard (as cited in Smith (2001))

As demonstrated in the Netscan sample reports shown in Figure 3, our goal is to present the social information embedded but obscured in these spaces to help people navigate and make sense of the discussions that take place there. Following the Loom concept of "social visualization," expressed by Donath et al.(1999), Microsoft Research has "created a system that provides access to the existing message bases of a large newsgroup feed—currently about 91,500 newsgroups—via an interactive Web interface composed of multiple visualization components. Drawing from a range of prior work in information and data visualization, our designs focuses on highlighting the social and temporal patterns present in the data." (Smith, 2001)

Data mining techniques were used against existing messages in newsgroups as the foundation for the Netscan project. "From these data—messages and the patterns of replies in threads—we may conjecture about or infer certain characteristics, such as the importance of a message within a thread or the role of a [respondent] in [an online group]. These characteristics are implicit in components like the interpersonal connections visualization, whose placement of authors on the plane reveals their likely role in the conversation. Relying only on the existing message data to infer such traits makes this approach automatic and passive from a user's perspective. There is no need for rating systems or feedback scores currently used by Web sites like Amazon.com, the online bookstore, and eBay, the auction Web site." (Smith, 2001) Though progress is being made in building interfaces to persistent conversations, it continues to be useful to survey users regarding information and data presented that is found to be of value. Combining this data with the measures developed from the message body itself to create detailed histories and "reputation scores" will in the future provide more accurate results. Microsoft Research is currently investigating unobtrusive ways to include this functionality in new interfaces for persistent conversations.

5   Viewing Online Tacit Indicators

The nature of online discussions, the messages, their timing, sequencing, amd authorship, often do not easily integrate. "Thus, grasping the nature and extent of interaction in a complex conversation from just one kind of interface is difficult or impossible. It is sensible, then, to provide multiple ways to view the conversational space in a single dashboard. Netscan, with its massive data warehouse of Usenet messages and techniques for extracting meaning from such data, has the potential to provide a common platform for the creation and integration of multiple visualizations and interface components by many authors. The components we have presented here begin to suggest the possibilities for novel conversational interfaces." (Smith, 2001) Similar interfaces would benefit KM valuation by providing a quantitative measure for online tacit behaviors in virtual communities.

The components described herein yield work behavior linked to detailed information about particular users and activities. If interfaces based on such tools become widespread, MS Research believes they will make persistent conversations, and related online activities, easier to navigate and even improve the quality of the virtual community work.

Marc Smith, Sociologist and Researcher at Microsoft Research, suggests important directions for future work in this area of "social accounting" could track the number of sessions users have had in each space and how often they interacted with others. He would like future work to explore the effects of presenting such data in the user interfaces of such spaces in real time. Smith believes that "social accounting data will add an important layer of context and history to online interaction environments that will improve their capacity to generate social cohesion" (Smith, 2000).

The activities that influence behavior can also be measured and linked to performance measures. The activity and behavior measures provide the leading indicators, or in-process measurements, to achieve the desired goal, or end-process performance measures. Companies should monitor and manage the in-process activity and behavior measures in order to make appropriate decisions that maximize contribution to business performance measures. Together these three measurements comprise the elements of the value model. The KM value assessment (KVA) framework, described in Figure 2, provides a way to link the activities to performance measures and allows management to focus attention on those enabling behaviors that positively impact the activity measures. To complete the KVA value model, activities are aligned to performance measures on the one side and KM-related behaviors on the other. A consistent review of a baseline study group will provide an organization with quantitative data to derive the value producing alignments. By means of a correlation study of activities-behavior combinations that associate with positive value generation, management can make proactive recommendations on work behaviors.

Figure 4 provides a graphical representation of a consulting group value model. This diagram shows the business driver to be an increase in profitability from each engagement. In this example, we have shown just a few of the work activities and related behaviors the consultants are charged with performing to complete a client engagement. In this type of service organization, assuming a fixed-price contract basis, time is profit. Thus, the primary measures in this case relate back to time and quality of delivery. Clarity in the statement of the performance measure is critical (% reduction time to delivery without loss of quality). Loosely drawn performance measures can result in incorrect result analysis and misdirection in the workplace.

Aligning appropriate KM behaviors (such as template reuse and consultation with skilled experts) to work activities (such as generation of proposals or cost estimation) should increase productivity, as well as customer and employee satisfaction (such as generating 10 percent faster response to customer quote requests). The majority of companies currently measure work activities by means of some form of performance evaluation tool. Utilizing this information in building the KVA data framework will reduce the amount of work required to do a KM analysis. By utilizing the same activities that appear on performance reviews, quality surveys and so forth, a company can increase employee understanding of the behavioral link between work performance, work behaviors, and company performance goals. Providing employees with a KVA demonstrating the alignment of the work activities they have been assigned with the specific performance drivers for their business unit and proposed KM related work behaviors would promote the

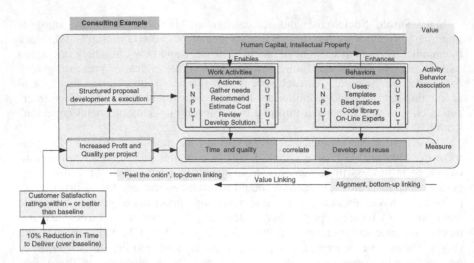

Figure 4. KM BV Role-Based Example

use of these behaviors. The KVA framework is designed to provide solid and on-going benefits analysis of knowledge management within a business using common performance goals as end-process measures. By linking KM measurement to the same goals utilized to measure performance throughout the company, management can achieve the alignment of KM to company success factors. We need to compare the predicted values produced by the KVA with actual business values and other end-process metrics developed by the company business managers.

6   Conclusion

The future is new ground and there is no certainty about how to get there. Because all strategy is a best guess at the time it is instituted, it is critical to review and renew the decision in light of achievements. After introducing the KVA and conducting reviews on a routine basis, process and behavioral changes may well surface as a result of real-time analysis. Every review period will produce new insights about results, employees, and processes. This continual process of real time analysis and change is, in reality, the real value of the KVA. The process of developing a KVA can, in and of itself, provide benefits, simply by improving the linkage of the key business drivers to the everyday work. Linking people, vision and data produces the real business value. Management "gut feel" is supplemented by trends and refined. Organizational learning takes place and knowledge assets are built within the organization.

KM is about how to manage better. Management and measurement are tied. If measurement does not make management better, there is no need for it. Therefore, measurement must reflect the goals and objectives of the business. In essence, knowledge management metrics are about how the organization manages its resources to achieve its goals.

References

Donath, J., K. Karahalios, and F. Viegas, "Visualizing Conversation," *Proceedings of the Hawaii International Conference on System Science*, 1999, 32.

Economist Newspaper Group, "A Price on the Priceless," *The Economist*, June 12, 1999, 61.

Itami, H., *Mobilizing Invisible Assets*, Cambridge, MA: Harvard University Press, 1987.

Kollock, P. and M. A. Smith, "Managing the Virtual Common: Cooperation and Conflict in Computer Communities," *Computer-Mediated Communications*, S. Herring (ed.), Amsterdam: John Benjamins, 1996.

Laing, J.R, "The New Math: Why an Accounting Guru Wants to Shake Up Some Basic Tenets of His Profession," *Barron's*, November 20, 2000.

Netscan Web site, 2002, URL=http://www.netscan.research.microsoft.com.

Polanyi, M., *Personal Knowledge, Towards a Post Critical Epistemology*, Chicago: University of Chicago Press, 1974.

Rasumus, D., "Key Trends for 2001: Information and Knowledge Management, Planning Assumptions," RPA-122000-00007 *Giga Information Group*, 2000, URL=http://www.gigaWeb.com.

Smith, M.A. and A.T. Fiore, "Visualization Components for Persistent Conversations," *Proceedings of ACM Conference on Computer-Human Interaction,* Seattle, March, 2001.

Smith, M. A., S.D. Farnham, and S.M. Drucker, "The Social Life of Small Graphical Chat Spaces," *ACM Conference on Computer-Human Interaction,* The Hague, March, 2000.

Sveiby, K.E., *The New Organizational Wealth: Managing and Measuring Knowledge-based Assets*, San Francisco: Barrett-Koehler Publishers, 1997.

Sveiby, K.E., "Measuring Intangibles and Intellectual Capital – An Emerging First Standard," URL=http://www.sveiby.com.au/EmergingStandard.html, August, 1998.

Sveiby, K.E., "A Knowledge-Based Theory of the Firm to Guide Strategy Formulation," *ANZAM Conference*, Macquarie University, Sydney, 2000, URL=http://www.sveiby.com.au/Knowledgetheoryoffirm.htm, 2000.

CHAPTER 25

A Framework for Security, Control and Assurance of Knowledge Management Systems

Rodger Jamieson and Meliha Handzic

School of Information Systems, Technology and Management, University of New South Wales, Sydney, Australia

Knowledge management systems are proliferating through organizations as management seeks to gain competitive advantage by enhancing and sharing knowledge across the organization. Unfortunately there are risks and consequences associated with knowledge management systems that may not be adequately controlled and audited, and may breach privacy concerns and legislation. This chapter addresses these issues and provides a framework and guidelines for management to provide assurance over their KM systems.

Keywords: Knowledge Management; Security; Control; Audit; Assurance; Privacy

1 Introduction

Knowledge is an extremely valuable resource that can contribute significantly to an organization's success. Key objectives of Knowledge Management (KM) are to facilitate, create, transfer and share knowledge amongst its employees and customers, and to foster organizational learning and intelligence (Liebowitz, 2000). KM is a "... multi-disciplined approach to achieving organizational objectives by making the best use of knowledge" (Standards Australia HB275-2001). KM is also defined as "... a broad collection of organizational practices and approaches to generating, capturing, disseminating know-how and other content relevant to the organization's business" (Denning, World Bank 2001).

Organizations operate in a fragile world and are subject to natural disasters, terrorism, cyber terrorism, e-crime, and a range of other threats to its information and knowledge resources and systems (CSI, 2001). Unfortunately there are risks and consequences associated with knowledge management systems, which if not adequately controlled and audited, may cause loss or damage to the organization and may breach privacy concerns and legislation. In order to protect knowledge assets from these threats, organizations should put in place appropriate security and control measures to counter these threats. One management process involved in considering threats and appropriate security measures is risk management. This chapter addresses these issues and provides a framework and guidelines for management to provide assurance over their KM systems.

This chapter first considers the senior management viewpoint from a KM governance and risk management perspective. The risks security and control mechanisms involved in KM are outlined using a knowledge management framework provided by Standards Australia. Assurance of knowledge management systems is then considered along with the continuous monitoring and audit of knowledge streams flowing in and out of an organization's knowledge repositories. Finally, the chapter considers privacy issues related to the capture and use of knowledge in an organization's knowledge management systems.

2   Knowledge Management Governance and Risk Management

Organizations are faced with continual technology evolution and new business models including virtual networks and the Internet, applications integrated with business partners, new business operations including e-business and m-business, and knowledge management. Concerns have continuously increased about the ability to keep this new environment aligned with business objectives. IT governance is key to facilitating and encouraging the business side of the company to work closely with technology managers and in line with board directions (Ramos, 2001). One aspect of IT governance should involve the governance of knowledge management to ensure that knowledge management strategies, knowledge infrastructure and technologies are in line with both IT strategies and organizational board directions.

First, it is important to ensure that knowledge management is an issue that is being considered by the corporate and IT governance committee's. Knowledge management governance should ensure that the objectives of knowledge management are part of the strategic planning process and both the corporate and IT strategic planning levels. When considering the key issues of KM security, controls, and audit assurance of KM infrastructure and systems, it is important that a risk management strategy be considered and that the internal and external IT auditors and security personnel be consulted in this process. These personnel will be able to provide advice on identifying risks and abuses within KM systems, and helping to place appropriate security and controls to mitigate these risks and threats. Guidance in this area may also be found from the IT Governance Institute in their document on Information Security Governance (IT Governance Institute, 2001).

2.1   Risk Management

Risk management is a broad process which identifies risks, security and controls for KM infrastructure and systems. The use of a Risk Management standard, for example AS/NZS4360 (Standards Australia, 1999), may also be considered by the KM governance committee. An illustration of this risk management process is shown in Figure 1. The KM governance committee needs to appoint persons to carry out this risk management process. We suggest the Chief Knowledge Officer of the organization together with the IT internal auditor and security managers are appropriate persons to carry out this task. IT audit standards (ISACF, COBiT 3rd Edition, 2000) and the IT governance framework developed by the IT governance Institute (ISACF, K-Net, 2001) should also provide guidance in this area.

To provide further guidance for KM, international bodies such as Standards Australia are developing frameworks to help in this area. For example Standards Australia's Framework refers to risk management in relation to Establishing Priorities and Sustaining Systems for Knowledge Management (Standards Australia International, HB275-2001, 2001: refer sections 3.2.1b p13-15; section 5.3.1 p47; and Appendix C p53-54). Standards Australia sees risk areas involving:

- Project – establishing a KM project within the organization;
- Strategy (Alignment) – alignment of KM with an organizations' objectives;
- Process – analysing the risks associated with creating, acquiring and sharing knowledge; and
- Foundations – risks within the enabling technology, the culture and sustaining knowledge systems of the organization.

The KM risk management team should first identify the KM assets (including personnel, systems, infrastructure and networks, locations) and then identify risks associated with these assets. The next phase involves identifying existing controls and security measures over these assets and then analysing the risks by determining the likelihood, consequence, and level of the risks. The risks are then evaluated and prioritised, and an action plan drawn up to implement the recommendations for additional KM security and control measures to counter or mitigate the identified KM risks. For some KM risks, management may accept the risk, thereby self-insuring against that risk. During this process, it is important to communicate with management and staff involved in KM about the findings from the risk management process, and solicit from them suggestions for improving KM security and controls. This process is not just carried out once and then forgotten, but should be monitored and reviewed on a continuing basis by the KM governance committee.

Detailed KM security and control mechanisms are covered in the next major section.

2.2 Knowledge Management Framework

The KM governance committee will also need to consider which KM technologies will be employed throughout the organization. Examples of KM technologies (Liebowitz, 1999) include:

- retrieval engines;
- content management;
- document and records management;
- learning systems;
- automatic classification systems such as neural networks, linguistic, or semantic processing systems;
- intelligent technologies including AI, intelligent agents, regression and correlation, expert systems, case-based reasoning, data and text mining, and rule-based systems;

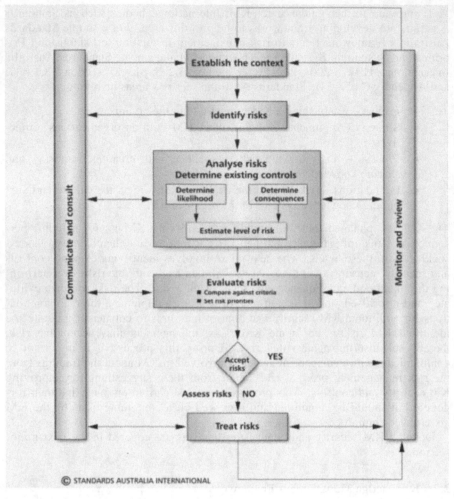

Figure 1. The Risk Management Process (Standards Australia International, 2001, p14)

- communication systems including email, discussion forums, groupware; and
- archiving.

Each of these technologies has its own risks and associated security and controls mechanisms. However, these technologies need to be considered in light of a knowledge management framework (Raich, 2000) and are just one part of the knowledge foundations required to support the knowledge processes within an organization. To illustrate, Standards Australia has formulated a knowledge management framework to guide practitioners setting up knowledge management within their organizations. Such a framework is depicted in Figure 2. Further details on the KM Framework are set out in Appendix 1.

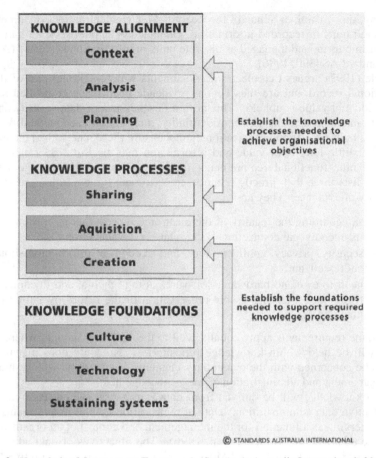

Figure 2. Knowledge Management Framework (Standards Australia International, 2001, p5)

2.3   Security Objectives for Knowledge Management

One of the fundamental components of knowledge repositories is the document, which will be the prime container in which most knowledge will be stored and shared. The NSW Evidence Act 1995 offers a document definition which is independent of the type of media upon which it resides:

"A document means any record of information, and includes:
- anything on which there is writing, or
- anything on which there are marks, figures, symbols or perforations having a meaning for persons qualified to interpret them, or
- anything from which sounds, images or writings can be reproduced with or without the aid of anything else, or
- a map, plan, drawing or photograph."

Similarly, the Australian Standard for Records Management defines documents as "structured units of recorded information, published or unpublished, in hard copy or electronic form, and managed as discrete units in information systems" (Australian Standard AS4390, 1996).

Doyle (1997) argues that electronic documents which make up part of the organizational record and are thus kept as evidence need to be controlled so that their evidential value is upheld. This notion raises issues of data security and the ability to maintain the tenets of confidentiality, integrity and accountability of the electronic holdings. If an organization cannot ensure these tenets, then documents will be of little long term value and information may be lost. Bearman (1994) identifies nine functional requirements for electronics records management, of these, he lists three that directly relate to integrity and the controls necessary for continuity of evidence. They are:

- safeguarding the legality of the electronic record, that is, it should retain its unequivocal connection to the related relevant action;
- security, privacy, confidentiality, and freedom of information should be addressed; and
- need to evaluate hardware, software, storage media, and documentation techniques to ensure usable preservation of the record over time (Bearman, 1994).

These same requirements apply equally well to the KM environment where documents will be held within knowledge repositories. Not only does management need to be concerned with the evidentiary elements of stored knowledge but with the management and administration of the knowledge held.

Often knowledge will be derived from data warehouses which required strong and effective data administration. Data administration is vital in an organization, and is emerging as a function for the management and control of an organization's corporate data resource (Martin, et al, 1996). The objectives of data administration as described by Horrocks and Moss (1993) may apply equally well to KM and have been adapted below:

- to support the business objectives of the organization;
- to promote the use of knowledge as a shared organizational resource;
- to aid efficient use of the knowledge resource;
- to ensure integrity and accuracy of knowledge;
- to ensure proper management of the knowledge resource;
- to improve co-ordination and integration in the organization by providing greater sharability of the knowledge resource;
- to improve availability of knowledge at all levels; and
- to control knowledge duplication and redundancy.

In order to achieve the objectives of KM relating to integrity, accuracy, availability, and control, management must consider the risks, security and controls over the knowledge repositories and environment. Examples of the types of risks security and controls are provided in the next section.

3 Risks, Security and Controls

This section first identifies the objectives involved in a management review of KM and then outlines a selection of risks faced in the KM environment. Security and controls necessary for protection and correct operation of KM systems are then considered with special reference to knowledge repositories.

3.1 Knowledge Management Audit Review Process

Prior to commencement of a review of this area, KM audit review objectives should be set. Review objectives may include:

- determining the extent of KM use and the impact of KM on the organization;
- identifying personnel relevant to an audit investigation and understanding their responsibilities;
- identifying locations where KM is used;
- understanding and documenting the KM technologies and components and how they inter-relate, both with each other and with other information technologies and systems;
- identifying risks associated with the KM environment, infrastructure, and systems;
- identifying types of security, control and assurance mechanisms in the KM environment;
- evaluating KM security, controls, and assurance/auditability mechanisms;
- reviewing KM documentation and legal consideration of KM systems development;
- gathering audit review evidence through the use of KM audit monitoring techniques; and
- concluding with an evaluation after the results of review testing are known.

After setting the KM audit review objectives, KM may undertake some of the major steps in this process, namely the identification of risks and the consideration of security mechanisms which are discussed in the following sections.

3.2 Risks in the KM Environment

The joint Computer Security Institute and the FBI Computer Crime and Security Survey (CSI, 2001) provide details of the types of risks, security breaches and attacks that organizations are facing in today's turbulent environment. Table 1 provides a selection of risks in the KM environment that need to be taken into account by management, security and audit personnel.

As well as these risks, KM management should be cognizant of the security and control considerations applicable to the KM environment.

3.3   Security and Controls in the KM Environment

Holsapple and Joshi (2000) provide an investigation of factors that influence the management of knowledge in organizations. One of the managerial influences on KM is *control* which involves two critical issues of protection and quality of the knowledge resources. They believe that the protection of knowledge resources from "... *loss, obsolescence, unauthorized exposure, unauthorized modification, and erroneous assimilation is crucial for the effective management of knowledge*" (Holsapple and Joshi, 2000, p240). They argue that management needs to consider knowledge validity (accuracy, consistency and certainty) and knowledge utility (clarity, meaning, relevance and importance) when establishing sufficient controls to govern knowledge quality. The security and controls discussed in this chapter are concerned with knowledge validity. Some of the considerations associated with operational KM systems are presented below and are summarized in Table 2.

In some organizations the trustees for KM systems are end user departments such as Research and Development (R&D) departments. This may be done order to qualify for tax deduction incentives in this area. One emerging issue concerns the appropriateness of the trusteeship, control and maintenance of the KM resting with R&D. In certain organizations this department is known for its flexibility of approach, creativity and informality – not great attributes for implementing and enforcing strict internal controls.

As with traditional information systems processing, *systems access security* is vitally important for KM systems. KM tools and environments need to be reviewed to determine the extensiveness of security features as some may be deficient in security and reliability. Management and auditors working in these environments will need to specify additional security features for their clients' KM systems and then pressure KM tool vendors to incorporate these features into their products. KM software houses may also want their products certified by major consulting/accounting firms, as to the provision of adequate security, control, and auditability features.

Table 1. Selection of Risks in the KM Environment

Selection of Risks in the KM Environment	
Strategic/Planning	• mismatch of KM strategy to corporate and IT strategies • unidentified or excessive costs especially maintenance and support • overlooked essential KM functionality

Accidental or intentional	<ul><li>damage</li><li>loss</li><li>modification</li><li>destruction</li><li>use</li></ul> to/of specialized KM or traditional IT hardware used to run KM systems, KM software, knowledge repositories, as well as feeder software and associated data bases. Loss or incapacitation of key KM experts, knowledge engineers, programmers, or knowledge maintenance personnel is also of concern.
Fraud and abuse	<ul><li>substitution/deletion of knowledge repositories</li><li>obscure placement of forward chaining demons in a knowledge base if expert systems or knowledge based systems are an integral part of the KM systems</li><li>unauthorized access to KM systems or KM management/audit trails</li><li>modification, deletion or insertion of KM information when passing through a network, communications or other layers of operating or support software such as data warehousing. This includes other application software when linked or integrated with KM systems.</li></ul>
Other Exposures	<ul><li>inability of imbedded KM software to recover/restart</li><li>KM hardware, infrastructure or software failure – especially real-time monitoring or imbedded systems</li><li>lack of knowledge use histories (audit trails) in hardcopy and/or magnetic/optical form</li><li>inadequate trace facilities in KM/KB software for debugging and KM/KB testing</li><li>KM systems knowledge not based on best expert's knowledge, reasoning, and explanations</li><li>Inadequate control of and access to KM repositories</li><li>poor quantity or quality of KM personnel</li><li>poor management, supervision, and control of the KM application and repositories if held elsewhere to IT department (e.g., under R & D)</li><li>inadequate training and supervision of KM personnel</li><li>inadequate KM hardware/software maintenance</li><li>legal liability for reliance on KM opinion when that opinion caused loss of life, damage, or monetary loss</li><li>inadequate KM documentation of tools, environment, and applications</li></ul>

Source: Adapted from Jamieson (1991)

Table 2. Selection of Security and Controls in the KM Environment

Selection of Security and Controls in the KM Environment	

KM Hardware :	Sensitive knowledge access:
	   ○ key locked equipment
	   ○ restricted/controlled boot up procedures
	   ○ biometric access controls
	   ○ encryption provisions
	Up-to-date documentation
	Regular audits of KM equipment
	Logging and follow-up of all reported faults
	KM back-up:
	   ○ strategy
	   ○ equipment
	KM maintenance:
	   ○ diagnostic aids
	   ○ documentation
	KM environmental considerations:
	   ○ uninterrupted power supplies or voltage regulators
	   ○ air conditioners
	   ○ physical protection barriers to restrict physical access
	Security infrastructure

KM Software	Automated procedures for KM access control
	Valid software license agreements
	Up-to-date documentation
	KM software integrity checks
	Appropriate KM maintenance strategy
	KM software upgrade controls
	Logging and follow-up of all reported software faults
	KM repository encryption
	KM explanation facilities if using expert systems or KBS:
	   ○ HOW facilities
	   ○ WHY facilities
	Help facilities
	KM repository integrity checking
	Restricted screen/report output and knowledge document delivery
	Separate development and run time versions
	Graphical layouts of KM repository
	Cross reference listings
	Knowledge dictionary or thesaurus maintenance access and controls
	Knowledge use trace facilities
	Knowledge use or consultation case history maintenance if KBS
	Audit trail logging of all activity
	Certified by major consulting/accounting firm

KM Systems Development	KM systems development methodology followed Separate KM systems development from production KM Appropriate design documentation Validation and testing of KM systems Quality assurance/control review Auditor involvement in KM systems development reviews Separate development and production KM source libraries Separate development and run time versions of KM software
KM Applications	Systems access security (password as minimum) & strong authentication Smart Cards Secure Client (IPSec) Digital Certificates Correct option setting for run time versions Edit facilities for data input Knowledge repositories/KB encryption Reasonableness checks Output review by competent personnel Hardcopy or magnetic/optical collection of case histories Management/audit review of audit trails Good application documentation Unauthorized copying protection Back-up and recovery
KM Network Controls	Internet, Extranet or Intranet access controls Virtual Private networks (VPN's) – site to site VPN Gateway Transmission encryption of Knowledge in transit Public Key Infrastructure (PKI) Dedicated connections Firewalls

KM Human Resources	Management commitment to KM strategy
	Assign responsibility for:
	   ○ KM systems development
	   ○ KM production operations
	   ○ KM disaster planning
	Adequate training of KM personnel
	Supervision and management of KM personnel
	KM Information Centre
	Segregation of duties
	Mandatory vacations
	Personnel security checks
	Maintenance supplier vetting

Source: Adapted from Jamieson (1991)

Traditional *input controls* such as appropriate edits, accuracy, completeness, and reasonableness checking will need to be refined in the KM environment. Input data validation may be simple, for example a range check (numeric 1 to 20), or context-sensitive, where the validation of the input data is dependent on other information already entered into the KM system. Most KM tools provide facilities for simple data editing but fall short on context-sensitive validation, especially of textual data in documents. For KM systems that included Knowledge Based (expert) Systems (KBS), such facilities as *'Whenever Modified'* slots (in object-based KM/KB tools) provide for the context-sensitive style to be programmed into the KM systems more easily. Other control features include ability to retract and backtrack in a consultation to enable corrections to be made. Care is required when programming these facilities, as practitioners comment that it is an area where many programming errors can be made. Also, facilities such as repeated data requests and using *'Are you sure?'* type of questions. Many KBS provide the facilities for entering *'unknown'* as an answer to certain questions. These KBS require rules to deal with unknowns, although with mature KBS unknowns would be infrequently used. From a management/audit perspective, we are concerned that these KBS receive a proper set of facts for the consultation under consideration, in order for it to arrive at an appropriate decision. Most interactions with KMs are via workstations where the user answers system queries by supplying numeric and symbolic facts and perhaps opinions. It is important that proper management and audit trails exist of the user-supplied input, which should be logged to a usage/case history file. Currently these facilities are provided by many KBS systems and may be used at the designer's or user's discretion. More sophisticated facilities are required to mandatory log all interactions with the KM/KB system into a proper management/audit trail.

During knowledge processing, the inference engine will usually provide a combination of forward and backward chaining control mechanisms to solve the goal state and provide a decision or judgment. For both management and auditors, the importance of having adequate *trace facilities* provided by the KM/KBS or processing environment is very important. These trace facilities show the consultation's questions and answers as well as the rule firing or instantiations, and the conclusions reached by the KM/KBS. This then provides a very detailed audit trail of the inferencing process and knowledge used to obtain to a decision or recommendation.

For *KM outputs*, which are usually in the form of documents or a report of the consultation and recommendation, there should be some form of reasonableness checking and knowledgeable user review prior to making decisions. Jamieson (1991) points out that there is a potential high risk of inadvertent reliance on the KM/KBS results by users, where after a period of time users may not question the systems judgments. This highlights the importance of continual validation and review of knowledge, especially in high risk applications.

If knowledge bases and repositories are of strategic importance to the organization then *encryption* of the KM repository may be considered.

Legal liability may arise from the use of a KM/KBS (Zeide & Liebowitz, 1987). Care is required to caveat the decisions made by the KM system so that the organization may not be litigated against for loss of assets or life as a result of someone acting on the system's decisions. The final responsibility must fall on a person in the organization, not on the system.

In a similar way to *controlling the amendments to source programs* for an application, alterations to knowledge, or KB system rule changes should also be approved, correctly updated and validated, and the KM repository maintained in such a form that unauthorized amendments to it are prevented. This involves maintaining a secure KM systems development library with versions of the KM system held that are equivalent to the released production versions. This also presupposes some sort of KM systems development section with abilities to modify copies of the KM systems source, fix errors and release new versions when appropriate.

Documentation is, and always will be, a perennial problem and KM systems are no exception. However, with these systems there is an ever greater need to correctly document the expertise that is encapsulated in the KM repository and its associated design. While systems design documentation has been mentioned previously, KM systems in operation should have, at the minimum, adequate on-line help facilities which are context-sensitive. An exception to this guideline is for KM systems embedded within other information systems where these types of facilities may never be required. In this case, system evaluation is performed during development and at periodic intervals by quality assurance or audit. A knowledge worker's or user's guide is useful as an introduction to the KM system, which could also be on-line. For KBS, when the operational version is used for consultations, then adequate documentation of the consultation, usually in hardcopy format is required, perhaps to give to the customer and to keep for statutory records purposes as proof of the business transaction or event. Optical or magnetic records may also be used to document case histories for later management or audit review. Adequate documentation of the operator's responsibilities at the end of the day is also required. This may include procedures for appropriate retention of magnetic, optical or hardcopy files and back-ups for the KM systems.

Contingency planning for KM is just as important as for traditional IT systems. Alternative locations and equipment, especially for specialized KM/AI hardware, must be found if KM systems requiring this equipment are critical to the organization. Regular off-site storage of development versions and KM production source is important for recovery purposes. Important requirements such as KM repository consultation case histories and documentation should also be stored off-site on a regular basis.

These security and controls are examples of the types of controls needed to be considered by organizations establishing KM systems (refer to the case study in section 6). The next sub-section focuses on one prime component of the KM system, namely security and control concerns with knowledge repositories.

3.4 Security and Control Concerns with Knowledge Repositories

There are a number problems associated with knowledge repositories. One of problems involves where the knowledge repositories are located and who is responsible for them and their security. If the knowledge repositories are controlled in the same way as corporate databases, then they may fall under the security that is given to all other major IT systems. However, if the knowledge repositories are located within an end user environment on a knowledge server then these systems may be inadequately controlled. As a result, knowledge management systems may have no systems access security, inadequate monitoring, and lack adequate backup and recovery procedures and facilities. If this is the case then management may need to review the security over these knowledge management systems and apply the same procedures as they would over their corporate IT systems. With knowledge repositories we need to ask questions as to who is responsible for placing documents within the repository, how is access to these documents controlled, and who is responsible for the disposal of the documents.

Some organizations have setup knowledge centres within the various divisions of their organization. Knowledge centres are responsible for the addition, maintenance and review of documents placed within the knowledge repositories. These knowledge centres should also be responsible for the security and accuracy of information and knowledge that is placed within the repositories. Personnel in these knowledge centres need be responsible for the setting up and maintenance of the knowledge dictionary or thesaurus for the organization. The knowledge dictionary may also relate to knowledge maps or taxonomies that may be purchased 'off the shelf', manually constructed, automatically generated or even a combination of all three. The knowledge dictionary is very important as it holds the key to accessing the many documents held within knowledge repositories. Knowledge held in documents within the knowledge repository is indexed and accessed by the terms set out in the knowledge dictionary. Therefore, protection over the knowledge dictionary is as vital as security over knowledge repositories. A person having access to the knowledge dictionary in a covert or incompetent manner may intentionally or accidentally destroy or corrupt key terms within the knowledge dictionary, or may in fact destroy the whole knowledge dictionary or substitute another in its place. Rebuilding of the knowledge dictionary may take many person days of effort and may even be impossible to reconstruct, thereby causing the organization significant losses due to an inability to access documents within the knowledge repositories.

Another concern is with the knowledge held within the knowledge repositories. Firstly, how are documents held within the knowledge repositories, are they encrypted or held in a clear text form? Secondly, are all documents held in a form that cannot be altered, or are these documents in an open form so that many people within the organization may have access to substitute, modify or delete them. If the documents are held in an Acrobat PDF form, then document security features may be enabled that provides protection on features such as content accessibility, print, change, extract or copy, altering author comments and fields, and document assembly. Adobe Acrobat also provides password protection and encryption over the document and over the document security features.

Three important concerns relating to security include confidentiality, integrity, and availability (IT Governance Institute, 2001). Confidentiality involves ensuring that the knowledge held remains confidential and is only used for the purposes to which that knowledge was collected. Confidentiality also implies that there may be degrees of confidentiality associated with a document. For example, there may be three levels of confidentiality namely, open access, commercially in confidence, or for senior management only. These levels of confidentiality need to be carefully thought through by an organization so that they formulate their own method of grading information, and access control information use, so that for example, only authorised personnel within the organization with appropriate security clearance will have access to the knowledge held at that security level. Confidentiality relates closely to privacy concerns discussed in a later section.

Integrity is an issue that may be overlooked by those responsible for the KM system. Integrity implies that the knowledge in the knowledge repository will remain current and correct (or accurate), overtime. This embodies the ideas of accuracy and currency of knowledge. In the knowledge management system a lack of accuracy or currency of knowledge may involve the organization in serious loss, damage to reputation, or severe financial exposure as a result of decisions made on the basis of that knowledge. Thus, it is important to audit the knowledge held within the knowledge repositories to ensure that that knowledge is current and correct overtime. Integrity also relates to the security of the knowledge held. If an unauthorised person has access to knowledge held within a document, then they may substitute, modify or delete knowledge and therefore compromised the accuracy and integrity of the knowledge incorporated within the document.

Monitoring of knowledge use is also an important concern. An organization needs to be able to track who has accessed the knowledge from documents in the repository, identify when that document was accessed, what was done to the document during the access, and if tracked, what use was made of the knowledge. Knowledge management systems may not yet have the monitoring and auditing facilities to allow this use to be tracked and captured. Others may have the facility within the knowledge management system but this facility may not have been enabled. In other cases, the logs from the monitoring system may not be kept for an appropriate length of time.

Availability of the knowledge repository is also an issue that needs to be addressed. It is of no use to have a knowledge repository that is unavailable to knowledge workers around the globe. This may arise through some unfortunate incident which may have destroyed the knowledge repository or prevented access to it. Examples include acts of cyber-terrorism or actual terrorism, accidental mishaps leading to the deletion of key knowledge repositories, or an attack that may render communication lines to the repository inoperative. Availability requires that an organization's knowledge infrastructure including communication lines, knowledge servers and knowledge systems are all operational and are securely protected from penetration. Should a disaster occur, it is important that a fallback facility is pre-arranged so that the organization may keep operating as usual following the disaster, by switching to those fallback facilities. It is a must that key knowledge systems and associated knowledge repositories are backed up and held securely off-site. Many organizations are using electronic vaulting as one of their backup and recovery strategies.

4   Knowledge Management Audit and Assurance

As well as identifying risks and putting in place security and control mechanisms to mitigate or control these risks, KM should also consider audit assurance of its systems and environments. This section will explain monitoring of knowledge flows, online alerting mechanisms and audit of knowledge systems to provide assurance to KM.

4.1   Knowledge Audit and Monitoring

Knowledge audit (Debenham and Clark, 1995; Tiwana, 2001) has traditionally involved the review of an organization to determine where knowledge is located within the organization and then look at the best methods of being able to retrieve, extract, capture, store, and disseminate the knowledge to others (Joseph, 1999). Doyle (2001) proposes a knowledge audit that involves a readiness assessment, then a gap analysis, followed by benchmarking to best KM practices. Knowledge auditing (Handzic and Jamieson, 2001) also has a different connotation which is to monitor the usage of knowledge within the organization. If the knowledge management systems do not have monitoring and auditing systems included (perhaps they were purchased as a package), then these need to be specified and programmed into the KM systems. KM auditing subsystems will provide continuous monitoring and auditing facilities to personnel in the knowledge centres, who have been allocated the responsibility for reviewing knowledge auditing reports. When a knowledge worker accesses a knowledge document in the repository the knowledge auditing system will record the date and time of access, which knowledge worker accessed the document, what document was accessed, and the use for which that knowledge access was put, if this feature was incorporated into the knowledge auditing system.

This knowledge access record then becomes part of an audit trail which knowledge centre management may review and the follow up at their discretion. Part of the continuous monitoring KM auditing system may involve an alerting component. There may be some access control specified on certain documents, for example, any access to a particular document or any change to a particular document. If such an access or change occurs to a document so marked, then not only will an alerting record be written to the knowledge auditing database, but an immediate alert will be sent to the knowledge centre's alert console for immediate follow-up by knowledge centre personnel. Such an auditing system may be named a *kSCARF* (knowledge System Control Audit Review File – refer to Figure 3). The *kSCARF* will also need to provide the facility for knowledge centre management to maintain the *kSCARF* system (Wong K., Ng, B., Cerpa, N. & Jamieson R, 2000), that is the ability to print auditing reports, maintain the alerting and auditing parameters, and archive knowledge auditing reports. These reports may be called on by management, police or other government agencies in the case of serious crime, abuse or other criminal acts. These knowledge reports need to be secured and held in a secure area as they may be called on as evidence. It is recommended that knowledge auditing reports should be held for a minimum period of seven years.

4.2   Knowledge Assurance

Knowledge assurance refers to a review of the knowledge management systems and infrastructure to ensure that these systems are adequately secured, controllable and auditable so that those who use the systems can rely on the results produced by those systems. This will involve having qualified knowledge auditors to perform quality assurance checks on the knowledge management systems. This func-

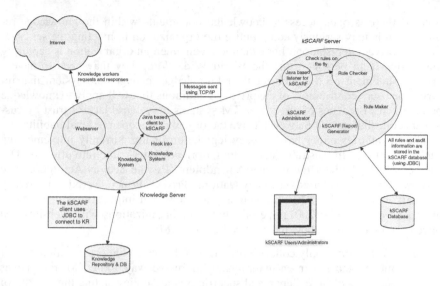

Figure 3. *kSCARF* Sytems for Knowledge Management (Adapted from Wong K., Ng, B., Cerpa, N. & Jamieson R, 2000)

tion may be carried out by an organization's quality assurance department or section if they have the required knowledge and abilities to carry out these audits. Knowledge assurance work may also be undertaken by many of the major audit/consultancy firms that operate globally. These reviews will consider not just the technology involved but also a review of the security and control structures that have been built in and around the knowledge management systems. Technical aspects will also be considered including security, backup and recovery facilities, a review of the knowledge management system itself, and a review of knowledge centre activities such as knowledge dictionary maintenance and control of the allocation of thesaurus/dictionary terms to documents.

5   Privacy Concerns for KM

Privacy is an important issue to address when discussing knowledge repositories. In many countries there exists privacy legislation for both public and private sectors. Privacy legislation usually requires that an organization informs all persons, from whom the organization is soliciting knowledge or information which is going to end in a knowledge repository, of certain key privacy tenets affecting how the information or knowledge solicited from them will be used and retained in the knowledge repository. Contributors need to be informed of what information or knowledge is being captured in the first place and then informed as the use for which that information or knowledge will be used in the future. It is then the organization's responsibility to monitor who has access to that knowledge, who maintains the knowledge, and how that knowledge is used a within the organization. If there is open access to knowledge documents within the knowledge repository, this may seriously compromise the organization in meeting the set criteria from privacy legislation. For example, even when an organization is capturing knowledge from persons using the World Wide Web, they may need to have a privacy statement on the Web for their knowledge management system that informs the users/contributors of the privacy conditions that will apply to knowledge being given. Breaches of privacy in KM systems may cause lack of trust by customers/contributors and may even leave the organization open to legal liability.

Many countries either have privacy legislation or are currently implementing such legislation. In Australia, new national privacy laws came into effect on December 21, 2001 under the Privacy Amendment (Private Sector) Act 2000. The privacy legislation is based on 10 key National Privacy Principles (NPPs) (Privacy Commissioner, 2001). The following explanations and implications of the NPPs are based on Braue's (2001) interpretations for organizations with websites and have been modified to show the implications for KM:

1. *Collection* – only collect information relevant to the organization by fair means and not in an unreasonable intrusive way. For KM, this means having a clear, coherent and specific privacy policy stating the identity of the organization and how to contact it, what knowledge will be collected, who will see the knowledge, why the organization needs the knowledge and what will happen if it doesn't have that knowledge.

2. *Use and disclosure* – the organization cannot disclose personal information unless it is for a specific need and customers/contributors would reasonably expect that disclosure. Knowledge users/contributors trust an organization when they give it personal information, and it is in the organization's best interest not to abuse that trust in any way. Any questionable ideas on use and disclosure should be run past the organization's privacy officer, legal representative or a privacy consultant.

3. *Data quality* – make sure any personal information collected, used or disclosed by the organization is accurate, complete and up-to-date. For KM systems, this involves ensuring that personal information or knowledge captured in knowledge repositories remains current and correct. This may involve offering a Web self-service portal to the knowledge repository so that customers/contributors can notify the organization of any changes or make changes themselves to their personal information or knowledge stored in the knowledge repository.

4. *Data security* – an organization needs to take reasonable steps to protect personal information from misuse and loss from unauthorised access, modification or disclosure. There is need to destroy or eliminate identifying details from information no longer needed for a specific purpose. For KM, this means implementing appropriate security measures that both protect personal data and knowledge stored in knowledge repositories (e.g. by encryption) and prevent unauthorised access to the repositories and/or use of that knowledge (e.g. by authentication, systems access control, and activity logging).

5. *Openness* – an organization must document its personal information management policy and make this policy available to anyone who asks for it. For KM, this entails publishing the KM personal information management policy on a web page prior to customers/users entering the KM site, and including links to the organization's privacy policy on its web site. An organization may also consider auditing and certification of the privacy policy, for example through such organizations as the Australian Privacy Compliance Centre (www.privacycompliance.org), and eTick – administrator of the Australian Privacy Seal Audit and Certification (APSAC) program.

6. *Access and correction* – organizations are to allow customers to see information held on them and must be able to correct any incorrect information held. For KM, this involves either an online self-service portal or a K-Centre providing procedures for customers/contributors to update incorrect or changed information/knowledge via email, fax or via a call Centre.

7. *Identifiers* – organizations cannot use the same identification number or code that another organization has assigned to a particular customer. This is in order to prevent aggregation of customer or client data from multiple sources. For KM, this means that the organization should develop its own process for identifying customers/contributors and ensure that they do not communicate customer/contributors identifiers when sharing this information with other organizations, including multiple divisions of a company.

8. *Anonymity* – where practicable individuals must have the option of not identifying themselves when entering into transactions with an organization. For KM, this entails that an organization must not demand personal information just to allow customers/contributors to enter their knowledge repositories site. KM systems should be built with basic level functionality available to all and then present a second tier offering extra value add-ons if a customer/contributor offers more knowledge/information about themselves.

9. *Transborder data flows* – organizations should not transfer information out of Australia unless the recipient is in a jurisdiction where privacy is at least equal to the NPP standards and the recipient is likely to uphold customer/contributor's privacy. Organizations should get approval for these transfers wherever possible. For KM, this means great care should be taken with whom knowledge and personal information is to be communicated outside national borders. Compromising customers'/contributors' privacy may seriously damage an organization's reputation and may even lead to legal liability.

10. *Sensitive information* – organizations should not collect sensitive information about any persons unless they have provided authorisation, or would authorise it but cannot, or the organization needs the information

to benefit public health or safety. Although the law does not define 'sensitive', this principle is intended to protect medical records and other health-care related information. So for KM systems holding personal information and knowledge about customers'/contributors' medical or health records, the organization should seek legal advice before implementing knowledge systems dealing with this type of information and knowledge.

Many knowledge management systems interact or form a key component of customer relation management (CRM) systems. The privacy principles and implications outlined above should be seriously taken into account by KM when developing and implementing these systems.

6   Mini-case: KM Security and Control Issues within Schlumberger

Schlumberger, a petroleum services and information technology company operating across 150 countries, provides global knowledge availability for the organization. This company uses a secure global infrastructure to enable widespread access to knowledge assets using both intranets within the company and extranet links to their customers. The infrastructure put in place by Schlumberger ensures high availability and connectivity for all stakeholders. With connectivity and availability the challenge is then to ensure there is accessibility by authorized parties while ensuring intruders are kept at bay. Schlumberger employs a range of security technologies including VPN (virtual private network), PKI (public key infrastructure), and smart-card based encryption services to help guarantee that only relevant parties gain access after proper authorization, and authentication while ensuring confidentiality, integrity, resource availability, non-repudiation and privacy. This is an illustration of an implementation of some of the security and control techniques suggested earlier in Table 2. Figure 4 provides an overview of the KM security infrastructure at Schlumberger.

At the heart of the circle in Figure 4 is the knowledge hub incorporating the knowledge repositories which require protection. These repositories contain high value content databases of best practices, lessons learned, answers to frequently asked questions, links to research, engineering material and expert content management helpdesks. Directory services like LDAP provide a database of people, listing with attributes that define privilege and even a listing of a public key for PKI. By using smart-card based 2-factor authentication an added layer of security is provided for access by legitimate parties.

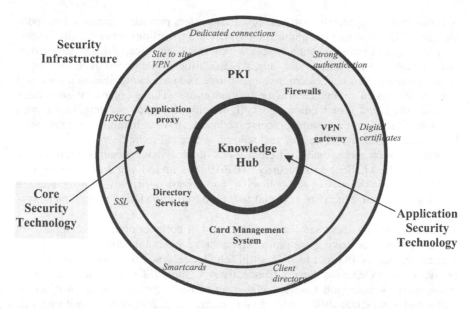

Figure 4. Schlumberger KM Security Infrastructure

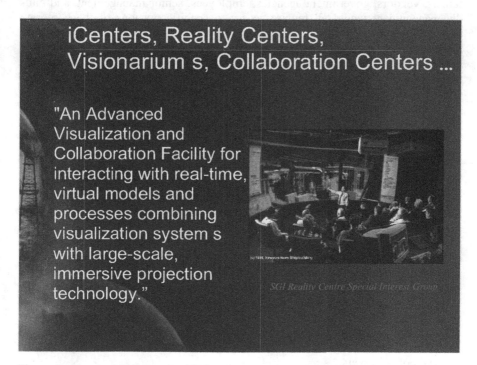

Figure 5. Advanced Collaborative Visionariums

iCentres in geographically disparate research centers provide a means where people can collaborate and communicate by providing facilities where multidisciplinary teams can discuss, share and review problems. Physically this means provision of high quality, large scale immersive facilities which reproduce the water-cooler situation, that is, the compression of time and space with ubiquitous v-c and plasma screens in reality centres or visionariums. These collaboration centres provide advanced visualization and collaboration facilities for interacting with real-time, virtual models and processes combining visualizations systems with large scale, immersive projection technology – refer to Figure 5.

With constant evolution of different types of knowledge systems, there is one constant – the challenge of security. TCP/IP, the underlying Internet protocol, provides little in the way of authentication, authorization, privacy, non-repudiation or integrity, all of which are essential to web-based knowledge management systems.

The rise in e-business and the growing trend of collaboration between partners and competitors is driving the rapid expansion of interconnection between intranets and extranets. In order to address this challenge, a solution that Schlumberger provides is the DeXa.Net Secure Connectivity Centers (SCCs) to facilitate multi-party, multi-organization knowledge sharing of repositories. Pre-defined access levels and sophisticated IP routing enable parties to access only repositories that they require with no compromise of confidential knowledge. For example, customers, vendors, government agencies, employees, senior management, and middle management would all require access to specific portions of the corporate knowledge that exists in organizations. The SCC is essentially a secure traffic management system that leaves an audit trail. On top of this is built a smart-card based PKI system with 2 keys (public and private) for secure access, both for digital signatures (for non-repudiation) as well as cryptography (for secure transmission of data). The key strength of the SCC is that it offers a reduction in deployment time, allowing Schlumberger to stay well ahead of the competition and the technology curve. It provides a quick time-to-market and the capability to rapidly add or remove new services and partner connections, which can be a powerful enabler in a growing E-business enterprise.

For Web applications accessing the knowledge hub, Schlumberger has a distinctive offering that provides both security and manageability for web-based applications and transactions. The DeXa.Port solution provides portal and application security and is a marriage of state-of-the-art technologies, such as directories, policy servers, certificate authorities, and optional secure tokens, as well as services, such as 24x7 help desk support and security consulting. Authentication, authorization, privacy, non-repudiation and integrity are provided over any standard Internet connection. As a result, Schlumberger knows with certainty with whom they are conducting business, leading to safe online productive and profitable collaboration, with Schlumberger's customers and knowledge workers confident that their transactions and knowledge use are genuinely private. Authentication is achieved using SecureID, smart cards, biometrics and/or passwords. Also, the DeXaPort solution provides complete hosting of the certificate authority, directories and policy servers.

Security Consulting Services provide controlled access to knowledge repositories and systems, secure KM connectivity, and reliable sharing of knowledge and proprietary information with partners and clients, by ensuring that security is incorporated as an integral part of every KM infrastructure, from design through implementation.

DeXaTouch Managed Services Support Centers offer user training, administrator training, system maintenance, and 24 × 7 help desk support for knowledge workers.

DeXaBadge Secure Web Access includes certificate and/or smart card-based authentication to knowledge web sites; directory architecture, implementation, and migration; policy server architecture, implementation, and migration; encryption of knowledge transfers and transactions; digital signatures; and non-repudiation of knowledge web-based transactions. *Certificate Authority* (CA) provides tools to authenticate and verify knowledge workers. Browsers such as Internet Explorer and Netscape Communicator are able to recognize the signature of the various CAs, making web-based knowledge access, transfers and transactions far more secure than ever before. *Web agents* are software applications installed on protected web servers to enforce access control to web content. They deliver a knowledge worker's security context directly to any knowledge web application being accessed by the user.

The DeXaPort user directory is managed using the Light-weight Directory Access Protocol (LDAP). It is where DeXaPort stores information about all end-users and knowledge workers. This user directory, along with other DeXaPort capabilities, enables single sign on for all the enterprise portals, including the knowledge hub. The user directory also provides knowledge workers and end-users with the ability to change their information (such as e-mail address and phone number) in one place and have this change be recognized by all of the enterprise's DeXa-protected portals. *Policy Server* – the knowledge users of enterprise portals typically have different access rights based on their role in the enterprise. Enterprise customers and knowledge workers might be given access only to selected web pages, while system/knowledge administrators and software developers may have another set of entitlements. These varying privileges are managed by the policy server.

End User KM – the DeXa End User Management site provides knowledge workers with a trusted, neutral place, not specific to a particular enterprise portal, where they can manage their user information, credentials, certificates, and smart cards. This user management site is not used during normal interaction with the Schlumberger enterprise web site. The DeXa.Port End User Management site enables knowledge workers to register with the enterprise, change passwords, manage personal profiles, order smart cards, and revoke certificates.

This combination of technical solutions, managed services and control provides strong authentication, authorization, confidentiality, integrity, non-repudiation and privacy of Schlumberger's knowledge repositories and systems and provides an illustration of KM security within an organization. Customers and knowledge workers information and knowledge privacy is protected by the above security mechanisms, and there is a privacy statement incorporated in the Legal Information link provided from the main corporate web page. While these tools and technologies are utilized in a significant manner in Schlumberger, it is imperative to note this organization recognizes and utilizes people as the central variable in the management of knowledge.

7   Conclusions

This chapter has presented the challenge of appropriate security, control, and assurance of knowledge management systems. KM needs to adequately understand and address the many and varied risks arising from implementing KM systems in an open Web-based environment. By considering KM governance and the use of appropriate risk management methodologies and techniques, the CKO and his/her team responsible for knowledge management should be able to put in place appropriate security and control measures over the knowledge management environment, systems, and repositories to counter these risks. The use of continuous monitoring audit techniques can help to ensure that the use of knowledge in the repositories is tracked to the users of that knowledge, and if possible, how that knowledge was used. It is important that KM also consider the important issue of privacy to personal information and knowledge held in the repositories. The privacy principles discussed above should present KM with suggestions how KM can deal with the implications of privacy for KM systems and repositories. The framework and guidelines presented here should provide knowledge managers with the ability to secure their knowledge management systems, repositories, and infrastructure, and to address the risks associated with KM.

While this chapter has addressed security and control issues within enterprise KM systems, discussion with colleagues reveal new security, control and audit challenges as increasingly KM systems are being deployed among multiple organizations as well as within each organization. Further, peer-to-peer (P2P) computing is affecting KM systems in several ways. First, a peer device can be a client as well as a server. P2P delivers a shift to decentralization and associated with this is a lessening degree of control for the MIS/Knowledge manager. This shift and lessening of control will add complexity to the auditing and control aspects of security. Second, the most prominent effects on P2P in KM are file sharing, brokered search, and virtual collaboration, either synchronous or asynchronous. Further research needs to be carried out into these areas to provide for cooperative security, audit and assurance of multi-enterprise KM systems.

Acknowledgements

The authors would like to acknowledge the valuable contribution of Ambrose Gerard Corray, General Manager of Schlumberger Network Solutions, East Asia for his contribution to the mini-case in this chapter.

References

Bearman, D., *Electronic Evidence*, Pittsburg, PA: Archives & Museum Informatics, 1994.

Braue, D., "The Privacy Debate: Customer Intimacy's Darker Side", *Webhead Magazine*, October, 2001, 32-40.

Capshaw, S.; "The Knowledge Audit," *Knowledge Management*, May, 2000, 25-26.

CSI, "2001CSI/FBI Computer Crime and Security Survey," *Computer Security Issues and Trends*, Computer Security Institute, 5, 1, 2001, 1-18.

Debenham, J.K. and J. Clark, "The Knowledge Audit," *Robotics and Computer-Integrated Manufacturing*, 11, 3, 1995, 201-211.

Denning, S., in Doyle, S. "A Little Knowledge Can be a Dangerous Thing: Issues in Knowledge Management," *Proceedings from Oceania CACS 2001*, Information Systems Audit and Control Association, Canberra, ACT, 23-26 September, 2001.

Doyle, S. "A Little Knowledge Can be a Dangerous Thing: Issues in Knowledge Management," *Proceedings from Oceania CACS 2001*, Information Systems Audit and Control Association, Canberra, ACT, 23-26 September, 2001.

Dolye, S., "Securing Electronic Documents," KPMG Global Knowledge Management Respository, 1997.

Handzic, M. and R. Jamieson (2001): "A Knowledge Management Research Framework for Electronic Commerce," *Proceedings of the IFIP TC8 Working Conference on Electronic Commerce*, Salzburg, Austria, 22-23 June, 2001.

Holsapple, C. W. and K. D. Joshi, "An Investigation of Factors that Influence the Management of Knowledge in Organizations," *Journal of Strategic Information Systems*, 9, 2-3, 2000, 235-261.

Horricks, B. and J. Moss, *Practical Data Administration*, Hertfordshire, UK: Prentice-Hall, 1993.

ISACF, *COBIT: Control Objectives for Information and Related Technology*, 3rd Edition, Rolling Meadows, IL: IT Governance Institute and Information Systems Audit and Control Foundation, 2000.

ISACF, *K-Net, Global Knowledge Network for IT Governance, Control and Assurance*, Rolling Meadows, IL: IT Governance Institute and Information Systems Audit and Control Foundation, 2001, URL=http://www.isaca.org/knet.

IT Governance Institute, *Information Security Governance: Guidance for Boards of Directors and Executive Management*, Rolling Meadows, IL: Information Audit and Control Foundation, 2001.

Jamieson, R., *Auditing Expert Systems*. Research Monograph No 3, Carol Stream, Illinois: EDP Auditors Foundation Inc, 1991.

Joseph, E.C, "Knowledge Management Audits," *Proceedings of the International Conference on Technology and Innovation Management*, PICMET, 1999, 1, 442.

Kalakota, R. and A. B. Whinston, *Frontiers of Electronic Commerce*. Reading, MA: Addison-Wesley, 1996.

Liebowitz, J., *Knowledge Management Handbook*. Boca Raton, Florida: CRC Press, 1999.

Liebowitz, J., *Building Organizational Intelligence: A Knowledge Management Primer*. Boca Raton, Florida: CRC Press, 2000.

Martin, E., D. Ferguson, S. Lewis, N. Lynch, and S. Doyle, *Data Administration Practice in Federal Government Organisations: A Pilot Study*. University of Canberra (unpublished), 1996.

Privacy Commissioner, *National Privacy Principles – Extracted from the Privacy Amendment (Private Sector) Act 2000*, 2000, URL=http://www.privacy.gov.au/publications/npps01.html.

Raich, M., *Managing in the Knowledge-Based Economy*. Switzerland: Raich Ltd., 2000

Ramos, D., "The Auditor's Role in IT Governance," *Information Systems Control Journal*, 5, 2001, 23-24.

Schlumberger, DeXa Port, 2001, URL=http://www.slb.com/Hub/Docs/tt/nws/

Standards Australia, HB275-2001, *Knowledge Management: A Framework for Success in the Knowledge Era*, Sydney, NSW: Standards Australia International Limited, 2001.

Standards Australia, *AS/NZS 4360:1999 Risk Management*. Sydney, NSW: Standards Australia International Limited, 1999.

Standards Australia, *AS4309 Records Management*. Sydney, NSW: Standards Australia International Limited, 1996.

Tiwana, A., *The Essential Guide to Knowledge Management: E-Business and CRM Applications*. Upper Saddle River, NJ: Prentice Hall, 2001.

Wong K., B..Ng, N. Cerpa, and R. Jamieson, "An Online Audit Review System for Electronic Commerce,", *Proceedings of the 13th Bled Electronic Commerce Conference 2000*, Bled, Slovenia, June 20-23, 2000.

Zeide, J. S. and J. Liebowitz, "Using Expert Systems: The Legal Perspective," *IEEE Expert*, Spring, 1987.

Appendix 1 – Knowledge Management Framework

PHASE	SUB-PHASE	STEPS	ACTIONS/PROCEDURES
Knowledge Alignment	Context	Understanding KM	Approaches to KM Understand KM Engagement Storytelling
		Establish the Context	Environment Strategy and Operation
	Analysis	Establish priorities	Planning Process Manage Opportunities and Risks (refer Risk Management AS/NZS 4360:1999)
		Set goals	The Process Approach Establish Goals
		Analyse Knowledge Processes	Analysis (Share, Acquire, Create, Import) Tacit Analysis
	Planning	Establish Implementation Requirements	Technology Change Management Plan-Do-Check-Act
		Determine the Benefit	Cost/Benefit Analysis Intangible Accounting
		Establish the Business Case	The Proposal SWOT Analysis
Knowledge Processes	Sharing	Share Tacit Knowledge	Tacit to Tacit Sharing Tacit to Explicit Sharing Explicit to Tacit Sharing Quality of Information Actively Encourage Sharing
		Share Explicit Knowledge	Information Discovery Taxonomy Metadata Structuring Information Quality Site Design
		Facilitate Learning & Training	Learning Methods Instructional Design Effective Knowledge Transfer

	Acquisition	Monitor the External Environment	Monitor Strategic Context Competitive Intelligence Market Research Customer Feedback Professional Participation
		Import Required Knowledge	Knowledge Resourcing Leveraging External Relationships
	Creating	Nurture Knowledge Creating Communities	Knowledge Creation Process Building and Nurturing Communities Community Platforms
		Learn from Experience	Activity Based Learning Pilot Projects Organizational Memory Exit Strategies Variance Analysis Act on Lessons Learned
		Innovate Continually	Prototyping Experimentation Research Joint Venture & Alliances Knowledge Mapping
Knowledge Foundations	Culture	Engage Staff	Engagement Knowledge Vitality
		Identify Challenges	Identify Challenges (Hording, no-one is interested, not invented here, reinventing the wheel, rigidity, power politics, resistance to change, denigration of roles, future blindness, leader dependency, change fatigue, digital divide, technology focus) Address Challenges
		Develop Change Strategies & Management	Articulate the Vision Develop Trust Manage Behaviour Communication Incentives Build into Normal Activities

	Technology	Technical Considerations	Explore the Options Information Management Simplicity Integration
		Specify the Requirements	Develop Specifications (technical needs, budget availability, staff involvement, develop KM suite, multi-channel delivery, balance KM requirements and technical limitations)
		Support the Implementation	Provide Training Provide Support Use Immediately Evaluate the Technology
	Sustaining Systems	Risk Management	Risk Management (quantitative, qualitative)
		Records Management	Standards in Record Management Records Management and KM Risk Management and Records
		Quality Management	Quality Management ISO9000
		Other Systems Complementing this KM Standard	Information Security Compliance Programs Documentation Standards B2B Information Exchange Outsourcing Management Complaints Handling

Source: Developed from Australia Standards, HB275-2001, 2001

Alternative Strategies for Leveraging the Knowledge Asset: A Framework for Managerial Decision-Making

John S. Storck and John C. Henderson
Boston University School of Management, Boston, MA, USA

Knowledge management has become one of the dominant themes of modern management, giving visibility to many examples of different approaches and best practices. In many cases, evaluation of these examples has focused on the processes of creating, capturing, storing, and transferring knowledge. As a result, explanations of success and failure tend to center around process improvements and associated technologies. These process models, however, often do not reflect the alternative implementation strategies available to the firm. In particular, there is a need to understand how the choice of any given approach affects the ability of the organization to leverage its knowledge assets. This chapter presents a framework for making decisions about how to leverage knowledge assets in a sustained manner over time. The framework integrates the cognitive dimension of knowledge access and the structural dimension of knowledge production. Different cognitive burdens, patterns of behavior, and biases characterize each of four quadrants in the framework. As a result, the framework allows managers to explore the strengths and weaknesses of strategic options. It also provides a means of learning from other knowledge management initiatives. Thus, we believe that the framework can help organizations successfully choose among alternatives for developing a knowledge management capability.

Keywords: Decision Making; Expertise; Knowledge Management; Organization Structure; Sensemaking

1 Introduction

British Petroleum, the Center for Army Lessons Learned, the Xerox Eureka project, McKinsey & Co., Buckman Laboratories, the World Bank – are all organizations among the presumptive members of the knowledge management hall of fame. Each has been recognized as a leader in making more effective use of its knowledge assets. By stimulating innovation and leveraging existing expertise, each has improved organizational performance. Their successes have been widely discussed, yet an integrated view of the factors that led to these successful initiatives is lacking. More generally, there is a need to improve our understanding of how the choice of any given knowledge management approach affects the ability of an organization to leverage its knowledge assets in a way that improves performance.

This chapter presents an integrative framework for making decisions about how to leverage knowledge assets in a sustained manner over time. The objectives are to help managers learn from other knowledge management initiatives and to provide a means for choosing among various options for developing a knowledge management capability. By using the framework to identify strengths and weaknesses of alternative approaches, managers can not only learn from the experiences of other organizations, but also make more appropriate choices from among the many alternatives available. The framework also facilitates the design of a knowledge management approach that has a sustainable impact on performance.

We arrive at the framework from the perspective of design, but not design as restricted to the myriad of organizational systems and processes that deal with knowledge. Instead, we add a structural dimension to the process dimension. This dimension more directly addresses the issues of accountability for the effectiveness of the knowledge management strategy and of sustainability of the solutions adopted. The framework also is grounded in a more theoretical set of constructs that move thinking about knowledge management from a cognitive processing view to a broader design view.

The chapter begins with a brief review of previous efforts to classify knowledge management initiatives. We then describe the framework and highlight some of the design issues associated with alternative strategies. The next section of the chapter explores the application of the framework, with a particular focus on the interactions that result from making choices within the dimensions of the framework. We conclude with a discussion of the strategic implications of using the framework to make these choices.

2 Prior Research

To date, two major themes have been prevalent in the knowledge management literature. Many people have focused on the value of knowledge to the organization, using the lens of organizational learning or of managing intellectual capital as a means of characterizing value (Senge, 1990; Leonard-Barton, 1992; Stewart, 1997; Davenport and Prusak, 1998). Many others have taken more of a process viewpoint, describing how creating, capturing, storing, and transferring knowledge can be accomplished effectively (Nonaka & Takeuchi, 1995; Davenport et al., 1998; Zack, 1999a). The concept of social capital is occasionally used to link the two themes. Social capital – the outcome of organizational learning or, alternatively, the result of effective management of intellectual capital – can be thought of as arising from knowledge management processes (Cohen and Prusak, 2000; Lesser and Storck, 2001).

Most knowledge management strategies have been designed from the process viewpoint. Dichotomizing knowledge as being either explicit or tacit has further reinforced the use of the process perspective. As a result, many organizations have made substantial investments in the development of processes to capture and store knowledge. Unfortunately, these investments generally have not met expectations.

Although empirical evidence is generally lacking because organizations do not like to report unfavorable news, our own fieldwork indicates that many of the large knowledge repositories that are the outcome of the investments in new processes are not being used or maintained. This outcome is reminiscent of a long history of research on information systems usage, where it has been shown that motivating use over time is a vital factor in realizing value from information systems investments. Discussions with senior executives in a variety of industries suggest that there is serious concern about how to achieve sustained usage of knowledge management systems. Because knowledge assets cannot affect performance unless they are captured and used, organizations have struggled to develop training programs, incentive schemes, and other behavioral change initiatives to encourage people to share and access relevant expertise.

A possible reason for this struggle is that there has been little focus on implications of alternative knowledge management strategies. One analysis of choices made by firms as diverse as Bain, Dell, and a major cancer research center suggests that there are two basic strategies: one that relies on definition of knowledge structures and population of a document database and another that is centered on development of networks of people who share tacit knowledge (Hansen et al., 1999). This analysis also states the proposition that firms cannot be effective at adopting both strategies, adding that the choice must be aligned with the competitive strategy and capabilities of the firm. A second article dealing with implications confirms the need for alignment of firm resources and needs (Zack, 1999b). This article also suggests that firms are either using or creating knowledge, and that they generate knowledge internally through, for example, R&D efforts, or acquire it externally. The choice results in what is termed either an aggressive or a conservative knowledge management approach. Although this analysis helps to delineate issues and options, neither the process view nor the obvious assertion that the knowledge management approach must be aligned with the strategic capabilities and objectives of the firm clearly informs a designer about how to identify the factors that lead to success.

Our approach builds on the options discussed above to define a framework for considering alternative knowledge management strategies. We are particularly concerned with the knowledge consumer, for it is the consumer who must use the knowledge assets over time in order to affect firm performance. Thus, the framework describes how the consumer can gain access to the knowledge assets, characterizing the link in both cognitive terms and structural terms.

3   A Framework for Classifying Knowledge Management Strategies

We motivate the need for a framework by presenting five brief descriptions of specific knowledge management initiatives. Each of these cases represents a substantial success for the organization involved, yet for the first four of the organizations listed below, each approach is substantially different from the others. The fifth organization used more of a composite strategy, as will be explained later.

1. All teams in the U.S. Army use an after action review (AAR) process to record lessons learned. The Center for Army Lessons Learned (CALL) collects, consolidates, and validates the results of the AARs, which include both high-level summaries as well as the details of operations orders. Staffed by a relatively small number of people, CALL also designs and operates the technology that allows Army personnel to access the knowledge that the AARs represent, using a variety of search engines and display techniques (Baird and Henderson, 1997).

2. A worldwide consulting firm begins implementing its knowledge management strategy by using Lotus Notes to capture documents that are the work products of each engagement. Responsibility for this system becomes centralized, with a 200-person staff providing overall coordination, database design and administration, and call center support. Some of the most critical information is packaged into downloadable files that are targeted to specific business objectives (Chard and Sarvary, 1997).

3. An office equipment manufacturer sponsors bi-monthly meetings of managers responsible for the 85,000 workstations that are the core of the IT infrastructure. Initially focused on one key corporate-wide objective, the infrastructure managers broaden their scope and develop a way of working together that facilitates innovation and knowledge transfer. Knowledge exchange typically takes place during the bi-monthly meetings, but document repositories and other community-defined processes serve as additional knowledge dissemination mechanisms (Storck and Hill, 2000).

4. An oil company forms a global team to reduce drilling costs. The team designs a means of accumulating knowledge about drilling that they call a "knowledge bundle." This creates a magnet that pulls in the knowledge of other members of a much larger community of drilling engineers. Web-based technology aids in the distribution of this knowledge around the organization (Storck et al., 1999).

5. Technicians working for an equipment service organization establish an informal network to share repair tips. Later, they capture these tips in a local database. In order to extend the reach of its accumulated knowledge, the organization implements new business processes and structure so that the tips can be classified, validated, and stored. (Orr, 1996).

Faced with this variety of successful initiatives, how does a manager embark on a design path that will result in an effective strategy? Two fundamental dimensions characterize the design dilemma. The first deals with the organizational structure employed to create, capture, and apply knowledge – the administrative strategy. This might be thought of as a governance structure for knowledge production, which we suggest is frequently the most important determinant of whether available knowledge is used. The administrative strategy defines the organizing mechanisms used to create and maintain the knowledge assets. The second dimension deals with how people access knowledge and make use of it – the sensemaking strategy. This is a cognitive dimension that is somewhat akin to the process view discussed above. The sensemaking strategy defines the extent to which the "knowledge consumer" is provided structured access to the knowledge.

The framework is portrayed in Figure 1, with the five knowledge management initiatives described above positioned to illustrate the point that any strategy can be characterized according to the two dimensions of the framework. Each dimension of the framework is described in more detail in the sections that follow.

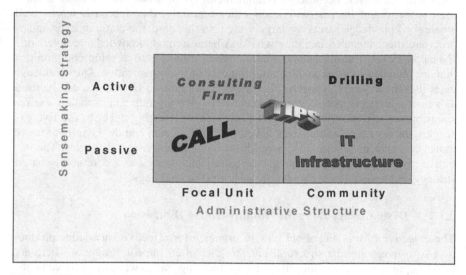

Figure 1. The Knowledge Management Strategic Framework

3.1 Administrative Strategy

3.1.1 Definitions

Knowledge production efforts are organized in the administrative dimension in one of two ways: either through a focal unit or by a community-based approach. Although the administrative dimension is a continuum, the two organizational alternatives represent real differences in strategy. Failure to recognize the differences can undermine an organization's efforts to sustain a successful knowledge management initiative.

A focal unit is tasked with the responsibility and authority to execute key knowledge management processes. Thus, it is a designated group of people that creates and sustains the conditions under which knowledge production takes place over time. This group does not need to be centralized at the corporate or divisional staff level. It could be discipline focused (e.g., a team of technical librarians drawn from different business units of a pharmaceutical firm who are responsible for managing information about competitors). It may even be one individual who is seen to be qualified because of expertise or role. Focal units can be comprised of people drawn from different functions, thus avoiding the potential bias of a single perspective. In the five brief descriptions presented, CALL and the centralized staff group in the consulting firm represent a focal unit approach.

In a community-based approach, control and responsibility for sustaining the knowledge production processes over time is in hands of a non-hierarchical, diffused group that is typically much larger than a focal unit. Forming such a loosely knit group – or community – almost always takes more time than establishing a focal unit. However, because individual members of a community share a common purpose and interact with each other regularly, this approach works well where the knowledge assets are largely tacit. In this case, the community is an appropriate mechanism to facilitate what has been termed "knowledge conversion" (Nonaka, 1995). The management challenge of course is to develop communities that are intended to achieve the strategic goals of the organization. Our work suggests that the emerging concept of strategic communities of practice can be used as a theoretical perspective to understand how such a group can execute these responsibilities effectively (Storck and Hill, 2000). Referring again to the five examples, the organization that established the drilling team and the IT infrastructure managers represent community-based knowledge management strategies. The initiative involving the equipment service technicians started as a community-based strategy, but evolved to become more of a focal unit strategy.

3.1.2   Design Issues along the Administrative Dimension

The objective of thinking about how to organize for effective knowledge production is to overcome the structural barriers that often impede progress. There are three important barriers: the difficulty of tracking and rewarding achievements, the design of incentives, and the need to provide appropriate leadership. The administrative strategy adopted will influence an organization's ability to deal with each of these obstacles.

Regardless of strategy, for many organizations the balance between obviously identifiable costs and customarily intangible benefits is the most persistent issue. In the focal unit approach, costs are more apparent and, as the benefits of the knowledge management investment are identified, it is usually difficult to allocate recognition for those benefits between the focal unit and the line business units that are the direct beneficiaries. The focal unit can be placed in the position of defending its costs, while line units take credit for successes. The costs of operating a community, on the other hand, are not as readily identifiable. As a result, there is less contention between the community and the line business units as to how to recognize contributions. However, community contention for resources – including resources as simple as dedication of employee hours to participate in community activities – results in tensions between line business leaders and community members. This was an important issue in the development of the community of IT infrastructure managers. Business unit leaders may not see a direct connection between participation of their employees and business value. Community members may be committed to enacting a knowledge management strategy by their participation in the community, but they also are benefiting individually. As their identification with the community increases, their desire to maintain or increase these individual benefits can result in conflicts with business unit objectives.

The community-based approach more directly addresses the issue of incentives than the focal unit approach. One might argue that incentives for a focal unit are inherent in its structure: as a formal creation of the organization, it is necessarily accountable to and consistent with overall organization strategy. It is important to note that a focal group does not directly enhance the ability of the knowledge customer to access knowledge assets, whereas the diffused nature of a community usually induces others to take advantage of the knowledge produced by it. In other words, because the knowledge is owned and controlled by the community, there is usually a greater willingness to use the knowledge. This is definitely the case in the community of service technicians, even after this grassroots initiative was transformed by the organization to become a focal unit. There is also better access to tacit knowledge because of a higher likelihood that, for example, a phone call will be returned. For the community, however, other important issues related to incentives arise. First, it is frequently difficult to motivate individuals to identify themselves around a set of common interests. Second, successful communities are those that can maintain themselves by absorbing new members and their knowledge. The community must be inclusive in order to encourage knowledge transfer. This means that its members must learn how to develop an awareness of others in the community and what they know, how to define and use a shared vocabulary, and how to develop and engage in norms of sharing knowledge.

The leadership issues related to managing a focal unit are little different from any team leadership role. However, the ability of the focal unit leader to exert influence over the prospective business unit knowledge providers and consumers is key. This role is a difficult one to execute effectively, requiring both detailed domain knowledge and well-developed interpersonal skills. The large consulting firm dealt with this obstacle by dedicating substantial human resources to its focal unit and by making the business processes highly visible. For the community-based approach, we see leadership barriers in several forms: there must be a willing and enduring sponsor, an effective facilitator of member participation, and often a visionary leader who can clearly elucidate a community mission with which members will identify. In a sense, the need is for a person who can provide the spiritual leadership that is essential to success.

3.2 Sensemaking Strategy

3.2.1 Definitions

From the perspective of an individual who wants to access organizational knowledge, the difficulty lies in making sense of what is available. The designer's objective is to make this an easy, effective process, taking into consideration two key factors: (1) the way the knowledge consumer thinks about and uses what he or she needs and (2) the nature of the knowledge itself.

Each individual interprets and internalizes knowledge differently depending on personality traits, prior experience, and expectations (Weick, 1995). Consider, for example, how a novice and an expert might make use of a procedures manual. With little experience and incomplete mental models, the novice would look for specific instructions, often applying these by rote. In contrast, an expert would be likely to engage in more interpretation, adapting instructions to the context of the problem and to his or her own way of working.

The nature of the knowledge that organizations deal with is wide-ranging along a continuum from phenomenological to highly abstracted (Thomas et al., 1993). There is clearly a tendency for knowledge management initiatives to attempt to turn all knowledge into information-like objects. But this is not possible for knowledge that is, for example, captured by a video of someone being served efficiently in a fast food restaurant. Thus, the designer must take into account the way the knowledge consumer gains access to knowledge, while recognizing the potential for influencing the way people interpret what they acquire.

Knowledge management initiatives can frame (or present) knowledge in a way that influences the kind of sensemaking strategy that the knowledge consumers use. An active frame sifts and sorts knowledge so that people see it as the designer intends. This is clearly the intention of the staff group in the consulting firm. Similarly, as processes and structures for dealing with repair tips became more formalized in the equipment service organization, this too has become an active framing strategy.

A passive frame may do some preliminary sorting, but basically presents the knowledge as is (perhaps as a detailed description of a phenomenon) and then lets the user make sense of it. Both CALL and the IT infrastructure managers' community use a passive framing strategy. CALL relies on technology to facilitate searching whereas the infrastructure managers' face-to-face meetings are framed by an agenda that they develop. The passive framing concept also applies to the way members of this community use their document repository to make sense of the artifacts of their meetings.

The term "frame" is used because of the physical analogy. An active frame is one that allows the designer to restrict the position of the viewer. A passive frame allows the viewer more latitude to develop his or her own interpretations. Continuing with the analogy, a frame includes boundaries as well as imparts biases if it restricts the perspective of the viewer. Note that there exists a continuum within each type of framing strategy, and indeed, a continuum across the entire vertical dimension of the framework.

It may be tempting to think of the passive frame as being applicable to tacit knowledge and, similarly, the active frame as applicable to explicit knowledge. This is not our intention. Instead, the notion of passive framing is one that is cognitively based: using a passive frame, the knowledge consumer sifts through explicit knowledge to make sense of it according to his or her experience and needs. The corollary behavior is for the knowledge consumer to be using an active frame to view, for example, a structured description of a phenomenon. The active frame guides the consumer's sensemaking of the tacit knowledge captured by the description. This is why the sensemaking dimension is different from the process viewpoint taken by others.

3.2.2   Design Issues along the Sensemaking Dimension

For the designer, the choice of a framing strategy depends on several factors, including volatility of knowledge, the need for the user to have tacit knowledge in advance of use, and efficiency goals.

Knowledge that is highly volatile will make it costly to maintain an active frame. This is perhaps an important reason why the Army developed CALL using a passive framing strategy. Although one might expect that the knowledge required to be effective in Army operations is largely contained in well-established doctrine and tactical manuals, in fact, history has shown that there is significant learning to be captured during every Army operation, at all levels. Volatile knowledge also implies that there will be a high probability of errors of omission, again another reason why CALL uses a passive frame. Nevertheless, developing a knowledge management strategy in an environment where knowledge is volatile is not a futile endeavor. Even a limited amount of codified knowledge can be a critical stimulant to capturing deeper knowledge. So, even if there are few stable knowledge assets, a "learn as you go" approach is feasible using an active frame.

Using an active frame, there is less use of tacit knowledge to access what is needed. This is so because an active frame channels the tacit knowledge that is relevant. Thus, the designer of the active frame defines a neighborhood of experiences that are assumed to be relevant to the requester. With a passive frame, the use of tacit knowledge is unconstrained and the neighborhood is defined through the interaction. One of the reasons why one would not design an active frame is the likelihood of a subtle selection bias: the knowledge consumer does not know what they don't know. In this case, the logical attribution that this user will make is that the knowledge management system doesn't have the required knowledge. Clearly, if this happens often enough, then people will stop using the system. On the other hand, there are clear reasons to design an active frame. The first justification would be based on an economic argument: assuming that the user is not naïve, an active frame is more efficient. A secondary economic argument would relate to *a priori* expectations about the cost of search. Users expect an active frame to be more efficient. Importantly, these expectations influence the probability of accessing the knowledge base again: success begets further attempts; failure reduces the desire to attempt further use.

One measure of the strength of a frame is the quality of content relative to a given problem context. An active frame will normally have a higher conversion factor (i.e., the knowledge acquired will have a more substantial impact on performance). Another way to express this is that an active frame also has a high relatedness factor (i.e., knowledge obtained by using an active frame will tend to be more closely related to the needs of the user than if a passive frame is used). This is certainly true in the case of tips made available to the service technicians, which is what motivated this organization to migrate toward the active framing quadrant of the framework. A passive frame normally has lower relatedness and a lower conversion factor. This is not to say that a passive frame is of less value. Indeed, when performance criteria are not clear – either because the situation is ambiguous or it is better for people to discover on their own how to improve their performance – the search should not be limited by an active frame. In this situation, the knowledge management system should be structured so that it is easy to go from one idea to another, to discern linkages and flows, and to spur rather than limit creativity. A data warehouse may be a way of implementing a passive frame, particularly with the use of search engines. The key design criterion for both the active and the passive frames is that knowledge conversion is the prime measure of success.

4   Application of the Framework

Given an understanding of the framework and therefore of the choices available to implement knowledge management initiatives, one can now consider how the choices along the administrative dimension and the sensemaking dimension interact with each other. First, we present an analysis of the strengths and weaknesses of each of the four quadrants of the framework. Then, we offer some ideas about the forces that might stimulate migration from one quadrant to another. This leads to a discussion about possible trajectories for development of a knowledge management capability.

Figure 2 presents a characterization of strategies corresponding to each of the four quadrants of the framework. We expand on this in the discussion below and highlight the potential biases imparted by each of the possible design choices. The discussion is not intended to position any single approach as the best one, but rather to allow the reader to weigh the advantages and disadvantages of each strategy against his or her own requirements.

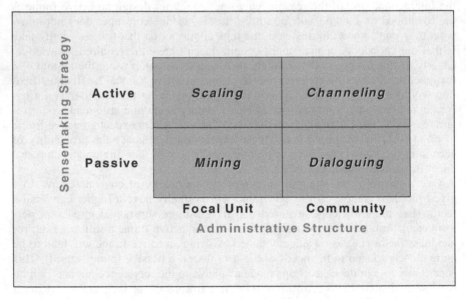

Figure 2. Characterizing Design Choices (adapted from Henderson and Baird, 2001)

4.1   Focal Unit/Active Sensemaking – Scaling

This is the starting point of the path followed by many firms to date: take explicit knowledge, codify it, and then distribute it. There are clear cost advantages to this approach, in part because people can be trained quickly as to how to use the codified knowledge assets and in part because of ease of scaling. In addition, it can be relatively easy to identify how the knowledge obtained creates value. As noted above, the focal unit/active sensemaking approach works best in a context where the knowledge assets are relatively stable. This was recognized by the equipment service organization, providing a reason to create a focal unit to enhance the benefits that had been obtained from the grassroots community. However, this approach suffers from the risk of low buy-in – a problem generic to any focal unit approach – and, perhaps more importantly, from the intrinsic bias of a knowledge taxonomy imposed by the focal unit, rather than one derived by the knowledge consumer. In this quadrant, the knowledge consumer will be likely to engage in "satisficing" behavior, which may result in suboptimal solutions.

4.2 Focal Unit/Passive Sensemaking – Mining

The principal strengths of this approach are that it is unbiased and unconstrained, in the sense that the knowledge consumer interactively defines the bounds of the sensemaking domain. The latter feature in particular increases motivation to engage in the sensemaking effort and thus the relatedness of knowledge obtained, although it also results in a greater workload imposed on the user. One important difficulty with this approach is that it requires the focal unit to devote substantial effort to ensure that the knowledge assets are comprehensively captured and that appropriate (and frequently costly) data mining and visualization technologies are available. On the whole, this is not a scalable approach and the focal unit must provide substantial training for knowledge consumers, adding cost and raising another kind of barrier. Nevertheless, for organizations in dynamic environments where knowledge assets are volatile and access requirements are unpredictable, the payoff of the focal unit/passive sensemaking approach comes in the form of greater innovation and interpretive coherence.

4.3 Community/Active Sensemaking – Channeling

In many organizations, this approach appears to be attractive because it combines the possibility of leveraging a community across organizational boundaries with the clear value proposition that is inherent to the active frame. Training requirements are low and the nature of the community-based structure leads to sustainability as wells as user buy-in. Building a community, however, is a slow process that requires special facilitation skills and management patience. The community/active sensemaking approach has worked well in situations where a community already existed so that its knowledge management processes could be channeled in directions that were valuable for the organization.

4.4 Community/Passive Sensemaking – Dialoguing

As with any community-based strategy, this approach is difficult to initiate, but once started is highly sustainable. There is substantial evidence that the dialogue that takes place within a community stimulates reflection and innovation. A community/passive sensemaking approach leads not only to individual learning and buy-in, but also to the establishment of the community as a credible knowledge source in the organization. This is clearly not an easily scalable approach and the unconstrained nature of the knowledge processing within the community can have unintended consequences for the organization. Without the guidance of an active frame, the community may move its dialogue in directions that are not consistent with organizational objectives. Moreover, control of intellectual property can become problematic. As a result, notwithstanding strong interest in communities as a core component of a knowledge management strategy, many organizations have difficulty accepting the value proposition underlying this approach.

4.5 Evolution of Knowledge Management Initiatives

We can build on the above analysis to consider how a knowledge management capability might evolve. This is not to say that an organization must necessarily change its approach over time. Rather, regardless of where an organization starts off, we believe that organizational dynamics and forces external to the organization will affect the development of the capability. What might be called knowledge management maturity will impact the amount of time it takes to move from one quadrant to another, but it is also interesting to ask whether an organization can build a capability that is designed to migrate.

We offer the following analysis of possible horizontal and vertical developmental paths (referring to the axis of Figure 1):

1. An organization will move from a focal unit to a community-based approach as people on the periphery of the focal unit become involved in knowledge production. This trend would be accelerated if the need for innovation became more dominant than the need for knowledge transfer.
2. An organization will evolve from the community-based approach to a focal unit when the need to scale the initiative becomes important because or when issues related to risk management arise (e.g, concern about intellectual property leakage or inconsistencies between the community's knowledge focus and organizational objectives).
3. A passive to active sensemaking strategy shift will take place when it is necessary to reduce cognitive load or decrease the cost/benefit ratio for the knowledge consumer. Although this will probably also result in increased bias, this shift is a natural response to pressures for more efficiency and for more knowledge sharing activity in critical areas. It could also occur as organizations shift their focus from identifying best practices to standardizing on current practices.
4. An active to passive move would possibly reduce both bias and efficiency, but could also be a result of a need to respond to rapid changes in knowledge requirements.

It is also important to note that technology may drive changes. For example, improved search engines – which could be thought of as a way of doing "dynamic framing" – will facilitate a transition to an active sensemaking strategy by increasing the denominator of the cost/benefit ratio. One could even conceive of attenuating bias by using multiple search bots that take on different perspectives while at the same time reducing cognitive load. Technology may also play a role in the evolution of a community-based strategy because the increasing sophistication of collaboration tools may provide organizations with greater ability to scale a community-based approach. Thus, in general, it appears that technology developments support the development of the knowledge management capability in a way that tends to the upper right-hand quadrant of the framework.

This review of the forces that cause a knowledge management strategy to evolve leads to thinking about development paths along the diagonals of the framework. One might view, for example, movement along the diagonal from focal group/passive sensemaking to community-based/active sensemaking as an indication of healthy development. In this case, after the organization establishes the focal unit, the community takes ownership, broadening the impact of the strategy and providing a community-defined structure for active sensemaking of the knowledge assets. An example of this might be a company that sets up moderated discussion groups that then are transformed in a series of community-owned bulletin boards. This development path is also one that might be stimulated by a change in the nature of business relationships (e.g., where an organization begins to adopt an alliance-based product development strategy in lieu of an in-house strategy).

Following the development path along the opposite diagonal (i.e., from community-based/passive sensemaking to focal unit/active sensemaking) could be construed as an effort to channel the work of a natural community. This may be a more challenging route, especially if the goal is to replace the community with the focal unit. Clearly, evolving the strategy along the diagonals implies changing both the control and cognitive aspects of the strategy at the same time. It is likely that this is inherently more difficult than shifting horizontally or vertically.

5   Conclusion

The purpose of the framework is to help organizations evaluate the experiences of others as well as their own goals, while they consider their options for implementing a knowledge management strategy. As managers search for an anodyne for their knowledge management needs, the framework will support their decision-making processes. Alignment with the organization's work processes, culture, and organization structure is definitely going to be a major factor in the decision-making process. Beyond "fit," however, is the issue of execution.

Although the dimensions of the framework are not "measurable" in the traditional sense, it seems clear from the examples that managers will be able to look at a proposed approach and determine how to classify the strategy. Thus, the framework will allow managers to consider how different strategies relate to differences in performance. For example, it is important to be able to consider the implications for innovation of a shift from a community-based strategy to a focal unit approach. Understanding that this could shift the balance of the administrative structure from creating knowledge assets to exploiting them is a valuable outcome of the application of the framework.

Gaining an appreciation for the notion of administrative structure as a critical component is also essential to effective development of a suitable knowledge management strategy. While this may not seem to be a difficult concept to grasp, the definitions in the framework imply that choices about administrative structure are more complex than making "simple" centralized/decentralized decisions. The perspective implicit in the framework is that the administrative structure choice is one of establishing a group that is organizationally determined or allowing a largely self-organizing group to emerge from the fabric of the organization with minimal guidance.

Many factors in today's economic and social environment make it necessary to have a systematic way of developing a knowledge management strategy. The implications of global distribution of people and therefore their knowledge have been widely discussed. Until recently, however, there has been less attention paid to the administrative options for organizing these people to accomplish the knowledge management objectives. Similarly, the role of technology as a means of building connectivity is well known. Less obvious, perhaps, is the trade-off between using an active framing strategy as means of providing structured access in a highly connected organization and using a passive framing strategy that is more readily adaptable to local needs. Now, with many examples of successful knowledge management initiatives and many tools available, a manager's responsibility is to choose an approach that will facilitate the creation, transfer, and use of knowledge to enhance individual and organizational performance. We believe that the framework described in this chapter will aid in identifying strategies that will lead to sustained use of knowledge assets and sustained impact on firm performance.

Acknowledgements

Several of the ideas in this chapter were developed during meetings of the Knowledge Management Working Group of the Boston University Systems Research Center during 1998 and 1999. The authors are grateful to members of this group for their insights and contributions.

References

Baird, L. and J.C. Henderson, "Learning from Action: An Analysis of the Center for Army Lessons Learned (CALL)," *Human Resource Management*, 36, 4, 1997, 385-395.

Baird, L. and J.C. Henderson, *The Knowledge Engine*, San Francisco: Berrett-Koehler, 2001.

Chard, A.M. and M. Sarvary, "Knowledge Management and Ernst & Young," Stanford Business School Case, 1997.

Cohen, D.J. and L. Prusak, *In Good Company: How Social Capital Makes Organizations Work*, Cambridge, MA: Harvard Business School Press, 2000

Davenport, T.H., D.W. De Long, and M.C. Beers, "Successful Knowledge Management Projects," *Sloan Management Review*, 39, 2, 1998, 43-57.

Davenport, T.H. and L. Prusak, *Working Knowledge*, Cambridge, MA: Harvard Business School Press, 1998.

Hansen, M.T., N. Nohria, and T. Tierney, "What's Your Strategy for Managing Knowledge," *Harvard Business Review*, 77, 2, 1999, 106-116.

Leonard-Barton, D., "The Factory as a Learning Laboratory," *Sloan Management Review*, 34, 1992, 23-82.

Lesser, E. and J. Storck, "Communities of Practice and Organizational Performance," *IBM Systems Journal*, 40, 4, 2001, 831-841.

Nonaka, I. and H. Takeuchi, *The Knowledge Creating Company*, New York: Oxford, 1995.

Orr, J., *Talking About Machines: An Ethnography of a Modern Job*, Ithaca, NY: IRL Press, 1996.

Senge, P.M, *The Fifth Discipline: The Art and Practice of the Learning Organization,* New York: Doubleday/Currency, 1990.

Stewart, T.A., *Intellectual Capital*, New York: Doubleday/Currency, 1997.

Storck, J., J.C. Henderson, and A. Cockerill, "Leveraging Expertise at British Petroleum: Drilling for Profits," Boston University Case Study Series, 1999.

Storck, J. and P. Hill, "Knowledge Diffusion through Strategic Communities," *Sloan Management Review,* 41, 2, 2000, 63-74.

Thomas, J.B., S.M. Clark, and D.A. Gioia, "Strategic Sensemaking and Organizational Performance: Linkages Among Scanning, Interpretation, Action, and Outcomes," *Academy of Management Journal*, 36,2, 1993, 239-270.

Weick, K., *Sensemaking in Organizations*, Thousand Oaks, CA: Sage, 1995.

Zack, M.H., "Managing Codified Knowledge", *Sloan Management Review*, 40, 4, 1999a, 45-58.

Zack, M.H., "Developing a Knowledge Strategy", *California Management Review*, 41, 3, 1999b, 125-145.

CHAPTER 27

The Leaders of Knowledge Initiatives: Qualifications, Roles, and Responsibilities

Alex Bennet[1] and Robert Neilson[2]

[1] U. S. Department of Navy Deputy Chief Information Officer

[1] Co-Chair, Government-Wide Knowledge Management Working Group

[2] National Defense University, Chief Knowledge Officer

[2] Institute for National Strategic Studies Faculty Research Fellow

Sponsored by the cross-government Knowledge Management Working Group, working sessions were held through the year 2000 and continuing into 2001 to build an understanding of the concepts, roles, and importance of Knowledge Management. Participants from these sessions came from government, industry, and academia. The "stories" of the processes used and the results of the sessions are detailed in this chapter. Results from these sessions have been used to define the roles of Chief Knowledge Officers in government, and are building blocks for certification programs emerging in the public and private sectors.

Keywords: Certification; Chief Knowledge Officer; Knowledge Manager; Knowledge Worker Roles; Knowledge Worker Responsibilities; Limits

1 Introduction

Over the last several years, organizational leaders have become increasingly aware of the rise of focused knowledge roles in both government and industry. As Chief Knowledge Officers, Knowledge Managers, and a myriad of other titles and roles have entered management literature, a collective understanding has emerged regarding what those roles entail, and how they contribute to the overall mission of the organization. Defining roles, responsibilities, competencies and skills helps embed a rising discipline into the organizational infrastructure. It also helps to redefine how we work. By their very essence, definitions impose limits, bounding and focusing, and providing the opportunities to build and share understanding, and stimulate new growth.

The concept of "limits" has a bad rap in the American language. Limits are often perceived in a negative connotation, but they can also facilitate positive growth. When referring to ideas, each of us lives in a field of possibilities. The limits imposed by defining ideas within a framework encourages deeper understanding and spurs the emergence of new ideas, with the potential for those ideas to go far beyond the defining framework of their birth. In other words, setting limits provides focus that can lead to new thought. A dramatic example of the value of limits can be found in the use of information technology. By placing limits such as open standards and protocols on enterprise systems, there is the opportunity for broader interoperability among and across organizational elements, giving more people data and information and creating the opportunity for greater efficiencies, effectiveness and innovation.

The U.S. government-wide Knowledge Management Working Group, sponsored by the Federal Chief Information Officers Council, held two government-industry-academia workshops at the Information Resources Management College, National Defense University, to define the roles and responsibilities of a Chief Knowledge Officer. These workshops focused on the breadth of knowledge and skills needed by knowledge managers. Along the way, these efforts surfaced current thinking on the importance of Knowledge Management. In a subsequent workshop, through identifying areas of competency, the Federal KM Working Group started to build an understanding of what those things are that make up the discipline of Knowledge Management. The stories (written in a story form) of how these workshops evolved introduce Sections 2 and 4 below.

2   The Importance of KM

2.1   The Process *Story*

Once upon a time, there was a group of three government employees, a professor at the National Defense University and executives from the General Services Administration and Department of the Navy, that recognized an opportunity. Now, in the course of doing a job, opportunities come along fairly often, but how many times do opportunities come along to help define a new emerging discipline? *This* was one of *those* opportunities.

Some few years ago, the group of three began a dialogue on whether there was any substance to the concept of knowledge management as a contributor to agency missions. As time and space began to pass, they had a continuing interest in learning more about why certain organizations paid attention to this thing called "intellectual capital" as a key factor of production. Organizational learning and intellectual capital literature pointed to a confluence of events occurring in the world. The systems thinking and learning organization work propagated by Peter Senge (Senge, 1990), coupled with the seminal work of Leif Edvinsson at Skandia regarding "intellectual capital" (Edvinsson, 1997) as a key determinant of organizational success, seemed to make sense. Additionally, everyone was touting the benefits of collaborative technologies as the next best thing since sliced bread, Tom Stewart was writing about intellectual capital as the new wealth of organizations, and conferences on the topic proliferated.

Concurrently, the U.S Federal Government passed the Information Technology Management Reform Act (1996) establishing Chief Information Officers (CIO) in federal agencies. Federal CIO's were primarily concerned with acquiring computer equipment and keeping networks up and running and secure, paying little attention to the data and information produced by the plethora of systems. Chief

Knowledge Officers (CKOs) arrived on the scene in the private sector touting the importance of tacit knowledge and communities of practice as critical drivers of success. Michael Earl's article "What is a Chief Knowledge Officer?" (Earl, 1999) piqued the group's interest. With all these disparate concepts and activities rattling around their respective heads, it seemed an opportune time to engage in some collective creative thinking to determine what roles CKOs play in public sector organizations.

In an attempt to put some boundaries and limits on the subject of KM as a useful concept in the U.S. Federal Government, a series of government and industry brainstorming sessions were held in May and June 2000. Participants in the first session included CKOs or equivalents from the federal government. The second session included CKOs or equivalents from the private sector, primarily from information technology and consulting businesses. Each group focused on the importance of KM, the role of a CKO in a public sector organization, the competencies that make a CKO successful, and the most important personal attributes CKOs must bring to the job. An overall result was a deeper understanding of the importance of Knowledge Management to organizations as seen through the eyes of both public and private sector Chief Knowledge Officers.

The results of these sessions, as discussed below, can also be viewed and downloaded from the Web at: http://www.ndu.edu/ndu/irmc/km-cio_role/km-cio-role.htm. Additionally, this material was used by the Department of the Navy to develop a career path for knowledge workers. See http://www.don-imit.navy.mil.

2.2   Results: What Is the Importance of KM to Organizations?

Responses to this question can be grouped in loose areas dealing with: eGovernment, productivity, best practices/processes, leadership and decision making, customer satisfaction, competitive advantage/market differentiation, innovation, collaboration, learning, social capital, human capital and structural capital. While organization into these categories is certainly an artificial construct influenced by the authors, it provides a useful way of thinking about and understanding the results to the question: What is the importance of KM to your organization?

Figure 1, "Importance of KM to Your Organization," graphically displays the combined findings of both brainstorming sessions in a hub and spoke diagram. The central question is located in the center of the diagram with enabling verbs located in oval shapes located on the spokes. The main idea or activities are located in rectangular boxes at the end of the spokes. Detailed information for each main idea or activity is located at the periphery of the diagram.

There are clear patterns that emerge from this material. For example, the responses focus on people and processes, with information technology clearly seen as an enabler. One of the key findings of this exercise was that the respondents anchored their responses into strategic organizational functions that drive mission or business goals. While there is little tactical information in these responses that would lead one to assume that KM is a strategic business enabler, the comments grouped under competitive advantage/market differentiation connect KM to business/mission goals.

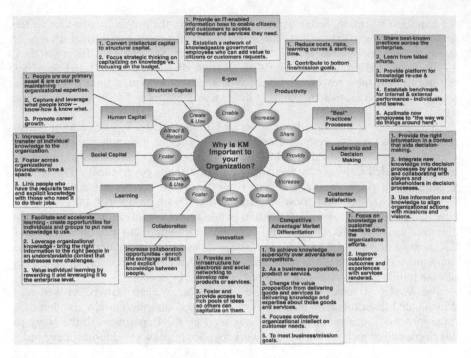

Figure 1. Why is KM Important to Your Organization?

3 Chief Knowledge Officer

3.1 Results: What Is the Role of a CKO in a Public Sector Organization?

Responses to this question show that Chief Knowledge Officers in the public sector play a markedly different role than that of a Chief Information Officer. While CIOs focus much of their activity on physical computer and network assets, CKOs focus their efforts on an integrated set of activities that address organizational behaviors, processes, and technologies. As illustrated in Figure 2, these activities loosely fall in the areas of: leadership and strategy, outcomes, best practices/ processes, knowledge-sharing culture, communities of practice, incentives and rewards, tools and technology, education, taxonomy, and resources

Analyzing the content for each activity indicates that a CKO's role involves leveraging the "soft stuff" in organizations. Creating a knowledge-sharing culture, championing communities of practice, providing leadership and strategy, and using incentives and rewards, are activities that are the province of the CKO, but are tough to measure using traditional and generally accepted business metrics. These activities mirror the activities of successful Chief Executive Officers (CEOs). Michael Earl remarks that CKOs are visionaries, able to see the big picture a CEO has in mind (Earl, 1999). Also, they are entrepreneurs within the organization, getting things done.

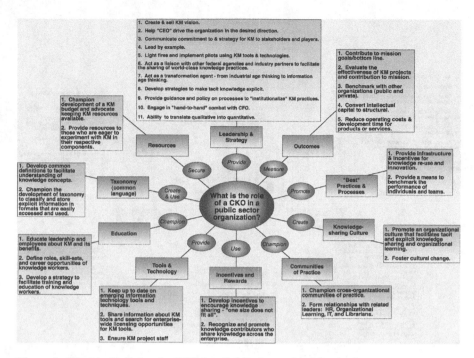

Figure 2. What is the Role of a CKO in a Public Sector Organization?

CKOs must also possess a working knowledge of the tools and technologies to leverage the extant intellectual base in organizations, though they are not necessarily technologists by training. In sum, their role is to create and maintain an environment and atmosphere within which all workers deliver value to the organization using existing and unexploited explicit and tacit knowledge sources. Frequently, CKOs fulfill this role by experimenting and partnering with business units. Additionally, they are charged with the task of charting clear processes, classification schemes, and tools to access and use existing data, information, and explicit and tacit knowledge in a manner that promotes sharing across time, space, and boundaries.

3.2 Results: What Competencies and Skills Make a CKO Successful?

This question attempts to probe beyond some of the existing literature addressing "what CKOs do" and determine what competencies help make CKOs *successful*, i.e., "How would you recognize a third degree black belt CKO if you bumped into one in the hallway?" Responses can be organized into six major competency areas that CKOs, or aspiring CKOs, should possess. These are: leadership and management, communications, strategic thinking, tools and technologies, personal behaviors, and personal knowledge and cognitive capability. See Figure 3 for a graphical representation of these responses.

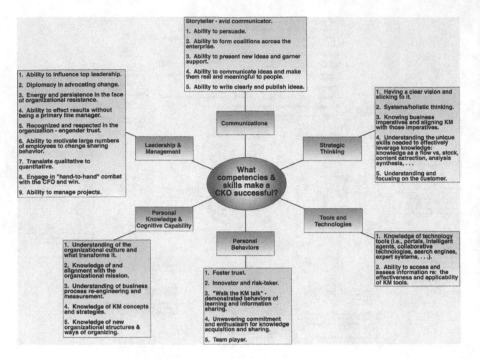

Figure 3. What Competencies and Skills Make a CKO Successful?

Both public and private sector CKOs felt that successful CKOs must think holistically and strategically and must be able to convincingly communicate the value of KM to skeptical audiences. CKOs need to move beyond what Tom Davenport calls "serious anecdote management" (Davenport and Prusak, 1998) and translate qualitative benefits of KM projects into quantitative benefits to win the hearts and minds of Chief Financial Officers (CFOs) and CEOs. Otherwise, many KM projects will fall into the management fad category.

In addition to the requisite leadership and management capabilities, and a working knowledge of tools and technologies, existing and aspiring CKOs need to possess an *a priori* personal knowledge base and cognitive capability set. Without a personal knowledge base and demonstrated personal behaviors, newly appointed CKOs lack credibility and have difficulty "selling" KM concepts to senior management.

3.3 Results: What Are the Most Important Personal Attributes CKOs Must Bring to the Job?

As Earl notes, CKOs come from diverse academic backgrounds and with cross-functional experience in areas including finance, human resources, marketing and academe, to name a few (Earl, 1999). Consequently the question: "What are the most important personal attributes that you as CKOs must bring to the job?" was posed to the participants of the brainstorming sessions to ascertain if there was a consistent list of attributes. Responses to this question included the following attributes: passion, patience, persistence, sensitivity, organizational savvy, smart, wise, life-long learner, "thick skinned," integrator, and depth and breadth of knowledge. With the exception of life-long learner, most of these personal attributes do not discriminate between a CKO and other senior leaders. Good chief executive officers, chief operating officers, and chief financial officers certainly possess the majority of the personal attributes in this list. Upon reflection, the question should have addressed what *unique* personal attributes CKOs should possess in addition to those attributes associated with senior leadership positions.

4   Learning Objectives for Knowledge Manager Certification

4.1   The Process *Story*

In the course of history, and as the world moved into a new era of global connectivity, it came to pass that the United States Government focused on the importance of intellectual capital, and the opportunity offered by knowledge management to help achieve eGovernment. As used here, eGovernment is government of the people, by the people and for the people in a virtual world, a collaborative government where technology meets human creativity, and where government manages and shares its vast stores of knowledge with, and for the benefit of, the citizen.

Out of the growing chaos engendered by the Internet and the nearly exponential increase in data and information, emerged a government-wide Knowledge Management Working Group dedicated to fostering interagency collaboration, interagency communities of practice, and the sharing of knowledge throughout the government. This group, starting from small beginnings, began to grow as more and more government agencies and organizations realized the potential KM holds. But even though each member realized and agreed on this potential, they all had different ways of defining KM, and different ideas about what it could do for their organizations.

At first this appeared confusing, but finally it began to dawn upon this learning community that the true value of KM was both what it held for each of their organizations **and** that it was bringing them together to build a connected and sharing government. Still, there was the realization **that if KM was defined as everything**, KM would, of course, fall short. Nothing can be everything. So the government-wide KM group devised a plan. They would partner with not only each other, but also with academia and industry associations, to figure out what those things were in KM that made sense for government knowledge workers – like Knowledge Managers and Chief Knowledge Officers – to know.

Now a great cry went up throughout the land to find those partners who already offered KM certification programs, those partners who had knowledge of and an interest in what a government KM certification program might look like. And lo and behold, they were found, and they agreed to participate in this important endeavor. Together, government, industry associations and academic organizations began to define a conceptual framework for KM through developing criteria for accredited government certification programs. The result was a draft set of learning objectives for government employees attending certification courses. And this end was the beginning.

4.2 Knowledge and Understanding

The learning objectives developed by the government-wide KM Working Group cover the breadth of what is needed to implement knowledge management successfully in the federal sector. The depth of knowledge and ability needed in each area is highly dependent on the specific job that needs to be done. Half of the learning objectives identified through the above process are concerned with the specific knowledge an individual needs in order to work effectively in the area of Knowledge Management. These are discussed in this subsection.

4.2.1   Have knowledge of the value added by Knowledge Management to the business proposition, including the return on investment, performance measures, and the ability to develop a business case.

Although Knowledge Management is capitalized in this sentence, we often speak to knowledge management as having a small "k" and a small "m." The intent is that knowledge management is not an initiative in and of itself, but supports the mission and business objectives of the organization. This objective positions KM as a strategic enabler at the enterprise level. Fundamental in this objective is tie-in to strategic business planning such as is accomplished with the Balanced Scorecard process. KM is an extremely broad discipline and using metrics brings solid management practices to the forefront of decision makers, thereby enabling choices. As KM matches corresponding effort with metrics in other domains of the firm, it will be recognized as a viable management practice.

Performance measures are the essence of good management practices. The progress of KM initiatives needs to be continually monitored to ensure progress toward their objectives. Given the complex and dynamic nature of modern organizations, KM – or any other organizational initiative – cannot guarantee that plans and strategies will succeed. Well-designed performance measures provide indications of the efficiency and effectiveness of people, processes, and programs, which in turn help managers understand and adapt their organizations. Indeed, performance measures are so integral to organizational success that the Federal Government has passed several pieces of legislation that specifically call for formal metrics. Legislation during the last ten years includes the Government Performance and Results Act (GPRA) of 1993, the Government Management Reform Act of 1994, and the Information Technology Management Reform Act of 1996.

4.2.2   Have knowledge of the strategies and processes to transfer explicit and tacit knowledge across time, space and organizational boundaries, including retrieval of critical archived information enabling ideas to build upon ideas.

Since Nonaka and Takeuchi first explored the interaction between tacit and explicit knowledge in *The Knowledge-Creating Company,* there has been a steady growth of interest on the capture of tacit knowledge. Aging workforce issues in the public sector have served as a catalyst for the development of processes and systems that facilitate understanding the role and importance of context in decision-making.

But this objective goes even farther. Transfer is the focus, not just understanding the nature of tacit and explicit knowledge. Increasing the dynamics of transfer by itself moves knowledge through the organization at an increased rate. The more knowledge is being transferred, the more it is available to the organization as a resource.

Understanding the relationship between tacit and explicit knowledge and its impact on the organization leads to informed decisions on an organization's knowledge management approach. A high ratio of *tacit* knowledge (knowledge held by the individual in his/her head) leads to a strong dependence on the individual and reliance on the connectivity between individuals for knowledge flow. The loss of that individual and his/her knowledge can have a serious effect on the organization. A high ratio of *explicit* knowledge requires an investment in the transfer of knowledge from tacit to explicit and may present issues regarding context, currency, and authoritative source. However, a high ratio of explicit knowledge leads to less dependence on the individual, and explicit knowledge can be stored and easily moved around.

4.2.3   Have knowledge of state-of-the-art and evolving technology solutions that promote KM, including portals and collaborative and distributed learning technologies.

We live in a world of technology. The exponential increase in data and information is both driven and enabled by information technology. We have the ability to reach further and further *within* domains and *across* domains for ideas and solutions. Knowledge repositories, automated libraries, computer services, databases, etc. offer the capability for not only storing large amounts of data and information, but also efficient and intelligent retrieval and assemblage capability. Powerful search algorithms, intelligent agents and semantic interpreters allow employees to rapidly retrieve information needed for problem solving and decision-making. Knowledge managers need to be aware of these capabilities, how they are used and how to integrate their operation with people to ensure knowledge availability and application.

In many organizations, portals are the principle delivery mechanism for an enterprise's knowledge sharing. Collaborative systems range from intranets to video teleconferencing to whiteboards. Their purpose is to aid groups of individuals, either co-located or dispersed, to work more effectively together to foster innovations, solve problems and make decisions. For example, distributed learning uses information technology to facilitate learning without having the instructor co-located. Individuals at different locations, using their own PCs, can learn via the Internet or computer-based training. The increasing rate of change necessitates the need for faster learning, forcing us to change our traditional concepts. Classroom-based learning may be supplemented or complemented with new virtual capabilities.

4.2.4   Have knowledge of and the ability to facilitate knowledge creation, sharing and reuse including developing partnerships and alliances, designing creative knowledge spaces, and using incentive structures.

Knowledge creation, sharing and reuse are the heart of Knowledge Management programs, and indeed these behaviors are intricately tied to each other. As people share knowledge within an organization, and others use it and find new ways to improve on it and innovate, the value of that knowledge increases for the entire organization. This process also provides the opportunity to identify integrators (knowledge leaders who connect people and ideas together) and subject matter experts (who provide a depth of thinking in specific areas). In turn, those involved in exchanges benefit from the exchange through a more complete understanding of the area addressed, thereby becoming a more valuable resource to the organization.

Three examples of facilitating knowledge creation, sharing and reuse are included in this objective to facilitate an understanding of the eclectic nature of KM. Partnerships and Alliances are means by which organizations can share information and knowledge while working together toward mutual goals. Knowledge spaces build on the concept of "open space," providing space and time for people to mentally explore events or thoughts and formulate ways in which to proceed. Open space, whether physical or virtual, provides a place to brainstorm and be creative. It comes in many forms: online chat rooms, threaded e-mail discussions, weekly in-person discussion forums, communities, discussion groups, coffee rooms, and water cooler encounters. Here knowledge workers can sort out complexities and receive feedback from others, hopefully resulting in new ideas and improved decision-making capabilities.

Senior leaders and managers may need to revamp incentive and reward structures and performance measures to help promote the creation, sharing and reuse of knowledge. Some organizations provide bonuses and other rewards to individuals who go out of their way to share knowledge with others. Event intermediations such as Knowledge Fairs have been successfully held in such organizations as The World Bank and the Department of the Navy.

4.2.5   Have knowledge of learning styles and behaviors, strive for continuous improvement and be actively engaged in exploring new ideas and concepts.

People learn differently. Some learn through reading, others through lectures or visual or graphic representations while still others learn by doing. Effective transfer of information requires understanding different learning styles and how people learn. Adults learn best from direct experience with real-world problems. How can this be extrapolated across a virtual environment? As learning becomes the mutual responsibility of leaders and workers, knowledge professionals must be constant learners, seeking new information and exhibiting behavior for others to model by continuously striving to improve the organization's use of information and knowledge.

This objective also sets the stage for capitalizing on new learning approaches including broadband web-based multi-media. As new concepts unfold, models and theories for learning will evolve. A foundation in this area will prepare Knowledge Managers for the future.

4.2.6 Have working knowledge of state-of-the-art research and implementation strategies for knowledge management, information management, document and records management, and data management. This includes project management of knowledge initiatives and retrieval of critical archived information.

Knowledge leaders and workers need to understand the conceptual linkages between Knowledge Management, Information Management and Data and Records Management. KM is part of a larger movement enabled by information technology, a movement that has brought us into the Information Age and is rapidly propelling us toward an age of increasing complexity where knowledge appears to be the only thing that can deal with complexity. There are continuing advances in data management, document and records management, and information management that will make information technology infrastructures more effective in supporting knowledge workers as they strive to make their organization more effective through the intelligent management of knowledge.

4.2.7 Have understanding of the global and economic importance of developing knowledge-based organizations to meet the challenges of the knowledge era.

We live in an omni-linked world. Anyone in the world can talk to almost anyone else in the world real-time. Technology has provided totally new ways of moving and transferring data, information and knowledge among individuals, organizations and governments. The results of these interactions are increased communication, and a corresponding increase in the flow of ideas and the making of decisions. Organizations are forced to scan, select and quickly respond to the increased flow of web-based exchanges and actions. Moreover, as the number of nodes in networks increase, the number of links increase, and as the links and their consequent relationships increase, so does the complexity. Critical thinking, the possession of deep knowledge and the ability to work collaboratively with others who think differently may help address issues of increasing complexity. Knowledge-based organizations need to provide time and space for critical thinking.

4.3 Abilities

The second half of the KM learning objectives deals with abilities, or skills. These are discussed briefly below.

4.3.1 Have the ability to use systems thinking in implementing solutions.

KM addresses powerful activities throughout environments, organizations, cultures and economies. As one considers the relevant issues and opportunities, Systems Thinking provides a means for looking at the "big" picture while examining the component parts.

Systems Thinking assumes that almost everything is a system, made up of connecting elements. Systems have boundaries and behaviors that are different from their individual elements. Systems Thinking emphasizes the importance of relationships and structure within the organization and makes individuals aware of the effects of their efforts on others in the organization, permitting them to understand and perform their roles more effectively.

The Learning Organization work coming out of the Massachusetts Institute of Technology includes a systems thinking approach to improve decision-makers' strategic thinking skills. Systems thinking helps manage complexity by providing a tool for decision-makers to map and understand cause and effect relationships among data, information and events in an organization. This is done through a process of identifying patterns that repeat themselves over and over again in decision-making and organizational life. This process forces decision-makers to consider the consequences of their actions and their impact on and relationship to other organizational functions. Systems thinking not only helps increase an individual's critical thinking skills, but also enhances collaboration and serves as a basis for collective inquiry by providing a common language and perspective for dialogue and understanding.

4.3.2   Have the ability to design, develop and sustain communities of interest and practice.

Communities are social constructs. In a primarily virtual world, communities provide a fundamental capability for developing and sharing expertise throughout the workforce. Communities of practice share a domain of practice, crossing operational, functional and organizational boundaries, and defining themselves by knowledge areas, not tasks. In like manner, communities of interest share a domain of interest. Communities are managed by establishing and developing connections between individuals and organizations, and focusing on value added, mutual exchange and continuous learning. Communities have an evolving agenda as participant knowledge builds and related areas of exchange emerge.

Collaboration, innovation, learning, and knowledge sharing are at the core of communities of practice and interest. Communities increase information flows in order to maximize knowledge, and exploit existing competencies to achieve maximum return. They also facilitate the transfer of best practices and lessons learned between organizational content centers, thus creating efficiencies while improving effectiveness. And Communities fill in the gaps where organizational knowledge falls short and where enterprise information is under exploited. In short, sometimes we do not know what we do not know. Communities encourage personnel to access key resources and build new knowledge to complete tasks faster, better and easier.

4.3.3   Have the ability to create, develop and sustain the flow of knowledge. This includes understanding the skills needed to leverage virtual teamwork and social networks.

The flow of data, information and knowledge moves around in the networks of systems and people. It is shared through team interaction, communities and events, and is facilitated through knowledge repositories and portals. This flow is both horizontal and vertical, including the continuous, rapid two-way communication between key components of the organization and top-level decisionmakers.

With increased connectivity, we reach further and further across organizations, communities, industries and the globe to tap resources. Virtual teamwork requires new skills of leadership, management and facilitation to create and maintain the trust, open communication and interdependencies needed for physically separated individuals to collaborate effectively.

Many companies and organizations invest a considerable amount of money in restructuring organizational charts and re-engineering business processes only to be disappointed with the results. That is because much of the work happens *outside* the formal organizational structure. Often what needs attention is the informal organization, the networks of relationships that employees form across functions and divisions need to quickly accomplish tasks. These informal relationships can cut through formal reporting procedures to jump-start stalled initiatives and meet extraordinary deadlines. However, information networks can just as easily sabotage the best laid plans of companies by blocking communication and fomenting opposition to change unless leaders know how to identify and direct them. Learning how to map these social links can help harness the real power of organizations.

4.3.4   Have the ability to perform cultural and ethnographic analyses, develop knowledge taxonomies, facilitate knowledge audits, and perform knowledge mapping and needs assessments.

As the amount of information and knowledge increases, tools such as taxonomies, audits and maps help organize information for decision-making. While search engines and agents keep improving, the bottom line is that the human brain is the final arbiter of effective relationships and patterns. Analytic techniques such as cultural and ethnographic analyses help leaders understand organizational cultures and their characteristics. Culture is often cited as one of the main barriers to successful implementation of KM.

A taxonomy is a framework for arranging or categorizing information and knowledge so that people can find and use it effectively. This is applicable when designing a knowledge base, but also applies to the wider knowledge system. For example, if knowledge is organized into groupings based upon a community of interest (or practice) on a web-site or knowledge base, then mentoring programs, training and other knowledge transfer processes should support these same groupings to facilitate knowledge flow. It is not necessary to pick just one way of arranging information and knowledge, but it is important to evaluate the many different ways before beginning any kind of knowledge base design.

Conducting a "knowledge audit" to find out how information is collected, stored and reported, and how the reports are used (if at all) can be beneficial in streamlining the information flow within an organization, saving time and effort. A knowledge audit examines what information is available and whether it is used. Simply put, the purpose of a knowledge audit is to help the organization "know what it knows" and then measure the quantity and usefulness of that knowledge base.

4.3.5   Have the ability to capture, evaluate and use best-known practices, including the use of storytelling to transfer these best practices.

The use of best practices across industry and government can provide efficiencies and increase effectiveness, if they are indeed best practices for the organization implementing them. How is the applicability of a best practice determined? How do you understand the context of the best practice, the simple rules that made it successful in some organizations?

Storytelling, the construction of examples to illustrate a point, can be used to effectively transfer knowledge, and best practices. An organizational story is a detailed narrative of management actions, employee interactions, or other intra-organizational events that are communicated informally within the organization. A variety of story forms exist and will arise naturally throughout organizations, including scenarios and anecdotes. Scenarios are the articulation of possible future states, constructed within the imaginative limits of the author. While scenarios provide an awareness of alternatives – of value in and of itself – they are often used as planning tools for possible future situations. The plan becomes a vehicle to respond to recognized key elements in each scenario. An anecdote is a brief sequence experienced in the field or arising from a brainstorming session. To reinforce positive behavior, sensitive managers can seek out and disseminate anecdotes that embody the value desired in the organization. The capture and distribution of anecdotes across organizations carries high value. Dave Snowden, a consultant and author in Great Britain who has investigated the use of storytelling in organizations for the past dozen years, has discovered that once a critical number of anecdotes are captured from a community, the value set or rules underlying the behavior of that community can be determined (Snowden, 1999). Understanding these values allows the use of informal as well as formal aspects of the organization.

Conveying information in a story provides a rich context. Context remains in memory longer and creates more memory traces than random information bites. Therefore, a story is more likely to be acted upon than other means of communication. Storytelling connects people, develops creativity, and increases confidence. The appeal of stories in organizations helps build descriptive capabilities, increase organizational learning, convey complex meaning and communicate common values and rule sets.

4.3.6   Have the ability to manage change and complex knowledge projects.

Management concepts, whether old or new, are about change management. And in today's world where complexity is increasing, according to Ashby's Law of Requisite Variety there must be as many or more ways to change a system as those things in a system that need to be changed.

Cultural change of any kind is a long, slow process. Accomplishing change requires daily support of sharing knowledge openly throughout the entire organization. KM initiatives are particularly challenging to change agents because of the uncertainty of outcome. Most managers like to change only one or two things at a time to mitigate against unintended consequences. When many factors within the organization are simultaneously changed, communicating, coordination and leadership become important in reducing resistance to change and maintaining motivation.

4.3.7 Have the ability to identify customers and stakeholders and tie organizational goals to the needs and requirements of those customers and stakeholders.

Total Quality Management brought to the forefront the tried and true values successful organizations have used for years, a focus on customers and stakeholders. No matter what new approach or initiative is popular, we must keep a focused eye on the needs of our constituents, and ensure all efforts underway contribute to fulfilling their needs. This makes good business sense.

5 Summary

The learning objectives developed for government certification programs serve as a candidate list regarding what should be included in educational programs and what is important in defining the boundaries of knowledge management in both the public and private sectors. While the results of the brainstorming and working sessions discussed above represent the views of participants, the sessions seem to confirm the results of similar studies and much of the work included in this collection.

The challenge for future research is to advance the theoretical understanding of knowledge management while at the same time applying practical KM concepts in organizations. The concept of *praxis* where practice builds theory and theory builds practice may apply to further exploration of KM. Searching for a single universal theory underpinning KM may well be a never-ending quest. But relying on a multiplicity of theoretical bases may well serve the academics and practitioners in their continuing quest to define and set boundaries on the field of knowledge management ... those limits that will allow us to collectively create new ideas and new directions for the organizations of the future.

References

Bennet, A. and D. Bennet, "Characterizing the Next Generation Knowledge Organization" *Knowledge And Innovation: Journal of the KMCI*, 1, 1, 2000, 8-42.

Davenport, T. and L. Prusak, *Working Knowledge,* Boston, MA: Harvard Business School Press, 1998.

Denning, S., *The Springboard Story: How Storytelling Ignites Action in Knowledge-Era Organizations*, Boston, MA: Butterworth Heinemann, 2001.

Earl, M. and I. Scott, "What is a Chief Knowledge Officer?" *Sloan Management Review,* 40, 2, 1999, 29-38.

Edvinsson, L. and M. Malone, *Intellectual Capital.* New York: Harper Business, 1997.

Department of the Navy, *The Knowledge Centric Organization Toolkit.* Washington, D.C.: DON, 1999.

Federal Government KM Working Group, "Minutes from Working Symposium,"
National Defense University, 2000.

Nonaka, I. And H. Takeuchi, *The Knowledge-Creating Company,* New York: Oxford University Press, 1995.

Senge, P., *The Fifth Discipline: The Art & Practice of the Learning Organization,*
New York, NY: Doubleday, 1990.

Snowden, D., "The Paradox of Story: Simplicity and Complexity in Strategy,"
Journal of Strategy & Scenario Planning, November, 1999.

CHAPTER 28

The 7 C's of Knowledge Leadership: Innovating Our Future[*]

Debra M. Amidon[1] and Doug Macnamara[2]

[1] Entovation International, Ltd., Wilmington, MA, USA

[2] Banff Executive Leadership Inc., Banff, Alberta, Canada

Leadership is a key influence on the conduct and outcomes of knowledge management in organizations and economies. This chapter advances and describes seven essential aspects of effective knowledge leadership: context, competence, culture, communities, conversation, communication, and coaching. It argues for the importance of leadership in measuring the results of knowledge initiatives. The chapter closes with a knowledge leadership litmus test.

Keywords: Coaching; Communication; Communities; Competence; Context; Conversation, Culture; Innovation; Knowledge Economy; Knowledge Leadership; Leadership

1 Introduction

> *"Few of the inventors responsible for the astonishing wave of innovation between 1750 and 1860 were scientists; most were artisans or engineers with little or no scientific training. They were men of common sense, curiosity, energy and a vast ingenuity, standing on the shoulders not of scholars but of similar practical types."* – Special Millennium Edition of The Economist, December, 1999

A new economic world order is emerging – one based on the flow of intellectual, not financial, capital. Every function, every industry, and every region of the world – developing and industrialized nations alike – is experiencing profound changes in the way we manage our most precious resource – human talent. Modern management concepts are evolving from practitioners – not the theoretical academic research base. Leading (and being led) is more a function of navigation and networking than the traditional command-and-control systems with which we are familiar.

Most astute executive managers have seen beyond the limitations of an information society, technology-enamoured strategies, and the dot.com phenomenon. Modern leaders do not fear the speed of change; they embrace an agenda of learning. They know that effective management is not a matter of having the most

---

knowledge; it is knowing how to use it. It is not enough to know modern management concepts. How do they get implemented (i.e., put into action)? Leadership is more an art than a science, but that doesn't excuse us from searching for appropriate metrics for a return-on-leadership (ROL). We must develop an innovation competence and how to measure the performance thereof.

At the heart of the current transformation is the human being within whom knowledge resides. And the path to a sustainable future is an ability to innovate – create knowledge, convert it into viable products and services, and apply it for the profitable growth of an enterprise, the vitality of a nation's economy, and the advancement of society. It is that simple and that complex.

There is certainly nothing new about the link of knowledge and progress. Since man began to interact with his environment, what he knew was essential for survival. What is different about the Knowledge Economy is our ability to focus on and manage knowledge – individual and collective – more explicitly. Because of the multiplier effect of knowledge – the more it is shared, the more it grows – we are now evolving a view of executive development demanding a new style of leadership behavior.

The agricultural, industrial, and short-lived information age utilized linear, competitive, market-share oriented management models. The new economy is far more a function of a system dynamic based on more intangible variables – intellectual capital, alliances/partnering, and global communications – both human and technical. Strategic plans – although essential – are not enough to command sustained market positioning. Progress is more a function of strategy; and strategy is the art of effective leadership.

2   How Does Leadership Differ in a Knowledge Economy?

Gone are the days when one measures the effectiveness of employee training and professional development based on the number of days or hours spent on courses. Most business resources are considered in a cost-valuation framework. Leadership must have an impact on the individual and the organization. Real value is created when connections are made between seemingly isolated elements. Margaret J. Wheatley (1999) suggests: "The literature on organizational innovation is rich in lessons…describes processes that are also prevalent in the natural universe. Innovation is fostered by information gathered from new connections; form insights gained from journeys into other disciplines or places; from active, collegial networks and fluid, open boundaries. Innovation arises from circles of exchange, where information is not just accumulated or stored, but created. Knowledge is generated anew from connections that weren't there before."

21st Century leadership demands more vision and visibility. It is not only a function of learned behaviors, but also how those behaviors demonstrate impact. With global communications, there will be a perceived levelling of competence. Knowledge obsolesce will accelerate. The 'Digital Divide' could exacerbate the gap between the haves and have nots; but the human (vs. the information or technology) agenda will place the emphasis on all people and all cultures – where it belongs! Real-time learning will become the critical success factor for prosperity in both the public and private sectors. Leaders used to focus on 'leading' the organization. Tomorrow's leaders will be perceived more of local, national, regional and international statesmen (and women) who are able to effectively balance economics, education and the environment.

3   Redefining the Management Agenda

We live in a world of kaleidoscopic change. It is not the speed of change of a variable, or the speed of change of multiple variables. It is the compounding effect of the speed of change of multiple variables creating a landscape for innovation that challenges even the most adept manager. There is a new Knowledge Value Proposition. Cost, quality, and time are no longer the differentiators for market positioning. It is a far more complex relationship between economics, technology, and behavior – sociological, psychological, managerial – that constitutes the "social capital" of an organization.

Here, we identify seven domains where we might (re)consider the implications for knowledge leadership.

3.1 Knowledge Leadership Is a Matter of *Context*

In the new Human Capital orientation, performance metrics are dynamic and based on measuring the intangibles. Table 1 contrasts this with the traditional orientation. Organizational structures are networked with self-managing knowledge workers. The processes transcend organization boundaries, linking all stakeholders (e.g., suppliers, alliance partners, distributors, customers, and even competitors) into a strategic innovation system. Information technology is used for knowledge processing – monitoring the flow of knowledge (i.e., how ideas are generated and commercialized).

Most important, it is not one orientation – Financial or Human – at the expense of another. Both are necessary to ensure optimal flexibility, adaptability, and agility.

Effective Knowledge Leadership is also a function of vision – and will increasingly be more so. Yet, according to Albert Hochleitner, Director General, Siemens Österrich, "Less than 2% of our time is spent on the future perspective. Some companies are even lower than 1%! Although the urgent business of everyday life is important, it is not as important as the future."[1] The reality is that executives know that visioning is important; but they haven't a clue how to effectively implement it, given such accelerating uncertainty.

It may not be that the 'Knowledge Leader' is the one to create the vision – far from it. He/she must, however, create the frame within which the vision can be created by a critical mass of organization stakeholders. The leader manages the innovation infrastructure within which ideas are generated and applied. It is a function of listening, guiding thought and cross-leveraging insights. Once created, the vision can/must be articulated broadly both inside and outside the firm.

---

[1] Observations presented in the ALPACH Conference, Austria. July 1999.

Table 1. Contrast in Management Styles (Amidon, et al., 1998)

	Traditional/Industrial (Financial Capital)	Knowledge/Innovation (Human Capital)
Performance Measures	• Financial • Static • $$$ as assets	• Comprehensive • Dynamic • Relationships as assets
Structure/Culture	• Competitive • Market share • Distrust of borders	• Collaborative • Sets of alliances • Value-adding
People/Leadership	• Cost/expense • Profitability	• Revenue/investment • Sustained growth
Process	• Independence • Cause-effect	• Interdependence • Value system
Technology	• Information processing • Data/information • Things/warehouse	• Knowledge processing • Tacit/explicit knowledge • Flow/process

Today's leaders must inspire passion for the work. They need to ensure that teams are stable enough to meet the high frequency burst of information and complex demands on decision-making. They must have an ability to help others maintain focus and balanced as they establish priorities. They lead by example, walk-the-talk, and understand fundamentally the 'whole.' They are able to convey context and meaning in ways that enable others to leverage their own talents.

3.2 Knowledge Leadership Is a Matter of *Competence*

Although Peter F. Drucker (1995) does suggest that innovation is the one competence needed to manage into the future, we know there are several sub-competencies that come into play. For the last seven years, The Banff Centre for Management has been researching and developing a competency-profiling system to assist managers in measuring the impact of their investment in the residential, experiential executive programs. So far, it has been tested with 5,000 executives from 500 organizations. 70% of organization competencies are generic and 30% are specific to the organization, its industry, and regional presence. Through customization, an organization can tailor and monitor its desired proficiency.

A Competency Map is an assessment tool that outlines the skills and behaviors required to successfully undertake a position or role. There are 35 identified competencies organized with the following categories: Direction Setting; Change Leadership; Critical Thinking; Organizational Development and Diversity; Personal/Organization Balance; Quality, Knowledge and Innovation. Each includes four levels of aptitude – an example of which is illustrated in Table 1.

   Through the profiles and learning contract, the process provides for a. Evaluation of a leader's competencies against researched standards, b. Agreement between the participant, their supervisor and the instructor (i.e., the learning triad)
and c. Measurement of successful changes in behavior.

Table 2. Sample Competency Map

UNDER-PINNING	LEVEL 1	LEVEL 2	LEVEL 3	LEVEL 4
A **Sales/ marketing customer service**	• "Pushes Product" • provides information in format they use	• listens for needs • provides solution options	• builds relationships • proactive idea and solution generation	• builds partnerships • focuses on customer's customer or strategic goals
B **Personal/ Team Leadership**	• personally competent	• able to get immediate team functioning competently	• works effectively inter-departmentally • can successfully lead an inter-departmental team	• works effectively inter-organizationally • often seen as an industry leader
C **Adult Development**	• focussed on "what's in it for me:"	• works well in defined parameters • employs cause & effect thinking/ analysis • traditional approaches	• 'Systems' thinker • analyzer • initiates new ideas, projects • takes responsibility for own career and activities	• self-directed • multi-systems thinker/ analyzer • systematizes external/ internal input and creative processes

It is almost impossible to be taught leadership. You have to learn it, experience it
and be supported in the process. Too often, we sign-up for courses and expect to
become a better leader. The truth is that the process can hardly be left to serendipity. The Banff Centre outlines a five-step learning process:

Step One – The Competency Profile: Assess the learner's competence in several
aspects related to their role. Peers and colleagues can offer observation and feedback. Some organizations, such as Royal Bank, Stentor, Canadian Occidental Petroleum, CP Rail and Alberta Agriculture Food and Rural Development have created such Maps as a basis for performance management. The more specific and
discrete you can be, the more relevance you can create with a prospective learner.

Step Two – The Learning Contract: Identify what is of most importance for the learner and focus. Capable individuals can generally only work on 4-5 major attributes at a time. By bringing together the learner, supervisor, and instructor, priorities can be established – identifying strengths, particular areas of focus, and strategies for testing learned competencies.

Step Three – The Learning Process: Whether pre-course, on-course or post-course, the Profile and Learning Contract provide focus. However, if the learning environment is simply academic or knowledge-transfer in design, results are suboptimal. Learning must be hands-on. It must provide participants with opportunities to experiment with new behaviors, receive feedback, and (re)focus their learning. The learning environment must support creativity, critical inquiry, and practical application – the same criteria necessary for successful implementation of new concepts.

Step Four – Re-entry Planning: Careful consideration of the return to the workplace is essential. Individuals who have experienced intense remote learning environments cannot be expected to return to their organizations and 'teach' others. Re-entry is far more of a listening exercise – identifying language, motivation and talent in others ready to be nurtured.

Step Five – Measurement of Impact: Successful demonstration of desired skills and learning competencies is essential. You cannot learn about management and leadership by 'talking' about it. These knowledge concepts seem new at first. The good news is that they are intuitively obvious and clarify many 'fuzzy, soft' management concepts by illustrating how they contribute to the bottom line when put into practice.

Of course, there are new competencies emerging as we write. Research into 33 case study examples of knowledge leadership in practice identified new roles and skills for the Knowledge Age. There are now position titles as knowledge architect, knowledge engineer, knowledge editor, knowledge analyst, knowledge navigator, knowledge gatekeeper, and knowledge brokers. There is considerable debate among knowledge professionals as to the relative merit of having a Chief Knowledge Officer (CKO). Regardless of your adoption of the knowledge nomenclature, it is essential that someone be designated to oversee the innovation process – how knowledge is created, exchanged, and applied in your organization for future sustainability.

3.3 Knowledge Leadership Is a Matter of *Culture*

Leadership training may be vested in the individual; but impactful leadership must start at the top and become an integral part of the organizational culture. Oftentimes, we see organizations investing in leadership development at he individual level, while the corporation values and culture remain unchanged.

Although in a survey administered in 1997, innovation was defined as the number-one advantage of a knowledge program, developing a culture of knowledge-sharing is unquestionably the greatest obstacle (Skyrme and Amidon, 1997).

Over the long-term, culture does more to influence the impact of corporate leadership than any other factor. It determines how individuals react and perform on a daily basis. Culture includes years of history – including successes and failures, good and bad decisions, individual and collective stories. All of these create a set of values – explicit and implicit – that constitute the underpinnings of the enterprise culture. The culture is what determines how leadership is or isn't manifested in an organization.

The two greatest obstacles to successful knowledge leadership are a lack of trust and inadequate communications – specifically regarding values, mission and critical success factors. These two elements, combined with a lack of vision, appear to be at the root of leadership duress.

Trust is a multi-faceted and elusive concept that pervades everything we do. It includes other attributes, such as accountability, integrity, honesty and ethics. Nothing erodes or destroys corporate leadership than mis-trust. Distrustful leaders may achieve mediocre improvements, but they will never effectively harness the passion for outstanding business results.

Poor communications – both human and technical – may be the greatest leadership weakness. It leads to the ineffective performance, poor morale, and internal confusion. With continuous downsizing, constructive knowledge-sharing ceases. Worse, organizations become paralyzed with a lack of responsible risk-taking – an essential criteria for innovation.

Without vision, the organization and its constituency – are at a loss for a sense of direction. Usually, visions are actually only missions. They do not provide an articulation of an organization's uniqueness, or its aspirations. They do not articulate stretch goals that fire the imagination of employees and customers.

Creating and sustaining a culture where knowledge is valued is one of the most difficult challenges in practice. Appropriate cultures are those that engender change, innovation, openness, and trust. People are recognized and rewarded for their knowledge contribution. Conditions for effective knowledge creation and sharing require more flexible, networked organizational structures, multiple teams, and a climate of intensive and purposeful networking.

Several factors help create the conditions that encourage knowledge-sharing – systems for moving people (e.g., job rotation), appropriate learning events, effective teaming, and a comprehensive technology infrastructure.

3.4 Knowledge Leadership Is a Matter of *Communities*

Over the years, various disciplines or schools of thought – and even functions – have begun to converge in scope of responsibility and practice. Each area has been broadening its theories and integrating core principles from the domains of others. There is a convergence of functional perspectives and a common agenda is emerging.

For instance, human resource professionals seek to develop more relevant performance measures as well as new ways to use information technology. Chief Information Officers, in order to justify investments in technology, are having to understand the organization structure, motivations of people, and cross-boundary processes. Quality experts are building training infrastructures for the transfer of knowledge and best practices. R&D managers are taking on new responsibilities for business development and reducing cycle time with increased customer interaction. Finance professionals are exploring ways to expand their audit capabilities to influence the business strategy of their clients. All are relying on emerging computer and communications technology advancements to do so.

There is a realization of – and respect for – alternative paradigms that did not exist a decade ago. Value is being created in the organization interfaces – the white space – the connections *between* individuals, organizations, and companies in the same industries and nations within regions of the world.

This notion of Communities of Practice originated with Etienne Wenger, Institute for Research on Learning, and John Seely Brown, Vice President of Xerox PARC (Palo Alto, California). Likely an outgrowth of quality circles and networked organizations, this is a concept that – when made explicit – helps harness the creativity and promote cross-fertilization of ideas necessary for prosperous innovation. "At the simplest level, they are a small group of people who've worked together over a period of time … not a team, not a task force, not necessarily an authorized or identified group … perform the same tasks … or collaborate on a shared task … or work together on a product. They are peers in the execution of real work. What holds them together is a common sense of purpose and a real need to know what each other knows" (Brown and Gray, 1995).

Even the best strategic planning process often does not provide for an understanding of such natural connections. However, modern managers must take notice of these streams of activity to optimize the innovation process. This is where knowledge leadership resides – where ideas originate, are exchanged, and eventually result in marketable products and services. Observing this convergence of competencies provides insights into how the entire operation may be effectively led.

Innovation becomes the glue that bonds together diverse constituencies. Knowledge and intellectual capital become the mechanisms to build synergy. Such a redefined focus on knowledge and innovation is not the latest consulting fad. It is the essence of sustainable organizations and economies of the future. Instead of operating from the pure perspective of competition, leaders will learn to collaborate and contribute to the success of one another. We are no longer managing a zero-sum game!

3.5 Knowledge Leadership Is a Matter of *Conversations* and *Common Language*

Of primary importance is the innovation language – a language that transcends the paradigm and biases of one particular function. Ideally, such a language would also encompass industries, sectors, and regions of the world and, therefore, be universal in scope.

There are several attempts to define the knowledge language with a glossary of terms – one such effort initiated by Skandia and Ericsson in Sweden – includes an on-line capability to add to the existing 400 terms. Of course, whatever terms or language is adopted must apply to the heritage, purpose, mission and strategy of the enterprise. Such language must pervade all operations and planning efforts.

Once connections are made among internal and external constituencies – with an explicit understanding of potential spheres of influence – attention should be given to purposeful conversations. Mastering the art of structured conversation and dialogue has been the focus of many academic consultants (e.g., Peter Senge, Fernando Flores, and Dan Kim).

Furthermore, there are many successful CEOs beginning to manage according to the quality and level of conversations (Amidon, 1997). One case in point is Ray Stata, Chairman of Analog Devices of Norwood, Massachusetts. In his quest for improvement, Stata began a quest for a common language and shared vision. In the process, he discovered that learning and improvement are really two sides of the same coin. Through a weeklong course for his senior executive team, he realized the value of conversations – the flow of meaning, if you will – among and between his senior management. The common bond was the quest for highly effective learning.

Stata's style is to encourage his employees to become a community of inquirer's, not advocates. With such a mindset, managers are encouraged to understand and leverage the diversity of knowledge, skills, experiences of one another. His organization is described as a 'network of conversations' – a theme he elaborates both internally and externally.

3.6   Knowledge Leadership Is a Matter of *Communications*

Given the dramatic increases in the functionality of computer and communications technology – including the explosion of the World Wide Web and e-commerce – companies must develop a strategy of how best to leverage the technology. There must take full advantage of both internal and external mechanisms (e.g., groupware, multi-media, cyberspace) to optimize results. Further, communications is not always technical. Keeping the organization and stakeholders apprised of priorities, changes in direction, success stories, and more is not only difficult, it is essential.

"As they say, "You do not get a second chance to make a first impression." These days, with companies being managed by chaos theory and the degree of complexity, simple but not simplistic communications should be the order of the day. A communication strategy must be fully integrated with any plans to leverage human capital – more specifically knowledge – of all stakeholders in the innovation process.

External messages must be consistent with internal culture, values, and vision. How companies are perceived in the marketplace – branding, ethics, direction, success stories, etc. – must be conveyed skillfully and on a regular basis. More and more companies around the world are using the platform of knowledge-type advertising campaigns:

> *"Knowledge is powerful medicine."* – Eli Lilly (Fortune, July 1995)
> *"Understanding comes with Time."*- Time Magazine (Fortune, July 1995)
> *"Prepare to have that idea shattered."* – Hewlett-Packard (Fortune July 1995)
> *"A brilliant deduction."* – Gifts in Kind America (Fortune, June 1995)
> *"Knowledge of the world on-line."* – Oracle (CNN ad, November 28, 1995)

"Old tradition, new thinking." – Harvard Funds (Fortune, June 1995)
"Your dog is smart" – Purina Dog Chow (CNN ad, February 26, 1996)
"Travel provides the power of knowledge." – American Express (CNN ad, Feb. 1996)

In the Knowledge Economy, taglines have taken on a deeper significance. Not only are they designed for marketing products and services, they serve as a concise vehicle to present a timely image to external stakeholders and a motivational tool for employees. Consider all the Federal Express communicated with "The World on Time." It was close to a stretch vision toward which all could relate. It was simple, memorable, substantive and visceral. Sometimes, we forget how important might be the right words in the right context.

Communication strategy may be as much of a learning process as a dissemination tool – perhaps even more so. We need to envision the innovation activity as a value-system, not a value-chain of events. For example, we may have more to gain from tapping into customer knowledge (i.e., what customers know) than approaching them as the end of a delivery chain. Communications may be more a function of operating a distributed learning network of expertise. It can be the source of an intelligence service as well as a business development function. Leadership is a function of listening – and acting upon insights – not merely a receptacle doe stakeholder contact.

3.7 Knowledge Leadership Is a Matter of *Coaching*

Coaching is a guided relationship process established between two parties. Both are responsible. The process is forward looking, change-oriented, and developmental. It is a tool to enable client success, productivity, revenue growth, and stakeholder value. Coaching is more about 'being' than 'doing.' Effective coaches engage in a process that involves trust, support, and shared values.

The coach's main role deals with expanding the ability to see contexts, rather than supplying content. The coaching process affirms the person, seeks to clarify choices, and acts as a catalyst for achieving both individual and organizational purposes. The coaching task connects the inner person (e.g., confidence, values, purpose) with the external manifestation of leadership (e.g., articulating vision, reaching targets, and achieving goals).

Coaching is the opposite of judging and the need for control. This is why its essence is congruent with the fundamental precepts of the Knowledge Economy. The coaching relationship enables people to work out issues and find answers through their own effective discovery process.

Effective leaders know they do not have all the answers. However, they do generally have a healthy curiosity, sense of direction, standards of excellence, and a track record of success. They genuinely value others and have a need to 'know what the others know.' They are constantly learning, not afraid to experiment with new ideas, nor afraid to make mistakes. They know that facilitating a process is almost always preferable to claiming answers and dictating action. Knowledge leaders will coach as well as be coached. They will navigate through uncharted territory with full confidence in the value of mutual talent.

With the shift to on-the-job learning, it is important to have others – not necessarily managers – guide them through their own innovation process. British Petroleum discovered that personal coaching was an important success factor when it introduced its video-conferencing for virtual learning.

4   Leadership in Measurement

Although many of these principles may have been around for decades, few organizations have implemented them in a major way. Fewer have discovered a systematic way to measure the results. Measurement in the management development field is uncomfortable and time-consuming. Now, with the significant research being done with the Brookings Institute and a variety of accounting/finance academic research centers and professional societies, we are beginning to comprehend the power behind the intangible value of the enterprise.

Today, we measure what we can measure, rather than ask the difficult questions. Courageous leaders such a Leif Edvinsson, notably the first Chief Knowledge Officer in the World and now a professor of Knowledge Economics at the University of Lund (Copenhagen, Denmark) said, "I'd rather be roughly right than precisely wrong!"[2]

The good news is that considerable progress has been made. There is a major research project affiliated with the Brookings Institute providing guidance. Accounting boards and professional organizations world-wide have placed the intangibles agenda as a priority. Best Practice Guidelines – even in this emerging field – are surfacing (Skyrme and Amidon, 1999):

- Draw up your own categories of intellectual capital and knowledge assets.
- Estimate ('guesstimate') for each their overall value, and future revenue-generating potential.
- Develop some form of balanced scorecard reporting.
- Explore, as an experiment, some of the newer methodologies (e.g., M'Pherson's Economic Value-added).
- Create a matrix linking the assets you have identified with business impact.
- Initiate pilot measurement and investment appraisal systems.
- Develop the value proposition.
- Don't despair if you cannot 'prove' bottom-line business benefit.
- Take the leap of faith, as are others.

Measurement is the area in this new knowledge field that shows the largest gap between management expectations and actual achievement of results. It may be the least understood and the most critical for future success. However, traditional accounting mechanisms developed over hundreds of years do not provide much

---

[2] Leif Edvinsson in response to an interview question. Published in "Global Momentum of Knowledge Strategy" available on-line:
http://www.entovation.com/momentum/globalmn.htm.

light on measuring intangibles. They are very effective in counting the past, showing where a company has been. They are not very effective in pointing the direction for future results and impact – precisely what is required by investing executives.

5   A Knowledge Leadership Litmus Test

In the *Knowledge Innovation® Assessment*, one of the ten dimensions of innovation strategy is leadership. Check your own capability:

1. *Can you define a map of your sphere of influence within your industry, across sectors and around the world?*
2. *Do you have an effective strategy to disseminate your knowledge and competencies to the marketplace?*
3. *Name the multiple methods of positioning your own intellectual leadership (e.g., articles, books, videos, professional visibility, and participation on committees/commissions)?*
4. *How are the learnings from your participation fed back into the organization and used to develop new business strategies?*
5. *Is there an internal mechanism to capture, codify and feed forward expertise in ways that might enhance the business performance of the organization as a whole?*
6. *Does your organization perceive external leadership activities as integral to the business? How are they leveraged?*
7. *Are there any formal mechanisms to legitimize, encourage, and reward people who impart knowledge and expertise to others?*

Use this sample diagnostic as a way to explore with others in your organization how effectively you are developing and leveraging your own leadership talent. Remember that leadership – in all of its facets – is a learning process. True leaders are learners first.

6   Conclusion

We are at the dawn of a new millennium. The leadership required to carry us forward may not resemble what was necessary in the past. Oh yes, we will always admire those who are now considered of innovation genius; but this is hindsight. What may be required for future leadership includes a novel skill-set.

Leaders will understand the nature of complex context – how to make sense of it and how to convey it (with magnetic vision) to others.

Leaders will know that competencies are based in experience and are more dynamic than static attributes.

Leaders will know the relationship between the motivation (psychology) of an individual and the culture (sociology) of an organization. They will value heritage (anthropology) and know that more than 2% of manager time need be dedicated to visioning – the lifeblood of a future generation business.

Leaders will understand the value of the collective – the teams and communities within whom work gets done and visions are realized.

Leaders will know how to evolve a common language and that there is more power in the dialogue than what gets documented in a particular planning process.

Leaders will value the communications process – both technical and human – but not as much for what gets conveyed as what might be learned.

Leaders will coach and be coached by people of similar values and vision. Trust will be placed in those able to care more about leveraging the competencies of one another.

Millennium leadership will not avoid the issues of measurement. They will embrace innovative mechanisms, tools and methodologies to navigate into the future. We will not avoid the issue of results on investment in building leadership capability. We will discover the human and humane methods to document progress. Our generations to come deserve nothing less.

References

Amidon, D.M., *Innovation Strategy for the Knowledge Economy: The Ken Awakening*, Waltham, MA: Butterworth-Heinemann, 1997, 68-72.

Amidon, D.M., et al., *Collaborative Innovation and the Knowledge Economy*, Toronto, Ontario: Society of Management Accountants of Canada, 1998, 21.

Brown, J.S. and S.G. Estee, "The People Are the Company: How to Build Your Company around Your People," *Fast Company,* November, 1995, 78-82.

Drucker, P., "Information Executives Truly Need," *Harvard Business Review,* January/February, 1995, 54-62.

Macnamara, D., "Competency Profiling and Learning Contracts: Building Partnerships in Leadership Development and Maximizing Impact," *Leadership Compass*, Winter/Spring, 2000,19-21.

Skyrme, D.J. and D.M. Amidon, *Creating the Knowledge-Based Business,* London: Business Intelligence, 1997.

Skyrme, D.J. and D.M. Amidon. "Measuring the Value of Knowledge," in *Handbook of Business Strategy*, New York, NY: Faulkner and Gray, 1999.

Wheatley, M. J., *Leadership and the New Science: Discovering Order in a Chaotic World*, San Francisco: Berrett-Koehler Publishers, Inc., 1999.

CHAPTER 29

Trust and Knowledge Management:
The Seeds of Success

Dianne P. Ford

Queen's School of Business, Queen's University, Kingston, ON, Canada

Within the practitioner literature, trust has often been noted as a key component for the success of knowledge management practices; however, trust is a very complex construct that has many different facets and definitions. This chapter reviews the trust literature to create an understanding of the different types and bases of trust. These types and bases of trust are then applied to the knowledge management processes (knowledge generation, knowledge codification, knowledge transfer, and knowledge application) to create better understanding of the possible relationships between trust and the knowledge management processes, and which processes require which type of trust for knowledge management success. Implications for practitioners are then discussed.

Keywords: Knowledge Management; Trust; Knowledge Management Processes

1 Introduction

For several years now, researchers and practitioners have been extolling the virtues of knowledge management (KM) and its role in organizational success through sustainable competitive advantage (e.g., Drucker, 1969, 2001; Matusik and Hill, 1998; Holsapple and Joshi, 2000). In line with this statement, knowledge management has been a hot topic. The processes knowledge management involves, knowledge management systems, and how an organization can successfully implement knowledge management are just some examples of how it has been studied (e.g., Alavi and Leidner, 2001; Jarvenpaa and Staples, 2000; Buckley and Carter, 1999; Gold, Malhotra and Segars, 2001).

Within the knowledge management literature, trust is often discussed as an important element for successful knowledge management ventures (e.g., Bukowitz and Williams, 1999; Rolland and Chauvel, 2000; Roberts, 2000). For example, statements such as, "Trust is, after all, the single most important precondition for knowledge exchange" (Rolland and Chauvel, 2000, p.239) are a common occurrence, particularly in practitioner oriented literature.

If trust is a key ingredient for the success of knowledge management, then it is important to understand how it relates to the various knowledge management processes, and how a manager may plant the seeds required for trust and knowledge management to grow (i.e., be successfully implemented).

Trust is a very complex construct, with multiple levels, bases, and determinants (Rousseau et al., 1998). The word is well known, and is frequently believed to be understood. Yet, throughout the years, trust has been defined in many different ways (e.g., Williamson, 1993; Zucker, 1986; Rotter, 1967). For instance, trust has been defined in terms of a personality trait (e.g., the propensity to trust; Rotter, 1967), but also has been defined as a behaviour (e.g., trusting behaviour; Mayer et al., 1995). Therefore, it is inappropriate to solely use the term "trust" and to assume its meaning is fully and properly understood.

Despite trust's claimed or apparent importance within the knowledge management literature, the construct of trust is typically left undefined and its meaning is assumed to be understood even though there is an extensive trust literature defining different types of trust. The types of trust are discussed even less frequently with respect to the various knowledge management processes. While there are some exceptions to this statement (e.g., Huemer et al., 1998; Kelloway and Barling, 2000; Roberts, 2000), none of these articles address the different types of trust and how these different types may relate to the various KM processes. Furthermore, they have not directly addressed the true necessity of trust, or how a manager may assist the development of the "proper" types of trust for each of the knowledge management processes.

Therefore, the purpose of this chapter is the following: 1) to briefly review the definitions of trust; 2) to explain trust's role with respect to the various knowledge management processes; and 3) to discuss the implications of trust's relationship with KM for practitioners. The literature for trust and knowledge management shall be discussed. Then, the types of trust will be discussed with respect to each of the knowledge management processes of knowledge generation, knowledge codification, knowledge transfer, and knowledge application, and how they assist knowledge management processes. Finally, the discussion will address the implications for practitioners.

2 Definition of Trust

Although trust has many possible definitions (see Table 1), Rousseau, et al., (1998) have noted several commonalities amongst different definitions, namely: (a) risk, (b) expectations or beliefs, and (c) a willingness to place oneself at risk with the assumption and expectation that no harm will come to oneself. One of the most frequently used definitions of trust is the following, "the willingness of a party to be vulnerable to the actions of another party based on the expectation that the other will perform a particular action important to the trustor, irrespective of the ability to monitor or control that other party" (Mayer, et al., 1995, p.712).

Mayer et al., (1995) differentiated trust from constructs such as predictability, cooperation, and confidence. As shown in Table 1, others have used these separate constructs as synonyms with trust (as highlighted) despite Mayer et al.'s (1995) convincing arguments that they are not identical. For example, if a person's harmful behaviour is highly predictable, then trust is less likely to occur be-

Table 1. A Sample of Trust Definitions

Definition of Trust	Source Citation
"Trust is a psychological state comprising the intention to accept vulnerability based upon positive expectations of the intentions or behavior of another."	Rousseau, 1998, p. 395
Trust is the "expectation of regular, honest, and *cooperative* behavior based on commonly shared norms and values." [Emphasis added.]	Fukuyama, 1995, cited from Doney, Cannon & Mullen, 1998, p. 603
"Trust is the degree to which the trustor holds a positive attitude toward the trustee's goodwill and reliability in a risky exchange situation."	Das & Tang, 1998, p. 494
"Trust exists in an uncertain and risky environment; trust reflects an aspect of *predictability* – that is, it is an expectance." [Emphasis added.]	Bhattacharya et al., 1998, p. 461
Trust is "one's expectations, assumptions, or beliefs about the likelihood that another's future actions will be beneficial, favourable, or at least not detrimental to one's interests."	Robinson, 1996, p. 576

cause the high predictability decreases risk, and the presence of risk is a required condition for trust (Mayer, et al., 1995). Deutsch (1958) stated that in order for trust to be meaningful, it must go beyond predictability (c.f. Mayer et al., 1995). Cooperation can occur without risk being present. For example, John could cooperate with Max because it would be to his benefit to cooperate, not because he trusts him. Hence, the presence of cooperation does not determine the presence of trust.

A second stream of literature discusses the bases of trust, or how trust is derived (e.g., Shapiro et al., 1992; Brewer, 1981; Williamson, 1993). Trust can be deterrence-based trust, knowledge-based trust, identification-based trust, cognition-based trust, relational trust, calculus-based trust, economics-based trust, institutional-based trust, or personality-based trust. See Table 2 for a summary of the definitions and citations.

In addition to different bases of trust, there are also different types of trust. For instance, Morris and Moberg (1994) make the distinction between personal and impersonal trust. Personal trust is based on person-to-person interactions; whereas, impersonal trust is based on positions (e.g., job titles, offices) not the actual person.

Another distinction made within the trust literature regards the target of trust. Interpersonal trust, and organizational trust (e.g., Rotter, 1967; Gilbert and Li-Ping Tang, 1998) are the most common ones identified. Other targets of trust are trust in groups, and trust in institutions (Rousseau, et al., 1998).

Table 2. Categorizations of Trust

Aspects of Trust		Definition
Common Research Approaches for Trust	Economics	e.g., economics-based trust (Williamson, 1993)
	Sociology	e.g., institution-based trust (Zucker, 1986)
	Psychology	e.g., personality-based trust (Rotter, 1967)
Bases for Trust	Deterrence-based trust (Shapiro et al., 1992)	Trust is derived through the presence of costly sanctions for opportunistic behaviour. Some contend that this is a form of control, not trust; however, others do, as someone trusts an individual because of the presence of the sanctions. (Rousseau et al, 1998)
	Knowledge-based trust (Shapiro et al, 1992)	Trust is derived through getting to know the other individual, and being able to predict his/her behaviour.
	Identification-based trust (Shapiro et al., 1992)	Trust is derived through empathy, and a sharing of common values (i.e., through identifying with the other individual).
	Cognition-based trust (Brewer, 1981)	Trust is derived through cognitive cues such as first impressions (Brewer, 1981)
	Relational trust (Rousseau, et al., 1998)	Trust is derived over time through information of trustee within the frame of the relationship (Rousseau, et al., 1998)
	Calculus-based trust	Trust is calculated on the basis of deterrents and intentions / competence (Rousseau, et al., 1998).
	Economics-based trust (Williamson, 1993)	Trust is derived from a rational decision based on costs and benefits (Kim & Prabhakar, 2000)
	Institution-based trust (Zucker, 1986)	Trust reflects the security felt due to guarantees, safety nets, or other structures (McKnight & Cummings, 1998)
	Personality-based trust (Rotter, 1967)	Propensity to trust; developed through childhood relations with caregivers. (Rotter, 1967)
Targets of Trust	Interpersonal trust	The "willingness of one person to increase his/her vulnerability to the actions of another person [e.g., Zand 1972]" (Aulakh, Kotabe & Sahay, 1996, p. 1007). Also defined as "generalized expectancy that the verbal statements of others can be relied upon" (Rotter, 1967, p. 651).

	Group trust (Rousseau, et al., 1998)	The willingness of one person to increase his/her vulnerability to the actions of a group of people.
	Organizational trust	"Organizational trust is a feeling of confidence and support in an employer... organizational trust refers to employee faith in corporate goal attainment and organizational leaders, and to the belief that ultimately, organizational action will prove beneficial for employees" (Gilbert & Li-Ping Tang, 1998, p. 322).
	Institutional trust	Institutional trust is a feeling of confidence and security in institutions (e.g., the law, organizations), that the laws, policies, regulations, etc. are to protect the individual's rights, and will not harm her/him.
	Trust in individuals	This is the same as interpersonal trust.
	Trust in firms	This is the same as organizational trust.
	Trust in institutions	This is the same as institutional trust.
Types of Trust (Morris & Moberg, 1994)	Personal	Trust is based on the person-to-person interaction; it is unique to each relationship. Violation of this trust is betrayal (Elangovan & Shapiro, 1998).
	Impersonal	Trust is based on the position within the organization, not the individual who fills the position. Violations of this trust are considered to be deviant, and are managed through formal reprimands and sanctions (Elangovan & Shapiro, 1998).

Several authors have defined different states of trust (e.g., distrust, conditional trust, and unconditional trust); see Table 3 for summaries. However, for the purpose of this chapter, Lewicki et al's (1998) definition of trust and distrust are used, such that they are separate constructs, and distrust is characterized by fear and skeptisim.

Table 3. Development of Trust

Characteristic		Description
States of Trust (Jones & George, 1998)	Distrust	Distrust is a difficult concept and its relation to trust is controversial within the literature. Two definitions are the following. • Distrust and trust are of the same construct, which is the experience of trust (Jones & George, 1998). Distrust is, therefore, the lack of trust within a relationship (i.e., the lack of belief that a person is trustworthy, and the unwillingness to expose oneself to risk with respect to that individual). • The other definition is that trust is a different construct of trust, and the two can coincide (Lewicki et al., 1998). Distrust is characterized by: fear, scepticism, cynicism, wariness and watchfulness, and vigilance (Lewicki et al., 1998).
	Conditional	*"Conditional trust* is a state of trust in which both parties are willing to transact with each other, as long as each behaves appropriately, uses a similar interpretive scheme to define the situation, and can take the role of the other (Jones & George, 1998, p.536). This trust is based on knowledge of the other and expectations. This is a common trust within organizations.
	Unconditional	Unconditional trust is characterized by "individuals abandon[ing] the "pretense" [sic] of suspending belief, because shared values now structure the social situation and become the primary vehicle through which those individuals experience trust (Jones & George, 1998, p. 536). This trust can be identification-based trust, relational trust.
Determinants of Trust (Mishra & Morrisey, 1990) versus (Mayer et al., 1995)	Open communication	Perceived trustee's ability
	Inclusion in decision making	Perceived trustee's benevolence
	Sharing critical information	Perceived trustee's integrity
	Sharing of feelings and perceptions	Trustor's propensity to trust
Determinants of Organizational Trust (Gilbert & Li-Ping Tang, 1998)	Work group cohesion	
	Friendship centrality	
	Receiving information through social integration and mentoring	

Finally, there have been different determinants of trust discussed within the literature (e.g., Mishra and Morrisey, 1990; Mayer, et al., 1995; Gilbert and Li-Ping Tang, 1998). Determinants of trust are behaviours and factors that increase the likelihood of trust incurring (see Table 3). The most pertinent determinants for KM are those proposed by Mishra and Morrisey (1990), which are: open communication, inclusion in decision making, sharing critical information, and sharing of feelings and perceptions.

In summary, trust is a very complex construct, which has many targets, bases, states, and definitions. The key aspects of trust that are discussed further in this chapter are the different targets of trust (e.g., interpersonal versus organizational) and the different bases of trust (e.g., institutional-based trust versus identification-based trust). It is important to understand how these different aspects relate to the knowledge management processes, as they suggest different management practices for implementing knowledge management.

3   Definition of Knowledge Management

Knowledge management has been defined in many different ways. A common view is that it is a business practice emphasizing the creation, dispersion, and use of knowledge (e.g., Davenport and Prusak, 1998; Alavi and Leidner, 2000). The purpose of knowledge management is to enable the organization to gain access to the knowledge held within the individuals of the firm. Knowledge has been defined as the following:

> "Knowledge is a fluid mix of framed experience, values, contextual information, and expert insight that provides a framework for evaluating and incorporating new experiences and information. It originates and is applied in the minds of knowers. In organizations, it often becomes imbedded not only in documents or repositories but also in organizational routines, processes, practices, and norms." (Davenport and Prusak, 1998, p.5).

Knowledge, like trust, has been differentiated into different types and levels (see Table 4 for a summary). For instance, different levels of knowledge would be knowledge as an object (separate from individuals), knowledge within the individual, knowledge within a group or community, knowledge within a firm (group and firm knowledge is also considered to be collective knowledge), and public knowledge (e.g., McLure Wasko and Faraj, 2000; Matusik and Hill, 1998; Davenport and Prusak, 1998). The key for an organization, which is focusing on knowledge management, is to maximize the collective knowledge, and to constantly be aware of and acquire public knowledge, but to not let the firm knowledge become public knowledge (Matusik and Hill, 1998).

Knowledge has been differentiated into two main modes: explicit and tacit knowledge (Nonaka and Takeuchi, 1995). Explicit knowledge, otherwise known as codifiable knowledge, is knowledge that is readily and easily codified into text, diagrams, etc. (e.g., Nonaka, 1991; Roberts, 2000). Tacit knowledge, on the other hand, is learned from experience, and can be very difficult to articulate and codify (Matusik and Hill, 1998). Others contend that the distinction between just explicit and just tacit knowledge is not as clear as it is believed to be, because they are not mutually exclusive, as Michael Polanyi (1966) states:

> "While tacit knowledge can be possessed by itself, explicit knowledge must rely on being tacitly understood and applied. Hence all knowledge is either tacit or rooted in tacit knowledge. A wholly explicit knowledge is unthinkable" (p. 7).

Within the knowledge management literature, there are at least two classifications of knowledge processes. Nonaka (1994) defines one in which there are four processes: internationalization, externalization, combination, and socialization. Internalization is the process in which an individual internalizes explicit knowledge to create tacit knowledge. Externalization is the process in which the person turns their tacit knowledge into explicit knowledge through documentation, verbalization, etc. Combination is the process where new explicit knowledge is created through the combination of other explicit knowledge. Finally, socialization is the process of transferring tacit knowledge between individuals through observations and working with a mentor or a more skilled/knowledgeable individual.

Another classification of knowledge processes is somewhat more popular within the literature (Alavi and Leidner, 2000; Davenport and Prusak, 1998). This classification focuses on the lifecycle of knowledge within a firm; whereas, the above classification focuses on different processes in which knowledge is created and transferred throughout an organization. There are essentially four knowledge processes in this classification: knowledge generation (creation and knowledge acquisition), knowledge codification (storing), knowledge transfer (sharing), and knowledge application.

Knowledge generation involves the discovery and resolution of opportunities or problems, and the creation of innovations for example (e.g., Gray and Chan, 2000; Matusik and Hill, 1998), and knowledge acquisition, which is the acquiring and integrating knowledge from external sources (Davenport and Prusak, 1998). Knowledge codification is the translation of knowledge into text, drawings, etc. for storage in a repository. Knowledge transfer is the sharing of knowledge between individuals within the organization. Finally, knowledge application is the use of knowledge to gain a competitive advantage (Alavi and Leidner, 2000).

For the purpose of this chapter, which is to examine the relationship between trust and knowledge management processes, the knowledge processes characterized by Davenport and Prusak (1998) are used to frame this examination. This classification of knowledge management processes was chosen as it relates directly to tangible business practices, and is thus pertinent to practitioners.

Table 4. Summary of Knowledge Classifications

Knowledge Classifications		Definition
Knowledge versus Data and Information	Data	Primary level, derived from transactions; building blocks for information (Davenport & Prusak, 1998).
	Information	Secondary level, derived from processing data or transforming knowledge into information. Information has meaning to the recipient (Davenport & Prusak, 1998).
	Knowledge	High level, derived from experience and processing information for example.
Levels of Knowledge	Knowledge as an object	Knowledge is an object that can be manipulated and transferred independent of people.
	Knowledge within an individual	Knowledge resides within an individual and is not always understood or even known by that individual.
	Knowledge within a group/ community	Knowledge resides within a group or community through shared experiences, discussions, discoveries; it is not within one single individual.
	Knowledge within an organization	Knowledge resides within an organization through culture, processes, and experiences; it is not within one single individual or group.
	Public Knowledge	Knowledge resides within the public, it is well known to everyone; it is not knowledge that resides with one individual organization, group or individual.
Types of Knowledge	Explicit Knowledge	Explicit knowledge is easily coded (e.g., documented, identified, articulated). Some argue that explicit knowledge does not exist independently of tacit knowledge; others argue that explicit knowledge, independent of tacit knowledge, is simply information.
	Tacit Knowledge	Tacit knowledge is extremely difficult to code (e.g., identify, articulate, document). Some consider this true knowledge and tacit knowledge may not be fully known by the individual who has the tacit knowledge.
Knowledge Processes I	Externalization	The translation of tacit knowledge into explicit knowledge.
	Internalization	The translation of explicit knowledge into tacit knowledge.
	Combination	The creation of new explicit knowledge through combining existing explicit knowledge.
	Socialization	The transfer of tacit knowledge through mentoring (for example).

Knowledge Processes II (i.e., Business Processes)	Knowledge Generation	The creation of new knowledge, either through creating it in-house, or through acquiring it from external sources.
	Knowledge Codification	Codification of knowledge into diagrams, documents, knowledge maps, etc.
	Knowledge Transfer	The sharing of knowledge between one individual to another (or between groups, etc).
	Knowledge Use	The application of knowledge to business practices (e.g., problem solving).
Knowledge Management Business Practices	KM Systems	Information systems and technology to assist in codification and transfer of knowledge (e.g., intranets, Lotus Notes, knowledge maps, executive support systems, artificial intelligence, neural nets, document management systems).
	Documentation	Organizational documents assist in codification and transfer of knowledge.
	Communities of practice	Communities of practice are groups (communities) of professionals or individuals with the same interest and goals. They are volunteer based communities in which knowledge is created, and transferred.
	Mentoring	Mentoring is a practice, which is best for the transfer of knowledge from an expert to a novice individual, through illustration, instruction, and active learning.
	Storytelling	Storytelling is a practice in which tacit knowledge is transferred through its illustration in context-rich stories.
	Serendipitous / Water cooler discussions	This is the business practice in which knowledge is created, and transferred through accidents / casual conversations between individuals.

4   Trust and Knowledge Management

This section discusses the importance of trust for each of the knowledge management processes recognized by Davenport and Prusak (1998).

4.1 Knowledge Generation

Within this conception of knowledge generation, there are two main processes whereby knowledge is "generated." These are knowledge creation and knowledge acquisition. Knowledge can either be generated through original knowledge creation within the confines of the organization, or it can be acquired from an external source and brought into the organization.

4.1.1   Knowledge Creation

Trust has not been discussed extensively with respect to knowledge generation; however, it has been suggested that trust is required for it to thrive. For instance, Probst, Raub and Romhardt (2000) discuss that there should be a trust in the tolerance for mistakes; this enhances the culture for knowledge creation. The trust discussed with respect to knowledge generation is organizational trust. In other words, the employees trust that the organization tolerates mistakes and will thus act accordingly (i.e., participate in more "risky" behaviour). Interpersonal trust may also come into play such that the employee will have to trust his/her supervisor to follow the policies; however, this form of interpersonal trust falls under organizational trust as defined by Gilbert and Li-Ping Tang (1998). Furthermore, this trust would be more knowledge-based, deterrence-based, or institution-based trust, not necessarily relational trust, because the trust would most likely be based on the employee's ability to predict and understand their supervisor's behaviours and motives, or through the rules and policies of the organization.

Knowledge generation not only occurs with individuals, but it also occurs within groups or teams. Knowledge generation within a group often requires individuals to share their knowledge and information (which involves the second knowledge process of knowledge transfer) in order for new knowledge to be created.

While it has not been extensively discussed, knowledge generation within a group or team setting is presumed to require trust. However, the more the organizational policies and regulations support knowledge generation for the group, then trust's importance decreases to the extent that controls and policies replace trust. On the other hand, if distrust is present, then knowledge generation will be blocked, as fear, cynicism, wariness will prevent an individual from sharing required knowledge or information with the team to generate new knowledge.

Conversely, the more trust that is present, the more information people will share with one another (Connelly and Kelloway, 2000), thus enabling the knowledge generation process. Therefore, while trust may not be a required component for knowledge generation, its presence would increase the success of the group/team in terms of knowledge generation. This time, interpersonal trust is the focus, as individuals within the group must trust the other individuals to share their information and knowledge, to generate the knowledge.

This trust may have different bases; for instance it could be relational trust, identification-based, knowledge-based, institution-based trust, deterrence-based trust, calculus-based trust, personality-based trust. However, if the interpersonal trust is relational trust or identification-based trust, then the group members will be more willing to share information, thus increasing the likelihood of knowledge generation (Bowles, 1999; Kramer, 1999). The reason for this elevated willingness to share information is due to the individual's identification with the group members' goals and the simple action of sharing information within a relationship creates relational trust. Therefore, the ideal trust for knowledge generation would be relational trust or identification-based trust.

The promotion of relational trust and identity-based trust is illustrated through the recommendation to create communities of practice for knowledge generation and sharing (von Krogh et al., 2000). Communities of practice are groups in which the social cohesiveness has been promoted, and the group assists in the generation of new knowledge (Davenport and Prusak, 1998). The promotion of social ties within these groups is related to the development of knowledge-based, identification-based and relational trust.

The above discussion suggests the following propositions for knowledge creation:

Proposition 1a: For individual-generated knowledge: the presence of organizational trust, which is either deterrence-based or institution-based trust, will be associated with more knowledge creation than with no trust at all.

Proposition 1b: For individual-generated knowledge: the presence of interpersonal trust with the supervisor, which is either deterrence-based, institution-based or knowledge-based trust, will be associated with more knowledge creation than with no trust at all.

Proposition 2a: For group-generated knowledge: the presence of organizational trust, which is institution-based trust, will be associated with more knowledge creation, than if there is no trust present.

*Proposition 2b:*For group-generated knowledge: the presence of trust in the group will be associated with more knowledge creation, than if there was simply organizational trust, or no trust present.

Proposition 2c: For group-generated knowledge: the presence of interpersonal trust, which is identification-based or relational trust, will be associated with more knowledge creation than if there was simply group trust, organizational trust, or no trust present.

4.1.2   Knowledge Acquisition

Knowledge acquisition involves accessing expertise from external sources in the knowledge market. Probst et al. (2000) suggest that personal trust is required within the knowledge market as it is difficult to assess the value of the knowledge being acquired. Acquisition of knowledge from an individual outside of the organization cannot benefit from organizational trust, as the individual is not a part of the organization. Impersonal trust also would not be effective as the trust is directed to a position or title within the organization; therefore, interpersonal trust is the best type of trust for knowledge acquisition. This interpersonal trust could have any of the following bases to be effective: knowledge-based trust, competency trust, relational trust, cognition-based trust, identification-based trust.

Therefore, the following propositions may be stated:

*Proposition 3a:*For knowledge acquisition, the presence of personal trust will be associated with more knowledge acquired than without personal trust.

Proposition 3b: For knowledge acquisition: the presence of interpersonal trust, which is either knowledge-based, competency, relational, cognition-based, or identification-based trust, will be associated with more knowledge acquired than without the presence of interpersonal trust.

4.2 Knowledge Codification

Knowledge codification is the translation of explicit knowledge into some written or visual format. Frequently, the codified knowledge is stored within knowledge management systems, or manuals. While there has been very little discussed with respect to trust in knowledge codification, there has been some discussion regarding trust in the quality of the data within the knowledge management systems and the use of these systems (e.g., Jarvenpaa and Staples, 2000; Probst et al., 2000). Therefore, it is possible to conceive that trust is required in the use of codified knowledge. This trust would be impersonal trust, as it is not directed toward a particular individual. This may also be trust in the system.

Similarly, when knowledge is being codified, the individual whose knowledge is being codified may need to trust the system such that the coded knowledge is stored as it is meant to be, and that it will be protected from those who should not have access to it. This can be an issue to not only the individuals within the organization, but it can also be a concern for individuals outside the organization (e.g., clients of that organization). Furthermore, the individual may need to trust the organization that the organization will use the knowledge properly. This will be discussed further in the knowledge use section.

In addition to the codification of explicit knowledge, some KM authors have proposed methods for categorizing tacit knowledge within the organization. One of the techniques is to create a knowledge map (i.e., "Yellow Pages") that identifies the experts and their field of expertise within the organization (Davenport and Prusak, 1998). To increase the level of trust in the users of the knowledge map, the inclusion of pictures or videos of the expert has been recommended (Davenport and Prusak, 1998). This relates to interpersonal trust as the trust is targeted towards the expert.

From this section, the following three propositions may be made:

Proposition 4a: The presence of impersonal trust of the data quality, which is trust in the system, will be associated with more knowledge codification.

Proposition 4b: The presence of organizational trust will be associated with more knowledge codification than if there was no organizational trust.

Proposition 4c: For knowledge maps: the use of pictures or videos in the knowledge maps increases interpersonal trust.

4.3 Knowledge Transfer

The most commonly discussed knowledge management process with respect to trust is knowledge transfer (i.e., knowledge sharing). It is frequently commented that in order for people to be willing to share their knowledge, they must have trust (e.g., Davenport and Prusak, 1998; Podolny and Baron, 1997; Kramer, 1999). It has even been commented, "trust is, after all, the single most important precondition for knowledge exchange" (Rolland and Chauvel, 2000, p.239). More specifically, trust has been discussed as a prerequisite for tacit knowledge sharing (e.g., Roberts, 2000; Rolland and Chauvel, 2000).

The importance of trust has been supported in a study by Connelly and Kelloway (2000). In this study, respondents noted that they would only be willing to share knowledge in contexts where they trusted the recipient of the knowledge (Connelly and Kelloway, 2000). While the type of trust was not specified, it can be inferred that the respondents were referring to interpersonal trust, as the trust was targeted towards an individual, not an organization; however, as with other studies, the bases of the trust were not discussed or investigated.

However, the relevance of trust (and the findings regarding the significance of the presence of trust) may be limited because of the uncertainty surrounding causal direction, as it has also been noted that the sharing of information also increases the level of trust (Bowles, 1999). In other words, as one shares information and knowledge with another individual, the perceived trust increases between these individuals. This implies that as people start sharing their knowledge because the company dictates it (and censures opportunistic behaviours), they will then start to feel interpersonal trust with those whom they share the information and knowledge. Therefore, interpersonal trust may not be required (as commonly believed) for the start of knowledge sharing, but it may develop as a result of knowledge sharing.

Sharing knowledge (and in particular tacit knowledge) is a risky behaviour, as the individual does not know for certain how the knowledge will be used. Furthermore, the trustor does not know for certain that the value that is associated with the knowledge will be transferred to the trustee. Therefore, to share knowledge is to assume risk by both parties (e.g., Kramer, 1999). As mentioned by Mayer et al., (1995), the assumption of risk is not sufficient to assume that trust is required. However, Mayer et al., (1995) claim "trust will lead to risk taking in a relationship" (p. 724). In situations in which there is little or no trust, the individual will rely on third parties to mitigate the level of risk. For instance, they will rely on organizational policies and rules to mitigate the level of risk. This is the case with deterrence-based trust, and institutional trust; controls are available to mitigate the likelihood of harm. To the extent that knowledge sharing is institutionalised, and sanctions exist for limiting opportunistic behaviour, then knowledge sharing should occur.

Without the sanctions, or policies and strong culture, interpersonal trust must replace external controls (e.g., Das and Teng, 1998; Edmondson and Moingeon, 1999). This interpersonal trust could be differently based trusts, such as: calculus-based trust, knowledge-based trust, identification-based trust, relational trust, cognition-based trust, economics-based trust, or personality-based trust. The literature does not differentiate between these types of trust and their implication on knowledge transfer. However, as noted earlier, if the interpersonal trust is relational or identification-based trust, then people will be more willing to share (e.g., Bowles, 1999; Kramer, 1999). Therefore, it is proposed that without a strong organizational culture regarding knowledge sharing, which may result in a lack of related policies, rewards, sanctions, then knowledge-based trust, identification-based trust, and relational trust become more important.

This proposition may explain the proliferation of recommendations for companies to support communication and sharing of personal information (Bowles, 1999), enhancing interdependency (Rolland and Chauvel, 2000), creating optimized networks (Burt, 1992), as these behaviours lead to an increase in knowledge and understanding, hence trust (i.e., identification-based or knowledge-based trust). Von Krogh, Ichijo, and Nonaka (2000) also make recommendations for creating trust for knowledge management. The recommendations are the following:

- Create a sense of mutual dependence;
- Make trustworthy behaviour part of the performance review;
- Increase individual reliability be creating a map of expectations;
- Sharing personal information for smaller groups;
- Use symbolic gestures for interdependency (von Krogh et al., 2000).

The first and last comments create interdependency. Interdependency produces one type of interpersonal trust (Rolland and Chauvel, 2000). The second relates to institutional sanctions; therefore, it is related to the development of institutional-based or deterrence-based trust. It also relates to organizational trust. The third increases knowledge of other's intentions, which can increase interpersonal trust based on predictability (e.g., knowledge-based trust). Sharing personal information increases interpersonal trust (Mishra and Morrisey, 1990). More specifically, it can assist in the development of knowledge-based trust, and/or identification-based trust. These recommendations suggest knowledge transfer can be encouraged by the development of interpersonal trust, and/or organizational trust. Since it can be difficult for managers to cultivate simply one type of trust within an organization, von Krogh et al.'s (2000) recommendations support the development of all types of trust.

It is possible that knowledge transfer can occur with limited interpersonal trust, provided that there are sufficient sanctions and policies to compensate for the lack of interpersonal trust. However, it is also possible for knowledge transfer to occur solely with interpersonal trust. Therefore, in order to optimise the amount of knowledge transfer within the organization, it is best to encourage all types of trust – that way individuals who lack strong interpersonal trust with others in the organization can still partake in knowledge sharing due to organizational trust or deterrence-based trust. It should be noted that if a person experiences distrust, then knowledge sharing will be blocked and will fail with that individual.

From this discussion, the following propositions are made:

Proposition 5a: For conditions of little or no interpersonal trust: the presence of organizational trust, which is institution-based trust, will be associated with more knowledge transfer.

Proposition 5b: For conditions of little or no sanctions or policies: the presence of interpersonal trust, which is knowledge-based, identification-based or relational trust, will be associated with more knowledge transfer.

Proposition 5c: For conditions of distrust: knowledge transfer will be blocked and will fail due to fear, cynicism and wariness.

Proposition 5d: A company in which there is strong organizational trust and interpersonal trust present will have more knowledge transfer than companies in which there is solely organizational or interpersonal trust.

Proposition 5e: The presence of knowledge transference will lead to an increase in interpersonal trust between the individuals of the organization; thus leading to more knowledge transfer.

Proposition 5f: The presence of distrust will be associated with knowledge blocks and failure in knowledge management if prevalent within an organization.

4.4 Knowledge Application / Use

Davenport and Prusak (1998) discuss the "not-invented-here" mentality, arguing that it creates a barrier to the use of knowledge that has come from a second source (i.e., someone other than the user). To overcome this barrier, it is important for the organization to have a culture and policies that condone the use of outside or borrowed knowledge (Davenport and Prusak, 1998). As with the tolerance of mistakes, the use of second source knowledge creates a need for organizational trust, and interpersonal trust with the supervisor. It is proposed that this type of trust would be institutional-based trust, or knowledge-based trust.

Therefore, the propositions are the following:

Proposition 6a: The presence of organizational trust, which is institution-based trust, will be associated with higher knowledge use and application.

Proposition 6b: The presence of interpersonal trust with the supervisor, with could be deterrence-based, institution-based or knowledge-based trust, will be associated with higher knowledge use and application than without it.

5   Discussion

Trust, as it pertains to knowledge creation, acquisition, codification, transfer, and use, has been discussed and propositions have been derived from the literature. The following implications for managers can be derived from these propositions and the above literature review.

These propositions suggest that in order for an organization to implement knowledge management successfully, they would need multiple types of trust promoted within the organization if they wish to be successful at all knowledge processes. The remainder of this section discusses the implications for managers, and directions for future research.

The above propositions suggest several implications for management regarding knowledge management practices. First, a manager of a firm cannot force employees to trust one another (i.e., interpersonal trust). This is partly because the trust is on the basis of the relationship of those two individuals, and second, trust is subject to a person's perception and willingness. Simply put, a third person cannot fully alter or enforce a person's perception; therefore, it is in management's best interest to focus its energy in areas where it has more influence. In other words, the manager should look at knowledge management as a flower that they seek to grow. Because a gardener cannot force a flower to thrive on its own without a plant and the right environment, the gardener is required in essence to create the best conditions and plant the right seeds to grow the flower *over time*.

The seeds for knowledge management are the components that define what practices should grow. These are the mission statement, valued behaviours, the reward structure, and policies. The seeds are only a start, because a seed will remain a seed without the proper environment. The environment is the organizational culture and organizational trust. Organizational trust is out of the manager's control (as it is the employee's choice to trust or not); however, a manager can influence the organization's trustworthiness provided the manager is consistent with respect to the policies, reward structure, valued behaviours, and his/her actions with respect to the employees. Together organizational culture and organizational trust should support the growth of knowledge management.

When the seeds are planted, the seeds start to turn into plants – albeit slowly. This would also be illustrated in the organization as knowledge management processes start to occur (albeit slowly). The more organizational trust there is (e.g., nourishing environment), the more knowledge management processes should flourish.

At this point, there should be a full-grown plant; however, the flower of the successful knowledge management is not yet blooming. This is where interpersonal trust enters the equation. Just as a plant's biology allows it to flower under the right conditions, so to does knowledge management's processes allow for successful knowledge management to develop. Interpersonal trust is the special ingredient that creates the most beautiful flowers. It is this extra condition that knowledge management requires to bloom fully. However, it must come from the plant (e.g., the people within the organization) and not from the gardener (e.g., the manager).

So, in business terms, let us revisit this process. A manager does have influence over policies and procedures. To some extent, they have control over organizational culture and the related expectations. This will assist in starting knowledge management practices within the organization. Due to the existence of these sanctions, policies, and organizational "laws", institutional-based trust can develop, and people will start to share their knowledge and generate new knowledge. This will occur due to people's understanding that there are safety nets protecting their self-interests (e.g., Jan can share her knowledge with Joe, because she knows that if he uses it against her in some manner, he will be reprimanded for such behaviour). Furthermore, this can also address and assist in the development of organizational trust (i.e., Bill knows that he is to share his knowledge, and that his success within the company will not be jeopardized by doing so – that Bill will not be harmed by the organization (lose his promotion, etc.) by following its rules).

The presence of institutional-based trust and organizational trust will assist in basic levels of knowledge management processes such as generation, codification, sharing, and use. However, as noted previously, knowledge generation, transfer, and use will be more successful and prevalent with the assistance of interpersonal trust. An interesting aspect of interpersonal trust is that it can be developed through the sharing of information between people. Furthermore, companies that are successful at knowledge management seem to have trust prevalent within the organization. It is suggested here that as knowledge transfer becomes more prevalent, interpersonal trust will naturally develop within the organization.

Mishra and Morrisey (1990) specify four determinants of trust, which are the following: open communication, inclusion in decision making, sharing critical information, and sharing of feelings and perceptions. Open communication and sharing of critical information are two factors that are inherent within the knowledge processes of knowledge generation and transfer. Sharing of feelings and perceptions also may occur within teams or groups (e.g., communities of practice). Therefore, it is very possible that as knowledge generation and transfer are occurring due to organizational policies, interpersonal trust is developing between these individuals.

As interpersonal trust develops, knowledge management practices get a "booster shot" – such that knowledge generation, use, and in particular transfer flourish even more within the organization with interpersonal trust present. The only knowledge process that does not benefit from interpersonal trust is knowledge codification.

Managers may wish to know how to create this booster shot effect of interpersonal trust, and may want to add this under their regime of control. As mentioned earlier, it is difficult if not impossible for a manager to force Person A to trust Person B; however, it is possible for a manager to create the setting in which interpersonal trust may develop. For instance, giving employees the opportunity to share their feelings and perceptions, critical information, and open communication should enhance interpersonal trust. Examples of such a setting would be communities of practice, office retreats, social events, and an open environment to "water cooler discussions".

The final key issue for trust and knowledge management is the issue of distrust. While there is the debate as to whether or not trust and distrust are the same construct or not, this chapter is going to take the stance that they are two separate constructs, where distrust is characterized by fear, scepticism, cynicism, wariness and watchfulness and vigilance (Lewicki, et al., 1998). If distrust is present within an organization, knowledge management cannot, and will not succeed. The reason for this failure is that when fear is present, people will not partake in "risky" behaviour (such as sharing critical information and their knowledge). They will be cynical regarding the organization's true intentions regarding the employee's knowledge. For example, Blair is cynical regarding the organization's claim that a person's success is related to their ability to share what they know with others and to document this knowledge; Blair thus believes that it is a measure to disempower him and thus it threatens his job security. As a result of this cynicism, Blair is very unlikely to participate willingly or fully in the knowledge management practices. Distrust is therefore the abort button of the knowledge management mission.

Finally, the knowledge management process that falls outside of this model is knowledge acquisition. This is because the person or organization from whom the knowledge is received is outside of the organization; therefore, organizational trust is null and void. This means that monitoring and interpersonal trust will be the key mechanism for this process. In other words, since there is no way to measure the true value of the acquired knowledge, conditional interpersonal-trust will be the key factor for the acquisition. The importance of interpersonal trust is evident through the importance of the company representatives of the respective companies. For instance when there is a strategic alliance, the employees who represent the respective companies and who work together create a relationship with one another, and changes in the representatives can disrupt the flow of knowledge and the firms' willingness to do business with one another.

6   Conclusion

Within this chapter, the constructs of trust and knowledge management have been investigated, and their relationship has been explored. This has addressed a weakness within the knowledge management literature, as it typically uses trust in a very generic sense, and does not address the issue fully. It should be noted that the propositions have not been tested empirically; therefore, it is recommended that studies be conducted to investigate this further.

Many different types of trust apply to the various knowledge management processes. In order for an organization to maximize the knowledge management efforts, they will need to support the various types of trust, primarily, organizational trust and, in turn, interpersonal trust. Kelloway and Barling (2000) similarly state that organizational trust is important for knowledge management, such that organizational trust assists in motivation. This chapter has extended this concept to include different types of interpersonal trust for the various knowledge management processes to supplement the organizational trust. Managers cannot force trust to occur; however, they can strive to create the conditions in which trust can interact with knowledge management seedlings to create successful knowledge management.

Acknowledgements

I would like to thank the following people for their feedback on this chapter: Jim McKeen, Brent Gallupe, Julian Barling, Peter Gray, Darren Meister, Yolande Chan, the participants of Queen's Knowledge Café, as well as Clyde Holsapple. Also, the author would like to thank Queen's Management Research Centre for Knowledge-Based Enterprises for it generous support of this project.

References

Alavi, M. and D. Leidner, "Knowledge Management and Knowledge Management Systems: Conceptual Foundations and Research Issues," *MISQ Review*, 25, 1, 2001, 107-136.

Aulakh, P., M. Kotabe and A. Sahay, "Trust and Performance in Cross-Border Marketing Partnerships: A Behavioural Approach," *Journal of International Business Studies*, 27, 5, 1996, 1005-1032.

Bhattacharya, R., T. Devinney and M. Pillutla, "A Formal Model of Trust Based on Outcomes," *Academy of Management Review*, 33, 3, 1998, 459-472.

Bowles, T., "Themes and Variations in Shared Cognition in Organizations," in Thompson, L.; Levine, J. and Messick, D. (eds.), *Shared Cognition in Organizations: The Management of Knowledge*, Mahwah, NJ: Lawrence Erlbaum, 1999, 328-348.

Brewer, M., "Ethnocentrism and Its Role in Interpersonal Trust," in Brewer, M. and B. Collins (eds.), *Scientific Inquiry and the Social Sciences*, San Francisco, CA: Jossey-Bass, 1981, 214-231.

Buckley, P. and M. Carter, "Managing Cross-Border Complementary Knowledge". *International Studies of Management and Organization*, 29, 1, 1999, 80-104.

Bukowitz, W. and R. Williams, *The Knowledge Management Fieldbook*, London: Financial Times Prentice Hall, 1999.

Burt, R., *Structural Holes: The Social Structure of Competition*, Cambridge, MA: Harvard University Press, 1992.

Connelly, C. and K. Kelloway, *Predictors of Knowledge Sharing in Organizations*, MSc Thesis for Queen's School of Business, Queen's University, Kingston, ON, 2000.

Cummings, L. and P. Bromiley, "The Organizational Trust Inventory (OTI): Development and Validation," in Kramer, R. and Tyler, T. (eds.), *Trust in Organizations: Frontiers of Theory and Research*, Thousand Oaks, CA: Sage, 1996, 302-320.

Crainer, S., "Prophet of the Information Age". *Management Today*, January, 1999.

Das, T. and B.S. Teng, "Between Trust and Control: Developing Confidence in Partner Cooperation in Alliances," *Academy of Management*, 23, 3, 1998, 491-512.

Davenport, T. and L. Prusak, *Working Knowledge: How Organizations Manage What They Know*, Boston: Harvard Business School Press, 1998.

Deutsch, M., "Trust and Suspicion," *Journal of Conflict Resolution*, 2, 1958, 265-279.

Doney, P., J. Cannon, and M. Mullen, "Understanding the Influence of National Culture on the Development of Trust," *Academy of Management Review*, 23, 3, 1998, 601-620.

Drucker, P., *The Age of Discontinuity: Guidelines to Our Changing Society*, New York: Harper & Row, 1969.

Drucker, P., "The Next Society: A Survey of the Near Future," *The Economist*, November 3, 2001, 2-20.

Edmondson, A. and B. Moingeon, "Learning, Trust and Organizational Change: Contrasting Models of Intervention Research in Organizational Behaviour," in Easterby-Smith, M.; Burgoyne, J. and Araujo, L. (eds.), *Organizational Learning and the Learning Organization: Developments in Theory and Practice*, London: Sage Publications, 1999, 157-175.

Elangovan, A. and D. Shapiro, "Betrayal of Trust in Organizations," *Academy of Management Review*, 23, 3, 1998, 547-566.

Gilbert, J. and T. Li-Ping Tang, "An Examination of Organizational Trust Antecedents," *Public Personnel Management*, 27, 3, 1998, 321-338.

Gold, A., A. Malhotra, and A. Segars, "Knowledge Management: An Organizational Capabilities Perspective," *Journal of Management Information Systems*, 18, 1, 2001, 185-214.

Gray, P. and Y. Chan, "Integrating Knowledge Management Practices through a Problem-Solving Framework," *Communications of the Association for Information Systems*, 4, 12, 2000, 1-21.

Holsapple, C. and K. Joshi, "An Investigation of Factors that Influence the Management of Knowledge in Organizations," *Journal of Strategic Information Systems*, 9, 2000, 235-261.

Jarvenpaa, S. and S. Staples, "The Use of Collaborative Electronic Media for Information Sharing: An Exploratory Study of Determinants," *Journal of Strategic Information Systems*, 9, 2000, 129-154.

Johnson, D. and P. Noonan, "Effects of Acceptance and Reciprocation of Self-Disclosures on the Development of Trust," *Journal of Counseling Psychology*, 19, 5, 1972, 411-416.

Jones, G. and J. George, "The Experience and Evolution of Trust: Implications for Cooperation and Teamwork," *Academy of Management Review*, 23, 3, 1998, 531-548.

Kelloway, K. and J. Barling, "Knowledge Work as Organizational Behaviour," *International Journal of Management Reviews*, 2, 3, 2000, 287-304.

Kim, K. and B. Prabhakar, "Initial Trust, Perceived Risk, and the Adoption of Internet Banking," *ICIS 2000 Proceedings*, Brisbane, Australia, 2000, 537-543.

Kramer, R., "Social Uncertainty and Collective Paranoia in Knowledge Communities: Thinking and Acting in the Shadow of Doubt," in Thompson, L.; Levine, J. and Messick, D. (eds.), *Shared Cognition in Organizations: The Management of Knowledge*, Mahwah, NJ: Lawrence Erlbaum, 1999, 163-191.

Lewicki, R., D. McAllister, and R. Bies, "Trust and Distrust: New Relationships and Realities," *Academy of Management Review*, 23, 3, 1998, 438-458.

Matusik, S. and C. Hill, "The Utilization of Contingent Work, Knowledge Creation, and Competitive Advantage," *Academy of Management Review*, 23, 4, 1998, 680-697.

Mayer, R., J. Davis, and F. Schoorman, "An Integrative Model of Organizational Trust," *The Academy of Management Review*, 20, 3, 1995, 709-734.

McKnight, D.H. and L. Cummings, "Initial Trust Formation in New Organizational Relationships," *Academy of Management Review*, 23, 3, 1998, 473-490.

McLure Wasko, M. and S. Faraj, "'It Is What One Does': Why People Participate and Help Others in Electronic Communities of Practice," *Journal of Strategic Information Systems*, 9, 2000, 155-173.

Mishra, J. and M. Morrisey, "Trust in Employee/Employer Relationships: A Survey of West Michigan Managers," *Public Personnel Management*, 19, 4, 1990, 443-463.

Morris, J. and D. Moberg, "Work Organizations as Contexts for Trust and Betrayal," in Sarbin, T.; Carney, R. and Eoyang, C. (eds.), *Citizen Espionage: Studies in Trust and Betrayal*, Westport, CT: Praeger, 1994, 163-187.

Nonaka, I., "The Knowledge-Creating Company," *Harvard Business Review*, 69, 1991, 96-104.

Nonaka, I., "A Dynamic Theory of Organizational Knowledge Creation," *Organization Science*, 5, 1994, 14-37.

Nonaka, I. and H. Takeuchi, *The Knowledge-Creating Company: How Japanese Companies Create the Dynamics of Innovation*, New York: Oxford University Press, 1995.

Podolny, J.M. and J.N. Baron, "Resources and Relationships: Social Networks and Mobility in the Workplace," *American Sociological Review*, 62, 1997, 673-693.

Polanyi, M., "The Logic of Tacit Inference," *Philosophy*, 41, 1966, 1-18.

Probst, G., S. Raub, and K. Romhardt, *Managing Knowledge: Building Blocks for Success*, Chichester, John Wiley & Sons, Ltd., 2000.

Ratnasingham, P. and K. Kumar, "Trading Partner Trust in Electronic Commerce Participation," *ICIS 2000 Proceedings*, Brisbane, Australia, 2000, 544-552.

Roberts, J., "From Know-How to Show-How? Questioning the Role of Information and Communication Technologies in Knowledge Transfer," *Technology Analysis and Strategic Management*, 12, 4, 2000, 429-443.

Robinson, S.L., "Trust and Breach of the Psychological Contract," *Administrative Science Quarterly*, 41, 1996, 574-590.

Rolland, N. and D. Chauvel, "Knowledge Transfer in Strategic Alliances," in Despres, C. and Chauvel, D. (eds.), *Knowledge Horizons: The Present and the Promise of Knowledge Management*, Boston: Butterworth Heinemann, 225-236.

Rousseau, D., et al., "Introduction to Special Topic Forum. Not So Different after All: A Cross-Discipline View of Trust," *Academy of Management Review*, 23, 3, 1998, 393-404.

Rotter, J., "A New Scale for the Measurement of Interpersonal Trust," *Journal of Personality*, 35, 1967, 651-665.

Shapiro, D., B. Sheppard, and L. Cheraskin, "Business on a Handshake," *Negotiation Journal*, 8, 1992, 365-377.

von Krogh, G., K. Ichijo, and I. Nonaka, *Enabling Knowledge Creation: How to Unlock the Mystery of Tacit Knowledge and Release the Power of Innovation*, New York: Oxford University Press, 2000.

Williamson, O., "Calculativeness, Trust and Economic Organization," *Journal of Law and Economics*, 34, 1993, 453-502.

Zucker, L., "Production of Trust: Institutional Sources of Economic Structure, 1840-1920," in Straw, B. and Cummings, L. (eds.), *Research in Organizational Behavior*, 8, Greenwich, CT: JAI Press, 1986, 53-111.

CHAPTER 30

Why Knowledge Management Systems Fail: Enablers and Constraints of Knowledge Management in Human Enterprises

Yogesh Malhotra

Syracuse University, School of Management, Syracuse, NY, USA

Drawing upon lessons learned from the biggest failure of knowledge management in recent world history and the debacle of the 'new economy' enterprises, this chapter explains why knowledge management systems (KMS) fail and how risk of such failures may be minimized. The key thesis is that *enablers* of KMS designed for the 'knowledge factory' engineering paradigm often unravel and become *constraints* in adapting and evolving such systems for business environments characterized by high uncertainty. Design of KMS should ensure that adaptation and innovation of business performance outcomes occurs in alignment with changing dynamics of the business environment. Simultaneously, conceiving multiple future trajectories of the information technology and human inputs embedded in the KMS can diminish the risk of rapid obsolescence of such systems. Envisioning business models not only in terms of knowledge harvesting processes for seeking optimization and efficiencies, but *in combination with* ongoing knowledge creation processes would ensure that organizations not only succeed in *doing the thing right* in the short term but also in *doing the right thing* in the long term. Integrating both these aspects in enterprise business models as simultaneous and parallel sets of knowledge processes instead of treating them in isolation would facilitate ongoing innovation of business value propositions and customer value propositions.

Keywords: Adaptive Systems for Radical Discontinuous Change; Business Model Innovation; Business Value Propositions; Customer Value Propositions; Design of Successful Knowledge Management Systems; Enablers and Constraints of Knowledge Management; Information Processing and Sense Making; Internet; Knowledge Harvesting and Knowledge Creation; Knowledge Management Failure; New Business Models; Strategic, Social, and, Behavioral Aspects of Knowledge Management; Transformation of Knowledge Work and Knowledge Organizations; Web

1 Introduction

The advent of the era characterized by high uncertainty was announced by a recent *Business Week* (2001) cover story that determined September 11, 2001, as the day of the watershed event. On this day, the unprecedented combination of *conventional* means of terrorism inflicted their wrath on thousands of human lives in the

World Trade Center twin towers despite policy-makers' preoccupation with *un-conventional* means of terror. The basic premises guiding the knowledge processes of the intelligence machinery and policy-makers' decision models surmised that:

- *unconventional* means pose greater risk compared with those posed by *conventional* means;
- *conventional* means cannot reconfigure in unpredictable ways to pose greater risk than *unconventional* means;
- impact of human and technology inputs can be determined with a safe margin of predictability;
- *hi-tech* inputs always have greater impact than *low-tech* inputs;
- human inputs play a lesser role compared with technology inputs and financial capital inputs in the input-outcome equation; and,
- inputs rather than the execution strategy primarily determine the outcomes.

In retrospective it was found that all these assumptions were questionable. A review of the above assumptions guiding policy-making decisions offers some interesting revelations listed below:

- Pre-specified and pre-determined notions of *unconventional* and *conventional*, and, *low-tech* and *high-tech* inputs may not necessarily be always applicable;
- Technology inputs and financial capital inputs may be less relevant factors in the input-outcome equation given unconventional *strategy of execution* that defines how creatively and innovatively inputs are deployed to produce unprecedented outcomes;
- Human inputs may not necessarily play a lesser role than technology inputs or financial capital inputs in the input-outcome equation – given highly committed and motivated humans and their leaders, technology inputs and financial capital may assume a lesser role in the input-outcome equation.

Extending the same analysis to understand the recent debacle of 'new economy' enterprises also offers some interesting insights. Given the euphoria about the Internet technologies and the pitch of the venture capitalists and tech stock analysts and underwriters, Internet technology based businesses were summarily branded as *unconventional* in contrast to the *conventional* enterprises of the brick-and-mortar economy. It was assumed that *conventional* enterprises must get up on the Internet bandwagon if they had to survive in the future. It was assumed that given enough investment of venture capital, technology, and hype, any company could create and sustain successful business performance outcomes within a very short time. In summary, the following premises guided the euphoria about the Internet based companies which was compounded by the over-exuberance of media network reporters and analysts:

- *unconventional* means pose greater risk compared with those posed by *conventional* means;
- *conventional* means cannot reconfigure in unpredictable ways to pose greater risk than *unconventional* means;
- impact of human and technology inputs can be determined with a safe margin of predictability;
- *hi-tech* inputs always have greater impact than *low-tech* inputs;
- human inputs play a lesser role compared with technology inputs and financial capital inputs in the input-outcome equation; and,
- inputs rather than the execution strategy primarily determine the outcomes.

Given the recent spate of Internet-based company failures, reversal of faith in the Net-based companies has been pervasive. This has happened despite the fact that widespread weaknesses are being observed in many sectors of the economy including many industries and companies that represent the tried-and-tested 'old economy'. It is time to reflect upon the lessons learned from the biggest failure of knowledge management in recent world history and the debacle of the 'new economy' enterprises. This is important to inform the prevailing myth about the intrinsic infallibility of 'old economy' enterprises in contrast with the 'new economy' enterprises despite dependence of both on the same fundamentals.

Based upon the earlier analysis, one can offer the following hypotheses that seem to provide a more robust basis for defining, implementing, and executing effective knowledge management systems.

- The impact of human and technology inputs cannot be determined with safe margin of predictability as the business performance outcomes are separated from these inputs by intervening variables. Such variables include effective acceptance and utilization of technologies by humans; motivation and commitment for adoption of these technologies and for achieving the specified performance outcomes; and, contextual interpretation of information resulting in diverse subjective decisions and actions. Pre-specified outcomes may also become marginalized with the changing business environment when the inputs are consumed for *doing the thing right* even though it may not be the *right thing* any more.
- *Lo-tech* and *hi-tech* inputs are constrained or enabled by knowledge workers who utilize these inputs as well as by the strategy of execution that may together produce different outcomes despite similar mix of the inputs. The contrast between *lo-tech* and *hi-tech* is based upon context-specific perspectives and as business contexts change, these contrasts may change or become immaterial with emergence of newer unprecedented inputs as well as innovative outcome propositions.
- Similarly, the contrast between *unconventional* and *conventional* means of producing business performance outcomes is based upon context-specific perspectives. As business contexts change, such contrast may become marginalized with emergence of newer unprecedented means as well as innovative outcome propositions. Such contrast may also become

marginalized if *conventional* means are configured in unprecedented ways to achieve unprecedented outcomes. As explained in the following discussion, unprecedented business performance outcomes are often realized as a result of innovative business value propositions and customer value propositions.

This chapter explains how both old and new economy enterprises having any mix of brick-and-click strategies are vulnerable to the above failures. Such failures result from the gaps between the input resources and the business performance outcomes, and, the gaps between the value these enterprises create and the value demanded by changing market conditions, consumer preferences, competitive offerings, business models, and, industry structures. KMS are often defined in terms of inputs such as data, information technology, best practices, etc., that may inadequately explain business performance outcomes if considered in isolation. Often, moderating and intervening variables play a significant role in skewing the simplistic relationships based upon correlation of the above inputs with business performance outcomes. Usefulness of such inputs and how they are strategically deployed are other important issues often left unquestioned as 'expected' performance outcomes are achieved, but the value of such outcomes gets eroded by the dynamic shifts in the business and competitive environments. The remaining discussion will explain why KMS fail; how *enablers* of KMS designed for the 'knowledge factory' engineering paradigm become *constraints* in adapting and evolving such systems for business environments characterized by high uncertainty; and, how risk of such failures may be minimized.

2 Knowledge Management for Routine and Structured Information Processing (Model 1 KMS)

Given the centrality of computerized information processing in most mainstream conceptualizations of knowledge management, most KMS primarily depend upon routines that are programmed in the logic of computational machinery and on data residing in data warehouses. [A detailed discussion about such definitions of knowledge management is available elsewhere (Malhotra 2000a, 2000b). A recent historical perspective of knowledge management is available in Prusak (2001).] Based on the pre-specification and pre-determination of the programmed logic connecting 'information inputs' and consequent 'information outcomes', such systems are based upon consensus, convergence, and, compliance to ensure adherence to organizational routines. The mechanistic model of information processing and control based upon compliance is not only limited to the computational machinery, but extends to specification of goals, tasks, best practices and institutionalized procedures to achieve the pre-specified outcomes. Motivated by emphasis on optimization and efficiency, this model has evolved from 'scientific' Taylorism and the assembly line techniques applied by Henry Ford in the production of Model T.

Even some Information Systems researchers apparently believe that technology inputs rather than knowledge workers would play the predominant role in the performance outcome equation discussed earlier, as illustrated by the following prescription from a popular text on Information Systems (Applegate et al., 1988, p. 44):

> "Information systems will maintain the corporate history, experience and expertise that long-term employees now hold. The information systems themselves – not the people – can become the stable structure of the organization. People will be free to come and go, but the value of their experience will be incorporated in the systems that help them and their successors run the business."

Business and technology executives trained in similar reasoning have been trying to push for adoption of computer technologies for *storing* their employees' *knowledge* in computerized databases and programmed logic of the computing machinery with mixed results. Many of them may not have realized that best practices, benchmarks, and rules that tended to define their assumptions about the 'theory of business' (Drucker 1994) not only become ingrained in information databases, but also in the organization's strategy, reward systems, and resource allocation systems.

A recent interpretation of the above rationale based upon pre-definition, pre-specification, and, pre-determination and illustrated in Figure 1, is offered in a definition popularized by the Gartner Group (cf: *Oracle Magazine*, 1998):

> "Knowledge Management promotes an integrated approach to identifying, capturing, retrieving, sharing, and evaluating an enterprises information assets. These information assets may include databases, documents, policies, procedures, as well as the un-captured tacit expertise and experience stored in individual's heads."

Such mechanistic and static representations of KMS do not adequately explain the prevalent gaps between the inputs and expected business performance outcomes. Nor do they suggest how to deal with "associated emotions and specific contexts" (Nonaka & Takeuchi 1995, p. 63) that epitomize tacit knowledge.

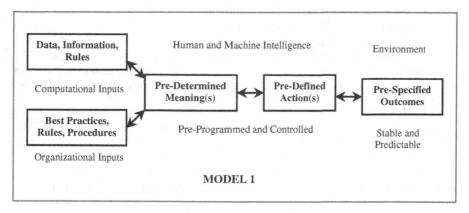

Figure 1. Knowledge Management for Routine and Structured Information Processing

Recent thrust of some organizational knowledge management consultants on archiving 'best practices' and 'what we know' (O'Dell, C. and Grayson, 1998) to guide future decisions and actions is based on a relatively predictable view of the business environment. Not surprisingly, this model, based upon pre-specification and pre-determination of business logic, has primarily focused on the *re-use of existing knowledge* [reified in best practices, computational logic, databases, etc.] over *creation of new knowledge*. The key managerial focus of this model is to ensure consensus and compliance for minimizing variance so that pre-specified business performance outcomes are achieved. Conformance to pre-specified and pre-determined business logic is expected to ensure pre-defined and pre-determined business performance outcomes are achieved.

Most knowledge management practitioners and researchers who identify with Model 1 treat both *information* and *knowledge* as synonymous constructs. In this view, both *information* and *knowledge* can be adequately expressed in the rule-based logic, data inputs, and data outputs that trigger pre-defined and pre-determined actions in pre-programmed modes. To ensure homogeneous compliance with rules, diversity of interpretations and multiplicity of *meanings* are either ignored or are subjected to additional controls. Homogeneity of information-processing and control logic is enforced with the belief that it will ensure that the pre-specified and pre-determined meanings will result in pre-specified and pre-determined actions to produce pre-specified and pre-determined outcomes. Feedback and feedforward loops may be included to fine-tune the inputs for optimal conversion of the inputs into outcomes.

Not surprisingly, the goal of KMS based on Model 1 is often characterized as "getting the right information to the right person at the right time." This model is based on the assumption that all relevant knowledge, including *tacit knowledge*, can be *somehow* stored in computerized databases, software programs, and, institutionalized rules and practices. The distinguishing features of this model are derived from the following assumptions:

(a) the same knowledge can be re-used by any human mind or computer to re-process the same logic to produce the same outcomes;
(b) the same outcomes will be needed and delivered again and again through optimal use of same input resources;
(c) the system's primary objective is to achieve the most efficient means for transforming pre-specified inputs into pre-determined outcomes; and,
(d) there is no need for subjective interpretation of information – criticism and conflict must be minimized to achieve conformance and compliance.

Model 1 KMS are based on *doing the thing right* where the pre-specified inputs, processing logic, and, the outcomes are assumed to represent *the right thing*. The overriding belief is that designers of the systems and the knowledge managers have accurate and reliable knowledge about the viability of the input-output transformation process as well as the viability of the pre-defined performance outcomes. [Information Systems researchers (cf: Churchman, 1971; Mason and Mitroff, 1973; Malhotra, 1997) have discussed limitations of this model, particularly for environments characterized by uncertainty and radical change.].

The next section explains the contrasting Model 2 of KMS that is more suited for non-routine and unstructured sense making when deterministic controls encounter 'wicked' environments (Churchman 1971) characterized by "wide range of potential surprise" (Landau and Stout, 1979) that defy predictive logic. Interestingly, many of the limitations of Model 1 may be considered as strengths in Model 2 as the premises of pre-determination, pre-definition, and, pre-specification of meanings, actions, and, outcomes become less relevant.

3   Knowledge Management for Non-routine and Unstructured Sense Making (Model 2 KMS)

In Model 2, *knowledge* is represented as *intelligence in action* as it is a composite construct resulting from interaction of data, information, rules, procedures, best practices and traits such as attention, motivation, commitment, creativity, and, innovation. Representation of knowledge as *intelligence in action* in contrast to the static computerized representations of Model 1 is the key distinguishing feature of Model 2. As discussed in this section, the *active, affective,* and *dynamic* representation of knowledge makes better sense from a pragmatic perspective and also represents a more accurate depiction based upon understanding of how humans process information to make decisions that influence their actions. In terms of influencing business outcomes, knowledge can be best understood in terms of behavior and actions rather than in terms of inert and static representations of Model 1. As affect plays an important role in focusing attention to specific information as well as in determining change in behaviors or actions based upon that information (cf: Bruner, 1986; Damasio, 1994; Kelly, 1969), emotions have an important role in transforming knowledge to performance outcomes. This process is *dynamic* as it is based upon ongoing reinterpretation of data, information, and, assumptions while pro-actively sensing how decision-making process should adjust to future possibilities (cf: Kelly, 1963). From a pragmatic viewpoint, the dynamic representation of knowledge provides a more realistic construct integrated within human and social interactions. An additional advantage of this representation besides its realism is that it helps in explaining the performance outcomes more directly while taking into consideration important intervening and moderating variables. [A detailed discussion about the active, affective, and dynamic representation of knowledge is available elsewhere (Malhotra 1999, Malhotra and Kirsch (1996), Malhotra (in press)).]

Model 2 provides a better representation of reality as it takes into consideration two key characteristics:

(a) what is done with data, information, and best practices depends upon subjective interpretation ("construction") of individuals and groups that transform these inputs into actions and performance; and,

(b) performance outcomes are continuously re-assessed to ensure that they indeed represent best business performance for the enterprise with respect to changing market conditions, consumer preferences, competitive offerings, and, changing business models, and, industry structures.

This view of knowledge management is consistent with some other perspectives that have attempted to address the limitations the previous model based upon "overdefinition of rules and overspecification of tasks" (Landau and Stout, 1979). For instance, Churchman (1971) has emphasized that: "To conceive of knowledge as a collection of information seems to rob the concept of all of its life ... Knowledge resides in the user and not in the collection." Likewise, Nonaka and Takeuchi (1995) have proposed the conceptualization of knowledge as *justified belief* in their argument that, "knowledge, unlike information, is about *beliefs* and *commitment*." Similarly, Davenport and Prusak (1998, p. 5) have defined knowledge as deriving from minds at work: "Knowledge is a fluid mix of framed experience, values, contextual information, and expert insight that provides a framework for evaluating and incorporating new experiences and information. It originates in the minds of knowers. In organizations, it often becomes embedded not only in documents or repositories but also in organizational routines, processes, practices, and norms."

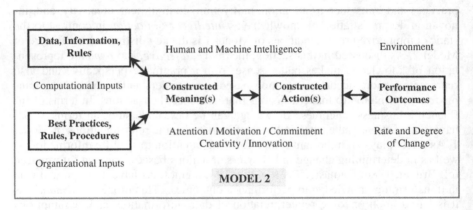

Figure 2. Knowledge Management for Non-routine and Unstructured Sense Making

As represented in Model 2, knowledge is a *dynamic* construct in contrast to *static* representations of Model 1 because diverse [individual and shared] meanings are possible based upon diverse interpretations of the same information inputs across different contexts and at different times. Processing of knowledge through the machinery of information technologies may still be represented by simplified, highly routine, and, structured forms that permit pre-definition, pre-programming, and, pre-determination of data inputs for achieving pre-specified performance outcomes. In contrast, human sense making is an active, affective, and, dynamic process influenced by attention, motivation, commitment, creativity, and innovation of individuals and groups. [Related discussion on how "construction of meaning" differs from "the processing of information" is available in Bruner (1990), Kelly (1963), Malhotra (1999), Morris (1938), Strombach (1986). Detailed conceptualization and empirical validation of commitment and motivation constructs is available in Malhotra (1998), and, Malhotra and Galletta (1999). Contrast between information-processing capabilities of smart technologies and sense-making capabilities of humans is explained in Malhotra (2001a).]

4   Continuum of KM Systems between Model 1 and Model 2

Model 1 works well in predictable and stable environments with primary focus on knowledge harvesting, knowledge re-use and replication. Under moderate levels of control, this model could be used for knowledge workers' goal and task specification to achieve pre-specified performance outcomes. This model may be susceptible to failure when creativity and innovation of knowledge workers overwhelms the controls inherent in the pre-specified logic of the input-output transformation process. It is also vulnerable to failure where attention and actions of knowledge workers are significantly influenced by their intrinsic motivation [rather than organizational or institutional rewards and punishments] and commitment to personal goals [rather than organizational or institutional goals]. The ideal scenario is to achieve perfect congruence between extrinsic motivation and intrinsic motivation, and, between organizational goals and individual goals, but this remains a formidable challenge for designers of most organizational KMS. [A detailed discussion about the contrast between extrinsic motivation and intrinsic motivation, and, contrast between various levels of commitment is available elsewhere (Malhotra 1998).]

While Model 1 and Model 2 represent the extreme archetypes of KMS, most organizations need some combination of both depending upon their emphasis on knowledge harvesting and knowledge creation. Also, organizations and inter-enterprise value networks contain some business processes that primarily depend upon knowledge harvesting and others that primarily depend upon knowledge creation. This point can be appreciated by considering the two world's of business that often co-exist in many organizations – the world of bulk-processing industrial economy and the "world-of-reeverything" of the knowledge economy (Arthur 1996):

> "The two worlds are not neatly split. Hewlett-Packard, for example, designs knowledge-based devices in Palo Alto, California, and manufactures them in bulk in places like Corvallis, Oregon or Greeley, Colorado. Most high-tech companies have both knowledge-based operations and bulk-processing operations. But because the rules of the game are different for each, companies often separate them—as Hewlett-Packard does. Conversely, manufacturing companies have operations such as logistics, branding, marketing, and distribution that belong largely to the knowledge world. And some products—like the IBM PC—start in the increasing returns world, but later in their life cycle become virtual commodities that belong to Marshall's processing world."

Model 1 is relevant to the industrial world of bulk-economy production and Model 2 is relevant to the "world-of-re-everything". Routinization of organizational goals and convergence is relevant for 'freezing' the meaning for achieving optimization-based efficiencies. However, 'unfreezing' of meaning embedded in information is critical for reassessing and renewing the routines embedded in business logic and business processes. Business enterprises will need to be facile in both modes despite the apparent contradiction in terms of the business logic and related assumptions. For instance, a key challenge for most organizations with institutionalized 'best practices' is to ensure that such practices remain open to critique, adaptation, and, replacement so that the enterprise is not caught in the death spiral (Nadler and Shaw 1995) of doing *more of the same better and better* with diminishing marginal returns (Drucker, 1994). Discontinuously changing environments impose upon the organization need for "creative synthesis" resulting from a "dialectical confrontation of opposing interpretations" (Mason and Mitroff 1973, p. 482).

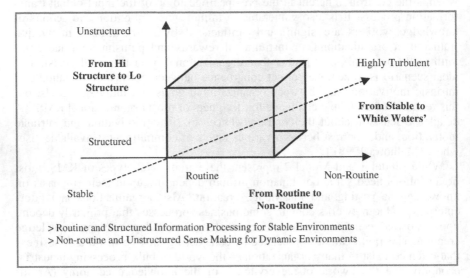

Figure 3. Continuum of KMS between Stable and Dynamic Environments

Although companies often separate the operations pertaining to the two worlds of business related to Model 1 and Model 2, both worlds need to be integrated in their enterprise business models. For example, given the diminishing margins in the PC markets due to increased competition, computer distributor Dell may need to shift its focus to distribution of servers or to hosting services. To do so effectively, however, it would need to start *harvesting* [using Model 1] knowledge that it *created* [using Model 2] earlier through experimentation, adaptation, and innovation related to servers or hosting when it is time to redefine the customer value propositions and the related business value propositions. [How the contrast between the two worlds applies to the use of information technology and knowledge management strategy is discussed in the context of business model innovation in Malhotra (2000d). How the worlds of 'old economy' and 'new economy' relate to their knowledge-based representations has been discussed in business literature on virtual organizations, virtual products, and, virtual services, see for instance, Davidow and Malone (1993). More recent research relating knowledge management to virtual organizations and business model innovation is available in Malhotra (2000c) and Malhotra (2001b), respectively.]

As most business environments would include a combination of both stabilizing factors and destabilizing factors, real world KMS implementations should contain combinations of characteristics of both models. The processes of *knowledge re-use* and *knowledge creation* need to be balanced by integration of routine and structured *information processing* and non-routine and unstructured *sense making* in the same business model. Figure 3 depicts this representation of business model that includes simultaneous and parallel sets of knowledge harvesting and knowledge creation processes.

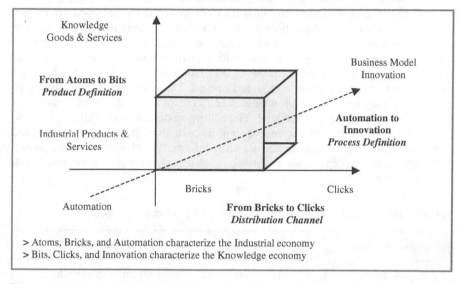

Figure 4. Continuum from Industrial Economy to Knowledge Economy

Prior arguments suggest the need for skepticism about the myth of intrinsic infallibility of 'old economy' enterprises in contrast with the 'new economy' enterprises despite dependence of both on the same fundamentals. Both old and new economy enterprises having any mix of *conventional* and *unconventional* brick-and-click strategies are vulnerable to the failures resulting from the gaps between their inputs and the business performance outcomes as well as from gaps between the value they create and the value demanded by their customers. Also, despite similarity of inputs and sought market shares, relative success of any business model will be determined more by its execution than by the inputs especially in case of rapidly changing environments. As illustrated in Figure 4, new business models for the knowledge economy need to consider Internet and Web simply as elements of the overall business strategy without getting caught in *irrational* exuberance or despair about these means of producing business value. Just like other inputs and intervening variables, inadequate understanding or application of Internet and Web should not become the basis for outright rejection or degradation of these technologies.

5   Enablers and Constraints of Knowledge Management Systems

Prior discussion has highlighted that knowledge management systems fail because of two broad reasons. First, knowledge management systems are often defined in terms of inputs such as data, information technology, best practices, etc., that by themselves may be inadequate for effective business performance. For these inputs to result in business performance, the influence of intervening and moderating variables such as attention, motivation, commitment, creativity, and innovation, has to be better understood and accounted for in design of business models. Second, the efficacy of inputs and how they are strategically deployed are important issues often left unquestioned as 'expected' performance outcomes are achieved, but the value of such performance outcomes may be eroded by the dynamic shifts in the business and competitive environments. These enablers and constraints are presented in the following discussion as seven *challenges* that need to be met for successful knowledge management. These are called challenges (see Table 1) as they represent *both* enablers and constraints in different contexts as represented by Model 1 and Model 2. The following discussion highlights how the seven challenges relate to the recent evolution in thinking about business and technology strategy, organizational control, information sharing culture, knowledge representation, organization structure, managerial command and control, and, economic returns.

Table 1. Enablers and Constraints of KMS: Model 1 and Model 2 Compared

Enablers & Constraints	Model 1 KMS	Model 2 KMS
Business & Technology Strategy	Pre-definition of Outcomes	World of re-everything
Organizational Control	Control for Consistency	Self-Control for Creativity
Information Sharing Culture	Based Upon Contracts	Based Upon Trust
Knowledge Representation	Static and Pre-specified	Dynamic and 'Constructed'
Organization Structure	Insular and Top-Down	Inclusive and Self-Organized
Managerial Command and Control	For Achieving Compliance	For Achieving Commitment
Economic Returns	Decreasing Returns	Increasing Returns

5.1 Business and Technology Strategy Challenge of Next Generation KMS

In the world of re-everything, automation of functions, rationalization of work-flows, and redesign of business processes that characterize Model 1 KMS will be inadequate (Malhotra 2000d). Rather, most organizations will need to develop adaptive capacity for redefining their *business value propositions* – that add great-est value to the business enterprise. Competitive survival and ongoing sustenance would depend on the ability to continuously redefine and adapt organizational goals, purposes, and the organization's "way of doing things." The digital business models will need to accommodate relatively rapid obsolescence of traditional con-cepts of industries, organizations, products, services and channels of marketing, sales and distribution (Mathur and Kenyon 1997). The critical challenge for most business enterprises will lie in the ability to redesign and reinvent their business processes and business models for realizing more interesting *customer value propositions*, while harvesting the knowledge flows embedded in the current setup.

Next generation KMS will need to accommodate the managers' need for ongo-ing questioning of the programmed logic and very high level of adaptability to in-corporate dynamic changes in business models and information architectures. De-signers of information architectures will need to ensure that they deliver upon the need for efficiency and optimization for knowledge harvesting while providing for flexibility for facilitating innovative business models and value propositions. They will need to provide loose coupling between technology architectures and business architectures so that existing technology infrastructure do not straitjacket the evo-lution of the business model. Greater technological integration will help in achiev-ing more efficient optimization for knowledge harvesting. There will be, however, a critical need for ensuring rapid adaptation of the business performance outcomes to the dynamic shifts in the business environment while keeping them loosely coupled with pre-specified technology architectures. The new paradigm of flexi-ble, adaptive, and scalable systems will accommodate real time changes in infor-mation and data across the business ecosystems network.

5.2 Organizational Control Challenge of Next Generation KMS

Organizational control is imperative in Model 1 KMS to ensure pre-determined meanings, pre-defined actions, and, pre-specified outcomes. Consistency is im-perative for ensuring homogeneity of processing of same information in the same manner to ensure same outcomes and is achieved by minimizing criticism and questioning of the status quo. This may, however, take its toll by suppressing in-novation and creativity. Even despite organizational control that demands absolute conformance, knowledge workers' attention, motivation, and, commitment may moderate or intervene in its influence. Control is often based on rules and hence difficult to maintain in a world where competitive survival often depends upon questioning existing assumptions. Given an environment characterized by radical and discontinuous change, the survival of the organization would hinge on ongo-ing assessment of assumptions underlying the business logic as well as ensuring that the definition of business performance outcomes is aligned with the changing market conditions, consumer preferences, competitive offerings, business models, and, industry structures.

Design of next generation KMS should ensure that they are not constrained by overemphasis on consistency. While the traditional business logic is based on control, dynamics of the new business environment require a business model that assumes existence of few rules, some specific information and a lot of freedom. Within the proposed model, the designers of organizational systems can at best facilitate the organization's 'self-designing'. In this organization design, not only would the knowledge workers define problems and generate their own solutions, the knowledge workers would also evaluate and revise their solution-generating processes. By explicitly encouraging experimentation and rethinking of premises, this model promotes reflection-in-action, creation of new knowledge, and innovation. Organizations will need to be comfortable with the *dialectic* of harvesting their existing knowledge *while* being able to rethink and redefine their current models of success before they are marginalized by environmental change.

Integration of data and processes across inter-enterprise value networks will also impose certain challenges of organizational control. On one hand, the players in the inter-enterprise supply chains and extended value chains will need to share information and collaborate with their upstream and downstream partners to ensure streamlined information flows. Ironically, they may also perceive the upstream and downstream players as potential competitors vying for the most attractive and dominant position in the value chain networks. While sharing of accurate information related to goods or services flowing across the supply chain will be necessary, it would increase the peril inherent in the paradoxical roles of collaboration and competition adopted by various players in the supply chain networks.

5.3 Information Sharing Culture Challenge of Next Generation KMS

Success of the next generation KMS will depend upon integration of not only data and processes across inter-enterprise supply chains and value chains, but also integration of decision-making and actions across inter-enterprise boundaries. Effectiveness of integrated information flows will depend upon the accuracy of information that is shared by diverse stakeholders across inter-enterprise boundaries. The challenge of information sharing will result from the potentially competitive nature of various enterprises across the value chains as access to privileged information may often determine the dominant position in the inter-enterprise value networks. Similarly, access to customer and supplier data residing in databases or networks hosted by outsourcing providers and ASPs may pose increased privacy and security challenges. This is particularly important in situations where sharing of proprietary strategic or competitive information about customer or supplier relationships needs to be safeguarded from third parties. This issue will be particularly relevant if the vendor's knowledge of the company's customers or specific customer relationships may be used against the best interests of the company. There will be need for trusting the vendor(s), however, given the changing business environment, the basis for trust will need to go beyond a simple contractual agreement that would have been sufficient in the deterministic and predictable logic of Model 1.

Often, individuals may not willingly share information with their departmental peers, supervisors or with other departments based upon the belief that what they know provides them with an inherent advantage in bargaining and negotiation. Despite the availability of most sophisticated 'knowledge sharing' technologies, such human concerns may often result in sharing of partial, inaccurate, or ambiguous information. Even more critical than the absence of information is the propensity of sharing inaccurate or ambiguous information because of competing interests that may not yield true integration of *information flows* despite very sophisticated integration of *enabling* information technologies. Integrated information flows depend upon motivation of people to share accurate information on a timely basis across intra-enterprise and inter-enterprise information value chains. Motivation of employees, organizations, customers, and suppliers to share accurate and timely information is based on trust, despite the potential of use of information in unanticipated ways. This in turn depends upon the overriding inter-enterprise and intra-enterprise information sharing cultures. As community and commerce paradigms increasingly intermingle, business enterprises will be challenged to inspire trust and motivation for sharing needed information with their stakeholders on which they may often have little formal control. Given the lack of these enabling factors, it will be almost impossible to ensure that accurate information is available for integration despite presence of *enabling* technologies that can facilitate such integration.

5.4 Knowledge Representation Challenge of Next Generation KMS

Static and pre-defined representation of knowledge is particularly suited for *knowledge re-use* and offers an interesting contrast against the dynamic, affective, and, active representation of knowledge needed for *knowledge creation*. The premise of the digitized memory of the past as a reliable predictor of the future success is valid for a business environment characterized by routine and structured change. While the digitized logic and databases can facilitate real-time execution of the inter-enterprise information value chains, their efficacy depends upon real-time adaptation of underlying assumptions to continuously account for complex changes in the business environment. Often such changes cannot be recognized or corrected *automatically* by computerized systems as they cannot be *pre-programmed* to detect an unpredictable future. The adaptability of a KMS is therefore dependent upon its capability of sensing complex patterns of change in business environments *and* using that information for adapting the digitized logic and databases to guide decision-making, actions, and resulting performance outcomes.

AI and expert systems based KMS can deliver the "right information to the right person at the right time" *if* it is known in advance what the right information is, who the right person to use or apply that information would be, and, what would be the right time when that specific information would be needed. Detection of non-routine and unstructured change in business environment would still depend upon sense-making capabilities of knowledge workers for correcting the computational logic of the business and the data it processes. A related challenge lies in tapping the tacit knowledge of executives and employees for informing the computational logic embedded in the KMS. It may be possible to gather information about the decision-making logic from human experts if such decisions are based on routine and structured information processing. AI and expert systems related technologies enable complex computation of specific and clearly defined domain expertise areas by compiling inferential logic derived from multiple domain experts. The challenge of 'scanning the human mind and its sense making capabilities' lies in the problem that most individuals may know more than they think they know. This is particularly true about their information processing and decision-making capabilities related to non-routine and unstructured phenomena and to knowledge that spans multiple domains. The meaning making capacity of the human mind facilitates dynamic adaptation of tacit knowledge to new and unfamiliar situations that may not fit previously recognized *templates*. The same assemblage of data may evoke different responses from different people at different times or in different contexts. Hence, storing explicit *static* representations of individuals' tacit knowledge in technology databases and computer algorithms may not be a valid surrogate for their *dynamic* sense making capabilities.

5.5 Organization Structure Challenge of Next Generation KMS

Developing an information-sharing technological infrastructure is an exercise in *engineering design*, whereas enabling use of that infrastructure for sharing high quality information and generating new knowledge is an exercise in *emergence*. While the former process is characterized by pre-determination, pre-specification and pre-programming for knowledge harvesting and exploitation, the latter process is typically characterized by creation of organizational cultural infrastructure to enable continuous information sharing, knowledge renewal, and creation of new knowledge.

Organizational routines embedded in standard operating procedures and policies can become formalized by their implementation in computer programs and databases as the firm's dominant business logic becomes reinforced. Such formalized information systems become inflexible when they are based upon *static* assumptions about the business environment. With increasingly rapid, dynamic and non-linear changes in the business environment, such systems are increasingly vulnerable because of out-of-date assumptions inherent in their processing logic and the data processed by them. To overcome these vulnerabilities, it is necessary to design technological systems that are sensitive to the dynamic and divergent interpretations of information necessary for navigating unforeseen changes in business environment. Subjecting the extant business logic to critique from diverse customer, supplier, and partner perspectives can help in defining innovative customer value propositions and business value propositions by early detection of complex changes in the business environment. Online and offline communities of customers, suppliers and partners could provide the means for enabling critical analysis of assumptions underlying given business models.

Expanded role of the customers, suppliers and partners includes their involvement in the creation of 'content', in generating product and service reviews, and in helping each other out on shared concerns. It is important to note that such roles *assumed* by *external* communities of customers, suppliers, and partners in the new world have been traditionally *delegated* to *internal* customer service representatives and technical support personnel. Hence, in the emerging business models, virtual communities could be rightfully treated as external extensions of the company's service and support infrastructure. Executives must understand the distinction between the lack of structure and lack of controls that characterize self-selected communities and the command and control systems embedded in their formal organizational structures. Such communities may defy compliance seeking tactics as they represent "self-organizing" ecosystems built upon self-control and autonomy. As knowledge work gets transformed and dissipated across the inter-enterprise value networks, enterprise managers will need to become more comfortable with the model of the enterprise as 'anything, anywhere, anyhow' *dynamic structures* of people, processes, and technology networks.

5.6 Managerial Command and Control Challenge of Next Generation KMS

Organizational controls tend to seek compliance with pre-defined goals that need to be achieved using pre-determined 'best practices' and standard operating procedures. Such organizational controls tend to *ensure* conformity by enforcing task definition, measurement and control, yet they may *inhibit* creativity and initiative. Enforcement of such controls is essentially a negative activity since it defines "what cannot be done" (Stout 1980) and reinforces a process of single loop learning with its primary emphasis on error avoidance (Argyris 1994). Given the premium on innovation of customer value propositions, business value propositions and business models, organizations in dynamically changing environments need to encourage experimentation. Design of new information architectures thus needs to take into consideration ambiguity, inconsistency, multiple perspectives, and impermanency of existing information. Such architectures need to be designed along the principles of flexible and adaptive information systems that facilitate exploitation of previous experiences while ensuring that memory of the past doesn't hinder ongoing experimentation and adaptation for the discontinuous future.

A key challenge for managers in the forthcoming turbulent environment will be cultivating *commitment* of knowledge workers to the organizational vision. As it becomes increasingly difficult to specify long-term goals and objectives, such commitment would facilitate real-time strategizing in accord with the organizational vision and its real time implementation on the frontlines. Knowledge workers would need to take autonomous roles of self-leadership and self-regulation as they would be best positioned to sense the dynamic changes in their immediate business environment. Compliance will lose its effectiveness as the managerial tool of control as managers removed from the frontlines would have less and less knowledge about the changing dynamics for efficient decision-making. Managers would need to facilitate the confidence of knowledge workers in acting on incomplete information, trusting their own judgments, and taking decisive actions for capturing increasingly shorter windows of opportunity. In the new world of business, the control over employees will be ultimately self-imposed.

Argyris (1990) has referred to the transition from traditional external control mechanisms to the paradigm of self-control as "the current revolution in management theory." Complementary views have been expressed by other scholars (cf:

Bartlett and Ghoshal, 1995; Ghoshal and Bartlett, 1996; Malhotra 2000e) to de-emphasize conformance to the *status quo* so that such prevailing practices may be continuously assessed from multiple divergent perspectives. The explicit bias of *command and control* systems for seeking compliance makes these systems inadequate for motivating divergence-oriented interpretations that are necessary for ill-structured and complex environments. Systems designed to ensure compliance might ensure obedience to given rules, but they do not facilitate the detection and correction of gaps between the institutionalized inputs, logic, and outcomes, and those necessary for the organization's survival and competence.

5.7 Economic Returns Challenge of Next Generation KMS

Some economists (Arthur, 1994) have argued that the production, and distribution of knowledge-based goods and services should create and sustain increasing returns in contrast to diminishing returns that are characteristic of the industrial goods and services. The traditional factors of production are constrained by a threshold of scale and scope as every unit increase in land, labor, or capital results in diminishing returns on every incremental unit beyond that threshold. In contrast, information and knowledge products seem to be governed by a different law of economic returns: investment in every additional unit of information or knowledge created and utilized could result in progressively higher returns. It is important to observe, however, actual realization of such returns requires fundamental rethinking of not only the nature of the product or service, but also its distribution channels as well as the processes underlying its creation, distribution, and, utilization. Increasing digitization and virtualization of business processes without rethinking fundamental premises of the traditional models of products and service definitions has been responsible for the demise of many over-hyped venture-capital funded enterprises.

While 'plug-and-play' technologies could enable rapid adaptability of integrated technology infrastructures, success of the business performance outcomes will be still dependent upon sustained business relationships with collaborators as well as potential competitors. Designers of the next generation KMS would need to understand how enterprise information architectures for intra- and inter-enterprise integration of business processes could enable relationship-building capabilities. This will facilitate sharing of accurate, complete, and timely information by stakeholders across inter-enterprise boundaries to achieve true integration of information flows. Understanding how information sharing occurs in emergent and self-designed communities of practice such as those supporting open-source technologies could perhaps facilitate this process.

A related issue is that of the incentives and rewards that are often used for justifying the economic rationale for knowledge sharing by employees as well as outsiders such as customers and suppliers. Knowledge managers responsible for success of KMS and knowledge sharing will need to reconcile contractual measures such as punitive covenants with the need for trust and loyalty of customers, employees, partners, and suppliers. This is particularly true about information-sharing environments that *emerge* from self-selection of organizations and entities that cooperate with each other based on shared concerns despite the absence of formal controls, rewards or incentives. These issues will gain greater importance with the emergence of Internet based exchanges for knowledge, expertise, skills and intellectual capital in which the free market of knowledge will be just a few mouse-clicks away. Design of incentives must consider that institutional controls as well as monetary rewards and incentives are inadequate and do not necessarily ensure desired knowledge sharing behavior. PricewaterhouseCoopers presents an interesting example of institutionalized formal knowledge harvesting and re-use existing side-by-side with informal ad hoc knowledge exchange and knowledge creation. In this company, the formal and institutionalized KnoweldgeCurve intranet has proven effective as a means for sharing routine and structured information relevant to worldwide employees, while the informal and ad hoc e-mail list, Kraken, has shown tremendous potential for hooking up "self-selected creatives" across various divisions and departments.

6 Summary and Recommendations for Knowledge Management Executives

Corporate executives are demanding better justification for investments in KMS infrastructures and expected business performance outcomes. They realize that the next generation KMS must be based on ongoing innovation of business value propositions and extended inter-enterprise value networks. Many of them want to know how investments in new KMS architectures and "solutions" would contribute to the adaptability of their businesses to unprecedented and rapid pace of change. Accordingly, in establishing the agenda for digitization of their enterprises, knowledge management executives must recognize that their companies can create viable KMS only by attending to the fundamentals of agility and flexibility.

Business environments characterized by uncertainty put premium on continuous business model innovation to deliver novel, sustainable, and competitively viable customer value propositions. Hence, the design of KMS should ensure that adaptation and innovation of business performance outcomes occurs in alignment with changing dynamics of the business environment. This would prevent the failure of KMS caused by the gaps between the value these enterprises create and the value demanded by changing market conditions, consumer preferences, competitive offerings, and, changing business models, and, industry structures. In addition, the design of KMS must give due consideration to moderating and intervening behavioral and sociological variables such as attention, motivation, commitment, creativity, and, innovation to ensure that computational inputs [including enabling technologies] and organizational inputs can more effectively determine business performance. This would minimize the risk of failure of KMS caused by the gaps between the data, information technology, best practices, etc., and the business performance outcomes. As explained earlier, conceiving multiple future trajectories of the information technology and human inputs embedded in the KMS can diminish the risk of rapid obsolescence of such systems as they can be readily adapted to innovative business value propositions and customer value propositions. The overriding challenge for the organizations is to effectively address the dialectic of knowledge harvesting and knowledge creation. This chapter provided some guidelines and suggestions for minimizing risk of KMS failures by meeting the challenges related to business and technology strategy, organizational control, information sharing culture, knowledge representation, organization structure, managerial command and control, and, economic returns. Further research, informed by KMS implementations in practice, is expected to contribute to better understanding of how these challenges can be effectively met.

The architects of next generation KMS cannot afford to treat strategic sustainability of business models, related organizational cultural challenges, and, dependence of these architectures on true integrated information flows as afterthoughts. To successfully manage these challenges, KMS designers must take a holistic approach to designing inter- and intra-organizational "systems" with due consideration not only for the technological design, but also for the design of strategic sustainability of these systems. This approach is expected to provide the needed balance of integration and flexibility required for next generation KMS architectures. Where 'disruptive technologies' *alone* fell short of expectations, the same technologies when coupled with 'disruptive customer value propositions' could provide the basis for self-adaptive enterprises. Organizational competence and success ultimately depends upon KMS architectures that can enable agile and adaptive enterprises skilled in creating innovative business models driven by unique, interesting, and competitive customer value propositions.

Acknowledgements

The content, discussions, and schematic representations in this chapter are based upon author's intellectual property including authored and in-print publications, working papers, keynote presentations, and speeches.

References

Applegate, L., J. Cash, and D.Q. Mills "Information Technology and Tomorrow's Manager," in McGowan, W.G. (ed.) *Revolution in Real Time: Managing Information Technology in the 1990s.* Boston, MA: Harvard Business School Press, 1988, 33-48.

Argyris, C., *Integrating the Individual and the Organization*, New Brunswick, NJ: Transaction, 1990.

Argyris, C., "Good Communication that Blocks Learning," *Harvard Business Review*, 1994, July-August, 77-85.

Arthur, B., "Increasing Returns and the New World of Business," *Harvard Business Review*, 74, 4, 1996, 100-109.
        URL = http://www.santafe.edu/arthur/Papers/Pdf_files/HBR.doc
        [last verified at the time of submission of the article.]

Bartlett, C.A. and S. Ghoshal, "Changing the Role of the Top Management: Beyond Systems to People," *Harvard Business Review*, 1995, May-June, 132-142.

Bruner, J., *Acts of Meaning*, Cambridge, MA: Harvard University Press, 1990.

Bruner, J., *Actual Minds, Possible Worlds*, Cambridge, MA: Harvard University Press, 1986.

Business Week, "Understanding A New World of Uncertainty And Risk," October 8, 2001.

Churchman, C.W., *The Design of Inquiring Systems*, New York, NY: Basic Books, 1971.

Damasio, A.R., *Descartes' Error: Emotion, Reason, and the Human Brain*, New York: Grosset/Putnam, 1994.

Davidow, W.H. and M.S. Malone, *The Virtual Corporation*, New York, NY: HarperCollins, 1992.

Drucker, P.F., "The Theory of Business," *Harvard Business Review*, 1994, September-October, 95-104.

Ghoshal, S. and C.A. Bartlett, "Rebuilding Behavioral Context: A Blueprint for Corporate Renewal," *Sloan Management Review*, 1996,Winter, 23-36.

Kelly, G.A., *A Theory of Personality: The Psychology of Personal Constructs*, New York: W.W. Norton & Co., 1963.

Landau, M. and R. Stout, Jr., "To Manage Is Not to Control: Or the Folly of Type II Errors," *Public Administration Review*, 1979, March/April, 148-156.

Malhotra, Y. and L.J. Kirsch, "Personal Construct Analysis of Self-Control in IS Adoption: Empirical Evidence from Comparative Case Studies of IS Users & IS Champions," *Proceedings of the First INFORMS Conference on Information Systems and Technology*, 1996, 105-114.

Malhotra, Y., "Knowledge Management in Inquiring Organizations," *Proceedings of the Association for Information Systems Americas Conference*, 1997, 293-295. [Available online at www.kmbook.com]

Malhotra, Y. "Role of Social Influence, Self Determination and Quality of Use in Information Technology Acceptance and Utilization: A Theoretical Framework and Empirical Field Study," in unpublished Ph.D. thesis, Katz Graduate School of Business, University of Pittsburgh, 1998.

Malhotra, Y., "Bringing the Adopter Back Into the Adoption Process: A Personal Construction Framework of Information Technology Adoption," *Journal of High Technology Management Research*, 10, 1, 1999, 79-104.

Malhotra, Y. and Galletta, D.F., "Extending the Technology Acceptance Model to Account for Social Influence: Theoretical Bases and Empirical Validation," *Proceedings of the Hawaii International Conference on System Sciences*, 1999, 6-19.

Malhotra, Y., "From Information Management to Knowledge Management: Beyond the 'Hi-Tech Hidebound' Systems," in Srikantaiah, K. and Koenig, M.E.D. (eds.), *Knowledge Management for the Information Professional*. Medford, N.J.: Information Today Inc., 2000a, 37-61.
[Available online at www. kmbook.com]

Malhotra, Y., "Knowledge Management and New Organization Forms: A Framework for Business Model Innovation," *Information Resources Management Journal*, 13,1, 2000b, 5-14. [Available online at www.kmbook.com]

Malhotra, Y. (ed.), *Knowledge Management and Virtual Organizations*, Hershey, PA: Idea Group Publishing, 2000c.

Malhotra, Y., "Knowledge Management for E-Business Performance: Advancing Information Strategy to 'Internet Time'," *Information Strategy: The Executive's Journal*, 16,4, 2000d, 5-16. [Available online at www.kmbook.com]

Malhotra, Y., "Role of Organizational Controls in Knowledge Management: Is Knowledge Management Really an 'Oxymoron'" in Malhotra, Y. (ed.), *Knowledge Management and Virtual Organizations*, Hershey, PA: Idea Group Publishing, 2000e, 245-257.

Malhotra, Y., "Expert Systems for Knowledge Management: Crossing the Chasm Between Information Processing and Sense Making," *Expert Systems With Applications*, 20, 1, 2001a, 7-16.

Malhotra, Y. (ed.), *Knowledge Management and Business Model Innovation*, Hershey, PA: Idea Group Publishing, 2001b.

Malhotra, Y., "Information Ecology and Knowledge Management: Toward Knowledge Ecology for Hyperturbulent Organizational Environments," in Kiel, D.L. (ed.), *UNESCO Encyclopedia of Life Support Systems* (EOLSS) Theme Knowledge Management, Organizational Intelligence and Learning, and Complexity, Paris, France: Eolss Publishers, (in press).

Mason, R.O. & Mitroff, I.I., "A Program for Research on Management Information Systems," *Management Science*, 19, 5, 1973, 475-487.

Mathur, S.S. and Kenyon, A., "Our Strategy is What We Sell," *Long Range Planning*, 30, June, 1997.

Morris, C.W., *Foundations of the Theory of Signs*, Chicago, IL: University of Chicago Press, 1938.

Nadler, D.A. and R.B. Shaw, "Change Leadership: Core Competency for the Twenty-First Century," in Nadler, D.A; Shaw, R.B. and Walton, A.E. (eds.), *Discontinuous Change: Leading Organizational Transformation,* San Franscisco, CA: Jossey-Bass, 1995.

Nonaka, I. and Takeuchi, H., *The Knowledge-Creating Company*, New York: Oxford University Press, 1995.

O'Dell, C. and Grayson, C.J., "If Only We Knew What We Know: Identification And Transfer of Internal Best Practices," *California Management Review*, 40, 3, 1998, 154-174.

Prusak, L., "Where Did Knowledge Management Come From?" *IBM Systems Journal*, 40, 4, 2001, 1002-1007.

Oracle Magazine, "Knowledge Management in the Information Age," May, 1998
URL = http://www.oracle.com/oramag/oracle/98-May/cov1.html
[last verified at the time of submission of the article.]

Stout, R., Jr., *Management or Control?: The Organizational Challenge*, Bloomington, IN: Indiana University Press, 1980.

Strombach, W., "Information in Epistemological and Ontological Perspective," in Mitcham, C. and Huning, A. (eds.), *Philosophy and Technology II: Information Technology and Computers in Theory and Practice*, Dordrecht, Holland: Reidel Publishing Co., 1986.

CHAPTER 31

Identifying and Transferring Internal Best Practices[*]

Carla O'Dell and C. Jackson Grayson

American Productivity & Quality Center, Houston, TX, USA

Many firms are devoting considerable effort to identifying, sharing, and using the knowledge and practices within their own organizations. However, the process of identifying and transferring practices is trickier and more time-consuming than most people imagine. This chapter examines why organizations are interested in transferring best practices, obstacles to doing so, and approaches to doing so. It discusses the creation of a climate supportive of transfer and offers seven lessons for firms about to embark on best practice transfer.

Keywords: Audits; Benchmarking; Best Practices; Culture, Knowledge Transfer; Leadership, Lessons; Measurement; Teams

1 Introduction

"If we only knew what we know at TI," lamented the late Jerry Junkins, former chairman, president, and CEO of Texas Instruments. Junkins was expressing what many managers are rapidly beginning to realize: that inside their own organizations lies, unknown and untapped, a vast treasure house of knowledge, know-how, and best practices. If tapped, this information could drop millions to the bottom line and yield huge gains in speed, customer satisfaction, and organizational competence.

While TI, like many corporations, has been vigorously pursuing knowledge and best practices by benchmarking with other organizations, it is now putting as much effort into "internal benchmarking" – the process of identifying, sharing, and using the knowledge and practices inside its own organization.

The need isn't new. Executives have long been frustrated by their inability to identify or transfer outstanding practices from one location or function to another. They know some facilities have superior practices and processes – and the results to prove it – yet executives continue to see operating units reinventing or ignoring solutions and repeating mistakes. In one well-known example, General Motors entered into a joint venture with Toyota at the NUMMI assembly plant in Fremont, California, to learn its approaches and transfer them to other locations in GM. Despite leading hundreds of "study missions" of GM managers and union

---

members through the NUMMI plant, practices didn't transfer to any great extent. GM had to create a completely new division, Saturn, to begin to capitalize on the new forms of work and labor relations created at NUMMI and elsewhere.

You would think that these better practices would spread like wildfire to the entire organization. They don't. As William Buehler, senior vice president at Xerox, said, "You can see a high-performance factory or office, but it just doesn't spread. I don't know why." One Baldrige winner told us, "We can have two plants right across the street from one another, and it's the damnedest thing to get them to transfer best practices." We see this in business, in healthcare, in government, in education.

Why? The process of identifying and transferring practices is trickier and more time-consuming than most people imagine. In 1994, many of our APQC International Benchmarking Clearinghouse members participated in research to understand what prevents the transfer of practices across a company. Gabriel Szulanski (1995) found that a practice would linger unrecognized for years in a company. Even when it *was* recognized, it still took more than two years on average before other sites began actively trying to adopt the practice, if at all. The barriers fell into three major categories: 1) lack of motivation to adopt the practice; 2) inadequate information about how to adapt the practice and make it work; and 3) lack of "absorptive capacity," the resources and skill to make and manage the change.

We have been working since the early 1990s with many of the 450 members of our International Benchmarking Clearinghouse to help them use benchmarking, internal and external, to achieve breakthrough performance. We define benchmarking as the process of identifying, understanding, and adapting outstanding practices from others, in order to improve your own performance. We know that external benchmarking has a powerful impact on organizations. It breaks established paradigms, creates a readiness for action, and provides models of excellence. The bottom-line results are significant as well. Our Clearinghouse members report a median savings from an external benchmarking study to be about $1.4 million per study, and two members each reported more than $1 billion savings from external benchmarking.

This may be the tip of the iceberg compared with leveraging internal and external knowledge. External benchmarking, with all of its power, overlooks the vast amount of untapped knowledge and best practices already residing inside our own organizations, which can be tapped through internal benchmarking.

The potential gains are enormous:

- TI recently avoided the cost of building a $500 million wafer fabrication plant by leveraging internal knowledge and best practices.
- Chevron has saved millions through sharing practices across its refineries and other business units.
- APQC awarded Eastman Kodak the Gold Award for Benchmarking a few years back for its global study of internal best practices in maintenance. Kodak not only improved uptime, quality, and customer satisfaction, but it also saved at least $12 million annually by implementing best practices.

- Chew, Bresnahan, and Clark (1990) reported performance differences of 3 to 1 between the best and worst of 42 almost identical food plants within a single company. The profitability of the top plant was more than 80 percent of the mean, and the bottom plant 40 percent below; yet their situations were virtually the same. Moving all plants to just the average level of performance would result in an increased firm profitability of 20 percent.

- Most of the large consulting firms, not prone to wasting their own time and money on unproven fads, have built huge systems for capturing and transferring internal engagement information and practices to consultants so they can sell projects and help clients design new approaches built on best practices.

What's going on? If this potential payoff is so great, why haven't more organizations seized the opportunity? Unfortunately, transfer of best practices is not as simple as picking up a wiring diagram or process flow chart and faxing it to another location, or exhorting everyone to become a "learning organization."

1.1 Why Is Internal Benchmarking and Transfer Tough?

We believe most people have a natural desire to learn, to share what they know, and to make things better. This natural desire is thwarted by a variety of logistical, structural, and cultural hurdles and deterrents we erect in our organizations. These include:

1. **Organizational structures that promote "silo" thinking, in which locations, divisions, and functions focus on maximizing their own accomplishments and rewards, hoarding information and thereby sub-optimizing the total organization.** As one manager put it: "When it comes to bonus time, we play a zero-sum game around here. To get my share of the bonus pool, I have to take it away from someone else. Why should I share my best ideas?" A leadership team and culture supportive of transfer requires a common focus and common fate. Without it, people have little incentive to overcome other obstacles that time and space create.

2. **A culture that values personal technical expertise and knowledge creation over knowledge sharing.** This is rampant in engineering and knowledge-based organizations, such as consulting and research firms. Another cultural barrier is the "not-invented-here" syndrome and the lack of experience in learning from outside one's own small group. Benchmarking has dramatically changed this culture in many of our member organizations.

3. **The lack of contact, relationships, and common perspectives among people who don't work side-by-side.** In most organizations, the left hand not only doesn't know what the right hand is doing, but it also may not even know there is a right hand. There is a need to create and catalogue the corporate memory of an organization's expertise and abilities so others can build networks and new solutions together.

4. **An over-reliance on transmitting "explicit" rather than "tacit" information.** Most of the important information people need to implement a practice cannot be codified or written down – it has to be shown to them or it requires dialogue and interactive problem solving. Just creating databases will not cause change to happen. Polanyi (1967) and Nonaka (1991) both have pointed out the importance and value of recognizing and trying to capture tacit knowledge – the know-how, judgment, intuition, and little tricks – that constitute the noncodifiable knowledge that may make the difference between failure and success in the transfer. Jerry Baker of National Semiconductor says that the company's research shows that 80 percent of the knowledge that needs to be transferred is in the noncodifiable arena: "It may be that somebody held their tongue just right as they pulled the wafers out of the oven, and that's what made things work."

5. **Not allowing or rewarding people for taking the time to learn and share and help each other outside of their own small corporate village.** All of these problems can be, and are being, overcome once they are recognized. In this chapter, we share lessons learned from companies as diverse as Chevron, Texas Instruments, Kodak, AMP, and many others that have been systematically leveraging internal best practices to create competitive advantage. We share our perspective and experience on 1) the reasons for the growing interest in the internal transfer of best practices, 2) a framework and approaches that appear to work, 3) cultural and organizational factors that help or hinder the process, and 4) lessons learned and recommendations to those who want to leverage their own knowledge and best practices to serve customers and to compete.

1.2 Why the Interest in the Transfer of Best Practices?

We have identified five instigators that launch organizations on the difficult quest to systematically identify and transfer best practices:

1. **A compelling call to action.** Chevron is an integrated energy and chemicals company with more than 37,000 employees and operations in nearly 100 countries. In Chevron's case, two factors drove the search for internal best practices: a focus by its leaders on the strategic and competitive need for significant cost reduction through sharing, coupled with a decentralized operating philosophy that presented both opportunities and barriers to transferring practices. The leadership support at Chevron cannot be overestimated. Ken Derr, chairman and CEO of Chevron, has been an untiring supporter from the beginning: "Every day that a better idea goes unused is a lost opportunity. We have to share more, and we have to share faster."

    In the case of TI, the stage was set when key customers threatened to take business elsewhere if TI couldn't improve its commitment to delivery dates and cycle time. Alarmed, TI launched a reengineering and benchmarking project on order fulfillment, including the search for best practices in cycle-time reduction and increased throughput. Ultimately, these findings actually created additional TI capacity equal to an entire wafer fabrication facility without the investment of $500 million to $800 million it costs to build that kind of facility. The company was able to increase yield dramatically, meet the market, and delay the huge financial investment that would have been required to build the new facility.

2. **A demonstrated success.** The success in TI's wafer fab operations opened the door to what is now a worldwide drive to duplicate this success by adopting best practice sharing approaches throughout TI. In 1995 TI was able to create "Free Fab No. 2," replicating its success in adopting best practices. For Chevron, the first success came from an early team in the U.S. oil and gas company. By comparing practices on the operation of gas compressors in fields in California, the Rockies, and offshore Louisiana, this team learned that it could save at least $20 million a year just by adopting practices already being used in its best-managing fields. In another case, Chevron's network of 100 people who share ideas on energy-use management has generated an initial $150 million savings in Chevron's annual power and fuel expense by sharing and implementing ideas to reduce companywide energy costs. These compelling examples of success have created great support for more internal sharing and transfer.

3. **Decentralizaiton and downsizing.** For decades, organizations have counted on functional or corporate specialties to be responsible for inventing, discovering, and transferring knowledge and best practices. But a decade of corporate downsizing has stripped out corporate support networks and forced operating units to take responsibility for improvement. There are fewer people at the "Mother Ship" to capture and disseminate knowledge (although their record was mixed anyway). Restructuring has also led to the demise of traditional management networks that served as one potential vehicle for the transfer of practices.

4. **Benchmarking evidence.** Both TI and Chevron had found, through external benchmarking, that better practices and results were being achieved among competitors and best practice firms. This created not only a sense of urgency, but also one of hope: If other organizations could achieve these results, so could they.

   Sometimes external benchmarking awakens a firm to its own internal achievements.

   - TI was trumpeting the performance of other companies, only to find equally world-class practices and results in its Sherman, Texas facility.
   - AMP Inc. had a benchmarking team conducting an external study on customer service. In its search for potential best practice partners, secondary research revealed not one but several AMP divisions noted for their practices in customer satisfaction and service. One AMP division had received national acclaim for exactly the practice being benchmarked. John Davis, benchmarking manager at AMP, was astounded by the information: "The realization that a wealth of internal knowledge and excellence was being overlooked has led AMP to a large-scale initiative to identify successfully demonstrated practices internally."

5. **Recognition of the potential gain.** Imagine the gains available if every similar operation were raised just to a median level of performance in your organi-

zation. One of our members in the delivery business calculated that bringing the lagging operations up to median performance would be worth more than $60 million a year on just five processes. Rank Xerox executives reported at a recent APQC meeting that their internal benchmarking showed a potential savings of $1.2 billion a year.

These companies are not alone their zeal in searching of internal best practices. Among the 450-plus organizations that are members of our APQC International Benchmarking Clearinghouse, internal benchmarking and the transfer of best practices is one of the hottest items on their improvement agenda. It is encouraging to note that, according to one of our recent member surveys, 55 percent of our members think their current culture is beginning to support internal benchmarking and sharing.

1.3 Knowledge Management: A Framework for the Transfer of Best Practices

We consider internal benchmarking and transfer of best practices to be one of the most tangible manifestations of knowledge management – the process of identifying, capturing, and leveraging knowledge to help the company compete. Sharing and transfer are also tangible evidence of a learning organization – one that can analyze, reflect, learn, and change based on experience.

The Knowledge Management framework depicted in Figure 1 was jointly developed between the APQC and Authur Andersen as part of our research in the area of knowledge management. APQC subsequently has been collecting data and conducting studies on the phenomenon. Some of these center cases and study results are shared in this chapter.

As Figure 1 illustrates, the environment – cultural and structural – necessary for successful transfer forms part of this knowledge management framework. Central to the framework is the process itself. This dynamic process often starts with finding and collecting internal knowledge and best practices. Second is sharing and understanding those practices so they can be used. Finally, the process includes adapting and applying those practices to new situations and bringing them up to best practice performance levels. Surrounding the process, and helping or hindering it, are what we call the enablers: technology, culture, leadership, and measures. These aspects of an organization's environment and infrastructure must be addressed in order for the transfer process to have a chance of working. One reason that internal transfer is so difficult is that these enablers have been poorly understood and were rarely addressed in earlier attempts.

1.4 The Process of Benchmarking and Best Practice Transfer

Before one can transfer best practices, it is necessary to define and find them. Of course, organizations have always had mechanisms, from R&D experts and technical audits to internal conferences and transfers, intended to identify and spread practices. Table 1 compares approaches to best-practice identification. Unfortunately, the mechanisms didn't always work well or as planned. As one executive

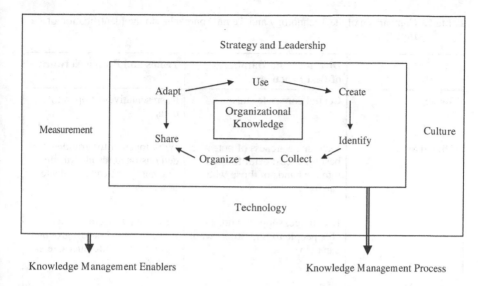

Figure 1. The Knowledge Management Framework

put it, "Research has good ideas, but they don't get used. The refineries don't talk to each other enough. We reinvent the wheel everywhere, and there is no way to pass on success stories."

Jim O'Brient, quality manager at Chevron's U.S. Production Company reflected on another common approach: "We had a long-standing process that was called "functional review." High-level managers used to circulate around the world and visit sites at least once a year to hear what was going on. We relied on those few key executives to make value judgments about what they were hearing and to pass along the news of what they were hearing to others. It was what I call the 'bumble bee' or pollination model for best practices." This approach can create sibling rivalry, holding up one unit as better than another, without providing enough information or motivation to adopt the practice.

The bumble bee approach has a second weakness. O'Brient continued: "It was all about sharing 'explicit' knowledge – the stuff that you could write down. There wasn't the conversation between the two groups that probably needed it to really implement change. But it did identify people who had created solutions, and [those people] became the ones transferred. *The actual transfer of people to another location was, and probably still is, the most effective way we have of transferring this kind of practice.* With a transfer, you move the implicit or tacit knowledge as well as the explicit."

While these earlier approaches had limitations, they provided a valuable departure point for the four approaches we have for identifying and transferring best practices: 1) benchmarking teams, 2) best practice teams, 3) knowledge networks, and 4) internal audits.

Table 1. Comparison of the Technology and Team Approaches to the Identification of Best Practices

	Directory and Databases of Best Practices	Teams and People Networks
Owner	Central corporate staff	Representatives of operating units
Objective	Increase awareness of potential best practices; get information into the hands of those who can use it	Work together to provide demonstrated results transferring best practices on selected processes
Role	Encourage, support, and enable people to find others who can help	Face-to-face meetings, electronic bulletin boards, groupware, video conferences, teleconferencing
Technology and Means of Access	Electronic databases and directories of sources and networks throughout the corporation	Detailed practice and problem resolution information
Information Shared	Pointer system – abstracts and contact names	Ongoing through life of project or team
Relationship Commitment	Short – potential single contact	High
Cost per Practice	Low	Demonstrable
ROI	Hard to calculate – track usage of databases	Can be lengthy depending on complexity of practice
Time Commitment	Low	Dedicated participants
Participation	Any interested party with access to online system	Process/practice experts and facilitators
Support Staff	Central corporate support with contributors in operating units	Find, adapt, and transfer best practices
Audit Process	Usually minimal – self-nomination or simple criteria	Usually a formal process

1.4.1   Benchmarking Teams

Benchmarking is the process of identifying, understanding, and adapting outstanding practices from organizations, including your own, anywhere in the world. As noted earlier, a corporate benchmarking team often takes on external benchmarking first, only to find that internal benchmarking is just as fruitful.

Like all novice benchmarkers, teams often start their benchmarking efforts by trying to compare measures and results in order to identify best practices. The first lesson teams learn is that comparisons of financial and operating performance alone are not enough. Other factors can affect performance outcomes. Teams can waste a lot of time trying to compare "apples with apples" and arguing about "who is really good" while they should be looking for breakthroughs in *practices*.

TI's quest for best practices actually started with eternal benchmarking, looking for breakthroughs and best practices in scheduling and throughput. The company found great examples of cycle time reduction and throughput in other manufacturing companies. At that point, TI's benchmarking and reengineering team thought the challenge was to implement these practices in all of TI's wafer fabrication plants. In 1993, experts went from fab plant to fab plant to train them, intending to use the bumble bee approach by using an emissary to cross-pollinate operations with good ideas.

But what the TI team found astonished and chagrined them. They found some of TI's facilities were actually using *better* practices and outperforming the external benchmarks. For example, their plant in Sherman, Texas was performing best in the class – better than any external partner.

Also, in late 1993, Tom Engibous, now TI president and CEO and then president of TI's semiconductor division, issued a challenge: "Build me a free fab in 1994 by creating capacity we are not using."

In response to this challenge and the threat of losing market share in a hot semiconductor market, TI formed a worldwide network of its managers and technical experts to find and use best practices throughout TI's wafer fab operations. Called the "Jonah Network" (from The Goal), this group created a common vocabulary around cycle-time reduction and a common language of business process improvement to communicate common processes in order fulfillment. This network identified and shared what worked and didn't work in the different fab plants. TI held sharing sessions and helped facilitators with special classes and outside speakers.

1.4.2   Best Practice Teams

While benchmarking teams usually have a clear life span, with start and stop dates, best practice teams may be an enduring part of the networking infrastructure of an organization. Chevron adopted best practice teams as one of its primary vehicles for transfer after almost four years of laying groundwork and trying alternatives. When Ken Derr became chairman of Chevron in 1988, he began requiring operating units to become more accountable for their performance, pushing authority for decision making to lower levels of the organization. That empowerment, combined with widespread adoption of the principles of quality and process improvement, triggered a readiness to search for best practices.

In 1994 a group of Chevron senior refining operating managers selected their six highest priority areas for process improvement and transfer, then formed teams around these six core processes: Crude Distillation, Reforming, Catalytic Cracking and Alkylation, Hydroprocessing, Delayed Coking, and Treating. Each best practice team immediately identified more than $10 million in potential improvement based on a comparison of its practices. Because of this early success, Chevron Refining added systemwide teams that focus on divisionwide infrastructure process areas that are not confined to a single operating process: Information Technology, Maintenance, Training, Energy, Process Control, and Reliability. These teams have a common charter, meet at least every other month, and are linked and work electronically between meetings. Chevron provides them with resources and expert support (see Appendix A).

1.4.3   Knowledge and Practice Networks

While benchmarking and best practice teams are often ordained from the top of the organization, knowledge and practice networks emerge as a grass-roots response to the breakup of former networks due to downsizing, reengineering, and restructuring. Without stable networks of practitioners and centers of excellence in technical and functional fields, the question becomes "How do you bring those people together in a virtual organization or community of practice so that expertise can be shared?" We have found that once an organization creates the environment and technology to support networks, they often emerge.

Chevron's approach has been to nurture and support these networks when they appear. Dozens of these "communities of practice" have sprung up over the last few years, including networks on customer satisfaction measurement, training, safety, quality, and a variety of technical issues. A corporate team at Chevron provides online technology networks, resource listings, and a Best Practice Resource Map. This colorful, fold-out map looks like a highway map (such as those you would get at a Chevron station, although the company claims it didn't intend the pun), with nodes and paths color-coded by Baldrige categories and by APQC's Process Classification Framework, designed to help people find their way to resources all over the company. The map's most important function may be to identify the doors into numerous networks throughout Chevron. It shows who is the primary contact for each one and lists phone numbers and e-mail addresses so people can find each other.

Hughes Space and Communications is building a similar "Knowledge Highway" with maps indicating where knowledge is located in the organization. National Semiconductor is trying to augment the knowledge pointers that exist in people's heads by using autonomous agent software that electronically pints toward interest profiles of individuals. When someone sends a pint-to-point e-mail to someone else, it automatically gets sent to others with that interest profile.

1.4.4   Internal Assessment and Audits

This fourth approach can range in form from formal technical assessments (often part of benchmarking and best practice teams) to internal award programs.

Perhaps one of the most dramatic examples of a combination of internal assessment and benchmarking team is Rank Xerox, winner of the European Quality Award. In 1994 Rank Xerox created a central team called Team C. Team C's job was to coordinate all internal benchmarking activity across Xerox and to come back with a business case as to what the opportunity for improvement might be. Team C analyzed the internal databases and operating reports and identified processes with high variation in results. Through internal audit work the team found very different performance levels throughout Europe in service-force productivity, customer service, and customer retention and loyalty. Second, it appointed experts – knowledgeable persons in each of the technical areas – whose job it was to identify where outstanding practices might lie. Then the team calculated what the payoff would be financially if the company were to adopt these best practices. Team C estimated that, in key areas, in one year the payoff would be $1.2 billion. Its task now is to form teams that can share and implement those practices.

UNISYS, Harris Corporation, and AMP are among many firms using internal award and recognition programs, often based on the Malcolm Baldrige National Quality Award criteria, to identify and recognize islands of excellence in key practices, as well as overall outstanding performance against the criteria. Chevron's Quality Fitness Review, which is based on the Baldrige criteria, is growing in popularity throughout the company as an improvement tool to spotlight best practices. For most, one of the requirements of internal award recipients is that they be willing to share with other units that request information or assistance.

These internal award winners are often showcased in internal conferences, but these and other practices can be highlighted through "share fairs." In 1995 AMP brought 1,700 of its top people together for its annual meeting devoted to communicating strategic quality initiatives. Integrated into this meeting was a successfully demonstrated practices share fair. Units with outstanding practices that might be broadly applicable across AMP had exhibit booths staffed by key personnel who knew the practice well. They handed out a two-page summary of the practice, along with business cards so people could call them later for more details. Those who hosted a booth received great recognition, and individuals who saw and talked to those using a practice found it compelling and had a personal contact for follow-up.

2   Creating the Environment for Transfer

None of these approaches to best practice transfer works unless the organization addresses the barriers and creates a supportive climate for transfer. Environmental enablers fall into four overlapping categories: technology, culture, leadership, and measurement. Let's start with technology, because reaping the benefits of technology requires addressing issues in leadership, culture, and measurement.

2.1 Technology in the Service of Best Practices: If You Build It, Will They Come?

Technology is no longer a major barrier to identifying and notifying the organization of best practices – all the necessary software solutions already exist, from Lotus Notes and other groupware to powerful and user-friendly databases to e-mail and internal Internets (intranets). Nor is technology the solution. Technology has a helpful role to play, but it will not be the driver of sharing best practices, for two reasons: 1) all the important information about a process its too complex and too experiential to be captured electronically, and 2) the incentives for and barriers to sharing are not technical.

Nonetheless, the first reaction to the desire to share best practices is frequently to create a technical solution, usually an online database of best practices, the theory being that if people only knew that the practice existed, they would adopt it. Dozens of companies have created internal electronic directories and databases, announced they were available, and waited for people to flock to them.

What happened? Often nothing. Despite sometimes massive internal corporate PR campaigns, few people entered information about their practices and few accessed it. Why? Because if access to information were the dominant barrier to change, there would have already been a run on corporate libraries. Besides, if you want to talk to someone, the telephone is easier.

Consider a few examples. Chevron Corporation started by creating an internal electronic database and expected people to enter their practices and contact others with intriguing solutions. The company experienced good access initially, but then usage began to trail off. Citibank developed a technical marvel of a database, but initially failed to create incentives for people to enter information into it. However, when the company assigned employees the responsibility of finding and entering those practices, then they began to get entered.

Best practices databases are becoming de rigueur in consulting firms. Their business strategy and raison d'être is the ability to get knowledge from people who have been through an engagement to those who are bidding on one. Arthur Andersen, Andersen Consulting, Price Waterhouse, McKinsey, Ernst & Young, KPMG, and other knowledge-based consulting firms have developed extensive databases for use by their consultants in the field, both to bid on projects and to bring the knowledge of the firm to bear on client issues. These firms have people devoted to finding, filtering, and entering information, as well as teaching the consultants how to use it. The most difficult issues in these firms are cultural and competitive. Their history of rewarding individual "experts" and stars, plus time pressures for billable days, make it difficult to convince people that success comes through taking time to share information, electronically or otherwise.

Both successful and languishing technological solutions have taught us a few lessons and given us realistic expectations about the real power of networking:

1. **The really important and useful information for improvement is too complex to put online; too much tacit knowledge is required to make a process work.** So, most firms have turned to directory and "pointer" systems that can supplement the search for best practices.

- Chevron Corporation's Best Practices Sharing Database is designed to promote the sharing of practices, knowledge, know-how, and experience that have proven to be valuable throughout Chevron organizations.

  The database is not designed to replace existing sharing mechanisms, but to enhance and support them. It is primarily suited to sharing generic information that is of broad application throughout Chevron Corporation.

  It is a place to seek help ("Requests") from other parts of Chevron and to reciprocate by offering assistance ("Offers") to others.

  The database recognizes that no single "best practice" is suitable for every circumstance. Each end-user will use unique criteria to judge what is best for each business.

  The database provides insight into what has already been done and what may be possible, rather than trying to provide "the right answer" at the touch of a button. It gives all users a wider range of information than has ever been available before, but does not offer a specific solution for every problem.

- AMP Inc. has had a centralized database or repository up and running since November 1994. Running on its mainframe system, entries follow a simple template, including: 1) the name of the source unit, 2) the name and a brief description of the practice and some of the reasons it is considered a successfully demonstrated practice, 3) the date it was entered, 4) who entered it, and 5) the person to contact to find out more about the practice. As John Davis said: "The database entry is just a pointer, not a cookbook. There's not enough information included [for you] to be able to adopt the practice. There's enough there to generate the interest to learn more, however."

- TI's Best Practices Knowledge Base is a global "card catalog" pointing to best practices, and delivered via Lotus Notes, intranet, and TI's mainframe systems. "We have learned that you have to be everywhere if you want to deliver best practices information," reflected Cindi Johnson in TI's Office of Best Practices.

2. **There has to be a framework for classifying information.** Many of our members, including Chevron, TI, and AMP, now organize the information in their best practices databases using the Process Classification Framework (PCF), developed by APQC, its Clearinghouse members, and Arthur Andersen (see Figure 2). The framework is organized around seven operating processes and six business and support processes. The PCF provides a common vocabulary for people from different businesses and industries to identify similar or analogous processes. This framework essentially serves the same purpose within companies, enabling diverse units to talk to each other more effectively about their business problems.

3. **Entering information into the system must be part of someone's job.** Busy managers and professionals will rarely take the time to enter a practice into a database unless it is part of their job. AMP has appointed people in each operating company to be responsible for entering practices when they find them. Additionally, AMP's global quality organization has become quite proactive

in both identifying and deploying the practices throughout the units and regions. UNISYS designated 30 people as the representatives from each of the operating groups involved to ensure that someone is concerned about entering and using information. Chevron, Harris, TI, UNISYS, and AMP – among others – have appointed people part time to find and enter information. Harris Corporation has also added a best practice screening committee. Divisions self-nominate, write up the ideas, and send them in; the screening committees then decide whether to pass them on or enter them in the database. UNISYS does not use a screening committee because its philosophy is that the person who enters the best practice has responsibility for verifying it. Chevron does not want to discourage entries at this point, so it does not screen but asks nominators to indicate the level of bests practice (see Appendix B).

4. **Culture and behaviors are the key drivers and inhibitors of internal sharing.** The real issues aren't technical: How do you get people to contribute to and use the system? What are the people systems surrounding the technology that support its use? Do you reward people for taking the time to share or seek out best practices?

    This leads us to the most influential category of environmental factors affecting transfer: the cultural and leadership issues.

2.2 Cultural Factors

Everyone embarking on internal benchmarking and transfer has to address a couple of critical cultural and leadership issues.

1. How can people be motivated and rewarded for sharing? Most managers have never learned "how to learn," especially cooperatively. American schools and colleges stress individuality and competition, not collaboration and sharing.
2. What can leaders do to help establish and reinforce a supportive culture? While tangible rewards are important, management and co-worker reinforcement is critical to achieving real cultural support for sharing and transfer. When Chevron's Best Practice Teams were formed, team members had to face their colleagues back in the plants who were asking, "Why are you spending your time doing this kind of thing? We need you here." According to Chevron's Jim O'Brient, employees don't recognize the investment in that longer-term payoff yet, because they don't see the gains for a long time. If units don't need to adopt a practice, they may never directly see the gains from a team.

"From a management perspective, I don't think we did near enough work to communicate to the teams our support for their making this kind of investment or our willingness to backfill for them," O'Brient said. "We just assumed that the teams would somehow support and take care of this."

When TI began its quest for a "Free Fab" facility, the company found that it had great practices but that they weren't known or shared. TI deduced four reasons for this:

Operating Processes

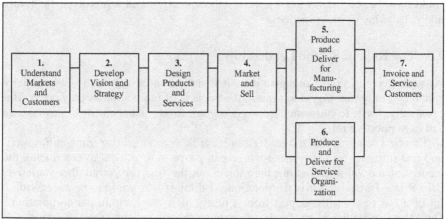

Management and Support Processes

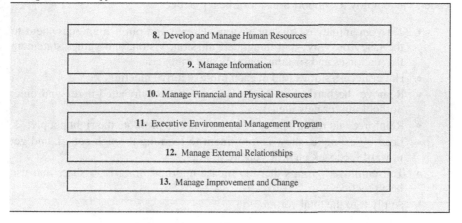

Figure 2. Process Classification Framework Overview

- Current financial measures incentivized competition among plants,
- Plant management had no responsibility for sharing,
- There was no common vocabulary to facilitate conversation, and
- There had never been a rallying cry for common purpose.

Unidimensional solutions are not enough. TI not only physically transferred people from high-performing plants to those that needed help, but also created a common business process map for wafer fabrication, reallocated funding to the least productive plants, gave plant managers common goals, and built sharing networks to support the process. It is critical to note that TI reinforced worldwide sharing by measuring and rewarding plant managers for overall wafer fab results, not just their own plant's performance. The result was more than the company could have hoped for: TI got its wafer fab capacity – and a prototype for future internal sharing of best practices.

2.3 The Role of Senior Leadership

As with change in most organizations, it is not essential that the leaders initially endorse it, only that they don't quash the pockets of innovation as they occur. But eventually, for it to blossom across the organization, management has to take an active, supportive role.

This first requires that the leadership itself be convinced that transfer has merit and real impact. An early success here can prove most critical to convincing the leaders of the value of putting themselves on the line for yet another initiative. Said Roger Burns of Harris Corporation, "I think if it is going to be successful, a lot of it has to do with support from a pretty high level within the corporation." Once that is established, the leaders themselves have to change their behavior.

Ken Derr of Chevron provides a dramatic example of what a leader can do to support a learning organization and sharing. Derr has suggested several tactics that leaders can employ to support transfer of best practices:

- Tie your initiatives to your vision: Create and publish an equivalent to the Chevron Way – an integrated mission, vision, and values statement that endorses and sustains learning and transfer.
- Have success stories told at each top-executive meeting.
- Remove the barriers to progress (e.g., the not-invented-here syndrome, not looking for new ideas).
- Reinforce and reward positive behaviors and promote the right people.
- Lead by example, show commitment to learning through action, and get upward feedback on how you are doing.
- Tell employee groups that the most important thing is to share and use best practices.
- Apply it to the total corporation.

The support in TI is also visible and tangible at the most senior levels. TI's corporate Quality Leadership Team (QLT), made up of the highest levels of senior management, is integrating best practices benchmarking and sharing into strategic planning as key tools to achieve their goal of Business Excellence. TI's Office of Best Practices has been chartered and funded by the QLT and provides more than 200 linking champions who support sharing initiatives across the corporation. They also support the TI Knowledgebase.

2.4 The Role of Measurement

There are two types of measurement issues involved in internal benchmarking and transfer: 1) measuring performance to identify a best practice, and 2) measuring the impact of initiatives and best practices transfer itself.

As we have discussed, measures of performance can help identify potential best practices, but they alone are not enough. The metrics indicate what level of performance is possible and help develop a business case for change, but they won't help units understand why an organization got outstanding results or how to do it themselves. A practice cannot be considered superior just because an operating unit has superior results. Many situational and extraneous variables (market, facility configuration, history, volume) may cause a unit to have better results. Conversely, a site working under adverse circumstances could be producing what appear to be average results with an outstanding process.

This is the same argument against relying solely on metrics in benchmarking: They can be misleading and are certainly not very illuminating. There is a risk that, by driving best practice benchmarking by comparisons of internal data, one may slow the actual transfer process and lead to competition. Jim O'Brient reflected on the use of comparative data at Chevron: "It is really a challenge to find the information that allows you to compare things across so that you can move to a more systematic look at these things, as opposed to the intuitive level. One of the biggest problems is that everybody's definition of what the process is – and what part of it they are measuring – is different. So there is a lot of room for denial in there. But you say, 'OK, even if it is a little different, the fact is we are talking about 30 percent, 40 percent, 50 percent variance in results.'"

How do you measure the effectiveness of best practice sharing? The answer is obvious when a benchmarking or best practice team has a clearly defined charter: Simply track the improvement results. But the measures become weaker and more hazy when you ask about the value of internal databases or networks. The current measurement systems used are still embryonic; they include:

1. **Measures of the frequency of use of the system and satisfaction with the information found in internal databases.**
2. **Reports of higher sales or more satisfied customers as a result of sharing of knowledge and best practices.**
3. **Cycle time to implement best practices.** Szulanski (1995) found, on average, it took 27 months for a process to be implemented. Do your approaches speed it up?
4. **The grass-roots growth in "virtual" teams and networks.** Chevron has found a dramatic expansion in the number and types of networks popping up all across the organization. The potential danger ere is mistaking activity for results.

Clearly, the measurement of the effectiveness of transfer systems is on the agenda for attention.

3   Lessons from the Front: Seven Keys to Effective Transfer

We have illustrated the approaches to transfer and the enabling technical, cultural, leadership, and measurement issues involved. Based on our experience across many organizations, we offer the following seven lessons for firms about to embark on best practice transfer.

1. **Use benchmarking to create a sense of urgency or find a compelling reason to change.** Competitive or best-in-class benchmarking can create a sense of urgency as well as demonstrate the value of looking outside for ideas and comparison. TI found that both customer threats and benchmarking created receptivity to external ideas. At Chevron competitive analysis and a few successful examples of internal transfer helped overcome cynicism. External benchmarking also helps avoid setting the bar too low. Measuring yourself against competitors helps keep people focused on the market.

2. **Focus initial efforts on critical business issues that have high payoff and are aligned with organization values and strategy.** Real action-learning and transfer is a time- and talent-consuming activity. Evaluate the potential ROI before focusing cross-company teams on the project. Focus your energies on projects most likely to improve long term organizational capabilities – you don't get many chances to demonstrate success.

3. **Make sure that every plane you allow to take off has a runway available for landing.** In the initial zeal and excitement that come from imagining the improvements and gains possible from the transfer of best practices, there is a tendency to forget that an organization can only invest in and support a finite amount of change at any one time. It is demoralizing to find best practices only to discover that the investment dollars have already been spent for this year or that a plant does not have the extra staff needed to handle another implementation. Limit the number of major projects to fit the resources that will be available for implementation.

4. **Don't let measurement get in the way. Most internal scoreboards are fraught with inconsistencies in data collection and open to interpretation about local causes for the differences in performance.** Rather than spend time debating "who's best" and why the measures are not fair, focus on those areas where dramatic differences in performance point to a real underlying process difference and not just an artifact of measurement. "Paralysis by analysis" is an easy pitfall to fall into, especially when management "sibling rivalry" is the historical norm. Comparative measures will improve over time, but only if you start to act on them.

5. **Change the reward system to encourage sharing and transfer.** Real internal transfer is a people-to-people process and usually requires personal generosity or enlightened self-interest. Leadership can help by promoting, recognizing, and rewarding people who model sharing behavior, as well as those who adopt best practices. It helps to design approaches that reward for collective improvement as well as individual contributions of time, talent, and expertise.

    It is necessary to constantly reinforce the need for people at all levels to take responsibility for voluntarily participating in this activity of sharing and leveraging knowledge. Managers can ask regularly what people are learning from others and how have they shared with management ideas they think worthy. Be sure to support teams that invest or "give up" resources to make this sharing happen, especially if they do not directly benefit.

6. **Use technology as a catalyst to support networks and the internal search for best practices, but don't rely on it as a solution.** People are no longer tethered to just their local organizational structure for information and knowl-

edge. They can step out and learn elsewhere to improve faster than those tied to smaller information sources. Use a combination of new information technology tools such as e-mail, "best practices databases," internal directories, and groupware to support employees seeking knowledge and collaboration across the organization. But, don't rely on the technology tools to create their own market. After all, although people have telephones, they don't automatically "reach out and touch" someone they don't know.

7. **Leaders will need to consistently and constantly spread the message of sharing and leveraging knowledge for the greater good.** We have found that the most effective transfer processes are those that are demand-driven (the pull to learn and change comes from the person or unit that has a problem or need) rather than push or laissez-faire (if you let them know about it, they will seek it out) approaches. Leadership can help create and support demand, but it can't make it happen. Leaders can encourage collaboration across boundaries of structure, time, and function. Some ways to do this are to:

- Promulgate success stories,
- Provide infrastructure and support, and
- Change the reward system to remove barriers.

4   Conclusion

In summary, we strongly recommend that every organization use these lessons to immediately begin to take advantage of the tremendous untapped reservoir of knowledge in their own backyard to reduce costs and increase revenue, speed, and customer satisfaction – whether calling this internal benchmarking, transfer of best practices, or knowledge management.

Three themes course through all the successful internal benchmarking and transfer efforts we have seen in business, healthcare, and education. First, internal transfer is a people-to-people process; relationships seem to precede and be required for meaningful sharing and transfer. Second, learning and transfer is an interactive, ongoing and dynamic process that cannot rest on a static body of knowledge. Employees are inventing, improvising, and learning something new every day. The wellspring of best practices need never run dry.

Finally, it all comes back to a personal and organizational willingness and desire to learn. A vibrant sense of curiosity and a deep respect and desire for learning from others may be the real keys.

Appendix A: How Do Best Practice Teams Operate?

Chevron's teams are composed of line management representatives from each refinery. Each member is sponsored by the refinery manager and is a midlevel process manager who "owns the process units" and has the authority to implement changes in practices. Each team is supported by a technical expert, known as the process master, who has both field and R&D experience in the practice under study.

Each Best Practice Team meets three to four times a year for two to three days. In their search for improvement, the teams look for three levels of opportunity for internal transfer:

1. Low-hanging fruit: These are short-term projects, known as "good ideas" or "good practices" that should be applicable to at least some refineries. Good ideas may have been tested in one Chevron refinery identified from R&D or from outside Chevron. A good practice is a good idea that at least one Chevron refinery has tested, that is working well, and for which there is someone who can tell you why and how. These practices don't require significant capital expenditure and can be implemented quickly.
2. Medium-term practices are those that have demonstrated value and are applicable to most refineries and worth pursuing due to the size of the opportunity and the demonstrated success in Chevron. A medium-term practice should require three to six months of noncapital-intensive effort and have significant systemwide impact.
3. Breakthrough improvements are those that will require significant operating changes and technology and will take longer to develop and implement.

The first half-day of the Best Practice Teams meeting is spent sharing hot issues, problems and how they were handled, safety issues, and lessons learned. The second part of the meeting is about identifying and closing gaps in low-hanging fruit and midterm practices.

The process master tracks minutes and assignments in the Lotus Notes groupware system used across Refining. Teams and their activities are also listed in Chevron's Best Practices Sharing system, it centralized online directory of practices and sources of information.

A Chevron Best Practices Team charter is not only to identify but also to implement best practices, unlike prior centralized approaches in which the R&D group identified a process, then distributed a memo and manual out to the field and left them to implement it. According to Ashok Krishna, one of the process masters for Refining, many ideas never got implemented. Why? The "process owners" were not involved in the development of the idea and were reluctant to implement it. R&D moved on to focus on the next invention while the earlier idea languished due to problems with implementation in the field. Practitioners needed direct access to the source – face-to-face meetings – and dialogue so they could get their operational questions answered about both the technical and field implementation aspects of the new idea.

Implementation is reinforced by biannual visits by the process master to the refinery to assist and evaluate and an annual visit by the vice president, who has read the audit reports.

External benchmarking still plays a key role in Chevron's best practices approach. For example, one team began by identifying "state-of-the-art" practice among leading competitors. This lead to the development of a business strategy for investing in new technology and upgrading antiquated hardware.

Appendix B: What Is a Best Practice, Anyway?

Labeling any practice as best immediately raises a hue and cry of dissenting voices in the organization. Not only is "best" a moving target in today's world, what is best is also situation-specific. Internal competition and management sibling rivalry real their heads as units start to quibble about whether they have been measured correctly. Others rightfully raise questions about spending significant resources to transfer a practice if the potential payoff has not been demonstrated in multiple locations.

One way to cope with these problems is to define levels of best practice carefully, as Chevron has done. The corporate group has adopted a simple definition of best practices: any practice, knowledge, know-how, or experience that has proven to be valuable or effective within one organization that may have applicability to other organizations. Chevron has also clarified levels of best.

Chevron recognizes four levels of best practices both in the corporate databases and in Best Practice Teams:

1. GOOD IDEA – Unproven: Not yet substantiated by data but makes sense intuitively; could have a positive impact on business performance. Requires further review/analysis. If substantiated by data, this could be a candidate for implementation in one or more Chevron locations.
2. GOOD PRACTICE – Technique, methodology, procedure, or process that has been implemented and has improved business results for an organization (satisfying some element of customers' and key stakeholders' needs). This is substantiated by data collected at the location. A limited amount of comparative data from other organizations exists. It is a candidate for application in one or more locations within the OpCo or Department and possibly at other locations in Chevron.
3. LOCAL BEST PRACTICE – A good practice that has been determined to be the best approach for all or large parts of an organization (OpCo, Department), based on an analysis of process performance data. The analysis includes some review of similar practices outside of Chevron (competitive intelligence data). This practice is applicable at most of all locations within the OpCo or Department and may be applicable to other Chevron locations.
4. INDUSTRY BEST PRACTICE – A practice that has been determined to be the best approach for all or large parts of an organization. This is based on internal and external benchmarking, including the analysis of performance data. External benchmarking is not confined to the organization's industry. This process may be applicable to other Chevron locations.

For the online Best Practices Sharing Database, Chevron holds the contributor responsible for deciding if the practice is worth sharing with others and into which category it fits.

Similarly, TI has defined best as "a practice that is best for me – that yields improvement and will fit in my business." The company has two measures: 1) the demonstrated improvement potential of a practice, and 2) how adaptable the practice is to other locations.

AMP Inc. took a different approach: finding another label and establishing criteria. AMP is the world's largest manufacturer of electrical and electronic interconnection devices, with more than 40,000 employees in 40 countries and 212 locations and sales of more than $5 billion per year. For years, AMP rather unsuccessfully promoted the transfer of "Best Demonstrated Practices" (BDPs). The label turned out to be counterproductive because it gave people the impression that there was only one best way to do something, and it provoked resentment among the laggards and fear of being accused of unjustified arrogance among good units. The label "best" was getting in the way of "better."

AMP switched the label to Successfully demonstrated Practices (SDPs) and added credibility by establishing criteria for successful demonstration. As John Davis, benchmarking manager at AMP, points out, resistance to learning from others in the firm hasn't disappeared, but it has decreased dramatically.

To ensure credibility, AMP only enters into its central electronic database those SDPs that can be verified in one or more of the following ways:

- Has the SDP resulted in measurable improvement for the organization?
- Has the SDP been recognized by internal/external experts or sources?
- Has the SDP been recognized through Malcolm Baldrige and/or European Quality assessments or ISO and MRP II Audits?

References

Chew, W., T. Bresnahan, and K. Clark, "Measurement, Coordination, and Learning in a Multiplant Network," in Kaplan, R. (ed.), *Measures for Manufacturing Excellence*, Boston: Harvard Business School Press, 1990.

Nonaka, I., "The Knowledge-Creating Company, *Harvard Business Review*, November-December, 1991.

Polanyi, M., *The Tacit Dimension*, New York: Doubleday Anchor, 1967.

Szulanski, G., *Appropriating Rents from Existing Knowledge: Intra-Firm Transfer of Best Practice*, Ann Arbor, MI: UMI Dissertation Services, 1995.

CHAPTER 32

Strategic Knowledge Managing within the Context of Networks

Sven A. Carlsson

Informatics, Jönköping International Business School, Jönköping, Sweden

The basic economic resource in the next economy is knowledge, but there is a lack in our understanding on how to manage knowledge and knowledge processes for competitive advantage. This chapter presents a conceptualization of strategic knowledge managing and a strategic knowledge managing (SKM) framework. The conceptualization is based on extensions of the resource- and knowledge-based view of the firm as well as ideas from inter-firm relationships and the "gift economy." We place strategic knowledge managing within the context of networks. Four types of networks for knowledge managing are defined: 1) intra-networks, 2) extra-networks, 3) inter-networks, and 4) open networks. The SKM framework can support organizations in strategically managing knowledge and knowledge processes to gain and sustain competitive advantage. The SKM framework comprises the activities: 1) strategic vision, 2) knowledge vision and key knowledge identification, 3) design, 4) knowledge protection and/or give away, 5) implementation, and 6) usage. The conceptualization and the framework open up new knowledge managing research areas and issues.

Keywords: Strategic Knowledge Managing; Knowledge-Based View; Networks; Strategic KM in Networks; Gift Economy

1 Introduction

Commentators on contemporary themes of strategic management stress that a firm's competitive advantage flows from its unique knowledge and how it manages knowledge (Barney, 1991; Boisot, 1998; Spender, 1996; Nonaka and Teece, 2001). It is argued that knowledge is displacing natural resources, capital, and labor as the basic economic resource in the post-industrial knowledge and information economy (Drucker, 1995).

Scholars have pointed out that for many firms, their ability to create, share, exchange, and use knowledge will have a major impact on their competitiveness in the future. Some researchers even state that the only sustainable competitive advantage in the future will be effective and efficient organizational knowledge managing (Wikström and Normann, 1994; Nonaka and Takeuchi, 1995; von Krogh et al., 2000a). Said Nonaka: "When markets shift, technologies proliferate, competitors multiply, and/or products become obsolete almost overnight, successful companies are those that constantly create new knowledge, disseminate it widely throughout the organization, and quickly embody it in new technologies and products" (Nonaka, 1991). This has led to an interest in idiosyncratic knowledge that is valuable, rare, immobile, and exploited by a firm to give the firm a competitive advantage (Barney, 1991).

Organizations have always "managed" knowledge intentionally. Although the concept of coding, storing, transmitting, exchanging, and using knowledge in organizations is not new, management practice is becoming increasingly more knowledge-focused (Truch et al., 2000; Collison and Parcell, 2001; Hatten and Rosenthal, 2001). Furthermore, organizations are increasingly depending on specialist competencies and employees using their cognitive capabilities and expertise (Blackler, 1995)—which Reich (1991) terms "symbolic analytical workers."

The recent interest in organizational knowledge has prompted consideration of the issue of how to manage knowledge to an organization's benefit and to the use of information and communication technologies (ICTs) for managing knowledge. These ICTs-based systems, called knowledge management systems (KMS), are presented and exemplified in section 5. Generally, knowledge managing (KM) refers to identifying and leveraging the individual and collective knowledge in an organization to support the organization in becoming more competitive; problems with maintaining, locating, and applying knowledge have led to systematic attempts to manage knowledge (Davenport and Prusak, 1998; O'Dell and Grayson, 1998; Cross and Baird, 2000; Baird and Henderson, 2001).

Although we have many answers to the question: "Why do firms invest in KM and KMS?" we have fewer answers to the question: "How can firms strategically manage knowledge to improve firm performance?" While we have some theories, frameworks, and models related to KM, there are large gaps in the body of knowledge in the area of how to gain and sustain competitive advantage through strategic knowledge managing.

The purpose of this chapter is threefold. First, we present a conceptualization of strategic knowledge managing based on extensions of the resource-based and the knowledge-based view of the firm. We also place KM within the context of networks—we argue that a main focus in strategic knowledge managing should be different types of networks. When addressing inter-organizational networks, the resource-based view of the firm in part breaks down. Ideas from inter-firm relationships, the "gift economy," and the open source movement are used to discuss how a firm can gain a competitive advantage from knowledge managing in inter-organizational networks.

Second, based on the conceptualization, we present a framework for strategic knowledge managing (SKM). The SKM-framework suggests that gaining and sustaining a competitive advantage through knowledge and knowledge processes is an effort involving: 1) strategic vision, 2) knowledge vision and key knowledge identification, 3) design, 4) knowledge protection and/or give away, 5) implementation, and 6) usage. The framework can support an organization in strategically managing knowledge and knowledge processes to gain and sustain competitive advantage.

Third, to discuss implications of the conceptualization and the framework for the use of ICTs for knowledge managing. The conceptualization and the framework also point out new research areas and issues in KM. Our approach is primarily conceptual-analytic (Järvinen, 2000), which means that we use previous empirical studies, theories, models, and constructs to develop our conceptualization and the SKM framework.

The remainder of the chapter is organized as follows: the next section sets the scene by briefly discussing knowledge, KM, and KMS. This is followed by a presentation and discussion of our conceptualization of strategic knowledge managing. Based on the conceptualization, we then present a framework for strategic knowledge managing. This is followed by a discussion of the roles ICTs can play in knowledge managing. The final section presents conclusions and further research.

2 Knowledge, Knowledge Managing, and Knowledge Management Systems

Although the concept of coding, storing, and transmitting knowledge in organizations is not new, different academic fields and managerial practice have recently become more knowledge-focused (*California Management Review*, 1998; Truch et al., 2000). This section briefly presents some of the numerous views of knowledge as discussed in the IS/IT, strategy, management, and organization theory literature. This enables us to uncover some (unstated) assumptions about knowledge managing and KMS. We also present the views on knowledge, knowledge managing, and knowledge management systems that form our starting point—in later sections we extend our views. (We do not enter the debate about whether knowledge managing is a novel idea or just a recycled concept. Arguments favoring the position that KM requires development of new theories, concepts, etc., can be found in, for example, Nonaka and Takeuchi (1995), Alavi and Leidner (2001), Alavi (2000), Spiegler (2000), Nonaka and Teece (2001), von Krogh et al. (2000a, b), as well as several chapters in this volume. On this issue, we adhere to the view of authors arguing that KM requires the development new theories, models, and concepts.)

Alavi and Leidner (2001) identified the following views of knowledge:

- Knowledge vis-à-vis data and information. Some authors, most notably in the IS/IT community, address the question of defining knowledge by distinguishing between knowledge, information, and data (Fahey and Prusak, 1998; Tuomi, 2000; Spiegler, 2000; Galliers and Newell, 2001).
- Knowledge as state of mind, where knowledge is described as "a state or fact of knowing" with knowing being a condition of "understanding gained through experience or study; the sum or range of what has been perceived, discovered, or learned" (Schubert et al., 1998).
- Knowledge as objects (things) that can be stored in knowledge repositories (organizational memories) and manipulated (Stein and Zwass, 1995; Wijnhoven, 2000).
- Knowledge as a process of simultaneously knowing and acting (Brown and Duguid, 2000, 2001).
- Knowledge as resource and capability with the potential for improving organizational performance (Carlsson et al., 1996; Meso and Smith, 2000).

The different views of knowledge lead to different perceptions of knowledge managing and of the roles of KMS (Carlsson et al., 1996; Alavi and Leidner, 2001). In accordance with the resource-based view (RBV) of the firm, our starting point will be knowledge as resource and capability. The main reason for this choice from among the different views is that this is the one that can be used to explicitly address the link between knowledge managing and firm performance.

Frameworks and models of organizations as knowledge systems suggest that knowledge managing consists of four sets of socially enacted knowledge processes, namely: 1) knowledge creation, 2) knowledge organization and storage/retrieval, 3) knowledge transfer, and 4) knowledge application (Pentland, 1995; Davenport and Prusak, 1998; Boisot, 1998). The frameworks and models represent the cognitive, social, and structural nature of organizational knowledge and its embodiment in the individuals' cognition and practices as well as the collective (i.e., organizational) practices and culture (Alavi and Leidner, 2001). The four processes do not represent a monolithic set of activities. They are interconnected and intertwined sets of activities.

According to Davenport and Prusak (1998), most knowledge management projects have one of three aims: 1) to make knowledge visible and show the role of knowledge in an organization, mainly through maps, yellow pages, and hypertext tools; 2) to develop a knowledge-intensive culture by encouraging and aggregating behaviors such as knowledge sharing and proactively seeking and offering knowledge; and 3) to build a knowledge infrastructure—not only a technical system, but a web of connections among people given space, time, tools, and encouragement to collaborate. Teece (2001) says that there are three broad aims frequently advanced by the "KM movement:" 1) the creation of knowledge repositories (data warehouses), 2) improvement of "knowledge" access, and 3) enhancement of knowledge environment. An underlying assumption in much of the KM-literature seems to be that "more is better", meaning, for example, that more knowledge sharing is per se good from an individual as well as an organizational point of view. Some scholars question this assumption and suggest that what is missing in the KM-literature is an attention perspective. The main argument of this view is that how knowledge is created, shared, and so forth is the result of how firms channel and distribute the attention of their knowledge-workers (Hansen and Faas, 2001; Davenport and Beck, 2001).

Knowledge management systems (KMS) refer to a class of information systems applied to managing individual and organizational knowledge. That is, they are ICTs-based systems developed and used to support and enhance the organizational processes of knowledge creation, storage/retrieval, transfer, and application. While not all KM initiatives involve the use of ICTs, and warnings against an emphasis on the use of ICTs for KM are not uncommon (Davenport and Prusak, 1998; O'Dell and Grayson, 1998; McDermott, 1999; Swan et al., 1999b), many KM initiatives rely on ICTs as an important enabler. The literature on applications of ICTs to organizational knowledge managing suggests four common applications: 1) the coding and sharing of best practices, 2) the creation of corporate knowledge directories, 3) the creation of knowledge networks, and 4) knowledge-based support of decision making and action taking. Our stance is that KMS is not a particular type of ICTs in a restricted sense, but primarily a perspective (vision) on KM, the role of ICTs as support for managing knowledge, and how to realize this vision in practice. There is room for different perspectives on KM and obviously also room for different perspectives on KMS. After we have presented our conceptualization and the SKM framework, we briefly discuss their implications for the use of ICTs for knowledge managing.

Summarizing, the KM-literature and chapters in this volume point out several reasons for KM initiatives, present different views on knowledge, describes KM and KMS in action, and describe the different activities in knowledge managing. The literature is sparse on how firms actually can manage knowledge to gain and sustain competitive advantage. In the rest of this chapter, we address this and take off from the resource-based view of the firm.

3   Conceptualizing Strategic Knowledge Managing

The conceptualization of knowledge managing we present takes its epistemological starting point in business strategy theory. It is, in part, based on extensions of the resource-based view (RBV) and the knowledge-based view (KBV) of the firm. The main proposition of the RBV is that competitive advantage is based on valuable and unique internal resources and capabilities that are costly to imitate for competitors. In the case of the KBV, the resources and capabilities are knowledge-related resources and capabilities. The RBV and the KBV are aimed at explaining, and in part predicting, a firm's market performance by addressing the role of the resources and capabilities on which product/service features are based. The RBV has been criticized. For example, Teece et al. (1997) point out that the RBV recognizes, but does not attempt to explain the mechanisms—dynamic capabilities—that enable a firm to sustain its competitive advantage. Also, research suggests that an important source for competitive advantage lies in an organization's network of external relationships (Gulati et al., 2000; Nohria and Ghoshal, 1997). Venkatraman and Subramaniam (2002) suggest that the viable view on strategy in the knowledge economy is strategy as a portfolio of relationships.

KM can be addressed from a strategic perspective: managing knowledge as strategic resources and capabilities. Strategy is about the direction and scope of an organization over the long term and strategy theory includes how to configure resources and capabilities of primary concern to senior management, or to anyone seeking reasons for success or failure among organizations (Rumelt et al., 1994; Johnson and Scholes, 1997). According to Barney, strategy is *"a pattern of resource allocation that enables firms to maintain or improve their performance. A "good" strategy is a strategy that neutralizes threats and exploits opportunities while capitalizing on strengths and avoiding or fixing weaknesses. Strategic management is the process through which strategies are chosen and implemented"* (Barney, 1997). Given these definitions, a strategic perspective on KM means addressing: 1) vision and direction for knowledge managing, and 2) how to organize and manage knowledge-related resources and capabilities for competitive advantage. If we believe that knowledge and knowledge processes are critical, theory and practice on strategic knowledge managing should address how important factors and activities in the management of knowledge and knowledge processes can lead to competitive advantage.

Given the above, the next sections are devoted to: 1) dynamic capabilities, i.e., an extension of the RBV, 2) an extension of the RBV and KBV to also include external relationships as a source of competitive advantage, 3) networks as a context for knowledge managing, and 4) a strategic knowledge managing framework.

3.1 Extending the Resource-Based and Knowledge-Based Views of the Firm

In the "new economy," the sustainable competitive advantage of business organizations flows from the creation, ownership, protection and use of commercial and industrial knowledge assets that are difficult to imitate (Teece, 2001). A knowledge-based view (KBV) of the firm has emerged in the strategy literature (Grant, 1996a, 1996b, 1997; Spender, 1996; Cole, 1998). This perspective builds on and extends the resource-based view of the firm (Penrose, 1959; Wernerfelt, 1984; Barney, 1991, 1995; Conner, 1991).

The RBV and the KBV postulate that the services rendered by tangible resources depend on how they are combined and applied, which is in turn a function of the firm's know-how (i.e., knowledge). This knowledge is embedded in and carried through multiple entities including organizational culture and identity, routines, policies, ICT-based information systems, and documents, as well as individual employees (Grant, 1996b; Nelson and Winter, 1982; Boisot, 1998). Because knowledge-related resources and capabilities are usually difficult to imitate and socially complex, the KBV posits that these knowledge assets may produce long-term sustainable competitive advantage. However, in many cases it is not the knowledge existing at any given time per se, but rather the firm's ability to effectively create new knowledge and to employ the existing knowledge to solve problems, make decisions, and take actions, that forms the basis for achieving competitive advantage.

The RBV makes two assertions. The first is resource heterogeneity, which means that resources and capabilities may be heterogeneously distributed across competing firms. The second is resource immobility, which means that these resource and capability differences can be stable over time. A firm's resources and capabilities include all financial, human, physical, and organizational assets utilized by a firm to develop, manufacture, and deliver services and products to its customers.

Descriptions of resource and capability attributes that give an organization a competitive advantage are plentiful. According to Kalling (2000), attributes are frequently cited are that resources and capabilities should be: 1) valuable, 2) unique, 3) spring out of factor imperfections and ex ante uncertainty, 4) costly to imitate, and 5) distributed in an optimal way internally within the organization.

1. *Value.* A resource/capability must enable an organization to respond to environmental threats or opportunities, for example, by lowering costs or raising the price for a product/service, or differentiating a product/service.

2. *Uniqueness or rareness.* In order to create a competitive advantage, a resource/capability must be unique and have an asymmetric distribution across competitors.

3. *Different fit and expectations.* Related to the issue of value are the different expectations on the future value of resources. In an SKM-perspective, this is related to what value specific knowledge-related resources and capabilities are expected to bring to an organization.

4. *Costly to imitate.* To gain and sustain a competitive advantage from a resource/capability, it must be costly to imitate. There must be a barrier to future duplication of the resource/capability. Hence, organizations without a resource/capability face a cost disadvantage in obtaining it, compared to organizations that already possess it.

5. *Resource organization and leverage.* This feature is related to how well a resource/capability is organized and is also related to the direct management of the resource/capability. Hence, it is related to structuring the organization, processes, routines, and so forth to make sure that the resource/capability is used "optimally."

Most RBV writings focus on stable rents that are costly, or impossible, to imitate. Recently, some writers have addressed the dynamic nature of resources (Grant, 1996a, b, 1997; Teece et al., 1997; Kogut and Zander, 1992; Eisenhardt and Martin, 2000). This can be viewed as an extension of the RBV as well as of the KBV. From an SKM-perspective this extension is critical in that it forces us to focus on the dynamic aspects of knowledge and knowledge processes. Also, we increasingly see that competition in the market gets displaced by the competition for the market (Teece, 2001). Said Teece: "The pay-off from market insight—figuring out where the market is heading and investing heavily to get there first—is high. ... The ability to sense and then seize such opportunities is in part an organizational capability" (Teece, 2001). This capability is often referred to as a dynamic capability and means a shift in focus (Teece and Pisano, 1994; Teece et al., 1997; Teece, 2001; Eisenhardt and Martin, 2000; Eisenhardt and Santos, 2002). It also means a shift in unit of analysis as well as unit of design.

The focus in RBV is on resources but in the dynamic capability view, focus is on processes, positions, and paths. Teece et al. (1997) define dynamic capabilities as "... the firm's ability to integrate, build, and reconfigure internal and external competencies to address rapidly changing environments. Dynamic capabilities thus reflect an organization's ability to achieve new and innovative forms of competitive advantage given path dependencies and market positions (Leonard-Barton, 1992)." A similar definition is given by Eisenhardt and Martin (2000): "The firm's processes that use resources—specifically the processes to integrate, reconfigure, gain and release resources—to match and even create market change. Dynamic capabilities thus are the organizational and strategic routines by which firms achieve new resource configurations as markets emerge, collide, split, evolve, and die. The dynamic capability view suggests that profits do not flow just from the assets structure of the firm and the degree of imitability, but also from the firm's ability to reconfigure and transform. This ability is especially critical for organizations in turbulent and high-velocity environments."

Our conceptualization is based on the RBV and the KVB, but extended by the dynamic capability perspective. To summarize, to gain and sustain a competitive advantage through KM includes:

- The creation and development, through knowledge processes, of knowledge assets.
- The design of strategic knowledge processes—knowledge creation, knowledge organization and storage/retrieval, knowledge transfer, and knowledge application.
- The "design" of means to redesign, reconfigure, and transform knowledge processes. This also includes the capability to decide which knowledge processes to retain, develop, or terminate. Consequently, it also includes how to evaluate knowledge processes.
- The capability of careful selections on what knowledge-related processes to manage and not to manage. This also includes how knowledge relevant for this capability is managed and how to evaluate this capability.

3.2 Strategic Knowledge Managing in Networks

Our second and third extensions are related to a move from an intra-perspective to an intra- and inter-perspective, and a focus on networks as the context for strategic knowledge managing. The inter-perspective differs from the RBV and the dynamic capability view, which argue that competitive advantage is an outcome of resources and capabilities residing within the firm.

More than fifteen years ago, Thorelli (1986) stressed the importance of networks and the need for research on networks. Thorelli used the construct network to refer to relationships between two or more organizations and argued that networks were hybrid intermediate forms and alternatives to markets and hierarchies. Other writers have used the term to refer to networks in an organization as well as between organizations. Following Laumann et al. (1978), we define a social network as "a set of nodes (e.g., persons, organizations) linked by a set of social relationships (e.g., friendship, transfer of funds, overlapping membership) of a specified type." In knowledge managing, the social network will be for enabling and supporting different knowledge processes. A network can be enabled and enhanced by the use of ICTs, but we do not view networks as technological networks.

A firm's inter-organizational networks differ in their importance and criticality. Because we focus strategic knowledge managing, our main concern is with strategic networks. These networks "...encompass a firm's set of relationships, both horizontal and vertical, with other organizations—be they suppliers, customers, or other entities—including relationships across industries. These strategic networks are composed of inter-organizational ties that are enduring, are of strategic significance for the firms entering them, and include strategic alliances, joint-ventures, long-term buyer supplier partnerships, and a host of similar ties" (Gulati et al., 2000). The durability requirement can be questioned. In some cases a network, for example, a supplier network, can be enduring, but the network will have participants (suppliers) entering and leaving the network.

Although the construct 'network' can be used to describe and explain observed patterns and processes, we advocate that it be used in strategic knowledge managing as a model and unit of design. We suggest that knowledge managing must become network-focused if knowledge intensive organizations are to gain and sustain competitive advantage from knowledge managing.

Support for our suggestion can be found in a number of empirical studies. Von Hippel (1988) found that organizations' suppliers and customers were their primary sources of ideas for innovations. According to von Hippel, a network with excellent knowledge transfer among users, manufacturers, and suppliers will out-innovate networks with less effective knowledge sharing activities. In a study in the biotechnology industry, it was found that the network of firms was the locus of innovation, not the individual firm (Powell et al., 1996). Dyer and Nobeoka (2000) showed that Toyota's ability to effectively create and manage knowledge sharing networks, at least in part, explains the relative productivity advantages enjoyed by Toyota and its suppliers. Liu and Brookfield (2000) found that Taiwan's successful machine tool industry has a number of network structures. They also found that the networks, in part, explain the tool industry's success. These, as well as other (e.g., Miles et al., 2000; Richter, 2000), studies demonstrate the importance of networks and that networks can be effective in all of the activities of knowledge processes—from knowledge creation to knowledge application and use.

New organizational forms have been proposed and in these the importance of using networks in knowledge and innovation processes is stressed—see, for example, Nonaka and Takeuchi (1995), Quinn (1992), Quinn et al. (1997), Richter (2000), as well as several of the contributions in Nohria and Eccles (1992). Castells takes the argument to its limits: "...the network enterprise is neither a network of enterprises nor an intra-firm, networked organization. Rather, it is a lean agency of economic activity, built around specific business projects, which are enacted by networks of various composition and origin: *the network is the enterprise*. While the firm continues to be the unit of accumulation of capital, property rights (usually), and strategic management, business practice is performed by *ad hoc* networks. These networks have the flexibility and adaptability required by a global economy subjected to relentless technological innovation and stimulated by rapidly changing demand" (Castell, 2001).

As noted by several researchers (e.g., Venkatraman and Subramaniam, 2002), the notion of inter-organizational relationships and networks is not new; firms do not conduct all their business activities internally. It is well known that firms, based on transaction cost criteria, use outsourcing to lower costs despite the firms having the necessary resources and capabilities internally. In the knowledge economy, inter-organizational relationships and networks are also created because firms do not possess the required knowledge-related resources and capabilities internally. Inter-organizational relationships and networks are also created to share and disseminate knowledge, for example, for the purpose of influencing emerging standards. Knowledge-based networks have also been discussed in the KM-literature (e.g., Newell et al., 2000; Swan et al., 1999a), but not, as in this chapter, from a strategic and competitive perspective.

As discussed above, networks can be of different types and forms. For our strategic KM conceptualization, we define four different types of networks for knowledge managing: 1) intra-networks, 2) extra-networks, 3) inter-networks, and 4) open networks.

An intra-network is an internal firm-specific network. That is, it does not transcend the firm's boundary (for example, a Lotus Notes-based intranet for disseminating "best practices" in the firm).

An extra-network is a network that transcends a firm's boundary. Participation in such a network is restricted, meaning that only specific individuals and organizations are allowed to participate (for example, an extranet for specific R&D personnel in specific telecommunication equipment firms engaged in the development of new Bluetooth applications).

An inter-network is also a network that transcends a firm's boundary, but participation in the network is not restricted. This type of network is open to anyone who wants to join and participate. An example is how Fiat used the Internet to test new design ideas for its Punto model. Fiat invited potential customers to select features for the car on its Web-site. More than 3000 replied and gave Fiat valuable design information—this is a good example of co-design using an Internet-based inter-network (Iansiti and MacCormack, 1997).

An open network is a network open for anyone interested and willing to participate in knowledge creation and sharing. A good example of this network type is the open source movement and the development of such results as Linux and Apache (Raymond, 2001). It is estimated that the worldwide development community for the overall Linux operating system exceeds 40,000 developers (Raymond, 2001). Although, we have used ICT-based examples, not all networks use ICTs; and in most networks, ICTs are only one of several critical components and aspects.

Scholars in the strategy field are concerned with explaining differential firm performance. As these scholars have searched for sources of competitive advantage, different views have emerged regarding the sources of above normal returns. Because the views are based on different, and in part contradictory, ideas concerning the primary sources of above normal profit returns and have different units of analysis, they have different explanatory and predictive power in relation to how to gain and sustain competitive advantage from knowledge-based networks.

The RBV, the KBV, and the dynamic capability view seem to be fruitful in explaining the competitive performance of knowledge-based intra-networks. The theories can also be used as foundations for designing and fertilizing knowledge-based intra-networks. Because the RBV, the KBV, and the dynamic capability view have an internal view, they are in their original form less fruitful for inter-organizational networks. Still, some scholars have extended the RBV to alliance formation (e.g., Eisenhardt & Schoonhoven 1996) and inter-organizational networks (e.g., Choudhury and Xia, 1999). This suggests that the RBV, the KBV, and the dynamic capability view can be used for designing knowledge-based extra-networks. For intra-networks, some researchers have suggested learning perspectives (e.g., Larsson et al., 1998; Edwards and Kidd, 2001) or a relational view (Dyer and Singh, 1998). Dyer and Singh's relational view suggests four sources of inter-organizational competitive advantage: "1) investments in relation-specific assets; 2) substantial knowledge exchange, including the exchange of knowledge that results in joint learning; 3) the combining of complementary, but scarce, resources or capabilities (typically through multiple functional interfaces), which results in the joint creation of unique new products, services, or technologies; and 4) lower transaction costs than competitor alliances, owing to more effective governance mechanisms" (Dyer and Singh, 1998). The four sources are related to the different activities in knowledge managing and tentatively the relational view can be used for designing knowledge-related extra-networks.

Moving to inter-networks and open networks, the views discussed above, in part, break down. Using a knowledge-based inter-network means, for example, that a firm will not be able to control who is participating in the network and the firm will not have specific and restricted agreements with the participants. Furthermore, the firm will not be able to control and manage the knowledge process: what knowledge is created, shared, disseminated, and used. Still, the firm has a degree of discretion in that it can set the agenda, in part manage the knowledge process by setting rules, and in part manage the knowledge process through intervening in the various activities. Given that the firm is able to exercise some discretion, some of the ideas from the relation view are valid for knowledge-based inter-networks. To exemplify, the inter-network can be effective for interfirm knowledge sharing, and the governance discretion used by the firm can be effective. According to the relational view, these two circumstances are primary sources of above normal returns—albeit, they are not the only sources of above normal returns. The firm can use different mechanisms to preserve profits, for example, time compression diseconomies and casual ambiguity. This means that the inter-network will enable the firm to be first in developing critical knowledge-related resources and capabilities and continuously improve these resources and capabilities. Using causal ambiguity means that the firm tries to "blur" the relation between a knowledge-related resource/capability and its effects (e.g., improved quality of a new product or faster to market with a new product). Using the causal ambiguity mechanism makes it hard for competitors to copy the resource/capability.

Moving to the open networks means even less discretion for a firm. The use and governance of this type of network is quite different from the other types of networks. It also means that the views discussed above are less useful. A view that might be informative for this type of network is based on a "gift economy" view (Hyde, 1999; Baird, n.d; Raymond, 2001). The gift economy has been proposed as an alternative to a market and commodity economy, especially in situations where creativity and ideas are crucial (Hyde, 1999). Hyde argues that gift economies are necessary for knowledge creation and dissemination. Gift economies serve to bind people together, which means that they create and maintain social groups within established social boundaries. To become a member of a gift community, a person or organization has to qualify by giving and receiving gifts. Exchanging gifts means initiating and maintaining interactions. As noted, strategic knowledge managing concerns firm performance and this means that the gift economy must also exist in a commodity economy. In turn, the gift economy and the market and commodity economy have to exist in a fruitful tension. Although, the gift economy view is, to a large extent, an unexplored view for describing and understanding open networks, it seems to be an interesting view to explore further.

Our extended conceptualization opens up new design and research issues in knowledge managing, for example:

- Under what circumstances are different types of networks effective in knowledge managing? Liu and Brookfield (2000) identified three basic types of networks: concentrated, dispersed, and multi-centered networks. Given the purpose of a knowledge managing initiative (e.g. knowledge creation or knowledge diffusion), each network type will be more or less effective and efficient. Within each basic type, they identified a number of different forms of networks. Their classification can be used in conjunction with our definitions of different types of networks. Related to different types of networks is the question of position in a network and network clustering. Venkatraman and Subramaniam (2002) suggest that the benefits of economies of knowing (expertise) come from firms' centrality in knowledge networks. This is an issue for empirical studies.
- Strong tie versus weak tie networks. Some studies suggest that a highly interconnected, strong tie network is effective for the diffusion of knowledge rather than for creating new knowledge, which is the strength of a weak tie network (Rowley et al., 2000; Dyer and Nobeoka, 2000). Although more research on when strong tie networks and weak tie networks are effective in knowledge processes is needed, the studies suggest when strong and weak tie networks are effective for knowledge managing.
- A problem with inter-organizational networks—especially inter-networks and open networks—is that in many cases there is no higher authority to orchestrate the design and management of the network. In some cases, a specific firm will not be allowed by other network participants to function as the governing body for the network (e.g. the open source movement). Research on how these types of networks can be designed and put to effective use is needed. Studies based on "the gift economy" might shed light on this issue.
- From a management and design perspective, we can distinguish between: 1) artificial (designed) networks, 2) and natural and emerging networks. Examples of designed networks include the design of an electronic communication network, using for example Lotus Notes, or the design of a knowledge repository where best practices from lab tests are registered. But design can also include the design of reward systems and education packages, as well as the design of physical meeting places. In and between organizations, some networks develop and emerge naturally or they are causally formed (i.e., they are not designed). An illustrating case is Gongla and Rizzuto's (2001) description of how different communities of practice emerged in IBM's Global Services and how the emerging communities were supported by different means. Von Krogh et al., (2000a) stress that an organization can and should take actions to enable knowledge creation and knowledge sharing. According to Gupta and Govindarajan (2000), a crucial requirement for effective knowledge managing is the development and support of an effective social ecology—the social ecology is the social environment within which people operate. Liu and

Brookfield (2000) point out that relationship-building and trust-building are critical in effective networks. At the same time, it should be noted that in many cases it is not easy to "build" knowledge sharing cultures, collaborative cultures, or trust (Huang et al., 2001; Hauschild et al., 2001; De Long and Fahey, 2000)—on these issues, see, Leidner (2002). In these situations, different organizational roles can be used to smooth things out and to function as communicators, negotiators, and brokers (El Sawy et al., 2001; Huang et al., 2001; Carlsson and Schönström, 2001). Research on how a firm can and should involve itself in fertilizing both designed and natural networks is another critical research issue. Research on related obstacles as well as how to deal with the obstacles is also needed.

- Future research is needed on how powerful (explanatory and predictive power) the views discussed above are and under what circumstances the views are useful for designing and fertilizing different types of networks.

To summarize, we suggest that the contexts of strategic knowledge managing should be networks. Consequently, strategic knowledge managing includes managing an organization's portfolio of strategically important knowledge-related networks. Our suggestion has implications for research on knowledge managing as well as for KM-practice. Although, theory and empirical studies support our suggestion, the KM-field, as noted, still need much more research on the above areas and issues.

4   A Framework for Strategic Knowledge Managing

Five resource and capability attributes, based on the RBV were presented, which when fulfilled render a firm a competitive advantage. Given our conceptualization of knowledge managing, a framework for strategic managing of knowledge-related resources and capabilities should support an organization in creating these attributes. This means that the framework should guide an organization in: 1) given the organization's vision, identifying its critical knowledge and knowledge processes, 2) developing and refining critical knowledge and knowledge processes to enhance value, 3) implementing and distributing critical knowledge and knowledge processes in an optimal sense, 4) making sure that knowledge and knowledge processes are used in an "optimal" way, and 5) deciding if and how it should protect knowledge and knowledge processes from imitation or if it should use a "give away" approach.

Our framework is, in part, based on a framework for IT resource management processes developed by Kalling (2000), who based on the RBV, developed his framework. We have adapted and extended Kalling's framework by: 1) focusing on knowledge and knowledge processes, 2) also using the dynamic capability view, interfirm relationship views, and the "gift economy" as foundations, 3) focusing on networks (intra-, extra-, inter-, and open networks), 4) renaming some of the tasks, 5) developing the content of the tasks to be specific for knowledge-related resources, capabilities, and processes, and 6) adding strategic vision.

As shown in Figure 1, the SKM-framework suggests that gaining and sustaining a competitive advantage through knowledge and knowledge processes is a process involving: 1) strategic vision, 2) knowledge vision and key knowledge identification, 3) design, 4) knowledge protection or/and give away, 5) implementation, and 6) usage. These are six distinct tasks that a firm has to manage in order to gain competitive advantage through knowledge and knowledge processes. Each task has certain purposes and certain problems; and certain evaluation issues are related to each of the tasks.

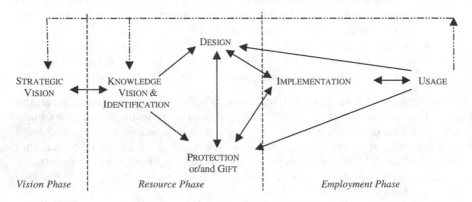

Figure 1. A Model of the Strategic Knowledge Managing Process

Based on the RBV, Barney (1997) generated four questions that can be asked about any resource or capability to assess whether or not it is or can be a source of competitive advantage. We adapt and enhance the questions to our conceptualization. The following questions form the foundation:

- *The question of value.* Does a firm's knowledge and network-based knowledge processes enable the firm to sense and then seize environmental opportunities, as well as respond to environmental threats?
- *The question of rareness.* How many competing firms already possess particular valuable knowledge and network-based knowledge processes?
- *The question of imitability.* Do firms without particular valuable knowledge and network-based knowledge processes face a cost disadvantage in obtaining them compared to firms that already possess them?
- *The question of organization.* Is the firm organized to exploit the full competitive potential of its knowledge and network-based knowledge processes?

Strategic vision. This is similar "traditional" strategic planning. The strategic vision can include: a) mission of the firm, the overriding purpose in line with different stakeholders' values and expectations, b) vision or intent, the desired future state which can include the aspiration of the firm, c) goal, general statement of purpose or aim, and d) objectives, quantification and operationalization or more precise statements of the goal(s). Whatever the strategic vision encompasses, it should, from an SKM-perspective, identify economies of knowing (expertise) as critical for the firm to gain and sustain competitive advantage. The strategic vision will identify the ultimate purpose of strategic knowledge managing. If strategic knowledge managing is not considered to be a critical means, the firm might be better off focusing on how to gain a competitive advantage through economies of scale and/or scope. (We lack studies showing a systematic link between economies of knowing and performance. Venkatraman and Subramaniam (2002) note that knowing may be a common cause of scale-based and scope-based effects, but they also point out the need for research on the issue.) The output of the strategic vision activity is the input to the knowledge vision activity.

Knowledge vision and identification of key knowledge-related resources and capabilities. To be able to manage knowledge-related resources and capabilities dynamically and continuously, a firm needs a knowledge vision. The knowledge vision should be aligned with the strategic vision of the firm (or a sub-unit of the firm). It should identify how the firm can fulfill its vision by managing knowledge and network-based knowledge processes strategically. Because the knowledge vision is related to the strategic vision it can transcend the boundaries of existing knowledge, knowledge processes, products/services, organizational units, and markets.

Using the four questions above we can ask:

- Can (or is) a specific type of knowledge and networked-based knowledge processes be valuable to the firm? The value should be evaluated in relation to the strategic vision.
- Do competing firms possess the specific type of knowledge and networked-based knowledge processes?
- Will firms without the specific type of knowledge and networked-based knowledge processes face a disadvantage in obtaining these compared to firms that already possess them?
- Will it be possible to design and implement different artifacts, artificial systems, physical and virtual spaces, etc. to exploit the full competitive potential of the specific type of knowledge and networked-based knowledge processes?

Using these questions will help an organization in assessing likely competitive implications of the specific type of knowledge and networked-based knowledge processes. Answering "no" to the four questions suggests that a specific type of knowledge and networked-based knowledge process will lead to a competitive disadvantage; answering "yes" to the four questions suggests that a specific type of knowledge and networked-based knowledge processes can lead to a sustained competitive advantage. A competitive disadvantage is likely to lead to an economic performance below normal; and a sustained competitive advantage is likely to lead to an economic performance above normal.

Consequently, the knowledge vision defines what network-based knowledge-related resources and capabilities the firm should develop in order to gain a competitive advantage through strategic KM, but the knowledge vision does not define how the network-based knowledge-related resources and capabilities should be designed, acquired, implemented, and used.

Design. The design activity addresses how the requirements identified in the previous activity can be fulfilled. Design is both about content and process, which can include the design of knowledge repositories, knowledge-intensive business and management processes, reward systems, etc., and even the design of physical places (Earl and Scott, 1999; Brown and Duguid, 2000; Hansen et al., 1999; Nonaka et al., 2001; von Krogh et al., 2000a; Gupta and Govindarajan, 2000). This can also include the design of environments for simulation (Schrage, 2000). Design is not only about the development of structural capital, but also about the development of human capital. It includes how knowledge can be used to enhance or amplify other existing (strategic) resources and capabilities that might be sources of competitive advantage (for example, how knowledge managing can enhance new product development (NPD) processes)—on knowledge managing around business processes, see, El Sawy and Josefek (2002) and El Sawy (2001).

At the core of design is the development of a strategic knowledge architecture, which is a combination of knowledge-related resources and capabilities within the context of networks to put the knowledge vision into effect. We can use the four questions to evaluate the design:

- To what extent can specific design alternatives of network-based knowledge processes be valuable—valuable in relation to the knowledge vision and the strategic vision?
- Do competing firms possess the specific design alternatives of network-based knowledge processes?
- Will firms without the specific design of network-based knowledge processes face a disadvantage in obtaining them compared to firms that already possess them?
- To what degree will it be possible to implement the different artifacts, artificial systems, physical places and virtual spaces, etc. to exploit the full competitive potential?

Using these questions will help an organization in assessing likely competitive implications of the design alternatives. A "no" in response to the four questions suggests that a specific design alternative will lead to a competitive disadvantage; and a "yes" response to the four questions suggests that a specific design alternative can lead to a sustained competitive advantage.

Knowledge protection and/or give away. The fourth activity is barely addressed in the KM-literature. According to the RBV, there are two purposes of knowledge protection: 1) protecting for imitation, and 2) protecting for value erosion. A firm can in some cases use contractual and legal protection measures, but for many knowledge-related resources, it can only use isolation mechanisms to protect its key knowledge-related resources. For a discussion of the use of contractual and legal protection measures see Oriel (2002) and Earl (2001). One of Earl's knowledge strategies is the commercial school. It focuses on how to both protect and exploit a firm's knowledge or intellectual assets (intellectual properties) to produce revenue streams—knowledge or intellectual assets comprise trademarks, know-how, patents, and copyrights. The commercial school addresses how intellectual properties as objects can be managed to generate rents.

Isolation mechanisms can be, for example:

- *Ambiguity.* This is a question of "blurring" the relation between a knowledge-related resource/capability (for example, an ICT supported network-based NPD process, and its effects).
- *Complexity.* This is a question of "embedding" a knowledge-related resource/capability in such a way that it becomes a socially complex phenomenon hard to describe, understand, and copy.
- *Time advantage.* This is a question of time advantage, trying to be first and continuously develop the knowledge-related resources/capabilities (a moving target for the competitors)—this is related to dynamic capabilities of a firm and to Teece's claim that increasingly competition in the market gets displaced by the competition for the market (Teece, 2001).

These mechanisms can complicate imitations and reduce value erosion. Again, it is possible to use the four questions to evaluate to what degree certain steps taken for protecting knowledge and network-based knowledge processes are likely to lead to a competitive advantage, and how well different design alternatives may function from a protection perspective.

As discussed above, open networks might be driven by a gift economy. This means that a protection "strategy" might not be viable. Instead open networks are driven by the idea about gifts and gift exchange. If a firm chooses a gifts and gift exchange "strategy" and the firm will try to participate in a gift network a number of issues have to be addressed, including:

- Is it possible for the firm to fulfill a stewardship in the "gift network"—by fulfilling a stewardship the firm will be in a better position to influence, and in part control, the network?
- Can the firm influence the way participants qualify to become members of the gift network?
- How can the firm strike a good balance between give (gift economy) and charge (market and commodity economy)?

Implementation. After the resource phase follows the employment phase. It is not enough to cleverly identify and design knowledge-related resources and capabilities. In most cases, there is a need for different interventions so that the knowledge and networked-based knowledge processes will be fully exploited. Implementation can include, for example, the development and implementation of a new reward system or unlearning and learning programs. The four questions can be used to evaluate different implementation tactics in terms of their likely competitive implications.

Usage. This is the actual use of the knowledge and the network-based knowledge processes. The four questions can be used to evaluate the effects of the actual usage of the knowledge-related resources and capabilities. The result of an evaluation can affect the strategic vision and the knowledge vision.

5   Knowledge Management Systems within the Context of Networks

As pointed out in Section 2, Knowledge Management Systems (KMSs) are not particular ICTs in a restricted sense, but primarily a perspective (vision and conceptualization) on knowledge managing and the role of ICTs as knowledge managing enablers and supporters. Strategic KM within the contexts of networks can be supported and enabled with an array of ICTs, including, the Internet, intranet, groupware and computer-mediated collaboration, data warehouses, knowledge discovery in data bases (including data mining), computer-based yellow pages, simulation tools, intelligent agents, video-conferencing, and so forth. (Different aspects of the use of ICTs in KM can be found in, for example, Liebowitz (1999), Alavi and Leidner (2001), Carlsson et al. (2000), Marwick (2001), and section 5.)

Generally, ICTs have been used to enable and support a firm in gaining competitive advantage through economies of scale or economies of scope. In the knowledge economy, ICTs will also be used to enable and support a firm in gaining competitive advantage through economies of knowing (expertise). As presented, strategic knowledge managing includes managing an organization's portfolio of strategically important knowledge-related networks. Above, we presented our conceptualization of strategic knowledge managing and the SKM framework. In light of what we have presented, we address the use of ICTs for strategic knowledge managing by discussing:

- Knowledge portals and the emerging digital knowledge workplace.
- KMS and mobility.
- Infrastructure and architecture for KMS.

5.1   Knowledge Portals and the Digital Knowledge Workplace

One consequence of our conceptualization is that enabling, building, and maintaining networks is a critical capability. ICTs can be a significant means for enabling and supporting networks. They can link different nodes (people, organizations) and reduce geographical constraints. Increasingly, we will see that the gateway to ICT-based networks will be one type of Enterprise Portal: Knowledge Portals (KPs) (Vering et al., 2001; Mack et al., 2001; Tsui, 2002). KPs are digital knowledge workplaces that have been designed to provide a single access point to internal and external desired applications, information, and services for an organization's knowledge workers, partners, customers, suppliers, and other persons and organizations with which an organization cooperates. Figure 2 outlines a Knowledge Portal. Often a KP is an entry point to information, applications, and services available via the Web; and in some cases accessed by a mobile device. The information and knowledge made available through a KP can be personalized depending on network participation.

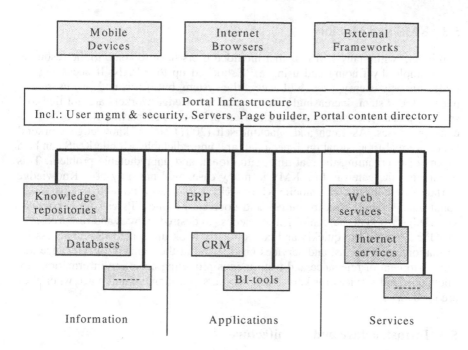

Figure 2. Knowledge Portal Components

Applications and services made available in a KP can include:

- Technologies to automatically capture and gather documents.
- Document analysis and document organization technologies (including technologies for categorization and clustering of documents).
- Technologies for browsing and searching documents.
- Support for analysis, synthesis, and authoring of information (including, for example, such systems as spreadsheets, project management software, and data mining tools).
- Communication tools, including, for example, e-mail, bulletin boards, instant messaging, IP telephone, audio- and video-conferences.

A KP keeps track of who in the organization and the extended organization is authorized to do what. The KP presents to each user only those resources and information the user is allowed to see and use, like information related to the specific network a person is a member of. Key elements in a KP are: 1) the width and depth of the KP in terms of what sources and resources can be accessed, 2) how changes can be made to the width and depth of the KP, and 3) how changes can be made regarding the network architecture (e.g., adding and deleting nodes).

5.2 KMS and Mobility

A problem with many KMSs is that intended users have to come to the resource, for example, by finding and using a PC hooked up to a LAN. If accessing the KMS this way is easy, users will access the system, but if it is not easy users will not use the system. Increasingly we see that knowledge workers are not tied to a specific place—e.g. sitting at a desk in an office—when participating in knowledge processes. As Keen and Mackintosch (2001) stress: knowledge workers' needs are real-time, situational, personal, and unpredictable. Mobile KMS can be a means of overcoming the real-time, situational, and unpredictable problem. This means that the gateway to a KMS in many cases will not only be a Knowledge Portal (KP), but actually a mobile KP (m-KP). KP makes it possible to have a personal gateway to desired resources and sources. Mobile-KPs can further reduce knowledge workers' burden of getting access to desired sources and resources. An m-KP can be used to quickly and conveniently hook up to a KMS and access information, applications, and services on demand at the moment of relevance and truth. Moment of relevance and truth means providing access to information, applications, and services for knowledge workers at a moment and place when they are needed.

5.3 Infrastructure and Architecture

In recent years, hardware and software companies, as well as service providers, have been promoting a new approach to organizational information systems. The approach is based on the idea that organizations in the future will buy an extensive part of their ICTs and services over the Internet rather than owning and maintaining their own hardware and software. The approach is launched under a number of different concepts: ".Net" (Microsoft), "Web services" (IBM), "network services" (Oracle), and "open network environment" (Sun). The firms are not only launching the concepts, but are investing heavily in making the new approach work. A result of this is that previous proprietary architecture—where companies built and maintained unique internal KMS—will to a growing extent be replaced by an open architecture where companies can rent data storage, processing power, specific applications, and other services from different types of external service providers.

Hagel and Brown (2001) describe the approach as an architecture having three layers: 1) software standards and communication protocols, 2) service grid, and 3) application services. The first layer contains different communication protocols and software standards, for example, SOAP, XML, and WML. This layer allows data to be exchanged easily between different applications and it also allows data to be processed easily in different types of applications. The second layer builds upon the protocols and standards and provides a set of shared utilities. An example of a utility provided by the second layer is data management containing directories, data brokers, repositories, and data transformation. This utility is critical for many KMSs. The application service layer contains different application services, for example, portals used in product development, business intelligence, and portals for cooperation. The approach suggests a number of changes regarding developing and maintaining KMS, for example:

- KMS will increasingly be built and maintained using non-proprietary hardware, software, and data.
- KMS built using non-proprietary hardware, software, and data can be more flexible and dynamic, which could make it easier to develop and change networks.

6 Conclusions and Further Research

Using a conceptual-analytic approach we developed a conceptualization of knowledge managing. We built our conceptualization on the RBV and KBV of the firm, but these were extended to also include: 1) the dynamic capability view, and 2) firm and inter-firm perspective. We also introduced networks as the context for knowledge managing and presented a strategic knowledge managing framework. Further theoretical work is needed to tighten the conceptualization and the framework. Empirical research will also be critical in helping us understand how firms get to be good at knowledge managing in network contexts, how they sometimes stay that way, why and how they improve their knowledge managing, and why sometimes knowledge managing decline. We also need both theoretical and empirical work on how ICTs can be used for strategic knowledge managing in networks.

Acknowledgements

Many thanks to Omar El Sawy, the late Bengt G. Lundberg, Mikael Schönström, Carol-Ann Soames, the Ph.D. students in the Knowledge Foundation Network on "Knowledge Creation in Organizations," Sweden, and the Ph.D. students in the "Articulating Research Issues in e-Business seminar, GSBA 610," spring 2001, at USC Marshall School of Business for their useful comments on earlier versions of this chapter.

References

Alavi, M. and D. Leidner, "Knowledge Management and Knowledge Management Systems: Conceptual Foundations and Research Issues," *MIS Quarterly*, 25, 1, 2001, 107-136.

Alavi, M., "Managing Organizational Knowledge," in Zmud, R.W (ed.) *Framing the Domains of IT Management Research: Glimpsing the Future through the Past*. Cincinnati, OH: Pinnaflex Educational Resources, 2000, 15-28.

Baird, D., "Scientific Instrument Making, Epistemology, and the Conflict between Gift and Commodity Economics," *Society for Philosophy & Technology*, 2, 3-4, n.d., URL = http://scholar.lib.vt.edu/ejournals/SPT/v2_n3n4html/baird.html

Baird, L. and J.C Henderson, *The Knowledge Engine: How to Create Fast Cycles of Knowledge-to-Performance and Performance-to-Knowledge.* San Francisco, CA: Berrett-Koehler, 2001.

Barney, J.B., "Firm Resources and Sustained Competitive Advantage," *Journal of Management*, 17, 1, 1991, 99-120.

Barney, J.B., "Looking Inside for Competitive Advantage," *Academy of Management Executive*, 9, 4, 1995, 49-61.

Barney, J.B., *Gaining and Sustaining Competitive Advantage.* Reading, MA: Addison-Wesley, 1997.

Blackler, F., "Knowledge, Knowledge Work and Organizations: An Overview and Interpretation," *Organization Studies*, 16, 6, 1995, 1021-1046.

Boisot, M.H., *Knowledge Assets.* Oxford, UK: Oxford University Press, 1998.

Brown, J.S. and P. Duguid, *The Social Life of Information.* Boston, MA: Harvard Business School Press, 2000.

Brown, J.S. and P. Duguid, "Knowledge and Organization: A Social-Practice Perspective," *Organization Science*, 12, 2, 2001, 198-213.

California Management Review, 40, 3, 1998.

Carlsson, S.A., P. Brezillon, P. Humphreys, B.G. Lundberg, A.M. McCosh and V. Rajkovic (eds.), *Decision Support through Knowledge Management.* Proceedings of IFIP TC8/WG8.3 conference, Department of Computer and Systems Sciences, University of Stockholm and Royal Institute of Technology, 2000.

Carlsson, S.A., O.A. El Sawy, I. Eriksson and A. Raven, "Gaining Competitive Advantage Through Shared Knowledge Creation: In Search of a New Design Theory for Strategic Information Systems," in *Proceedings of the Fourth European Conference on Information Systems*, 1996, 1067-1075.

Carlsson, S.A. and M. Schönström, "The Birth, Death, and Resurrection of a Knowledge Managing Initiative," in *Proceedings of the Second European Conference on Knowledge Management*, 2001, 93-104.

Castells, M., *The Internet Galaxy.* Oxford, UK: Oxford University Press, 2001.

Choudhury, V. and W. Xia, "A Resource-Based Theory of Network Structures," in Venkatraman, N. and Henderson, J.C. (eds.) *Research in Strategic Management and Information Technology*, Volume 2. Greenwich, CN: JAI Press, 1999, 55-85.

Cole, R.E., "Introduction," *California Management Review*, 45, 3, 1998, 15-21.

Collison, C. and G. Parcell, *Learning to Fly: Practical Lessons from one of the World's Leading Knowledge Companies.* Capstone Publ., 2001.

Conner, K.R., "A Historical Comparison of the Resource-Based Theory and Five Schools of Thought within Industrial Organization Economics: Do We Have a New Theory of the Firm," *Journal of Management*, 17, 1, 1991, 121-154.

Cross, R. and L. Baird, "Technology is not Enough: Improving Performance by Building Organizational Memory," *Sloan Management Review*, Spring, 2000, 69-78.

Davenport, T.H. and J.C. Beck, *The Attention Economy*. Boston, MA: Harvard Business School Press, 2001.

Davenport, T.H. and L. Prusak, *Working Knowledge*. Boston, MA: Harvard Business School Press, 1998.

De Long, D.W. and L. Fahey, "Diagnosing Cultural Barriers to Knowledge Management," *Academy of Management Executive*, 14, 4, 2000, 113-127.

Drucker, P., *The Post-Capitalist Society*. Oxford, UK: Butterworth-Heinemann, 1995.

Dyer, J.H. and K. Nobeoka, "Creating and Managing a High-Performance Knowledge-Sharing Network: The Toyota Case," *Strategic Management Journal*, 21, 3, 2000, 345-367.

Dyer, J. and H. Singh, "The Relational View: Cooperative Strategy and Sources of Interorganizational Competitive Advantage," *Academy Management Review*, 23, 4, 660-679.

Earl, M., "Knowledge Management Strategies: Toward a Taxonomy," *Journal of Management Information Systems*, 18, 1, 2001, 215-233.

Earl, M.J. and I.A. Scott, "What is a Chief Knowledge Officer?" *Sloan Management Review*, 40, 2, 1999, 29-38.

Edwards, J.S. and J. Kidd, "Knowledge Management when 'The Times They are A-Changin'," in *Proceedings of the Second European Conference on Knowledge Management*, 2001, 171-183.

Eisenhardt, K.M. and J.A. Martin, "Dynamic Capabilities: What are They?" *Strategic Management Journal*, 21, 2000, 1105-1121.

Eisenhardt, K.M. and F.M. Santos, "Knowledge-Based View: A New Theory of Strategy?" in Pettigrew, A.; Thomas, H. and Whittington, R. (eds.) *Handbook of Strategy and Management*. London, UK: Sage, 2002, 139-164.

Eisenhardt, K.M. and C.B. Schoonhoven, "Resource-based View of Strategic Alliance Formation: Strategic and Social Effects in Entrepreneurial Firms," *Organization Science*, 7, 2, 1996, 136-150.

El Sawy, O.A., *Redesigning Enterprise Processes for e-Business*. New York, NY: McGraw-Hill, 2001.

El Sawy, O.A., I. Eriksson, A. Raven and S. Carlsson, "Understanding Shared Knowledge Creation Spaces around Business Processes: Precursors to Process Innovation Implementation," *International Journal of Technology Management*, 22, 1/2/3, 2001, 149-173.

El Sawy, O.A. and R.A. Josefek Jr., "Business Process as Nexus of Knowledge," in Holsapple, C.W. (ed.): *Handbook on Knowledge Management*. Heidelberg, Germany: Springer-Verlag, 2002, this volume.

Fahey, L. and L. Prusak, "The Eleven Deadliest Sins of Knowledge Management," *California Management Review*, 40, 3, 1998, 265-276.

Galliers, R.B. and S. Newell, "Back to the Future: From Knowledge Management to Data Management," in *Proceedings of the Ninth European Conference on Information* Systems, 2001, 609-615.

Gongla, P. and C.R. Rizzuto, "Evolving Communities of Practice: IBM Global Services Experiences," *IBM Systems Journal*, 40, 4, 2001, 842-862.

Grant, R.M., "Prospering in Dynamically-Competitive Environments: Organizational Capability as Knowledge Integration," *Organization Science*, 7, 4, 1996a, 375-387.

Grant, R.M., "Toward a Knowledge-Based Theory of the Firm," *Strategic Management Journal*, 17, Winter Special Issue, 1996b, 109-122.

Grant, R.M., "The Knowledge-Based View of the Firm: Implications for Management Practice," *Long Range Planning*, 30, 3, 1997, 450-454.

Gulati, R., N. Nohria and A. Zaheer, "Strategic Networks," *Strategic Management Journal*, 21, 3, 2000, 203-215.

Gupta, A.K. and V. Govindarajan, "Knowledge Management's Social Dimension: Lessons from Nucor Steel," *Sloan Management Review*, 42, 1, 2000, 71-80.

Hagel, J. and J.S. Brown, "Your Next IT Strategy," *Harvard Business Review*, 79, October, 2001, 105-113.

Hansen, M.T. and M.R. Faas, "Competing for Attention in Knowledge Markets: Electronic Document Dissemination in a Management Consulting Company," *Administrative Science Quarterly*, 46, 2001, 1-28.

Hansen, M.T., N. Nohria and T. Tierney, "What's Your Strategy for Managing Knowledge?" *Harvard Business Review*, 77, 2, 1999, 106-116.

Hatten, K.J. and S.R. Rosenthal, *Reaching for the Knowledge Edge: How the Knowing Corporation Seeks, Shares & Uses Knowledge for Strategic Advantage*. New York, NY: AMACOM, 2001.

Hauschild, S., T. Licht and W. Stein, "Creating a Knowledge Culture," *The McKinsey Quarterly*, 1, 2001, 74-81.

Huang, J.C, S. Newell and R.D. Galliers, "The Myth of a Collaborative Culture: Component-based Development and the Dynamics of Organizational Subcultures," Working paper no. 102, Department of Information Systems, London School of Economics and Political Science, London, 2001.

Hyde, L., *The Gift: Imagination and the Erotic Life of Property*. London, UK: Vintage, 1999.

Iansiti, M., and A. MacCormack, "Developing Products on Internet Time," *Harvard Business Review*, 75, 5, 1997, 108-117.

Järvinen, P.H., "Research Questions Guiding Selection of an Appropriate Research Method," in *Proceedings of the Eighth European Conference on Information Systems*, 2000, 124-131.

Johnson, G. and K. Scholes, *Exploring Corporate Strategy*. Hemel Hempstead, UK: Prentice-Hall, 1997.

Kalling, T., *Gaining Competitive Advantage through Information Technology*. Doctoral dissertation, Lund University, Sweden: Lund Studies in Economics and Management 55, 2000.

Keen, P.G.W. and R. Mackintosch, *The Freedom Economy*. Berkeley, CA: Osborne/McGraw-Hill, 2001.

Kogut, B. and U. Zander, "Knowledge of the Firm, Combinative Capabilities, and the Replication of Technology," *Organization Science*, 3, 3, 1992, 383-397.

Larsson, R., L. Bengtsson, K. Henriksson and J. Sparks, "The Interorganizational Learning Dilemma: Collective Knowledge Development in Strategic Alliance," *Organization Science*, 9, 3, 1998, 285-305.

Laumann, E.O., L. Galskeiwicz and P.V. Marsden, "Community Structure as Interorganizational Linkages," *Annual Review of Sociology*, 4, 1978, 455-484.

Leidner, D., "Culture and Infrastructure as Knowledge Resources," in Holsapple, C.W. (ed.): *Handbook on Knowledge Management*. Heidelberg, Germany: Springer-Verlag, 2002, this volume.

Leonard-Barton D., "Core Capabilities and Core Rigidities: A Paradox in Managing New Product Development," *Strategic Management Journal*, 13, Summer Special Issue, 1992, 111-125.

Liebowitz, J. (ed.), *Knowledge Management Handbook*. Boca Raton, FL: CRC Press, 1999.

Liu, R.-J. and J. Brookfield, "Stars, Rings and Tiers: Organizational Networks and their Dynamics in Taiwan's Machine Tool Industry," *Long Range Planning*, 33, 3, 2000, 322-348.

Mack, R, Y. Ravin and R.J. Byrd, "Knowledge Portals and the Emerging Digital Workplace," *IBM Systems Journal*, 40, 4, 2001, 925-955.

Marwick, A.D., "Knowledge Management Technology," *IBM Systems Journal*, 40, 4, 2001, 814-830.

McDermott, R., "Why Information Technology Inspired but Cannot Deliver Knowledge Management," *California Management Review*, 41, 4, 1999, 103-117.

Meso, P. and R. Smith, "A Resource-Based View of Organizational Knowledge Management Systems," *Journal of Knowledge Management*, 4, 3, 2000, 224-234.

Miles, R.E., C.C. Snow and G. Miles, "The Future.org," *Long Range Planning*, 33, 3, 2000, 300-321.

Nelson, R.R. and S.G. Winter, *An Evolutionary Theory of Economic Change*. Cambridge, MA: Harvard University Press, 1982.

Newell, S., H. Scarbrough, J. Swan and D. Hishop, "Intranets and Knowledge Management: De-centred Technologies and the Limits of Technological Discourse," in Prichard, C.; Hull, R.; Chumer, M. and Willmott, H. (eds.) *Managing Knowledge: Critical Investigations of Work and Learning*. London, UK: Macmillan, 2000, 88-106.

Nohria, N. and R.G. Eccles (eds.), *Networks and Organizations: Structure, Form, and Action*. Boston, MA: Harvard Business School Press, 1992.

Nohria, N. and S. Ghoshal, *The Differentiated Network*. San Francisco, CA: Jossey-Bass, 1997.

Nonaka, I., "The Knowledge-Creating Company," *Harvard Business Review*, 69, 6, 1991, 96-104.

Nonaka, I. and H. Takeuchi, *The Knowledge Creating Company*. Oxford, UK: Oxford University Press, 1995.

Nonaka, I. and D.J. Teece (eds.), *Managing Industrial Knowledge: Creation, Transfer and Utilization*. London, UK: Sage, 2001.

Nonaka, I., R. Toyama and N. Konno, "SECI, *Ba*, and Leadership: a Unified Model of Dynamic Knowledge Creation," in Nonaka, I. and Teece, D.J. (eds.) *Managing Industrial Knowledge: Creation, Transfer and Utilization*. London, UK: Sage, 2001, 13-43.

O'Dell, C. and C.J. Grayson, *If Only We Knew What We Know*. New York, NY: Free Press, 1998.

Oriel, S., "Intellectual Property: A Key Knowledge Resource," in Holsapple, C.W. (ed.): *Handbook on Knowledge Management*. Heidelberg, Germany: Springer-Verlag, 2003, volume 2.

Penrose, E.T., *The Theory of the Growth of the Firm*. New York, NY: Wiley, 1959.

Pentland, B.T., "Information Systems and Organizational Learning: the Social Epistemology of Organizational Knowledge Systems," *Accounting, Management and Information Technologies*, 5, 1, 1995, 1-21.

Powell, W.W., K. Koput and L. Smith-Doerr, "Interorganizational Collaboration and the Locus of Innovation: Networks of Learning in Biotechnology," *Administrative Science Quarterly*, 41, 1996, 116-145.

Quinn, J.B., *Intelligent Enterprise*. New York, NY: The Free Press, 1992.

Quinn, J.B., J.J. Baruch and K.A. Zien, *Innovation Explosion*. New York, NY: The Free Press, 1997.

Raymond, E.S., *The Cathedral and the Bazaar* (revised edition). Sebastopol, CA: O'Reilly, 2001.

Reich, R., *The Work of Nations: Preparing Ourselves for 21st-Century Capitalism*. London, UK: Simon & Schuster, 1991.

Richter, F.-J., *Strategic Networks: The Art of Japanese Interfirm Cooperation*. Binghamton, NY: International Business Press, 2000.

Rowley, T., D. Behrens and D. Krackhardt, "Redundant Governance Structures: an Analysis of Structural and Relational Embeddedness in the Steel and Semiconductor Industries," *Strategic Management Journal*, 21, 3, 2000, 369-386.

Rumelt, R.P., D.E. Schendel and D.J. Teece (eds.), *Fundamental Issues in Strategy. A Research Agenda*. Cambridge, MA: Harvard Business School Press, 1994.

Schrage, M., *Serious Play: How the World's Best Companies Simulate to Innovate*. Boston, MA: Harvard Business School Press, 2000.

Schubert, P., D. Lincke and B. Schmid, "A Global Knowledge Medium as a Virtual Community: the NetAcademy concept," in *Proceedings of the Americas Conference of AIS*, 1998, 618-620.

Spender, J.C., "Making Knowledge the Basis of a Dynamic Theory of the Firm," *Strategic Management Journal*, 17, Winter Special Issues, 1996, 45-62.

Spiegler, I. "Knowledge Management: a New Idea or a Recycled Concept?," *Communications of the Association for Information Systems*, 3, article 14, 2000.

Stein, E.W. and V. Zwass, "Actualizing Organizational Memory with Information Systems," *Information Systems Research*, 6, 2, 1995, 85-117.

Swan, J., S. Newell, H. Scarbrough and D. Hislop, "Knowledge Management and Innovation: Networks and Networking," *Journal of Knowledge Management*, 3, 4, 1999a, 262-275.

Swan, J., H. Scarbrough and J. Preston, "Knowledge Management–the Next Fad to Forget People?," in *Proceedings of the Seventh European Conference on Information Systems*, 1999b, 668-678.

Teece, D.J., "Strategies for Managing Knowledge Assets: the Role of Firm Structure and Industrial Context," in Nonaka, I. and Teece, D.J. (eds.) *Managing Industrial Knowledge: Creation, Transfer and Utilization*. London, UK: Sage, 2001, 125-144.

Teece, D.J. and G. Pisano, "The Dynamic Capabilities of Firms: an Introduction," *Industrial and Corporate Change*, 3, 3, 1994, 537-556.

Teece, D.J., G. Pisano and A. Schuen, "Dynamic Capabilities and Strategic Management," *Strategic Management Journal*, 18, 7, 1997, 509-533.

Thorelli, H.B., "Networks: Between Markets and Hierarchies," *Strategic Management Journal*, 7, 1986, 37-51.

Truch, E., J.-N. Ezingeard and D.W. Birchall, "Developing a Relevant Research Agenda in Knowledge Management—Bridging the Gap between Knowing and Doing," in *Proceedings of the Eighth European Conference on Information Systems*, 2000, 694-700.

Tsui, E., "Knowledge Portal Technologies," in Holsapple, C.W. (ed.): *Handbook on Knowledge Management*. Heidelberg, Germany: Springer-Verlag, 2002, this volume.

Tuomi, I., "Data is More than Knowledge: Implications of the Reversed Hierarchy for Knowledge Management and Organizational Memory," *Journal of Management Information Systems*, 16, 3, 2000, 103-117.

Venkatraman, N. and M. Subramaniam, "Theorizing the Future of Strategy: Questions for Shaping Strategy Research in the Knowledge Economy," in Pettigrew, A.; Thomas, H. and Whittington, R. (eds.) *Handbook of Strategy and Management*. London, UK: Sage, 2002, 461-474.

Vering, M., G. Norris, P. Barth, J.R. Hurley, B. MacKay and D.J. Duray. *The E-Business Workplace*. New York, NY: John Wiley & Sons, 2001.

von Hippel, E., *The Sources of Innovation*. New York, NY: Oxford University Press, 1988.

von Krogh, G., K. Ichijo and I. Nonaka, *Enabling Knowledge Creation*. Oxford, UK: Oxford University Press, 2000a.

von Krogh, G., I. Nonaka and T. Nishiguchi (eds.), *Knowledge Creation: A Source of Value*. London, UK: Macmillan Press, 2000b.

Wernerfelt, B., "A Resource-Based View of the Firm," *Strategic Management Journal*, 5, 1984, 171-180.

Wijnhoven, F., *Managing Dynamic Organizational Memories: Instruments for Knowledge Management*. Pacific Grove, CA: Boxwood Press, and Enschede, Netherlands: Twente University Press, 2000.

Wikström, S. and R. Normann, *Knowledge and Value: A New Perspective on Corporate Transformation*. London, UK: Routledge, 1994.

Keyword Index

Page numbers in italics refer to Volume 2 of the Handbook.

S